ON THE WATERFRONT:

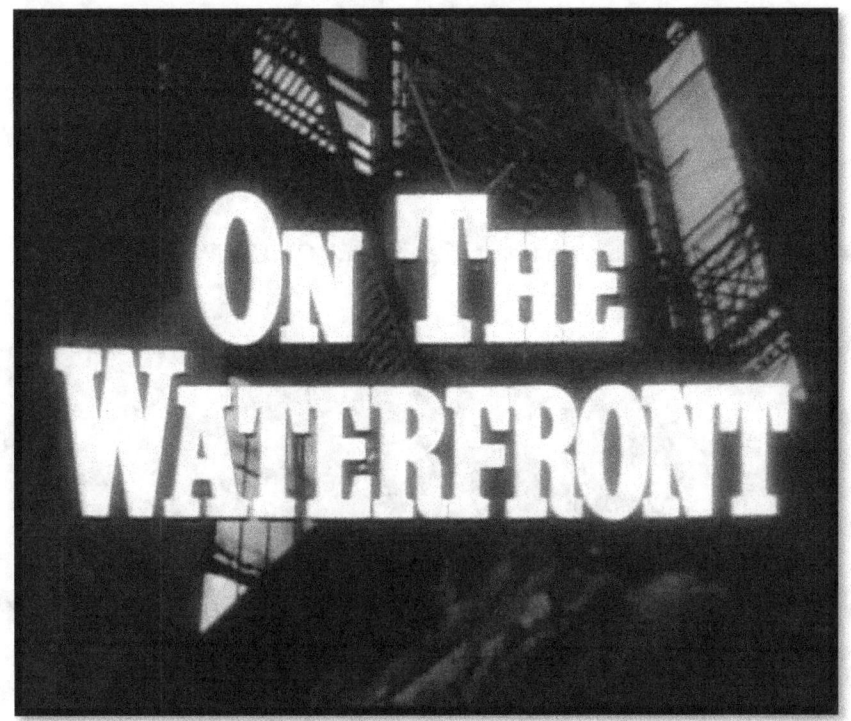

THE MAKING OF A GREAT AMERICAN FILM

By

John William Tuohy

INTRODUCTION

The Waterfront

"The waterfronts tougher, Father, like it ain't part of America**." On the Waterfront**

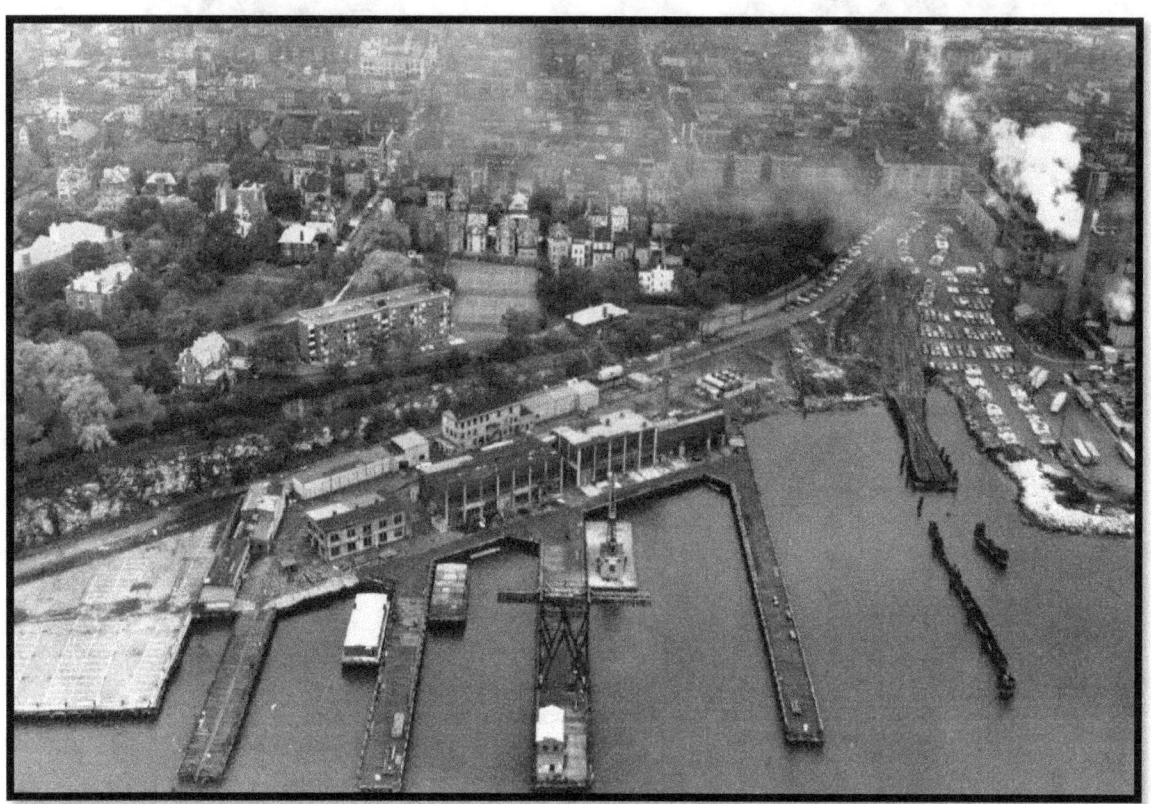

On January 8, 1947, at 7:00 AM, Andy Hintz, a hiring boss on Pier 51 in Manhattan, stepped out of his front door and while his wife and children watched in horror, he was shot to death by a waterfront hood named Cockeye Dunn. Just before he died, Hintz identified his killer to his wife "That was Johnny Dunn. You tell them that Johnny Dunn shot me"

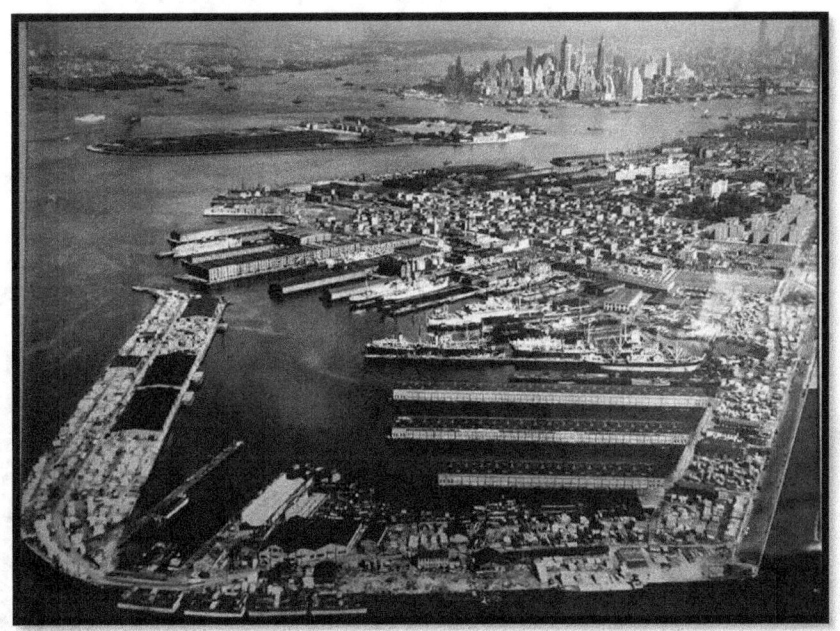

Red Hook

Within hours, police arrested Dunn, his partner Andrew Sheridan and a Danny Gentile, a one- time prize fighter turned enforcer and charged them with the Hintz shooting, learning that Hintz was murdered because he refused to be replaced as hiring boss by Dunn's handpicked man "Ding Dong' Bell, a well-paid enforcer for the violent International Longshoremen's Association, (ILA) the corrupt union that represented New York's dock workers.

According to witnesses "Dunn sent around one of men to tell Hintz he was out, but Hintz replied, "You tell Dunn that I said he should go to hell"
They murdered him the next morning.

No one on the waterfront expected Dunn or his gunmen to do any jail time over the murder of Andy Hintz. If anything, it bewildered most that the killers had even been arrested. It was commonly assumed on the docks that those who had ordered the killing, the Mob and the all-powerful ILA were not only above the law; they were, in, fact, a law unto themselves, at least on the waterfront.

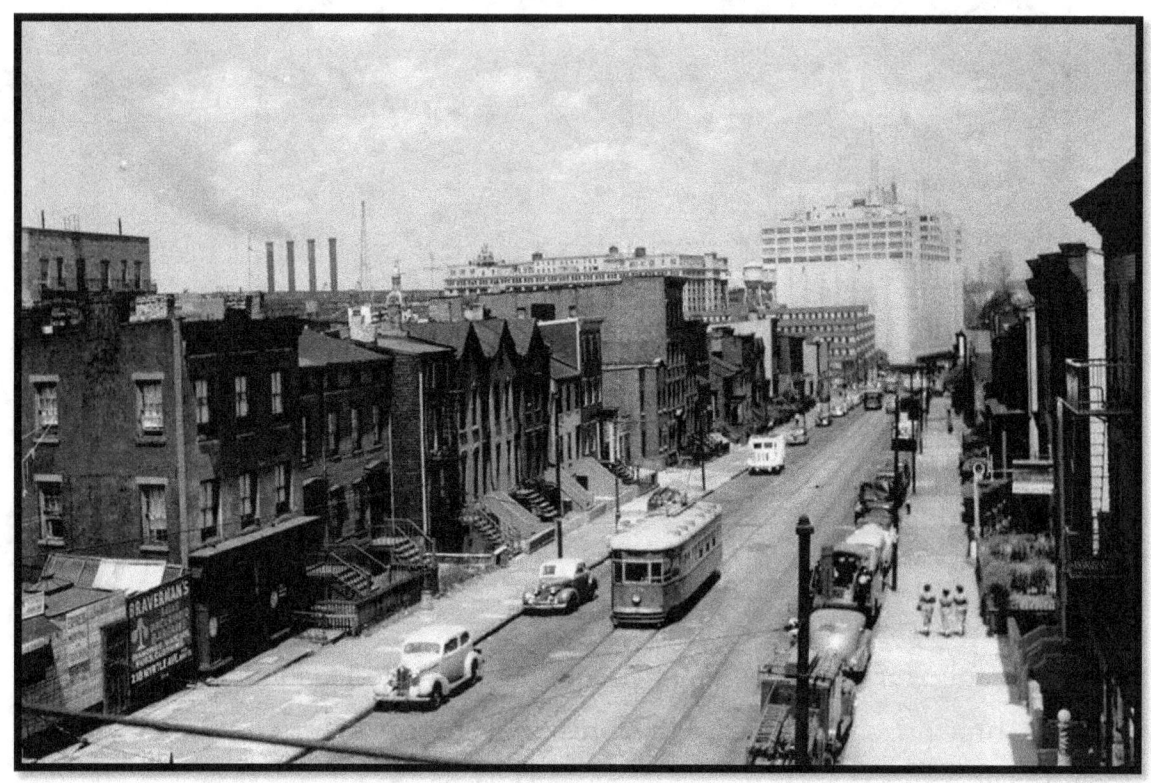

Red Hook, the docks are located at the end of the street where the large white building sits

In 1948, the New York- New Jersey waterfront was home to the largest, busiest Seaport in the world. Every fifty minutes, 24 hours a day, seven days a week, massive seagoing ships cleared its passages that were spread out through 750 miles of shore line, dotted by 1,800 piers, of which 200 were so large they served 400 ships at one time.

Every year, one million passengers departed from the waterfront on luxury liners, 35 million tons of cargo passed in and out of docks with a 1948 value of eight billion dollars. The waterfront was home to 2,500 tugboats, barges, derricks and scows. It was where 1,250,000 tons of fresh fruit arrived to feed Gotham, most of it carried by the12 major railroads' companies that were headquarters in its vast lots. The waterfront of 1948 was a bastion of free enterprise that reeked with cash.

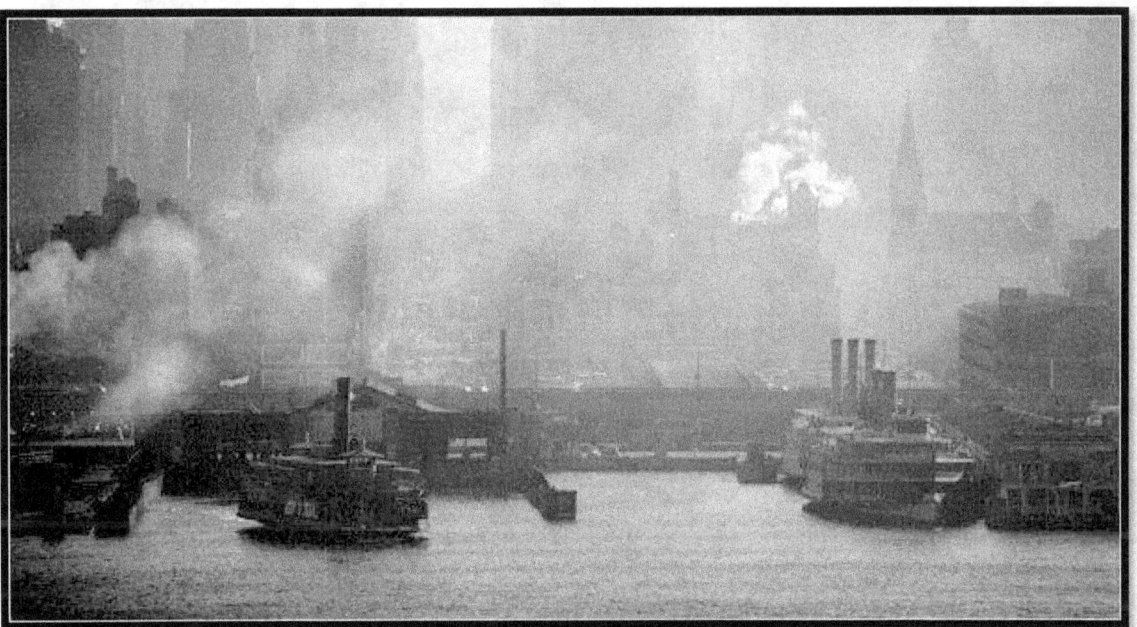

There was another waterfront. A poorer, shabbier waterfront that housed over 50,000 ill paid workers in run down brick row houses. A crime invested, closed little world rarely seen from the outside and known to few. It hadn't always been like that. Before the days of the American Revolution, New York's waterfront was the finest residential district in North America. Here, the best families and rich merchants built enormous, fine homes along wide, tree-lined streets. It was where George Washington resided when he was inaugurated President of the United States, not far from the elegant mansion of John Hancock.

The waterfront held to much promise for riches to remain a fashionable resting place for the new nations' elite. Manhattan was becoming the leading port in North America, largely because ships could use the ports to reach further inland, the Mohawk Valley and the Erie Canal.

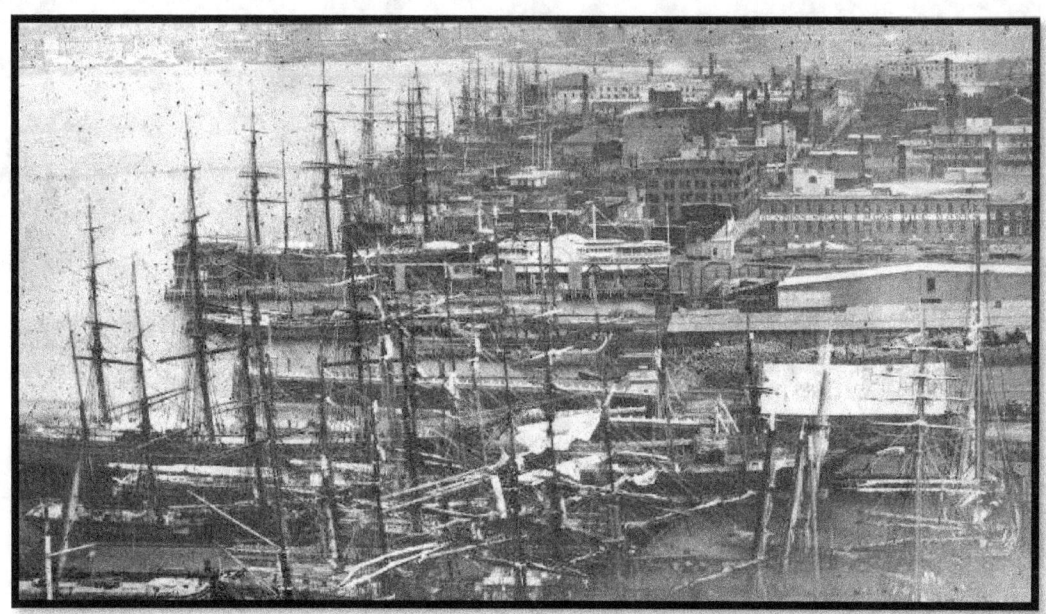

As the ports grew, wave after wave of German, French and English immigrants flooded into area in search of work, forcing the aristocrats to flee deeper into Manhattan. Eventually the Germans and English gave way to the Irish and Italians who arrived by the hundreds of thousands and settled into what was, by the mid-18th century, the dismal and miserable existence of life along the waterfront.

In South Brooklyn, Columbia Street was the boundary between the Italians and Irish longshoremen, two warring tribes so much alike and yet so far apart. What they shared was the boarder of filthy water that was oily, the harbor bottom rose several feet each year in a thick blanket of sludge.

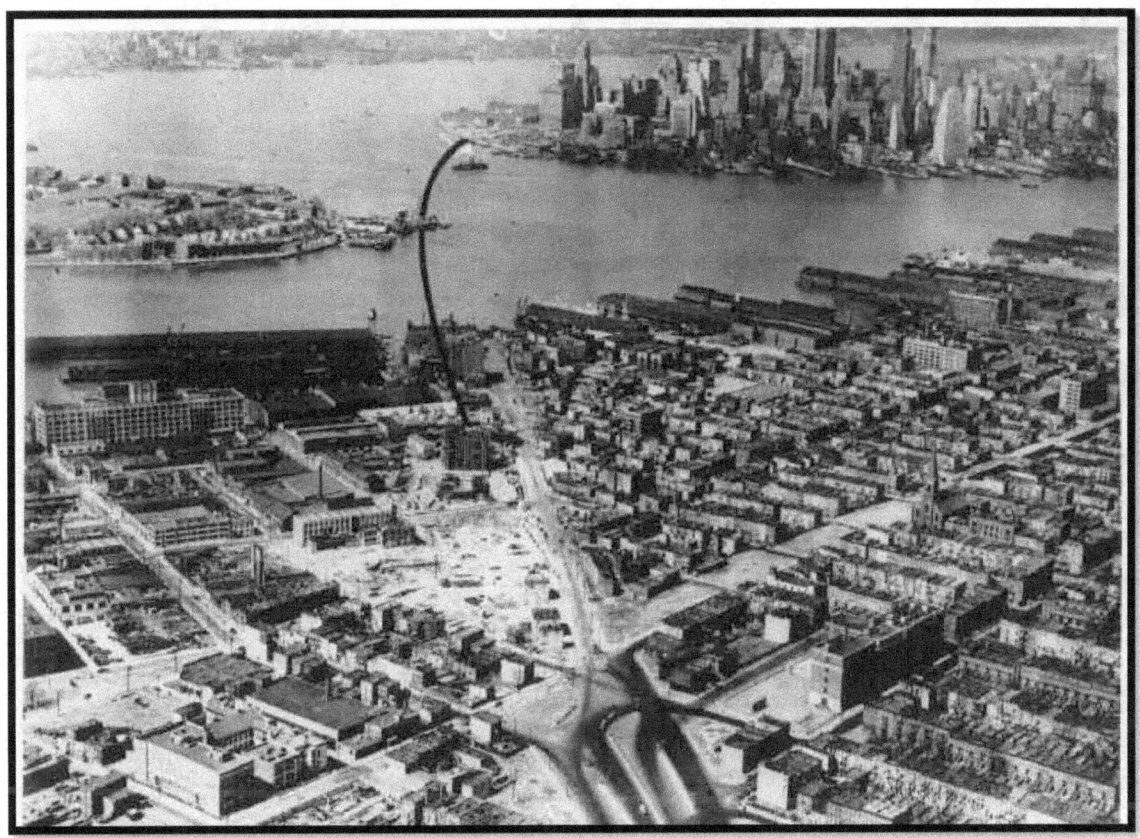

The sailors who ran the big harbor dredges used to say that they could bottle the harbor water, they'd sell it for Poison.

It wasn't just longshoremen's ghettos of South Brooklyn that had surrendered its once pristine beauty to the air of defeat and depression. The Catholic Labor activist Dorothy Day recalled the Docks of 1944 as; *Mott Street, New York, is a mile long, extending from Houston Street down to Chatham Square. It is a curved street, very slightly and gently curved. It turns into Chatham Square where the Bowery ends and becomes Park Row, where East Broadway, New Bowery, Bowery, Park Row, and Mott Street all run together.*

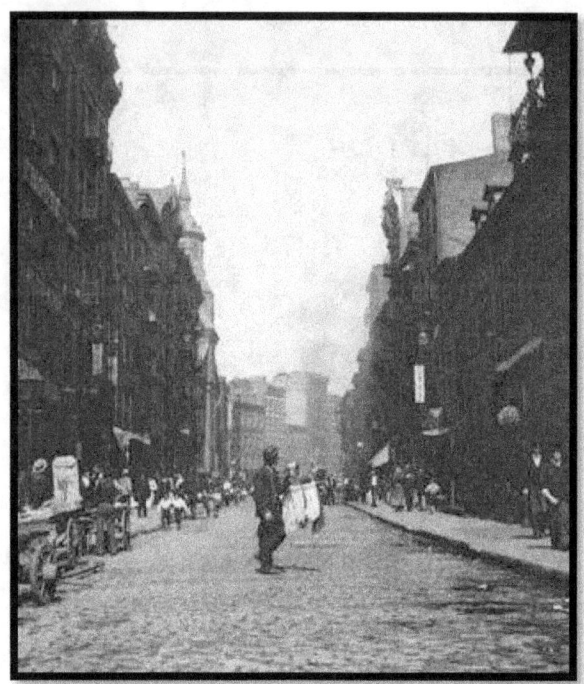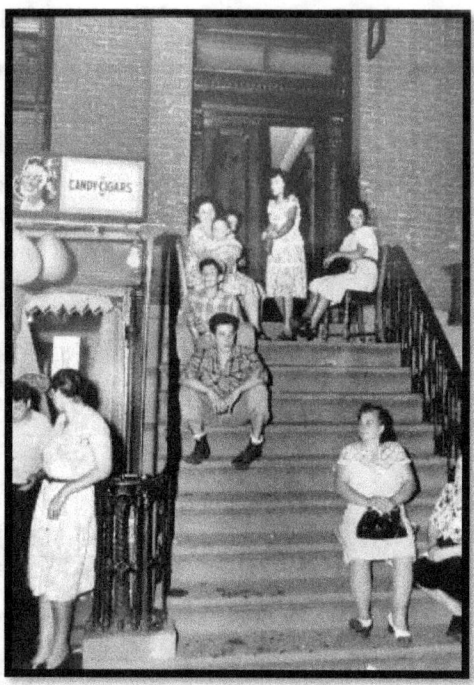

Mott Street

*All of Chatham Square is dark and dank under the elevated lines, for here the
Third Avenue line branches out and goes down Park Row to Brooklyn Bridge,
and down New Bowery to South Ferry, a mile or so away. Here Chinatown and
the Bowery meet, and the Bowery used to be like a bower, and lovers used to
walk there. Now it is a street of the poor, a street of cheap hotels, where men can
lodge for twenty or thirty cents a night. In all the larger cities of the country
they have such streets, and the migrants call them Skid Roads, and the term
originated in the northwest among the lumber workers who came to town from
the woods with their pay envelopes and either put the skids under themselves or
had them put under them by the liquor they drank or the company they kept.*

The Bowery is the street of the poor, and there are pawnshops and second-hand clothes shops. Here sailors and coal heavers and dock workers without families come to live because they have not enough money to live elsewhere. Here are their cheap amusements, movie houses, penny arcades and taverns. Here also the unemployed congregate, and there is a thieves market, where everything can be sold, from a razor to a pair of pants.

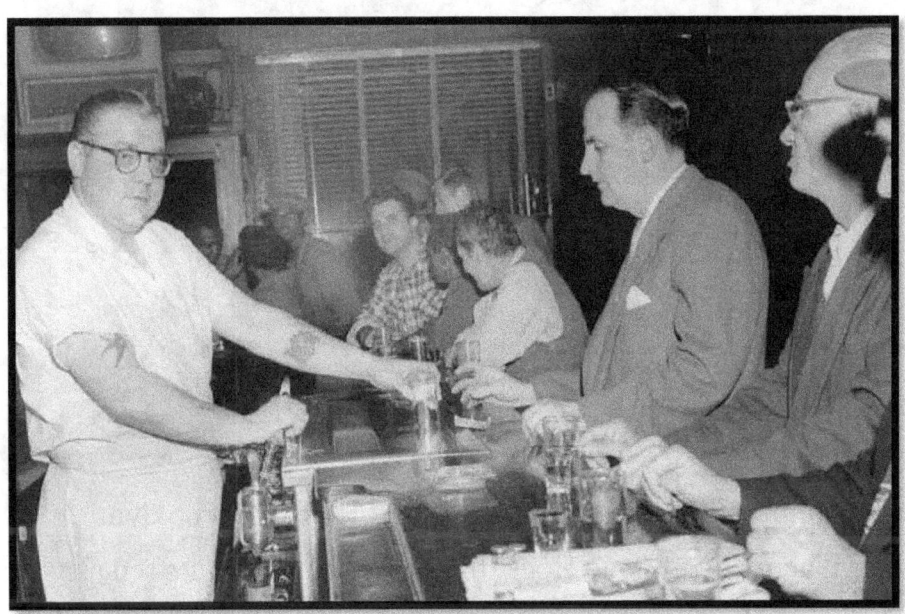

The very clothes on one's back can be sold and substituted for overalls or dungarees. Here, too, men lie prone on sidewalks, sleeping in doorways and against the house fronts. Here, too, are fights; and because of this the street now has the name of a street of bums and panhandlers, drunks and petty thieves. But it is the street of the poor, the most abandoned poor.

It is the street of missions, where for a confession of faith, men are given a bed, and thus religion is dragged, too, in the mire, and becomes an attempted opiate of the people. Here is Christ in His most degraded guise, spat upon, buffeted, mocked, and derided. This is not a glamorous neighborhood. There is no romance or beauty here in the Waterfront neighborhoods.

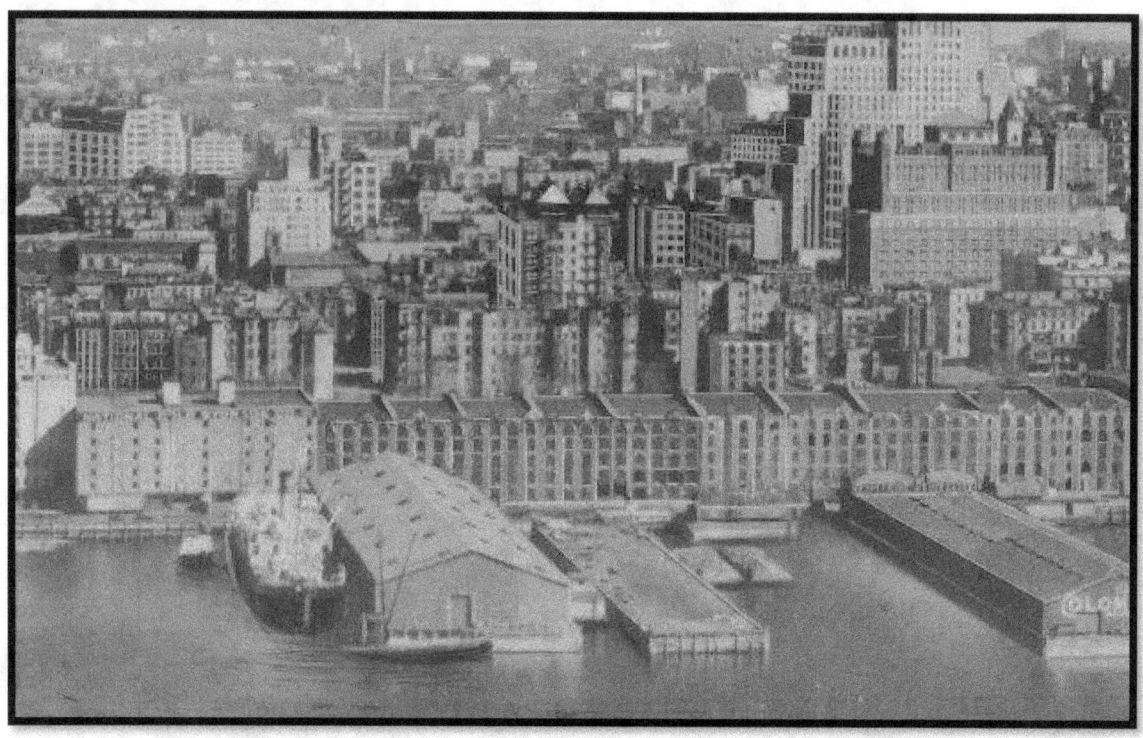

The largest longshoremen's neighborhoods were Red Hook, in Brooklyn. Originally a Dutch village called Roode Hoek, the name came from its red clay soil and the hook shape of its peninsular corner of Brooklyn that still projects itself.

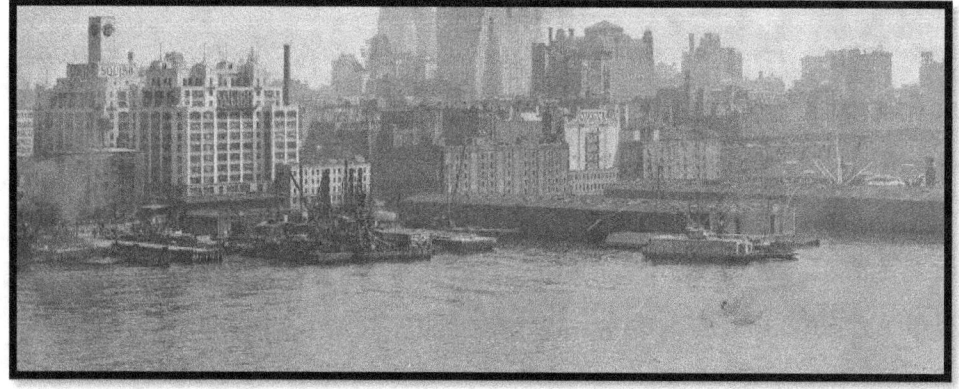

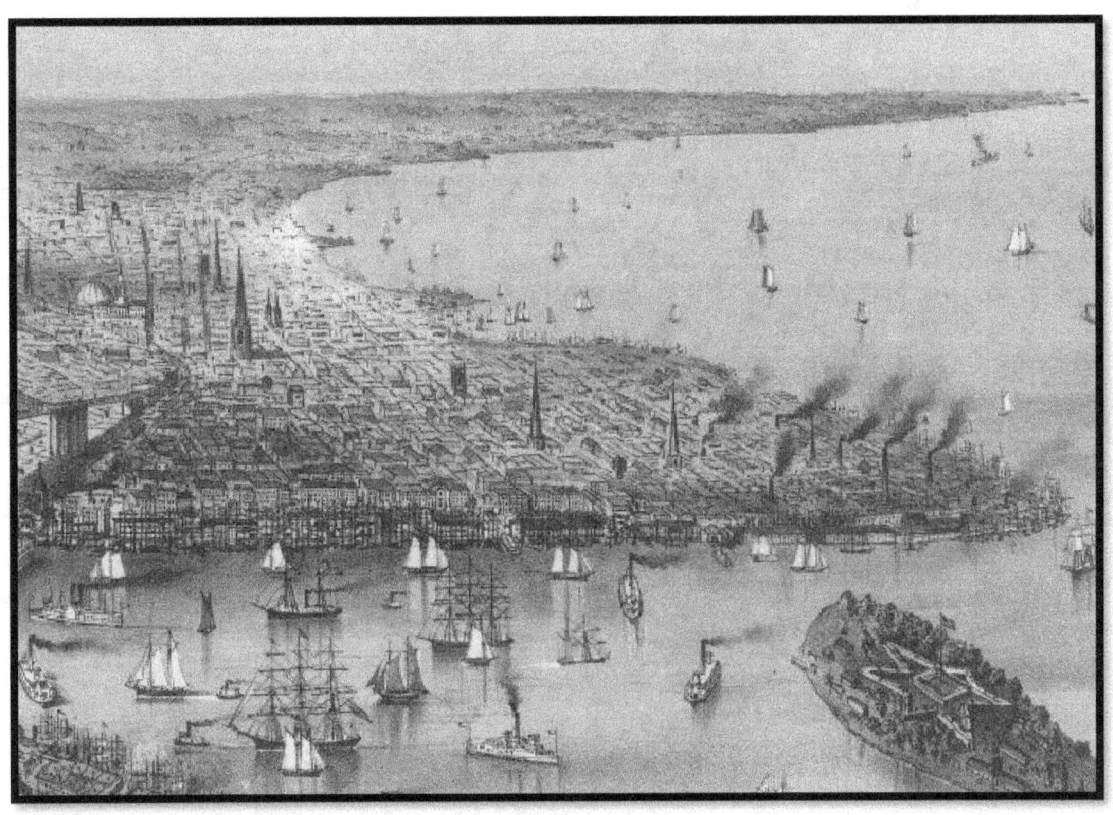

Roode Hoek

Out into the East River. While most of the longshoremen's enclaves left the outsider with the sense of sinister otherworldliness, it was truer in Red Hook than anywhere else. In 1946, the opening of the Gowanus Expressway and the 1950 opening of the Brooklyn Battery Tunnel cut the neighborhood off from the rest of the borough of Brooklyn, giving it an other worldly aura.

In the 1850s Red Hook became one of the busiest ports in the country. Grain barges from the Erie Canal would wait at the mouth of the Gowanus Canal for their turn at the active piers.

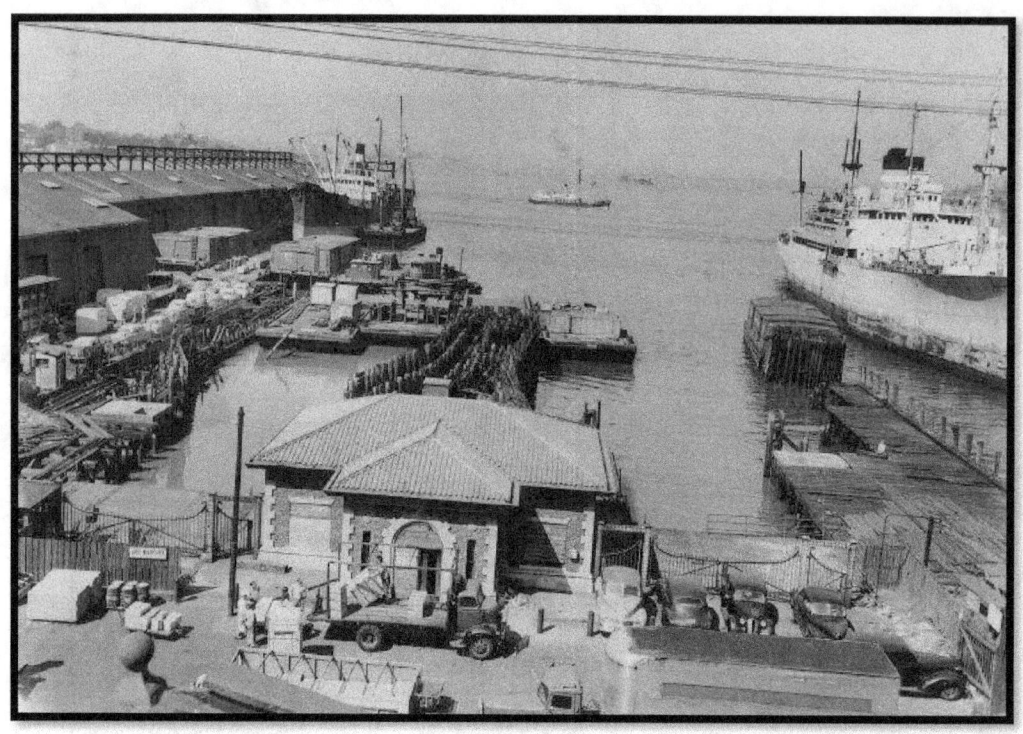

At its peak, in the early 1950s, Red Hook housed 21,000 people, almost all of the longshoremen or the family or longshoremen, who got by in cheaply built so-called Red Hook Houses, built in 1936 for the growing number of dock workers who were priced out of the city, as part of one of the first and largest Federal Housing projects in the country. Among its residents were Al Capone (38 Garfield Place, it still stands) and Lucky Luciano.

In 1948, Red Hook pulsated with activity, with droves of seedy workingman Bars and restaurants that were open 24 hours a day, seven days a week all catering to longshoremen and sailors, places where checks were cashed, credit was granted and the prices were low.

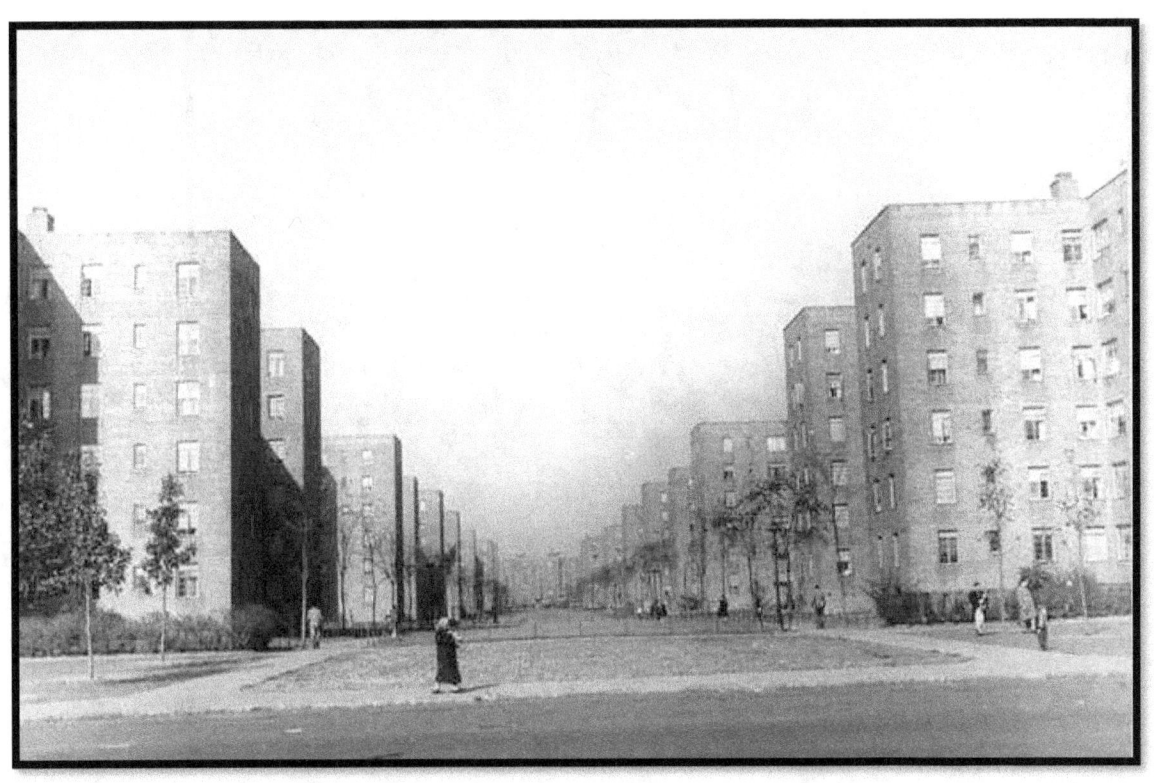

The Brooklyn Waterfront Projects

A saloon owner remembered: *Red Hook in those days sounded like maybe what took place in the Tower of Babel. You know, and people can hear crickets now. In those days, you couldn't-, you would hear the sound of steel against steel, all your pile drivers going, and ships coming and going, and horns blowing, and just so much activity. Then people getting off of ships and-, and running to get to what-, wherever it was they could get to after having traveled from wherever they came from. That 12 o'clock whistle would blow and all the gates - and there were many - all the gates, and the whole of the neighborhood would open up. It was like a stampede*

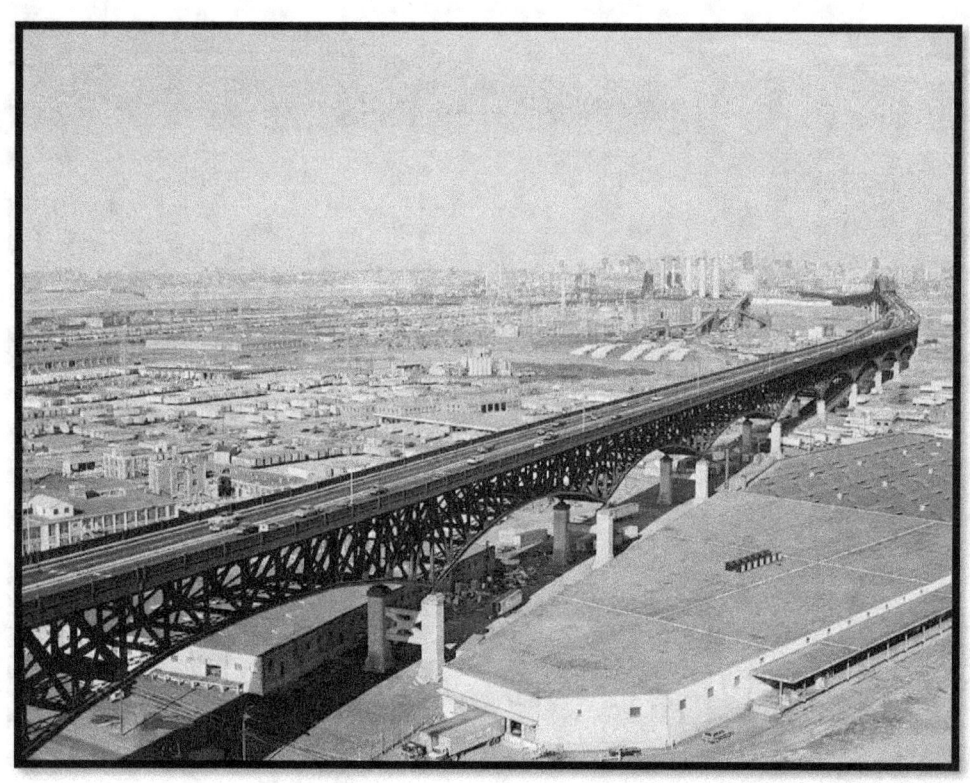

Before he gained fame as the author of the international best seller, *Angela's Ashes*, writer Frank McCourt worked on the docks in Red Hook *"You had to be careful you're not takin' jobs from longshoremen because they think nothing of sinking a baling hook in your skull and pushing you down between ship and dock, on the chance you would be crushed beyond recognition.*

They make better money on the docks than we do in the warehouses, but the work is unsteady and they have to fight for it every day. I carry my own hook from the warehouse, but I've never learned to use it for anything but lifting.

I'm glad to be getting decent wages again. Seventy-five dollars a week, going up to seventy-seven for operating the forklift truck two days a week. Regular platform work means you're on your feet in the truck, loading pallets with boxes, crates, sacks of fruit and peppers. Working the forklift is easier. You hoist up the load of pallets, store them inside, and wait for the next load.

No one minds if you read the paper while you wait. But if you read The New York Times, they laugh and say, "Oh, look at the big intellectual on the forklift."

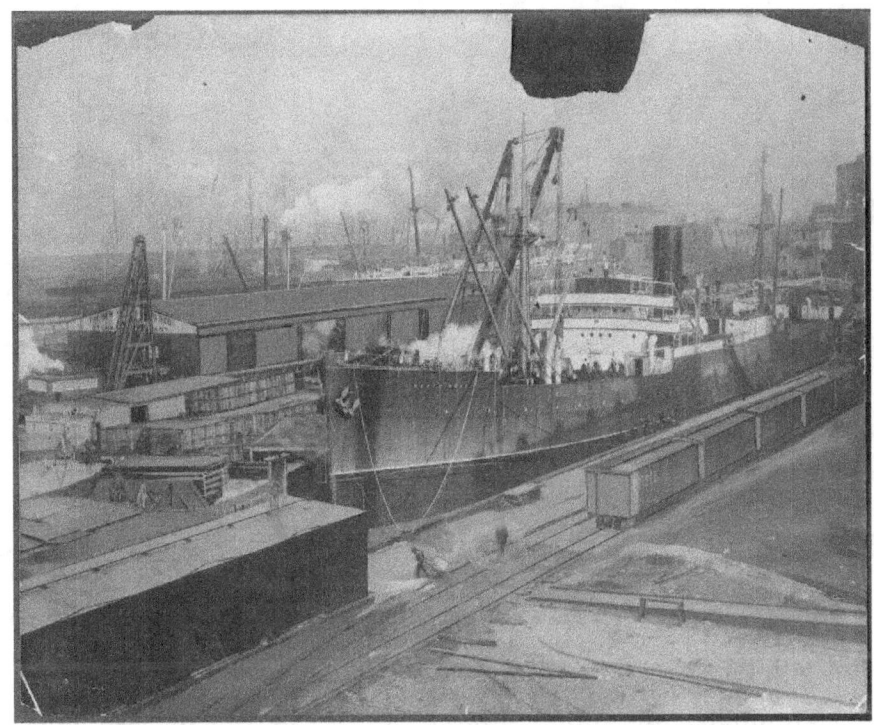

It's gone now. All that remains of Red Hook, as it was, is the name and the staining red clay and foul smell of the oily water. But while it lasted, Red Hook and the docks gave New York's massive pool of unskilled laborers, generations of them, steady, reasonably well paying work and right to belong to the almighty, all powerful I.L.A, the International Longshoreman's Association.

As the dock workers had predicted, the murder of Andy Hintz went unsolved despite a positive identification of the killers by the victim. Hintz's killers walked free and the world outside the secluded world of the waterfront was no wiser for it. However, there was one person on the waterfront who had refused to allow the Hintz murder slip away.

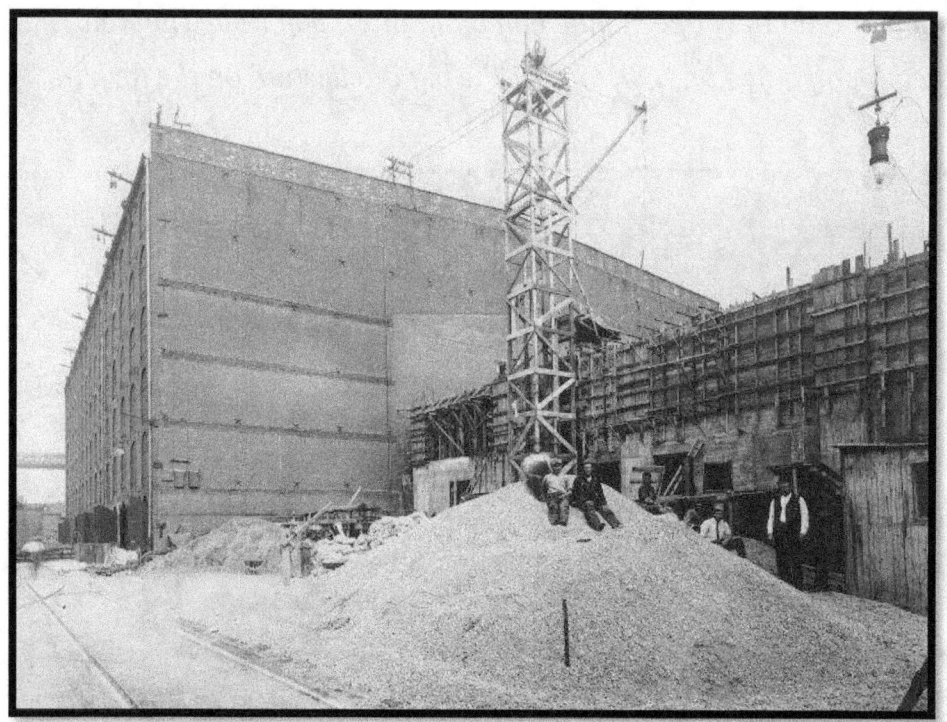

He was Father John Peter Corridan, a "rangy, ruddy, fast-talking, chain-smoking, and tough-minded, sometimes profane Roman Catholic priest" who was sent to the docks by the church to open a Labor School, St. Francis Xavier Labor School, near the west-side piers of Manhattan, in 1946.

The name "Labor School" was somewhat misleading. The Jesuit order, which ran the schools, distinguished itself by its theme of bipartisanship rather than a union-only focus, an outgrowth of the Catholic social welfare movement which called for the curbing of excessive profit-taking through regulation of the rates, return to ownership of public utilities, progressive taxation, participation of labor in management decisions, and a wider distribution of ownership through cooperative enterprises and legal enforcement of the right of labor to organize.

Although the social vision program was widely opposed by most members of the American hierarchy and by the broader Catholic Church community in general, it provided some legitimacy for social justice initiatives including the labor schools. Founded in 1936 as the Xavier School of Social Studies, held its focus.
To the labor movement with a goal was to concentrate its efforts on organizing Catholic workers in New York City by shepherding them away from the growing influence of the Communist Party since, as one Xavier priest said, "the Communists seemed to be spending most of their money and their energies on the unions...."

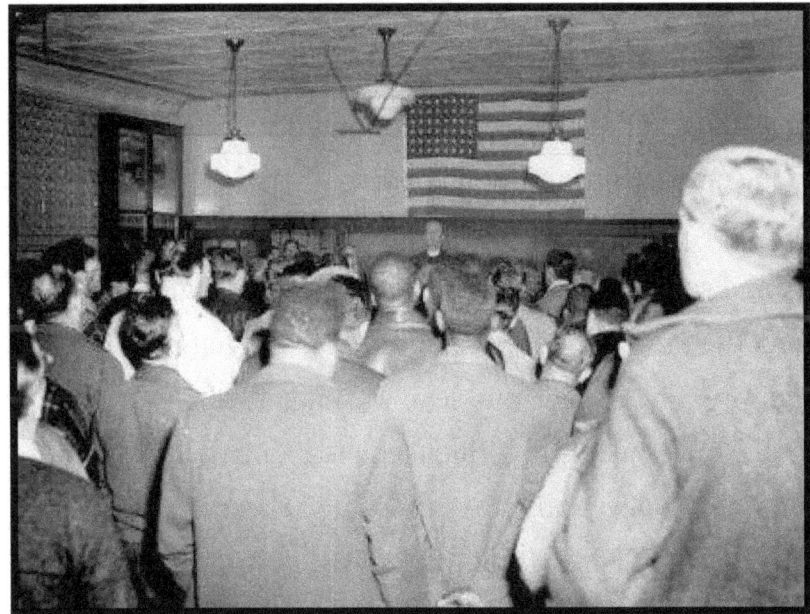 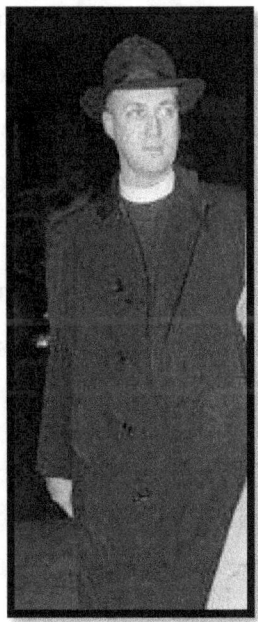

Corridan conducts a longshoreman's meeting

Throughout the late 1930's and into the war years, the target union for the Xavier School was the Transport Workers' Union (TWU) whose Communist leadership held steady sways over its overwhelmingly Catholic membership. However, by late 1948, the Communists were losing their grip in the TWU and the Xavier School shifted its attention to the waterfront. A shift that coincided with the arrival of Father Corridan in 1946.

Classes at the schools were held one or two nights per week for eight to ten weeks; running one hour, with two to three class periods per night; a set of core courses consisting of ethics, public speaking, parliamentary procedure, and labor problems. The faculty consisted of largely lay practitioners: union leaders, labor attorneys, school teachers all of who volunteered their services. Clergy or religious normally handled the ethics course.

The cost was minimal ($1- $5) or, at times, free. Sometimes enrollment was restricted to Catholics or unionists, but in the case of the Jesuit programs, open to all. St. Xavier's was somewhat different, in that it sponsored forums addressing broader issues such as the criminal justice system, public education, communism, etc., appealing to the entire community. They also offered workshops or extended courses tailored to special occupational groups such as lawyers, public school teachers, and senior labor relation's management staff. However, the essential mission of the these schools was improving the material and social well-being of the largely impoverished American working class; overcoming the growing Communist presence and influence in the United States work force. Lastly, their mission was the deepening the faith-life of the American Catholic worker in an increasingly secular culture that tended to divorce religion from economic life.

In a speech given on June 6, 1937 during the "Little Steel" strikers in Youngstown, Ohio, Msgr. Charles Rice told the strikers: *"Because I have come here at this moment I shall be accused of injecting religion into the labor issue, and I reply: It is about time that religion was introduced into that issue. The reason we have labor strife today, the reason we have had it for generations, the reason six men lost their live in Illinois last week is that religion and religious principles have been kept out of the labor question. Because religion was forgotten, no not forgotten but deliberately thrown aside, too many industrialists have conducted their affairs as if Christ had never lived and died, as if there were not just god in heaven, and have tried to rule like the absolute Pagan Emperors of old, forgetting that they were dealing with human beings, endowed with human rights by the God who made them."*

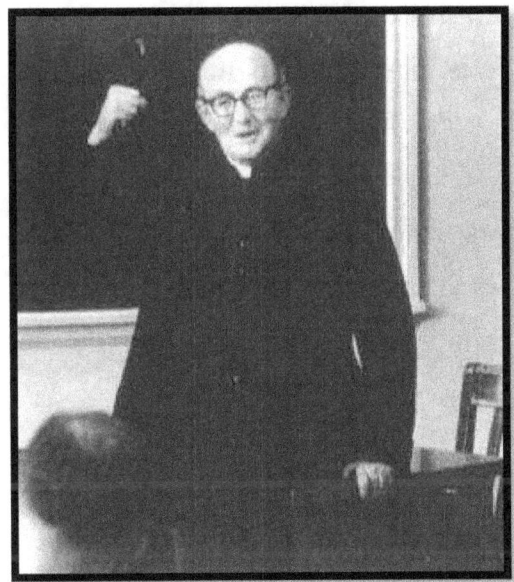 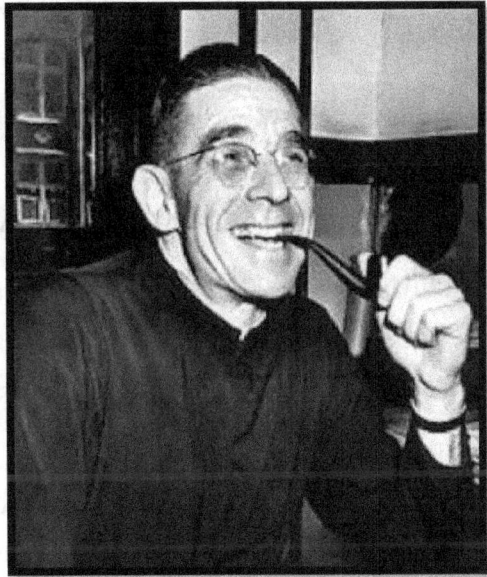

Left, Monsignor Charles Owen Rice, known as "Pittsburgh's Labor Priest" and right, Twomey

The work of the Jesuit directors, like as Corridan, ranged widely, from mediating/arbitrating labor management disputes, to lecturing to Church, business or civic organizations, to service on government boards overseeing employee relations.

Corridan was one of many Jesuits active in social issues in the 1950s. In 1937, Rice founded the Catholic Radical Alliance and organized the first picket line at the Heinz Food plant. He was an early supporter of Rev. Martin Luther King, Jr. in the Spring Mobilization for Peace in New York in 1967, he protested against America's involvement in Vietnam in 1969.

Father Lou Twomey, SJ, at the Loyola University Institute in New Orleans moved into the racial issue in the late 1940s well in advance of the decisive court cases and early protest marches of the mid-'50s. He also authored the newsletter "Christ's Blueprint of the South" which for almost two decades served as basic social justice reading for all the seminarians.

The St. Joseph's Institute in Philadelphia, led by Dennis Comey, SJ, staked out an image of a sophisticated, academically demanding, labor-management program, while Comey himself became known as the Waterfront Peacemaker through his extensive arbitration work.

Fr. Willie Smith, SJ, after starting the Crown Heights Labor School in Brooklyn in the late 1930s, introduced the most diverse range of labor/management educational programs of any Jesuit Institute. He also published articles for the national media on this labor school tradition. Most importantly, in the waterfront school, the director was to be high profile.

At a time when so many working people were labeled as communists because of their pro-union views, the priest's presence was an important affirmation by the Church to the working community. This was especially true on the docks, where, under the reign of the ILA's Joe Ryan, being *Red Smeared* was a long favored tactic.

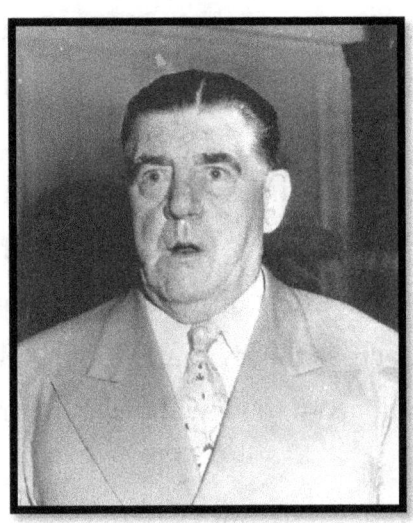

Boss Joe Ryan

Like most New Yorkers, Corridan knew little of life on the waterfront. Under the tutelage of Father Philip Carey, Corridan learned how to deal with the longshoremen and to recruit activists that could confront both the ILA leaders and Communist militants. It was dangerous work, for the priests and the activists alike, and Corridan's organizing was done with painstaking slowness.

A native New Yorker who had entered the priesthood late in life, Corridan knew all about the mob and he fully understood the dangers inherent in taking on the longshoremen' struggle as his own. It would be three years before he had established himself enough as a public figure in the media before he felt completely safe on the waterfront. The mob probably wouldn't harm him bodily, but they would (and did) use their considerable influence from within the Catholic Church and New York politics to do whatever they had to do to stop him. At first, Corridan appeared at the docks but realized the tactic was useless, no one wanted to be seen talking to him. Afterwards, he and Father Philip Carey dropped leaflets advertising the classes in all of the locales frequented by longshoremen.

Father Carey claimed that leaving leaflets in toilets "served a double purpose, it gave a man freedom from fear while he was reading it and number two it gave him sufficient time to reflect on its contents."

Contacts with longshoremen were sometimes made in alleyways and basements away from the ILA and mob snitches who were everywhere on the docks. Over the next few months, Corridan learned everything he could about the waterfront. He walked every pier, took a ferry across the river and looked at the docks from angle, even once traveling into Manhattan to view the waterfront from the Empire State Building.

He concluded that problems on the waterfront were not insurmountable and that he would change them. He began by building an extensive intelligence network made up of a handful of longshoremen, altar boys, reporters, housewives and anyone else that would provide him with accurate information on the ILA and the mob. By the end of his first year on the docks, Corridan had collected sixteen filing cabinets full of information. What Corridan learned was that the ILA, the International Longshoremen's Association, was the union controlled virtually all of the hiring on the New York-

New Jersey waterfront. The ILA was begun in 1877, by a Dan Keefe, Irish tugboat worker (or possibly a tug boat owner) from Chicago who formed the first local of the Association of Lumber Handlers and then successfully expanded membership to include dock workers.

Keefe set the iron fisted management style that would rule over the ILA for the next century. Keefe also established the ILA's ruthless methods to achieve its ends. Under his rule, the ILA eliminated independent stevedores by threats and intimidation and secured the ship owner's loyalty with a guarantee of uninterrupted work in return for a closed dock. When Keefe resigned in 1908, and then due only to his advanced years, the ILA had just over 100,000 dues paying members, mostly in the Great Lakes states. His hand-picked replacement, TV O'Connor, another Great Lakes tugboat man, would have a far shorter reign, just under twelve years, but would use that time to establish the ILA as New York's leading stevedore union.

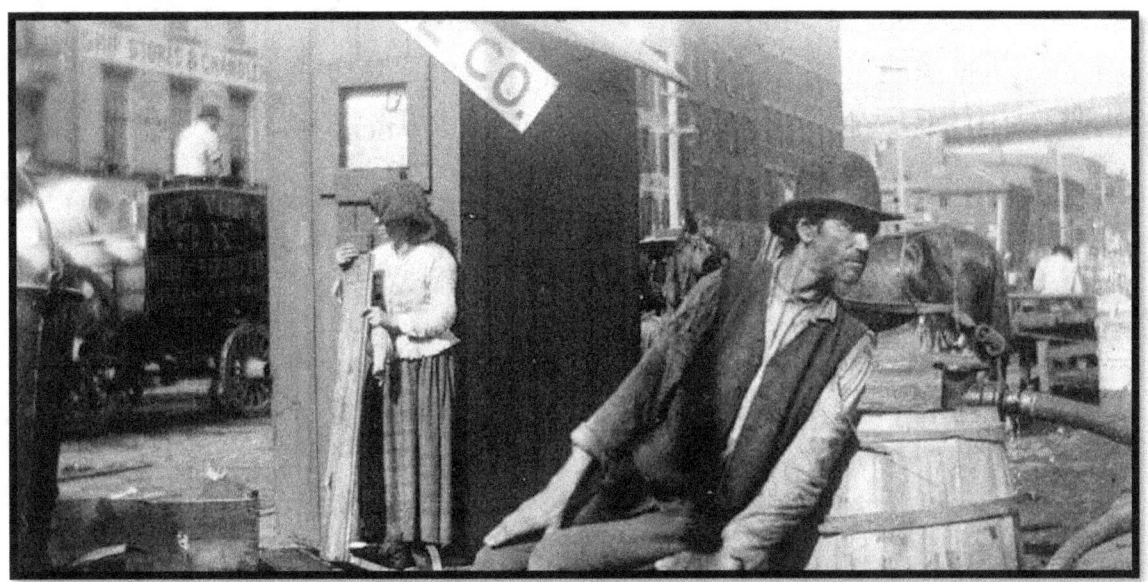

Brooklyn waterfront circa 1870

As the ILA grew, power shifted increasingly to the Port of New York, where, in 1949, 30,000 longshoremen moved more than 6.5 billion in cargo through the New York-New Jersey Ports.

By the late 1940s, Joseph Patrick Ryan, AKA The King, was running the New York docks as the ILA's International president. Ryan, a crude, obnoxious little man, had come to power in 1927 and stayed there through his deep connections inside New York's political machine, Tammany Hall. For a cut of the unions' profits, Tammany assured Ryan protection from the police and other criminal investigations. Furthermore, in exchange for control of a handful of his

Manhattan and New Jersey locals, the powerful New York mobs paid Ryan and Ryan paid Tammany.

Joseph Patrick Ryan was born on May 11, 1884 in Babylon, Long Island, the son of Irish immigrants, both of who died before he reached age nine. He moved to Manhattan with his stepmother and grew up in the Chelsea neighborhood, taking his elementary educated at St. Xavier Catholic parish, which would later be headquarters to the labor school that would bring about his demise.

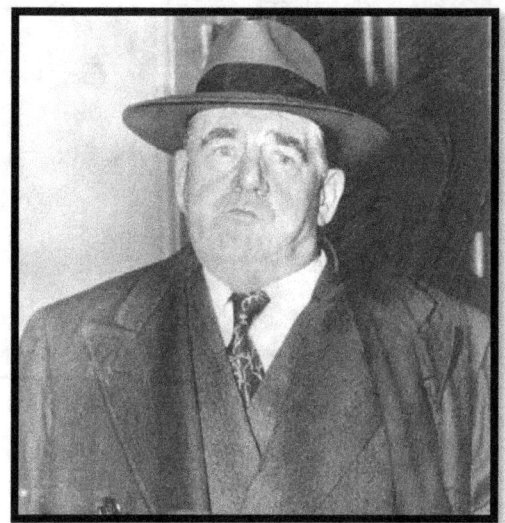 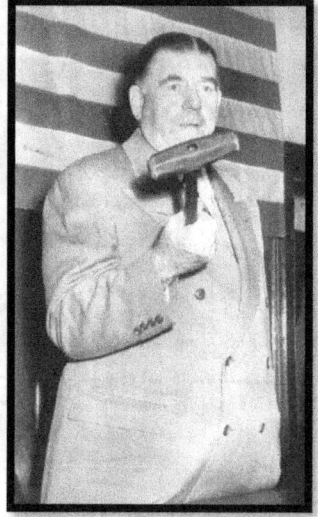

Ryan left school at age 12 to work as a janitor and stock boy in Manhattan. In 1912, at age 28, he got his first job on the docks, in the hold of a ship, at 25 cents an hour for a mandatory 60-hour week. In 1916, he joined the ILA, buying his union book for $2.50 "The finest investment I ever made" he said.

With time, Ryan was promoted to financial secretary of Local 791 and then to organizer, for $30 a week. A natural and gifted speaker, he was the ideal organizer and soon came to the attention of Tammany Hall, New York's Tammany Hall, New York's entire powerful, thoroughly corrupt Democratic machine.

With political clout behind him, in 1927 he was appointed president of the ILA. Despite the fact that he was extremely unpopular with the rank and file, Ryan was eventually made, self-appointed actually, the unions "president for life" in 1943, a tittle, which he insisted, was "an honorary title reflecting my stature and prominence with the working men"

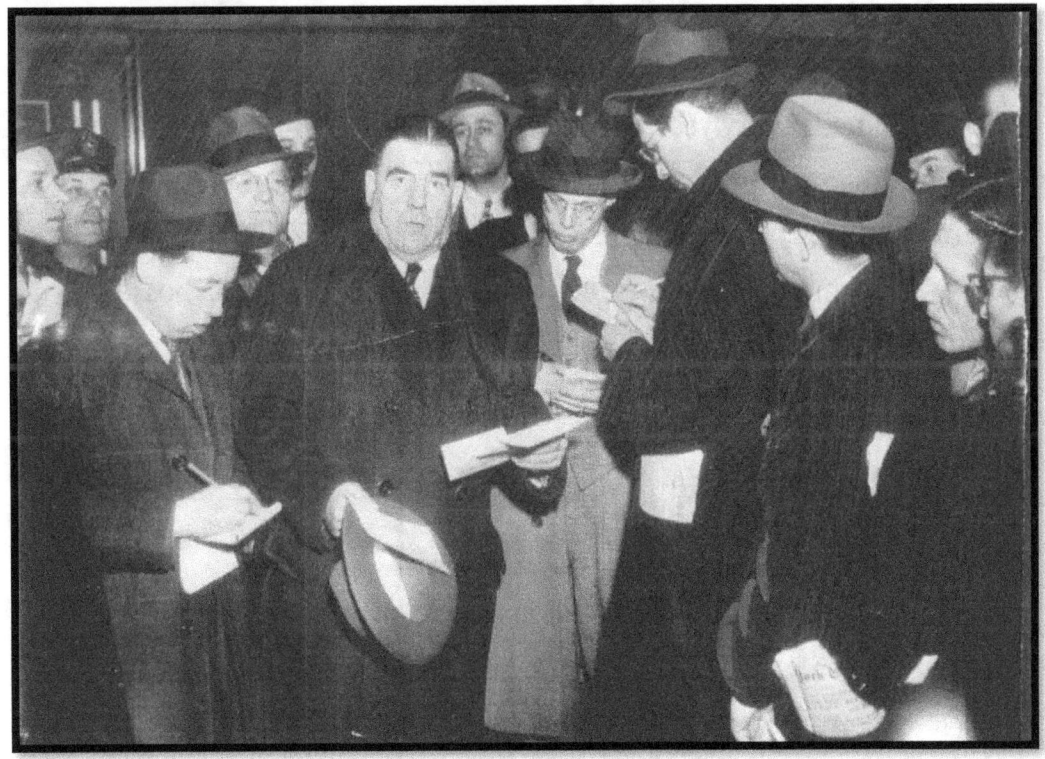

Ryan, center

Officially, his salary was less than $28,000 a year. However, according to the state of New York, his off the books' earnings were probably ten times that amount. He lived well on the wages earned by the sweat and labor of his membership. An indulgent father to his two daughters and an attentive husband to his wife of forty years, he had no use for other women and held an Irishmen's puritanical contempt for other married men who wandered from the bonds of matrimony. The family seldom missed Sunday mass or an evening at *Toots Shors* or *Cavanagh's*, the Tammany meeting place on West 23rd street. They belonged to the best clubs, including the exclusive Winged Foot Country Club in Westchester County.

With loot taken from the ILA, he formed the Joseph Patrick Ryan Association; a Catholic political club that eventually became the mouthpiece or the powerful Trades and Labors Council. Every year, the Association held a dinner dance in his honor, a must attend on every politicians schedule.

At one dinner in 1937, New York's reform Mayor, La Guardia, found himself sitting an elbow away from the ILA's top killer *Cockeye* Dunn and Mafia boss Phil Mangano. The following year, La Guardia canceled his reservation.

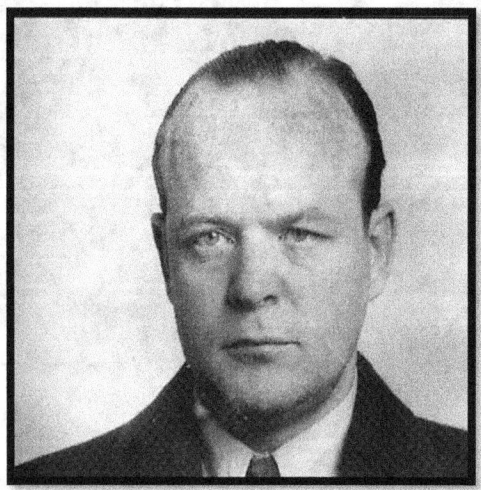

Cockeye Dunn

While Ryan may have been president of the ILA, he wasn't the ultimate power on the waterfront. In fact, there were a myriad of powers on the Docks consisting of Ryan, the Mafia, independent Irish gangsters, the shipping companies and the Democratic parties of Tammany Hall in Manhattan and Frank Hauge in Jersey. However, directly over Ryan was William J. McCormack AKA Big Bill.

It was from McCormack's political patronage that Ryan drew his power. In turn, Ryan acted as McCormack's eyes and ears on the waterfront, inside Tammany and the Mob. Everyone who was anyone knew Ryan, because Ryan wanted it that way, however only a handful of insiders knew who McCormack was or how powerful a force he was.

Like Ryan, McCormack was an Irish-American from Manhattan, the son of immigrant milk wagon driver and like Ryan, and he sprang up from grinding poverty.

Always an enormous size, even as a child, McCormack, who left school as a 13-year-old boy, was able to handle of team of horses as a wagon driver on the Jersey waterfront. Tough and fearless, by age 23, McCormack and his brother owned their own trucking company and were early supporters of Jersey City's colorful but hopelessly corrupt Mayor, Frank "Boss" Hauge (Once, while he was supposed to address a group of young criminals with an uplifting speech on proper citizenship, Hauge told the children *Yous didn't do nothin different from me when I was a young stud, cept, yous got caught and I became Mayor*)

During World War One, McCormack, working for the Jersey waterfront, made a fortune as a meat shipper, using that money to buy out several other trucking firms to create the US Trucking Corporation of America. When Tammany's Al Smith lost his bid for Governor, McCormack (A Republican) was shrewd enough to appoint Smith President of US Trucking. When Smith was elected governor in 1922, he made McCormack the States Boxing Commissioner.

Five years later, McCormack sold US Trucking and entered the sand and gravel business. Using his considerable labor and political power, McCormack and his partner, Italian publisher Generoso Pope, almost cornered the ready mix concrete market in Manhattan.

By 1932, McCormack had investments in banks, railroads, contracting, sand, harbor dredging, oil tankers, a race track and, most importantly, a Stevedoring firm that employed thousands of longshoremen. His estimated cash worth in 1950, not including real estate holding and stocks, was $20 million dollars. With his money, came more political power and enormous clout within the shipping industry and control of Joe Ryan and the ILA.

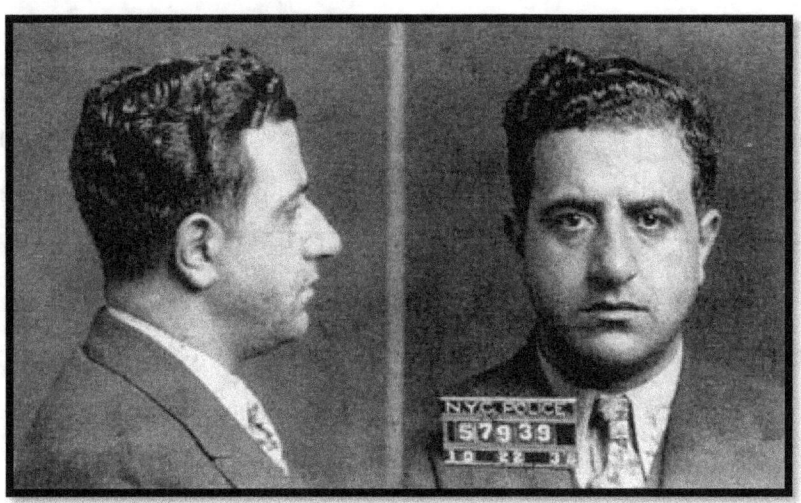

Ryan's partners on the dock was Mafia chief Vincent Mangano and his underboss, Albert Anastasia (**above**) who, in turn, controlled Emil Camarda, vice president of the ILA. Likewise, Camarda controlled Dr. Tom Longo, who ran a powerful political organization, the City Democratic Club, located at 33 President Street in Brooklyn. (Camarda owned the entire block) just a few minutes' walk from Pier 11. Longo was the Mobs and ILA's contact to William O'Dwyer, the Brooklyn District Attorney.

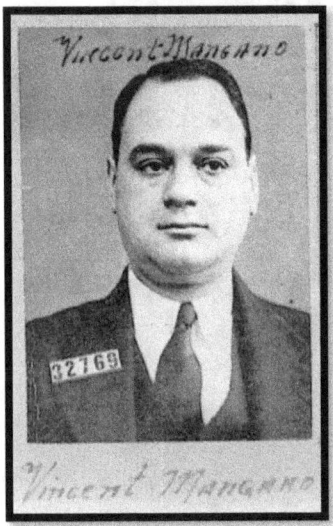 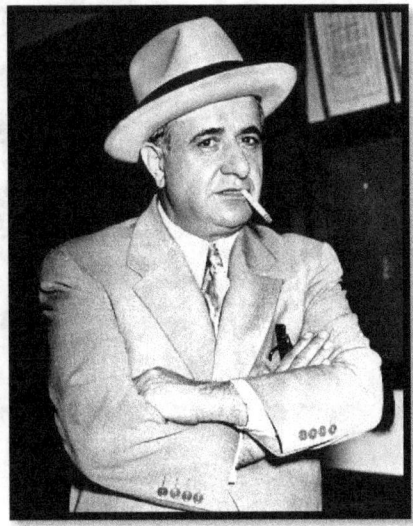

Vincent Mangano and Albert Anastasia

Vincent Mangano, the ultimate power, was an old style Mafia boss whose power within the ILA was unquestioned although virtually unknown outside that secular universe. Vincent Mannino, a lawyer who represented six ILA "pistol locals" testified before the state of New York's crime commission that he was "shocked" to learn that his position had been granted only after the personal recommendation of Mangano. Nino Camarda, brother of ILA Vice President Emil Camarda told him "Of course it's true. Without Vincent Mangano's okay, no-body could work here."

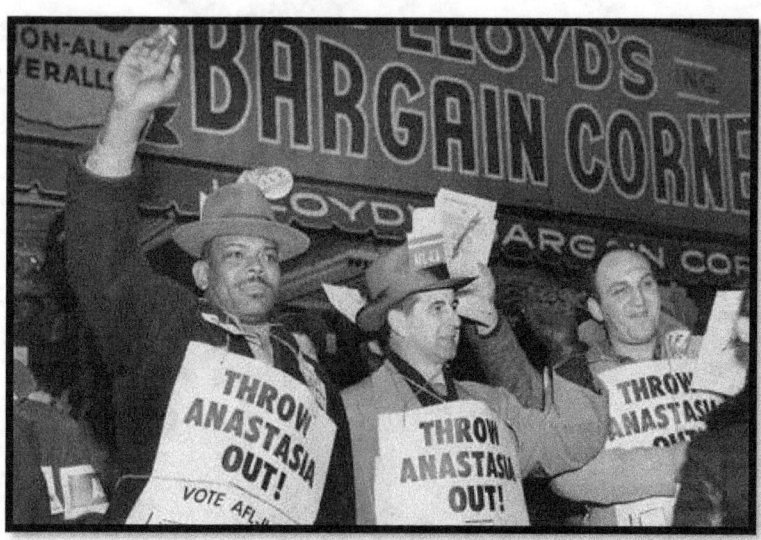

While Mangano was certainly ruthless, he wasn't ruthless enough. In 1951, his Underboss, Albert Anastasia, tired of Mangano's careful, old world ways, murdered him.   He then took control of his organization and all twenty miles of the Brooklyn docks, stretching from Pier One just below the Brooklyn Bridge, south to the end of the Bush Terminal Docks all the way into Hoboken, New Jersey.

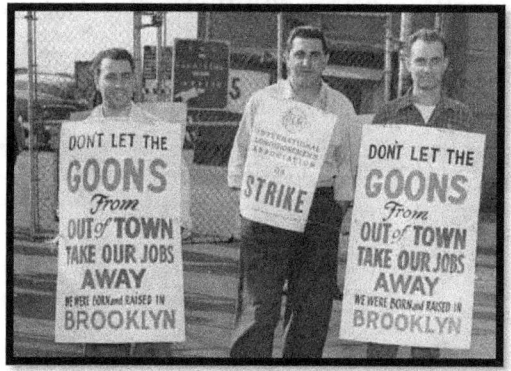

No one ever doubted that Albert Anastasia, dubbed "The Mad Hatter" by the press, was insane. Just how insane he was, was made clear one night in 1952, when Anastasia was home listening to the news on the radio, when he heard that bank robber Willie Sutton had been recognized and turned in by one of his neighbors in Brooklyn, a young man named Arnold Schuster. Anastasia got up from his chair and called one of his men, an escaped convict named Frederick Tenuto, told him about the news story and said, "I hate squealers, find this fucking Schuster and kill him." On March 8, Tenuto walked up behind Schuster on a New York Street and shot him to death.

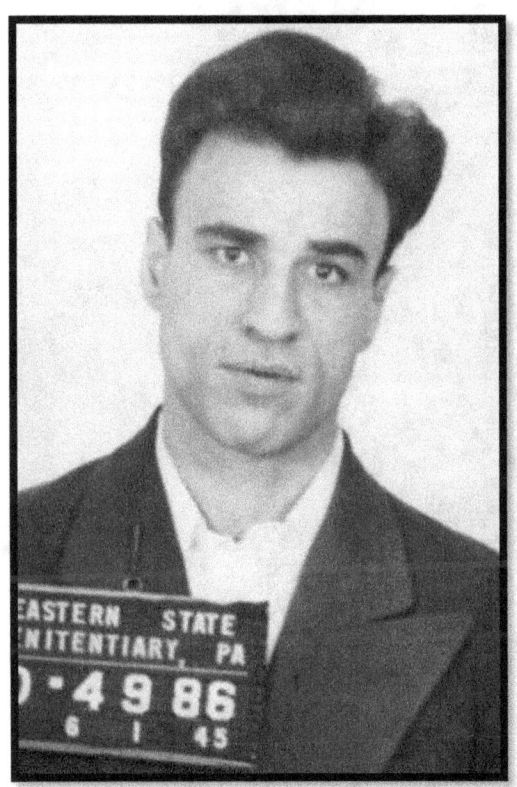
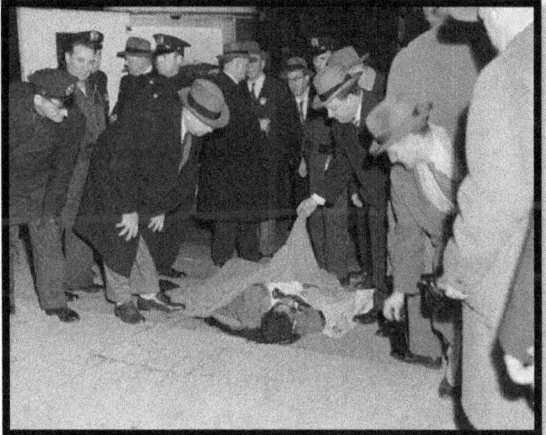

Tenuto (left) and Schuster, dead.

When sanity returned to Anastasia, and he realized what he had done, he ordered Tenuto's death as well. His body has never been found.

Anastasia long, often spectacular criminal career had started as a labor terrorist on the waterfront. He was once arrested for the stabbing/strangulation murder of a longshoreman named Joe Torino in a dispute over unloading cargoes. There were several witnesses to the killing and Anastasia was convicted and sentenced to death, spending 18 months in the death house of Sing Sing. However, just before he was to be executed, he won a new trial when several witnesses reversed their statements. The state dropped the charges and Anastasia walked out of jail a free man.

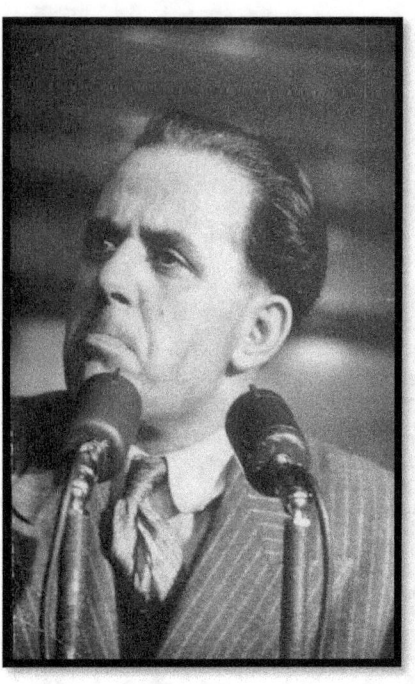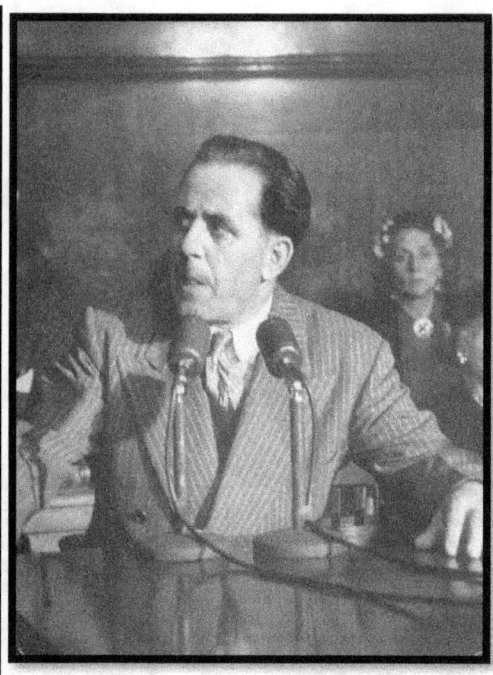

Anastasia's enforcer on the Brooklyn docks was his brother, Tough Tony Anastasia (above) who was also a Vice President of the ILA and boss over the very powerful ILA Local 1814. He was also on salary with the Jarka Stevedoring Corporation as an executive, a major employer on the waterfront.

When Jarka's president, Frank Nolan, was pressed by state investigators to explain why the near illiterate Anastasia was on the company's payroll as a senior executive, Nolan replied, "He is resourceful and tireless on the job. He preserves discipline and good order on the part of the men."

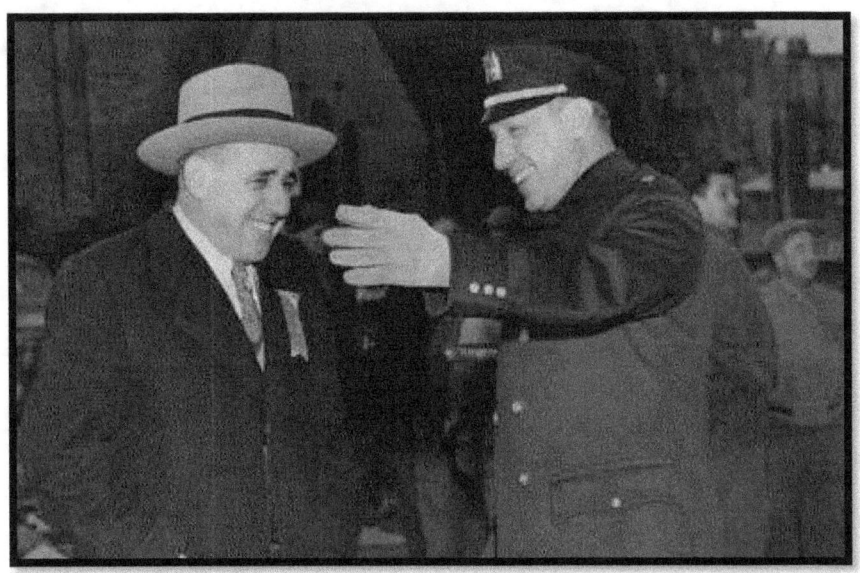

Tough Tony Anastasia, above talking to cop. He can also be seen in the photo below, behind the man with the Anti-Anastasia sign.

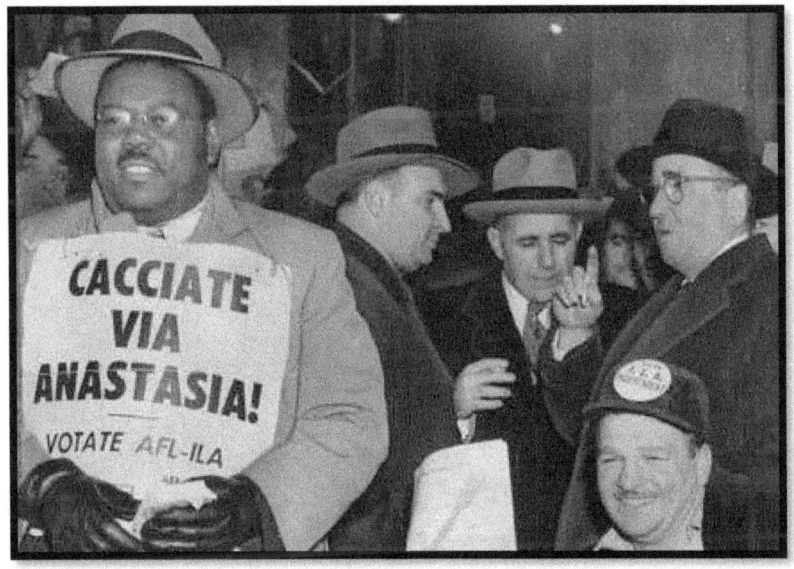

He preserved discipline on all levels through fear. Once, when a reporter from the New York Sun had written an unflattering piece on his brother Albert, Tony cornered the reporter and asked "Why do you keep writing all of those awful, terrible things about my brother? He ain't killed nobody from you're family" and then added "Yet"

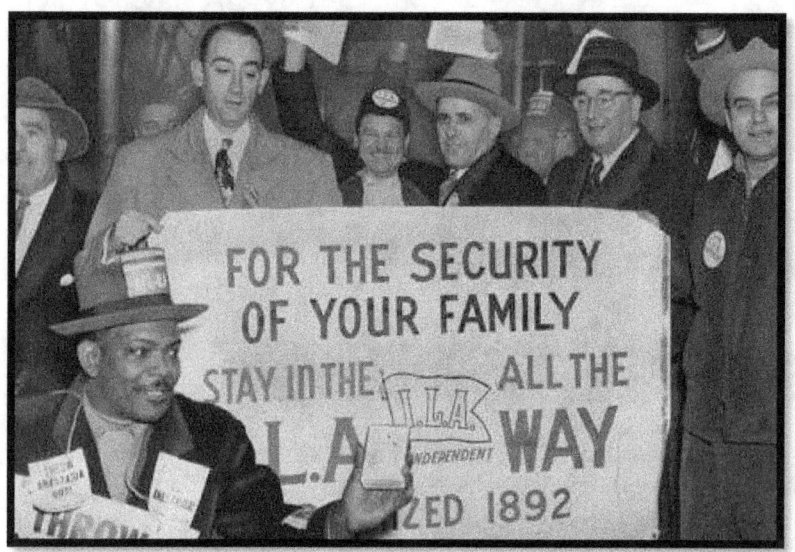

Tough Tony, center, light felt hat.

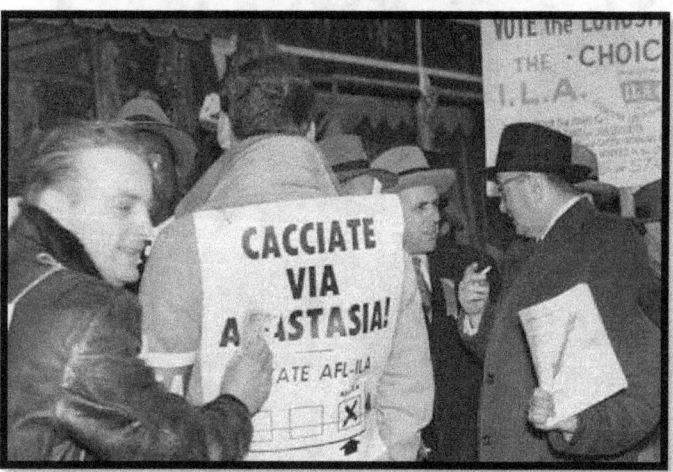

Tough Tony, to the right.

During the Second World War, Tony claimed to have arranged the sinking of the French luxury liner *SS Normande* inside New York harbor, as leverage to release Mafia boss Lucky Luciano from far away Dannermore state in prison in upstate New York, to a jail closer to the city where he could still run things from behind bars.

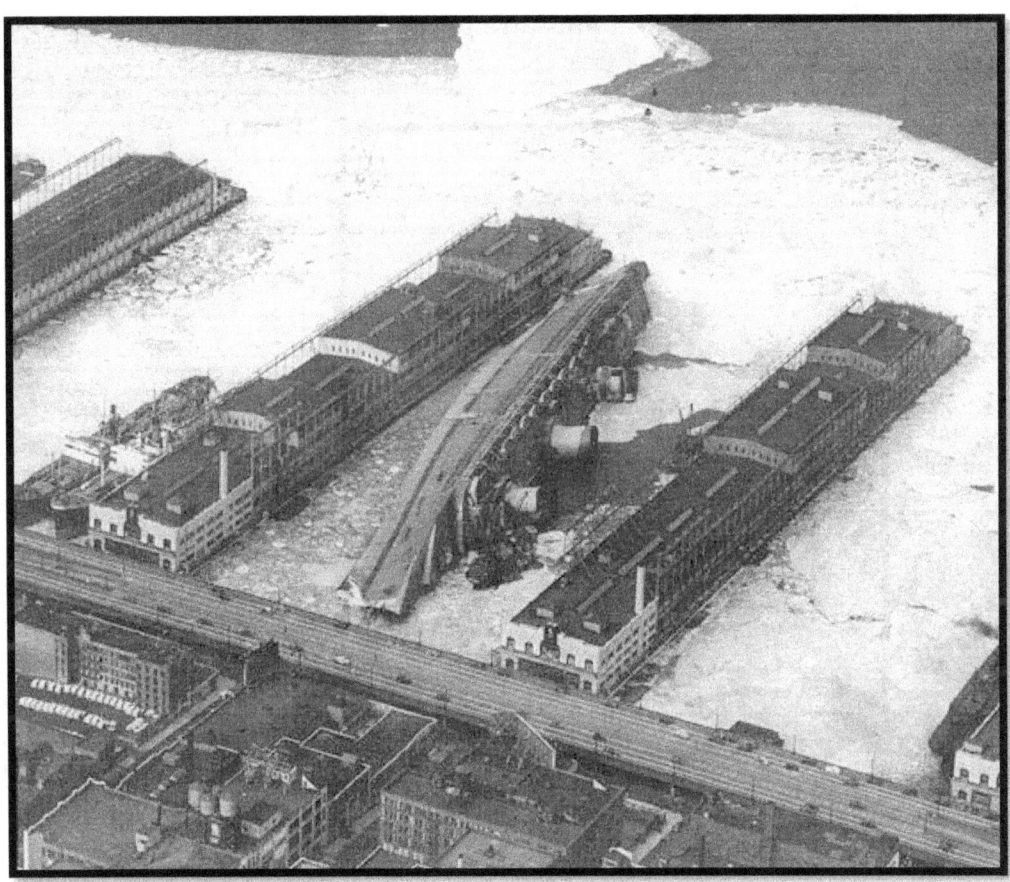

Under pressure from Naval Intelligence, New York State relented, and Luciano was released. The mob stayed to its unholy bargain and for the remainder of the war; through their help, there was never any Nazi infiltration or sabotage in the harbor.

One of the reasons that the hoods were able to run the locals with such ease was due to the high number of illegal aliens within the local. A longshoreman explained " If you have an all-Italian local and a lot of the men working there are young men who've jumped ship, may be illegal immigrants in many cases-and very likely to do what they're told".

On the Irish West Side there was Edward J. "Eddie boy" McGrath who had risen up the ranks of Irish gangdom under Manhattan's powerful celebrity gangster "Little Owney" Madden.

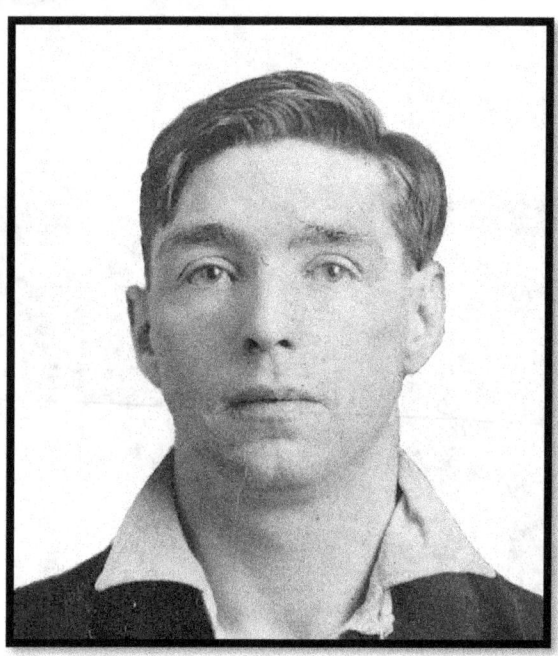

Madden

Officially, McGrath, who had a record for twelve arrests for crimes ranging from petty larceny to murder, was a salaried officer for the ILA and carried the title of "Organizer at Large", a position he was appointed to by ILA president Joe Ryan. His actual duty was front line political and police corruption and running a crew of thugs that included Johnny "Cockeye" Dunn, and Andrew "Squint" Sheridan who controlled the lucrative numbers racket throughout the port of New York.

In 1942, Dunn made a play to control the hiring on Pier 51, a massive and important dock on the waterfront. The hiring boss who ran the pier, a hood named Eddie Kelly, held out against Dunn who then called a strike against the Pier until his own man was voted into to replace Kelly. When the rigged election was over, Dunn followed Kelly to a saloon on West and 10th streets and beat him senseless. Kelly survived the beating and pressed charges, which led to Dunn's eventual conviction and return to prison.

Letters of support for Dunn came in from Adam Clayton Powell, then a powerful New York City councilman from Harlem, US Representative George Tinkham of Massachusetts and the heads of the U.S. Transportation Department. The US Army Transportation Corps also intervened and demanded Dunn's release as being vital to the war effort.

Mayor La Guardia, never a friend to the mob, called the Secretary of Defense and demanded an explanation. None was given and the Army withdrew its request to free Dunn from prison. In the end, Dunn only served two years of an eight-year term. He was released on September 16, 1944 and went back to work on the docks.   Also working under Dunn as a leg breaker was Barney Baker, a legend in the underworld who later worked for Jimmy Hoffa.

In 1937, George Donahue, a Catholic Trade Unionist, noticed several thugs at a local meeting. He approached the Local president and asked him to remove the thugs from the meeting "What?" the president asked "Are you nuts. They'll kill me"

Donahue wouldn't let it drop. He complained to ILA officials. Several days later, Barney Baker and two other men cornered Donahue on the pier and said "I'll blow your head off and throw you in the river if don't mind your own business" and then beat him up. Donahue filed a complaint with the police and Baker was arrested. Since he was on parole at the time of the assault he was returned to prison on a parole violation.

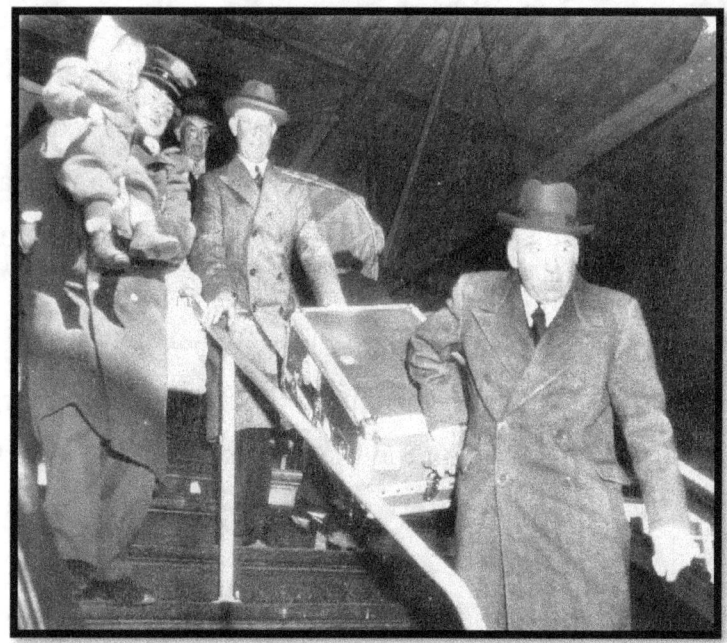

Passengers carry their own luggage during the 1948 strike

During the dockworker's wildcat strike of 1948, Joe Ryan's top enforcers, Squint Sheridan and *Cockeyed* Dunn were permanently put of business. Sheridan was given a life sentence for murder and Dunn was executed by the state.

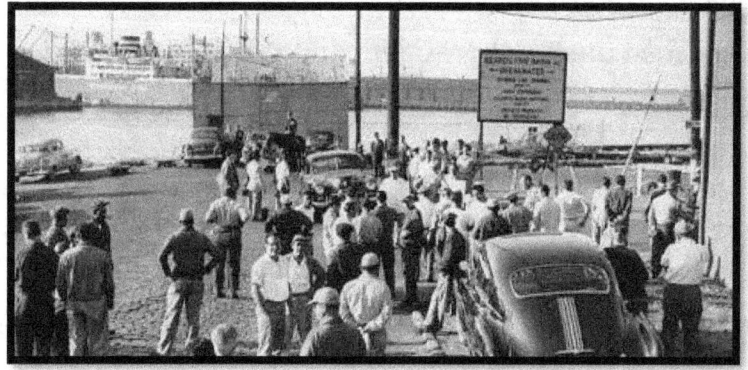

He passed up a chance to save himself when the New York Anti-Crime Commission met to investigate the origins of the strike, it subpoenaed the mobster.

Dunn, on death row, tried to work a deal that would allow him to walk free if he would name the so-called "Mr. Big" who ran things on the docks. The Commission suspected Mr. Big to be either financier Big Bill McCormick or mayor William O'Dwyer, however, the strike was settled and Dunn lost his opportunity to stay alive.

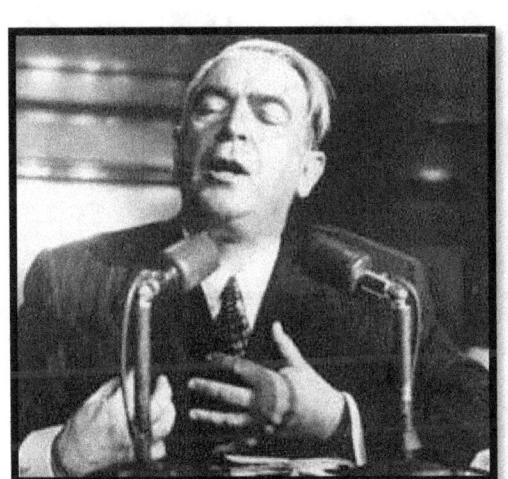 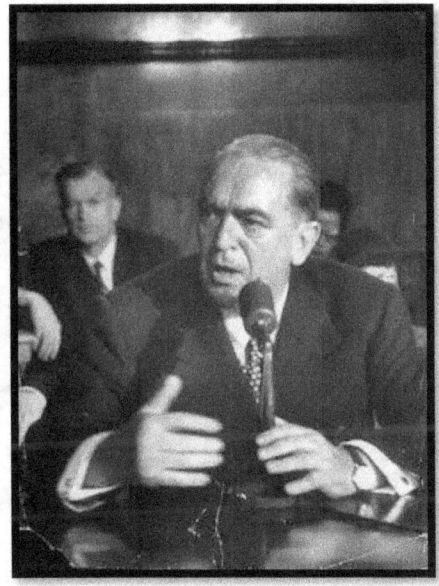

O'Dwyer

Schulberg later used a part of the incident in the film. There is one shot of a respectable man watching the Crime Commission hearings where the mob is exposed as Lee J. Cobb's character; Johnny Friendly loses control of the wharfs. Mr. Big turns to his butler and says, "If Mr. Friendly calls me--I am out."

One interesting explanation of the line "If Mr. Friendly calls I'm out" is that the line referred to New York Mayor William F. O'Dwyer, who announced, when Dunn was threatening to talk, that he would not seek re-election, although had he run he would have won.

Then on July 7, 1949, Dunn and Sheridan were both electrocuted to death and O'Dwyer changed his mind and announced that he would, in fact, run.

McGrath, aside from controlling Dunn, also controlled Mickey Bowers and his cousin, Johnny. Micky Bowers, a one-time bank robber had served a ten year prison term, and had a record for grand larceny (Three charges) assault with intent to kill, robbery with intent to kill and parole violation. Bowers had control of the so-called "Pistol local" 824 on Manhattan's heavily Irish West Side Docks whose officers included the snaked eyed Johnny Keefe, a convicted bank robber who served 12 years in prison on an assault with intent to murder charge. His other arrests included two assault charges and one for illegal possession of handgun.

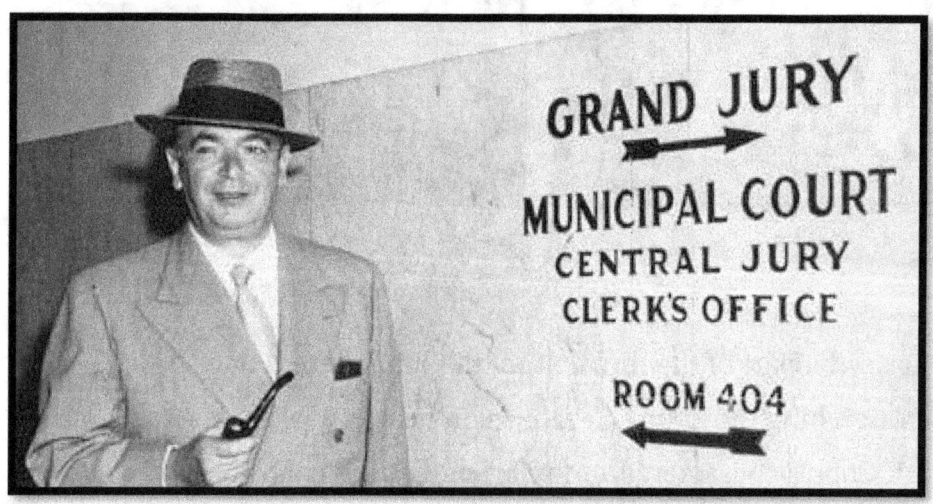

O'Dwyer

Also employed by local 824 was Johnny "Apples" Applegate, a convicted burglar who had served a term in Sing Sing and was a material witness to a homicide, and John T. "Sudden Death" Ward who had served time for carrying a concealed weapon. Controlling the Staten Island for Ryan and the ILA was Alex "the Ox" DiBrizzi, who had been convicted on 23 gambling charges.

By 1956, little had changed on the waterfront. The mob still ran the ILA. Tough Tony Anastasia punched, shot and stabbed his way into control of the Brooklyn waterfront locals as he intended to do back in 1952.

Mickey Bowers's mob was still in power along the piers, there were more loan sharks than ever before and to many persons looking for work where there were fewer jobs to be had.

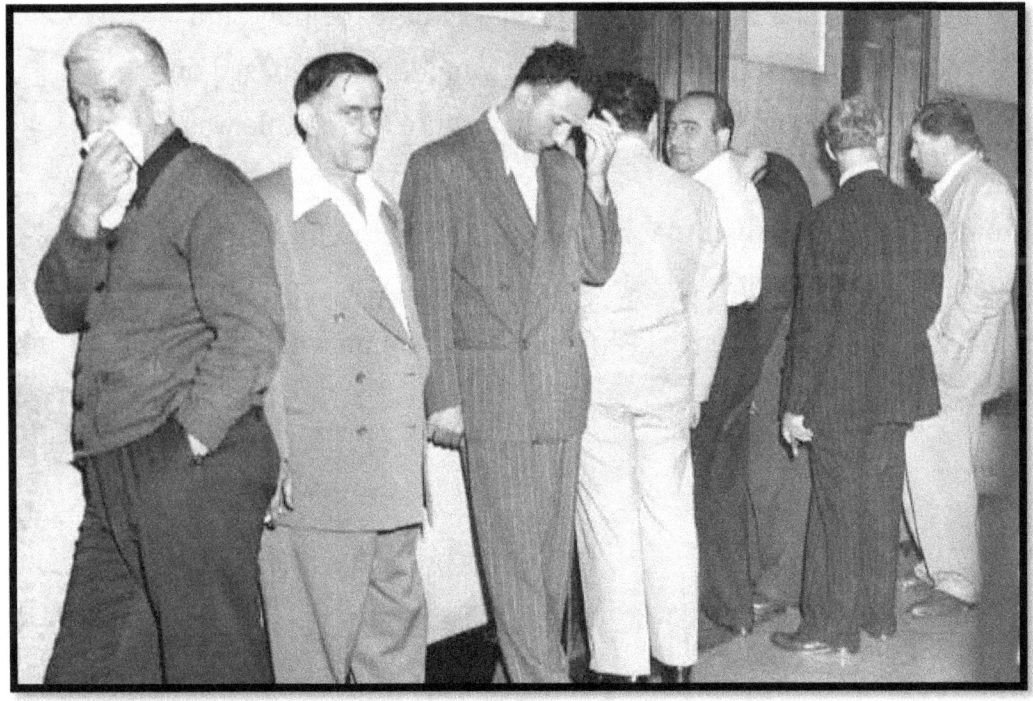

Mob bookies/loan sharks operating on the waterfront. The bookies paid a percentage to Anastasia in order to operate on the docks.

Mob Boss Albert Anastasia eventually fell from power as a result of plot-counter-plot Mafia power play. On October 25, 1957, the Gallo brothers, working on orders from the National Mafia Commission, killed Anastasia as he sat in the barbershop's chair at the Sheraton Hotel, a hot towel wrapped around his face. There were eleven people in the tiny shop, five barbers, a manicurist, three shoe shine boys and two customers who watched the two young hoods quickly enter the shop and put at least ten bullets into his head and neck.

In 1962, a year before he died of a heart attack, Tough Tony Anastasia told the FBI that his brother deserved to die "I ate from the same plate, I hate from the same table, we both came from the same womb. But my brother deserved to die. He killed to many men"

Ryan and the mob got away with it because they controlled hiring on the docks through the morning "Shape up" a humiliating process where the hoodlum connected bosses decided who would work and who wouldn't work based on the amount the hiring dockworker was willing to pay to be sure their name was called.

One longshoreman testified in 1952 that he paid the hiring foreman two dollars per week and "once in a while on Fridays--buy him a pint of whiskey [It was] more than I could afford, but in order to keep the job and support my family you got to do those things."

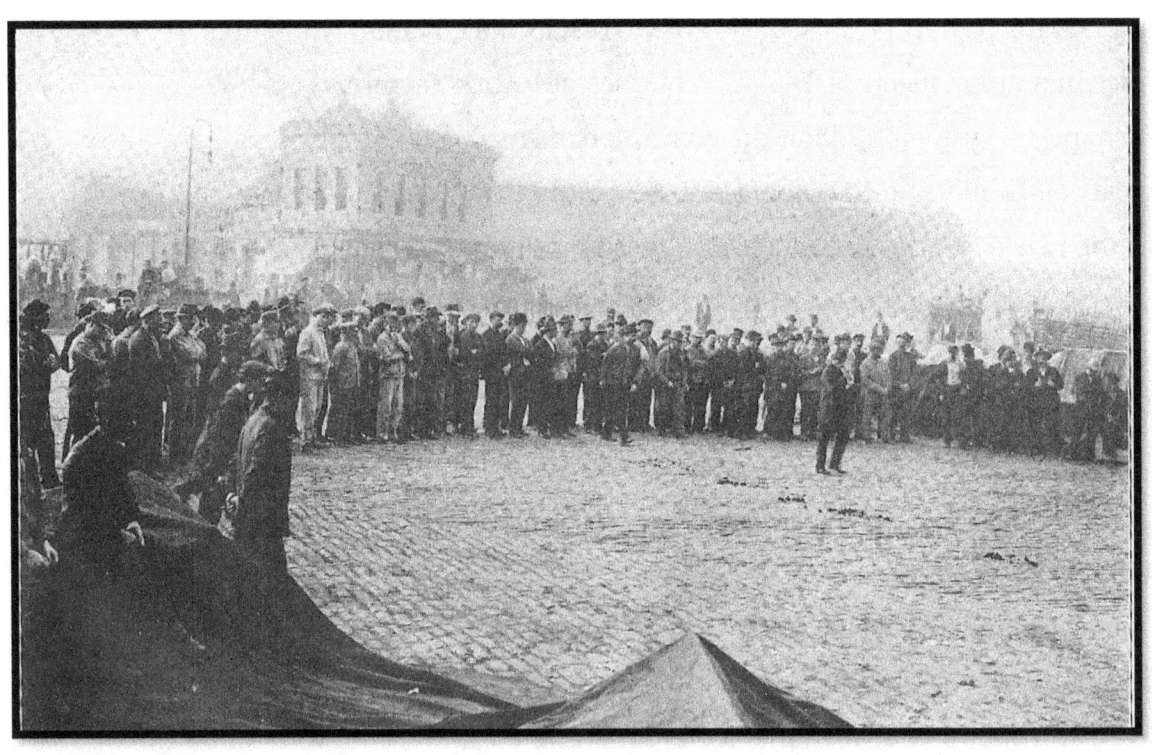

A Shape up at Chelsea Piers, New York

The Shape up's, where between 75 and 150 longshoremen were huddled into horseshoe formation in the cold morning air, been exclusive to the New York docks. There was no shape up for longshoremen on the west coast. Joe Ryan and the ILA not only allowed the shape up's to continue; they actually sanctioned them because the shape up gave the union its power. Through shape up's the locals controlled who was hired. Any longshoreman, or even any member of his extended family, or caused trouble for the union or the hoods, was overlooked at the shape up. He didn't work.

An attorney representing rank-and-file longshoremen testified in 1948 to the Senate Committee of Labor and Public Welfare that a union leader successfully maintained his power "because he is able to discipline any man who dares to raise his voice in a union meeting.... That man does not work anymore."

The shape-up system, built on the guarantee of surplus labor, also made for Job insecurity "I think" said the Chief Counsel for the ILA, Louis Waldman "this is one of the rare exceptions in modern industrial relations to have men come to the employer's establishment [each day] and make themselves ready and willing to work with no obligation on the part of the employer whatever to take them. You will find that". Another testified that "99 out of a hundred times... names were submitted to that hiring boss before the men go to the shape-up. You pretend to shape-up...and the other fellows waiting there think they have a chance. But they don't."

Shape up's were also used to justify the hiring of "Ghosts", fictitious names given the hiring boss to call. Each week the wages of the fictitious worker were collected and split up between the hoods and union officials who were in on the scam. In one typical case, Timmy O'Mara, a boss loader, regularly collected the wages of a non-existent longshoreman named Ross whose pay totaled $25,000 for the period 1943-1951. The shipping company, who paid the wages, knew about the scam but continued to pay O'Mara to guarantee labor peace. Commercial extortion was another moneymaker on the waterfront. In the summer of 1948, the mob and corrupt officials called the ILA out on strike against the powerful New York Daily News, whose management had refused to pay a tribute of $100,000 on newsprint being brought in from Canada. The mob/ILA

Countered by demanding one dollar a ton on all newspapers shipped into the city. The paper still refused to pay and eventually had their shipments brought into the port of Philadelphia and then trucked to New York. Over the next two decades, other firm's doing business on the docks followed suit, leading to the eventual demise of the largest, busiest port in the world.

Union leaders also took money from the membership by selling "charity tickets" to non-existent events. Those who refused "might find he couldn't get work, or he might get kicked around. A man soon gets the idea; he doesn't refuse more than once."

Mob loan sharks were everywhere and were so powerful, that they were able to demand the workers' pay card, the device used to pay the workers, to collect there Loans. The sharks took out there percentage from the pay (Which was usually in cash) and then turned the balance, if any, over to the dockworker. A mob loan of $100 cost $360 in interest, paid weekly.

One of the few changes on the waterfront that came after the war years was standard use of the sling load, or the standard measure of cargo in the sling, which was increased with the introduction of heavier bearing winches.

Before the war, Longshoremen worked with a one-ton draft, or 2,240 pounds. After the war, there was no limit. The results were that most men over age 30 couldn't handle the weight on a continuous basis and the heavier sling loads increased the threat of serious injury one hundred fold, in part because there were no safety provisions and in part because of rotten ropes that frayed and broke, sometimes causing tons of cargo to land on three or four longshoremen at once.

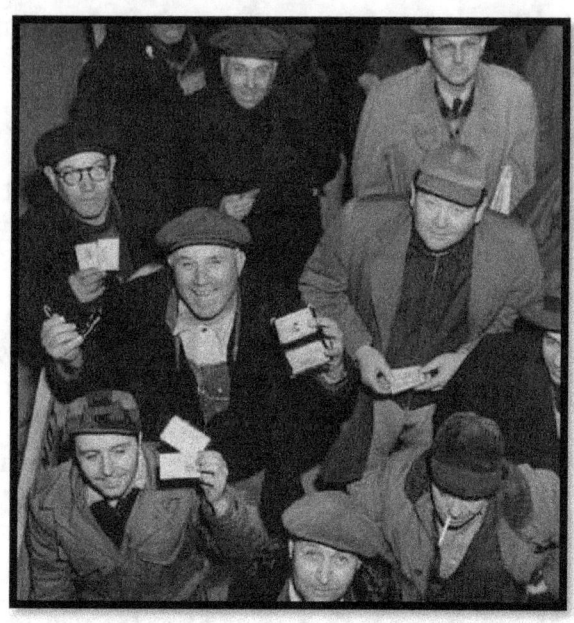

Longshore workers hold their Pay Cards

As a result, Long shoring held the dubious distinction of being the most dangerous occupation in the nation. Hernias, falls, cuts, fractures and death were common, in fact, expected, on a daily basis.

This was the world that Father John Corridan stepped into in 1948, a demoralized and extorted work force, mob control of one of the nation's largest ports and a hopelessly corrupt and violent union. Corridan was determined to bring the situation on the waterfront to light and decided that the murder of Andy Hintz was the vehicle he needed to press his case.

Ten months after Cockeyed Dunn and his men murdered Andy Hintz, Malcolm Johnson of the New York Sun newspaper began investigating Hintz murder and penned a piece about the 1948 strike as well as the general situation on the waterfront.

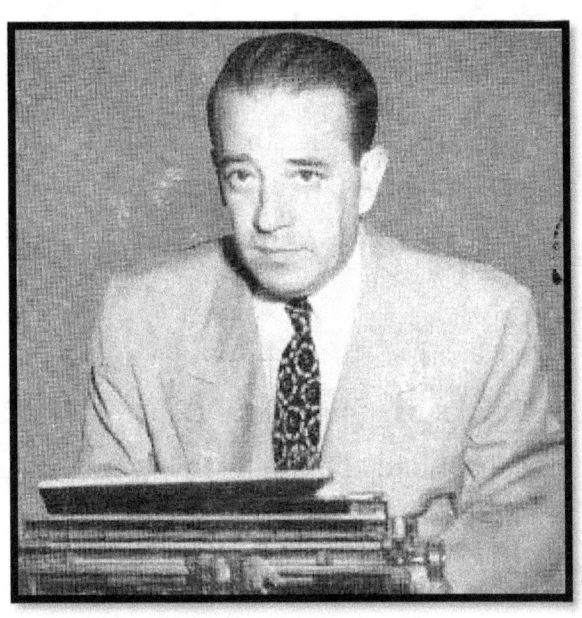

Malcolm Johnson

Corridan read the Sun piece and contacted Johnson's editor by letter in November of 1948. Corridan, a former salesman, had been very successful in bringing the plight of the longshoremen to the media. He had managed to have pieces written in the *World Telegram, Fortune Magazine, The New York Post, The New York Times, Look Magazine, Collier's, Jubilee, True Detective, Life Magazine, the Readers Digest* and the *Brooklyn Eagle*. He had also been covered by CBS, NBC and ABC news.

The editor at the Sun turned the letter over to Johnson "You'd better go on over and contact this guy, he seems to know what he he's talking about"

Malcolm Malone Johnson, called Mike, hailed from Gainesville, Georgia. He left Mercer University in 1924 to start work as a newspaper reporter *The Macon Telegraph*. Four years later, he wrote a series of articles on criminal activities of the powerful Klu Klux Klan in Toombs, County. An editor at *The New York Sun*, heard about the piece and hired Johnson to come and work the metro beat in Manhattan.

In New York, Johnson covered most of the big stories of the day, including a popular Broadway and Nightclub column. In the early 1930s, he was one of a handful of reporters who met in Heywood Broun's apartment to found the Newspaper Guild of America.

At the outbreak of World War Two, the *Sun* made Johnson its Pacific theater correspondent. He covered the invasions of Iwo Jima, Okinawa, the first task force raids against the Japanese mainland and finally the Japanese surrender aboard the U.S.S. Missouri. Months before, he had been one of the first newspapermen to tour Hiroshima after the atomic bomb was dropped there. He returned to the Pacific again in 1946 to cover the atomic bomb tests at Bikini Island.

After meeting with Corridan, and using the priest's considerable contacts on the waterfront to establish his leads, Johnson penned a series on the ILA, the Mob, Joe Ryan, the Communists and their influence on the little known world of the waterfront. There had been other media pieces on the waterfront, but Johnson did what no other reporter had ever done in the past when writing about the waterfront, he named names, *Cockeye* Dunn, Eddie McGrath, Johnny Applegate, *Big Moe* Nizich, *Richie the Bandit* Gregory, *Socks* Lanza and Charley *The Jew* Yanowsky, Albert Anastasia and Meyer Lansky. He detailed criminal records and outlined the control the mob had over the ILA and the ILA had over the longshoremen.

In the days prior to the public's understanding of the Mafia, Johnson explained, in an understandable way, how the cash taken from the waterfront financed mob owned investments across the United States and how the various Mafia family's ran narcotics, gambling, prostitution and smuggling throughout North America as a result of controlling the ILA and the waterfront.

Writing the series and naming names was fraught with danger. Even though he worked for a major metropolitan newspaper, by no means whatsoever was Johnson or any of his family safe from a beating, a maiming or murder by the mob. In broad, very general terms, the mob in Chicago had decided that policemen and reporters were exempt from retribution from doing their jobs, in so long as they were honest. The New York-New Jersey Mob, however, had no such understanding with the upper world. Everyone was fair game when it came to self-protection as national columnist Victor Riesel found out.

In 1956, Riesel, an acclaimed journalist who specialized in labor affairs, was one of the nation's leading reporters. His column was syndicated in almost 200 newspapers nationwide and his opinions were highly regarded from the White House to Wall Street.

On April 5, 1956, Riesel appeared on a national radio program and revealed the abuses of the Long Island based Local 138 of the International Union of Operating Engineers and its leader, William DeKoning, who had just been released from state prison on an extortion-threatening charge. After the program, Riesel walked to Lindy's restaurant on 51st street and left at about 3:00 A.M.

As he walked along the street, a hood named Gondolfo Miranti fingered Riesel to 22-year-old Abe Telvi, who walked up to the reporter and tossed a vial of liquid sulfuric acid in his face and eyes that left Riesel blind for the rest of his life.

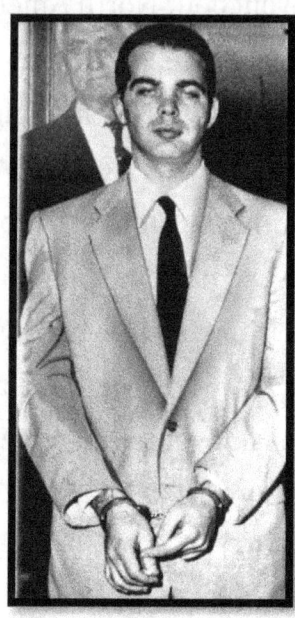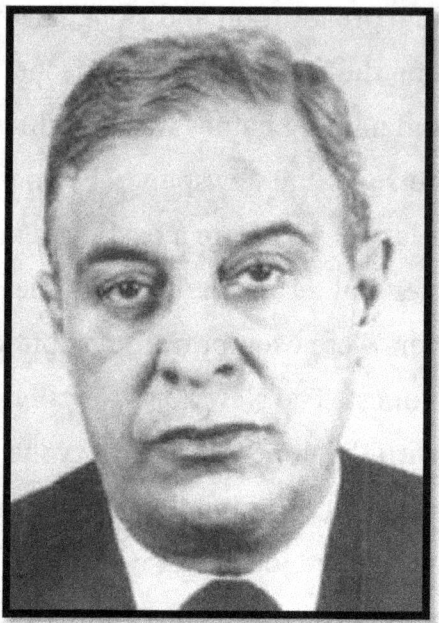

Telvi and Johnny Dio

According to investigators, Telvi was paid $1,175 for assault by Lucchese family garment district labor terrorist Johnny Dio, who promised the Telvi he would bring him into his organization if the job was done right.

The blinding caused a national incident and eventually polices Miranti and another hood that was involved in the plot. Both agreed to identify Dio as the hood that gave the orders for the attack by changed their minds before the case went to court. However, police did learn that Dio had allegedly ordered the assault to please Teamster boss, Jimmy Hoffa. Telvi, who may not have realized who Riesel was when he blinded him, he demanded more from Dio. On July 28, he was shot to death on the Lower East side of New York.

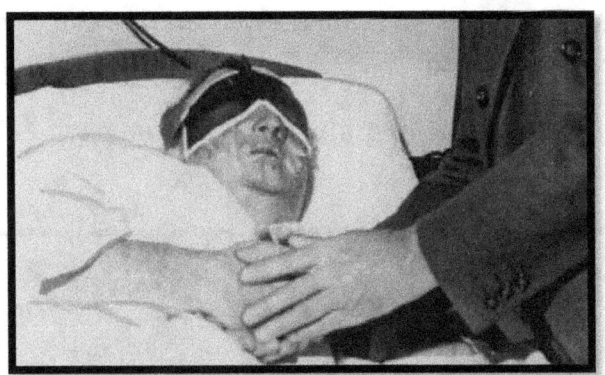

Riesel after the attack

The Malcolm Johnson series sparked no less than nine investigations into the waterfront, most of them little more than whitewash, although some brought a few indictments and jail terms for small time hoods along the docks. It did have some immediate positive results however. Among other things, the series made the waterfront a hot political issue in an election year.

In the meantime, the Priest continued to conduct his labor-unionism classes at the Xavier School. By the end of first semester, each of his classes was filled And the mob started to send informants to the school to watch Corridan and take the names of anyone else who appeared there regularly. Eventually it became unsafe for longshoremen to attend the classes and more often than not, the longshoremen had to sneak in through a back door to avoid being seen by informants and union enforcers.

Once, after Corridan found a pair of thugs waiting outside the school, he told them "If anything happens to the men I'm trying to help here, I'll know who's responsible, and I'll personally see to it that they are broken throughout this port. They'll pay and I'll see that they pay. Now get lost"

Corridan's openness campaign was starting to take effect. In January of 1949, Johnny Dwyer, the leader of the rebels from pier 45 went to Father Corridan for help and advice. Several months after Corridan arrived on the waterfront, in the winter of 1948, there was a wildcat strike, caused by a contract, signed by Joe Ryan, which involved sling loads, the shape-up, and overtime payments.

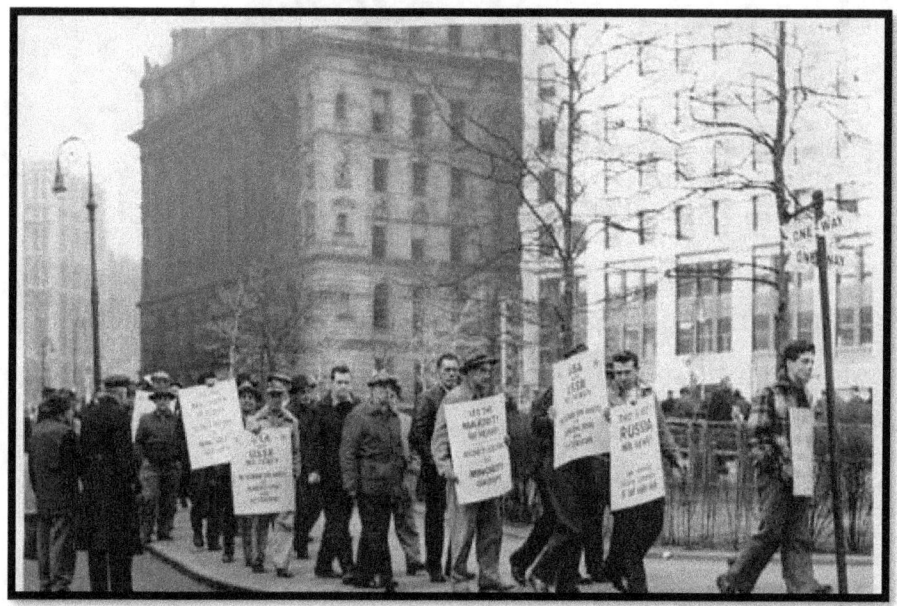

The year before the strike, the rebels and their attorney, paid for by the Communist party, inaugurated a series of suits demanding back pay owed through the 1938 Fair Labor Standards Act, which established that regular working hours on the docks would be from 8:00 A.M. to 12 M. and from 1:00 P.M. to 5:00 P.M.

Any work time over those hours, was over time, or paid at a rate of time and a half. However, under Ryan's rule, most longshoremen work a 12 hour day, some as many as 14 hours, all of it at regular pay rates.

The lawyers and the Communist saw the overtime issue as a means to cut into the ILA's power, sued on behalf of the longshoremen and formulated Back Pay Committees in Brooklyn, Hoboken, New Jersey, and Baltimore.

Father Corridan, recognizing the Communists leadership of the strike, traveled to Washington to meet with Harry Truman's labor advisor John Steelman, explaining that if the strike was successful, the Communists foothold on the docks would be secure. The strike, Corridan argued, needed to be averted (During the meeting, Joe Ryan, who must have been informed of Corridan's visit through his intelligence network, phoned Steelman and tried to talk him. Steelman refused the call.)

Steelman turned the problem over to Cyrus Ching, Director of the Federal Mediation and Conciliation Service, and Corridan filled him in on the tense situation on the docks. Ching did nothing and a day later, on November 10, 1948, strikes erupted on the waterfront in Boston, Philadelphia, and Baltimore.

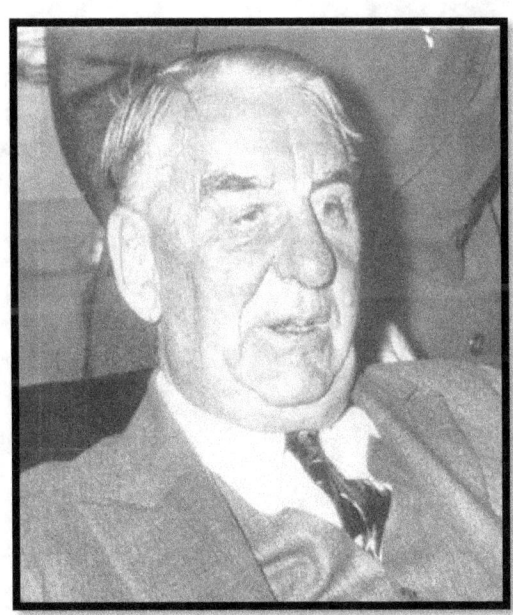

Ching

As a result of the strikes, which were well executed, Joe Ryan, lost considerable amount prestige within the international labor industry and the mob. With no other choice left, he declared the strike legal and joined the walk out, enabling him enough time to dismantle the rebels from within.

The true strikers, the rank-and-file, were relegated to meeting in bars and on street corners to further organize the strike. But, at best, they became a scattered force and as a result were unable to organize and formulate their demands, especially after outside pressures brought on by the ILA and federal government, chased the Communists organizers from the picket lines.

Twenty-six days after the strike had erupted, the federal government had secured an agreement giving the men a thirteen-cent raise, vacation time, and a welfare fund.

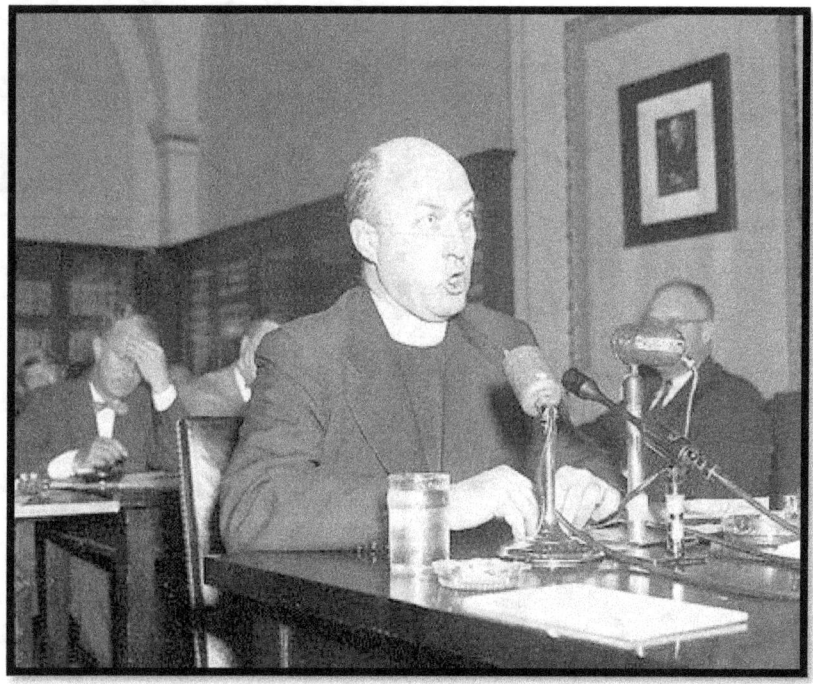

Corridan testifies

The rebels accepted the agreement and returned to work the following day.

Corridan didn't see the end of the strike as a victory for the workers, but for the Communists, "The stench rising out of the waterfront" as he called them, and predicted that with more victories, even minor, they would eventually take over the docks, or at the least push out the labor schools and any chance of an effective union.

As he saw it, the only answer was to rid the waterfront of the ILA and the Mafia. When the strike ended, Corridan began a campaign to urge Congress and the State of New York to investigate the waterfront conditions. Appearing before the U.S. House Committee on Education and Labor on June 15, 1949, Corridan contended that reform could "be brought only by a Federal and State investigation resulting in remedial action."

Much to his annoyance, he had to share the Congressional stage with Communist activists. Frustrated that they're to many voices pretending to speak for the Longshoremen, Corridan and one of his followers, Christy Doran, created a newsletter, *The Crusader*.

"It had to be" the Priest said "underground. At the outset I didn't even want people generally to know where it was put out. I didn't want the longshoremen associated with me to become masked men. I used to evade some questions as to where publication office was and who was putting it out. It was real cloak and dagger stuff. The paper we used was without a watermark and we never bought it twice at the same store. The typewriter we used was never used for any other job...we mailed from different parts of the city so they couldn't trace back the mailing office"

Corridan and followers, working with a very limited budget mimeographed the single sheet publication that was published bi-weekly and mailed it out to 500 longshoremen.

By 1953, the newsletter was being sent out to 3,000 longshoremen, politicians and newspaper reporters. The most damaging aspect about the newsletter, which was written in slang and local lingo, was that it named Joe Ryan's informers who were operating on the waterfront, the names provided by Corridan's intelligence network on the waterfront, rendering the squealers useless.

Much to Father Corridan's delight, Joe Ryan immediately called *The Crusader* "A Communist publication from top to bottom, a real product of Moscow, let me assure you " and that the paper was put out under the guidance of "a religious fanatic with communistic leanings"

The tiny paper annoyed Ryan so much that he commissioned the creation of a counter paper, The Longshoremen's News "At least we accomplished that much" Corridan said "Ryan and the mob were beginning to have to use propaganda of their own to keep their own men in line. The guns and blackjacks weren't enough anymore"

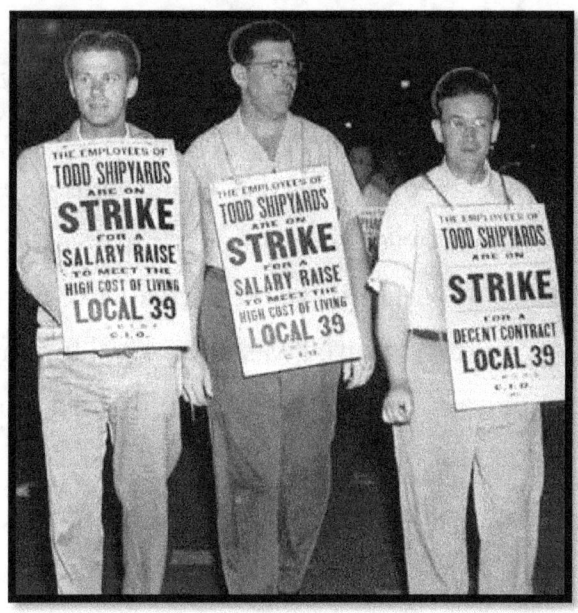

Now, a year later, the priest advised Dwyer and his men to pitch another wildcat strike. Instead, he argued them to take the problem public in a meeting, if they did that, he assured them, he would get Malcolm Johnson to cover the meeting. Dwyer agreed and a public forum was held at St. Veronica's parish on the waterfront. Corridan sent out invitations to the media as well as to Joe Ryan and Big Jim McCormack and Mayor O'Dwyer. They all declined.

At the start of the meeting, Teddy Gleason, an ILA officer in three locals. He had served a term in Sing Sing. His record included arrests for receiving stolen property, attempted robbery, assault with intent, robbery and illegal possession of a machine gun.

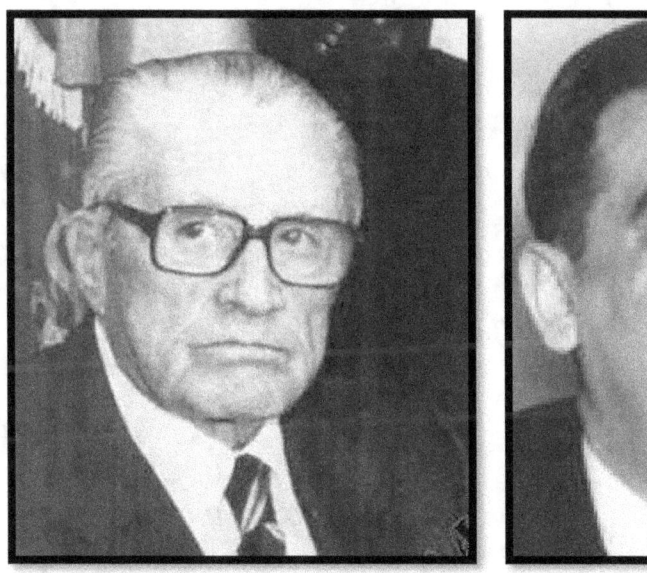

Teddy "Steady Teddy" Gleason, (left) later President of the ILA and O'Dwyer

He worked directly under Joe Ryan, was the first to speak, defending Ryan and the ILA. While Gleason was in mid-sentence, Johnny Dwyer stood up and denounced Gleason as "A stooge not only for Ryan but for Big Bill McCormack the waterfront czar.... I'm walking out and everybody who agrees with me can follow me out"

As promised Johnson covered the story on the front page of the New York Sun. That same afternoon, Mayor O'Dwyer called the rebel longshoremen into a meeting at city hall. The next day Johnny Dwyer and his crew were running the pier under police protection and the ILA hoods were gone.   It was the beginning of the end of the mobs control over the waterfront.

THE HOOK
SPRING 1951

"By whatever means it is accomplished, the prime business of a play, a story, is to arouse the passions of its audience so that by the route of passion may be opened up new relationships between a man and men, and between men and Man. Drama is akin to the other inventions of man in that it ought to help us to know more, and not merely to spend our feelings." **Arthur Miller**

He was a causality of his time and a victim by his own design and it all happened in less than 48 minutes. It also happened at the worst possible time. It always does.

Elia Kazan, an artist who had always sought greatness and approval, was riding higher than he had ever dreamed he could. His screen production of *A Streetcar Named Desire* and his Broadway presentation of "All My Sons" and "Death of a Salesman" had earned him a fortune, given him his much sought after fame and made him a living show business legend.

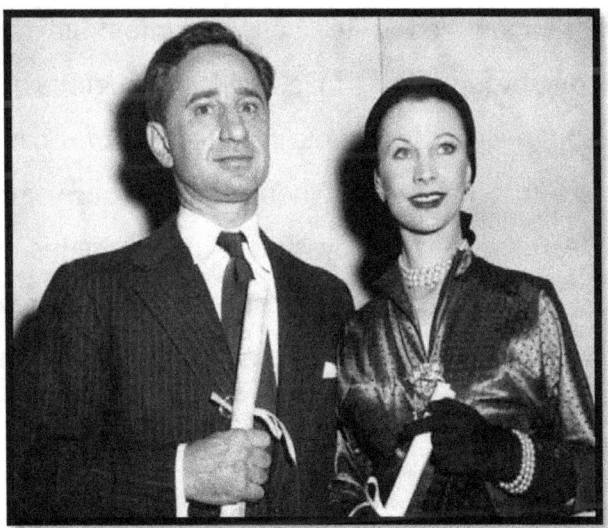

Kazan and Vivien Leigh hold the New York Film Critic's awards they won for A Streetcar Named Desire. January, 1952

Then it all collapsed around him. He named names before the House Committee on Un-American Activities, effectively telling the committee what it already knew; the names of writers, director, producers in Hollywood who were members of the Communist Party or who had expressed sympathy with the Communist view.

Until the day he died, he claimed that this one small act, in a long and glorious career, had brought him peace of mind but the truth is, that 48 minutes before an ancient government microphone in a dimly lit room, would torment him for the rest of his days. Kazan would remain a man haunted by the ghosts and conflicts of his past that were as real as they imagined, a man who used those images to create his greatest work, *On The Waterfront*, a masterpiece film based in an iconoclastic political essay whose artistic message is still being heard, still being debated, still evoking emotions and passions.

****

Elia Kazan was born Elia (pronounced Ee-lee-yah) Kazanjoglous on September 7, 1909, in Constantinople, one of four sons of George Kazanjoglous and Athena Sismanoglou, both Anatolian Greeks whose roots reached back for centuries to the village of Kayseri in rural Turkey. In 1913, when Elia was four years old, the family immigrated to the US and settled in New York City, where his father became a rug merchant working under his older brother who had already Americanized himself from Avraam-Elia Kazanjioglou to A.E. Kazan, otherwise known simply as Joe Kazan.

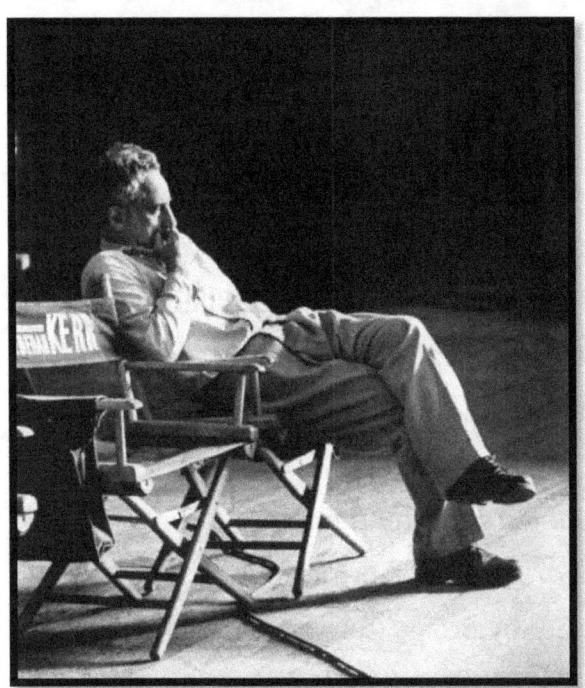 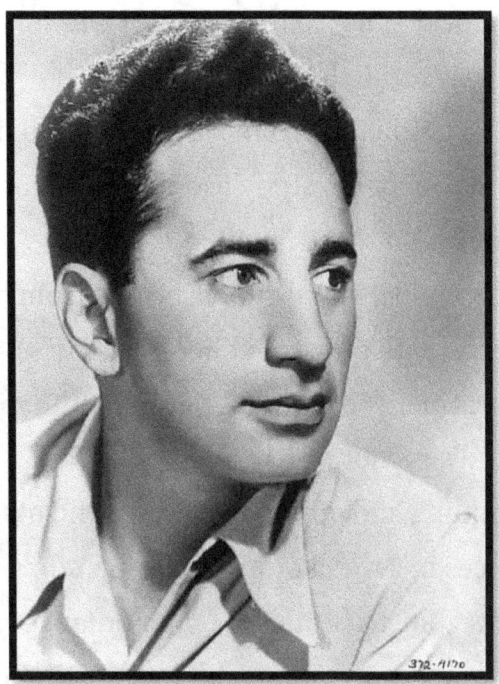

Elia Kazan

Together the brothers eventually founded the prestigious George Kazan Inc. Oriental Rugs & Carpets, the preeminent provider of imported carpets to New York's wealthy set. During the summers, Elia worked in the store, rolling out carpets for customers and other menial tasks. Otherwise, he attended local public schools in New York City and later in suburban New Rochelle, N.Y., without distinction.

Elia grew to fear his, father, a base character with a brutal side who nicknamed his shy and intelligent son "Mister. Good for nothing." Despite his constant badgering of his son, the father expected that after high school, Elia would enter the family's continually prosperous carpet business. When his wife told him husband that their son had decided to attend Williams College in Massachusetts, a decision the father had not been a part of, his response was to punch her in the mouth, knocking her to the floor.   It was moments like that and his endless sarcasm that scalded his son like acid.

After Elia graduated from college and told his father that he was entering the Yale Drama School to study acting, his father's response was 'Didn't you look in the mirror?'

All of the child's moral support came from his mother who encouraged her son's creative side with or without her husband's approval. Elia would willfully carry those resentments and memories with him for the rest of his life, setting the stage in his mind's eye forever.

A demanding and oppressive father and a troubled son would make appearances in several of his films, including *Waterfront,* where Johnny Friendly is the protagonist's brutal and manipulative father by proxy. Conversely, each of his films would present an understanding and encouraging female tossed into the rough-hewn shadow of a crude and remorseless man or surroundings.

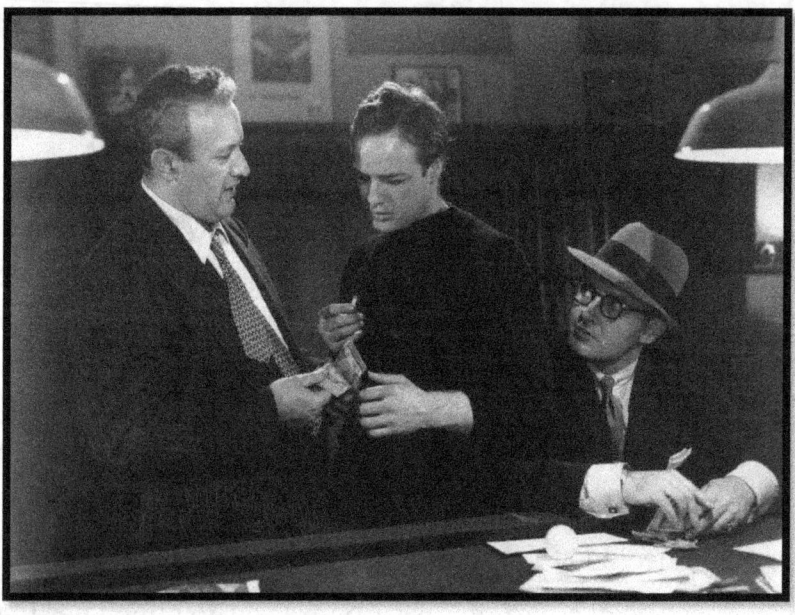

****

Thanks largely to the efforts of his mother; Elia grew into an energetic and optimistic young man with a genuine care for those around him, an eye for women who found his honesty and sensitivity charming. To help pay his tuition at Williams College, he waited tables, washed dishes or tended bar at the Greek fraternities who barred him from membership because, oddly enough, he was Greek.

After graduating cum laude, he entered the Yale School of Drama and returned to New York after graduation where he joined the progressive and left leaning Group Theater as an actor and assistant stage manager. At the time, the group was one of the focal points of artistic life and radical thought and activity in New York City.

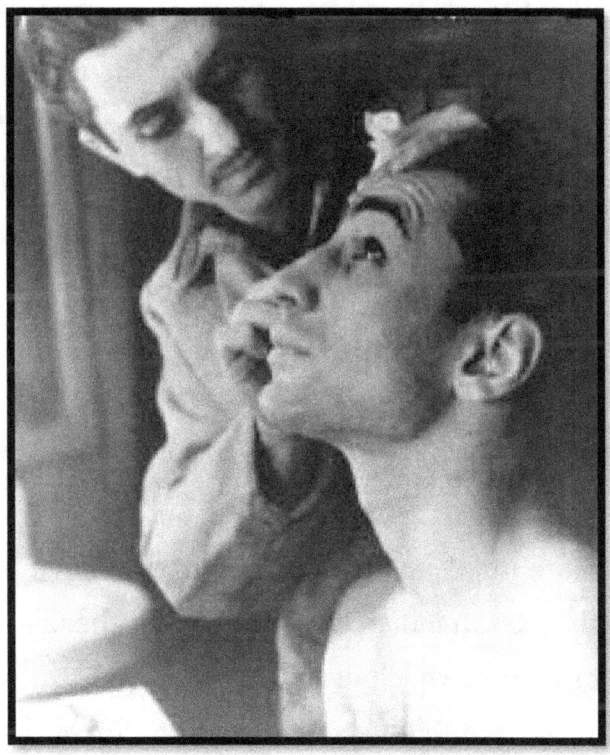

Kazan in makeup at the Group Theater.

It attracted the best actors and directors, as well as a variety of writers who specialized in the Stanislavsky's Method form, in which the actor is experiencing internally the emotion he is to emulate onstage, relating the character's feelings to his own experience.

Although Kazan was an eager disciple of the practice, he took on another theory, embodied by the actor Osgood Perkins, in which in acting and film creation, there is no emotion only skill. Unlike many in the art, Kazan understood that while both forms...the psychological and the professional (Technical).... were strong, if the two forms were combined in the right hands, the result would be magical. And in his hands, it was. That, the emotional and technical, melded together would become his trademark in filmmaking.

Although never even a remotely handsome man, despite his staggering success with woman, Elia considered himself acting material and in the 1930s, talked his way into several small roles in a dozen plays, including *Waiting for Lefty* (1935) and *Golden Boy* (1937) by Clifford Odets and *The Gentle People* by Irwin Shaw (1939)

****

"All of a sudden I had a family of people that worked in the same way and had the desire to reveal themselves." **Kazan**

At that time, in the mid to late 1930s, the Group Theater contained a small but influential communist cell that Kazan joined. At the time, for the practical and overly ambitious Kazan, it probably seemed like a logical move because he saw the tightly knit group of armchair communists as a means to forward and guide his theatrical career.

The Theaters communist cell was made up by the best the group had to offer, and no doubt, exclusivity and snob appeal, always-strong attractions in Kazan's life, played a larger role in his decision to commit to the party's ideals then did a radical change in the core values of this rug merchant's son. In fact, throughout his life, Kazan always made it clear that he was highly dedicated to fat paychecks, dual coastal mansions and the privileges that came with being a card-carrying member of the artistic elite.

While the Group Theaters Communist group was lofty and idealistic, the national American Communist Party was an authoritarian, iron fisted organization determined to succeed. Controlling the influential Group Theater fit into that goal and the leadership ordered Kazan (and others in his cell) to seize control of the Group. Kazan refused, in part because of his ideals that theater and art were sacred and in part because he was headstrong and simply had a lifelong problem with authority.

He was denounced by the national party, no small thing at the time, and ordered to repent and submit to party authority. He resigned instead and so ended the young man's foolish 17-month association with the communist party. It was a small, youthful, meaningless side journey in a long and fascinating life that he would pay for in the years to come, very dearly and very deeply.

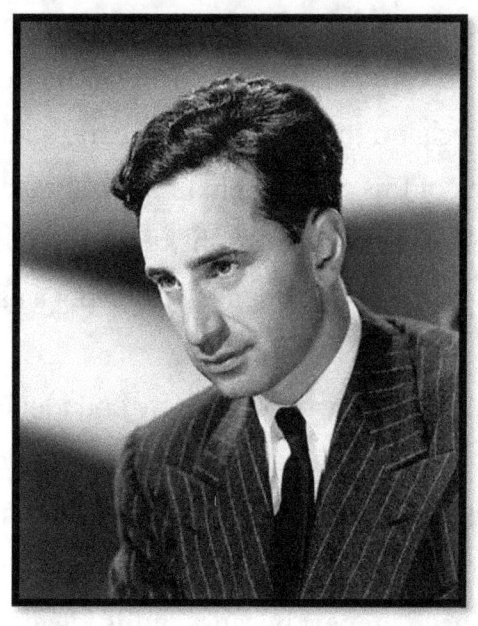

*****

He became one of the founding members of the Actor's Studio, a place where thespians could grow and develop their craft with the psychological awareness that was increasingly needed for the plays that were dominating Broadway Theater.

It was here, that Elia began directing more main line, commercial plays winning critical notice for his energetic delivery of the popular comedy, *Cafe Crown*. More success came with *The Skin of Our Teeth*, with Tallulah Bankhead, Florence Eldridge, Frederic March and Montgomery Clift. The play was a huge box-office hit, won a Pulitzer Prize and brought Kazan his first New York Drama Critics' Circle Award for direction.

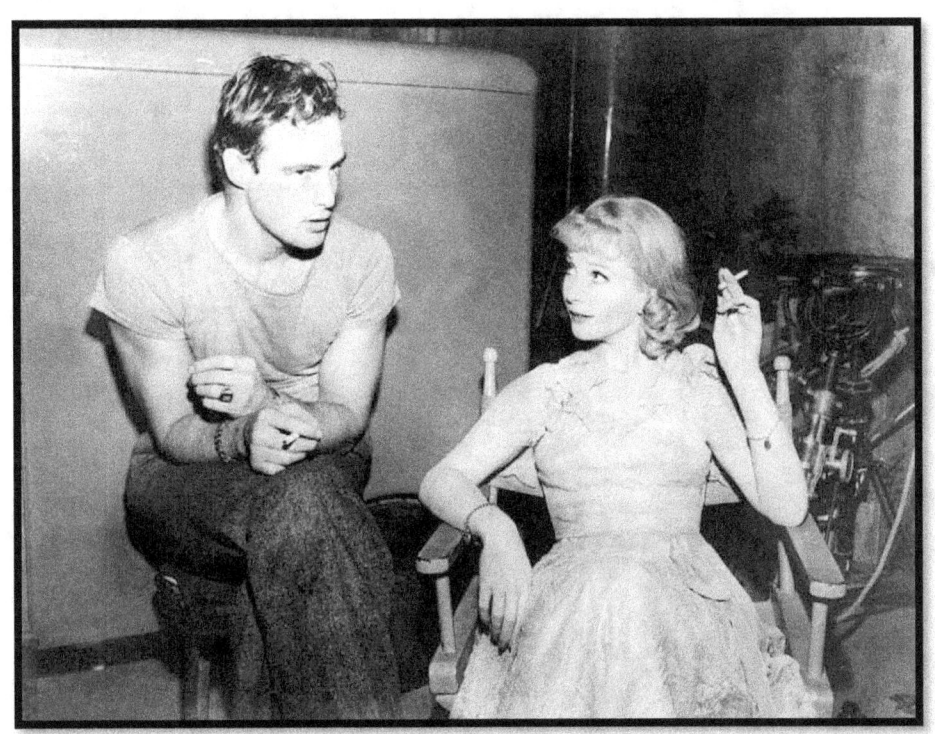

Brando and Vivien Leigh pause for a smoke on the set of A Streetcar Named Desire

After *The Skin of Our Teeth*, he became a major force on Broadway through his collaborations with Arthur Miller and Tennessee Williams. His strong direction of two of Miller's plays, *All My Sons*, and *Streetcar Named Desire*, established Kazan as Broadway's preeminent director and made a star of 23-year-old Marlon Brando who was largely a Kazan discovery. He followed these successes with another powerful theatrical milestone, Arthur Miller's *Death of a Salesman*, with Lee J. Cobb as Willy Loman.

Having conquered the stage, he turned his considerable talents to the silver screen as a director. (His first work was a forgettable film called *The People of Cumberland*).

Occasionally, in his salad days, Kazan employed himself from time to time as actor, first with a bit role as a character named Googi Zucco in the 1940 Cagney film *City for Conquest* and then *Blues in the Night* (1941) as a bit character named Nickie Haroyen.

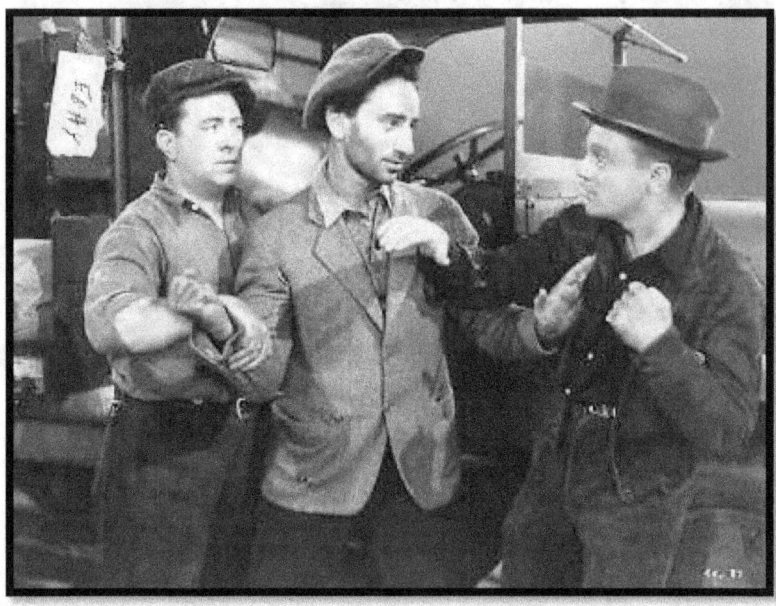

With Cagney in *City for Conquest*

Kazan had also taken a role in the 1935 independent film short called *Pie in the sky* made by the left wing *Public Theater* during the depression.

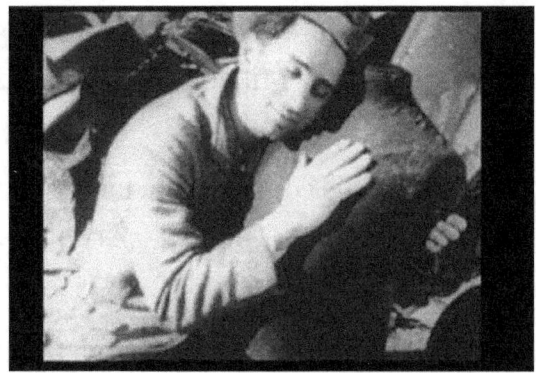

Kazan in *Pie in the Sky*

His first major film as a director, in 1945, was *A Tree Grows in Brooklyn*, a tale about a working class Irish family coping with poverty and an alcoholic father. (Kazan had attended Yale with Betty Smith, the books author.) The film won James Dunn an Academy Award as best supporting actor.

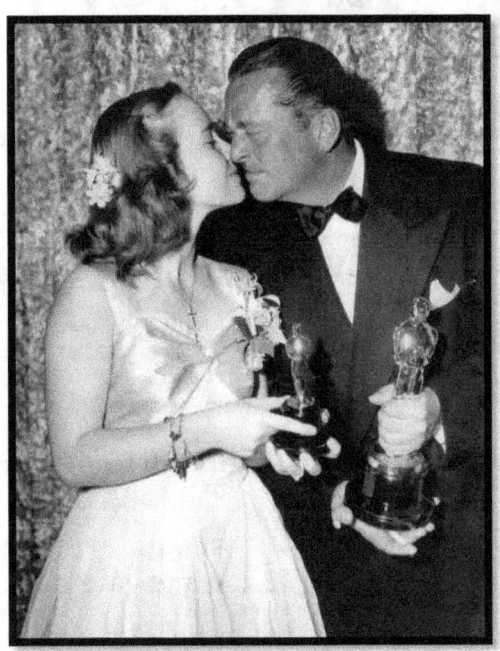

Peggy Ann Garner and James Dunn with the Oscars they won for A Tree Grows in Brooklyn

He followed with *Gentleman's Agreement*, starring Gregory Peck, which won Kazan an Oscar, beating out George Cukor (*A Double Life*), David Lean (*Great Expectations*), Henry Koster (*The Bishop's Wife*), and Edward Dmytryk (*Crossfire*).

Gentleman's Agreement was a creation of Fox Studios boss Daryl Zanuck, one of the first films to deal with the subject of anti-Semitism. Zanuck, who was not Jewish, admitted to having commissioned the film over his deep regret for making the remarkably racist *Ham and Eggs at the Front* (1927) with Myrna Loy who was also disgusted with herself for being aligned to the project.

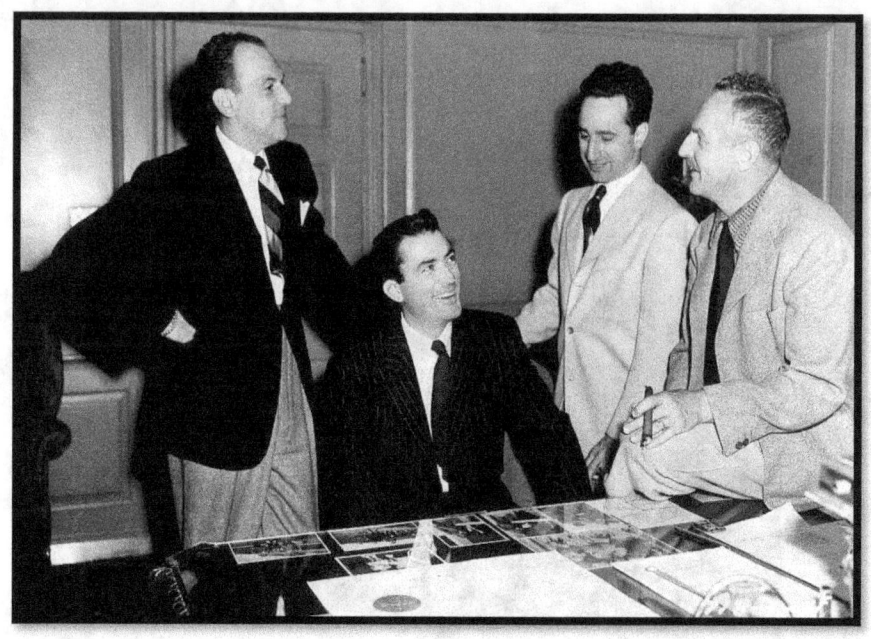

Kazan (third from the right) and Darryl F. Zanuck (fourth from the right) on the set of Gentleman´s Agreement

The film was a major project for the young Kazan and gave him a chance to work with Gregory Peck, who was given the lead in the film over John Garfield who wanted the lead so badly he offered to change his stage name, John Garfield, to his given name, Julius Garfinkle. However, the studio bosses, who were largely Jewish, campaigned against making the film, preferring to leave the subject alone. Instead, Garfield took a supporting role in the film at a leading star salary.

Kazan later added a scene in the film that reflects Zanuck's woes with the other studio bosses over creating the film. The movie was the top grossing film of the year and opened to wide critical success.

Based on the box office success of those works, other films followed including *Boomerang*, a 1947 thriller about small-town corruption starring Dana Andrews, Lee J. Cobb, and Karl Malden.

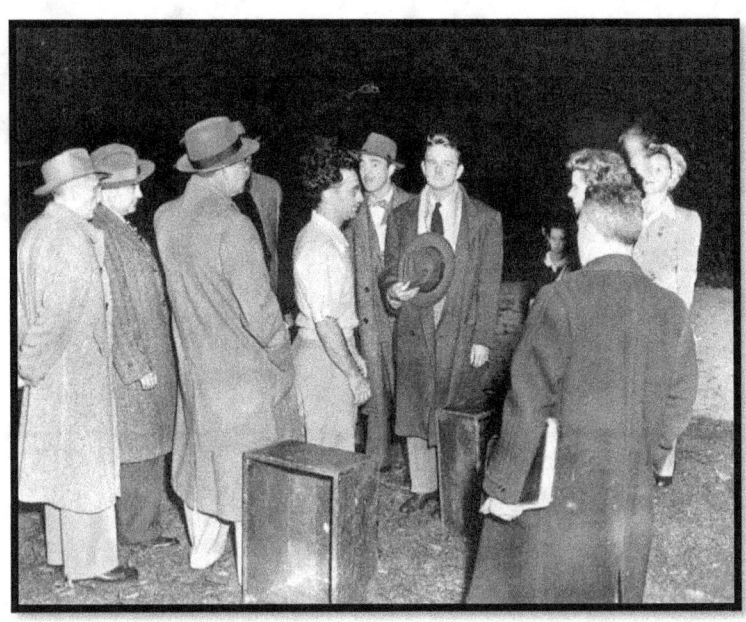

Kazan (Middle) on the set of *Boomerang*

That same year he directed *Sea of Grass*, a horse and cowboy opera with major stars Tracy and Hepburn.

This was followed by *Pinky* (1949) dealing with racism and miscegenation and was yet another atonement film by Zanuck, whom despite the best of intentions, turned down the light skinned African American Actress/ singer Lena Horn for the role of a white women. (Horn filmed much lighter than she actually was and probably could have carried the part)

Zanuck felt that America was not ready for a Black actor in a lead role that involved several love scenes with a white actor. The film did moderately well at the box office and Fox gave Kazan *Panic in the Streets* (1951), with stars Richard Widmark, Jack Palance, and Zero Mostel in a taut drama about a manhunt in New Orleans to find the carrier of a plague. Also in the film are *Waterfront's* "Tiger" Joe Marsh and Kazan who hired himself for a small role in the film as a mortuary assistant.

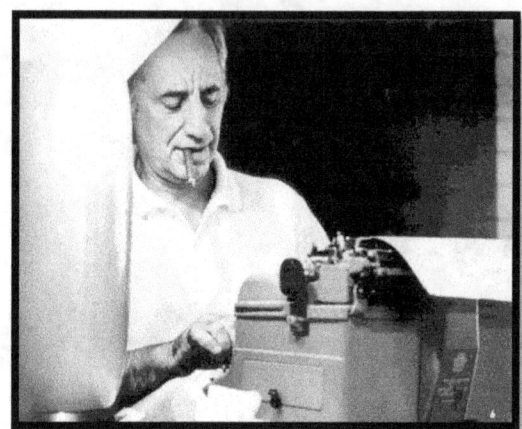 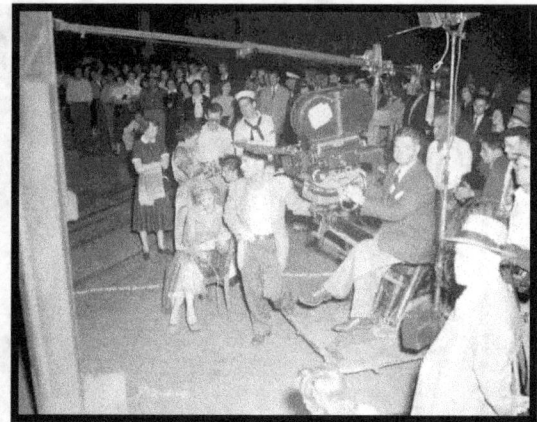

Kazan (left) and On the set of *Streetcar*

In 1951, Elia joined with Brando for the filmed version of *A Streetcar named Desire*, one of only two films in history to win three Academy Awards for acting. The studio had favored John Garfield for the role of Stanly Kowalski but Garfield did not want to take second billing to the films female lead, Vivian Lee, and passed on the role.

The part was then offered to Anthony Quinn. Quinn had played the role of Stanly on the road tour and was widely credited with delivering a stronger performance then Brando did on Broadway.

In the end, Kazan managed to get Brando for the role with the understanding that Brando would take second billing to Vivian Lee. Another Brando film followed, *Viva Zapata!* (1952) which the studio had originally pegged Tyrone Power for the lead. Following *Zapata*, a good film but a commercial flop, he directed Man on a *Tight Rope*, also a commercial dud.

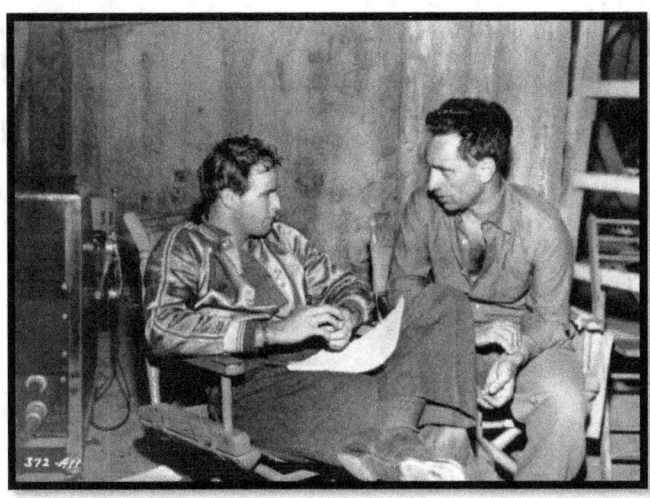

Brando and Kazan on the set of *A Streetcar Named Desire*

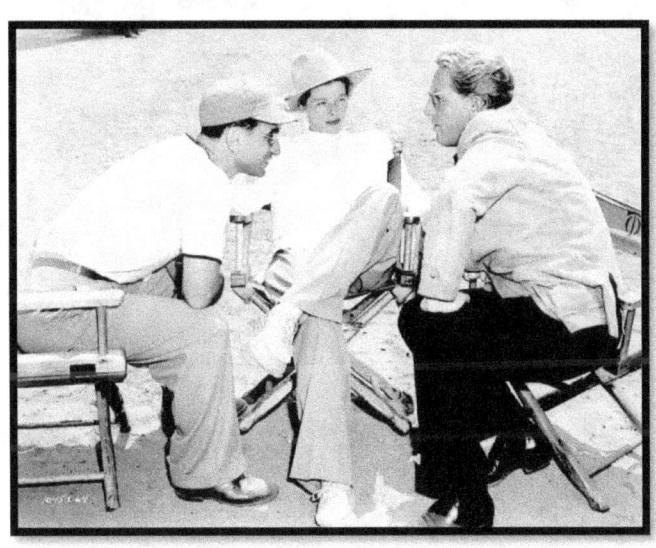

On the set of *Sea of grass*

Aside from those few snags, it was an amazing career for such a young man. Most of the time Kazan's films not only made money for the studios, they were completed on time and without problems. It seemed that everything Kazan touched, from screen to stage, even the actor's careers that he touched, turned to gold.

He had already won an Oscar and two Tony's (He would earn three in his lifetime) He was on the inside, a mover and shaker on his way to becoming a Hollywood power. What he needed to assure his lasting position in Hollywood, to fulfill his dream for greatness as a businessman and artist, was a great film, an epic, a classic. He would find it in *On the Waterfront*.

THE MIILER-KAZAN COLABORATION,
SUMMER 1950

"If I have any justification for having lived it's simply this, I'm nothing but faults, failures and so on, but I have tried to make a good pair of shoes. There's some value in that." **Arthur Miller**

In the early 1950s, the true-life dramatic events on the New York docks with its violent wildcat labor strikes and mob violence had caught the attention of hundreds of writers who saw it as an exceptional story in the making.

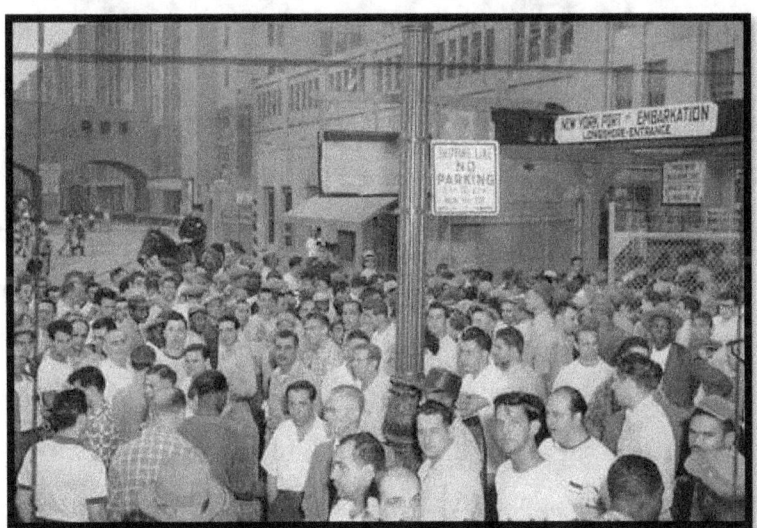

Over the next five years, the waterfront saga would spur the creation of at least three major screenplays, one novel, and four nonfiction books and four local, state and federal investigations. Among those watching was Kazan's close friend, confidant, and sometime business partner, playwright Arthur Miller, who was at the pinnacle of his career. In early 1950, Miller approached Kazan with the idea of filming a treatment he had written called The Hook, which followed a loner named Marty, a longshoreman who battles the mobs control of the docks.

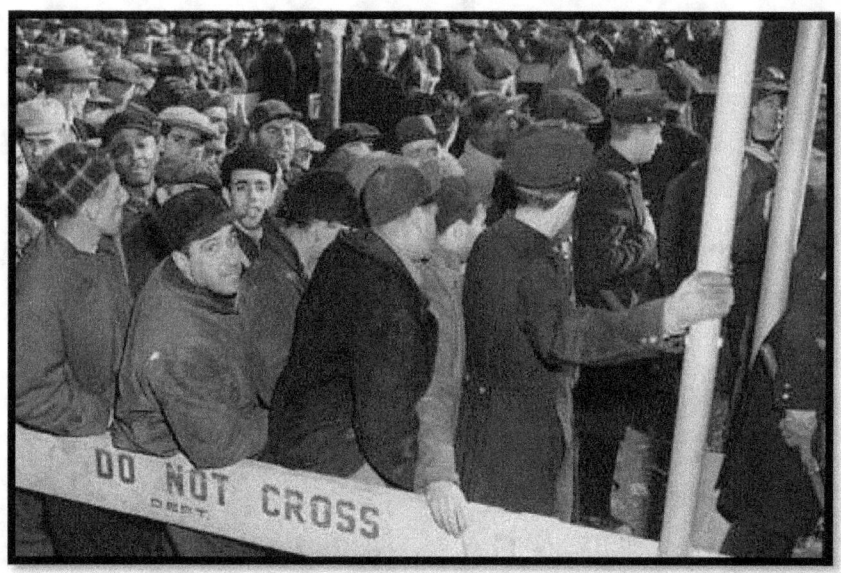

Miller had taken the idea for The Hook from the 1947 waterfront murder of labor activist Peter Panto. Miller recalled: "I knew two guys who were trying to organize a movement in the longshoreman's union, which was notoriously corrupt and completely under the Mobs control. They were trying to organize a counter-movement in the union, at grave danger to themselves. In fact, the preceding organizer ended up murdered by the union. I lived in Brooklyn Heights, on Willow Street, and I see signs all over the place, chalk signs, saying "Dov'é Pete Panto?" (Where is Pete Panto?)

Panto was that he was a self-appointed labor leader on the Brooklyn waterfront, perhaps a communist, and was effective enough to raise the anger of the Mafia boss Albert Anastasia. Burton B. Turkus, who had been Assistant District

Attorney for Kings County (Brooklyn), wrote "In mid-summer 1939," Turkus and Feder wrote, "Peter Panto was waging a determined war against gangster rule on the water front. For months, he had been whipping up the longshoremen to shake off the mobster grip. Panto was only twenty-eight... 'We are strong,' he urged the union men. 'All we have to do is stand up and fight.

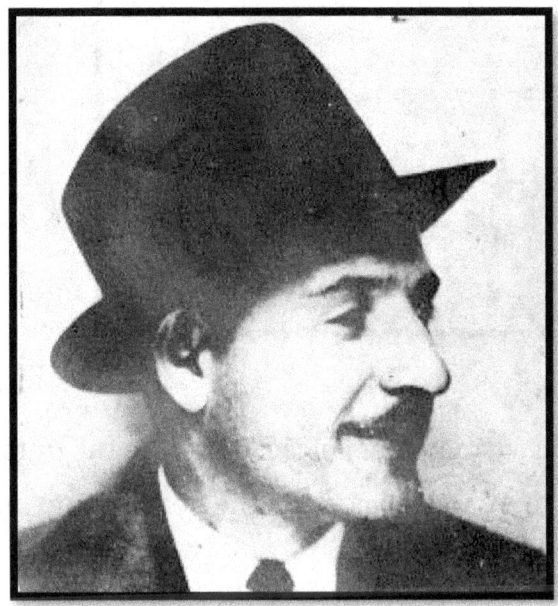

Panto

Panto's fate was sealed after he called a meeting of ILA local 929 on July 8, 1939, attended by 1,250 members, where Pantos insisted on an honest election for the local. The Longshoremen stood to their feet and cheered him as the Mafia's enforcers looked on, stupefied.

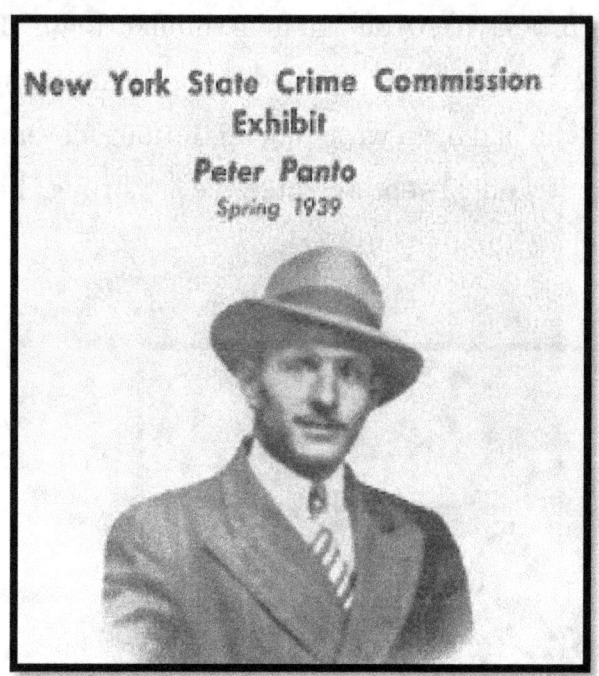

New York State Crime Commission
Exhibit
Peter Panto
Spring 1939

   On Friday July 14, Panto was visiting his fiancée, who bore the unfortunate surname Maffia. At 10 p.m., there was a knock on the door. Panto answered it and then stepped outside to talk to two men.

   According to Organized Crime contract killer Abe Reles, the men insisted that Pantos come with them to meet union officials who wanted to offer him cash to leave the docks. When Pantos refused, he was beaten, tossed into a car and driven to an isolated spot.

   Although Panto's was slight in build, weighing less than 163 pounds, he fought the gangsters and according to Reles, nearly biting off the finger of killer Mendy Weiss before he could be overpowered and strangled to death. He was covered in quicklime and buried in a New Jersey lot.

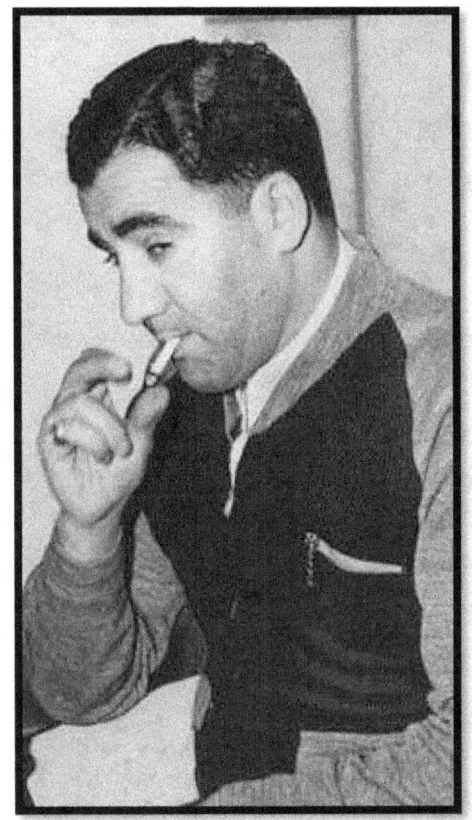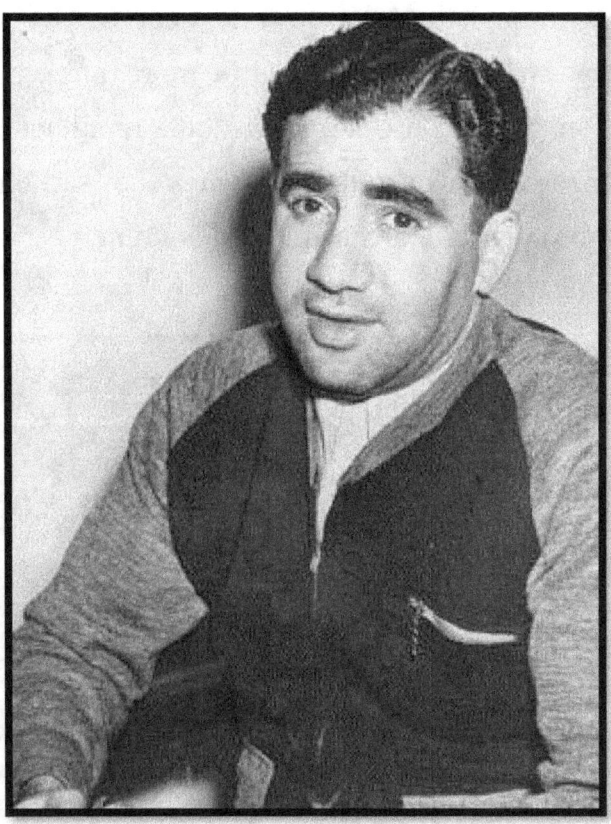

Reles

Kazan and Miller, both part-time New Yorkers, were following the waterfront events through in the New York Sun newspaper written by reporter Malcolm Johnson.

There had been other media pieces on the waterfront, but Johnson's story did what no other reporter had ever done when writing about the waterfront, he named names, detailed criminal records and outlined the mobs control over the dock workers union, the remarkably corrupt International Longshoremen's Association, the ILA.

The twenty-six part, Pulitzer Prize winning series, entitled "Crime on the waterfront" was followed by a second, equally damaging series also written by

Johnson. Although the Johnson series sparked no less than nine investigations into the waterfront, most of them little more than whitewash, for the most part, the battle on the dramatic New York docks remained an east coast story. Kazan and Miller recognizing a great story when they saw one decided they would retell the longshoremen saga on an epic scale in film.

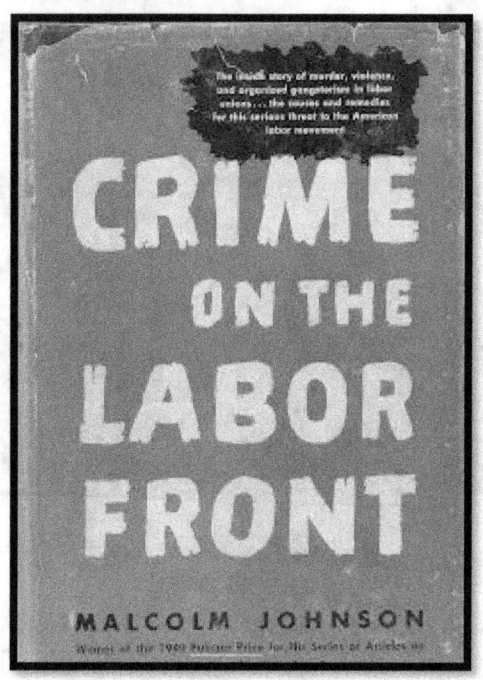

It was a plausible notion. Both Miller and Kazan were at the apex of their careers. Their works were almost guaranteed moneymakers and, as Kazan continually pointed out to the studios, the waterfront was a film ready story.

A film-ready story of not, as far as the Hollywood studios bosses were concerned, the events on the waterfront happened at the wrong time in history. The cold war mind set had gripped the nation and Hollywood was high the list of right wingers who saw the film community as holding a lenient, soft, view of the communist menace.

A story about unionism, a subject tinged with leftist themes, had no place in the film industry in the early 1950s. There was something else wrong with the waterfront story; it was not glamorous. It was the direct opposite of glamorous, it was dreary and miserable and blue collar a subject that Hollywood had never warmed too.

As Budd Schulberg said when it was his turn to introduce his version of the Waterfront to the studios "Having been raised in Hollywood, and knowing its reluctance to embrace blue-collar, hard-hitting material, I had my doubts" Hollywood wanted what the public wanted after the war years, cheerful escapist films with uplifting themes and vibrant colors not moralistic stories about oppressed workers and half-crazed gangsters.

Kazan knew that of course, he was an inside Hollywood player but he was tired of the genre he had helped to create through maudlin heart wrenching tales A tree grows in Brooklyn or high handed moralistic quasi-dramas like *Gentleman's Agreement*. He wanted to create something with social merit, something with meat on its bones and despite what the studios believed Kazan felt strongly that a film like Waterfront would work.

Even before Miller approached him, Kazan had been working on a draft that was similar to the unfolding story on the waterfront, this one about a Jewish garment manufacturer, a one-time gangster, who was working to free the industry of hoodlums. He had shopped it around and studios liked it but the concept died at birth after it was learned that Kazan intended to hire a communist screenwriter, Walter Bernstein to pen the script and hire communist actor, John Garfield for the lead. Both Garfield and Bernstein had refused to testify before the House Un-American Activities Committee (HUAC) looking into communist influence in American films and both were bound to be blacklisted within the year. It was something Kazan should have considered since his new creative partner, Arthur Miller, was not far from being blacklisted himself.

Working on a 30-page draft of Miller's concept for the waterfront film, Kazan enthusiastically encouraged Miller to complete the work, which he did by January of 1951. However, the completed draft fell far below Miller's usual high standards and they both knew it. Even after several rewrites, the script was still lacking. Miller may well have been the best stage writer of his time but the nuances of screenwriting seemed to escape him. There was also the factor that Miller simply did not understand his subject. Still Kazan felt that as weak as the work was in its artistry, the overall theme was good. He decided that could sell the work to the studios based on their joint resumes.

It did not quite work out. When Fox Studios President Darryl Zanuck read the Miller script, he recoiled. Perhaps as a means to stay out of the project while not angering two of the most creative men in the business, Zanuck turned the script over to the FBI for review. As he expected, the Bureau suggested that he pass on the script because it might foment unrest on the docks and hamper the war effort in Korea.

Undaunted, Kazan brought the script to Harry Cohn at Columbia Pictures. While Cohn probably shared the same doubts about the script as other film executives, he also understood that Kazan and Miller were moneymakers. As for the annoying themes in their latest work, would do what he always did; agree to the everything the creative side wanted, sign the deal and then do everything his way. It usually worked.

*****

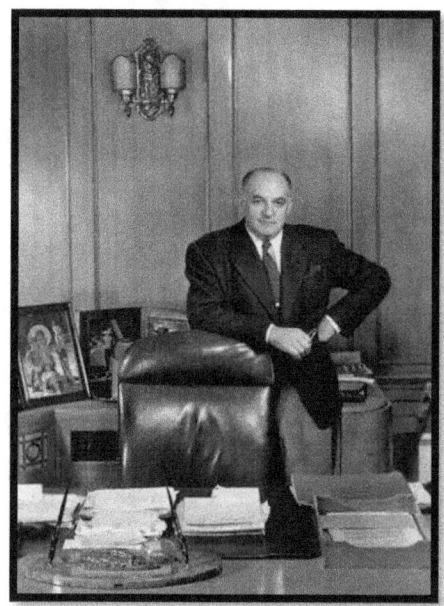 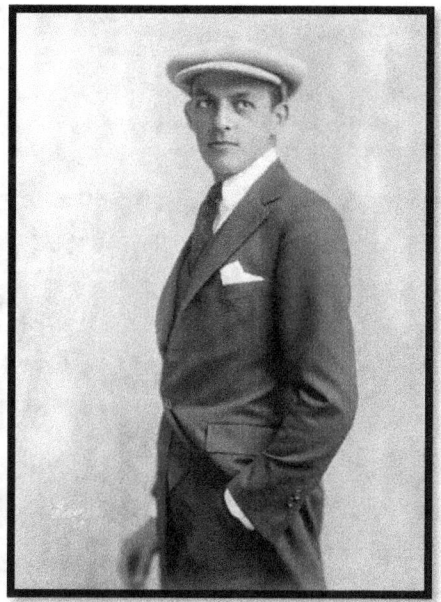

Harry "King" Cohn, a nickname he had given himself, crawled his way up from the streets to fabulous wealthy and success but the streets never left him. He made his first bit of extra cash with composer Harry Ruby when they had a hot with *Ragtime Cowboy Joe.*

In 1918, while his brother Jack, was working at Universal Pictures, Harry hustled his way into a job as a secretary-assistant to Universal's president, Carl Laemmle.

In 1920, the Cohn's and friend Joe Brandt struck out on their own and formed C.B.C. Productions, a film company that churned out one-reel comedies and questionable documentaries. While the industry looked down their collective noses at C.B.C, the fact was that the company was profitable.

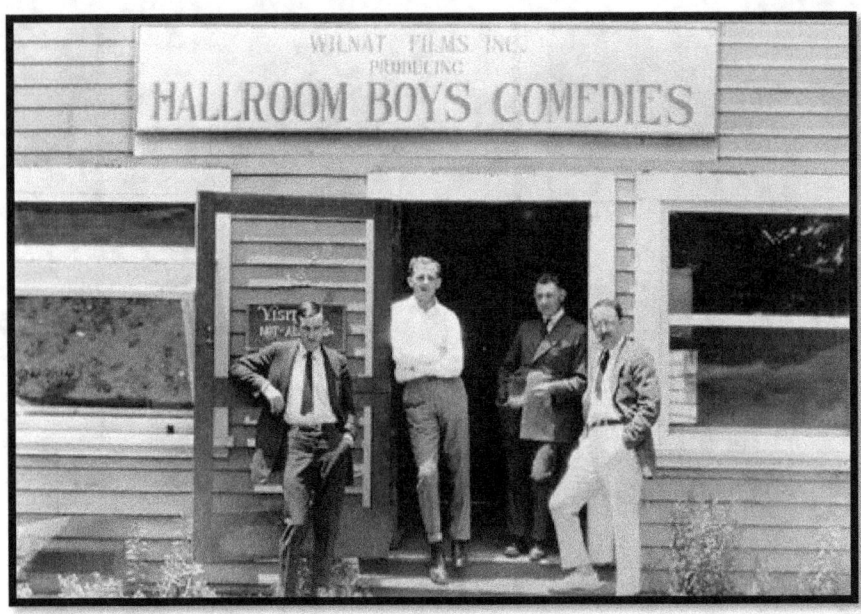

Harry and Jack Cohn on Poverty Row as producers

Columbia Studio's was born in 1924, when the Cohn brothers and Brandt bought a tiny film studio and an adjoining apartment building in a run-down part of Los Angeles.

The new company used inexpensive talent and cut corners at every possible turn and gave the people what they wanted. That, compounded with Harry Cohn's ability to get great distribution for his films, made Columbia one of the few studios to turn a profit during the Great Depression.

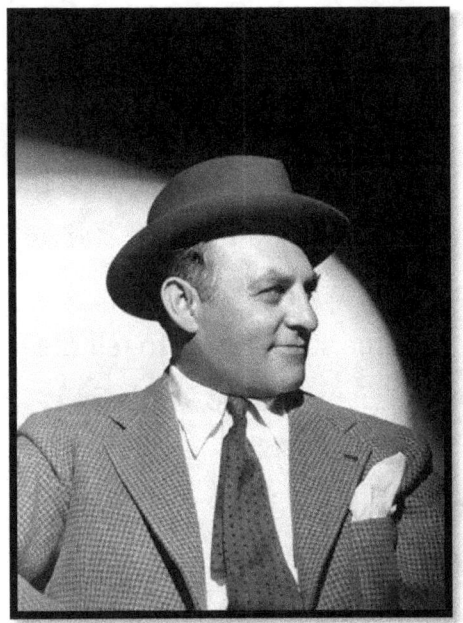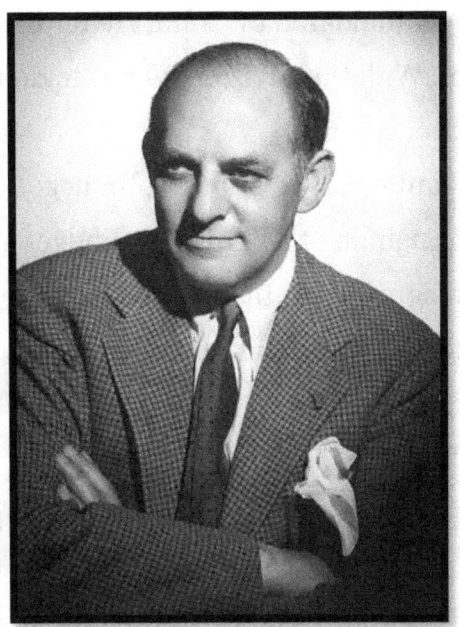

Cohn

He was intentionally rude, crude and vulgar and regaled in his own ignorance and his ability to offend, so much so that director Charles Vidor took him to court for verbal abuse.

Cohn's unpopularity was legendary. One story had it, that when he died, the studio ordered its employees to attend his funeral for fear that no one would attend.

Looking at the lines of dismal mourners one acted quipped, "See? Give the people what they want, and they'll come!" a take that was Cohn's maxim on filmmaking. For all his faults, Cohn helped to create some of the finest films in history, including *Waterfront, The Caine Mutiny, From Here to Eternity*, and others.

After a week, Kazan phoned Cohn and asked him what he thought of Miller's screenplay. "Burn it" he said, "Throw it in the ash can!"

Kazan wasn't intimidated by Cohn. He understood the importance of the ritual dance with him. With that, Kazan offered to do the film without pay, taking 25% of the profits after release.

After more banter, the standard Cohn negotiating tactic, Cohn agreed to do the film if it was brought in at a minuscule budget and had at least one major star in the cast. Kazan agreed. Not that he had any intention of living up to that agreement. Like Cohen, Kazan's tactic in dealing with the studios was to tell them what they wanted to hear and then do exactly what he wanted to do in the first place. It usually worked.

Besides, having a star in the film would only up the films budget.

Miller and Kazan approached Marlon Brando to take the lead. Brando owed his fame to Kazan's directing and agreed to read the outline and give it serious consideration. However, by that time, although everything seemed to be moving along perfectly, word drifted back to Kazan that the script was going to be sunk by the studios because of a man named Harry Bridges.

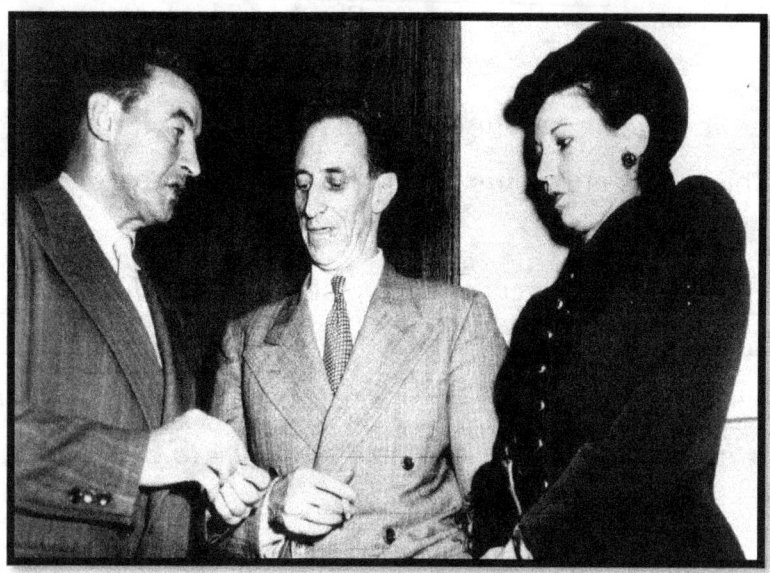

Bridges, center, with his wife and their lawyer.

The West Coast Longshoremen's union, the ILWU, was dominated by the Communist and led by the militant Harry Bridges. Bridges had constantly sought to disrupt and control the Hollywood film making unions and in 1950, his ILWU had been expelled from the Congress of Industrial Organizations for its pro-Communist record.

The entertainment union bosses and the HUAC operatives in Hollywood were suspicious with the notion that Miller, known for his pro-communist sympathies, would pen a left leaning script that might glamorize the likes of Harry Bridges.

A few weeks after the rumors started, Kazan was called in to see Harry Cohn and Roy Brewer of the Mafia dominated International Alliance of Theatrical and Stage Employees. Brewer was a man to be listened too. Even the obnoxious Cohn was respectful and deferential to him. As well as he should have been. If Brewer wanted, too he could pull his union from the production of any film, or several films, shutting it down and costing a studio millions.

The Mobs control of the IATSE eventually led to the so-called Bioff scandal and gave the Mafia a permanent foothold in Hollywood. Now, in 1950, with Hollywood Mob front men Willie Bioff and George Brown in jail, nothing had changed inside the IATSE.

Brewer had already testified to HUAC as friendly witness in 1947 where he publicly "encouraged and supported Mr. Kazan to testify against the Communist Party"

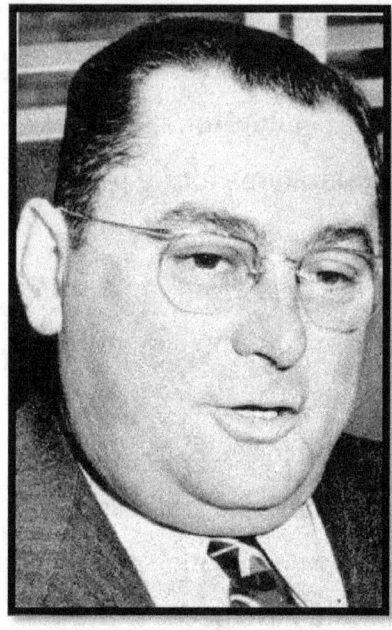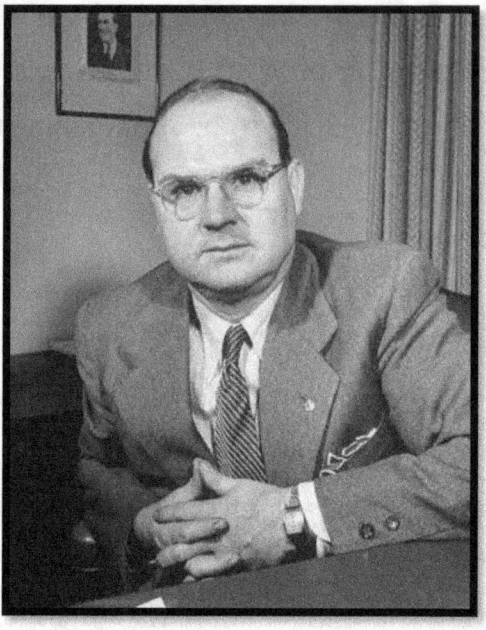

Bioff (left) and Brewer

The same seven members of the executive board, who had sat there when the Chicago mob ran the union, were still in place, one of whom, Richard Walsh, then unions President. There had been no house cleaning inside the union since the government had not locked up Bioff and Brown, nor would there be under Walsh's administration.

Instead any charges that the mob still ran the union was answered with counter charges by Walsh that the accuser was a communist. When asked about the mob dealings inside his enormous and powerful union, Walsh responded, "That's a problem I don't talk about at all…. A good president never takes responsibility for anything"

Working under Walsh was the more competent Brewer who carried the official title of International Vice President, a job he had been appointed to in 1945.

A Nebraskan who had studied law through the LaSalle Extension University, Brewer had joined the IATSE in 1926 as a projectionist. Over the next few years he was elected to various positions within the union, working briefly as Tom Clark's compliance officer under the National Recovery Administration before he accepted the position as IATSE's International Vice President in Hollywood.

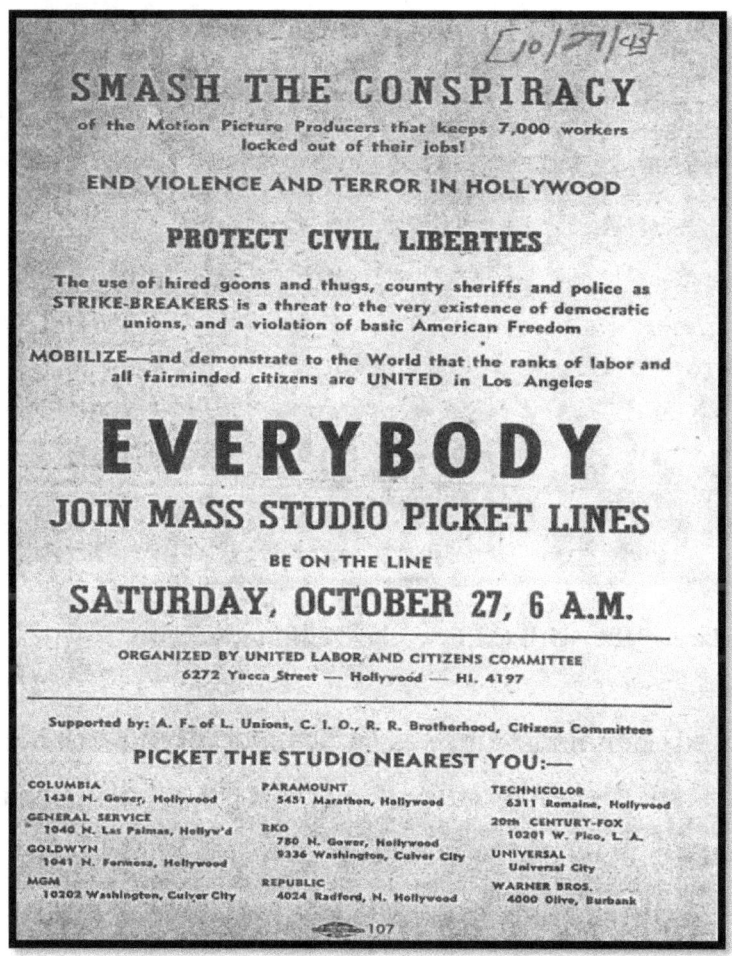

From the very start, Brewer made it clear that he had no intention of ridding the union of gangsters "When Brown and Bioff went to jail" he said "That ended any connection with the Mob in the IATSE" and then added that although his boss Richard Walsh "went along with them (The Mob) and that "He did some things" he was quick to add that "Walsh had done a good job of cleaning up the mob" One person Brewer did get rid of was Jeff Kibre, the IATSE progressive who had risked his life to uncover the Mafia's control of his union under Bioff and Brown.

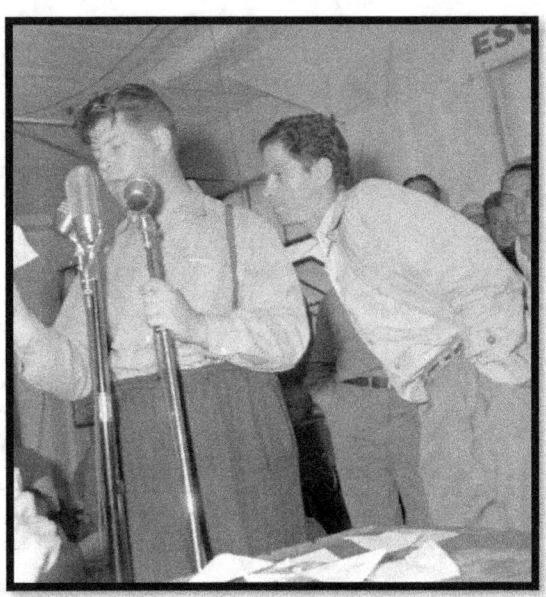

Jeff Kibre, right, with C.I.O leader William Elconin

Kibre was a self-avowed Communist and was immediately blacklisted in the industry by Brewer's forces. Brewer continued to take out his petty vendetta' where and whenever he could. When the Blacklisted director Jules Dassin, who Brewer particularly hated, fled to France to direct a film starring Zsa Zsa Gabor, Brewer phoned the film's producer and warned him that if Dassin wasn't fired, the film would never be released in the United States nor would any of the producers future films be released in the states. He then called Zsa Zsa Gabor and threatened her as well.

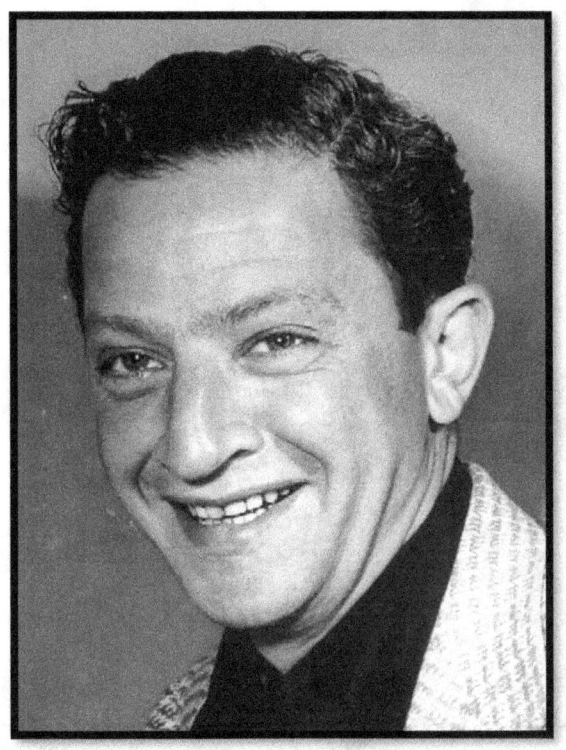

Jules Dassin

Brewer was pro-producer, pro-management and held a healthy dislike for Miller and all other Hollywood writers, since they had backed his rival the Conference of Studio Unions, which Brewer was absolutely convinced was little more than a communist front.

The more radical leaders of the Screen Writers Guild.... Lester Cole, John Lawson and Ring Lardner Jr.... had tried to rally their colleagues in support of the Conference of Studio Unions, rising money for them and hailing their professionalism. But the Screen Writers Guild was the only talent guild to support the Conference, which led people in the business, like Brewer, to believe that the Guild had been behind the conference's activities all along.

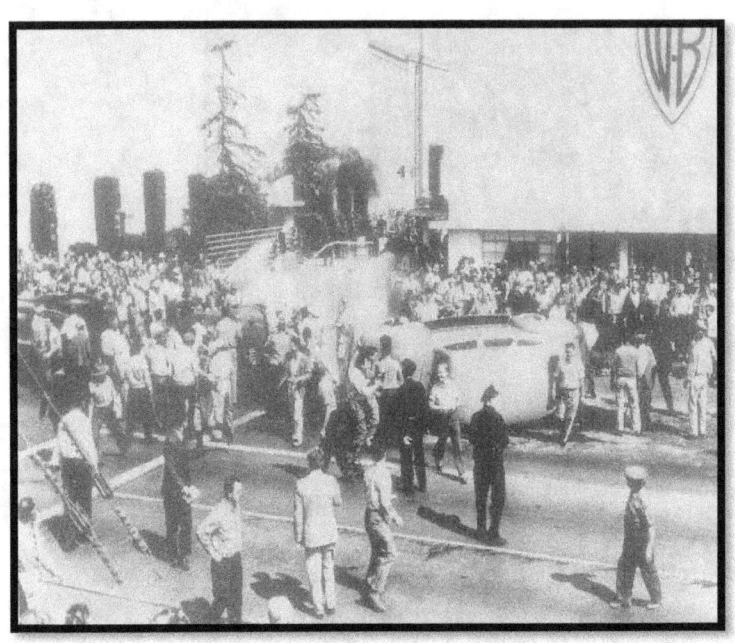

Hollywood studio strike

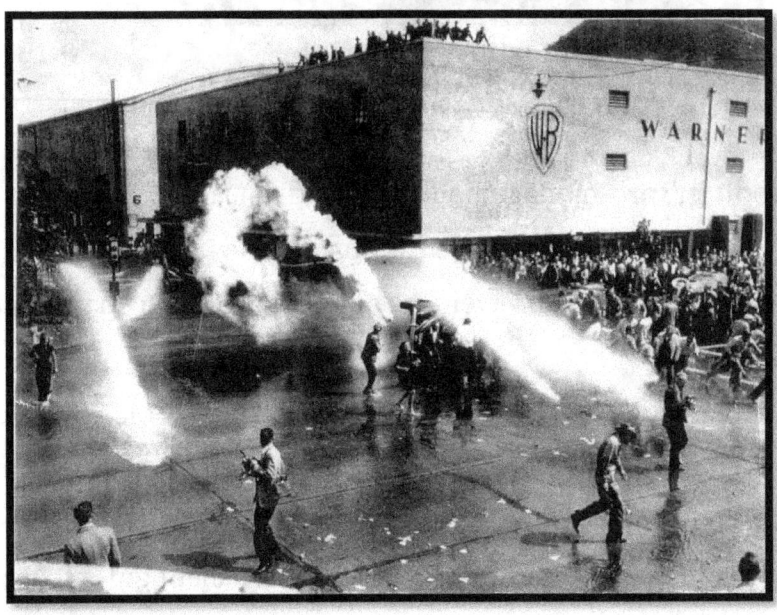

Brewer's revenge was to take writers like Miller and others apart at every turn.

The meeting was bound to go wrong for Kazan. Brewer was pro-producer, pro-management and held a healthy dislike for Miller and all other Hollywood writers, since they had backed his rival the Conference of Studio Unions, which Brewer was absolutely convinced was little more than a communist front. Harry Cohn and Brewer sat next to each other in Cohn's office facing Kazan and Arthur Miller.

Cohn was nervous. Brewer was calm and reasonable. Brewer had seen the manuscript for *The Hook* and felt that it needed a voice over forward. Kazan, knowing that forwards were usually cut from the final edit anyway, agreed.

Then Brewer, a future ring leader of the Blacklisting gang, told them that he thought that the hoods in the film should be rewritten as Communists. At this point, it's not clear if Brewer had gambled that Miller and Kazan would balk and change and walk away from the film, which is perhaps what the union boss wanted.

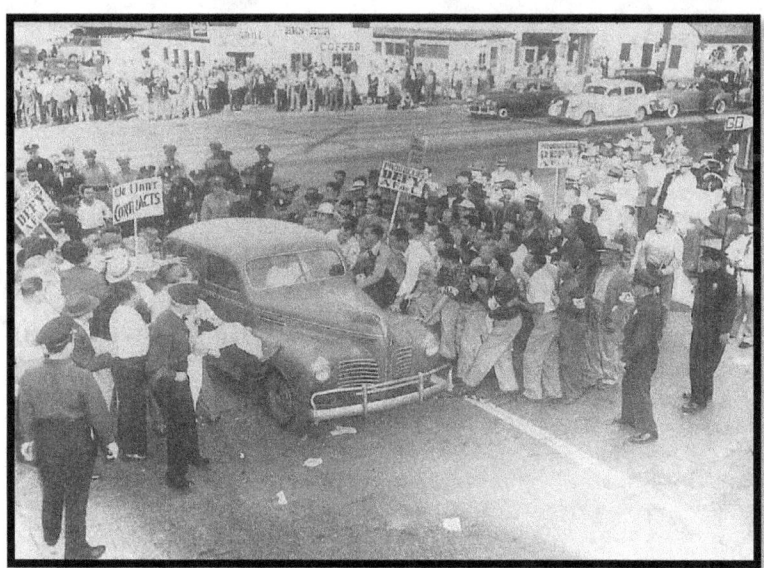

Hollywood studio strike

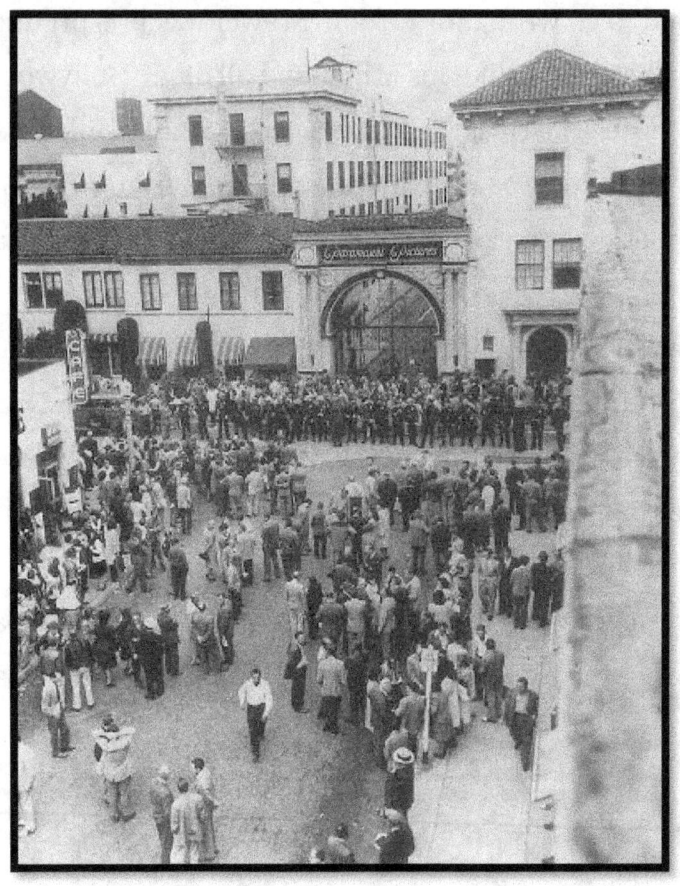

"The racketeers" he said "are much less a menace to labor than the Communists"
It is probable that Brewer may have been gambling that Miller and Kazan would balk at the changes and walk away from the film. But they did not balk, nor did they accept it. They agreed to think it over and get back to Brewer with their decision.

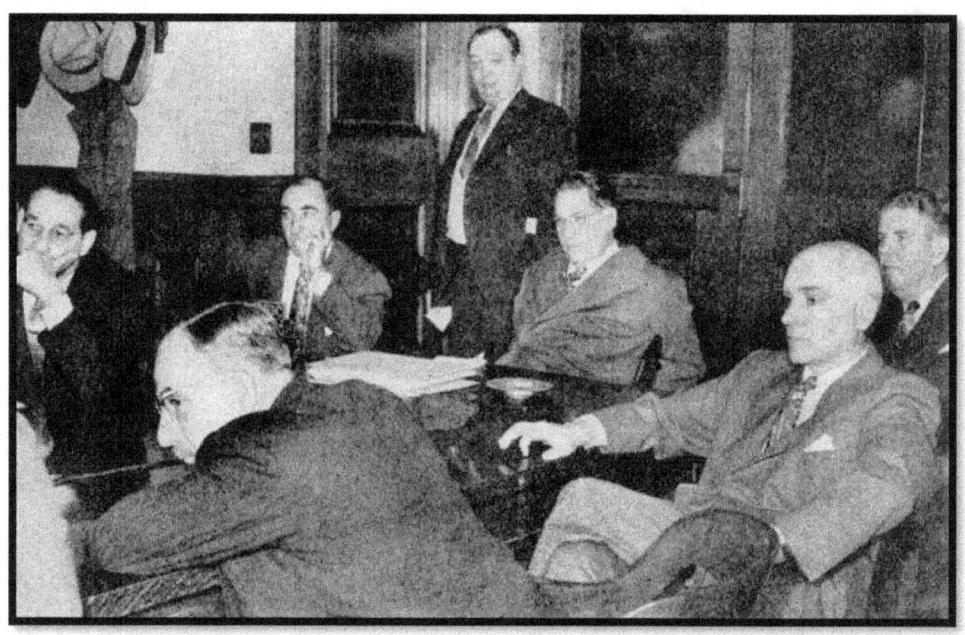

Chicago Mobsters indicted in the Bioff-Hollywood scandal

The meeting dragged on for a while longer before Cohn brought it to a close and asked Brewer "How do you think we stand on this, Roy?" to which Brewer answered "There is a certain amount of danger doing a picture of this particular type at this particular time"

"Do you mean" Cohn asked, "Unless the changes you brought up are made?" "Even with those changes" Brewer replied, "there is still a certain amount of danger doing this film, at this time"

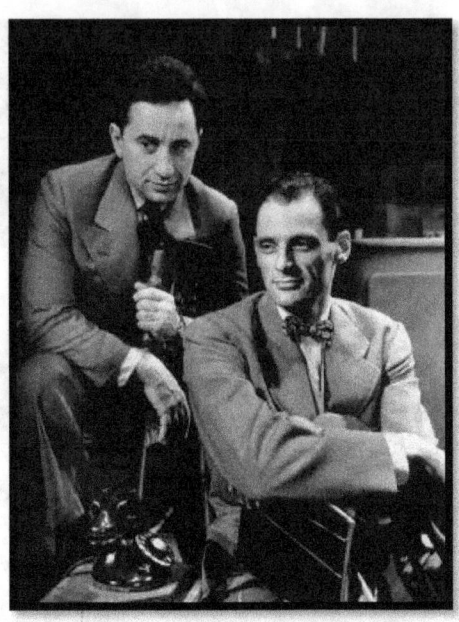

Kazan and Miller

Even with Brewers near condemnation, in the weeks that followed, all signals were clear that the film had been given the green light for production. Cohn kept the scripts budget meeting was in place, meaning he still planned to move along with the film and Kazan went about the business of setting up a production schedule.

For his part, the sometimes-difficult Miller, who was not used to so many voices editing his work, stalled over changes in the script, most of them very heavy-handed edits by Brewer and HUAC operatives within the studio system as well as by jittery studio lawyers.

A few weeks later Miller called Kazan and told him that he was dropping out of the project. Harry Cohn greeted the news as a confirmation that Miller was a communist. "Strange" he told Kazan "how the minute we want to make a script pro-American, Miller pulls out" Miller had a near completely different recall of the incident.

96

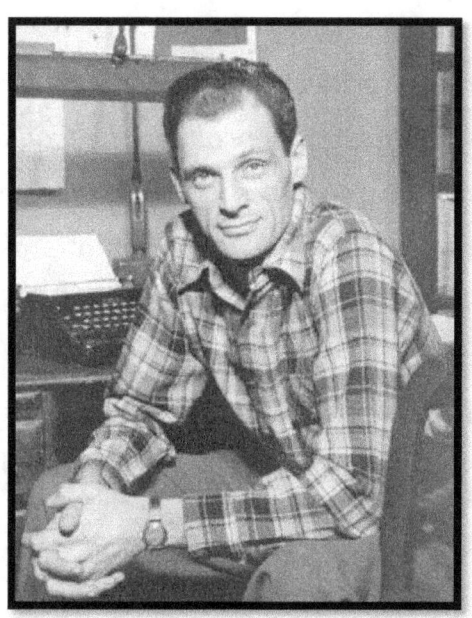

Miller

"In the early 50s, along with Elia Kazan, who had directed All My Sons and Death of a Salesman, I submitted a script to Harry Cohn, head of Columbia Pictures. It described the murderous corruption in the gangster-ridden Brooklyn longshoremen's union.

Cohn read the script and called us to Hollywood, where he casually informed us that he had had the script vetted by the FBI, and that they had seen nothing subversive in it.

But the head of the AFL motion picture unions in Hollywood, Roy Brewer, had condemned it as untrue communist propaganda, since there were no gangsters on the Brooklyn waterfront.

Cohn, no stranger to gangsterism, having survived an upbringing in the tough Five Points area of Manhattan, opined that Brewer was only trying to protect

Joe Ryan, head of the Brooklyn dock workers (who would serve time in Sing Sing prison for gangsterism).

Brewer threatened to call a strike of projectionists in any theatre daring to show the film. Cohn offered his solution to the problem: he would produce the film if I would make one change - the gangsters in the union were to be changed to communists. This would not be easy; I knew all the communists on the waterfront- there were two of them (both of whom in the following decade became millionaire businessmen).

So I had to withdraw the script, which prompted an indignant telegram from Cohn: "As soon as we try to make the script pro-American you pull out."

On his way out the door, Miller also implied that Kazan had jeopardized his own artistic value by agreeing with the changes that Brewer demanded. The fact is, Kazan had also stood against the Brewer inspired changes in script and had told Miller as much, telling him not to fret over the details.

Understanding the film making processes better than Miller, he knew he could find a way around most of the changes added to the script. But the often-sanctimonious Miller refused to cooperate or even wait for Kazan perform his standard magic in dealing with the studios. A by-product of Miller pulling out of the project under the anti-communist cloud set by Brewer, was that he may have by association, dragged Kazan into the light of political suspicion since shortly after Miller backed the script, and both he and Kazan were called before the House Un-American Activities Committee.

Several years later, when Waterfront became a blockbuster hit, a bitter and angry Miller used the anti-Kazan crowd to propel a story about Kazan stealing his unproduced screenplay, *The Hook,* and using it as the basis for On the Waterfront. Miller himself never directly made the accusation, but made a point of comparing his script to Kazan's script. Although he never accused Kazan of stealing his idea, he came close to it by describing the two plays in such a way that the similarities of a story- longshoremen who are victimized by gangsters, a corrupt union and ship owners- would be impossible to miss.

All of this forced Kazan to defend himself, having to admit that he and Miller had worked together in a failed attempt to get *The Hook* produced in Hollywood and explaining that no matter how Miller explained it, The Hook had very little in common with *Waterfront* except the setting.

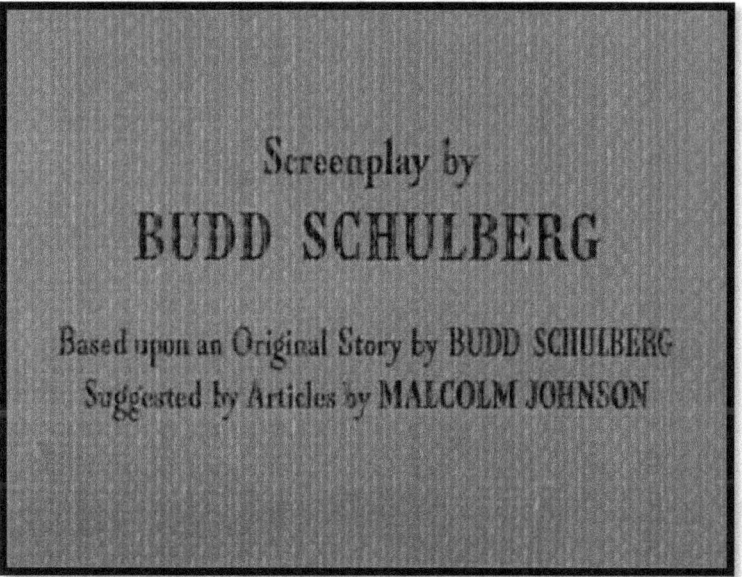

Kazan and Schulberg's characters are authentic working men whose authenticity was created through observation, quality of writing and a real insight into the lives of the working poor. By contrast, Miller's view of the working poor in *The Hook* is, to be kind, elitist. (The fact of the matter is, Miller's screenplay was awful. Several reviewers have termed it "Tedious" Kazan was more direct calling it "A half-assed screen play")

If there is a similarity to be found between *Waterfront* and any other work, it would Sean O'Casey's powerful play, *Shadow of a gunman*, which would fit with the Irish-American themes of Kazan's waterfront in its representation of family loyalty and personal desire thwarted by external events.

O'Casey's Ireland and Kazan's waterfront are filled with hopelessness, tragedy, and poverty and pending disaster. Both places are fraught with danger where the IRA is the final authority as are Johnny Friendly and his gang. Kazan's idealistic Edie Doyle is not terribly different from O'Casey's Minnie Powell, a flighty dreamer who cannot, or will not see her surroundings for what they are. Large parts of O'Casey's lost, confused and indifferent Seamus Shields character are found in Kazan's Terry Malloy.

Miller and Elia Kazan never regained the close friendship they shared in the late 40's and early 50's. The Red Scare that sidetracked both their lives and careers changed everything between them and eventually too much happened to the nation and between them to close the gap. Instead, they came to embody the deep divisions that separated the country during the McCarthy era.

In popular culture, Miller took on an aura of saintliness under the guise of the artist who defied the HUAC by refusing to answer their questions. Kazan would become to the once brilliant playwright and director who threw his dignity away in a devils bargain made with the inquisitors. And thus, sadly ended the relationship between two brilliant creative minds who had once called themselves brothers.

Time, wisdom, and maturity heal all wounds. In 1999, forty-six years after they had last spoken to each other, Elia Kazan was presented with a special Academy Award. The presentation was controversial, due to Kazan's cooperation with the HUAC, and caused uproar within the film community. Miller came to his old friend's defense, telling The Guardian newspaper "My feelings toward that

100

terrible era are unchanged but at the same time history ought not to be rewritten. Elia Kazan did sufficient extraordinary work in theater and film to merit acknowledgement."

Kazan replied with a short note "Thank you. I hope all is well"

With or without Miller, Kazan was still captured by the idea waterfront film and it was obvious by the studios commitment to the Miller script, as weak as it was that they were interested in producing a similar formula. And that fact was not missed by the film colony. If he did not produce the right outline in a short amount of time, someone else would.

What Kazan needed a script, a strong script. He went back, reviewed the Johnson expose series and tried, in vain, to write his own version of the script. It was that point that he learned through the Hollywood grapevine that Budd Schulberg, whom he did not know, had purchased the rights to the Malcolm Johnson expose series. In late 1951, the director reached out to Schulberg the screenwriter and suggested they meet.

In the meantime, the situation on the waterfront, despite the advances made by Father Corridan's work, continued to deteriorate. In 1951, four years into Father Corridan's tenure on the waterfront, the workers revolted against Ryan's rule again and caused a 25-day work stoppage.

Again, the cause of the strike was an agreement reached by the ILA leadership with the shippers, which was rejected by the rank-and-file. This time, there were no communists in the strikers leadership, rather, the longshoremen were led by Corridan's people, insurgents Johnny Dwyer, and Ryan's chief ILA rivals Gene Sampson of Local 791 in Manhattan and Salvatore Brocco in Brooklyn.

Starting on the west side of Manhattan, the strike quickly spread to the Brooklyn docks. Ryan responded with his usual charges of Communist influence on the strike, which had the desired results and inflamed the situation. Corridan countered the charges by pressing New York Governor Thomas Dewey to examine the causes of the strike. It worked.

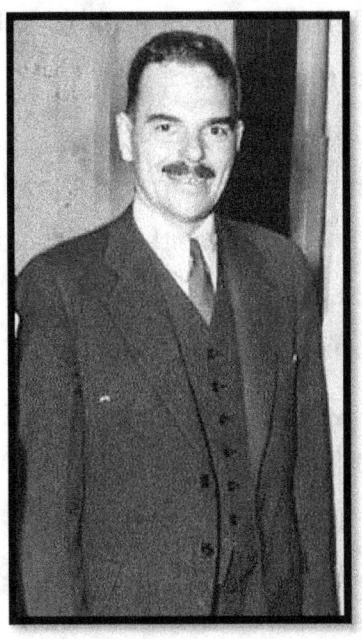

Dewey

Dewey ordered an investigation, the first of several. New York State Industrial Commissioner Edward Corsi headed the investigation. Heroically, Corsi extended the investigation beyond its original mandate and his final report attacked the fraudulent voting procedures which Ryan had forced into place and the absolute and complete corruption of several of Ryan's mobbed up locals.

Additionally, the Corsi Report captured the public and the national media's attention, forcing Governor Thomas E. Dewey to ordered the New York State Crime Commission to conduct a full investigation of the ILA which ended with the complete condemnation of both the ILA and Ryan as corrupt beyond all hope.

As a result of the Corsi report, in 1953, the Waterfront Commission of the New York Harbor was created with almost dictatorial powers, to do something, anything, to stunt the corruption of the ILA. Among its other reforms, the commission banned the hated shape-up.

Under pressure from the States of New Jersey and New York, in August 1953, the ILA was suspended from the American Federation of Labor and replaced with the AFL created the International Brotherhood of Longshoremen (IBL-AFL) Corridan campaigned hard to gather support for the new union which was run in New York by one of Corridan's, Xavier Labor School, Johnny Dwyer.

Then Dewey ordered the New York Crime Commission to hold hearings as well, through 1951-1952.

The Commission relentlessly questioned a string of ILA officials, each of the swearing under oath that they knew nothing or could not remember anything about the Mafia on the docks and kick back payments from shippers and longshoremen. Most of the officials didn't know how many locals they had in the unions or the number of card carrier's longshoremen that worked on the docks.

One of the first witnesses called before the hearings was Joe Ryan's boss, Big Bill McCormack, after the powerful national columnist Westbrook Pegler named McCormack as the waterfront "Mister Big" McCormick rushed to lift himself above the mudslinging and hired a press agent to clean up his faltering image but to no avail.

McCormack, whom the commission saw as the ultimate power on the waterfront, was grilled like the common criminal in a public hearing for several hours. However, on the stand, McCormack proved to be a great actor. He was well spoken and dignified and, essentially, told the Commission nothing. He denied that the accusation that his company, Penn Stevedoring, had promised New York State Parole Board officials employment for no less than 200 convicts while they were still in prison, that he controlled Joe Ryan and swore under oath that he knew nothing about the Mafia's control of the waterfront.

While McCormick may have thought that he won the battle, he had actually lost the war. While he was virtually unknown outside the waterfront, almost everyone connected with that world, from the average beat cop to the long shore worker, knew who McCormick was and the power that held over their lives.

For them, his forced appearance before the committee, no matter how well it had gone for him, was a victory for the longshoremen and the waterfront.
The final witness before the Commission, number 209, was Joe Ryan, who also came across as the worst of the lot that were cross-examined.

For several long hours, Ryan stumbled, lied contradicted himself and generally fumbled his entire testimony. Like McCormack, he told the commission nothing, but unlike McCormack the Commissions lawyer viciously attacked him for almost eight hours.

He admitted to taking over $31,000 from the union which he used to purchase lunches at the Stork Club, car repairs, a trip to Guatemala on a cruise ship and clothes. He insisted that he was absolutely shocked to learn that 30% of the ILA's officials had police records that 45 locals had no accounting system in place and that ILA officials granted themselves an average pay increase of 60% a year.

He admitted knowing Mafia boss Albert Anastasia, that he often dined with him and that he liked him but that the gangsters under him were "Communists" and that as head of the ILA "My life is in constant risk for fighting them at every turn"

He stepped down from the stand visibly shaken. As he left the hearings surrounded by the press he said "I've done nothing wrong. Look, when a teller of a bank pleads guilty of something, they don't lock up the bank president do they?"

Father Corridan refused to testify before the Commission, stating that most of the information he had about life on the waterfront had been given to him in confidence. "Any testimony (That I give) would weaken the belief of people around the waterfront in my trustworthiness" Few people believed the priest. It was widely assumed that Corridan ongoing feud with New York's ultra-conservative Cardinal, Richard Spellman.

Spellman was passionate anti-communism, a conviction that led him to make one of the most ill-considered decisions of his career in 1949. A strike by gravediggers at Calvary and Gate of Heaven cemeteries had resulted in more than 1,000 unburied bodies. Convinced that a communist-controlled union was responsible for the situation, he brought in seminarians from Dunwoodie as substitute gravediggers and used them to break the strike.

Spellman publicly and privately questioned Corridan's role in the 1951 strike, kept the priest from testifying. Spellman summoned Corridan to his palatial office behind St. Patrick's cathedral in Manhattan. Waiting for him there was Corridan immediate boss, the Provincial of the Jesuit order and several other Jesuits from across the city who also worked in labor schools. The men waited for two hours while Spellman conducted a special mass in the church before twenty Bishops and Arch Bishops.

When the meeting started, Spellman sharply informed Corridan that "persons and another priest" had made charges against Corridan for misconduct during the strike, namely that he had discarded his priest's uniform, dressed as a longshoreman and engaged in several fist fights on the docks. The second charge was even more ridiculous.... namely that Corridan had actually organized and then sparked the strike.

Exactly who the accused the priest remains unknown, but Spellman was, above all else a businessman first and a church leader second. Joe Ryan, the ILA's president had always been a major contributor to Spellman's causes. He was a trustee of the Shrine of the Scared Sea and reliable backer of Spellman's often odd political posturing.

Ryan's staunchest ally in the church was Monsignor John O'Donnell, whom Ryan put on the on the ILA payroll as chaplain. In turn, Spellman appointed O'Donnell director of the Shrine of the Scared Sea.

Corridan claimed later that he denied the charges and was not ordered by Spellman to be silent for the remainder of the strike and to never appear before a Public hearing again. But the fact of the matter is, Corridan did sit out most of the tail end of the strike and refused several requests to testify at the hearings, although he provided the Commission with information, contacts and leads, all of the record, while at the same time encouraging the state and the city to help reform the ILA by opening a hiring hall, which would do away with the dreaded shape up, licensed registration of all longshoremen, and institution of a seniority system.

One of the less known results of Corridan's behind the scenes work was that the Waterfront Commission also barred many of the militant Communist and Communist sympathies barred from the waterfront.

THE PRINCE OF HOLLYWOOD

"If life is a series of disenchantments through which we prepare ourselves then I was richly endowed, for our castles were built on glamorous quicksand" **Budd Schulberg, Los Angeles Magazine 1965**

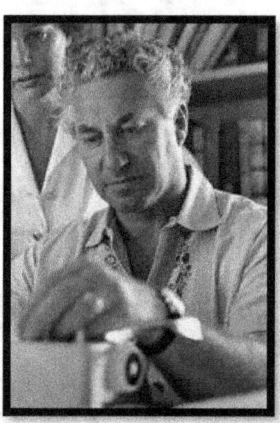

Budd Schulberg was a prince of the Hollywood elite, the ultimate industry insider and in many ways, the direct opposite of his future creative partner Elia Kazan.

His father, Benjamin Percival Schulberg, known on the back lots as "B.P," was head of production at Paramount's Lasky studio (a position he held until 1932) BP Schulberg was not the typical ill-educated crass immigrant that founded Hollywood. Born in Bridgeport, Connecticut in 1892, he was the last of fourteen children.

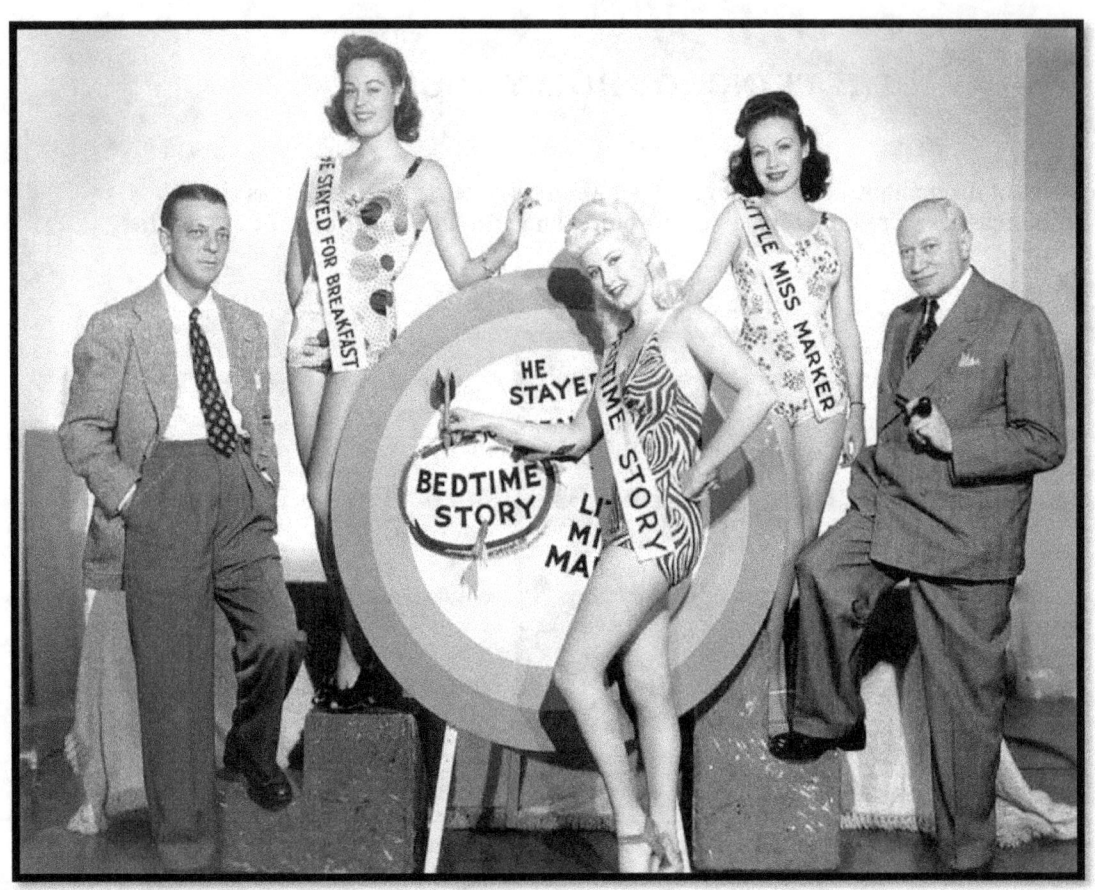

B.P Schulberg, far right, on the set for *Bedtime Story*.

The family eventually moved from Bridgeport to New York's lower east side, where B.P., still a teenager, attended City College. He gave up college to become a copy boy for Franklin P. Adams on the Evening Mail and eventually promoted to beat reporter.

At age 20, he became the editor for *Film Reports*, a trade paper where he met director Edwin Stratton Porter and became his scenario editor of Rex Films Production Company. (Later absorbed into present day Universal Films) Porter was the most prominent innovator in the early years of motion pictures. While Thomas Edison was content to film mundane, everyday events, Porter the realized the means to tell a story on film was by the use of editing. Through his technique of physically splicing the story together, Porter put the word "move" in movie scenario. He created a fictional scenario with two groundbreaking films that absolutely mesmerized the public.

By being astute enough to be in the right place at the right time, B.P. became one of the industry's original screenwriters who delivered his first film script in 1913, In the *Bishop's Carriage* and would be involved in a scattering of film over the next three decades including the 1923 classic, *The Virginian* and *Little Miss Marker* (1934).

BP was one of the first to understand that films had to be sold to the public. Schulberg dubbed Mary Pickford "America's sweetheart." He discovered Clara Bow and dubbed her *"The It girl"* ("It" being a euphemism for the word "sex")

He also discovered Gary Grant, Claudette Colbert, George Raft and Frederic March. It was BP who brought Marlene Dietrich from Germany, made the original *Dr. Jekyll and Mr. Hyde* and started the gangster film genre with Ben Hecht's *Underworld*. He also helped produce the antiwar film *Wings,* that won the first Academy Award in 1928.

His son Budd suffered from fainting fits and speech impediment, stammering his way "from therapist to therapist." But while he did not speak well, he compensated by becoming a good listener and, in turn, a better than average writer. His writing talent was encouraged by his mother, Hollywood agent Adeline Jaffe Schulberg a vivid, attractive and intelligent woman with a crisp understanding of the film business.

It was Adeline who discovered the actor Sylvia Sidney, an early glamour star, when Sidney was appearing in a Broadway play called *Bad Girl*. Ad pushed her husband to sign the young actor to a contract but he was unreceptive but Ad persisted and eventually BP gave the young starlet a long-term Paramount. He also started a love affair with her, which eventually broke up the marriage.

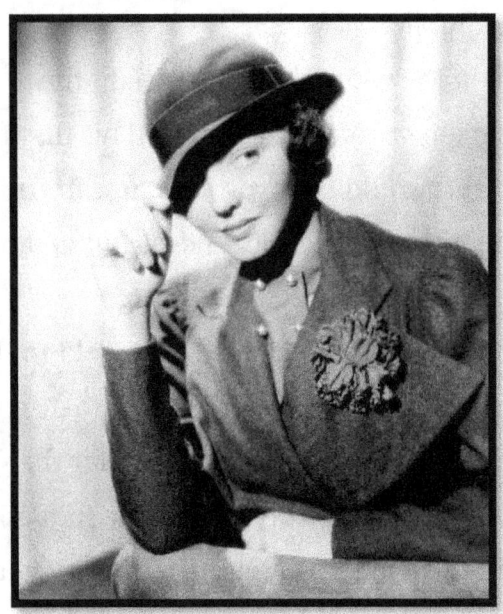

Sylvia Sidney

BP Schulberg declined well before Sidney's film career ended. Towards the end of his term at Paramount, when his salary was $10,000 a week, it was clear that the world had outpaced him. Many factors led to the downfall of BP Schulberg.

The advent of talkies was one of them. B.P. had come to the top of his form in silent films, he did not adjust well to the change (neither did his protégée, Clara Bow who flopped in talkies) Then the depression hit and ticket sales fell. Distracted by his torrid love affair with Sylvia Sidney, BP slipped out of control. He slowly became unstable. A lifelong teetotaler, he started to drink and gamble, sometimes losing as much as $25,000 in a night.

He tried independent producing for a while and then bounced from studio to studio. Nothing worked for him. In the ultimate humiliation, in 1949, he took out an ad in Variety begging for work. No one responded. He died in 1957 a virtual unknown in the industry he created. (BP was later given a Star on Hollywood Blvd.)

Budd Schulberg graduated from Dartmouth in 1936, (A.B. cum laude), at the age of seventeen. He returned to Hollywood and worked as a publicist at Paramount, writing bright and airy stories about the ambitions of the stars before they had become famous.

That same year he married actor Virginia Ray. Ray, called Jigee was one of Hollywood's most glamorous women who had been courted by, as Walter Bernstein said, all of the left wing screenwriters in the community and "any other man with common sense and eyes."

Budd won her heart despite being what Sheilah Graham described as a shy young man who strutted, painfully, always knocking things over and apologizing in a mumble of words. Like his father before him, Budd eventually began writing screenplays for Paramount. In 1938, he wrote the script for Paramount's, Little Orphan Annie, followed by the romantic comedy, *Winter Carnival* (1939) co-written with F. Scott Fitzgerald. The film flopped and both Schulberg and Fitzgerald were fired.

The film would be produced Walter Wagner, who had just released Stagecoach and had hired Fitzgerald and Schulberg to write a pleasant script about the Dartmouth Winter Carnival. Both Schulberg and Wanger were Dartmouth graduates and considered Fitzgerald's work, *This Side of Paradise*, to be one of the finest novels ever written.

It was about the only thing they had in common. Schulberg, then 24 years old, considered Wanger "A Dartmouth drop out with intellectual pretensions" and later added that Wanger was a fraud who smoked a pipe, discussed great books and tried to make himself seem more cultivated than other producers, but was essentially a crass and tactless little man who abused his writers.

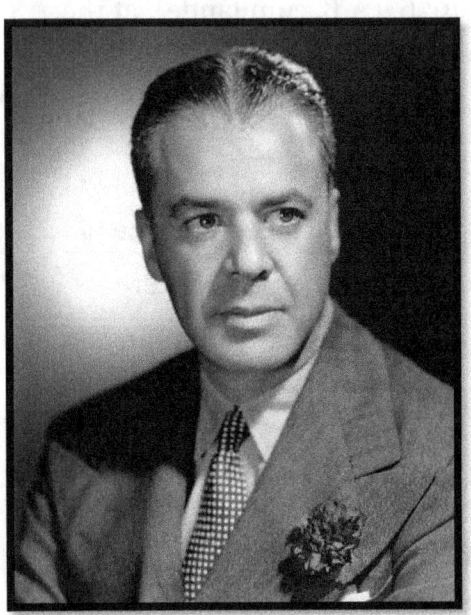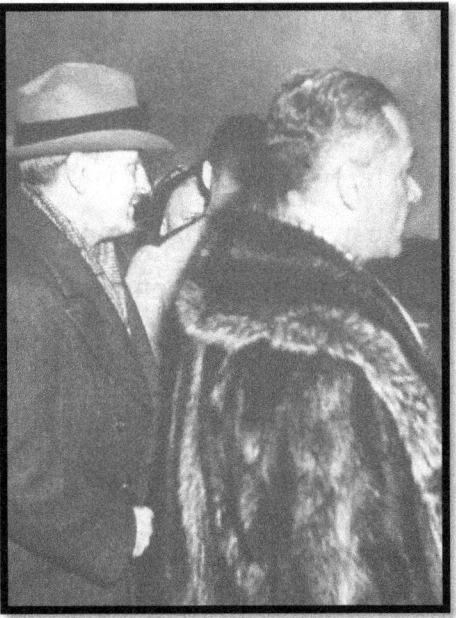

Walter Wanger (left) and Wanger and Fitzgerald on the shooting set of *Winter Carnival*

Schulberg, according to his friend Maurice Rapf, had already been on the film for a year but was having a difficult time with the script and Wanger was getting desperate. He wanted to start shooting and had already missed one Winter Carnival at Dartmouth and was determined to make the next one. Fitzgerald was brought into give Schulberg a boast.

When he learned that he was going to be working with the great novelist, Schulberg said, "I thought he was dead,"

"If he is," Wanger said, "He must be the first ghost who ever got $1,500 a week."

Schulberg was honored to be working with Fitzgerald but was sadden by how anxious the great man looked. Alcohol had taken its toll and Fitzgerald looked a full decade older than his forty-two years. They spent hours together talking about literature, overlooking the hapless script they were supposed to pen about winter frolics in New Hampshire, a painfully boring chore for two such highly gifted men.

Relaxed and comfortable around the young Schulberg, Fitzgerald reminisced and discussed his future work, although he saw his better days behind him "You know" he told Schulberg " use to have a beautiful talent once, baby. It used to be a wonderful feeling to know it was there, and it isn't all gone yet. I think I have enough left to stretch out over two more novels. I may have to stretch it a little thin, so maybe they won't be as good as the best things I've done. But they won't be completely bad either, because nothing I ever write can be completely bad."

Wanger insisted that Fitzgerald go east and see the Dartmouth Winter Carnival first hand, an unneeded trip at best. But Fitzgerald, accompanied by Schulberg, went anyway. Before they left, Schulberg's father provided them with two bottles of champagne, which Fitzgerald quickly drank, setting off a weeklong binge. Unable to find a hotel room near the school, they secured the servants quarters at the Hanover Inn.

That night at a cocktail party, Fitzgerald made his entrance by dead drunk by falling face dunk a flight of stairs. The college staff, disgusted with Fitzgerald's drunken state, did little to cloak their disgust for him, a point not lost on the great writer who told Schulberg "Wanger will never forgive me for this because he sees himself as the intellectual producer and above all he wanted to impress Dartmouth with the fact that he used real writers, not vulgar hacks, and here, I, his real writer, have disgraced him before all these people"

Wanger, who was already at Dartmouth with his film crew, was disgusted with Fitzgerald as well. When he discovered that virtually no work had been done on the script, he fired both Fitzgerald and Schulberg.

Wager to get them out of sight as quickly as possible, Wanger had them tossed on the first train out of New Hampshire, where Fitzgerald continued to drink, so much so, that when they arrived in New York, unshaven, without luggage and Fitzgerald completely out of control, no hotel would take them in. Finally, friends entered the writer into a private hospital for three days to dry him out.

It was the last Hollywood script Fitzgerald would work on. Schulberg, with his all-powerful father behind, was rehired by Wanger to finish the script, which he did, horribly bad as it was.

Fitzgerald and Schulberg remained friends, but just barely. Once, when the writer dropped by Schulberg's house to discuss books, Schulberg excused himself to keep a minor dinner engagement that he could have broken. It troubled the young man to do, but Fitzgerald could be fatiguing when sober. When Schulberg released his book, *What Makes Sammy Run*, Fitzgerald commented only by saying "Budd, the untalented" Schulberg was further hurt when Fitzgerald used the Schulberg's early years in Hollywood as the model for the miserable Cecilia Brady in his novel, *The Last Tycoon*. Actually, Fitzgerald liked the book, although he found it amateurish.

Schulberg responded with a very negative portrayal of Fitzgerald in his work, The Disenchanted, which was essentially the story of the great man's drunken binge at Dartmouth. The book became a Broadway play, but Hemingway had the final say when he called *Disenchanted* "Grave robbing" Carnival, a romantic comedy dealing with collage romances, failed at the box-office and Schulberg was fired again.

Schulberg, disgusted with Hollywood, left California for the rolling hills Norwich, Vermont, where he completed his first novel, *What Makes Sammy Run?* (1941). The work, a satirical story of corruption of an office boy, Sammy Glick, who rises to head of a major motion picture studio, won National Critics' Choice as Best First Novel of the Year in 1941. It was his first critical and financial success.

The Second World War returned Schulberg to Hollywood, this time as a member of director John Ford's documentary unit. It was Schulberg who wrote the narration for Oscar winning documentary December 7 (Schulberg was assigned to gather war crime evidence for the Nuremberg trials)

With the war over, he returned state side and published a second a novel, *The Harder They Fall* (1947) which was eventually turned in to boxing film starring Humprey Bogart (Schulberg, a lifelong fight fan, was later honored by being inducted into the Boxing Hall of Fame) A short time later he released his third novel, *The Disenchanted*, loosely based on his screen writing experiences in Hollywood. By 1949, Schulberg was looking for a new project, something with social significance and box office potential. Like Kazan and Miller, he found it on the waterfront.

WATERFRONT PRIEST
SPRING 1949

"The fight is never about grapes or lettuce. It's about people" **Cesar Chavez**

"You want to know what's wrong with our waterfront? It's the love of a lousy buck. It's making love of a buck, the cushy job - more important than the love of man! **On the Waterfront**

The Malcolm Johnson expose series about crime and exploitation on the waterfront that had captured Kazan and Miller's attention had come to Schulberg attention by way of Joe Curtis, the nephew of Columbia Picture studio boss Harry Cohn.

In early 1949, Curtis had come to see Schulberg on his farm in New Hope Pennsylvania. With him was Robert Siodmak, who had directed the cult classic film *The Killers* based on the Hemingway story. Although underrated during his career, cinephiles have come to consider Siodmak the primary architect of the American film noir genre.

Curtis and Siodmak had been watching the dramatic events unfolding on the New York waterfront, saw a film in it and wanted Schulberg to write the script. Curtis, as Cohn's nephew, felt he could get the financing for the film based on Siodmak's considerable directing abilities and Schulberg's skill as a screenwriter. Schulberg liked the concept and considered writing the script, but first wanted to do some background research.

He drove down to New York and met with Malcolm Johnson who directed him to see a Priest, Father John Corridan, the man who had sparked Johnson's interest in the waterfront.

In November of 1948, Corridan had contacted Johnson's editor by letter. The editor turned the letter over to Johnson "You'd better go on over and contact this guy, he seems to know what he he's talking about"

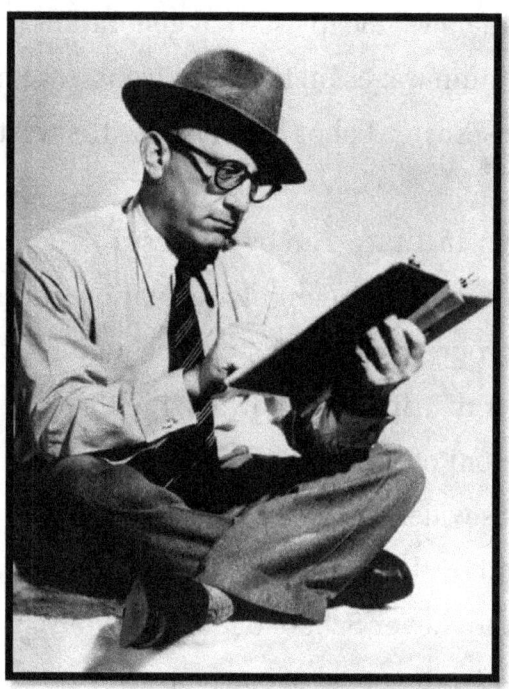

Robert Siodmak

Johnson spent time with the Priest and learned that he had been raised in the tenement slums of New York, the son of Irish immigrants. His father, a New York City Policeman, died in 1921 when Corridan was nine years old, leaving the family with a $25 a month pension.

His mother worked three part time jobs as a charwoman, but still the family was forced to enter the welfare rolls. Corridan, who worked several part time jobs through high school and New York University, eventually took a position on Wall Street as a financial correspondent. However, at the age of twenty, he read Rene

Fullop Miller's *The Power and Secret of the Jesuits* and decided to join the order. After fifteen years of study, in 1944, he was ordained a Priest and assigned, at age 35, to the Crown Heights Labor School in Brooklyn.

There, his job was to recruit Catholic activists on the docks, with an emphasis on those "from the bottom of the pile" mostly second generation Irishmen and Italians toiling for below minimum wages on the waterfront. A year later, in 1946, he was moved to the St. Francis Xavier Labor School, near the west-side piers of Manhattan.

The school was actually policy institute, run by the Jesuit order, and called for the curbing of excessive profit-taking through rate regulation, return to ownership of public utilities, progressive taxation, participation of labor in management decisions, a wider distribution of ownership through cooperative enterprises and legal enforcement of the right of labor to organize.

A social vision program, it was widely opposed by most members of the American church hierarchy and by the broader Catholic Church community in general. Founded in 1936 as the Xavier School of Social Studies, the school held its focus on the labor movement with a goal of concentrating its efforts on organizing Catholic workers in New York City away from the growing influence of the Communist Party.

Like most New Yorkers, Corridan knew little of life on the waterfront but under the tutelage of Father Philip Carey, rector of St. Xavier's parish (which was affiliated with the labor school) Corridan learned how to deal with the longshoremen and to recruit activists that could confront and regulate both the corrupt ILA leaders and Communist militants. It was dangerous work, for the priests and the activists alike, and as a result, Corridan's organizing was done with painstaking calculation. It would take three years before he had established himself enough as a public figure in the media that he felt completely safe on the waterfront. The mob probably would not have harmed him, bodily, but they could (and did) use their considerable influence in New York politics to do whatever they had to do to stop him.

At first, Corridan made his presence known at the docks but realized the tactic was useless, no one on the waterfront wanted to be seen talking to him in fear of losing their jobs or worse. As a result, contacts with longshoremen were often made in alleyways and basements away from the ILA and mob snitches who were everywhere on the docks.

Over the next few months, Corridan learned everything he could about the waterfront. He walked every pier, took a ferry across the river and looked at the docks from every angle, even once traveling into Manhattan to view the waterfront from the Empire State Building. He began building an extensive intelligence network made up of a handful of longshoremen, altar boys, reporters, housewives and anyone else that would provide him with accurate information on the ILA and the mob.

By the end of his first year on the docks, Corridan had collected sixteen filing cabinets full of information and reached the conclusion that the Mob and the ILA union had formed an unholy alliance to control the waterfront and the workers. In a meeting arranged by Johnson, Schulberg met with Father Corridan. He recalled, *"I went down and had lunch with Corridan at Billy the Oysterman's, and he told me how men were getting killed, right there on the waterfront, and how nobody would talk about it. I swear Karl Malden looks like him, walks like him, talks like him. Corridan was a very tall man. Very tall and strong. Vigorous. Looked like a longshoreman. Talked like a longshoreman. Swore like a longshoreman. Worse than that. He called Big Bill McCormack, the Mister Big of the whole waterfront 'a son of a bitch' McCormack was a power behind the mayor of New York, Impelliteri. Whenever McCormack called city hall, (The mayor) would stop what he was doing and take the call"*

He gave me lessons on where to go, where not to go. There were rebel bars where Father John's people would take me. They told me: Don't ask. Don't talk. Just listen. Father John had revolutionized my attitude towards the Church. In Father John, I found the perfect antidote to the stereotyped Barry Fitzgerald-Bing Crosby "Fah-ther" so dear to the hearts of Hollywood.

In west side saloons, I listened to Father John, whose speech was unique blend of Hell's Kitchen, baseball slang, an encyclopedic grasp of waterfront economics and an attack on man's inhumanity to man based on the teachings of Christ as brought up to date in the papal encyclicals on the reconstruction of the social order. I was there so much that Walter Winchell in one column said that I was taking instructions on becoming a Catholic. The Jewish organizations got on my case.

Father John had ticked off for me the various mobs controlling different sections of the harbor named the hiring bosses with criminal records and described the evils of the shape up system. He gave me chapter and verse on the wholesale pilferage from the ships cargoes and explained how ILA hoodlums extorted payoffs from the shipping companies...highly vulnerable to threats of work stoppages since the idle ship can earn no money.

Longshoremen who were trying to change things had been coming to Father John up at St. Xavier's Labor school after dark for advice. "Father John knows the score" had become a popular saying by the time I came to know him well. Father John was furious that the waterfront story was so untold. Even The New York Times ignored it."

What Corridan explained to Schulberg was that the ILA controlled virtually all of the hiring on the New York-New Jersey waterfront, 30,000 jobs, and that the ILA was completely, hopelessly corrupt, and dominated by the mob.

Its President, Joseph Patrick Ryan, AKA "The King" Ryan, a crude, obnoxious little man, had come to power in 1927 and stayed there through his deep connections inside New York's powerful political machine, Tammany Hall. For a cut of the unions' money, Tammany assured Ryan protection from the police and other criminal investigations. Furthermore, in exchange for control of a handful of his Manhattan and New Jersey locals, the powerful New York mobs paid Ryan and Ryan paid Tammany.

Directly over Ryan was William J. McCormack AKA Big Bill. It was from McCormack's political patronage that Ryan drew his power. In turn, Ryan acted as McCormack's eyes and ears on the waterfront, Tammany and the Mob. Everyone who was anyone knew Ryan, because Ryan wanted it that way, however only a handful of insiders knew who McCormack was or how powerful a force he was.

Ryan and his partner, the mob, got away with so much on the waterfront because they controlled hiring on the docks through the morning "Shape up." The Shape up was a humiliating process where the front line hoodlum bosses decided who would work and who wouldn't work based on the amount the dockworker was willing to pay a kick back to be sure their name was called. This was the waterfront of 1949 that Budd, Schulberg, the prince of Hollywood, had strolled into.

THE COLABERATION, KAZAN AND SCHULBERG
FALL 1952

"I often think of film-making as a horse race in which teams of three or four or five horses must run together. If they run at all, it is rather remarkable. If they run as well as they can, manage not to trip each other up, and cross the finish line together, it is a not-so-small miracle. This may explain why the most gifted of film-makers, Ford, Stevens, Huston, Kazan, may achieve only three or four truly memorable films in a lifetime of hard work." **Budd Schulberg in Writing in America**

In late 1951, after three years of prowling the docks, Schulberg started writing the screenplay for *On the Waterfront*. But when he finished the script, both Joe Curtis and Robert Siodmak had backed out of the project. They had shown the play to Curtis's uncle, Harry Cohn of Columbia Studios, who called it "Communistic" a Cohn-ism meaning, essentially, that a Hollywood haunted by the HUAC and a Red Baiting public, would never make the film.

As Schulberg explained: *A few months later, in the early spring of 1951, my script was finished. Robert Siodmak, who was to direct it, seemed happy about it, and I thought my days on the waterfront were done. But the months melted away without production. The little film company was something less than a financial rock. In fact, it was unable to get up the "scratch." The subject matter was a little too hot to handle. If the longshoremen's locals were gangster run, how could our picture company get on the docks? Why not make a nice Western or a musical? Prospective backers backed away.*
Another year passed. Now the rights to the script had reverted to me. And, when Johnson's option with the original company lapsed, I took plunge number two

and bought his material. Truth was I couldn't get the waterfront out of my mind.

By the spring of 1952, Curtis, Siodmak and Miller had pulled from the project. Fox Studios had turned it down once and Columbia Studios had turned it down twice. Regardless, Kazan, a director and Schulberg, a screenwriter, knew the story would make an excellent film, a great film. What they needed was the spark to make it happen.

Kazan, who had never met Schulberg, wrote to Schulberg to discuss building a film built around the Malcolm Johnson articles and suggested that they meet. Schulberg wrote back and invited Kazan to his farm in Pennsylvania. Kazan leaped on the offer, however, what he found was that Schulberg was willing to discuss the film but was reluctant to commit to the project. He told Kazan that he had quit films because he had never been permitted to make a film in his own way.

"Because the writer" said Schulberg "Is always the low man. They take his script and everybody rewrites it, the director rewrites it, the actor rewrites it, the producer rewrites it. To hell with it" and that the recent bad experience with Joe Curtis had further soured his outlook on Hollywood. Kazan listened and said "Budd, I promise you this, if you'll do this film, I promise I will treat the script with the same respect I would give to an Arthur Miller play or a Tennessee (Williams) play or a Bill Inge play. I'll make all kinds of suggestions, I'll criticize it, I may be hard on it, but you will have the final say. I won't change a line without you.

"And" Schulberg recalled five decades later "He lived up to it too, he really did" Convinced that Kazan was serious about making a meaningful film, Schulberg shared his recent creation with the director, a play based on his experiences on the docks, entitled, *On the Waterfront*. They read it on the floor of the writer's living room. Kazan was enthralled. He pushed Schulberg to convert the play into script. Schulberg agreed and the rewrites began. They produced 8 script drafts over the next 2 years before completing a final draft with the working title "Golden Warriors" a name Schulberg was enamored with but was later changed by Kazan who saw it as a potential trouble spot with the HUAC as glorification of the working man. Schulberg kept it in the film, naming Terry Malloy's racing club *The Golden Warriors.* (Another explanation, offered by Kazan, was his attempt to resurrect Clifford Odets' *Golden Boy* the stage play that had brought Kazan so much early success.)

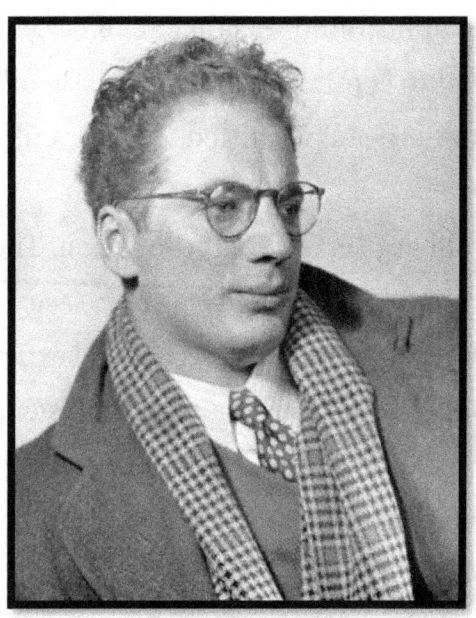

Clifford Odets

Kazan did make his own "original golden warrior," in the character of Terry Malloy, a warrior who will take on the mob, rise from temporary defeat and depose of his corrupt adversary, Johnny Friendly. That optimistic theme, to face seemingly overwhelming adversity and win, was wholly suited to the outlook of the scrapping and determined immigrant inside of Kazan. In prior stage work, especially Tennessee Williams' *Streetcar* and of Arthur Miller's *All My Sons* and *Death of a Salesman*, Kazan often added bits and pieces that spoke out against exploitation, degradation, pointless materialism while advocating moral responsibility. However, the pessimism infused in those dramas by the playwrights was suited to Kazan's true outlook on the American way of life as it would be in Waterfront.

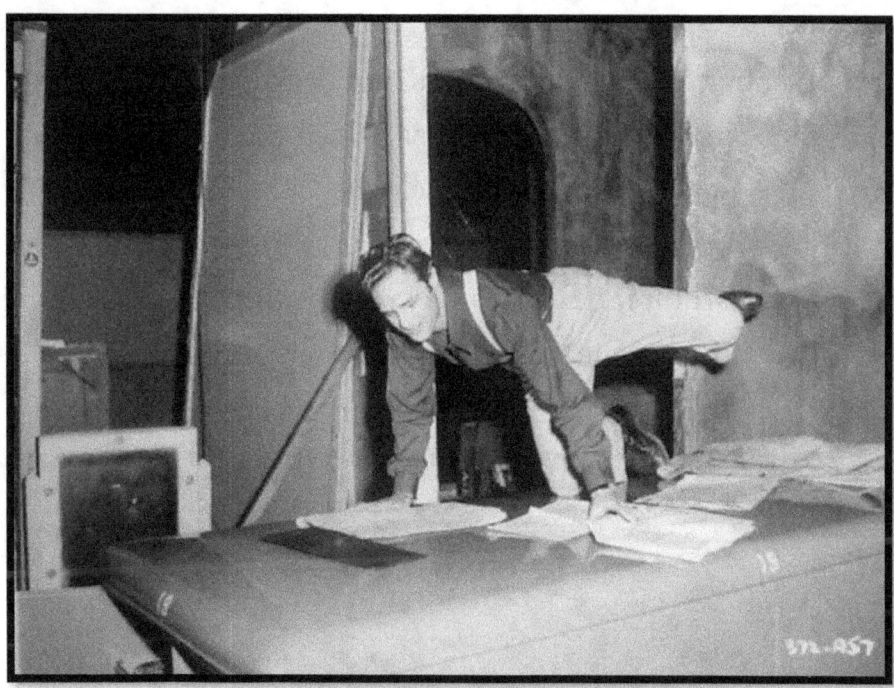

Brando on the set of *Streetcar*

To accomplish that, he turned to what he knew best and what had been his highest success to date, *Streetcar*. He would revive and meld Tennessee Williams' characters from *Streetcar* into his Waterfront script. Blanche DuBois "an ambivalent figure who is attracted and repulsed to the harshness and vulgarity surrounding her, became in, some part the character of Edie Doyle. Her ambivalence, however, is transferred to the character of Terry Malloy (The original Terry Malloy as written by Schulberg was anything but ambivalent) and Terry shared several characteristics with Stanley Kowalski including the inability to control his violence or to comprehend his situations and actions.

Terry, like Kowalski is vulnerable with a thin coat of sensitivity. However, unlike Kowalski, Terry holds the facility to grow and change. (The original Terry Malloy, in both Siodmak's and Miller's versions, are driven, somewhat educated men on a mission.)

In the final script of Waterfront, Schulberg and Kazan delivered a three-part structure, each marked by a death. In part one, Terry goes along with corruption revealed in the "shape-up" scene and helps set up the death of Joey Doyle. In part two, Terry discovers depth of his corruption. This part ends with the death of Kayo Dugan. Part three, the martyrdom scene with Father Barry's sermon, Terry is resurrected and fights back after death of his brother Charlie.

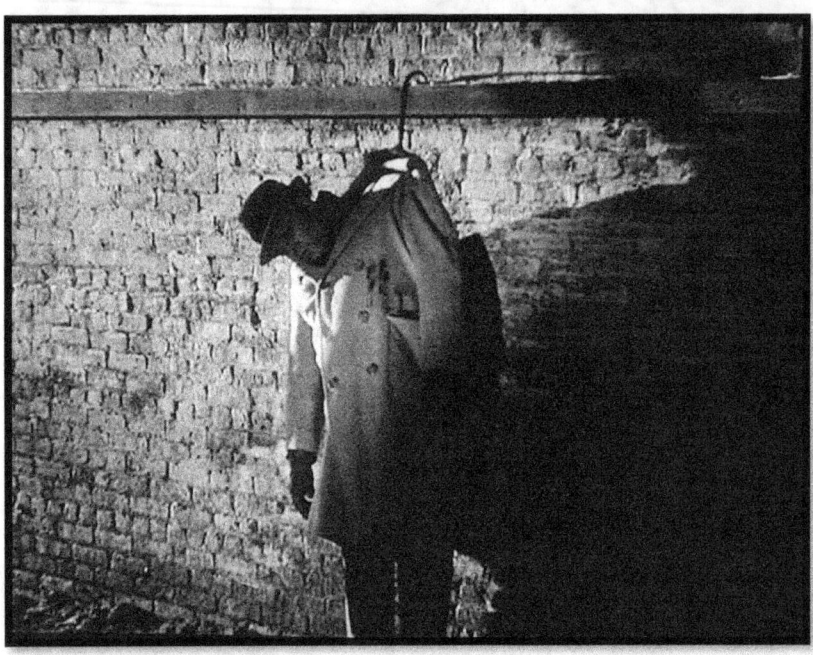

"That picture is terribly simple. It's all up front" Kazan said "It's mostly about this dumb kid who's unprepared and to whom it's painful to do what he did, who realizes through the girl and through what he knows in his heart and sees with his eyes, that telling on his friends was the better of the two choices facing him. The early death of Joey Doyle, who had obviously caused enough trouble within the rank and file to have the corrupt union bosses order his killing, signals, for Kazan, the birth of a new labor leader "In the labor movement" Kazan said "a new movement starts with the death of a person, through the memory of a martyr."

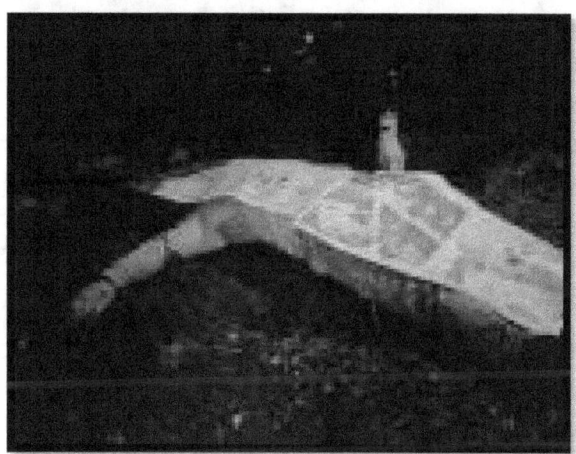

This again is a possible allegory for Kazan's testimony before the HUAC. While the reworked *Waterfront* script clearly displays Kazan-the -immigrants belief that determination of purpose leads to positive change, (his own remarkable life is a testament to that)

There was also in the Kazan credo, a lack of moral judgment. In immigrant Kazan's view, there was no room for such lofty notions, as his testimony before the HUAC clearly showed.

He had, like so many of his characters, a moral ambivalence. Clearly, the social consciences influence of Miller (and probably Schulberg) would define the scripts clear notion of good and evil, right and wrong. Conversely, it was this combination of Kazan's optimism and moral ambivalence and Miller /Schulberg's social conscious, which would blend to make the script so perfect.

Kazan had also reviewed the script that Schulberg had outlined for Curtis a few months before and determined that although the Curtis script although it had many similarities to the Waterfront script, it was, as Schulberg recalled, not as good.

In the Curtis script, the protagonist is a reporter who finds himself facing the Mobs vengeance for reporting about the real conditions on the docks.

In the new script, written by Kazan and Schulberg, the character was changed from a news reporter working on the outside of the docks to a dockworker thug working on the inside of the operation.

Even with those changes, there is a slight hint of the influence of director Rickard Siodmak left in the final Waterfront script. Most prominent (as it is in many of Siodmak films) domestic strife, such as sibling rivalry, is a key component that resonates in *Waterfront* in the relationship between Charlie and Terry Malloy.

Another Siodmak trademark is the uneasiness in the family unit. Something either has gone wrong or is changing at a disturbingly rapid pace and one member of the family manipulates the other for material gain, as Charlie Malloy did with his brother Terry; fixing the fight of his life so Charlie can earn a fortune from Terry's defeat. When change comes between the brothers, it comes fast and it comes violently.

It is also interesting that in Siodmak's brilliant film, *The Killers*, with its hard-boiled realism, a promising young boxer turns criminal and works with gangsters whom he later betrays and is killed as a result.

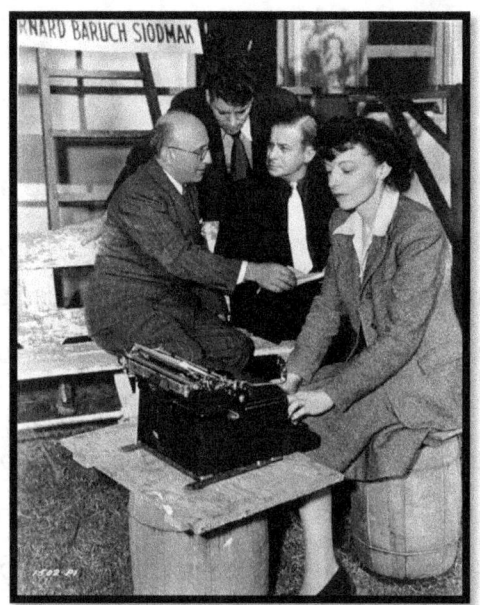

Siodmak on the set of *The Killers*

Both films, *Waterfront* and *The Killers*, open with a graphic murder scene by gangsters. The ever-present powerful mother figure in Siodmak's films warns the protagonist of impending danger. In *Waterfront*, hoodlum Johnny Friendly is clearly the father figure to Terry Malloy and Charlie Malloy, who warns Terry of the contract to murder him, is the Mother-side of the relationship.

Waterfront also echoes *The Killers* grimly purposeful mission and employees the same simple sets, atmospheric lighting and nightmarish nocturnal world of shadowy streets, seedy bars and brutish gangsters. The Killers also includes a network of professional hoodlums, a devastating double cross, the spirit of heavy fatalism and a hard-boiled protagonist doomed by existential fate

Like Kazan, and probably not lost on Kazan, Siodmak was the benefactor of great actors and outstanding filmmakers and by his own ability to inspire stellar performances from minor characters.

Siodmak was also notorious for creating sets full of other psychological tensions, use of music, visual images and the expressionistic montage to convey sexual energy. Siodmak's use of deep-focus, like Kazan's in Waterfront, is also notable.

Siodmak's influence is also found in Terry Malloy's jacket, the films motif noir, which symbolizes a form of lost identity. Siodmak frequently had his male characters wear uniforms as a means to help male characters reclaim their lost identity. In Terry Malloy's case, the jacket symbolizes his lost innocence, his goodness.

On a less symbolic stance, the jacket also serves another, more practical purpose, to keep the wearer warm. Kazan's longshoremen are working poor and the script is filled with remarks about making ends meet and keeping food on the table. In their world, a fine leather jacket is expensive and not to be tossed aside because two men were murdered in it.

None of these similarities was lost on Siodmak who entered suit against On the *Waterfront* producers shortly after the film was released. Although the details of the suit were not made public was awarded $100,000 in a settlement.

Before Kazan went back to California, Schulberg took him on a tour of the Waterfront and introduced him to his friends down there including Father John Corridan.

As Schulberg recalled; *"The day I brought Kazan, Father John was yelling, "I'm going to stop (New York's powerful Cardinal) Spellman." He was cursing--"that son of a bitch"--and shouting. Kazan could not believe a priest would talk like that. That day he was going up in smoke. He was furious that (Powerful New*

130

York Cardinal) Spellman was giving an award to John McCormack--the "Mr. Big" of the waterfront. Mr. McCormack was a respectable man. He had lots and lots of money. He put Mayor Impellitteri in office. Nevertheless, the people under McCormack were monsters and killers. Kazan asked Schulberg "Are you sure he's a priest? Maybe he's working there for the waterfront rebels in disguise." Assured that Corridan was in fact a Priest, Kazan shook his head in amazement and said, "We have to make him the centerpiece of the movie."

PITCHING THE SCRIPT, AGAIN
SPRING 1953

"Goodbye Mr. Zanuck: it certainly has been a pleasure working at 16th Century Fox. " **Director Jean Renoir**

In the late Spring of 1953, Kazan felt that he was ready to introduce the Waterfront script to the major studios for consideration, especially to his mentor Darryl Zanuck, the head of Twentieth Century Films. "I assured Budd" Kazan said "that it was the kind of material Darryl couldn't resist. Budd was less sure; having grown up in the betray-your-brother society of the film world (he) seemed to distrust the whole movie colony"

Schulberg, who was eventually paid $5000 for his work on the film, was not in a position to gamble financially. His farm was mortgaged and his primary source of income was from his recent novel, *The Disenchanted*, which was then number one on the *New York Times* best seller list for the sixth straight month, but a film could take years to finish and there was no telling if the end product was saleable. The script was sent to Daryl Zanuck at 20th Century Fox Studios. Four weeks went by without a reply or even an acknowledgment.

Kazan soothed a jittery Schulberg by telling him that he believed that Zanuck was in Europe. "or perhaps" he recalled, "that's only what I told Budd." Finally, a letter from Zanuck arrived.

"I have struggled with the problem of the waterfront story as this means a decision of great importance to the company. I like the basic material

enormously, as I told you when I read the treatment (a 35-page outline sent earlier) but I continue to worry about labors support (for the project)

We must not hit everything on the nose and get up on a soapbox. If we do that, we will certainly have a failure. We must stick to the personal story (Something that Kazan took to mean, the love angle) and let the picture speak for it.

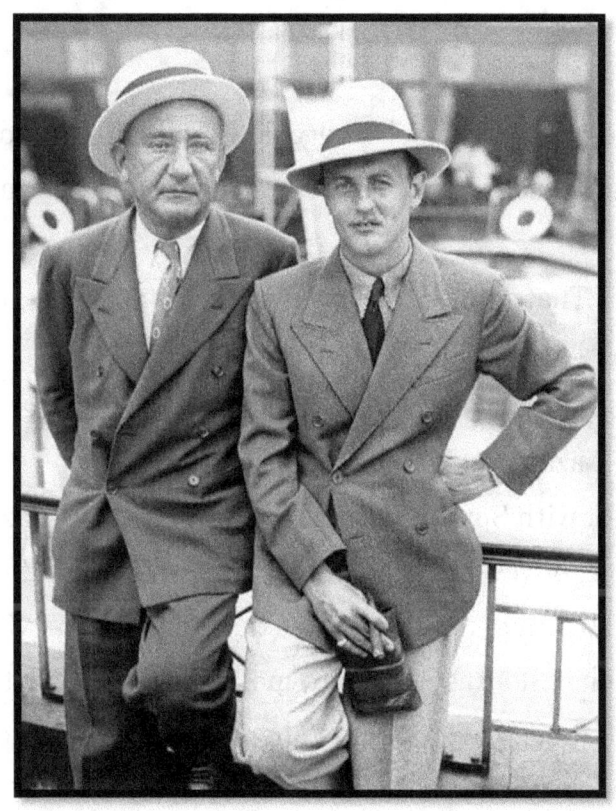

Joseph M. Schenck and Darryl F. Zanuck in 1934

I am certain that the picture as a whole, by what it shows and not by words, will reveal the corruption of the waterfront. We don't have to make speeches about it. I believe that the evil of the waterfront situation should be the background as it was in Pinky and that the personal story must predominate.

There is no use in making a wonderful picture like Zapata, which nobody came to see except the intelligentsia.
I recommend that Budd and you come out here next week for one or two days. I believe I have some valuable story contributions, which will help the girl from looking like an amateur detective who is out to right wrongs of the world. This is an important undertaking and if we are to go ahead with courage, we have to know conclusively that we understand each other"

The normally Hollywood-pessimistic Schulberg flew out to Hollywood, twice to meet with Zanuck on the proposed script changes and came away certain that the film would be made.

"We found" Zanuck said "That some of Darryl's suggestions, when put to the test, helped our story, others did not and we didn't use them"

The corrected script was sent back to Zanuck. Kazan and Schulberg waited another four weeks before Kazan and Schulberg decided to

Fly out to California to meet with Spyros Slouras, a fellow Greek to Kazan and president of Fox. Over wine, olives and cheese, they discussed the film and again, came away with the understanding, that they had a deal for the film with Fox. Years later, Kazan figured that Slouras wanted to make the film, in fact, intended to make the film, but that Zanuck never intended to make it and had lied to Slouras about his commitment to the project

They returned East and shortly afterwards were summoned out to California, this time to meet with Daryl Zanuck.

Schulberg said, "Kazan swore that Darryl Zanuck owed him a picture, so we mailed him the script and got on the train and went west...tripping to Hollywood - Kazan and me. Kazan who directed this film, who already won an Academy Award for *A Gentleman s Agreement* - all the way out telling me what a great script we had. He was saying we were so lucky because I had Arthur Miller and Tennessee Williams *Streetcar* and I think that is one the best three scripts I've ever had. And I was worried... I told him I was worried about coming back (to Hollywood). I told him I didn't think they would like it out there. Kazan was annoyed with me."

On the cross-country trip, Kazan would sit in the club car reading the script repeatedly making a few changes. The character of Terry Malloy, Brando's character, was originally called Joey Doyle. Kazan changed that on the train, probably out of simple boredom.

In the first draft, the charter of Edie Doyle originally lived with her sister May Doyle, May's daughter, Pop and her brother. The family name was Monahan later changed to the more mainline Doyle. The sister was later written out, as was her daughter.

Kayo Duggan's name was changed from Petey (Peter Pantos?) and was originally killed when a crate of fish falls on him, not Irish whisky. The character "J.P.," (Johnny Friendly's loan shark) was given the line "When I'm dead and gone, you'll know what a friend I was." The original response, from Dugan, (although originally the response came from a character named Murphy who was dropped from the finished film script) "Drop dead so I can see if you're right." But changed in the film to "Why don't you drop dead now so we can test your theory?"

In the original script, the hero was a WASP reporter named Al Chase who was also Edie's love interest. The Al Chase character was determined to seduce Edie (Unlike Terry Malloy, who, at best is unsure of his feelings for her) but is rebuked by her because he refuses, out of fear, to report on the waterfront mob. However, he changes his mind, reports on the mob and is shot as a result, but survives. Kazan dropped the Al Chase character completely and changed him into ex-fighter. The place where the Al Chase character meets Edie is in a nice nightclub, not the dreary docks. In the finished film, Terry takes Edie to a local bar for shots and beers.

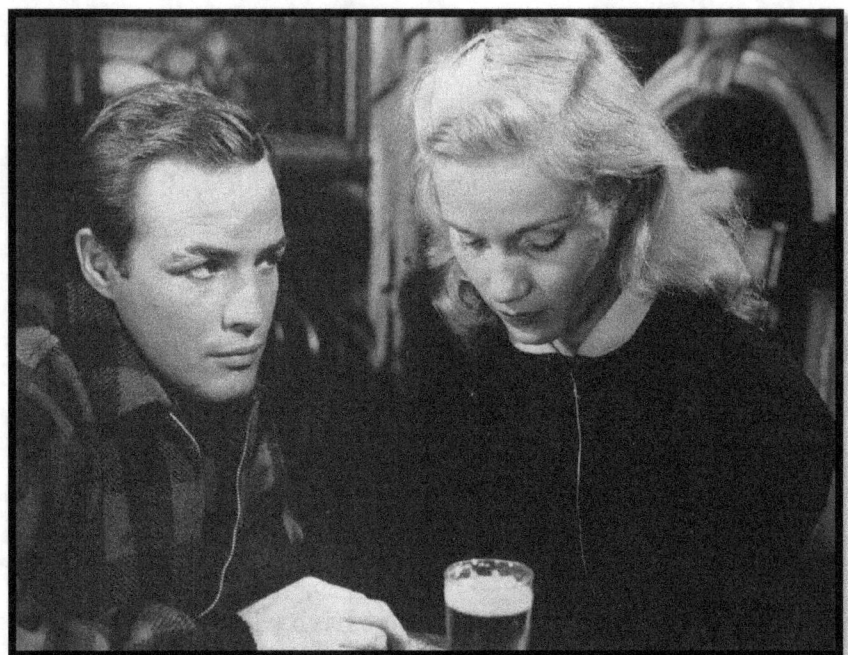

Father Barry was originally Father Moran but the church meeting that he holds to discuss the union was kept in both scripts except originally it took place during Joey Doyle's funeral mass.

Another scene, also centered on the now rewritten funeral scene, had the gangsters arriving en mass and tossing $500 into the coffin, which Edie promptly throws back at them causing a fistfight in the church. The Al Chase character rescues Edie from the Parish Hall, as Terry Malloy does in the film.

Moose, the African American dockworker was a Johnny Friendly thug in the first script. The character of Charlie Malloy does not exist not is there any mention of Terry Malloy having been a boxer or taking a dive for the mob, Johnny Friendly was Mickey Friendly. The essence of the cab ride scene made it from one draft to the other.

Schulberg recalled *He's be savoring it. He'd say 'It's one of the best scripts I ever had' and then he would turn to me and say 'Budd I don't understand you, why aren't you more excited? I said 'Gadge, I have a terrible feeling that Zanuck is not going to like it' and Kazan said 'Budd, what is wrong with you? He's going to love it!' He said that all the way out. But coming from there (Hollywood) I knew what kind of movies they had made and were making and I didn't think they were going to love it'*

"When we got off the train... and there was no one to meet us and I said, "Kaz, there's no limo".

Now Kazan is a very down to earth guy and he said, "We don t need a limo, I hate limos."

So we went up to the Beverly Hills Hotel and got there, checked in and no invitations from Daryl Zanuck - it was a film to be made for Zanuck - no invitation to come down to Palm Springs and play croquet. I said "there's no invitation to play croquet".

Kazan says "I hate croquet!" and I said, "Yeah, I don't but we're still not being invited"

And we went up to the room, we had a little suite, and there weren't any flowers. I looked around and didn't see any flowers. And I said, "Katz, we have no flowers". Kazan says, "What it is with you, I don t need flowers. To hell with the flowers".

It was beginning to sound like a vaudeville act"

And I said, "Kaz, you come from New York, I come from Hollywood. And I know the unspoken language of Hollywood and Zanuck is telling us something. I tell you Gadge, I think we're in trouble"

And he really got mad at me. He said "Jesus Budd, you're such a worrier. Let's go out and enjoy it. Let's go to the Polo Lounge, have a drink" He didn't drink much. I enjoyed drinking, he didn't. But he wanted drink"

Kazan didn't believe me. But Monday morning we called and we had no set appointment. The secretary said "DZ is not back from Palm Springs yet. He's coming around lunch time. Why don't you come in and we'll give you an office

By this time Kazan was worried. When Zanuck finally arrived, Schulberg and Kazan still had to wait while Zanuck worked his way through several meetings before they were called in. This was not the treatment that Hollywood's favored director had become accustomed to.

"Daryl Zanuck met us" Kazan said "raving about Cinemascope, he said "I'm so excited, I'm so excited, we have this great new medium, Cinemascope, he said that as the great thing about our business. First it was flickers and the films jumped, and then we learned how to make them more smoothly. And then we had color and then we had sound and now we have the Cinemascope. The screen almost wraps around you. The girls in cinema scope! The tits 'll practically be in your face!"

"Kazan and I looked at each other" Schulberg said "because we had written that this film should be something in flat black and white. As he went on about what could be done, he said, "Can you imagine what Prince Valiant would look like in Cinemascope?"

And I thought, uh oh because our script was specifically in black and white. And finally Kazan said, "Daryl, what about our picture?"

There was a long, pregnant pause and Mr. Zanuck said, "Boys, I'm sorry, but I don t like a single thing about it".

And I think I was quiet and Kazan said not a single thing.

Kazan and Schulberg sat in shocked silence. Zanuck did nothing more than to stare at them. Finally, Zanuck said "You mean Darryl, that you don't like anything about it? Anything? It's exactly what the audiences want to see now"
He said; "Whatta ya got except a bunch of sweaty longshoremen".

"And that stabbed me in the heart because when Kazan came to talk with me about doing this movie, I went down on the Lower West Side, in the Chelsea area - and I got involved with and amazing man, one of the most amazing I ever met, the waterfront priest - Father John Corridan.

I mean, we've learned now that the ILA - the International Longshoreman s Association - was totally in the hands of the mob. They were killers and thieves. Corridan was really filling the vacuum and trying to guide the rebel longshoremen into making some effort to win back their young and make a real living.

This went on for several years and I hung in with these people. I love these people and when Zanuck said that all you got is a lot of sweaty longshoremen... my heart was broken.

Zanuck's fascination with Cinemascope and his commitment to make all of the studios pictures in the wide screen process was a decision was not made with any artistic venue in mind but rather it was made out of survival. The studios were competing with television, and theater attendance was down, way down. Television was the first serious competition Hollywood faced. The industry had drafted the films industries best writers, directors and technical people. As a result, the entertainment it offered was well written and produced and it was free. However, television was still a black and white medium, if Hollywood was going to compete it needed to offer something completely different for the paying public, hence wide screen Cinemascope.

Zanuck was such a big promoter of Cinemascope that when theater owners refused to make the significant investment required to install Cinemascope equipment, they felt it was another fade like the short lived 3-D, Zanuck pledged that all future 20th Century Fox releases would be in Cinemascope. He had already licensed the process to Metro-Goldwyn-Mayer Walt Disney Studios, Warner Brothers, Universal and Columbia. Now Kazan and Schulberg sat before him offering a black and white film shot in documentary style.

Kazan again offered the argument that Waterfront offered a tightly written story line with social significance "It's unique–something different–it catches the whole spirit of the harbor–the way you caught the Okies in Grapes." (The film *Grapes of Wrath*, a Zanuck success) To which Zanuck replied, "But the Okies came across like American pioneers. Who's going to care about a lot of sweaty longshoremen?"

Until the day he died, Kazan believed that Zanuck's rejection was based in Hollywood's anxiety about representations of social class in stories and its reluctance to deal with the labor unions issue. He also pointed out that when Fix rejected the script, that Zanuck was having his own problems with Hollywood trade unions.

There is no doubt that Zanuck was wrong and Kazan was right. However, the interesting speculation is--- what if they had accepted Zanuck's financing for the film with the stipulation that it be filmed in wide screen Technicolor? According to Kazan, Zanuck then added, "And who gives a shit about longshoremen?" as almost a challenge to Kazan's statement as fact that the people wanted films about labor problems and longshoreman. He then added "I even tried to make Terry (Brando's part) a member of the FBI, but it didn't work" and rambled on about the general poor state of the film industry and returned to his plans to film Prince Valiant in Cinemascope.

Kazan stood abruptly and started to leave the room with Schulberg in tow. Zanuck stopped them and tried to smooth things over by offering to pay Schulberg for the time he had put in on the script's rewrites but added, bluntly, that Fox didn't owe Kazan anything because he was "already rich"

Kazan, who had never learned the art of overlooking a slight,   would never forgive Zanuck for turning away from the script and for decades spread a story that if Zanuck had produced film, it would have been a dud.

When the meeting ended, Schulberg and Kazan went back to the Beverly Hills Hotel the manager informed them that Zanuck's office had already called and taken them off of the Fox studio account. If they wanted to stay another night, they would have to pay for it out of their own pockets. They paid.

Once back in their room, Schulberg confronted Kazan "God dam it Gadge, I'm furious with you! I was really happy where I was in New Hope (His farm) I was living a nice peaceful life. Now I'm all torn apart, I'm upset; I'm back in the goddamn Beverly Hills Hotel! You pulled me out of my comfortable little world!"

Kazan was indulgent. "Budd, I'll tell you this, I'm going to make this picture if I have to get a handheld camera and shoot it myself. I'll use actual longshoreman and get some guys from the actor's studio who'll work for nothing, or a piece of it. I'll make it like a home movie. I'm going to make this damn thing."

"Budd wasn't speaking to me" Kazan recalled, "I knew what he felt…. Budd was furious and it was at me. He felt that I had led him into a trap where all his work had come to nothing. "

Schulberg said that he intended to return to his farm and write Waterfront as a novel (Which he eventually did do) however, convinced him to wait. With the initial shock of rejection over, slowly, their confidence in the Waterfront script returned and they began to market the concept around town, but to dismal results.

Schulberg recalled: *"After that, (The meeting with Zanuck) every studio in town had the same reaction. We went to Warner s, Paramount, MGM, every single one said no. They wouldn't make the picture. And as I said... what we were talking about a few minutes ago, one thing that really warmed me to Kazan... and I tried, I really tried... and I turned on him. Back at the hotel... I was so mad.*

I had spent about two years, I had actually mortgaged my farm, I was going broke doing this movie... and I turned on him and I said, "God dam it, I told you there weren't going to make this movie". And Kazan said, "Budd, I promise I'll make it. I have to get on the docks with a hand held IMO and use the actual longshoremen" - the rebel longshoremen who were working with Ed Xavier and some of the actors out of the (Actors) Studio and make this movie. And that's pretty much how it was made . It really was the longest of the long shots. It was almost accidental that the movie ever got made at all. It was a long shot. We couldn't stop. It was like the reflexes of a dead animal that keeps kicking and twitching. We kept making adjustment to the script" Kazan said "I remember we carried off a typewriter from Fox and a great stack of blue paper, the floor of our suite was littered with crumpled balls of blue paper"

THE PRODUCER

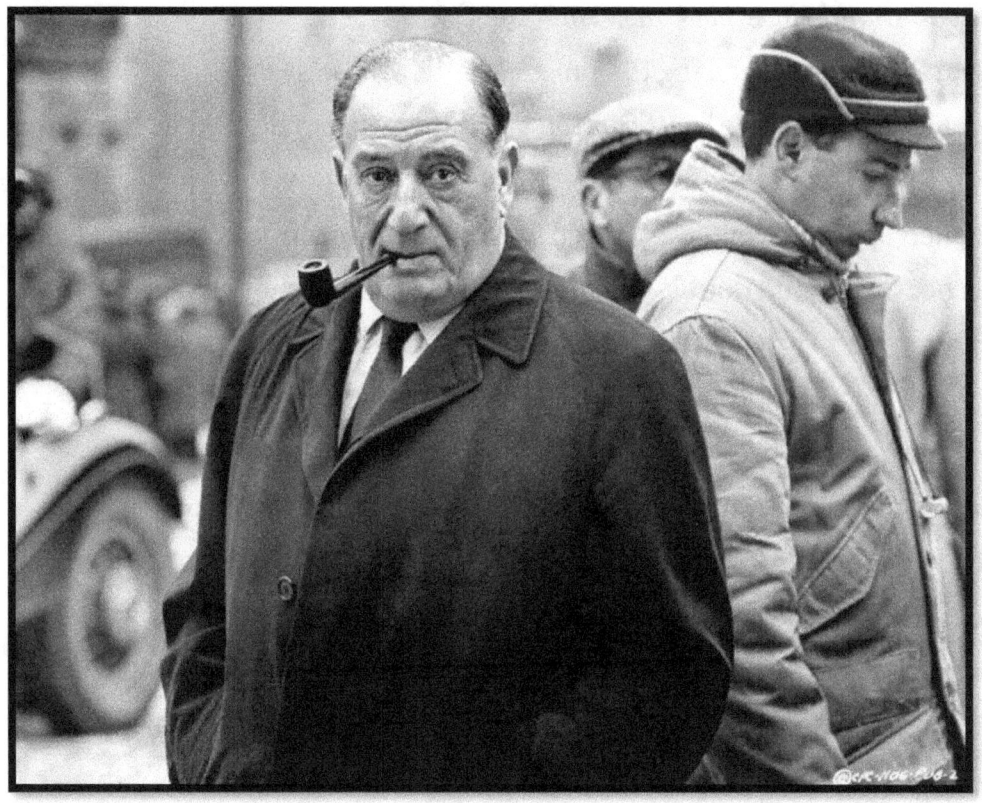

"A gambler is nothing but a man who makes his living out of hope." **William Bolitho**

"Sam Spiegel was a modern day Robin Hood, who steals from the rich and steals from the poor" **Billy Wilder**

   Independent film producer Sam Spiegel was, as Marlon Brando so aptly called him "a colorful, manipulative freebooter". Spiegel had produced *The African Queen* and *The Stranger* and would later be responsible for bringing such classics as *The Bridge on the River Kwai* and *Lawrence of Arabia* to the big screen.   Before that, he had backed a number of very forgettable but very profitable films over the years, including the horrific *Melba* (1953) *The Prowler*,

(1951) *When I Grow Up* (1951) *We Were Strangers* (1949) *Tales of Manhattan* (1942) *The Invader and Invisible Opponent* (1933).

Spiegel rose to prominence during the tail end of the studio system. He was, said historian Kevin Brownlow, "perhaps the last authentic movie tycoon" who arrived in Hollywood a generation too late. He was also a Hollywood survival story. His sudden appearance in the United States from Europe was followed by a trail of bad checks, lies and double crosses, a pattern that did not change during his time in Hollywood. Through it all, the great wealth and the brink of bankruptcy, he had a reputation in Hollywood as a man who would do whatever he had to do to make a project work.

"He learned, for instance" Kazan wrote, "to lie without betraying tremor of his facial muscles" 25   It came to be called "Being Spiegeled", the Hollywood equivalent of being left holding the check for an enormous dinner one assumed they had been invited to by Spiegel. Still, his films worked because Spiegel managed to attract a top-notch cast with profit participation and salary plan.

In one plan, for African Queen, Humphrey Bogart received 25 percent of the profits, and Katherine Hepburn took 10 percent. John Huston, as director and partner with Spiegel in Horizon pictures, received 50 percent of profits. The financing came from a British distributor Romulus Films, Ltd. which put up production costs in exchange for the exclusive rights to distribution in the eastern hemisphere.

Unfortunately, for everyone involved, except Spiegel, no money arrived from The African Queen, which was a box office smash. Teams of lawyer showed that Spiegel had managed, on paper, to lower the gross receipts to the point where the film actually lost money. The only one who made money on the film was Spiegel, who took his share from distribution rights and production expenses. He got away with it because he was a great salesman. He had an enormous charm and a seemingly irresistible gift for persuasion. It was Spiegel who convinced Jordon's Prince Hussein to allow parts of Lawrence of Arabia, filmed in his country based on the highly improbable argument that the Jews and the Arabs are actually blood cousins separated by slightly different cultures.

He was a man with quirks and deep emotions. In both his personnel and professional life, he was said to be generous and protective to those he loved and vicious, and vindictive to those he hated or who hated him.

Legends abound in Hollywood over Spiegel. He spread most of them. The rumor mill said that he had escaped Nazi Germany through blackmail and bribery, that he was a front for the gangster Meyer Lansky, that he had been smuggled into the US through the Mexican border in the trunk of a car. He was a man who left the impression that he was hunted. Kazan once noticed that inside Spiegel's suite at the New York St. Regis hotel there were "two flat rolls of American Express checks. This suggested that he was ready to make a quick getaway at a moment's notice"

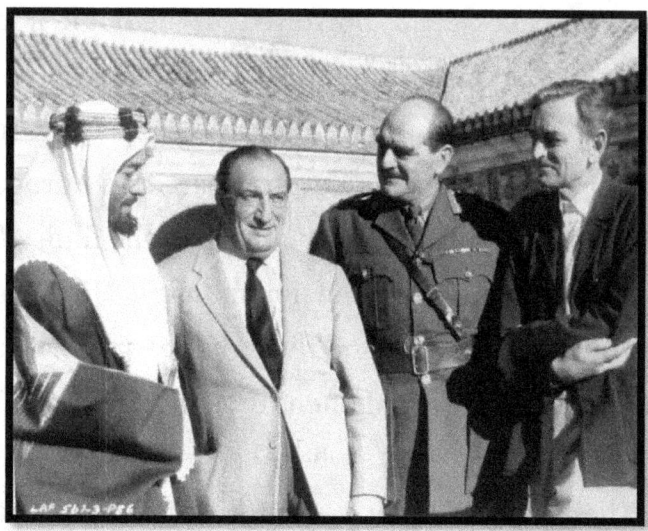

Spiegel, second from the left, on the set of _Lawrence of Arabia._

Placing aside the dozens of fascinating legends and tall tales about him, Sam Spiegel, the son of a Zionist tobacco merchant, was more than probably born on November 11, 1903, in Jaroslau, Galicia, then part of the Austria-Hungarian Empire and now Jaroslaw, Poland. But even that simple fact was distorted by the ever status conscious Spiegel who claimed he was born and raised in far more fashionable Vienna, Austria. But he was, in fact, born in Jaroslau within a 100 mile radius of Hollywood legends Sam Goldwin, Louis B. Mayer, Harry, Jack Warner, and Adolph Zukor.

However, and as Spiegel was very quick to point out, unlike those men, he was born and raised as an assimilated Ashkenazi Jew and by his own frequent admission was far more educated and cultured than the crass Warner or the belligerent Goldwin. Actually, the statement was factual. Spiegel did speak spoke nine languages and held a degree from the University of Vienna.

At age 18 was a leader in the Zionist youth movement that helped to settle Palestine on a farm inhabited by Bedouins. He had his share of legal problems in Palestine as well. He stole bank check's and "borrowed", as he put it, a friend's white Mercedes which he claimed to have "forgotten to return".

He left there in 1925, abandoning a young wife and child and a cattle importing business and a slew of Israeli creditors, to pursue a film career in Europe. He wound up in Berlin where he helped with the publicity of the film, *All Quiet on the Western Front,* Spiegel's paying job in the film industry. He fell in with Berlin's Jewish filmmakers and bounced around the industry until he was eventually arrested in London, on a variety of offenses, and deported to France. Undaunted, he arrived in the US in the 1920's where he passed himself off as a diplomat and economist. That guise led to his arrest for diplomatic fraud while in mid-negotiation for a $3,000.00 a week contract with a top film studio. The US deported him to Germany but the ever-resourceful Spiegel managed to land a position at Universal Studios' German office. During this time, he produced several German films (One featuring Peter Lorre) before fleeing the Nazi's. (One version has him escaping with Otto Preminger, although Preminger denied the story).

He lived in Europe and Mexico before finally landing back in the US in 1939, the rumor being that he came over the boarder hidden in the trunk of a tourist's car. He arrived in Mexico speaking fluent Spanish. He would later convince the Mexican government to put up money for a musical stage production called Mexicana. Spiegel got the play all the way to Broadway but quickly ran afoul of the Mexicans and was forced to flee the country in the dead of night. The director Otto Preminger later accused him of selling dope and running a white slavery racket in Mexico City.

Over the next two decades, he would be fabulously wealthy and dead broke. Schulberg had his own memories of Spiegel. "My mother at one point, soon after I got out of college, was in London, renting a house from some Lord, putting on airs, having a very successful career as an agent. She's rented as big house and was putting on some huge fancy party when, in the midst of this, the butler came in and said ; Madam, Brixton Prison is on the telephone" It was Spiegel, broke, in debt, caught in some funny business, calling to beg for money"

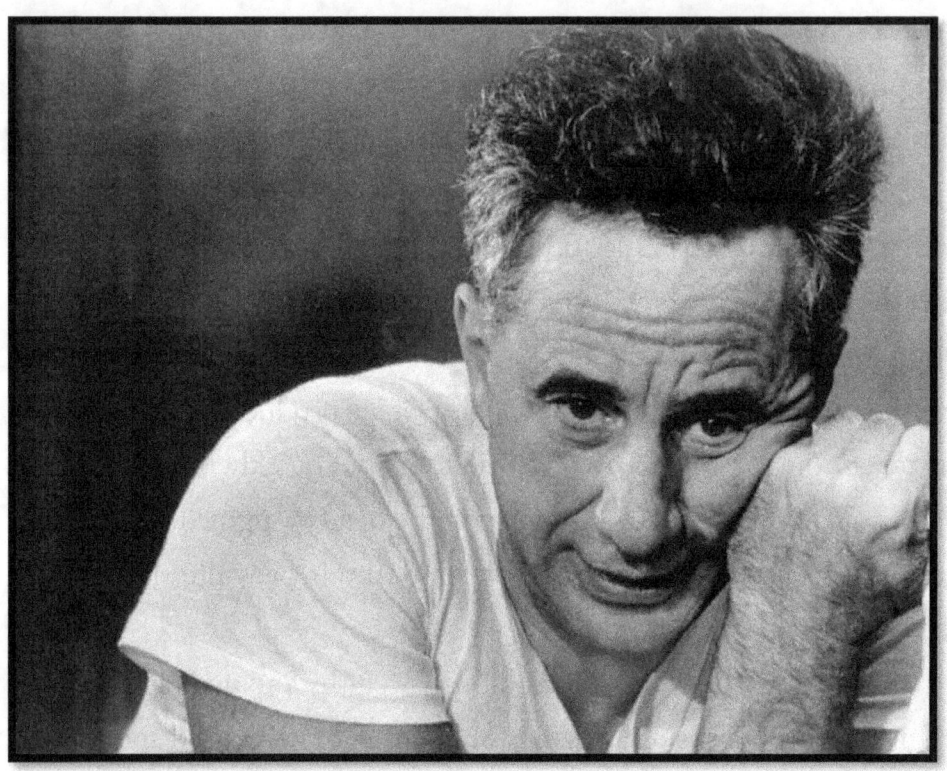

Unknown to Schulberg and Kazan, at the time he had agreed to produce Waterfront, Spiegel was dead broke. The IRS had taken his Beverly Hills estate for back taxes owed and his wife, from whom he was separated, had attached virtually all of his other assets.

His latest venture, a film called *Melba*, about an opera star, was a complete disaster. No one would release it and Spiegel had lost a small fortune on the production.

It was odd chance that brought the trio together. While Kazan and Schulberg sat in their hotel room working on rewrites, Spiegel's hotel room was directly across for theirs. The reason Spiegel was there was to throw a party. Although penniless again with no hope in site, Spiegel was true to form; he was throwing an expensive party and invited the Hollywood elite and allowing them the opportunity to bid on Melba's distribution rights.

Spiegel knocked at Kazan's door and found the writer and director in their bathrobes, unshaven and depressed "Boy's" announced Spiegel "Come to the party, I'm giving a very nice party tonight"

They declined and explained the situation to Spiegel who listened and said, "Why don't we meet tomorrow and you can tell me the story? (Of the script)" At 7:30 AM, on the morning after Spiegel's big party, Schulberg went to Spiegel's room, stepping over cigarette butts and empty glasses until he found a hung over Spiegel in bed, the silk sheets pulled up to his eyes.

"I said 'Sam I hate to wake everyone up' and he didn't stir. "Sam we're taking a morning plane out" but he groaned, just sort of groaned, very hung over. But he finally sort of nodded and said, "All right, so tell me the story" I walked around the bed for twenty minutes telling the story of the Waterfront script. Sam looked dead. I didn't know if he was listening or if I was talking to a corpse. Suddenly he pulled the sheet down to his chin and said "I'll see if I can do it' and later added 'If you guys think you can do it for $800,000 and do it fast, 35 shooting days, I'll try to raise the money from United Artists"

The next morning Spiegel high-pressured United Artists to put up $500,000 for the film, an almost insulting low budget given on Spiegel's agreement that the film would be filmed, edited and ready for pre-release in less than three months, a point Spiegel agreed to without Schulberg or Kazan's knowledge or consent. Few things travel faster than gossip in Hollywood.

The rumor, probably planted by Spiegel or perhaps the egotistical Kazan, already making the rounds in the studios was that Waterfront was slated as a grade A production by United who expected the film to gross record numbers. It was a complete fabrication of course, if anything, United executives probably saw the film as a creative tax lose, but nonetheless, a fabrication that could cause the equally egotistical Daryl Zanuck to lose face.

On the day Kazan and Schulberg flew back to New York, Daryl Zanuck released a press statement that he had dropped *On the Waterfront* from Fox's shooting schedule "Because he does not believe it adaptable to the wide screen technique." In New York, Kazan blew the remark off privately telling friends and supporters that the remark was nothing less than a "last ditch knifing" by Zanuck.

THE LEADING MAN
SUMMER, 1953

"Would people applaud me if I was a good plumber?" **Marlon Brando**

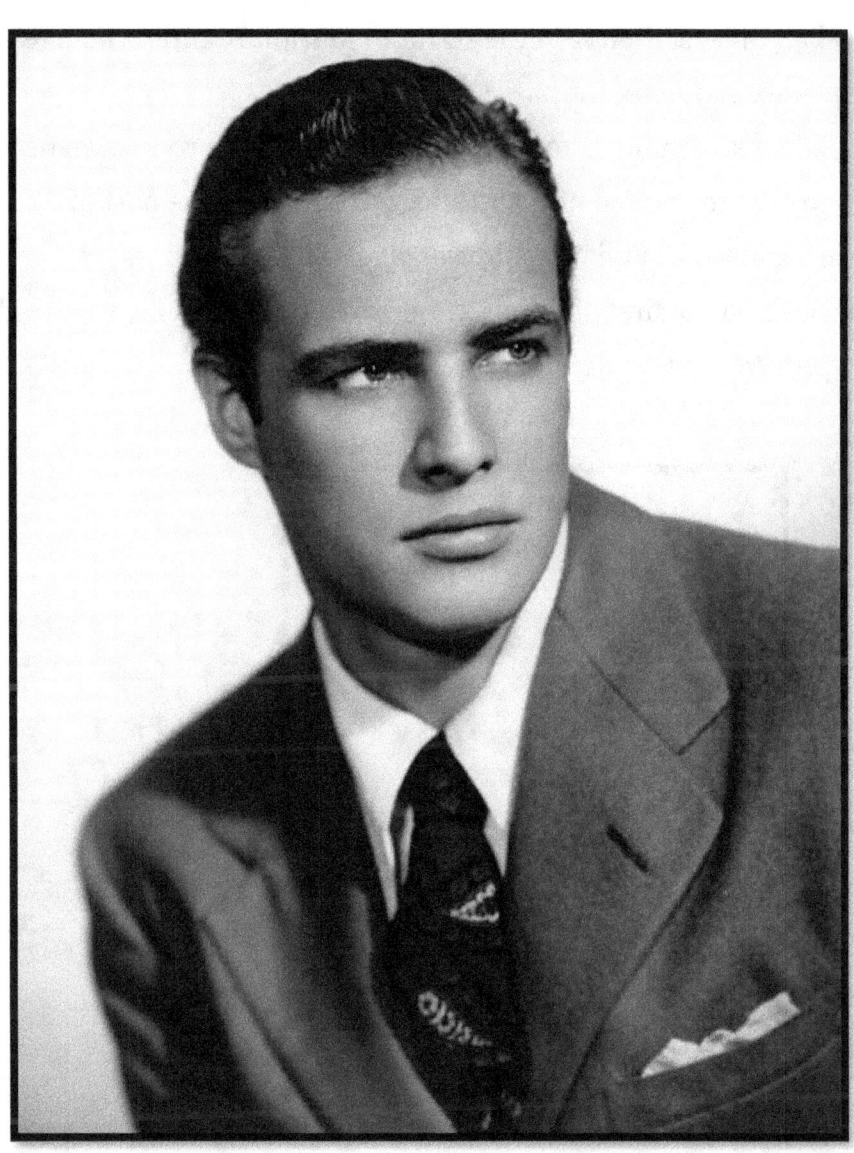

They had a great story, a great script, a visionary director, an above average screenwriter, and a producer who would stop at nothing to get the job done; now they needed star power.

Sam Spiegel had Montgomery Clift in mind for the role of Terry Malloy, but the troubled and troublesome Clift was involved with another project and unavailable much to Kazan's relief. Spiegel then sent the script to Marlon Brando who had worked with Kazan twice in the recent past.

In 1946, Brando, still a struggling actor, appeared in the stage production of *Truckline Café* where Kazan spotted him and suggested Brando the part of Stanley Kowalski in Tennessee Williams *A Streetcar named Desire*. After *Streetcar* Brando collected the first of his eight Oscar nominations, he appeared in Kazan's *Viva Zapata!* (1952) and *Julius Caesar* (1953)

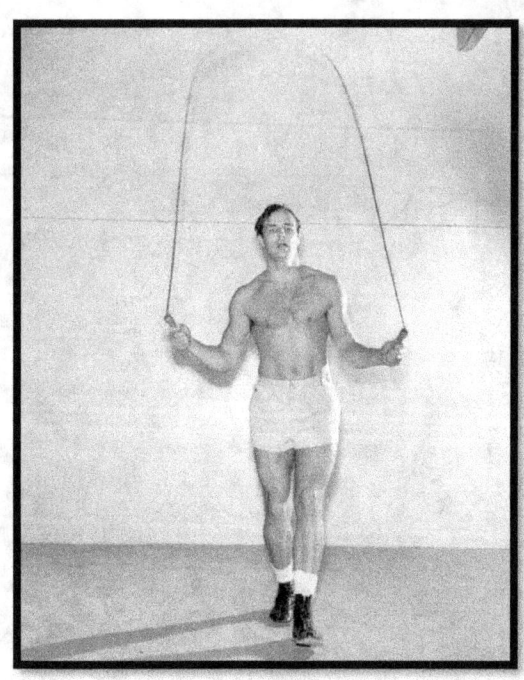

It was the beginning of the age of Brando and Kazan had ignited it. However, Brando sent the Waterfront script back to Kazan with a refusal with a terse note that the role was not right for him. However, before the script arrived, Schulberg placed bits of paper between the pages, an old Hollywood agents trick probably learned from his mother. When the bits of paper came back undisturbed, they knew that Brando had not read the work.

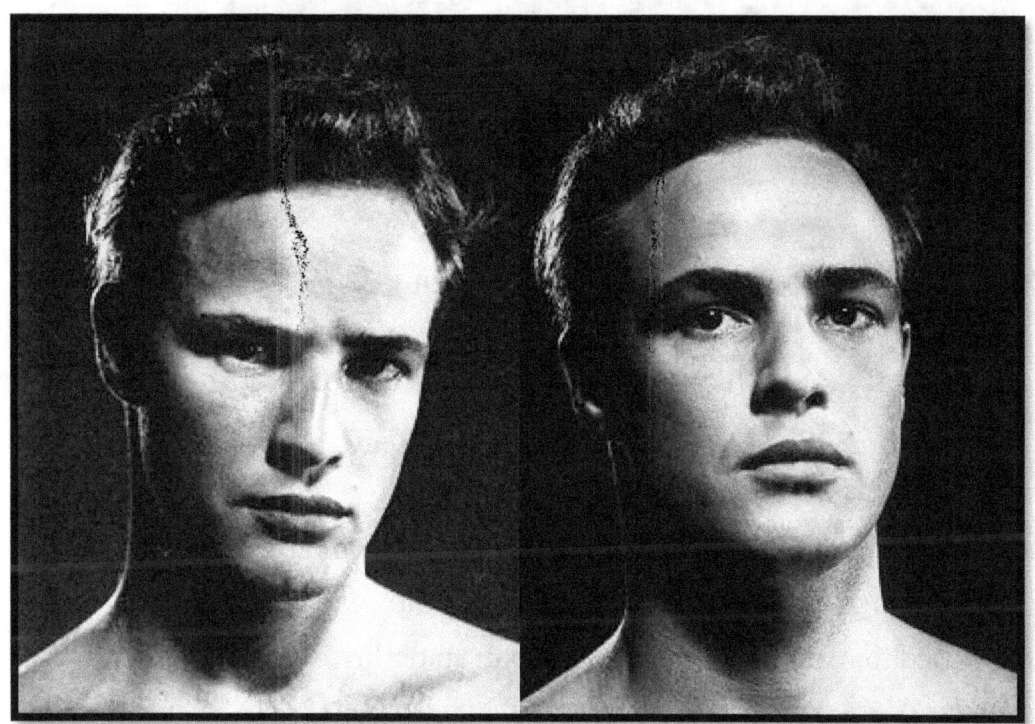

While Kazan and Schulberg were taken aback by the stars rejection, Spiegel, in typical Spiegel fashion, moved ahead and as usual, he did it with consulting with his partners.

Although Kazan owned 25% of the pending film, he seldom knew what Spiegel was doing with the film or what deals he was making with it. One afternoon without warning, Spiegel called Kazan and suggested he call Frank Sinatra to discuss the lead in the film.

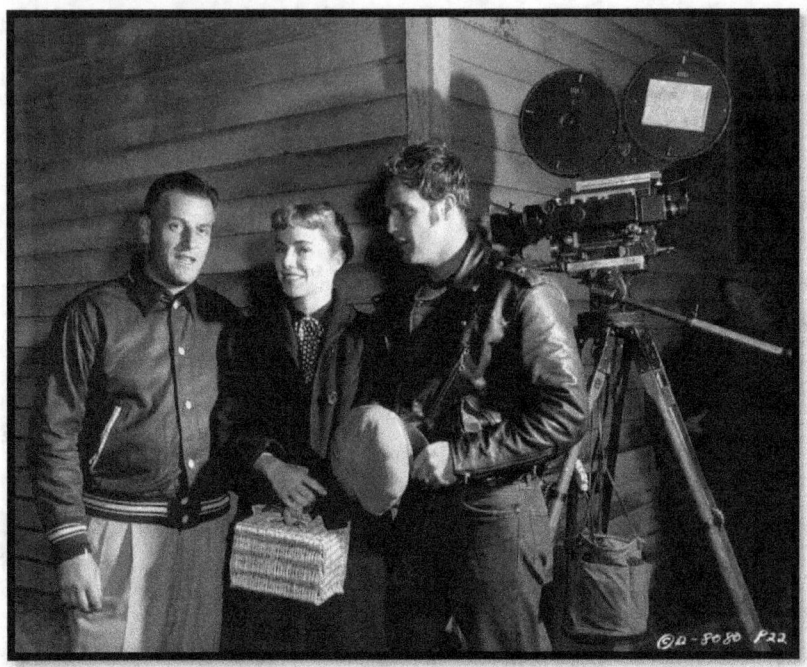

Brando, right, on the set of *The Wild Ones*.

Sinatra was, Kazan knew, perfect for the role. He was born and raised on the waterfront in Hoboken, New Jersey. His family had political and mob ties there, which could be used to make location shooting, run smoothly.

"And" said Kazan "He spoke perfect Hobonense"

The script was sent to Sinatra who agreed to do the film. While Sinatra did not have a written agreement with Spiegel, he did have a formal oral agreement and as one of Hollywood's most bankable stars, Sinatra probably logically felt he did not necessarily need a written agreement so early in production. However, Sam Spiegel was not a man who conducted business in the normal fashion. Then Spiegel called Kazan and asked, "Why did Marlon turn down such a wonderful role? I think this role is perfect for Marlon"

154

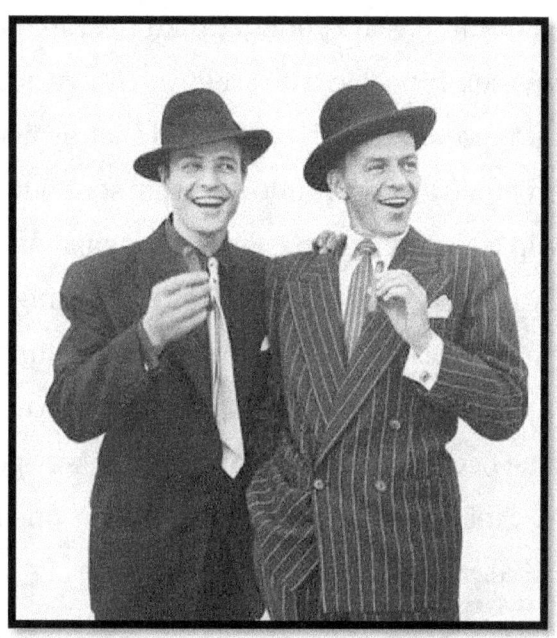

Kazan could almost see the wheels turning in the producers head.
As Kazan had so correctly assumed, Spiegel had secretly arranged with United
Artist to bank the film because Sinatra would have the lead.

At the same time, he was secretly working with Columbia Pictures to underwrite
the film if Marlon Brando had the lead role. Kazan learned afterwards that
Spiegel had managed to get more money for the film from Columbia Studios with
Brando in the lead then

United Artists was willing to put up with Sinatra in the lead. Of course, Spiegel
had negotiated all of this without a signed agreement with either star, something
the two studios probably did not know when they agreed to finance the film.

In the end, Spiegel and Columbia went with Brando because it all came down to
drawing power.

In 1951, although Brando still wasn't the established box office draw that
Sinatra was, Brando was far more popular than Sinatra to the right group of

movie goers that the studios needed to stay alive, the under thirty crowd. Brando, at age 30, was fifteen or more years younger than the top male box-office stars of the fifties, he had a raw sex appeal and sex sells in Hollywood.

Spiegel's next move was to get Brando to sign on. He did that by using the professional jealousy between Sinatra and Brando. Spiegel sent out his usual flood of news releases to gossip columnists and celebrity magazines raving about Sinatra's attachment to the project while at the same time attacking Brando with an onslaught of Spiegel charm. It worked. Brando changed his mind and agreed to do the film for $100,000 the same amount Kazan was making yet far more than Sinatra was willing to take because he believed the script was perfect for him. Motives did not matter. Sinatra was unceremoniously dropped from the project, so unceremoniously that he learned about Brando's hiring from a fan magazine.

Schulberg recalled: *"Harry Cohn agreed to do the picture at Columbia. Barely. He sort of backed into it. I didn't like him at all. He was almost like a gangster. When Spiegel got Brando, Cohn changed his mind if Spiegel promised to keep the budget under $800,000. He was reluctant. But with Brando he did not have much to lose ....After the role (of Terry Malloy) went to Brando, Sinatra wasn't very happy. I felt badly. Morally, we had offered the part to him. He had a lot to say. There was screaming. He was being Frankie. I never thought of him. It was Sam Spiegel, the producer, who gave Marlon the script. Brando turned it down. I don't think he read it. So we went to Frank Sinatra. He was a Hoboken kid. Kazan thought he could do it. But Spiegel kept wooing Brando even after verbally agreeing with Frankie"*

Perhaps in an effort to placate Sinatra, or simply to avoid a lawsuit, Spiegel offered Sinatra the part of Father Corridan in the film. However, Sinatra turned it down and insisted on getting the Terry Malloy role. In fact, on the advice of lawyers, Sinatra actually showed up for the first day's script reading, ready for work. Eventually he sued Spiegel for $50,000, claiming breach of contract. Although the exact terms are unknown, the suit was settled out of court without any exchange of cash.

While Spiegel was offering the role to both Sinatra and Brando, Kazan entertained the idea of handing the role to actor John Garfield and even discussed the part with him.

"Garfield" said Schulberg "Would have been good in it and was pissed off when it went to Brando" A member of the original Group Theater and a suspected communist, Garfield was, more or less, blacklisted anyway and probably would not have gotten the part. He died suddenly a few months before filming started anyway.

Once Brando accepted the role, he let it be known that he had taken it reluctantly since both Kazan and Schulberg were out with Hollywood for their testimony before the HUAC. He made sure his camp spread the story in Hollywood that he had turned the role down at first because the money was too low (Leaving the assumption that he had held out for top dollar, which he did not). He even went so far as to tell Kazan, the director who had given him start and made him a star that the only reason he had agreed to make the film was that it would bring him closer to his psychoanalyst in Manhattan.

ON LOCATION
FALL 1953

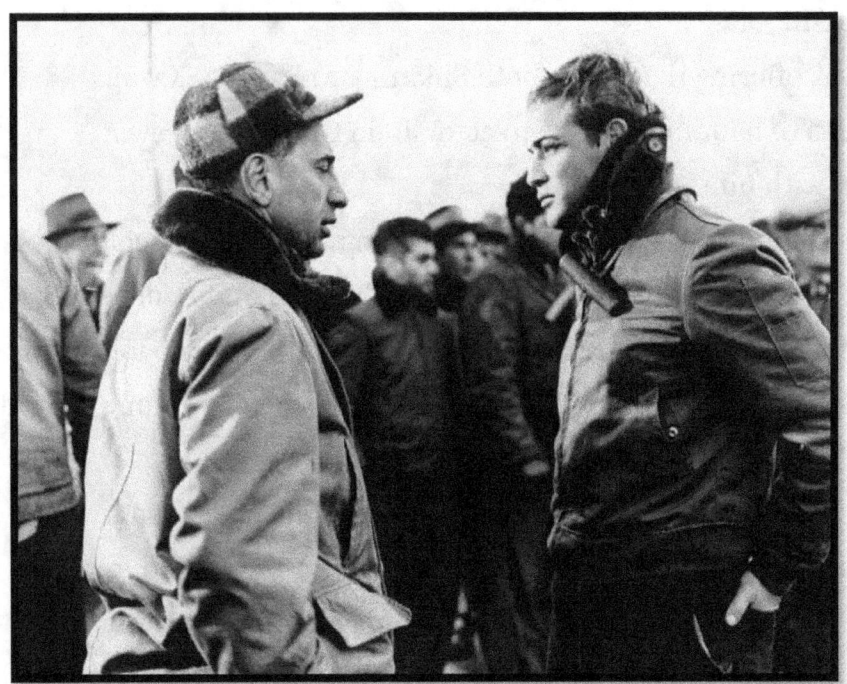

By June of 1953, everything was in place including the site location to film the picture, Hoboken New Jersey. Kazan's request (later a demand) for location shooting did not sit right with Columbia's boss Harry Cohn.

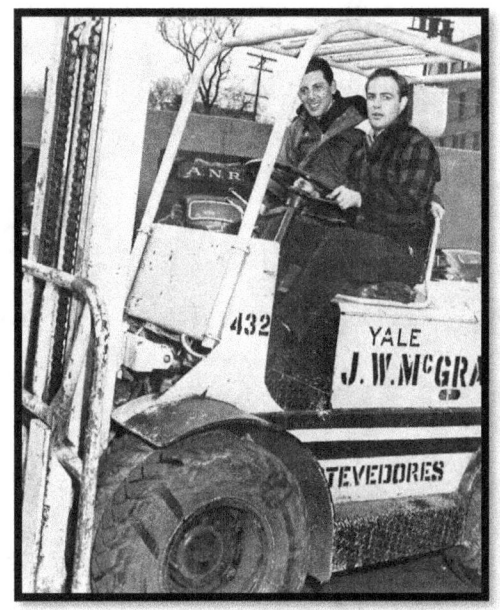

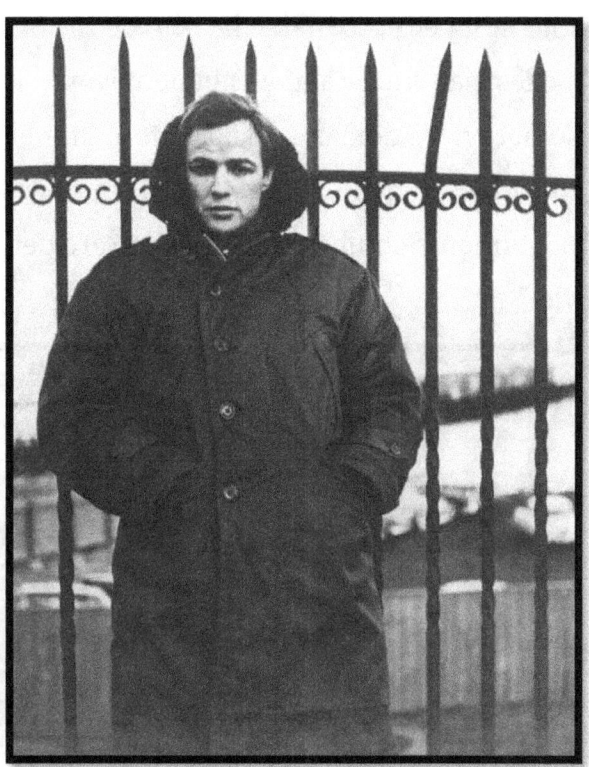

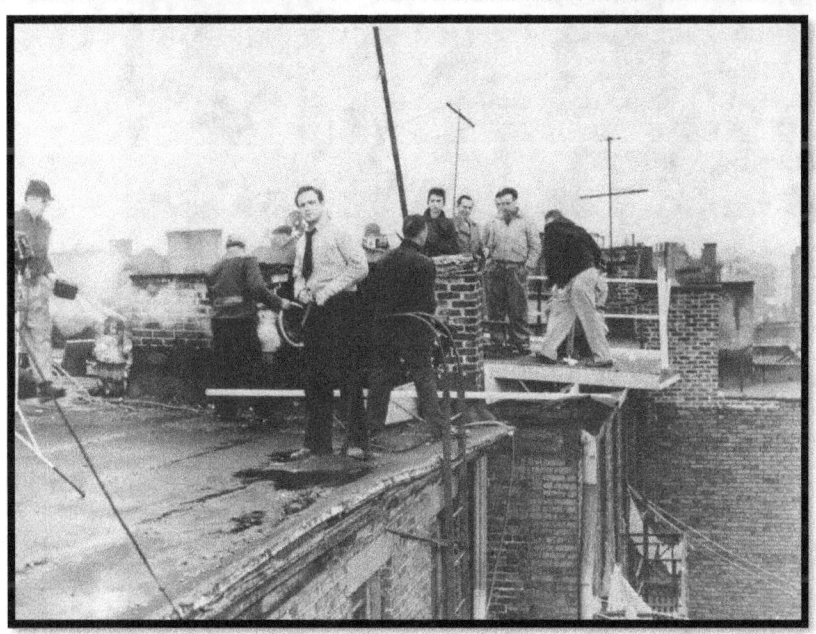

Cohn thought it better to make the film on his back lot in California where weather, pedestrian traffic and local talent would not slow down production. Kazan held out on his demand, like Huston, Mankiewicz and Zinnemann, believed the atmosphere in Southern California was detrimental to the films theme. In addition, Schulberg and Kazan were determined to make "An east coast movie."

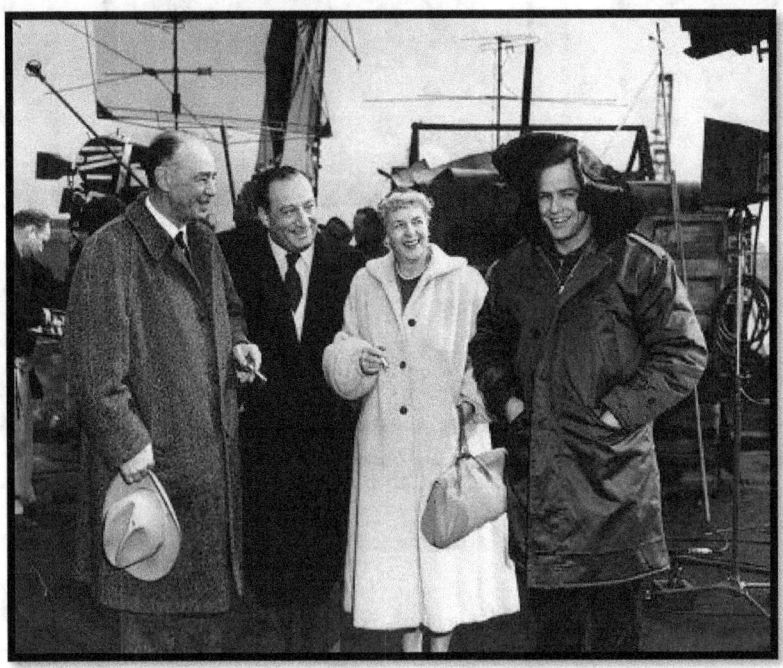

Brando, his parents and producer Spiegel on set

That is, a film that would be developed and shot entirely on the east coast as opposed to the back lots of Los Angeles, which is how most films of the 1950s were developed with transparencies (imposing a film shot of an actual location as a background for the actors) *Waterfront*, Kazan decided, would use the actual locations.

160

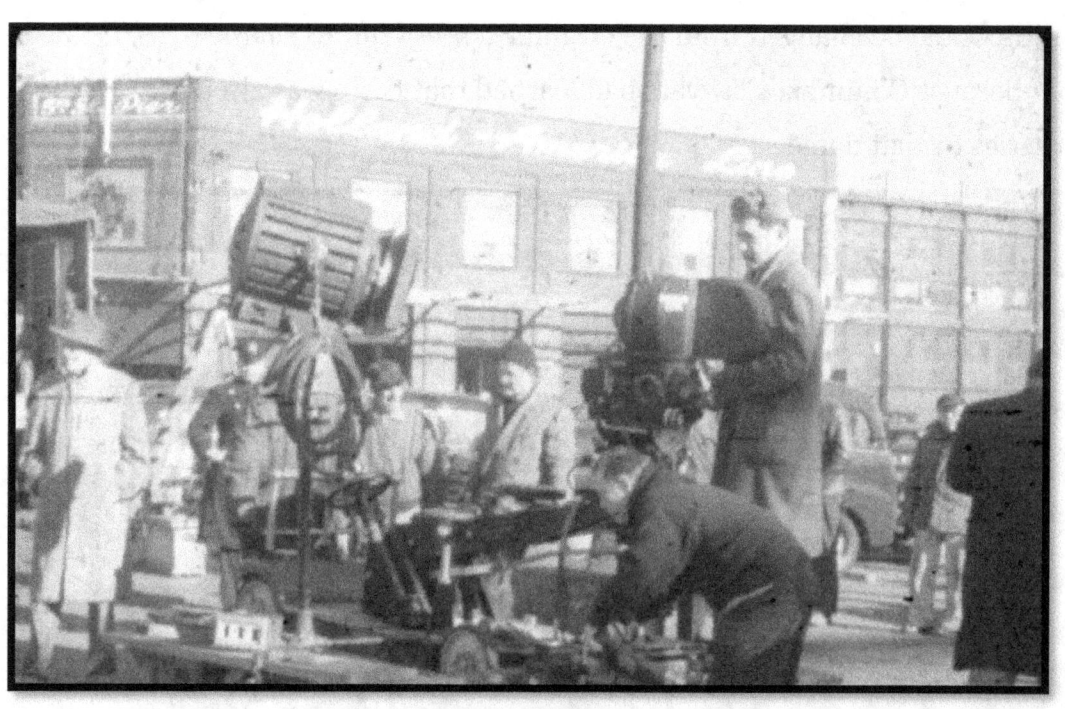

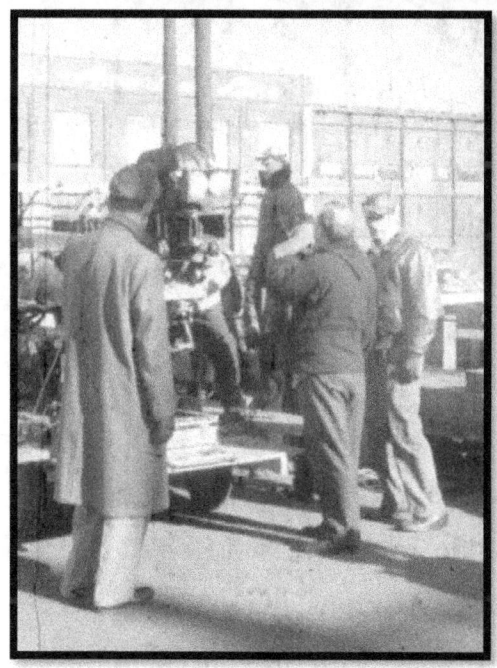
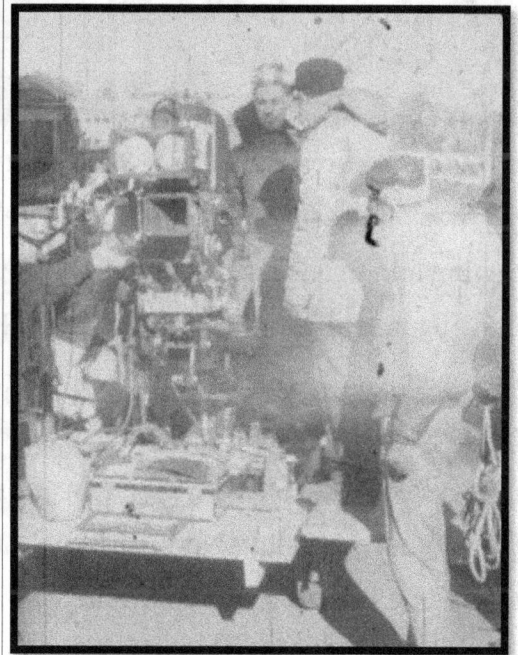

Reluctantly Cohn agreed to location shooting but with two demands of his own; the film's title would be changed from the original *Waterfront* to *On the Waterfront* because Columbia's lawyers had learned that there was already a television series by that name.

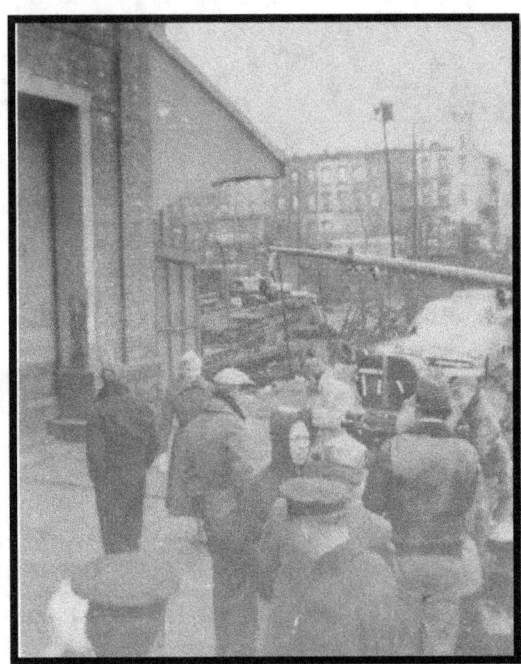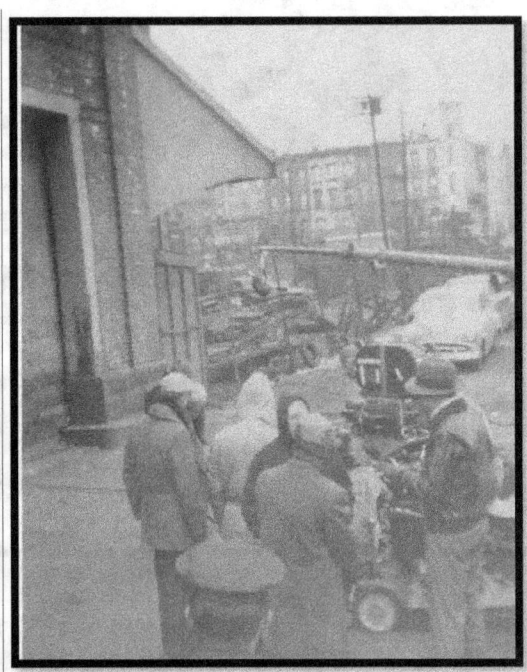

In addition, Cohn wanted the entire shoot completed in 30 days. Sam Spiegel, whose money was on the line, was completely behind the time rush demands. With his pushing and prodding the film, shooting was completed in 37 days.

During shooting in Hoboken, he would phone Kazan and Schulberg each night at midnight or even two or three on the morning, with the same message 'Go faster, speed up production, get it done, wrap it, we're losing money'

Hoboken was a secondary choice as the location shoot. Kazan and Schulberg had done all of their research in New York's West Side, in the areas of Hell's Kitchen and Chelsea but they passed on the New York locations due to the high expense, the traffic and the Mafia, which was clearly upset with the concept of the film. They looked across the river and saw Hoboken.

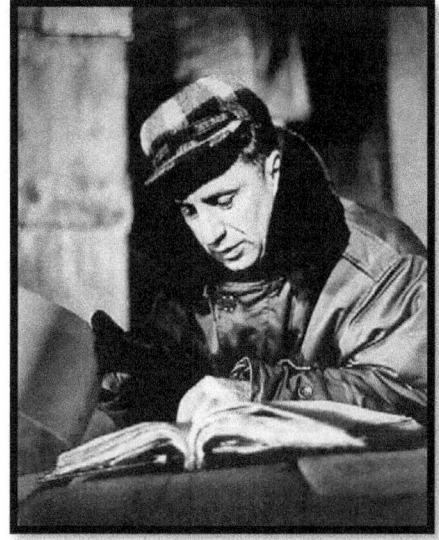 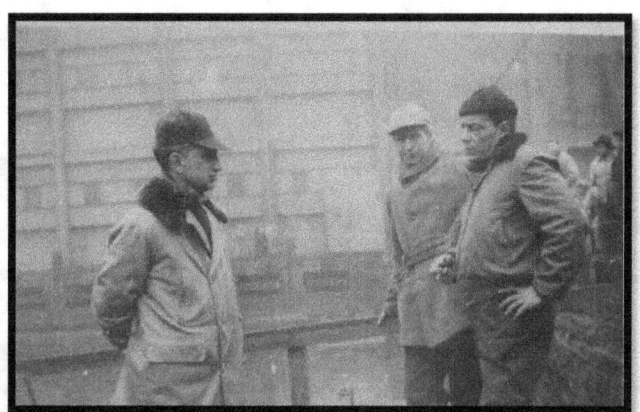

Kazan reading the script on location and on set

They drove over the bridge to New Jersey and talked with the local Chief of Police, Arthur Moretta. They told him about their problems or least their perceived problems with the mob. Moretta, delighted at the idea of his city in a major motion picture, promised them a safe filming in Hoboken and appointed his brother to protect the cast and crew.

There was probably never any real danger from the Mafia to the cast and crew on the location, but there was a sense on the set that they were doing something daring not the least of which was denying the mob that still ruled over the waterfront.

There was only one minor incident during the filming. When the crew broke for lunch, some thugs, local teenagers who were upset at the way their town was being portrayed, grabbed Kazan and started to rough him up, the police managed to pull them off.

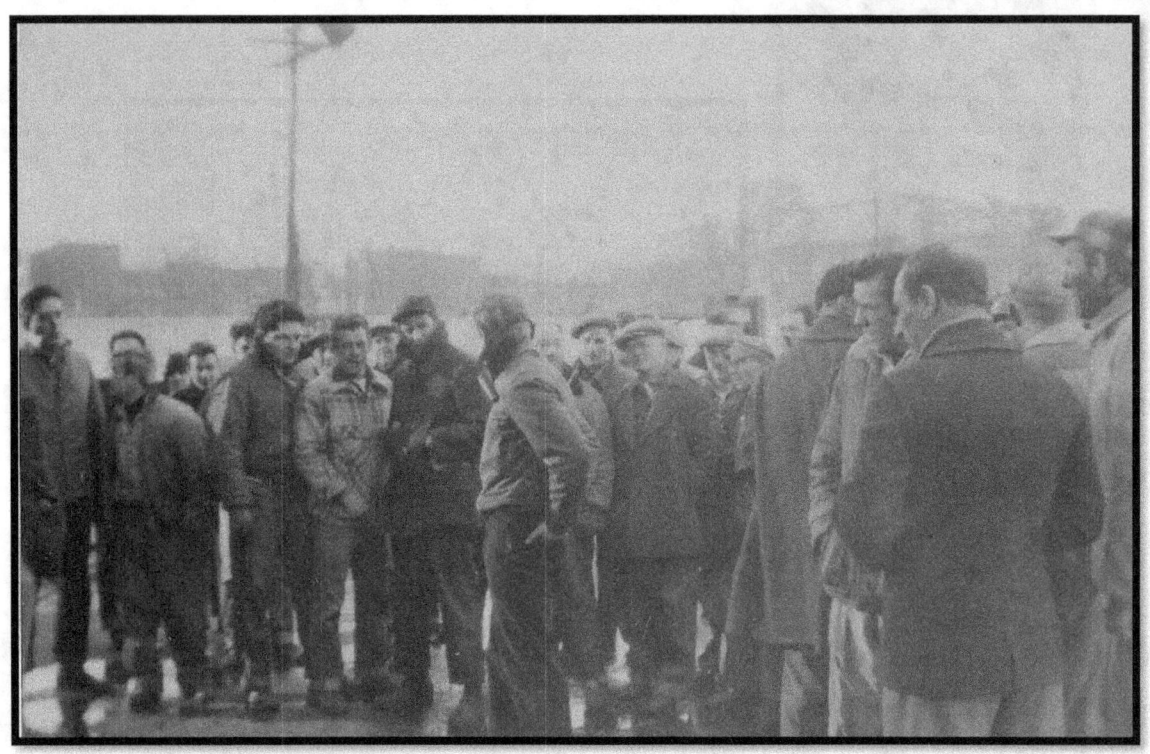

Overall, that was one of the few negatives from the locals, aside from adding $30,000 to the budget to cover payoffs to Hoboken property owners who charging exorbitant rents and fees to the film crew.

The production was one of the great events in the city's history. In its long history, the tenement city of Hoboken, dwarfed by its prestigious neighbor, Manhattan, had but a few claims to fame. It was the birthplace of Frank Sinatra, G. Gordon Liddy, five-foot actor Pia Zadora and troubled but extremely talented, singer Jimmy Roselli. (Considered by many to be the inspiration for the character of Johnny Fontane in the *Godfather* films) Hoboken was where Steven Foster, in sober moment, penned a few of his classic American songs and Willem de Kooning began his career as an artist (Of sorts, he was a house painter) The first game of organized baseball was played here, the ice cream cone was invented there and so was the Locomotive engine.

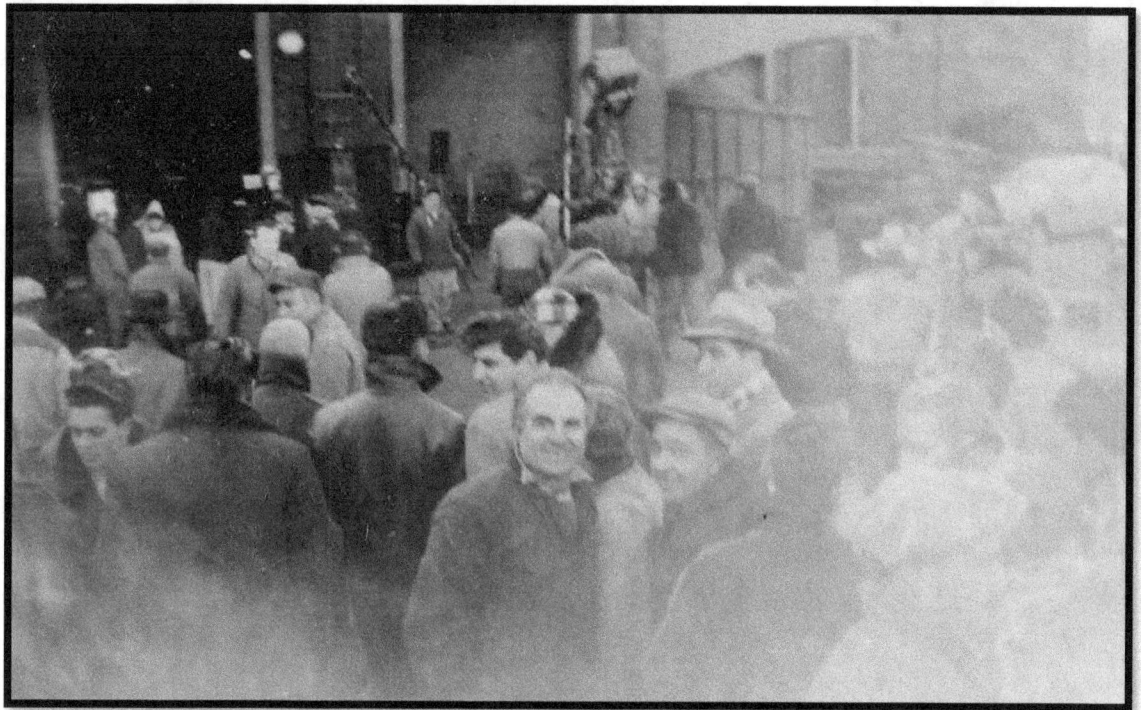

By the mid- 1930's and despite the films depiction of the city as an Irish enclave, Hoboken's largest ethnic group was Italian. The city itself was a rough, grimy seaport town, dangerous in some places, a closed community that did not welcome outsiders and the Waterfront film crew was no exception.

"It was" said a former resident "Ten minutes from Manhattan, filled with people who never went there" another added "We were right across the river from Manhattan but we might as well have been in Detroit, it was that different"

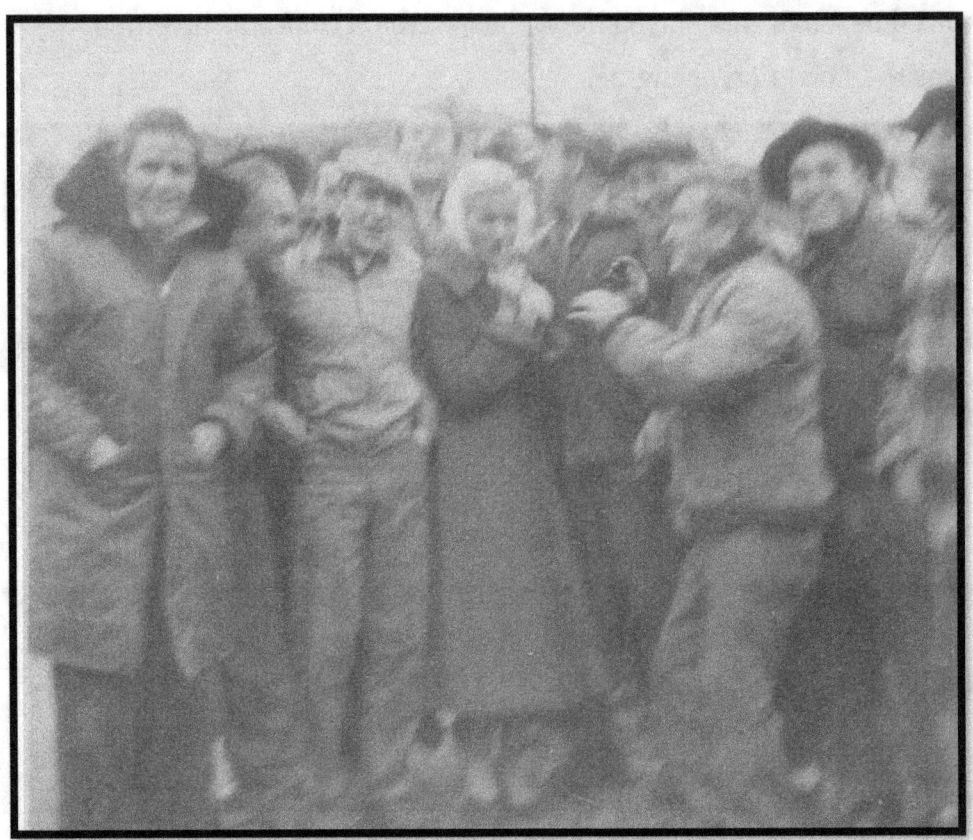

Only one square mile in size, Hoboken became a living part of the film and no amount of careful art direction could have resulted in the set Hoboken gave Kazan with its view of Manhattan, its seedy smoke filled crowded bars, the dank cramped apartments where the dock workers lived and the inner cargo holds.

While Hoboken gave Kazan the setting he needed, drab and worn, his primary concern was to make an exciting, successful commercial feature film, the fact that it showed the deplorable working conditions for the long shore workers and allowed mainstream America and eventually the world to better understand cultural and class differences is an admirable by product of the production.

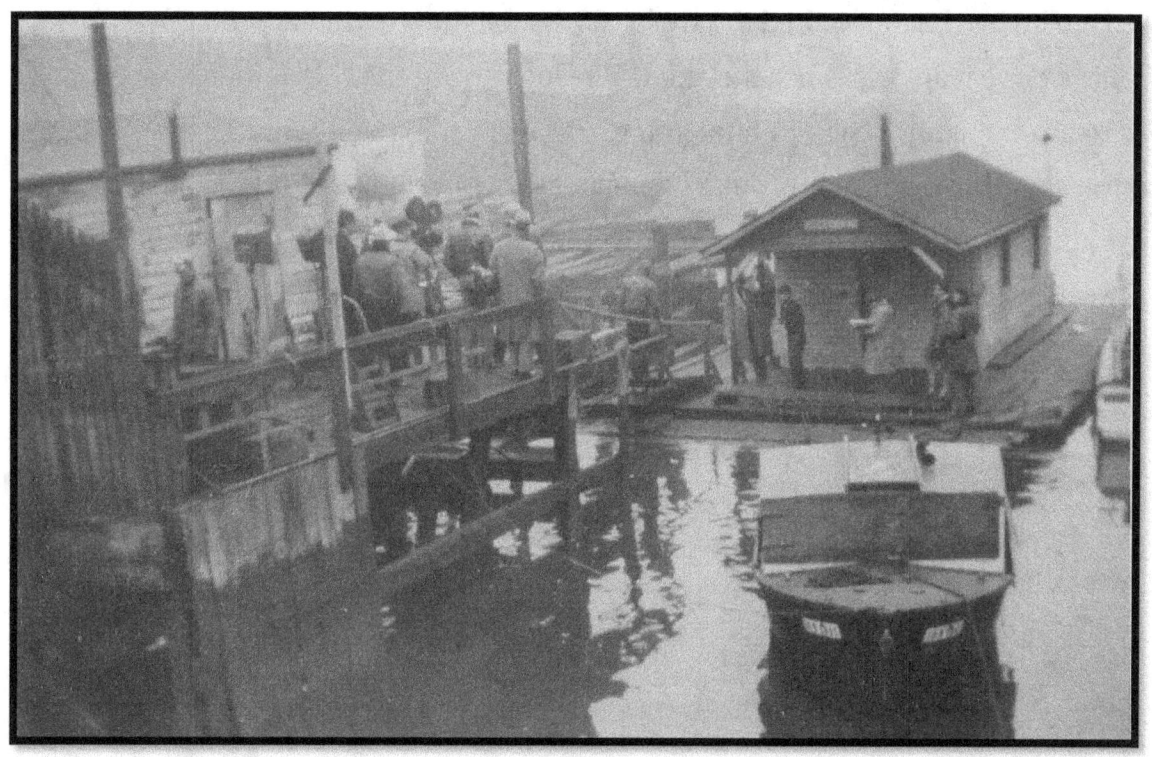

While the film succeeds somewhat in its depiction of the dockworker's life, it is entertainment, a love story. What Kazan needed to do, and what he did do, and brilliantly, was to create spontaneity and the illusion of reality. (which is why the outdoor shooting in Hoboken in the freezing cold that showed the actors breath on film pleased him so.)

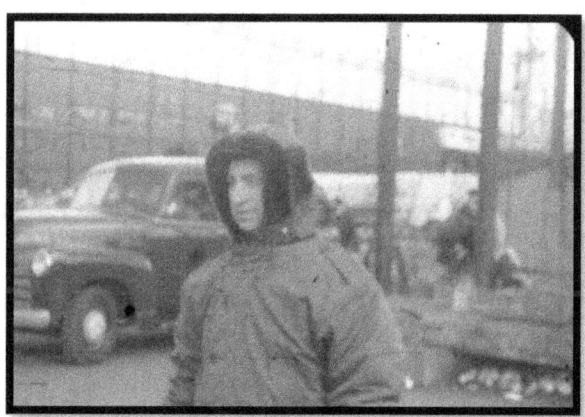

Although he had been required to hire locals for the films extra, he probably would have done it anyway since they had "The look" he needed. Another reason he had to hire so many locals (In total 500 extras were paid to either be in the film or on standby) the winter of 1952 happened to be one of New York's coldest in years and professional New York actors weren't interested in a trip out of the city to work in the freezing winds of Hoboken.

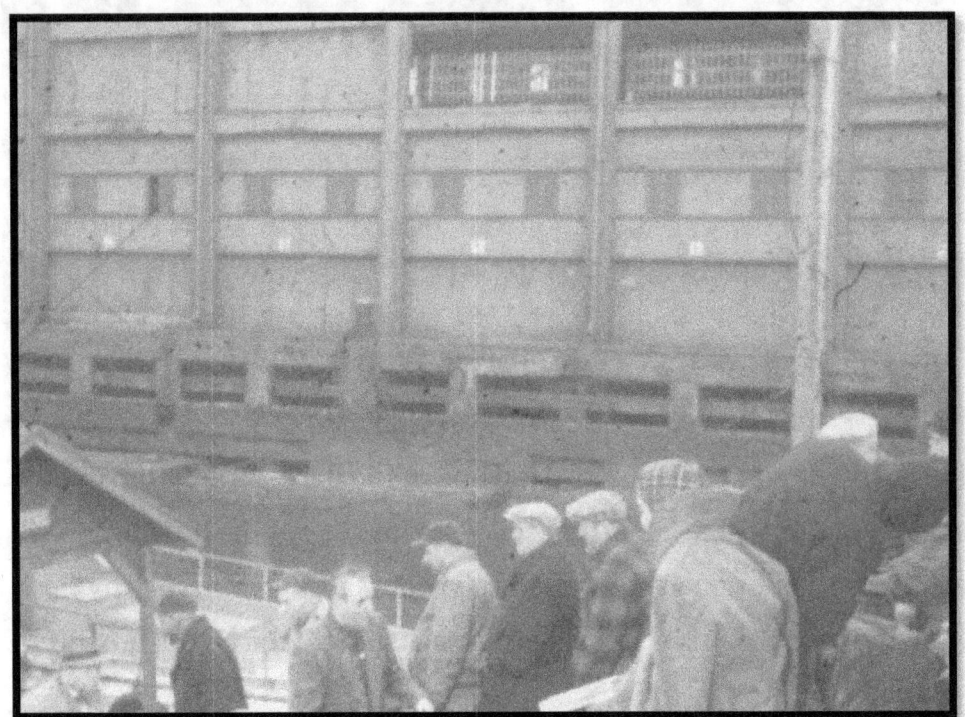

The weather was wet, bitter cold, overcast and gray and in several scenes, the metal barrels that the crew used to warm themselves can be seen in several shots throughout the final edit of the film. Breath is visible on screen, a detail Kazan loved and spoke of often because it suggested the brutal lives of the Dock workers against both corrupt union officials and the elements.

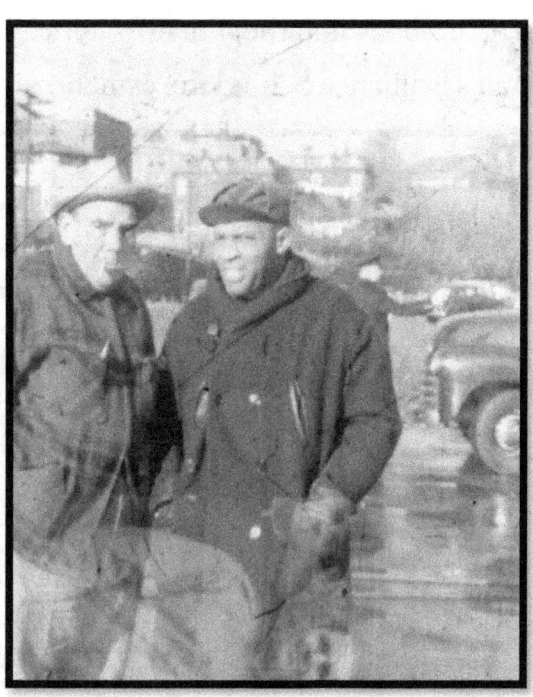

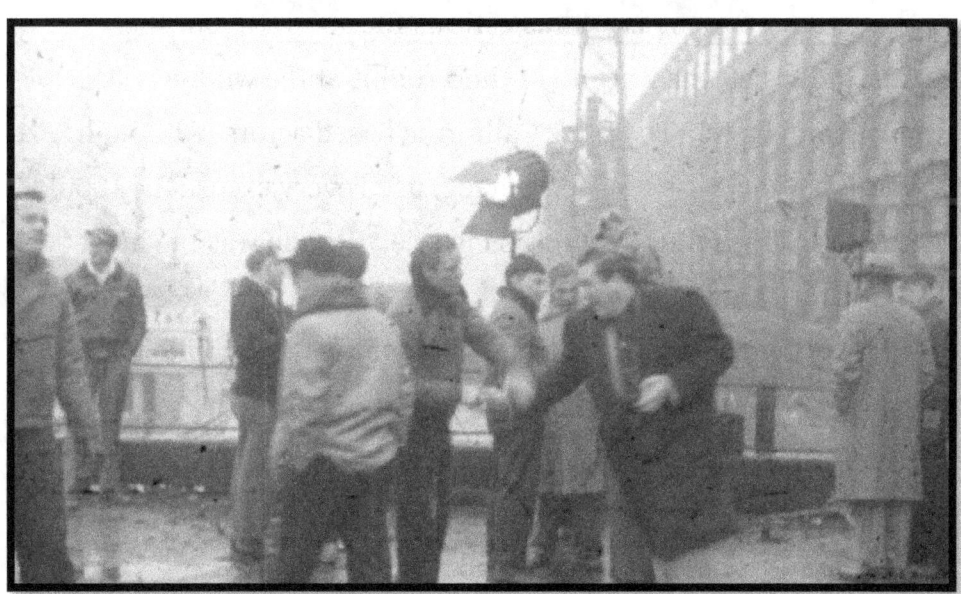

With so many natural elements, the actors were free to focus entirely on their characters' emotions. Making conditions worse was the fact that most of the film was shot at night which few people who watch the film ever notice, a tribute to cinematographer Boris Kaufman's brilliance behind the camera.

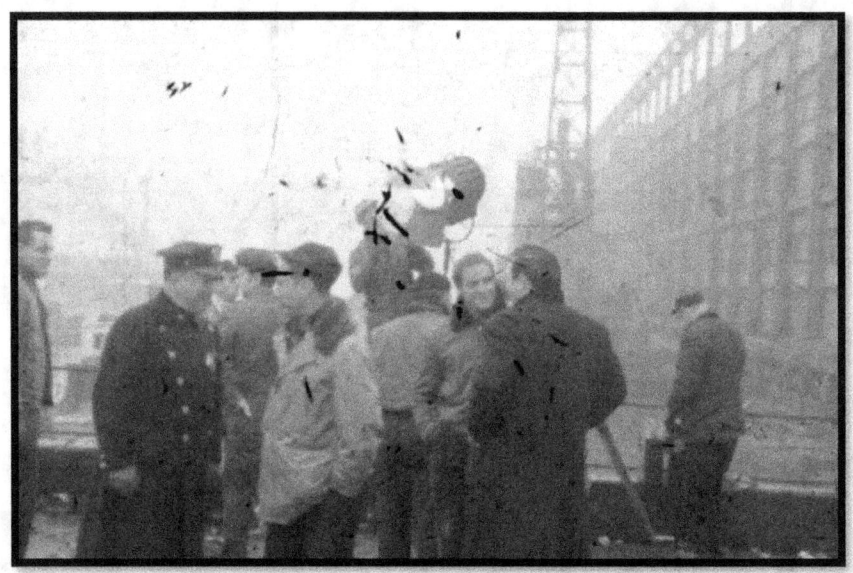

For their part, the actors were not as enthusiastic as Kazan was about the freezing weather and rarely left the warmth of their rooms at the wildly misnamed Majestic Grand Hotel. The films California based actors (Although Eva Marie Saint was born and raised in New Jersey) used every excuse they could think of to delay the early (5:30 AM) shooting schedule. Brando was the most difficult to get out into the frigid morning air.

Schulberg recalled, "The temperature was near zero and the wind chill blowing up the frozen river was often 10 below. Teeth were chattering and the cold crept into our bones. On the roof one day, Marlon made a classical remark. "Ya know, it's so fucking cold out here there's no way you can over act."

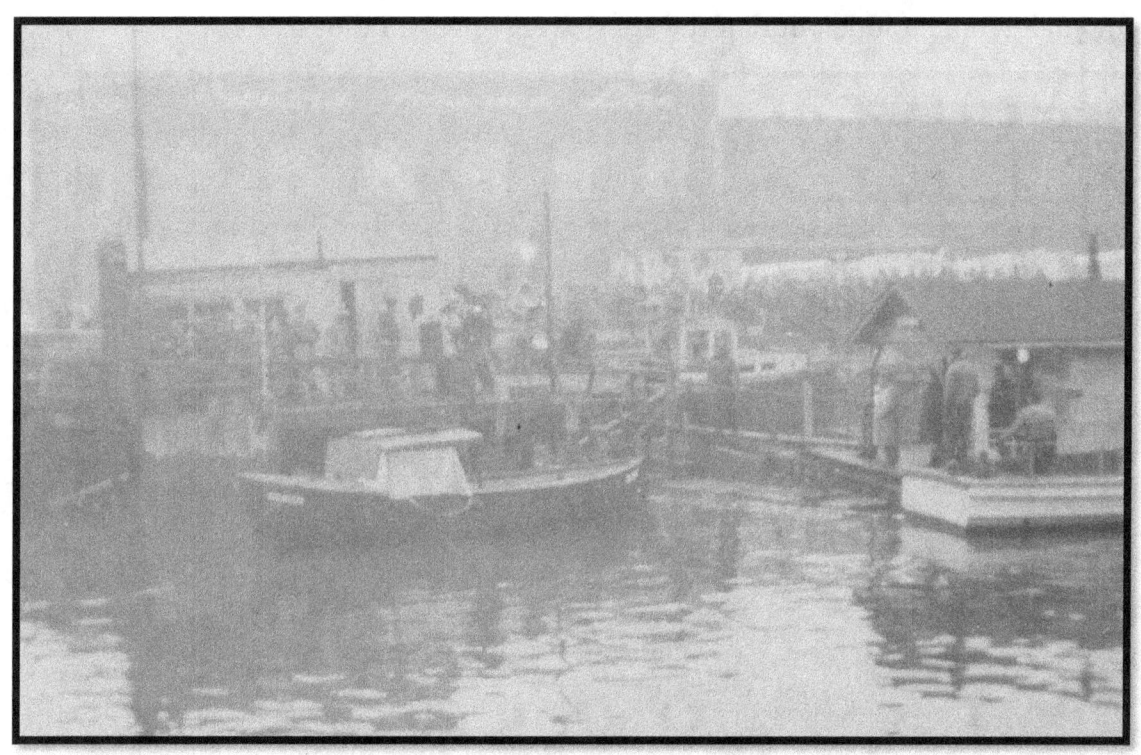

"In that case" cracked the ever Spiegel "you're in your element" However, the wind and the cold had a positive effect on the picture "it made them look like people" Kazan wrote "and not actors, in fact, like people who lived in Hoboken and suffered the cold because they had no choice."

Of course, the weather, as a part of the film, could be a double-edged sword. Hoboken offers one of the best skyline views of New York in the entire tri-state area and Kazan wanted to shot it from Hoboken's view... distant, cold and foggy... the opposite of the picture postcard image of the Big Apple that most American knew. On the first day of shooting, Kazan ordered his crew, tossed together on a moment's notice, up to a rooftop to shoot the New York City skyline as a backdrop opening to the film. However, on the very moment that they were about to begin filming, a fog rolled in from the ocean and covered their angle.

Kazan had taken the precaution of setting up crews on other rooftops, from different angles, only to find out that the crews were down on the street.

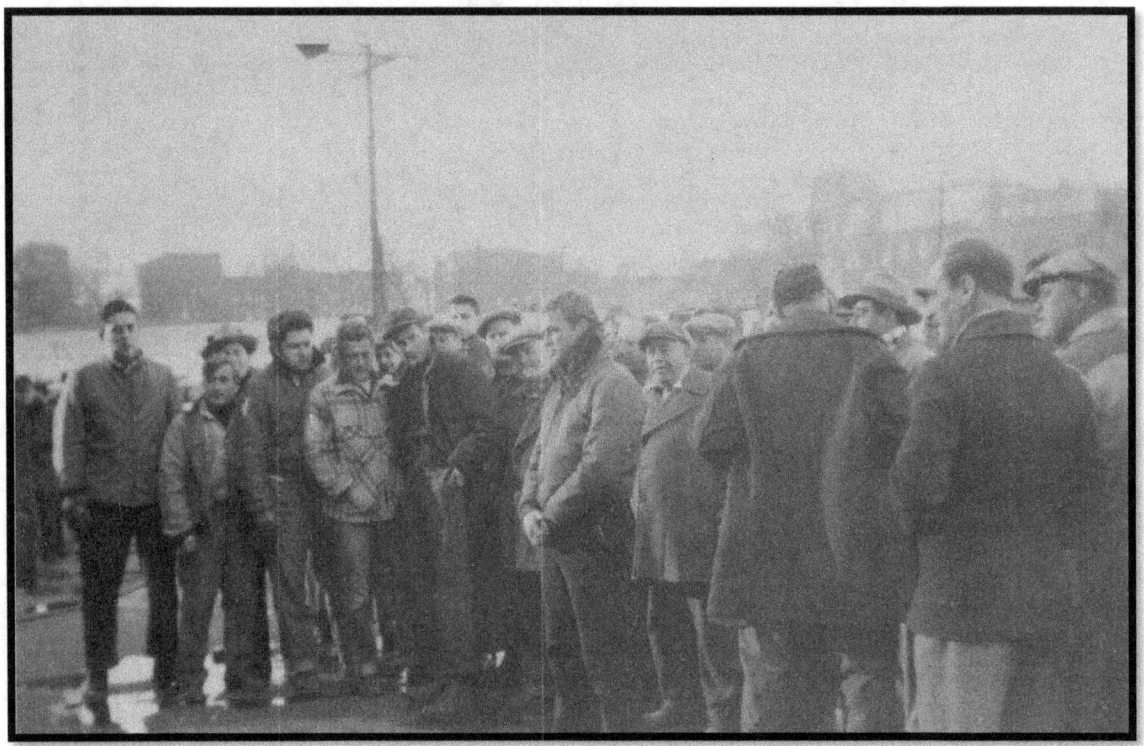

"What the hell are they doing down there?" he screamed at his assistant director. Spiegel, the answer came, had refused to rent the two roofs from the owners because they had asked for too much money. "He chiseled on every cost and took it out of our hides and legs and patience... Where Sam chiseled was on crew costs and every insignificant thing he could come up with or cut down"

In between, during and after set shots, Kazan was flooded with calls from Sam Spiegel, demanding that he rush through the film and cut costs. Kazan was positive that the majority of the calls were to impress "Whatever teenager was on his arm this week" (Spiegel was a firm believer in the casting couch)

Spiegel was an endless problem for everyone. Brando suspected that the driver Spiegel had provided for him was a spy. It turned out he was right. Nor was Brando's driver the only spy on the set.

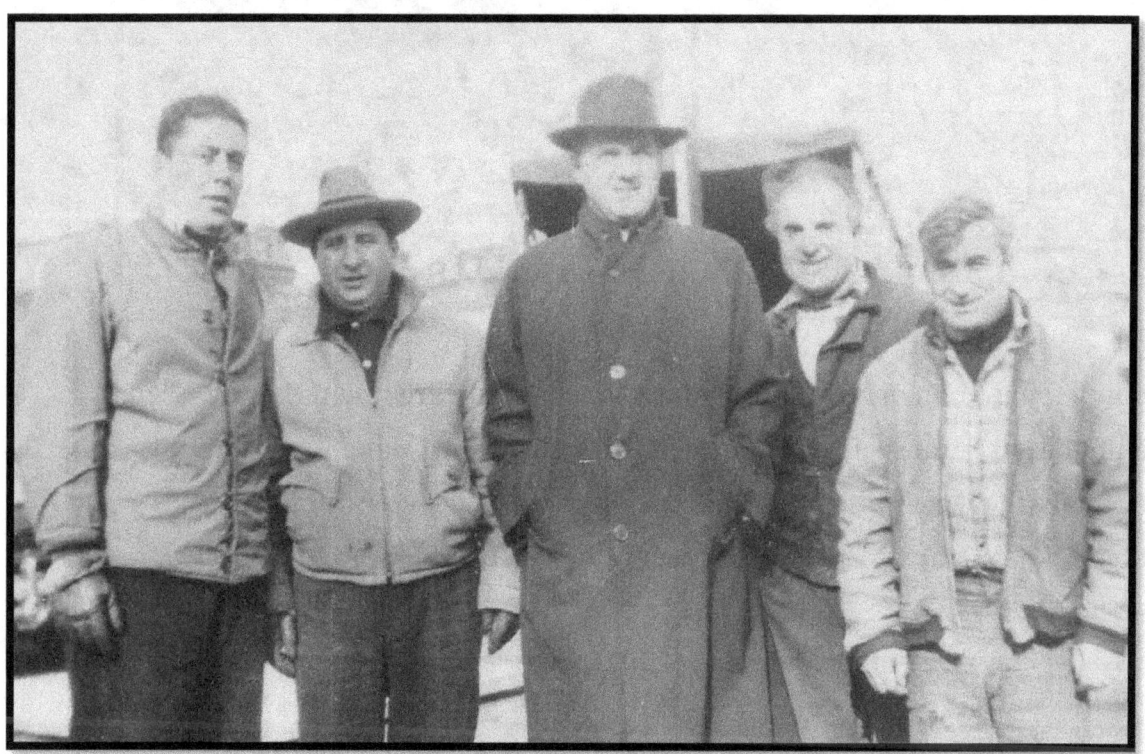

Schulberg and Kazan were plagued with calls from Spiegel complaining about a miner expense they had made only minutes after they had made. He also insisted on cutting line after line and scene after scene in an effort to hurry production along. While some of the cuts were drastic, others, Kazan and Schulberg agreed, were good and needed. The problem was, when they would consent to one small cut, Spiegel would see his opening and push for several more. One of the cuts he demanded was the core of the film, the sermon in the cargo hold by Father Barry. "You can't give a sermon" he shouted "in the movies! It just doesn't play in the movies and it has to be cut!"

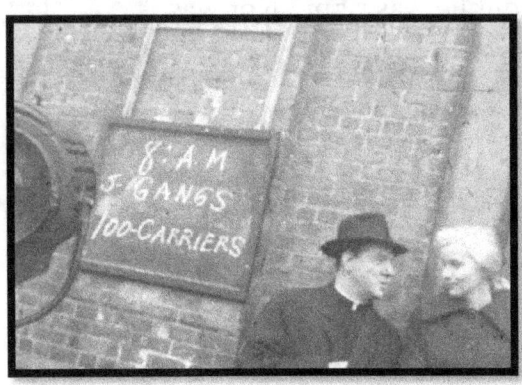 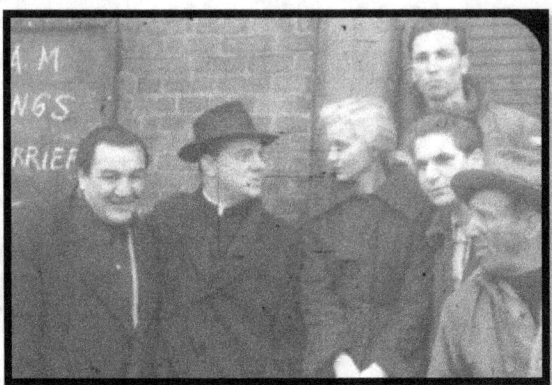

Schulberg fought him on the cuts making the legitimate argument that the scene could not be cut because so much of the films underlying theme is spiritual.

The ritual of Spiegel's attempted cuts was reenacted each morning when Schulberg, Kazan and Spiegel would meet in Kazan's hotel room to go over the script changes.

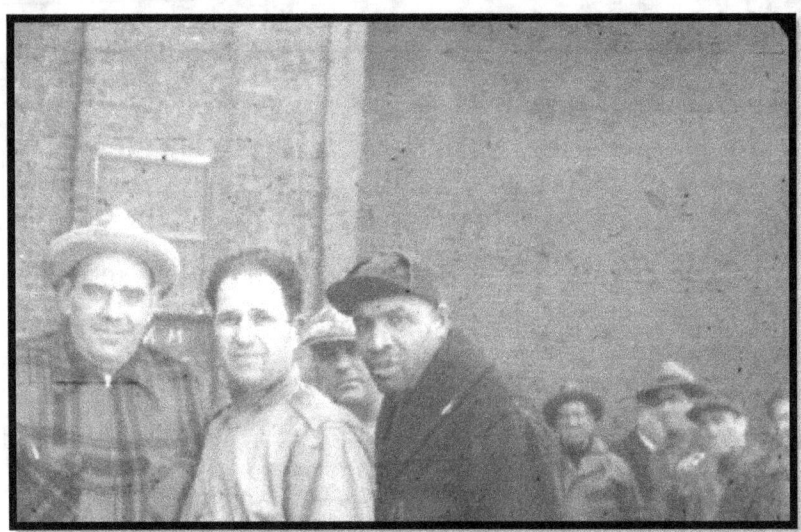

Each morning, Spiegel would start the meeting by asking to see the cuts and revisions in the script only to be told there were not any. At this point, Spiegel would looked shocked and hurt and ask why his director and screen writer had reneged on their promise to him to cut a scene or a line only to have the pair remind him that they had never agreed to cut anything. He was, said Kazan "A great actor and a masterful liar"

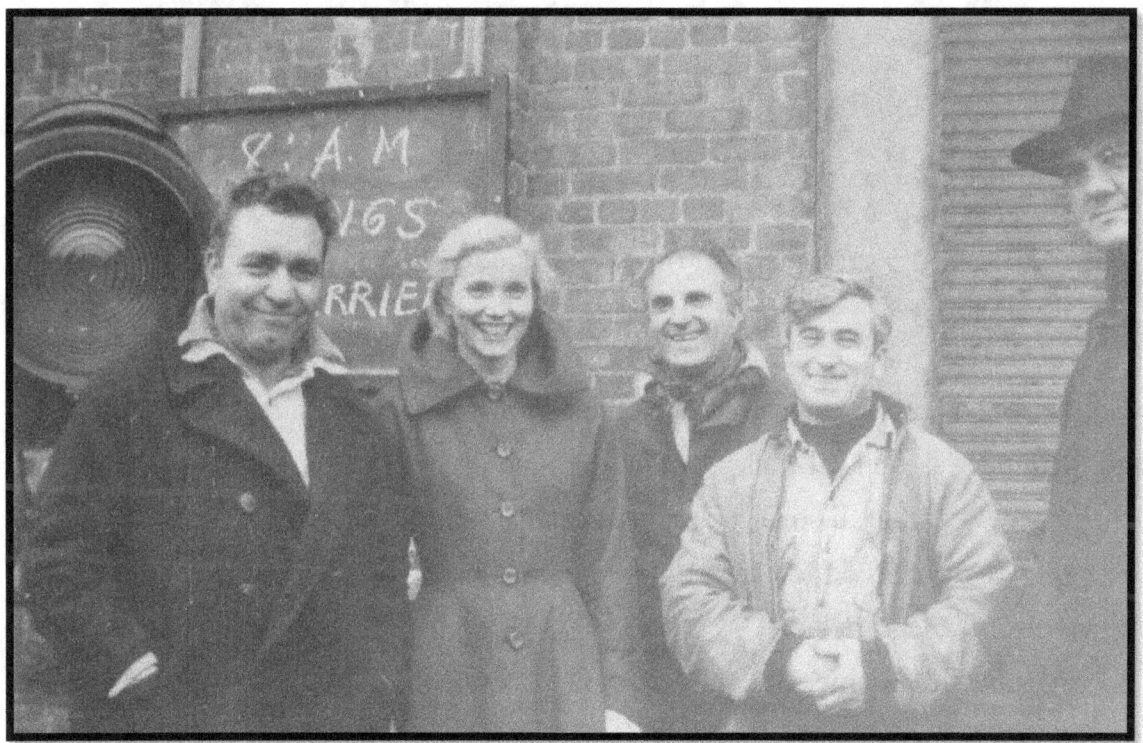

   As to Spiegel's argument that some of the films dialogue would run to long on screen, Kazan would counter with the argument that Spiegel was reading the lines from a page, on screen, the camera would cut to different actors as lines were spoken to draw their reaction.

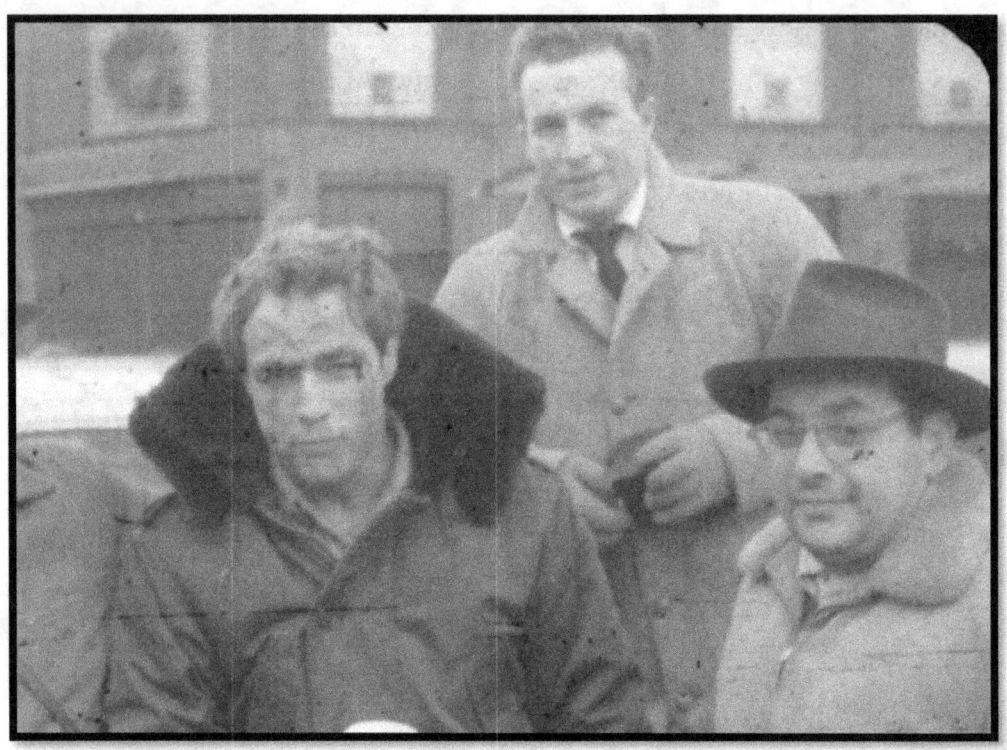

Eventually Spiegel managed to run down the generally easy going and good-
natured Schulberg as well with his constant demands for rewrites on the script.

   On the first weekend of the project, Schulberg decided to fly up to Dartmouth
College to plan a memorial for a teacher he had known. A panicked Spiegel called
"Budd, where are you going?"

 Schulberg explained to which Spiegel countered "For how
Long?"

"The weekend"

"How are you getting there?"

"By small airplane" Schulberg told him

"But" Spiegel asked "What about the script?"

"Don't worry" Schulberg said, "I have the script with me"

"But what of the plane crashes?"

One night Schulberg's wife awoke at three in the morning to find her husband shaving.

"What are you shaving for?" she asked

"I'm driving to New York," he answered

"Why?"

"To kill Sam Spiegel"

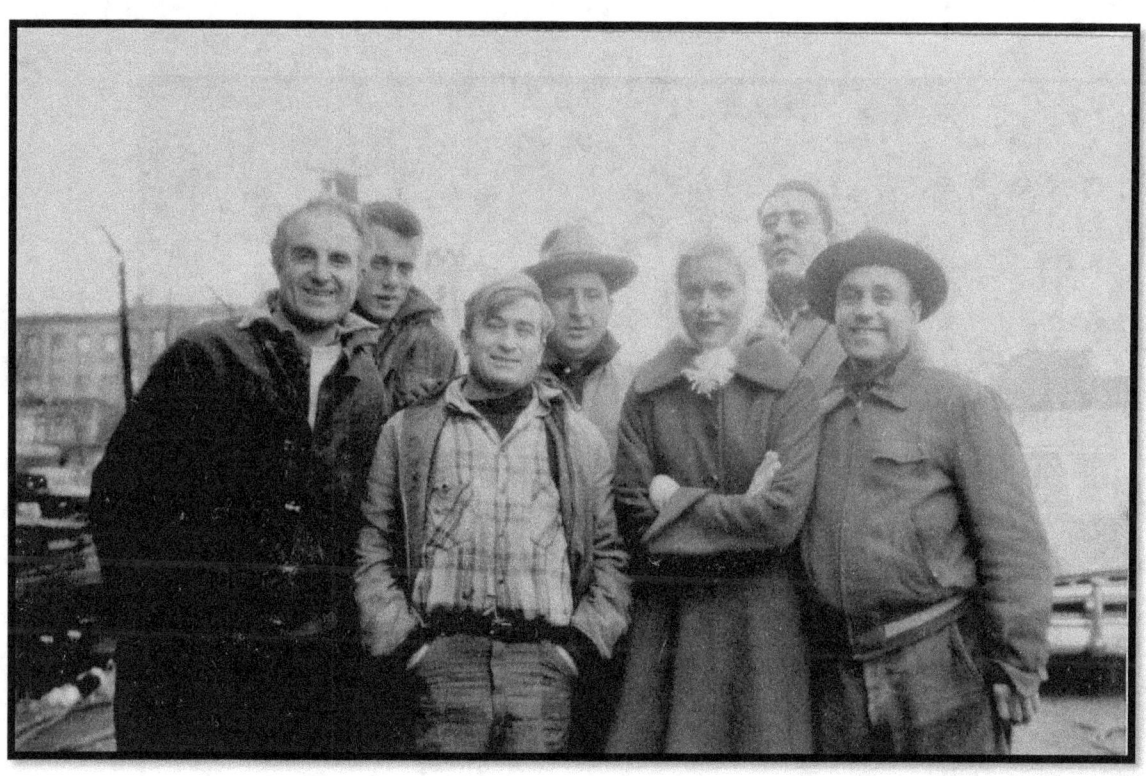

*****

While Kazan and company filmed in Hoboken, the real life waterfront drama continued to unfold. Immediately after the result of the fixed union election were in, New York's Governor Dewey waged a campaign to overturn the election results but trying to buy time against the results which he, and virtually everyone else, knew were rigged.

He refused to recognize the ILA as the collective bargaining agent for the longshoremen and ordered a report on the ILA actions during the election in an effort to build a case for fraud. New York City Police Commissioner George Patrick Monaghan submitted a report showing what Dewey had suspected, wide spread violence and scare tactics by the mob during the election had kept many of the anti-ILA forces home on election day.

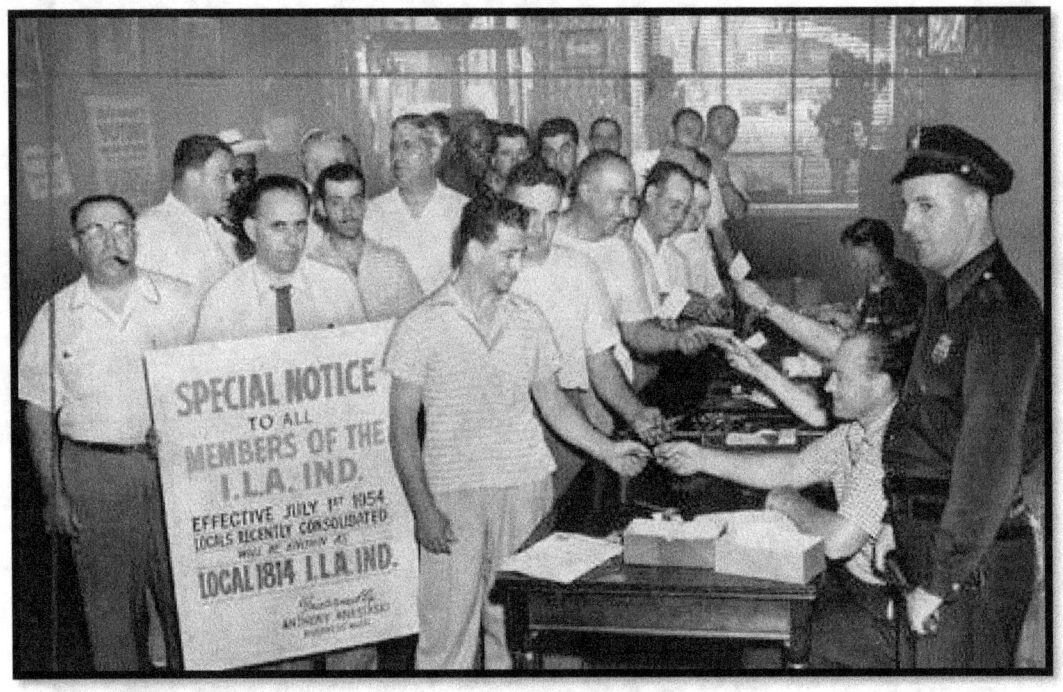

ILA vote: Above, Tough Tony Anastasia is at the front of the line carrying sign

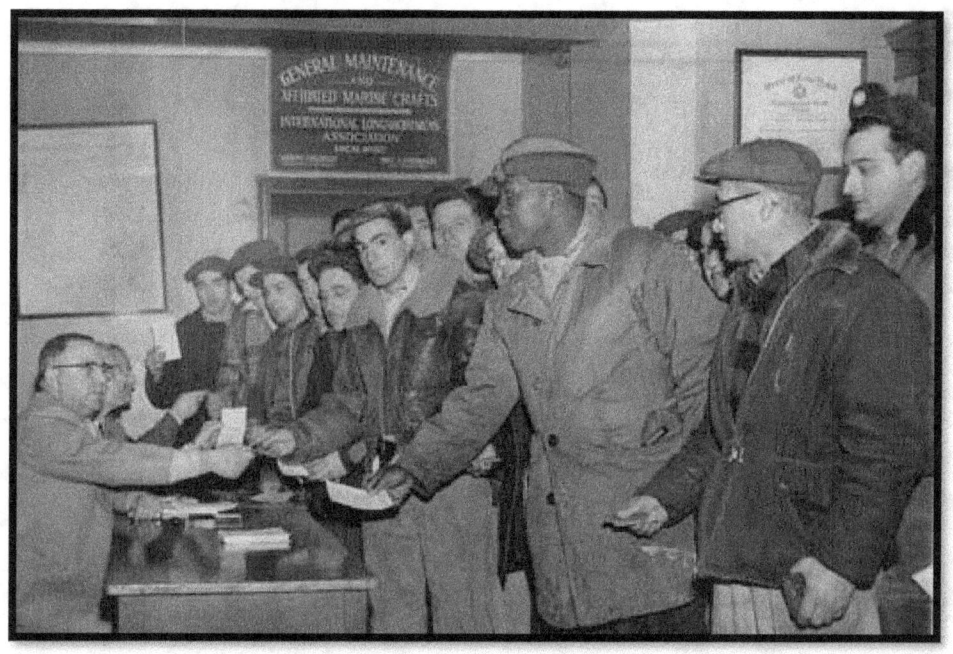

The results were further challenged by the AFL rebels who simply refused to sit down with the ILA to count the disputed votes, a tactic they hoped would buy their legal team time to find a means to void the election and call for another.

However, the best their lawyers could come up with was a weak argument that since the ILA had been "adopted" by United Mine Workers of America and the top management at the Miners had refused to sign non-Communist affidavits as they were required to do under the Taft-Hartley Act, that the election results were null and void. Understandably, the judge disagreed.

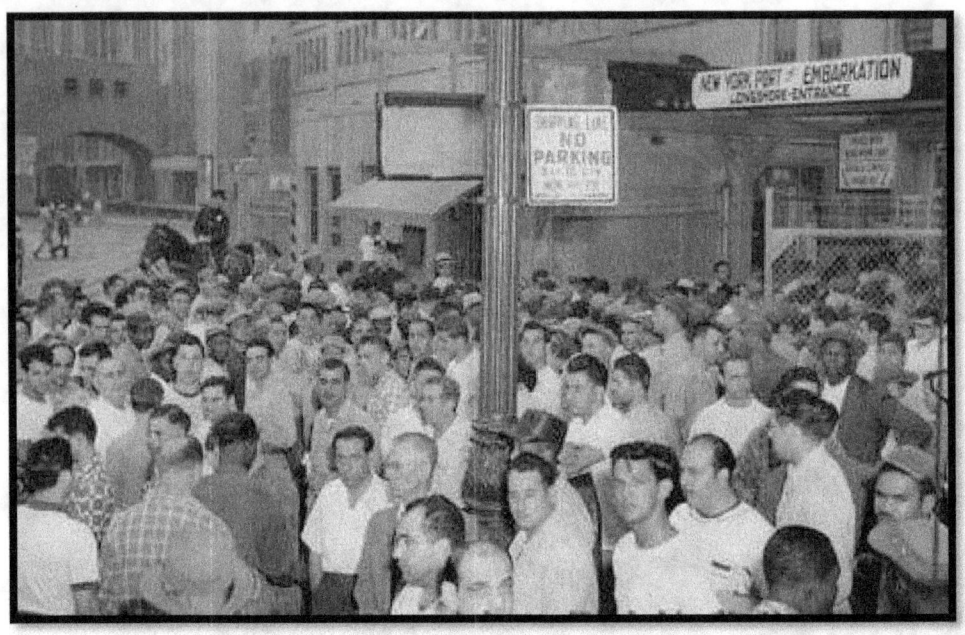

 In the meantime, the ILA legal team hired dozens of private detectives to investigate the pasts of the AFL-Seafarers and Rebel leaders who were opposing the election results. The longshoremen took another tact; they walked off the docks and called a strike. In early March 1954, just months after the release of the film Waterfront, Teamster boss David Beck refused to cross the rebel's picket line. News spread and on piers up and down Manhattan, and the rebel Longshoremen came back to life. However, the ILA sent out a division of enforcers who threatened to murder any worker who touched Teamster deliveries and the Port of New York was crippled by the wildcat strikes.

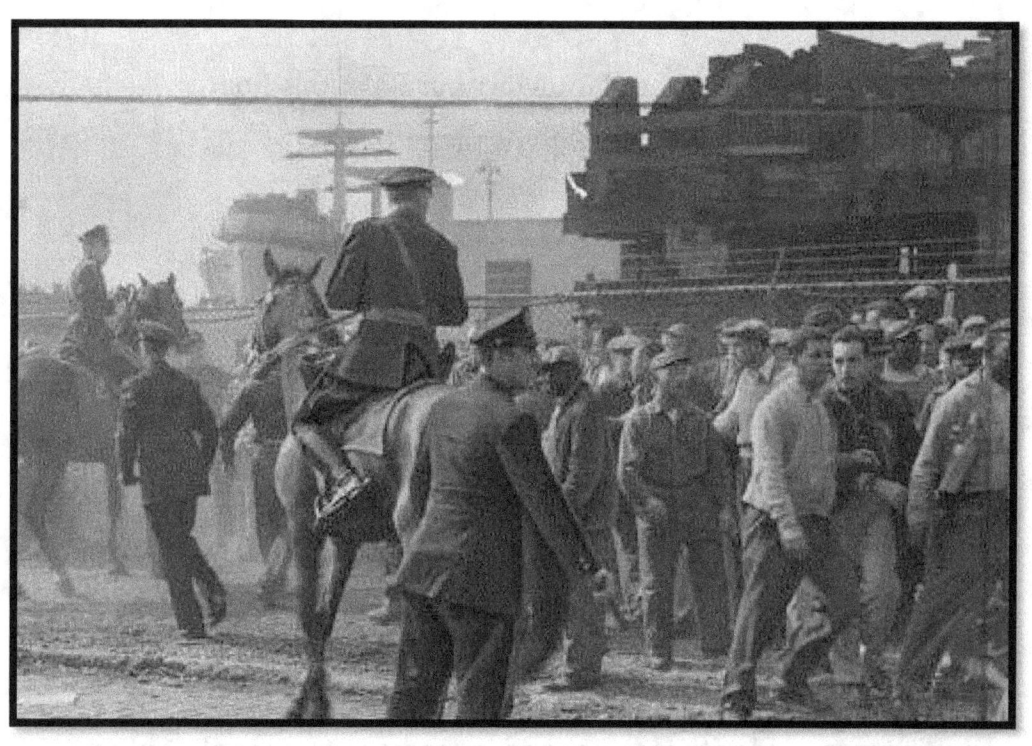

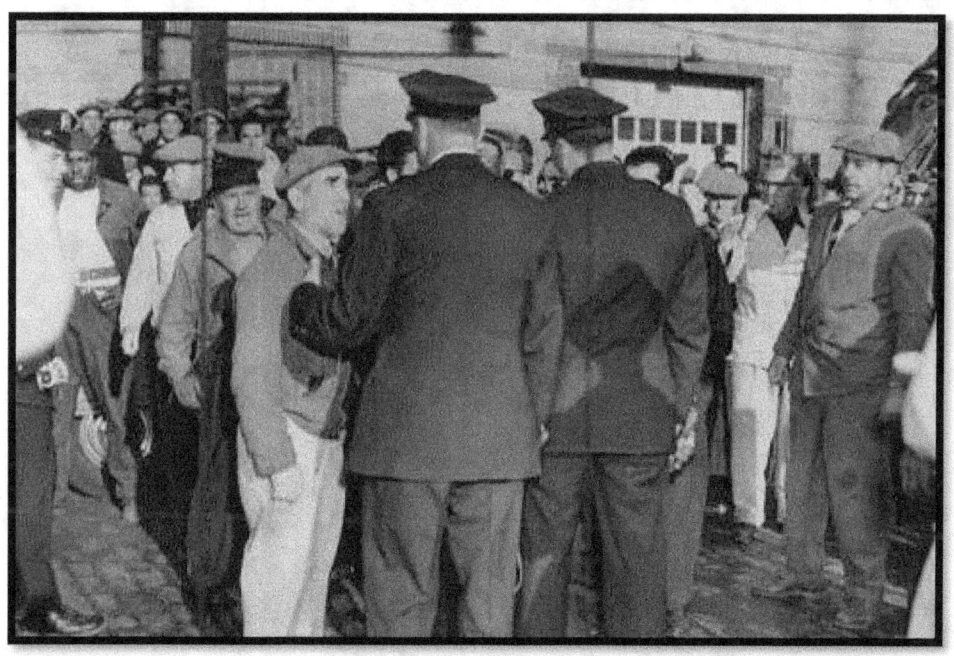

On March 4, 1954, an injunction by the National Labor Relations Board Forbade ILA from striking or disrupting freight transportation.

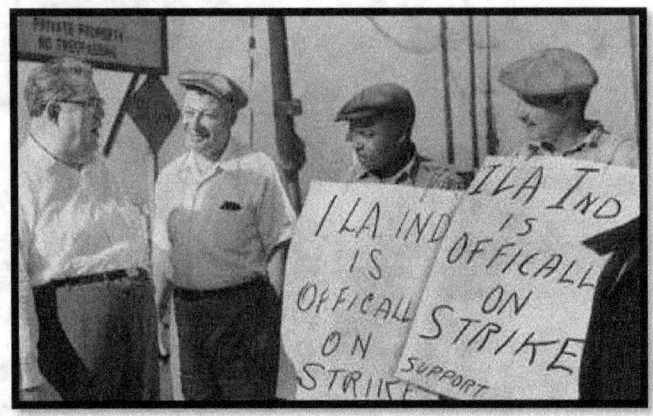

 The ILA leadership responded with violence and sporadic warfare broke out on the docks between the ILA goons and the rebel longshoremen who were backed up by the Teamsters might which eventually smashed the ILA's picket lines and, on March 8, 1954, NLRB examiner effectively overturned the ILA elections based on the findings that they were conducted "in an atmosphere of terror, coercion, and intimidation..."

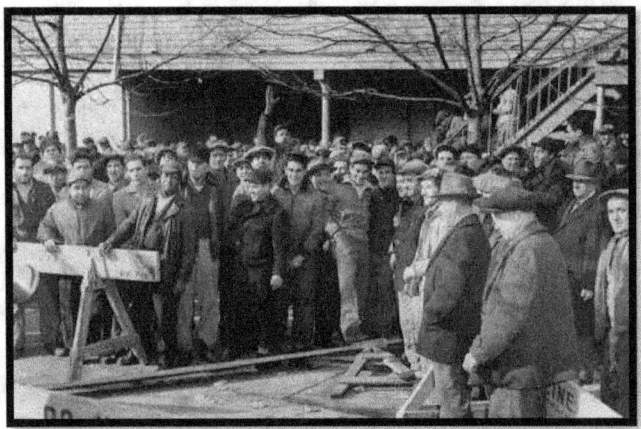

By March the 19, Three thousand six hundred and sixty longshoremen had returned to work under police protection, crossing the ILA picket lines. The ILA responded by taking the battle from the docks into the neighborhoods. Longshoremen's wives and children were stopped and threatened, car tires were slashed, bombs were thrown into homes, and one rebel was stabbed.

To slow down police protection, nails were tossed out under the hoofs of the horse's carrying the mounted police and police escorts bringing rebel longshoremen to the docks were ambushed from rooftops with bricks and from the work sites.

In the meantime, work slowed to a snail's pace and the decline of once great New York harbor began. Several massive shipping lines, disgusted with the extortion and violence, gave up on the harbor and docked elsewhere. President Eisenhower sent his Secretary of Labor to New York with a threat that he would call out the United States Army to bring peace to the waterfront and had the Justice Department brand the ILA strike a criminal conspiracy. The ILA answered by sending 600 trouble makers to Washington to picket the White House.

The State of New York, with the full backing of Governor Dewey Answered with a series of lawsuits against the ILA leadership. At the same time the, in April of 1954, the NLRB officially set aside the results of the December elections and called for a new vote but announced that the ILA would be banned from future elections unless it ended its work stoppage...which the ILA denied existed... "Forthwith."

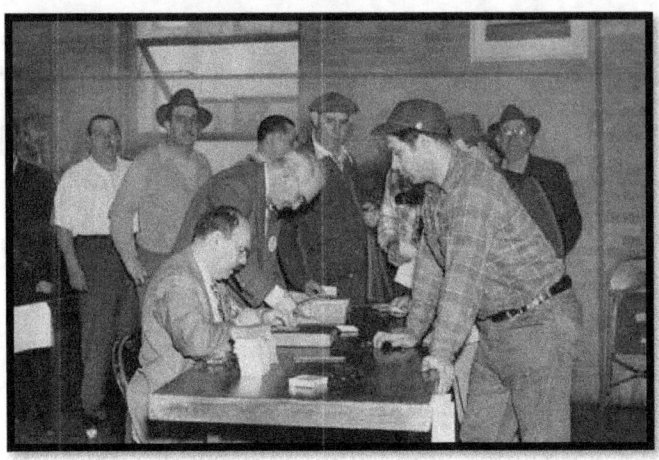

The ILA relented, the election was held, and again, the ILA slugged its way into a very slim victory.

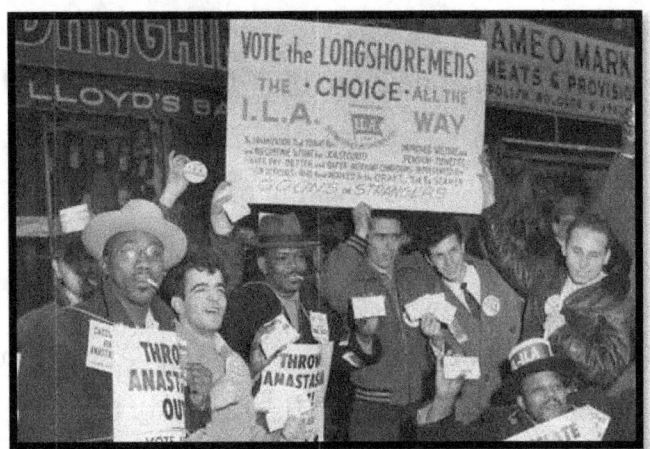

However, the rebels refused to go quietly and forced a third representational election in 1956, in which, again, the ILA won under curious circumstances and by a very narrow margin.

THE CAST AND CREW

Waterfront works because of its extras. The viewer is left with little doubt that these people have lived through the harrowing experiences of the Waterfront. The extras, like most of the professional actors Kazan uses in the film, are not the typical handsome, sun drenched faces of 1950w Hollywood productions. His extras are gritty, defeated and course. Nor do they behave like extras in other films of the day. They are the types of people one would expect to encounter when wandering into a blue-collar working atmosphere of Hoboken or Red Hook. Waterfront's strong, richly developed secondary characters help to create a wonderful film. Pops Doyle is a loving doting father who raised a heroic and fearless son and a compassionate, loyal daughter. He is a hard workingman, a good provider who has one arm longer than other from tossing bails to provide for his family.

Charley Malloy, with two years of college gives him an intellectual edge over Terry and the rest of the Johnny Friendly gang. He has a nickname, an all telling one at that, Charlie the gent. His taste in clothing is expensive and more refined then Johnny Friendly's. We know that he has the will power to claw his way up from poverty and beneath his tough-guy exterior is a deeply passionate man.

Mack, the otherwise mean spirited gang boss from the docks shows a human side by hiring a lazy brother in law because he is evidently afraid of his wife "Who will kill me" and he protects his brother law from JR, Johnny Friendly's merciless loan shark.

Profound inner conflicts confront each central character's conscience creating a motivating background for each. Edie cannot choose between honoring the memory of her murdered brother and loving the man who betrayed him. Terry

Malloy believes that he can remain simultaneously loyal to his brother, Johnny Friendly and himself. The film does not dash to the truth it gropes for the truth and rises from a slow awakening to find it.

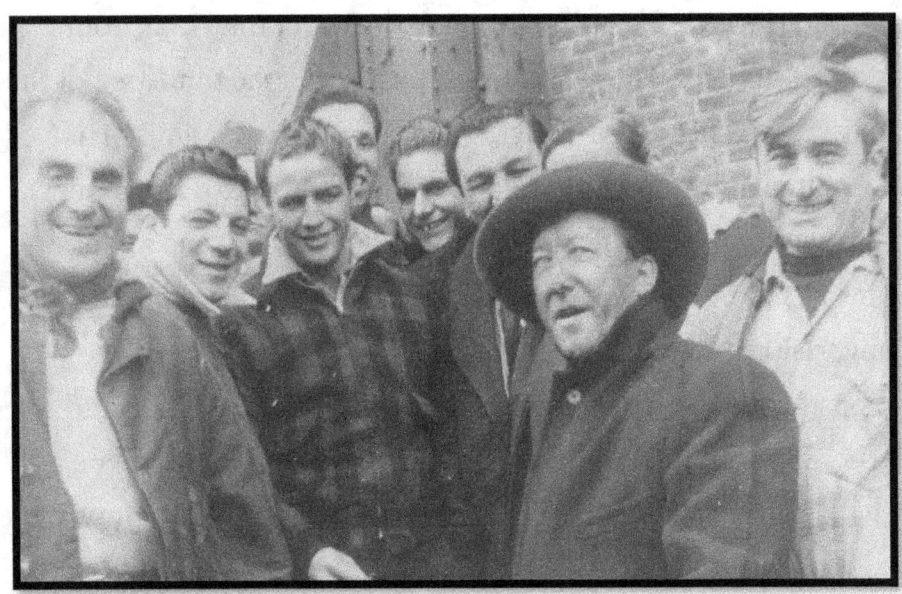

While most of the cast was recruited from the Actors Studio, Hoboken police officers would play Hoboken police officers. Kazan insisted that real Longshoremen be hired as extras to play actor dock workers. It did not always work out.

The longshoremen had been promised four hours of work, paid in cash the following day. In the first week of shooting, the cash did not arrive. Two enormous dock workers took Kazan's assistant director behind a building and promised to toss him off a pier if they were not paid, when, at that exact moment, Spiegel and his paymaster arrived in his limo. They had stopped for coffee and were late.

To play the role of Father Corridan, Kazan chose Karl Malden.

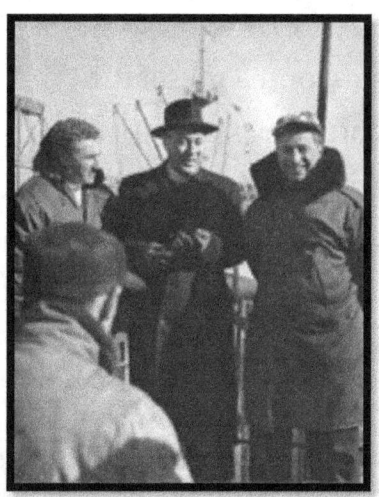

Schulberg, Corridan and Kazan.

The two had first worked together in 1946 in a play *Truck line Café* that started the career of another relatively unknown actor, Marlon Brando.

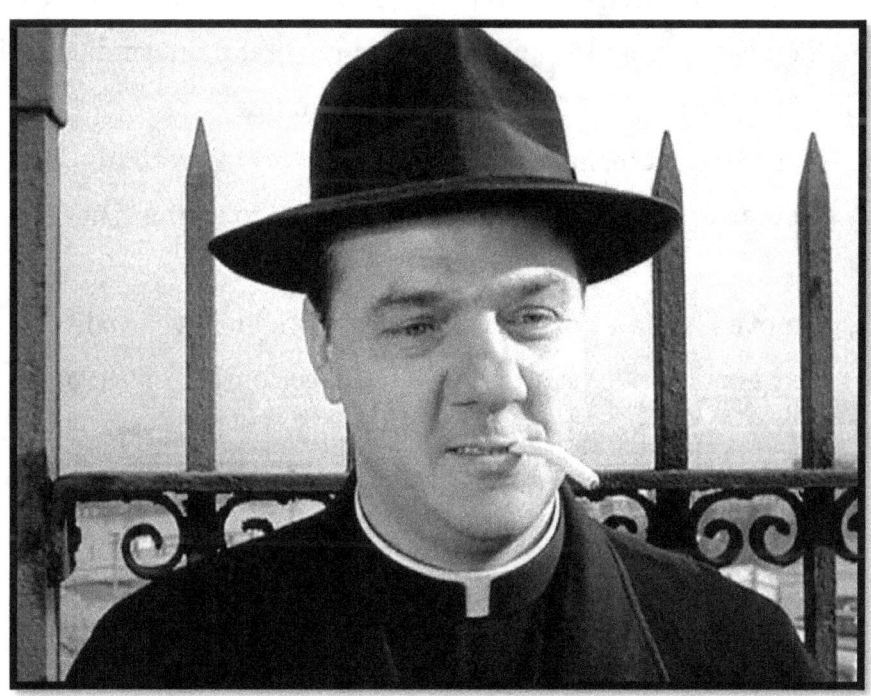

Sinatra had originally been in mind for the role of the Priest, but he turned it down and it is doubtful that at a $900,000 asking price for the role, that he would have gotten it anyway. By that time, Malden had over 18 films to his credit including the much-heralded *A Streetcar Named Desire* (1951) again with newcomer, Marlon Brando. The role won him the Oscar for Best Supporting Actor in that film.

Of the role, Malden said, "Father Corridan was a great orator and a remarkable man. No other person I've portrayed in my film career has had such a profound impact on me as a human being. I can't express how much I admired Father Corridan. He was just like Hoboken—cold and tough on the edges, but filled with integrity and a helluva lot of dignity."

Malden was the son of a Serbian father and a Czech mother, neither of whom spoke English, (he never heard a word of English until he got to first grade.) he was born Malden George Sekulovich on March 12 1912 in Gary, Indiana. (The stage name Karl Malden came from dropping the "l" in his first name and using it as his last name. For Karl, he borrowed his grandfather's name)

After graduating from high school, he spent three years working with his father in the dismal Gary steel mills, saving up enough money to go to acting school in nearby Chicago.

Four years later, he moved to New York to find acting work and eventually landed a series of bit parts on Broadway, which led to bigger parts. In the 1930s, he moved into radio parts where he befriended actor Richard Widmark.

In 1947, Widmark helped Malden land a role in Widmark's movie debut, *Kiss of Death* (Oddly enough, the favorite film of gangster Joey Gallo, the man who would gun down dock boss Albert Anastasia's. Gallo modeled his insane and bloody career on Widmark's character.)

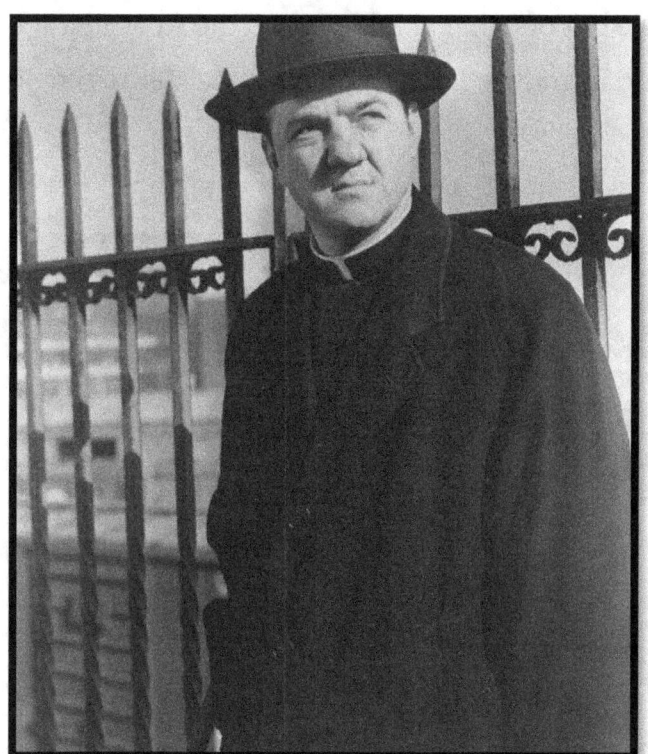 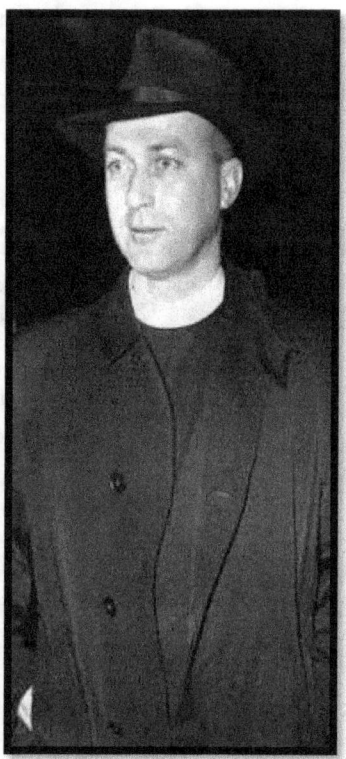

Malden and Corridan

Schulberg said, "We brought Karl to meet Father John" "He sat around and drank with the priest. In the movie, Karl walks like him, talks like him. The Priest liked him so much he gave Malden his black hat and overcoat, which the actor wore throughout the production."

We were the same size, so I bought his coat and hat from him to wear in the film," Malden said. "The wind off the river was ferocious. I was freezing, but somehow I felt a little warmer in his coat and hat."

Malden used the real Father Corridan's chain-smoking in his characterization; the more the priest becomes involved in the docks, the more he smokes, the more he smokes, and the more resolved he is to change the waterfront.

189

For the role of Edie Doyle, Kazan chose the unknown Eva Marie Saint after deciding that the script's romantic angle but one that would tie into the story in a realistic way. The draft was rewritten to introduce Edie, the innocent sister to the murdered hero Eddie Doyle.

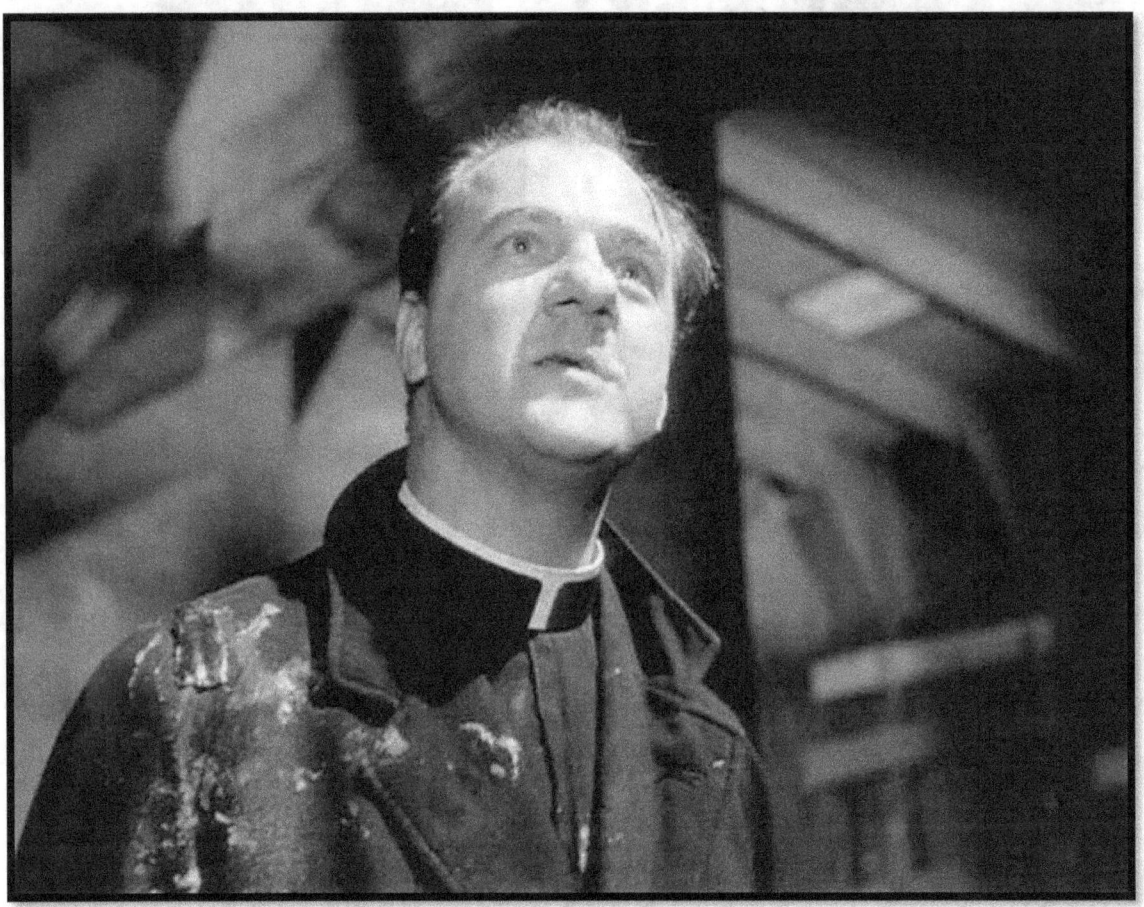

"Eva Marie Saint" said Schulberg "we found in the Player's Directory, it was her first picture." Saint had studied acting at Bowling Green University, afterwards finding quick work in radio and TV drama's which was restricted to a May 29,

1950 CBS television drama *The Man Who Had Influence* starring Robert Sterling.

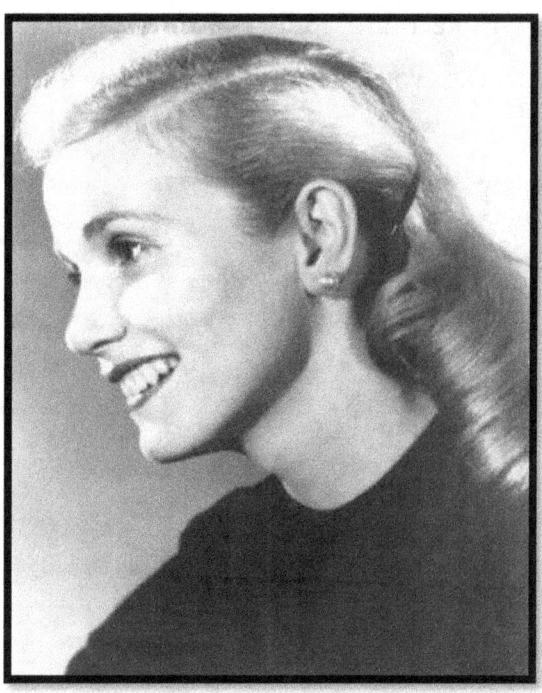

 Kazan had actor Elizabeth Montgomery in mind for the part and although her screen test was flawless, she had, as Kazan wrote "an air of genteel Connecticut finishing school about her"

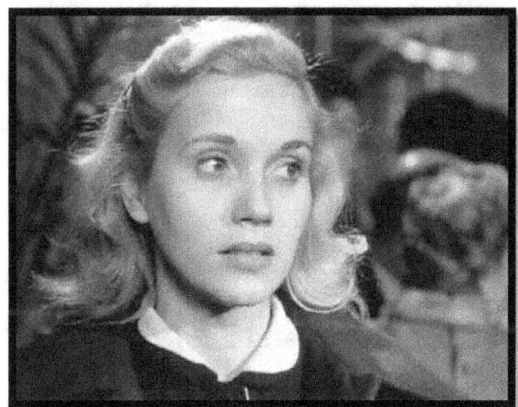 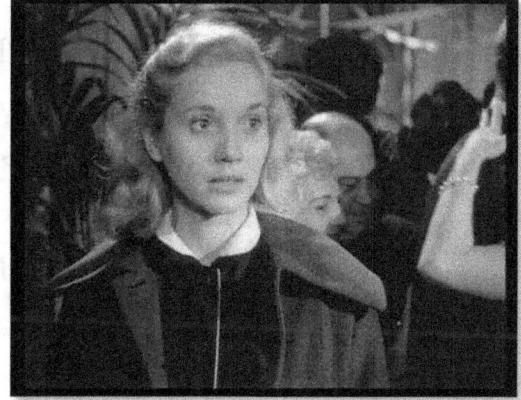

Saint

Another name tossed around for the role was Grace Kelly, who withdrew herself from consideration since she had consented to take the lead female role in *Rear Window*. Despite her wealthy background, Kelly was only a generation from the rough-hewn Irish dock workers and would have given the role an interesting dash.

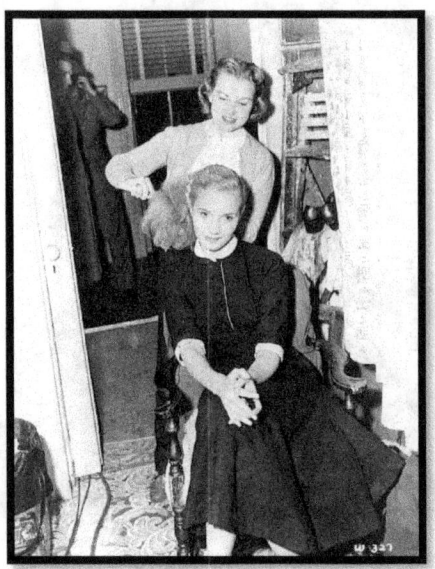

"We had more trouble casting that part" Schulberg said, "We went through the whole screen actors guild book, kept turning pages, getting nowhere. Eva Marie Saint was working in a play on Broadway with Lillian Gish, and had one small scene (The Play was *The Trip to Bountiful* playing at the Henry Miller Theater 1953-1954) Gadge said, "You go" I went and I was very impressed by her. She had never been in a movie before"

Even with its sterling screenplay, the film would not have had the same impact without the strong acting skills and screen presence of Rod Steiger and Lee J. Cobb (with Cobb in particular deserving more credit than he is often given.)

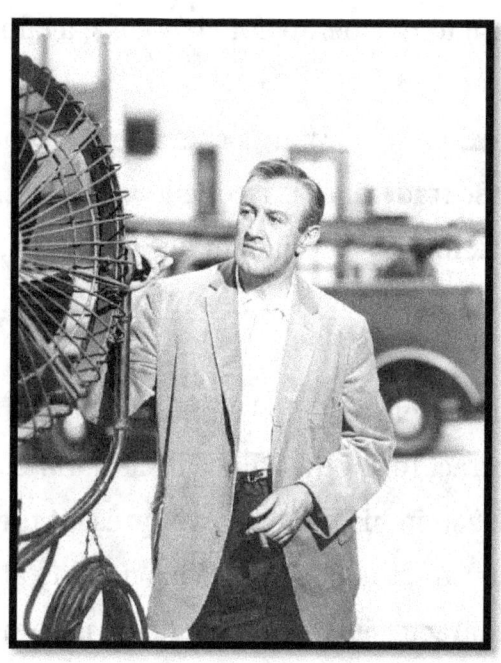

Lee J. Cobb.

Kazan chose Cobb for the role of waterfront gangster Johnny Friendly. It is a remarkable performance as the strangely likable yet brutal mob boss. The performance is even more remarkable considering Cobb's state of his mental health at the time of the filming, the pressure of new film, working with Kazan and Schulberg, both identified as informants for the HUAC, his wife's failing health and mental condition (She had suffered a nervous breakdown) and Cobb's precarious financial situation strained him during the entire filming.

Eight months after the release of *Waterfront*, he suffered a massive heart attack that almost killed him. Frank Sinatra moved in pulled the actor from despair. The two had worked together in the 1949 release, *Miracle of the Bells*. Sinatra, who felt that Cobb should have won the Academy Award for his role in Waterfront, paid for all of actors medical bills not covered by his insurance and then moved him into a rest room to recuperate for six weeks, again paying all of the bills from his own pocket.

Rod Steiger starred as Charley Malloy, Brando's characters brother, the beefy, round-faced Method actor whose trademark is a coiled-spring intensity was already known through his work in the early days of live television, especially in Paddy Chayefsky's *Marty* and the anthology series as *Philco Television Playhouse* (1948-56).

However, Kazan had wanted the role to go to Laurence Tierney but the Celtic looking Tierney was under contract to another film. It was a difficult role. Schulberg in his writing and Kazan in his filming never present the Malloy brothers as more than what they are, thugs. Despite his nobility at the films end, Charley Malloy is a repulsive character just as Terry Malloy is pathetic figure as the ex-boxer of promise reduced to as mascot status to the hoods because of his low mental capacity. The brilliance of both Brando and Steiger's performance is that they molded their characters, through body language and facial expressions, into sympathetic characters.

Added to the stress of the role, Steiger's Charlie Malloy is forced to deal with a wide variety of emotions but again, truth is the primary motivator behind his actions. Steiger plays the role with a gauntlet of emotions, showing his growing anxiety of Terry's relationship with Edie with narrowed eyes, or nervously slapping his gloves in hand during the taxicab scene.

For Brando's part, Kazan gave him complete freedom in his role as Terry Malloy. Brando took the opportunity to become Terry Malloy to the point that the viewer is not watching Brando embody Terry Malloy the viewer is watching Terry Malloy in the flesh. The impression left is so real that the viewer could easily believe that Kazan's camera has simply shown up at a time in Malloy's life when he is confused and troubled.

It is also impressive to watch Brando's body movements. He makes them as important as his lines by pushing Malloy's personality quirks into the limelight. Terry walks like the prizefighter he is, head forward, chin down, and the attention to his scarred eyebrow. Before Brando's Terry Malloy appeared, few actors considered incorporating body language or building characters quirk into their roles.

It was not the performance that viewers in 1954 expected to see, but it is the performance that modern viewer have come to expect, the result being that the performance that once defined the cutting edge, loses some of its energy. Brando's performance, his visionary flair, have been replicated so many times over the decades that it has, unfortunately, lost its freshness, due, oddly enough, to the dominance of method acting in films that Brando and Kazan helped to introduce.

THE FILM AS A MORAL MESSAGE

"Art, like morality, consists in drawing a line somewhere." **Gilbert Chesterton**

Although Kazan was not a particularly religious man in his personnel life, he understood the power of religious imagery, specifically Roman Catholic imagery; desperate souls, an evil betrayal of the moral messenger and then ingeniously (or self-servingly) inverted the act of betrayal into a near saintly form of enlightenment.

Budd Schulberg, who was Jewish and not Catholic, also understood the Catholic churches intrinsic power of appeal to morality, conscience and justice. As a result, almost every scene shot by Kazan and every bit of dialogue written by Schulberg, happens only to contribute to Terry Malloy's transformation from complicit bystander to active witness against evil.

The films spiritual morality causes Brando's characters arch, his dramatic transformation. At the same time, the arch for the other characters is equally impressive and tied to Brando's arch. Johnny Friendly is reduced from unquestioned head of the union and the local mob to a common street thug, Charlie Malloy goes from smug mob accountant to a noble soul who loses his life to save the life of his brother. Like Terry Malloy's character, Father Barry's character also changes and develops as the film progresses, transforming from a Priest sheltered away in his church to a man of the street willing to fight for what he believes in.

The priest's transformation comes directly after Joey Doyle is pushed to his death, The martyrdom scene Father Barry kneels over his dead body, whispering the Last Rites of the Church, Edie is sobbing over her brother. Kazan and Schulberg handle the death of Joey Doyle in a realistic fashion.

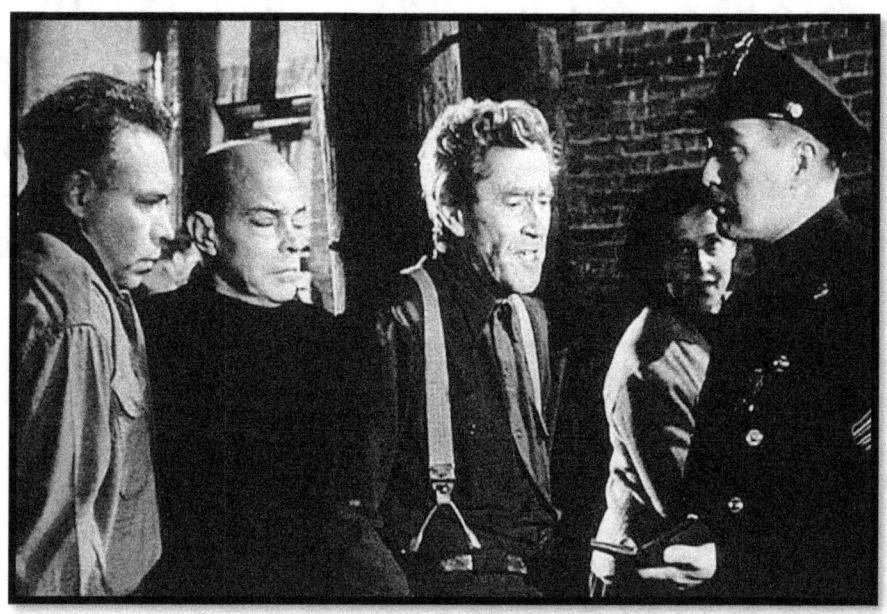

Pop Doyle is stoic over his son's death and mutters "Kept telling him. Don't say nothin'. Keep quiet. You'll live longer.' At the same time, his daughter, Edie is distraught. Kazan shows that people, even in the same families, have different reactions to death.

During the scene, Edie chastises the priest for hiding in his church while his flock suffers. In the scene that follows, the next morning Edie apologizes to Father Barry for his outspokenness. Barry response by asking if she thinks that he is a freeloader looking for an easy duty. When she does not answer, he answers the question himself.

He says that he had thought about what she said and that she was right, he would never what he could to right the wrongs on the waterfront unless he left the rectory and found out what the situation is.

Thereafter Father Barry then extends the parameters of his parish to the waterfront but he never loses site of his primary mission, to spread the word of God and advocating peaceful resistance to the evil on the docks. When Terry waits in a bar room with a loaded pistol to kill Johnny Friendly, Father Barry disarms him and advocates peaceful resistance by telling the truth.

Father Barry condemns the longshoremen to account for their inaction in the face of evil (Johnny Friendly) which he considers a sin, thus elevating Joey Doyle and Kayo Duggan to the realm of enlightenment since they have both died for the sins of the longshoremen.

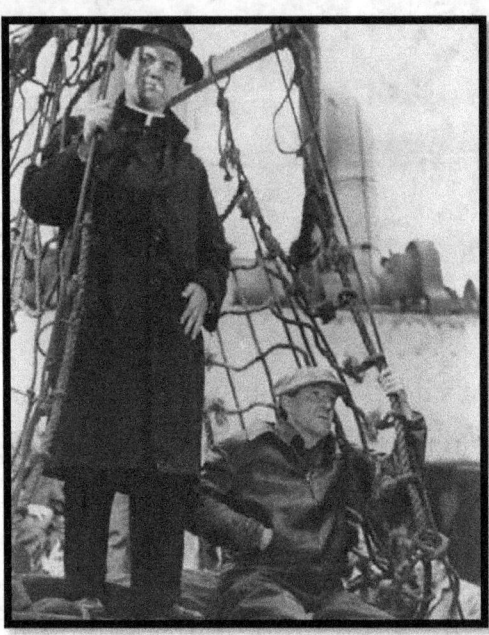

Kazan follows the scripts strong spiritual themes with equally strong religious imagery in Doyle and Duggan's deaths scenes. Edie cradles Joey's corpse as Madonna cradled Jesus' body, Father Barry rises out of the cargo hold with Dugan's body as if ascending to heaven, and Charlie's corpse hangs by a hook, all of which are visual references to Christ's body on the cross.

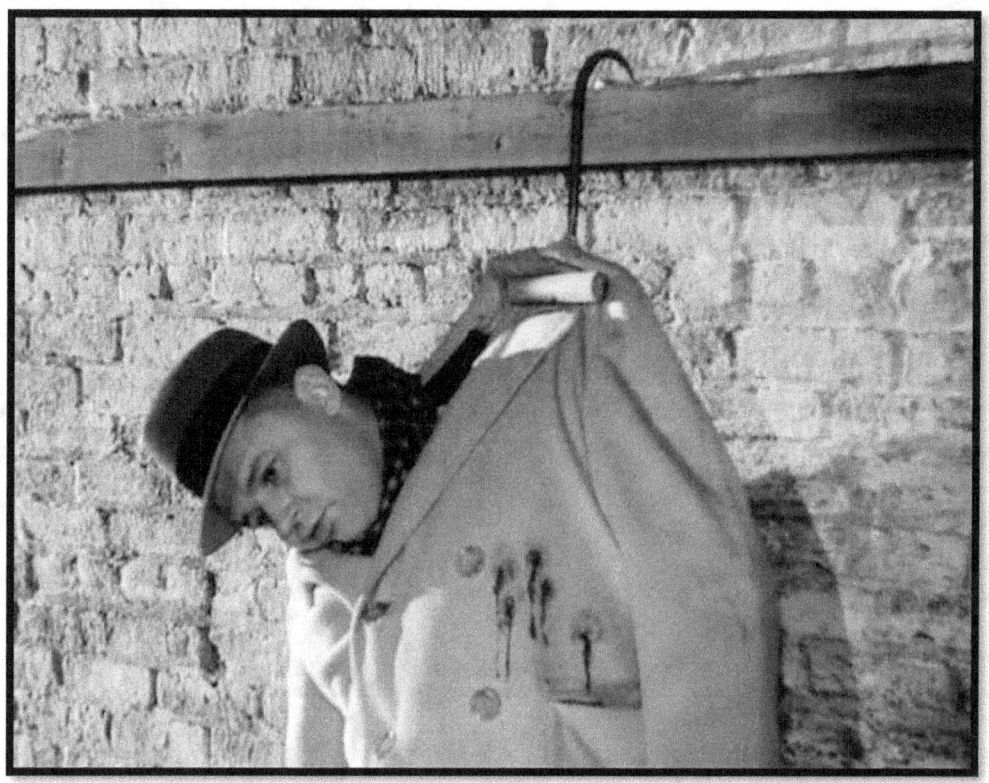

More religion, specifically Christian religion, is laid on thickly throughout the film, especially from the "Christ is in the shapeup" speech given by Father Barry in the cargo hold.

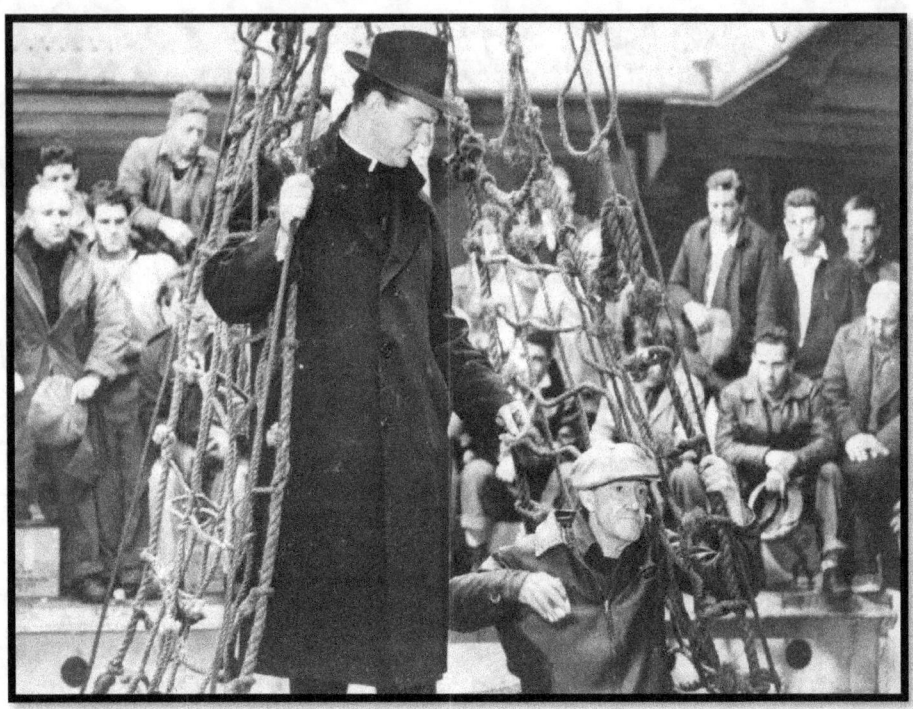

"Christ is always with you," Father Barry tells the dock workers

"He's in the hatch, he's in the union halls"

In the cargo hold scene Johnny Friendly and his men are positioned high above the hold, above Father Barry and above the longshoremen, his position of power on the docks has not changed.

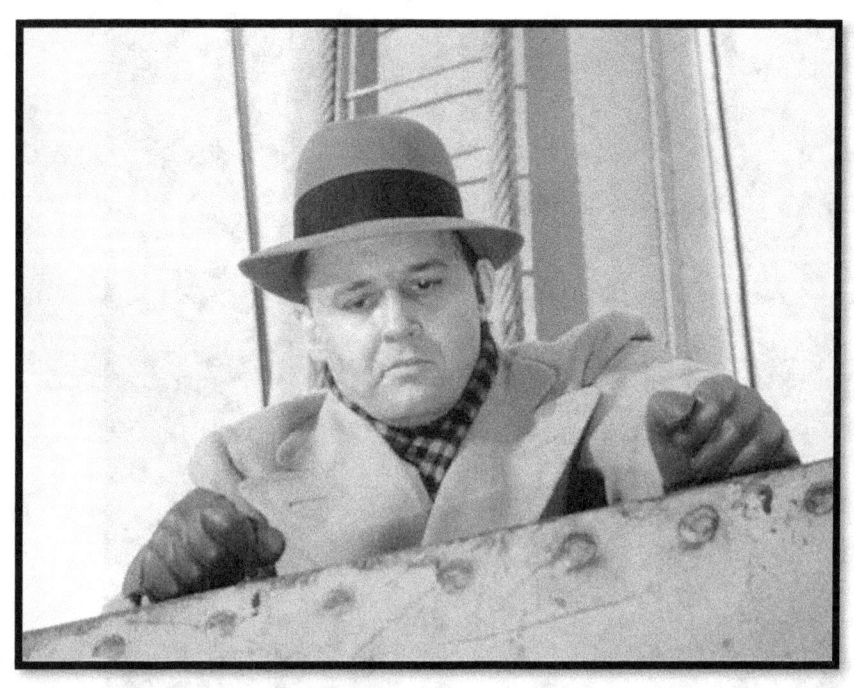

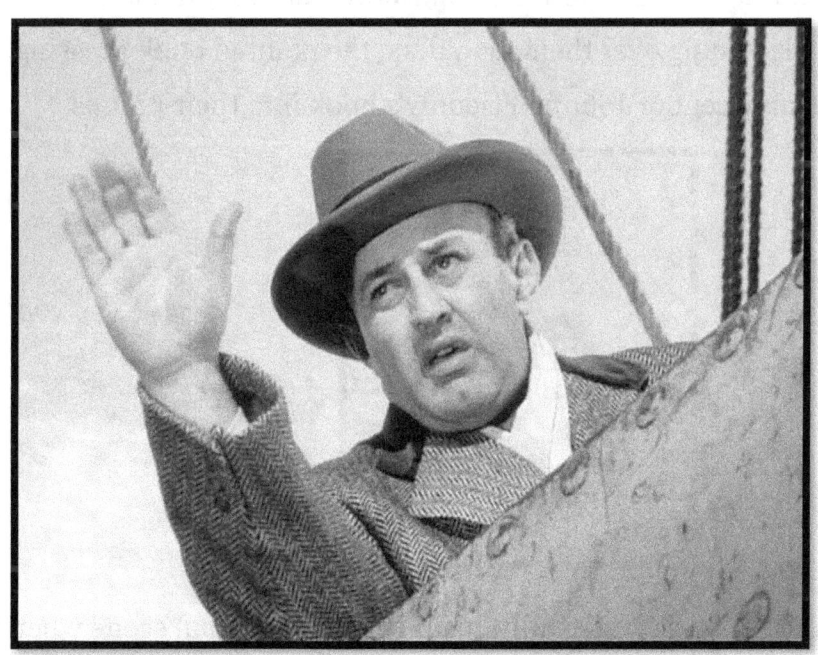

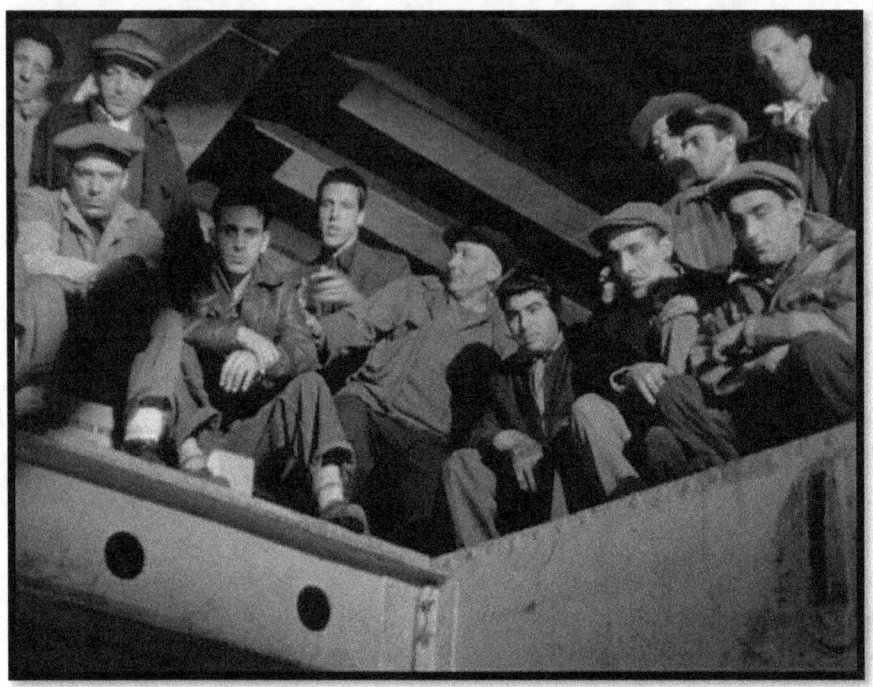

Intentional or not, throughout the film the Longshoremen wear their metallic loading hooks swung over their shoulders, the pointed hook pressing into their chests, reminiscent of Johnny Friendly's hook into their unions.

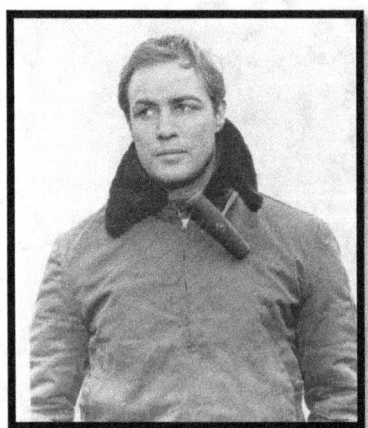

The loading hooks are used wonderfully again in the film's final scene when the now Christ like figure of Terry Malloy, beaten and bleeding from the head, carries his hook, cross like, as he leads his new flock, the longshoremen, back to work.

Following the religious themes of the film, the story stresses the power of faith, intangible faith. Edie and Father Barry, who rise Terry up from the docks and open his conscious, are both people of faith who want nothing more than to do the right thing and eventually that faith in doing the right thing validates their values and principles. Edie's faith transforms Terry's faith who eventually transforms his Brother Charlie's faith. As a result, the characters grow, Brando's Terry Malloy, transforms before the viewer's eyes.

Opposing them are the corrupt union officials and mobsters whose only faith is in worldly good, terror and fear.

The hot air steam seeping up through the sewers and creates a misty visual of an otherworldly atmosphere. The steam is most effective in the scene where Terry confesses to Father Barry in the park. The steam swirls around them, almost engulfing them. It is interesting to note that Terry's confession takes place outside of the church.

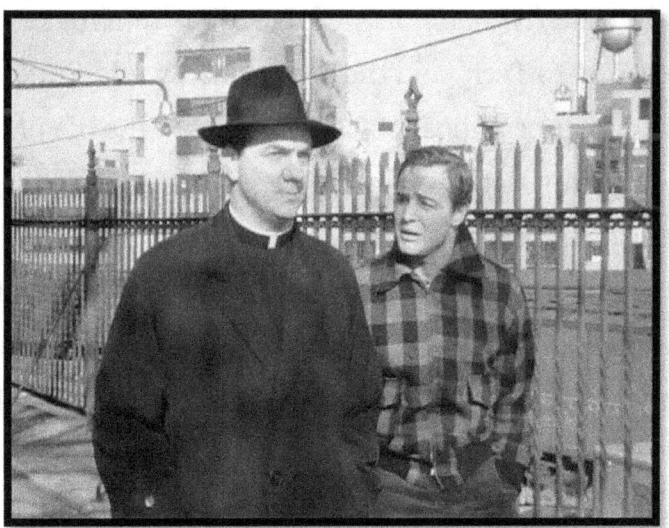

Even though Terry wants to talk to Father Barry inside the church, (The church used in the film is the towering Gothic Revival, Our Lady of Grace Roman

Catholic Church. Directly across the street is the Willow Avenue Park, called Church Park by the locals, where Terry and Barry speak.) the machinations of the plot draw them outside to the waterfront.

The location shades the scene Kazan is telling the audience that Terry's confession is not religious. Instead of hiding in a confessional, the waterfront becomes a living part of the film. The scene also carries through with the message that throughout the film, Father Barry never seems to take to Terry.

He obviously does not like him. He is never Terry's father- confessor and repeatedly indicates to Terry that merely talking about his sins on the waterfront will not absolve his sins, only action will set him free, fitting into the Jesuit maxim seen in the real life Father Corridan's actions, through action faith, through faith, action.

In *Waterfront,* Father Barry is not a Catholic guide to Terry but a mentor of the soul. However, at times, Father Barry's sermonizing to Terry seems sanctimonious because the underlying moral message of the film makes Barry's religious parallels unnecessary to Terry and the audience. By mid film, the viewer already recognizes the films philosophical stance; that the life of even an ordinary man can become a living act of moral change. (Johnny Friendly, unfortunately for Terry, also realizes this)

Through his contacts with the forces of light (Edie, Pop Doyle, Father Barry) Terry listens to his conscience and reconsiders his life and decides to be the man he thinks he is but it took the love of Edie Doyle and the persuasion of a Father Barry to show Terry how low he has fallen. He comes to understand what is going on around him, and understands how he has been an unwitting ploy in Joey Doyle's death.

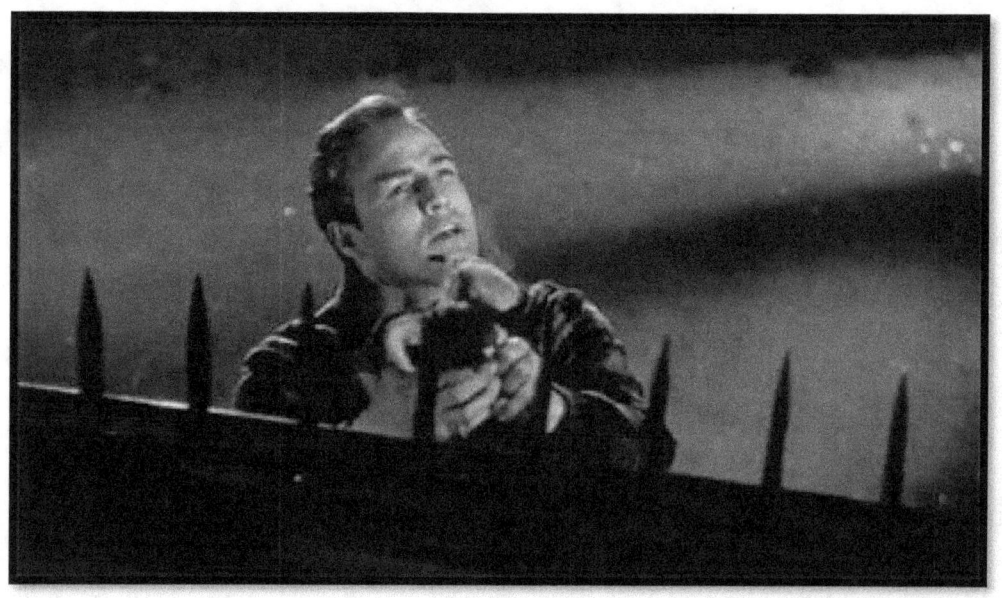

Through a process of reflection, Terry experiences a Lenten journey of repentance and conversion, of sort. He follows his conscience and is prepared to suffer his decision to do the right thing. His is a journey from darkness to light, from lies to truth.

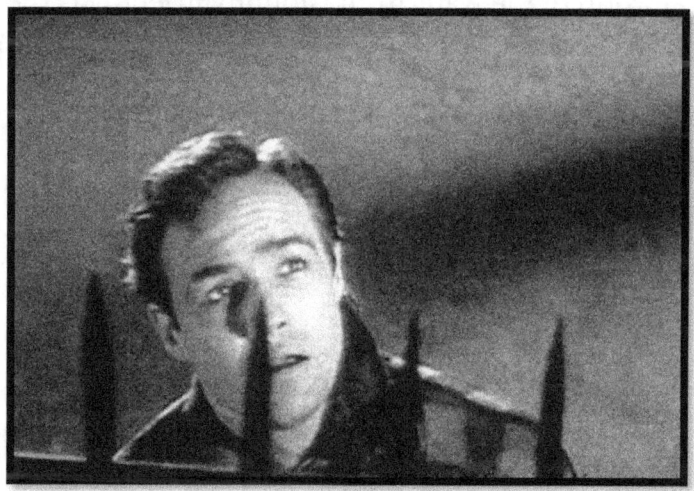

His testimony before the waterfront commission and telling Edie about his role in her brother's death, he articulates his repentance for his part in the waterfront conspiracy. The truth sets him free. Just as the truth is the primary catalyst for Father Barry and Edie's actions and in the end, Terry Malloy stands ready to die for the truth.

Terry's journey to find the truth changes not only himself but also the community of the waterfront, fitting into the Catholic-Jesuit social action movement of the times, which placed the community at the center of all moral action.

This admirable principle is neatly corrupted by Kazan and Schulberg; informing is the correct moral choice because informing (In this specific case) is done for the good of the community.

The film also stresses that power; the tool of the unsaved in this case, corrupts. Virtually every one in the film who has any power at all is morally bankrupt except Father Barry whose power is moral and has not corrupted him because it has little effect in the real world of the waterfront. Johnny Friendly is the ultimate definition of corrupt power. There is not a single decision he makes in the film that does not establish his power or further it. Even stuffing $50 down Terry's t-shirt obligates Terry to repay the favor later.

In Kazan's view of power, there are no friendships. Mr. Big turns on Johnny Friendly as soon as he is exposed by the Waterfront Crime Commission, Friendly kills Charlie Malloy, even though he has known him for decades.

Because Kazan made the films themes so clear, it becomes equally clear to the audience and Brando's Terry Malloy, that forcing him to a take a dive in the contender fight establishes his minimal importance in the mob. To the mob, Terry's brother and Johnny Friendly, the man who took him to ball games as child, are indifferent to Terry's personal emotional needs. In fact, they are more than willing to subordinate his interests to their own.

Failure and Terry's sense of unfulfilled life, fueled by resentment, give the character psychological depth. In the taxi-cab scene Terry complains to his brother that he 'could've been a contender' and could have had class, had not Charley and Johnny Friendly ended his chances of a title shot by forcing him to throw fights for 'the short-end money'.

Later, on the roof, the Crime Commission investigator reminds Terry of his lost boxing career and the viewer senses how deeply the betrayal affected him when Terry breaks the code of Deaf and Dumb and explains that he was forced to throw the fight.

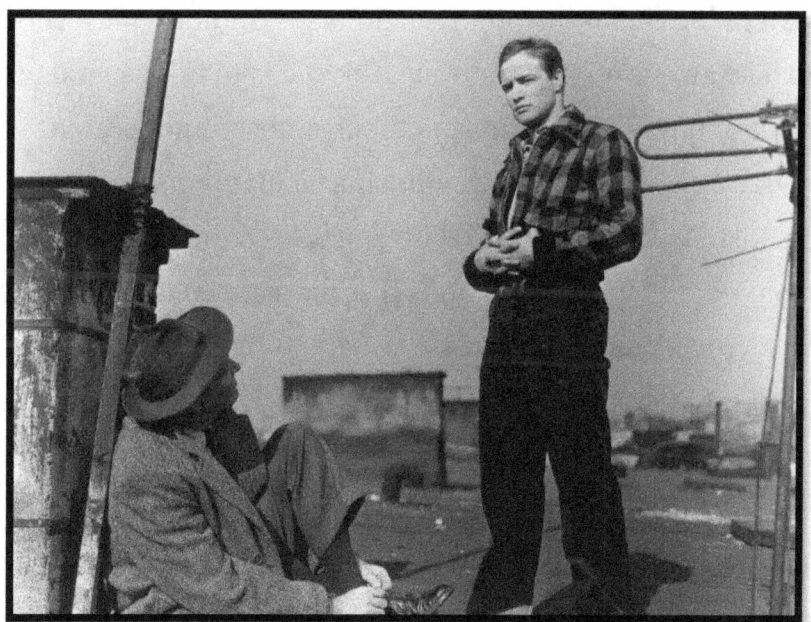

Working within the confines of the script, Schulberg and Brando created a sympathetic protagonist in Terry Malloy. Life happens to him, he is a little man with no control or seemingly no care over his ambivalence and powerlessness.

Terry Malloy is not naturally mean, like Johnny Friendly, or hardened like Charlie Malloy. His participation in Joey's death was unintentional as opposed to Charlie and Johnny Friendly's participation, while marginal, was still direct. As a result, the character of Charlie Malloy while in the end is actual quite noble, he is not as sympathetic as Terry's. As much as anyone else, Terry is a victim of the mob. Unlike Johnny Friendly, his flaws are human, forgivable.

Terry is a man with troubles that are eating away at him. He is boiling just below the surface. Several times in the film, he picks fights with those around him. He is sarcastic to the police, the crime investigators, Father Barry, the longshoremen, the bartender where he takes Edie for a drink.

The film remains a powerful film because its subtext is the revelation of character through psychological motivation. What makes Brando's performance so brilliant is that to take an eye off him for even a second is to miss a vital telling sign. Through a gamut of physical acts, most of them almost unnoticeable Brando presents a Terry Malloy who is a brooding inarticulate confused little man who is seething, just under the surface, with a massive bundle of contradictory emotions who slowly understands that his actions have definitive results. His roof top racing pigeons, located in the heaven like retreat above the docks are his only outlet for devotion, love and gentleness. In the scene with the pigeons, Terry mentions their loyalty to their mates a quality he admires and needs because he lacks it in his own life.

In his reality, even his brother has sold him "For the short money" Later in the same scene he mentions that the pigeons are nervous because a hawk is in the area and that the city is filled with them. The words echo his life and the danger that surround him from the Johnny Friendly gang. The film is filled with references to birds, pigeons, canaries, birdseed, hawks and stoolies with the implication that everyone on the waterfront are little more than pigeons.

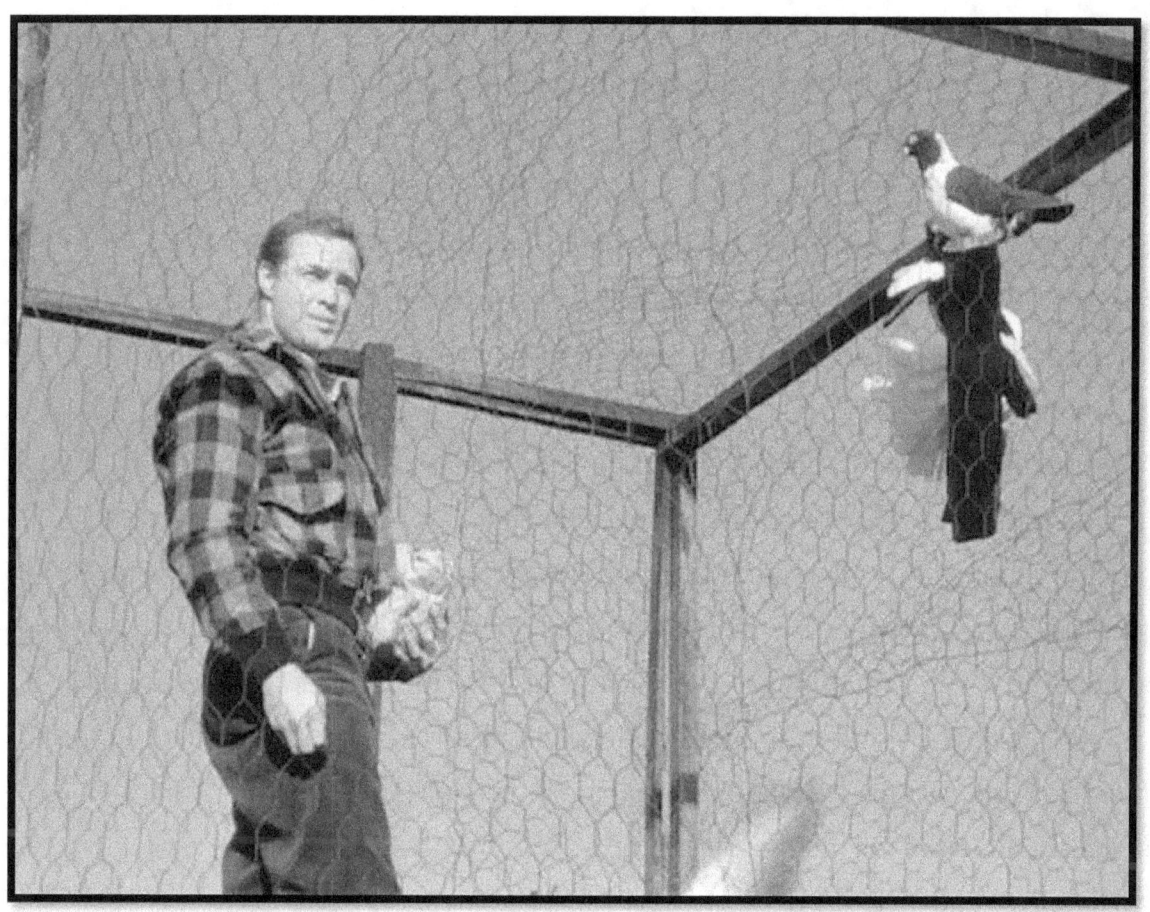

However, it is Brando's physical portrayal of Terry Malloy is the key for the audiences understanding of Terry Malloy character, he shuffles his feet and looks away from whomever he's speaking to, (except his brother) his hands nervously rub the back of his neck and when he is adamant or hurt, he shoves them into his pockets.

Brando's use of mannerisms are complete throughout the role, leaving the audience to guess what his true emotions are, sometimes to surprising results, such as playing with a piece of lint when his brother pulls a pistol on him in the cab or toying with his zipper when he learns that Joey Doyle was killed.

Kazan emphasizes on the gamut of Terry's emotions by consistently focusing the camera's attention on Brando's face, Brando's narrowing eyes narrow or the slackness to his face when faced with a truthful reality or his hesitant smiles for Johnny Friendly and Edie.

Brando became Terry Malloy. Kazan said, "We drove in from New York to Hoboken every day together when we were shooting On the Waterfront. We'd talk and laugh on the way to work, but as soon as we arrived, he would transform himself into Terry. The intimacy and nuance that he brought to the role were breathtaking."

As the film progresses, Brando's Terry Malloy physically changes before the camera, an indication that his priorities have changed and signals to the audience that he now completely understands that actions have results. Slowly he faces the complexities of the decisions before him, spurred on by his complete understanding of his role in Joey Doyle's death, his love for Edie and her feelings for him, the barrage of guilt from Father Barry and his own brother's murder. Brando has Malloy communicate his confusion in his new, threatening surrounding, all in the neighborhood he grew up in, by stressing his inarticulateness and an array of nervous, evasive gestures.

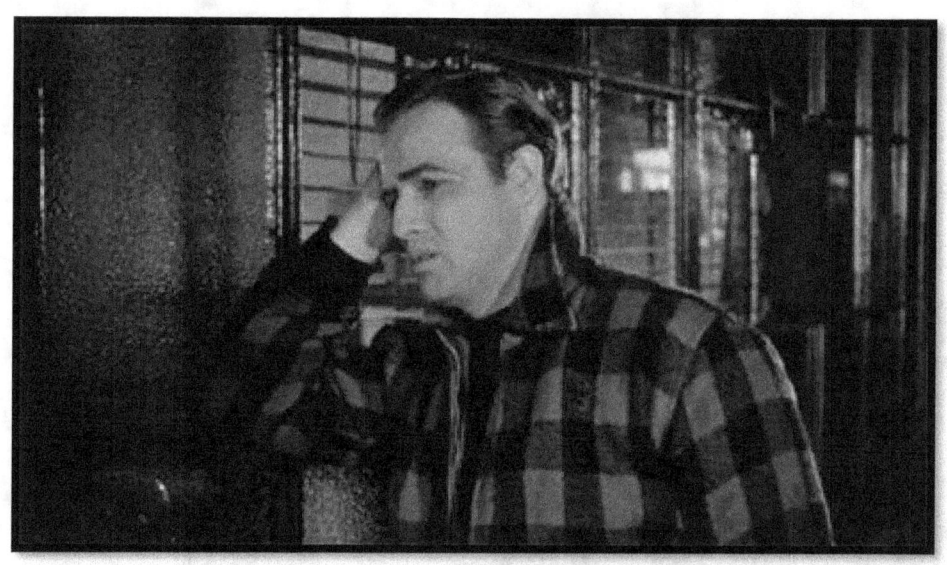

Terry's inability to look a person in the eyes is countered by Johnny Friendly's determination to stare into the eyes from only inches away or his henchmen, in solid colored hats and overcoats staring blankly into the speaker. Brando's Malloy is one of them and he is not.

When John Friendly slaps around the bookie named Skins for cheating him out of $50, he gives the money to Terry, sticking it in his turtleneck collar. Brando's Terry winces when the money is shoved into shirt, he is already unhappy with his role in Johnny Friendly's world.

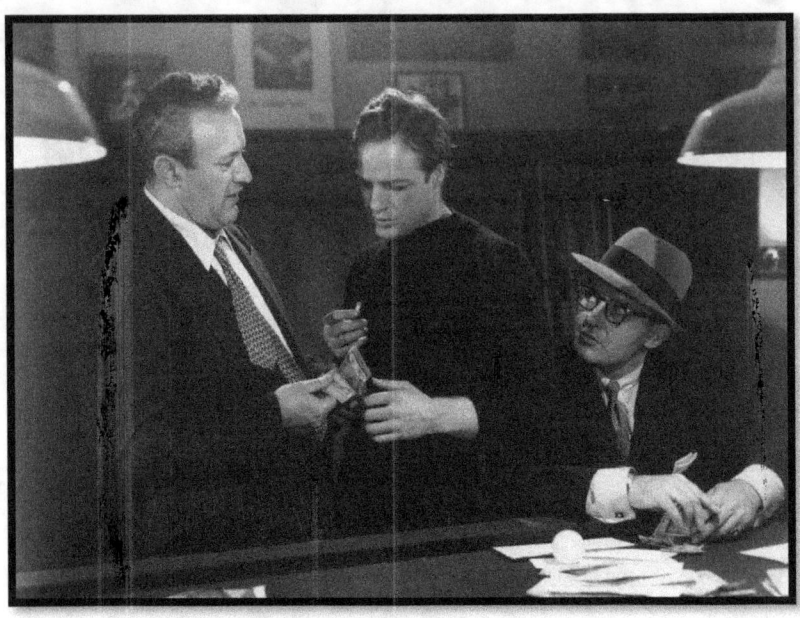

The wince was not scripted but because of it, within seconds we have a better understanding of Terry Malloy's character. What is lost in the scene is the fact that the $50 stuffed in Terry shirt was a substantial amount of money in 1953.

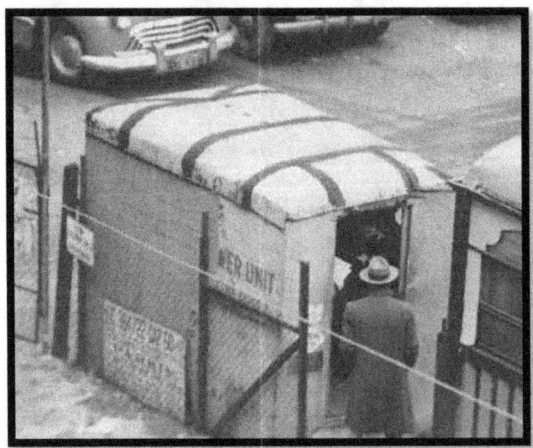

Bookies and loan sharks operated out in the open on the dock. The photo above, a Brooklyn bookie opened his bet shop in a storage shed in the parking lot.

In the film, the rooftop is Terry's sanctuary, here we see him very relaxed, lying down on the roofs edge, the pressure from the outside world, always the factor that drives Terry to the roof, are gone.

On the roof he's far away from the docks and Johnny Friendly's bar (The tavern used in the film still stands and operates as an upscale saloon) he's in the heavenly clouds, much the same way that we assume Joey Doyle, who kept racing pigeons and finally dies while being thrown from the roof, sought his sanctuary on the roof.

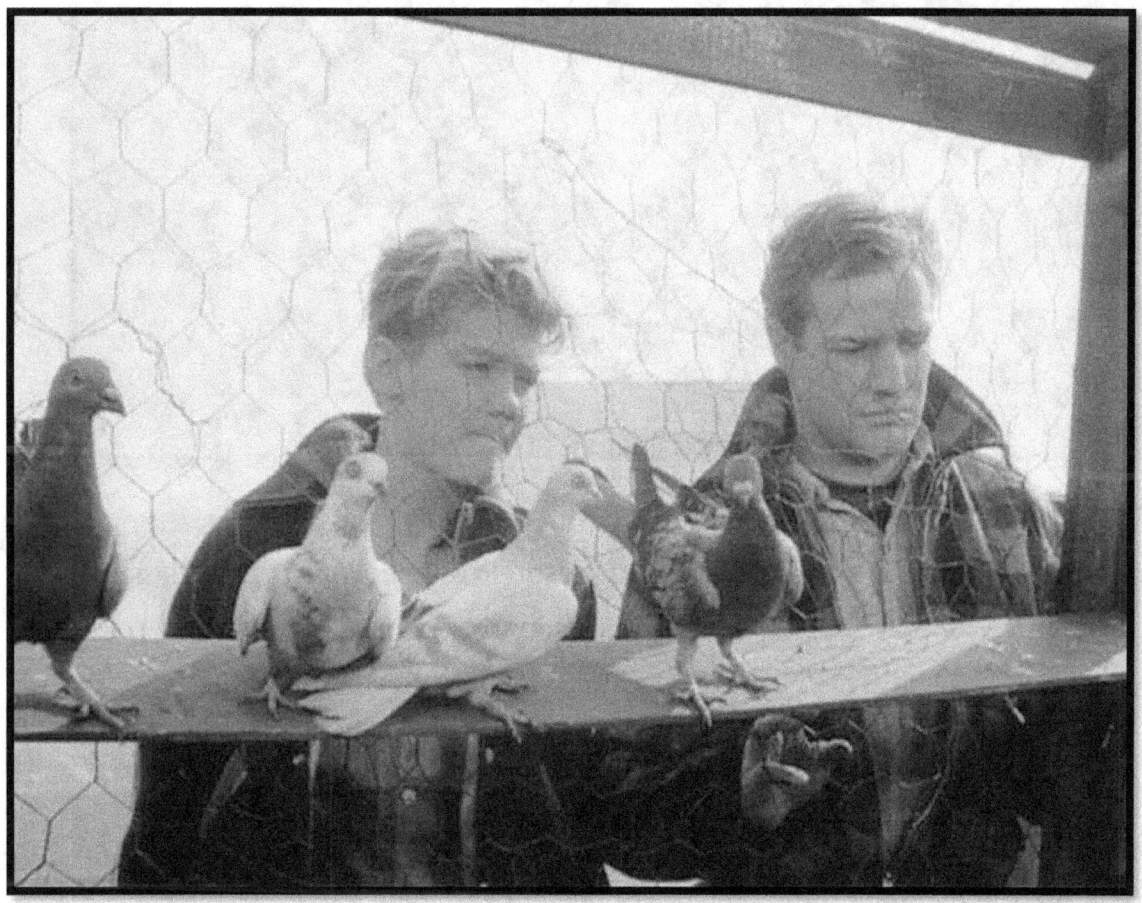

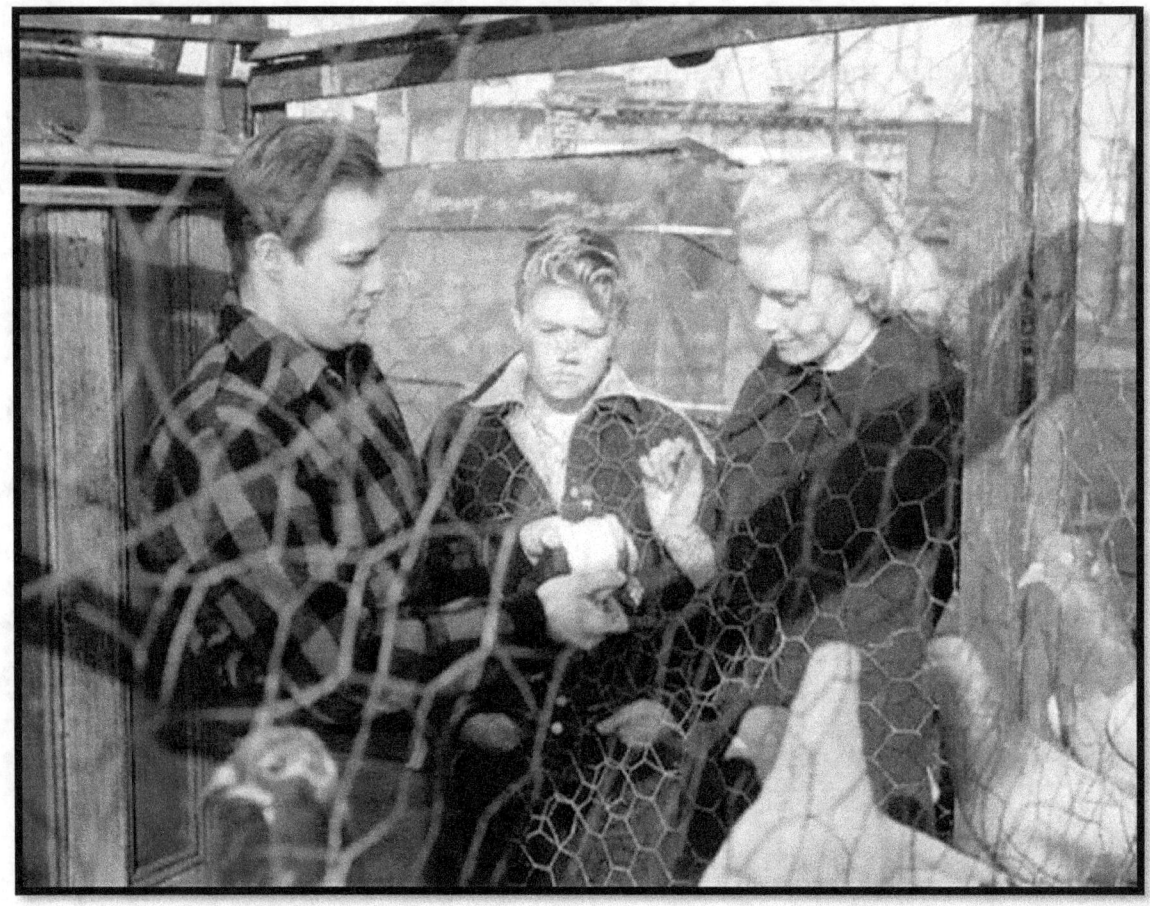

From the roof tops the audience sees the Hudson River, shown so often in the film, is a border, an edge that to the longshoremen world where corrupt local Union runs everything. The Empire State Building, the tallest building in the world 1954, looms in the distance to represent the dreams of a better, richer life, yet it is only occasionally glimpsed in the fog over the weather beaten gray rooftops of a poverty stricken waterfront.

Fitting into the roof top motif is the use of pigeons that play a reoccurring role in the film. A the films start, Terry is able to lure Joey Doyle onto the roof by returning one of his pigeons who has gone astray, in much the same way, Joey has gone astray in his decision to testify against the flock.

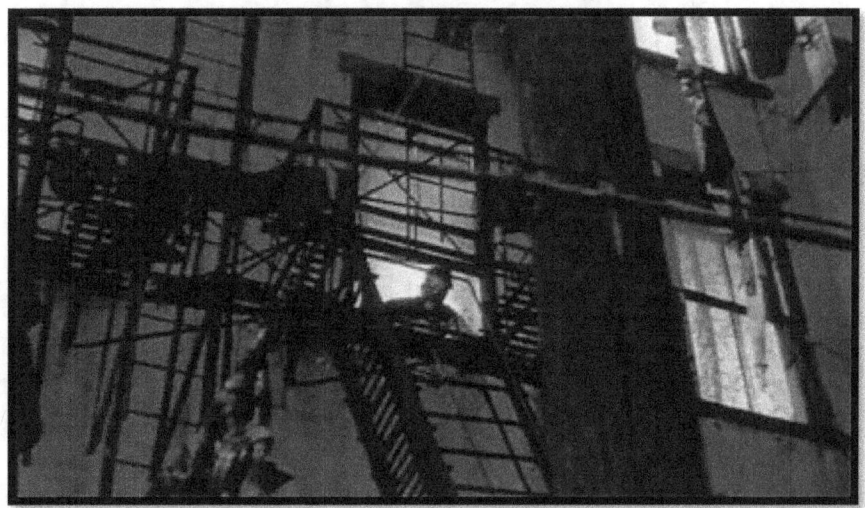

Joey Doyle death scene

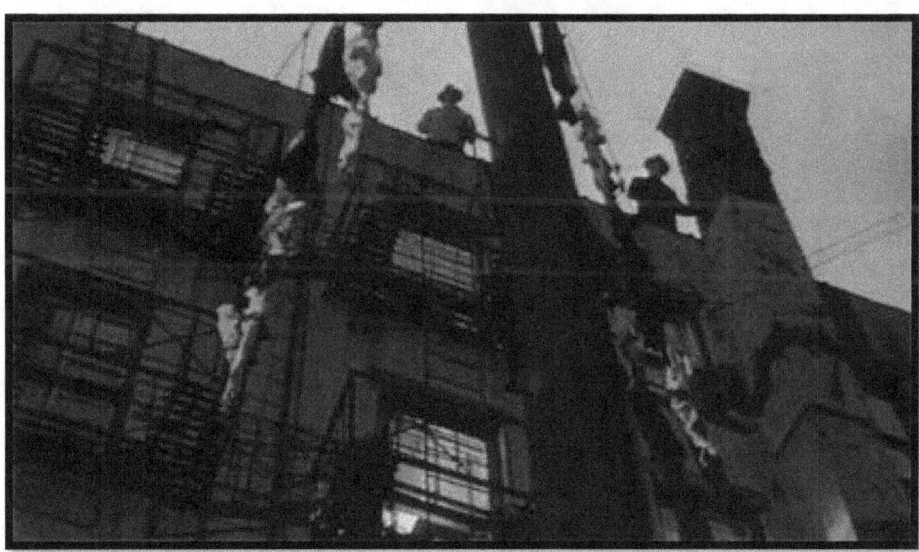

The pigeons are copped, unable to fly because they have been trained not to fly, not dissimilar to Terry's predicament. He is stuck on the waterfront, a flunky to his brother and John Friendly. The imagery of Terry inside the cage when he tends the birds shows his affinity with the animals. Terry's excessive care for the birds is his only outlet for affection. There is also, of course, the negative connotation, stool pigeon, an informer.

Finally, the transformation is complete when Terry Malloy's stands up to Johnny Friendly on the docks, wearing Joey Doyle's jack, an indication of how deeply the death affected him, the character stands tall and confident, swaggering even.

He looks around the pier openly, calmly, without his fear or shyness so clearly established in the opening of the film. Now he chews gum with a cocky, slow steadiness, his speech is clear the whining mumbling voice of the early Terry Malloy is vanished.

THE ROLE OF EDIE DOYLE

"The world is a dangerous place, not because of those who do evil, but because of those who look on and do nothing." **Albert Einstein**

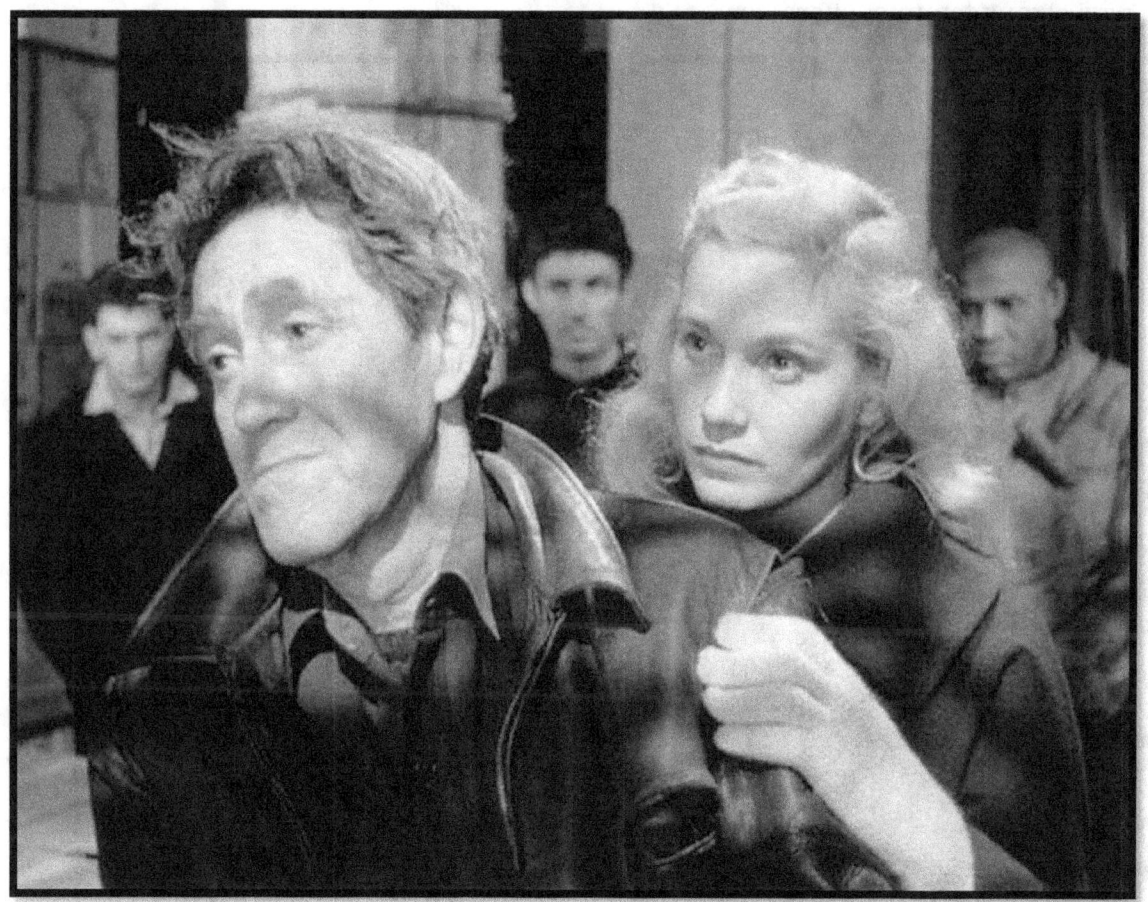

   Edie Doyle, the films leading lady is Kazan's primary vehicle to propel the story through by her determination to find her brothers killers. She is the films catalyst for action.

Edie, although her poverty was near equal to Terry Malloy's, comes from a protective and nurturing environment. Her dockworker father and his deceased wife struggled to collect coins for their daughter's education. As a result of that nurturing Edie character is not the brainless one-dimensional female character role women were so often relegated to in the 1950's and her part flirts with creating a strong feminist character.

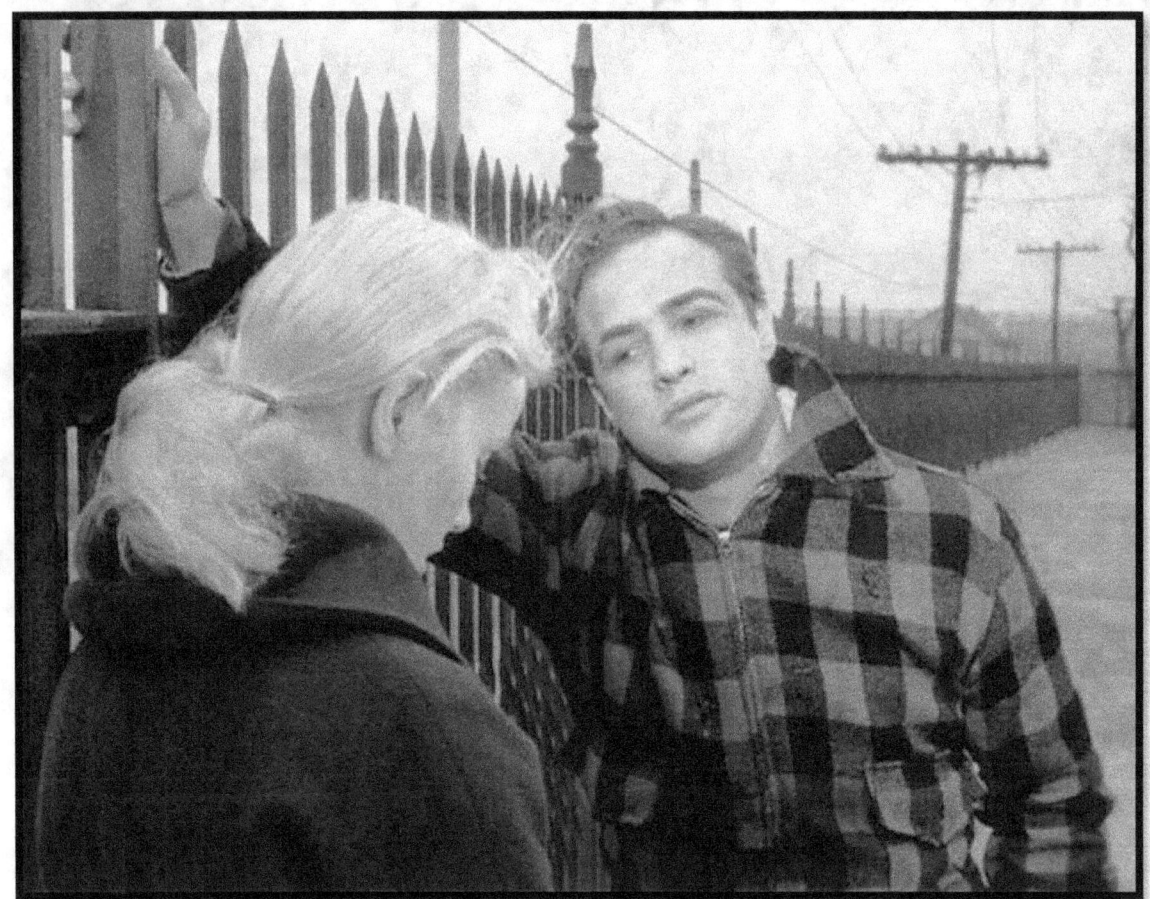

She is college educated with professional aspirations. She speaks out. She demands to know who killed her brother why they killed him. She demands action from the Priest and the community. She is as forceful as she is brave and confronts Terry's moral ambivalence by demanding he take a stand in his life.

Conversely, Kazan does not allow the character to go too far. She wants to run away after Terry's brother is killed leaving the impression of the standard Hollywood female character, a powerless woman who will run from confrontation rather than face it.

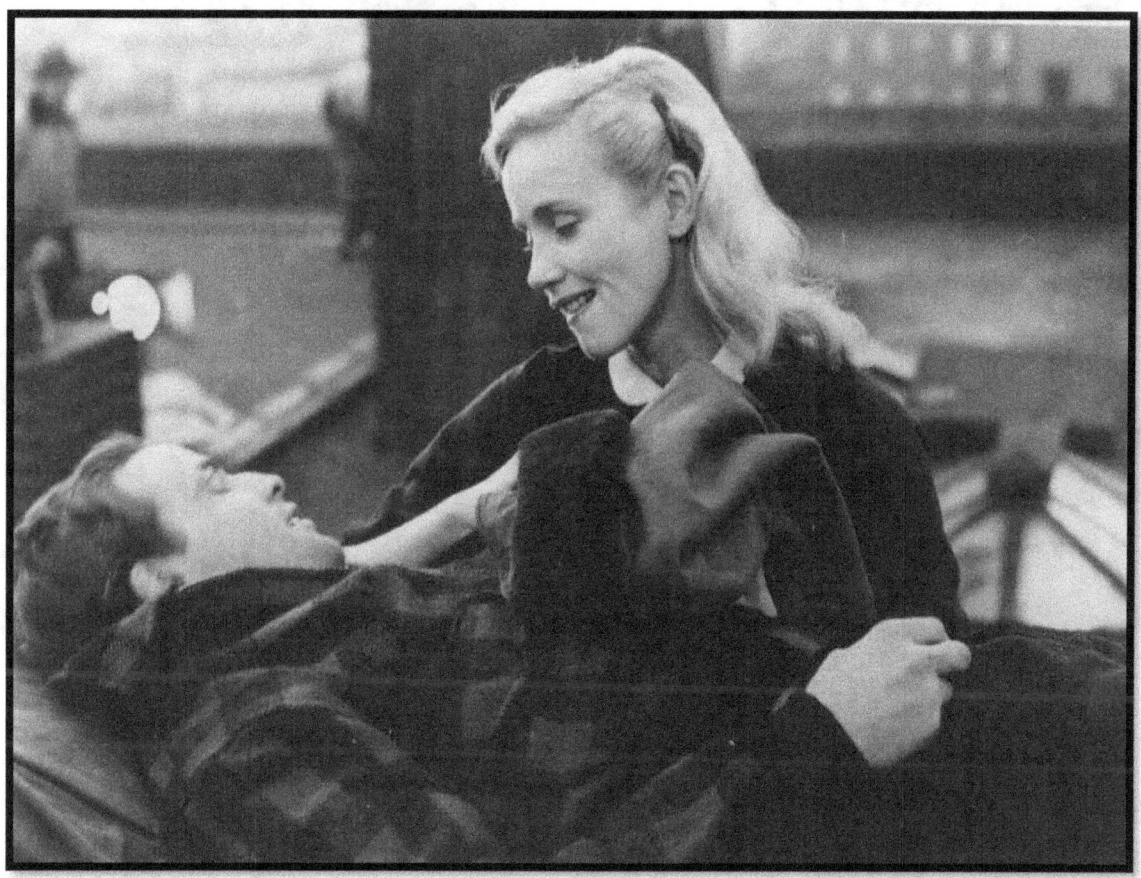

However Edie's doesn't want to flee because she is frightened. Rather, her character sees the hopelessness of the situation on the docks that the docks will never change. Instead of being weaker than Terry, she simply smarter than he is.

Terry is a far less complicated character then Edie Doyle. He is a likable, ageless Neanderthal, a man-child completely uneducated and from a tough poverty-stricken childhood. It is evident he sees more in her then a beautiful face, he sees in her a morally clean soul, a way out. Edie has class, which is what he wants.

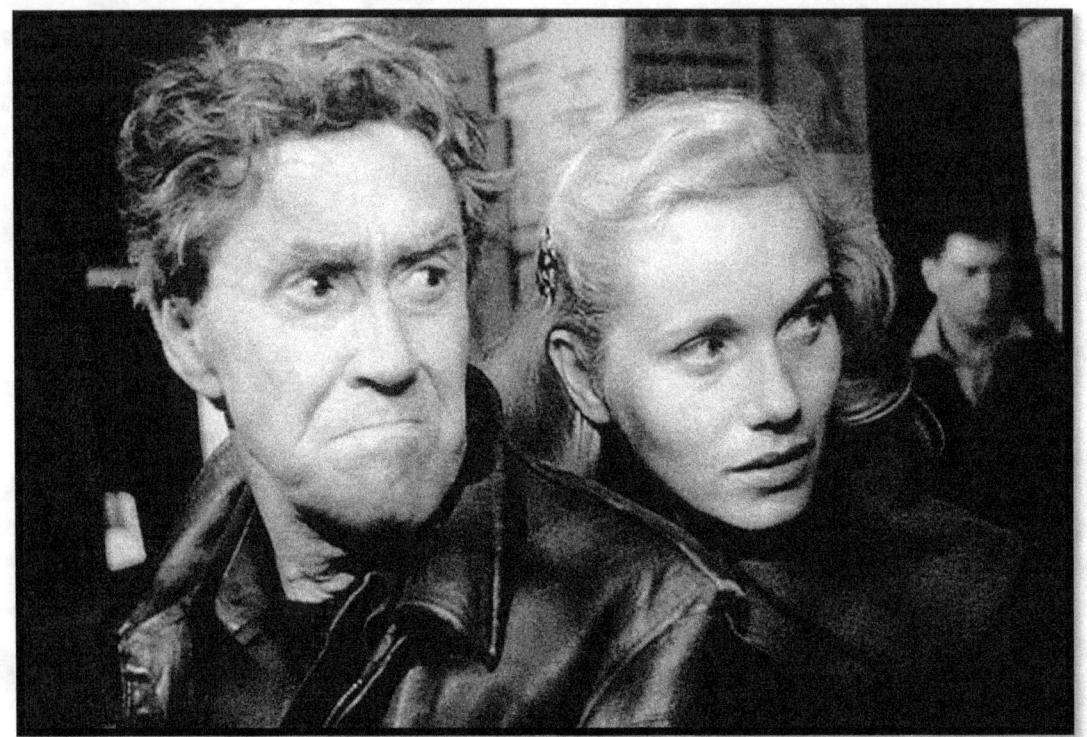

Edie Doyle's innocence and purity helps Terry to reclaim his conscience and her acceptance of him for what he is, opens his heart to a flurry of new emotions and thoughts. Her devotion to her dead brother's memory, which is the driving force behind all of her actions is actually her own demand for respect of human life, is a new world to Terry.

At first, for Terry, Edie offers a way out of the docks, a new life somewhere else but it becomes apparent to him that his moral cowardice will always be what it is and her moral strength will always be what it is, unless he takes a stand in the here and now.

Before Terry decides to finally cross the moral and take a stand, he decides to test Edie's faith of good will in others by telling her the truth about his role in her brother's murder. Although disturbed by the information about Terry's part in the murder, Edie eventually holds true to her ideals, her faith in humanity. The story line elevates her moral grounding above everyone else in the film and it is only fitting then, in the bar scene, that when Terry pours out his feeling for Edie, she turns the conversation to conscience.

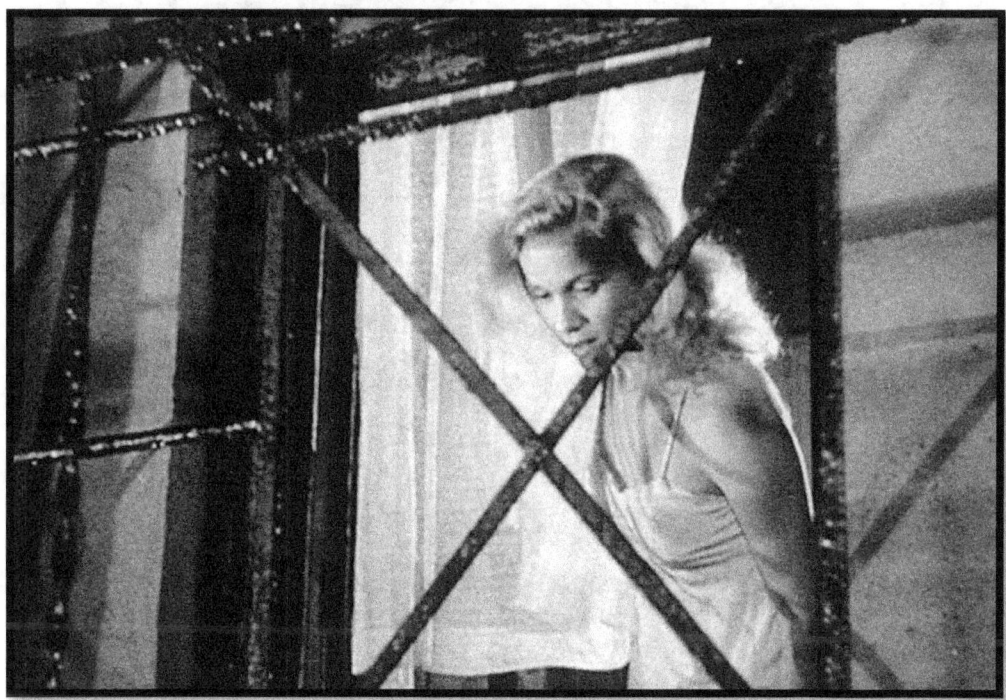

At that point, the films cinematographer Boris Kaufman, shots an angelic close up of her face in the upper right hand corner of the screen, lowering Terry to the center of the screen, a guardian angel dangling slightly above him.

The idea that Edie offers more than just physical beauty is told again in the playground scene when it appears as if Terry is actually speaking more to himself then to Edie when he reminds her that she was once "A real mess" He is not teasing her, he admires that she is now beautiful.

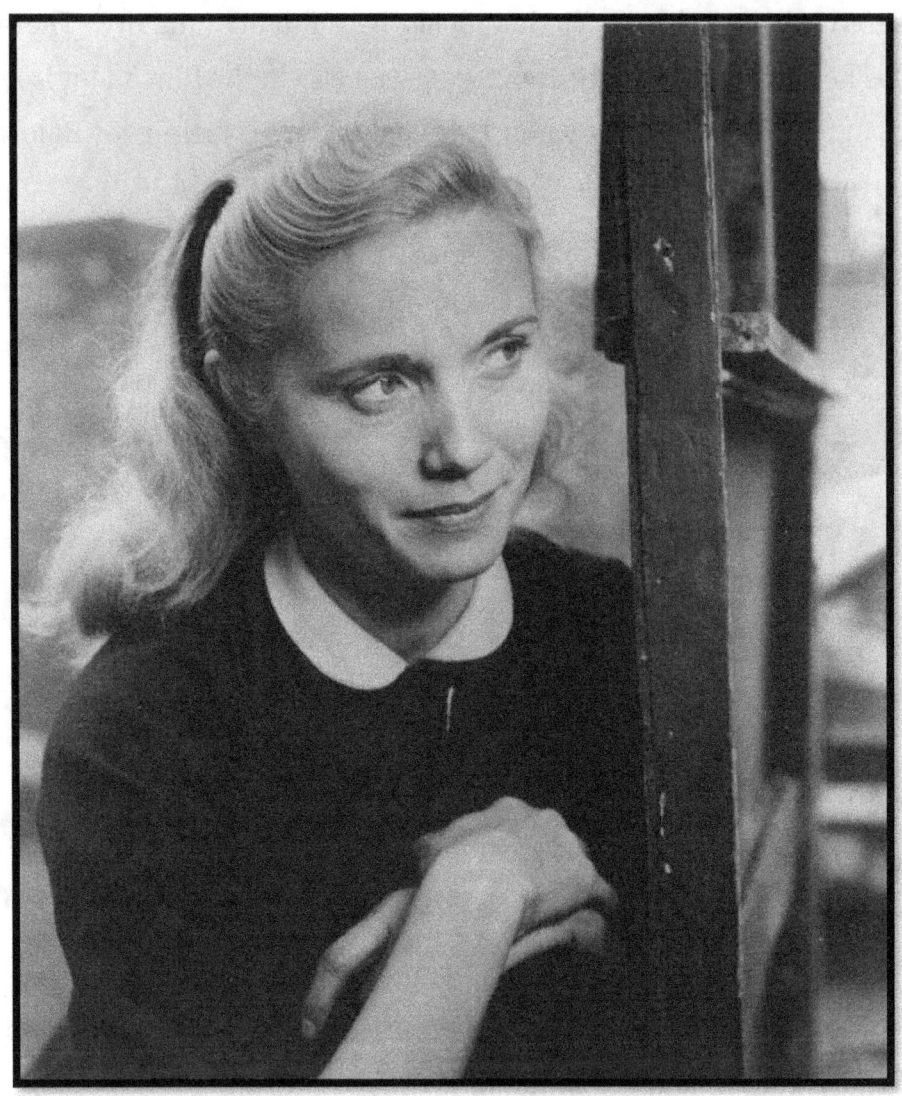

Although it is obviously the remark of a man in love, it is, equally, the remark of a man who admires the will power and determination it takes to transform oneself into a person of dignity.   She is no longer "a real mess" Edie has self-respect, Terry had no self- respect.

Things have changed since the schoolyard. Now he is the one who is "a real mess." Terry feels he gave up his self-respect when he allowed himself to take the dive in the title contender fight. Terry wants what Edie has, dignity and self-respect, something he is trying to reclaim but does not know where to start.

The crucial role of Edie Doyle was for Kazan, signifying "The deepest of human needs, redemption" and logically, the sympathetic Edie Doyle is Terry Malloy's father confessor unlike the films priest who refuses to hear Terry's confession and is almost completely unsympathetic to Terry throughout the film.

Schulberg denied that the role of Edie Doyle was as the redeemer, for him the character was little more than the films required love sequence, however, he was shrewd enough to insist that the relationship between Edie and Terry take center stage in the film.

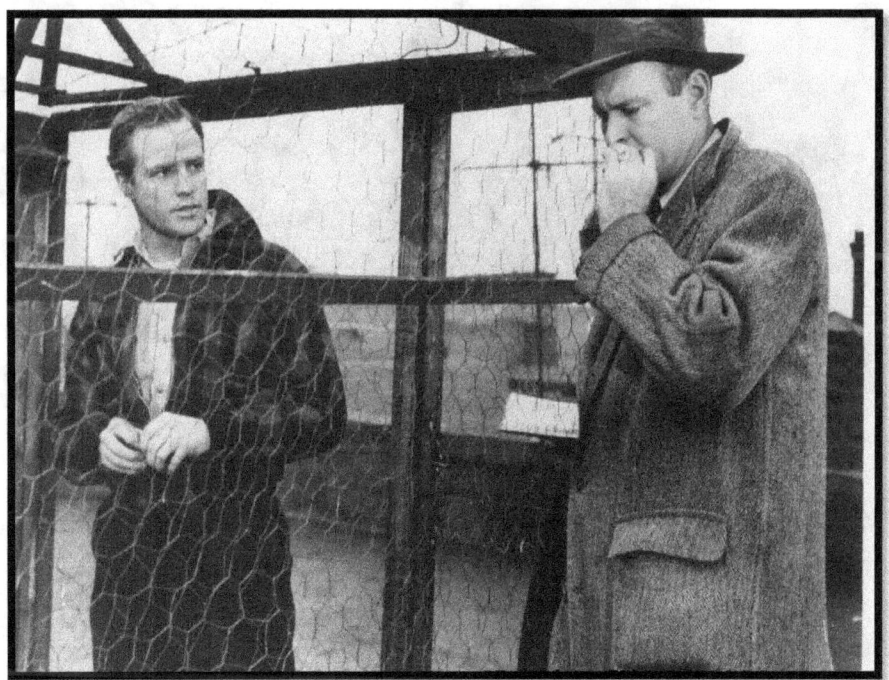

If Edie and Father Barry are the films religious authority, the Tweedy, waspy Crime Commission investigators are the secular moral authority and the roles are played with an evenhanded, even icy delivery by actors Martin Balsam and Leif Erikson. The Crime Commission investigators are truth seekers. Like Edie and Father Barry, it is their job to push Terry closer to the light of truth.

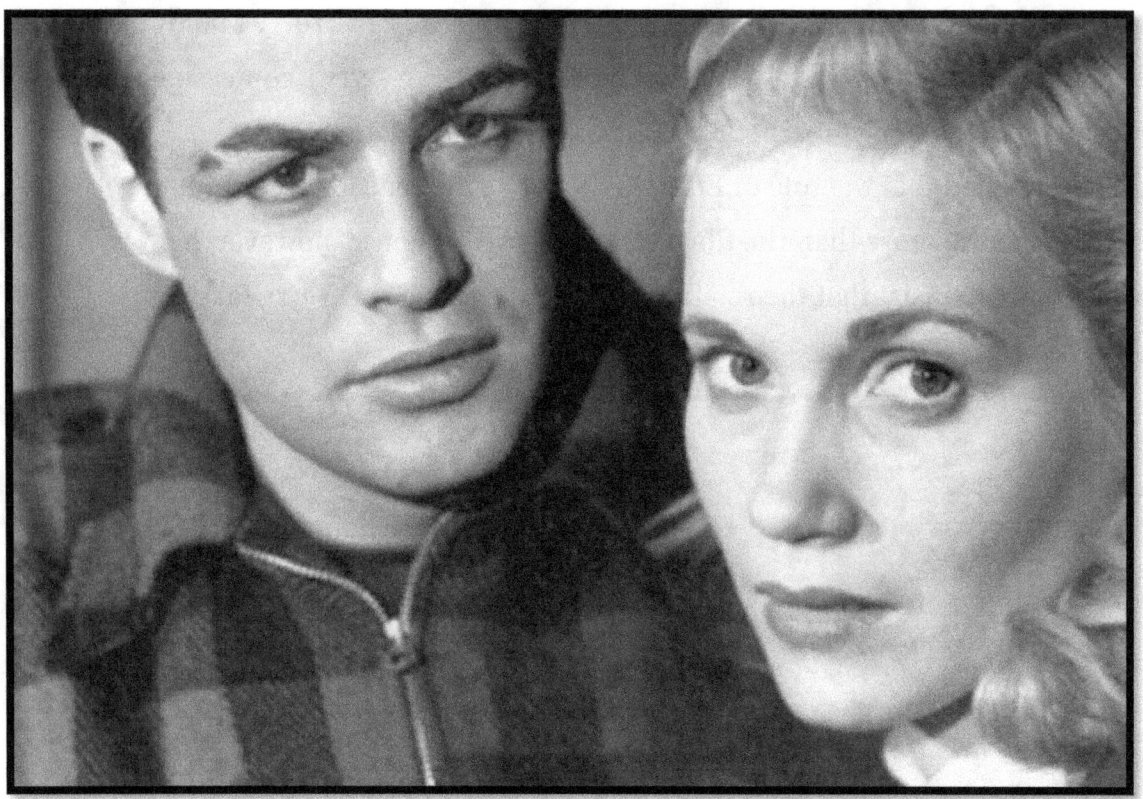

THE ROLE OF JOHNNY FRIENDLY

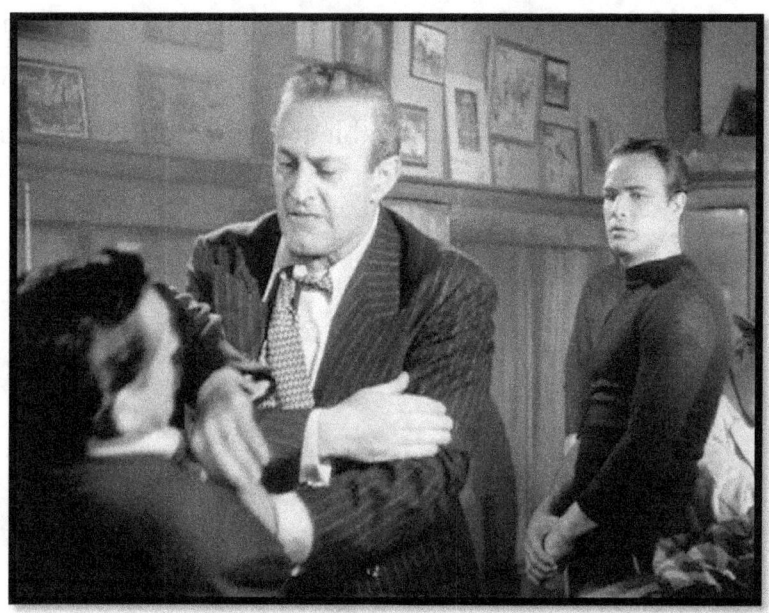

"When I was sixteen, I had to beg for work in the hold. I didn't work my way up out of there for nuthin'...You know, takin' over this local took a little doin'. There's some pretty rough fellas in the way. They gave me this (he displays an ugly scar on his neck) to remember them by...I got two thousand dues-payin' members in this local - that's $72,000 a year legitimate and when each one of 'em puts in a couple of bucks a day just to make sure they work steady - well, you figure it out. And that's just for openers. We got the fattest piers in the fattest harbor in the world. Everything moves in and out - we take our cut...You don't suppose I can afford to be boxed out of a deal like this, do ya? A deal I sweated and bled for, on account of one lousy little cheese-eater, that Doyle bum, who thinks he can go squealin' to the Crime Commission? Do ya? Well, DO YA? **On the Waterfront**

Both Kazan and Budd Schulberg had been branded as Reds during the government's inquisition into Communist infiltration into the film industry. Indeed, they had both been active members of the party in their youth.

In 1934, Budd Schulberg and childhood friend Maurice Rapf joined a group of other Dartmouth Students for a three-month summer trip to the Soviet Union, sponsored by the Communist National Student League. While there they met screenwriter Ring Lardner Jr who would be blacklisted by the HUAC twenty years later as was Rapf. The boys returned to the states, their heads shaven to rid them of the lice they had caught on the trip, and hailed the Communist system as the way of the future. Kazan's brush with the Communist party started when he studied drama at Yale where he met a talented young writer named Albert Maltz, a Columbia grad, who wrote to him, "We may be able to help with the Communist theatre which is starting."

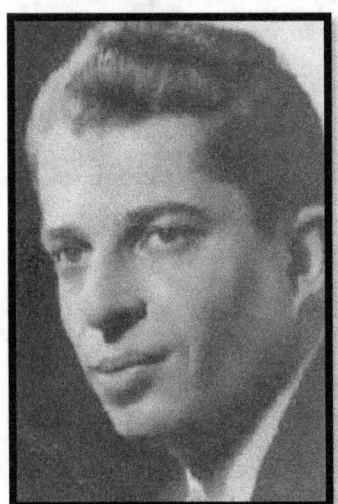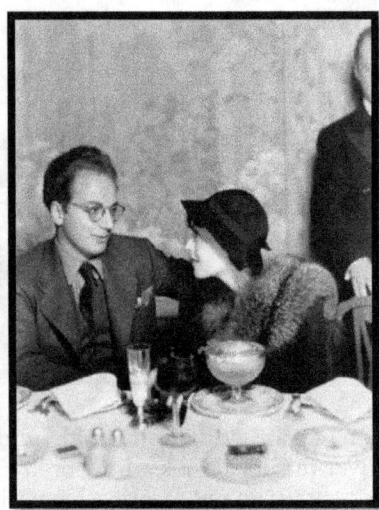

Maltz (left) and Odets with Luise Rainer

Like so many others who would later make the move to Hollywood, Kazan learned his craft in a world dominated by the Communist Party, which praised his early effort in directing and encouraged him to do more. For them, Communist Party doctrine held that art was a weapon, and that unless a dramatic work sent the audience home with sweeping revolutionary insight, it amounted to mere bourgeois decadence

In 1932 Kazan joined the Group Theatre in New York led by Lee Strasberg. Members of the group tended to hold left-wing political views and wanted to produce plays that dealt with important social issues. Those involved in the group included John Garfield, Howard Da Silva, John Randolph, Joseph Bromberg and Lee J. Cobb. Kazan joined the American Communist Party in 1934 and the following year appeared in *Waiting for Lefty*, a play by a fellow party member, Clifford Odets.

When Kazan finally joined the party, he said he did so...*for spiritual reasons. My hostility was no longer alienation. The Party had justified it, taught me that it was correct, even reasonable. I could be proud of it; it made me the comrade of angry millions all over the earth. I'd reacted correctly to my upbringing, to my social position, to the society around me, to the state of the world. I was a member of what was sure to be the victorious army of the future. (Membership) made me into another person. I felt reborn, or born for the first time. The days of pain were over. I was an honored leader of the only good class, the working class, and the only real theater, the Group.*

Kazan was a major force in the New Theater League, a Communist front organization, where he taught directing classes and played the lead in Clifford Odets' *Golden Boy* with Frances Farmer, "the blonde that you dream about," who had also been cultivated by the Communist Party. The government later blacklisted Farmer.

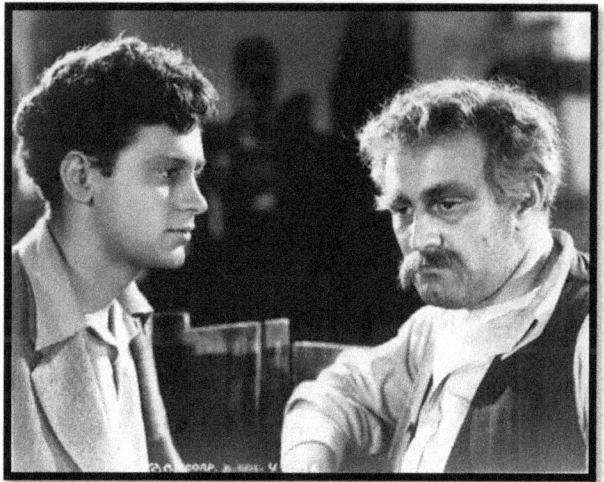

William Holden and Lee J. Cobb in *Golden Boy*

The American party's owl faced Cultural Commissar V. J. Jerome vetted plays, scripts, and novels to ensure their political correctness. "The duty of writers and directors" he said "was to accept the dictates of Party leaders"

Those who showed too much independence were attacked until they crawled before the party and recanted their wicked ways. Most of the party faithful submitted. Others, like Budd Schulberg didn't and left. Kazan soon followed after he called the party "A police state for the mind"

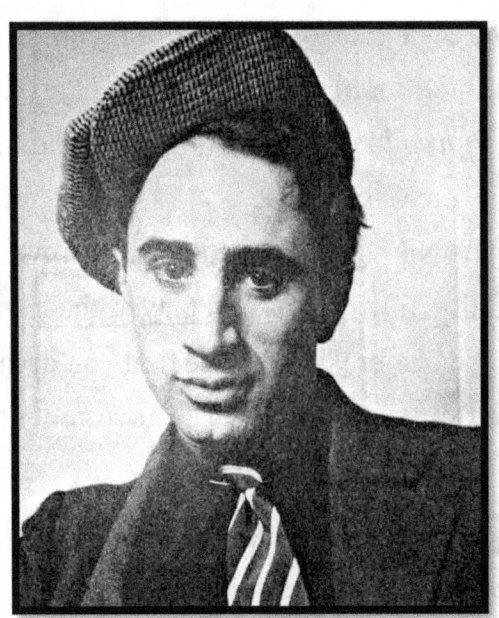

Kazan in the 1930s

When he appeared before the House of Un-American Activities Committee on April 12, 1952, Kazan explained how the Communist Party had attempted to take over the Group Theater in the 1930s.

"I was instructed by the Communist unit to demand that the group be run "democratically." This was a characteristic Communist tactic; they were not interested in democracy; they wanted control. They had no chance of controlling the directors, but they thought that if authority went to the actors, they would have a chance to dominate through the usual tricks of behind-the-scenes caucuses, block voting, and confusion of issues.

This was the specific issue on which I quit the Party. I had enough regimentation, enough of being told what to think and say and do, enough of their habitual violation of the daily practices of democracy to which I was accustomed.

The last straw came when I was invited to go through a typical Communist scene of crawling and apologizing and admitting the error of my ways. I had had a taste of police-state living and I did not like it.   From there on, he was transformed him into a premature anti-Stalinist, though he remained politically far left of center.

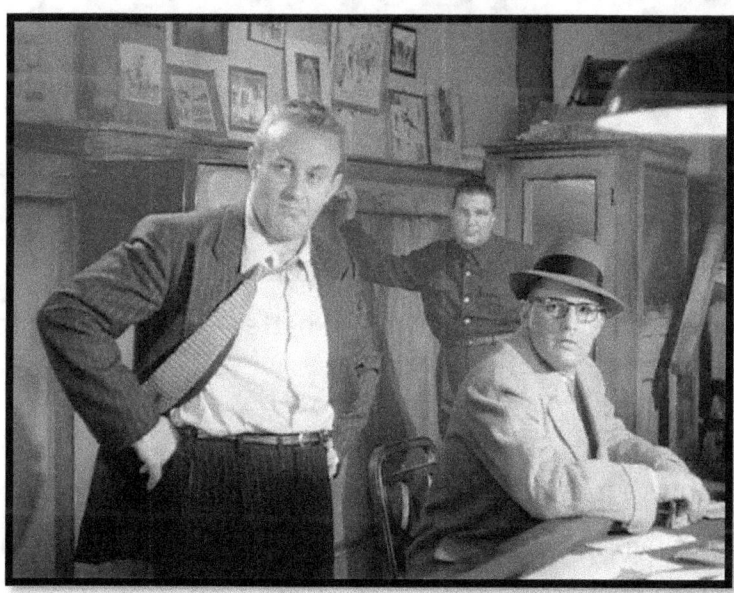

While Kazan hired Cobb for the role, the Johnny Friendly character has the earmarks of a Schulberg creation, in his novels Schulberg provided at least one powerful character whose existence depends upon weaker characters that he exploits, in the case of *Waterfront,* this would include virtually everyone around Johnny Friendly including his gangster friends who virtually kneel before him.

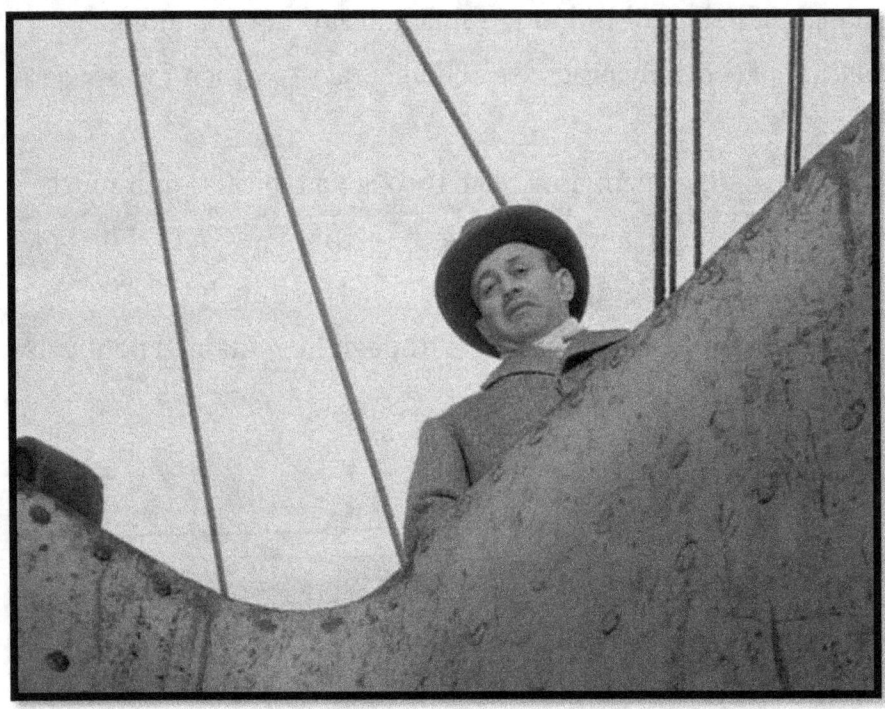

At the same time, each Schulberg work portrays the slow and agonizing climb of a victim who fights to maintain his or her dignity in hostile, graceless environments that protect and empower the wicked better enabling them to crush the weak.

Johnny Friendly's position of power is on the waterfront is established with the opening shot that shows a massive ship in the background as Friendly and his men strut out of the tiny shack in the foreground, dwarfed by the scale of the ship. This visual contrast tells the viewer how much power they really have. In the background, composer Leonard Bernstein's *Murder Theme* plays aggressively giving an unsettling sense of danger.

Cobb's portrayal of mob boss Johnny Friendly is defined by his heartfelt speech at the bar when we first meet the character when he describes his life before making it big in the grimy little world of the waterfront, the poverty stricken youth, the violence the rose him to the top.

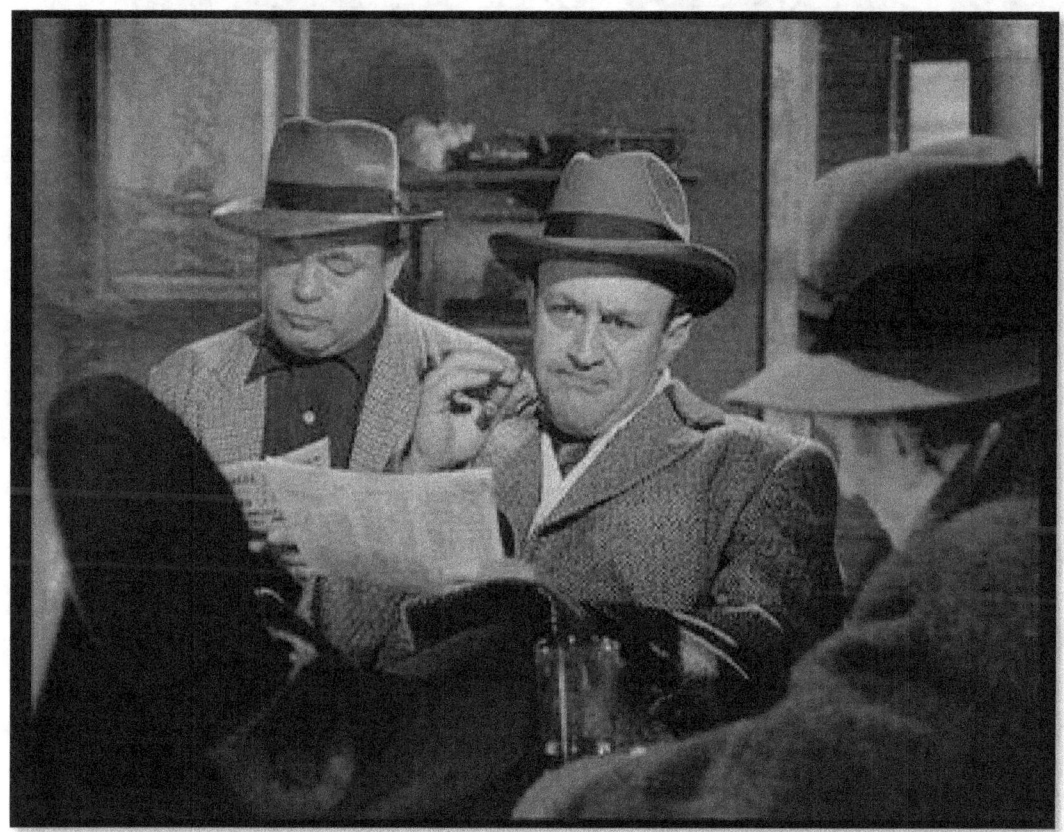

However, the speech rings empty because he is and empty wicked man who uses his poverty-stricken background to justify his actions. Friendly's background is not dissimilar from Edie Doyle or the Malloy brothers, who stand for righteousness or who will eventually stand for righteousness.

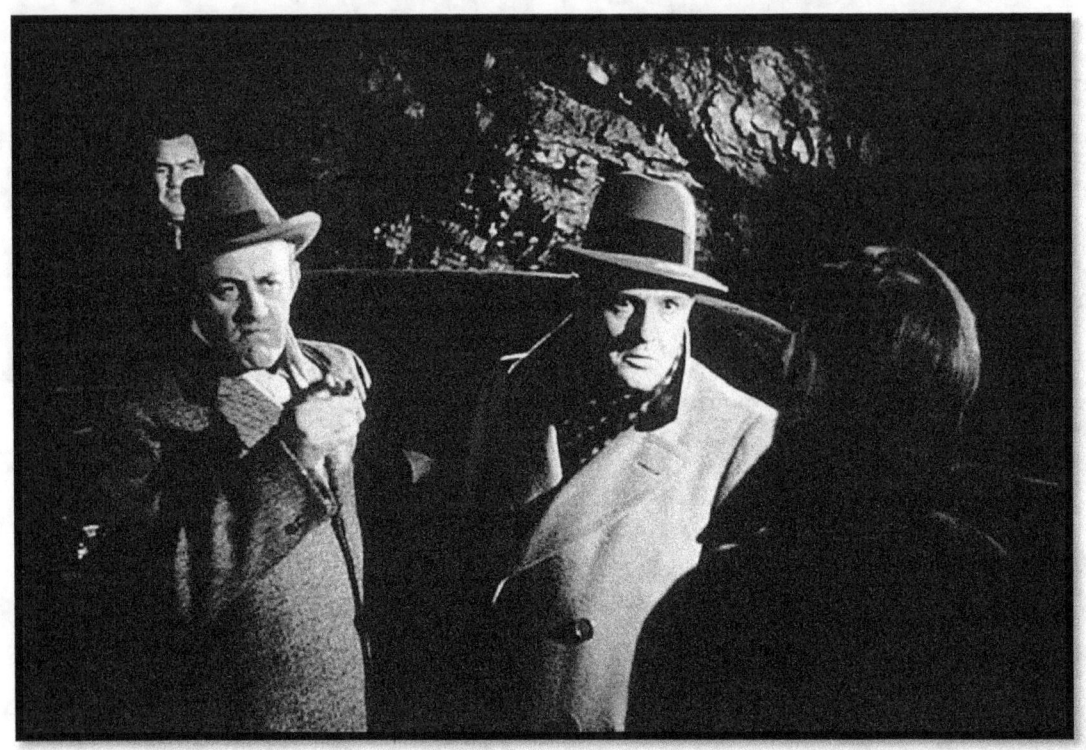

Cobb, Kazan and Schulberg understood the characters mind set. When Johnny Friendly sees Father Barry's sermon in the ship's hold is effective, he signals his men to stop tossing garbage at the priest and the corpse so more martyrdom does not accrue to them, an act any street-smart gangster would have understood.

At first, it's easy to like Johnny Friendly's character, he smiles, he hugs, he encourages and he gives a seemingly dense Terry Malloy and extra $50 and a good slot as a cargo unloader.

Nevertheless, when anyone's objective differs in the least from his, we see the true Johnny Friendly; a man driven by complete self-preservation at the cost of anyone who gets in his way, a man driven by money, quick to flex his muscle and lay down his awesome authority.

While Cobb's character never changes priorities in the film, even to the very end, ("I'll be back" he roars in defeat) the way he is seen by the other characters in the film and by the audience changes dramatically once he is defied by Terry at the waterfront hearings. He begins to weaken in the face of goodness and moral courage.

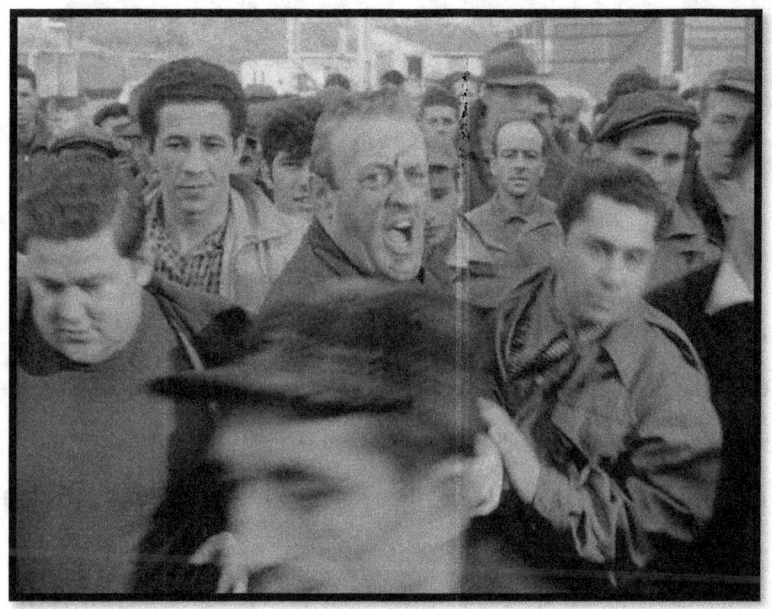

The scene shot in Johnny Friendly's bar Establishes the gangsters closed world, kept tense and real through Kazan's blocking choices. Kazan gives a few seconds of underworld business to several characters while in the background a half dozen minor characters stand around and even without lines, offer a perfect defining presence.

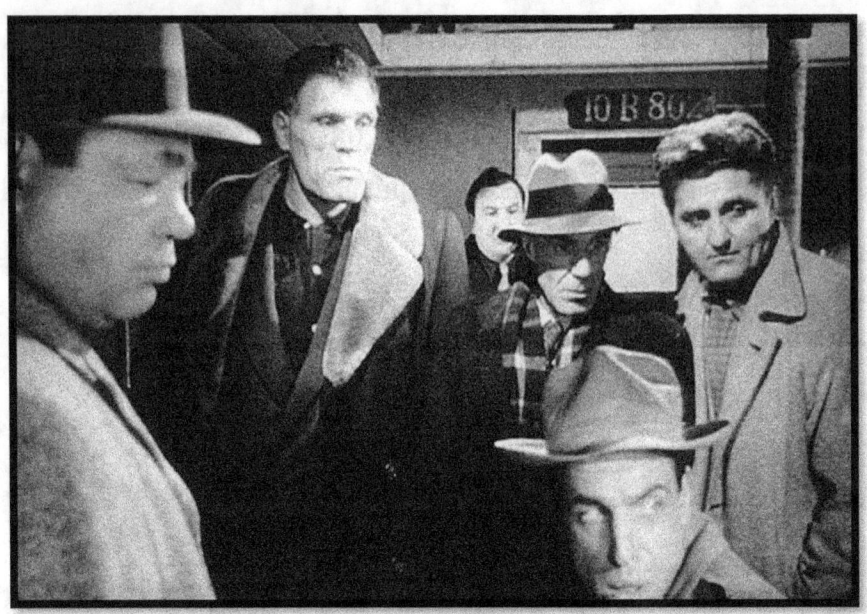

It is clear within minutes of the scene that each of these men owes an obligation of some sort to Johnny Friendly, as does virtually everyone else on the waterfront. The hoodlums owe him their income. The long shore workers owe him money and their jobs. At this point, the viewer also learns Terry and Charlie Malloy owe even more to the gangster. They owe him their souls.

Charlie has been, for the most part, a loyal brother to Terry, a father figure to him, just as Johnny Friendly has been a father figure to both, Charlie and Terry Malloy, even promoting Charlie to second in command on the docks.

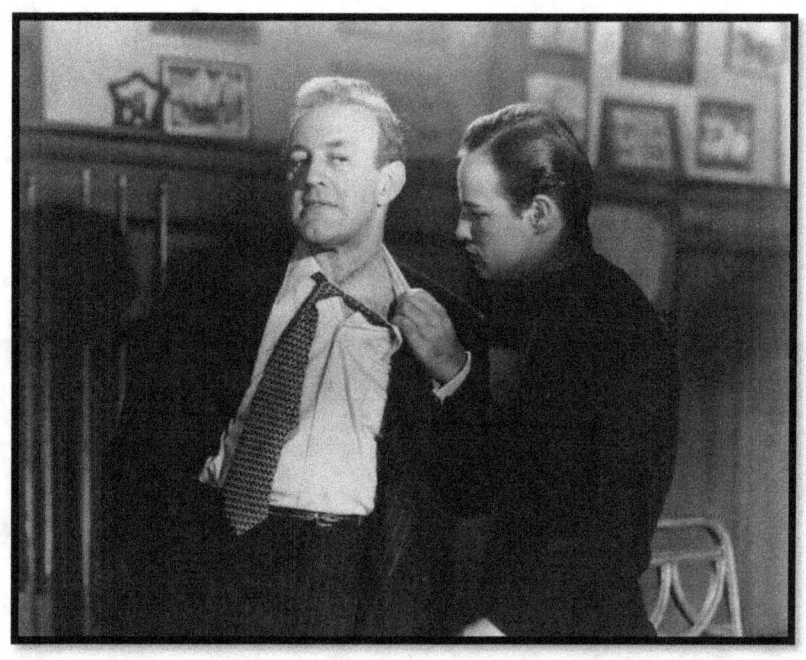

Once the brothers were joined by the hope of climbing out of their poverty-stricken childhood and united in their care and concern for each other's welfare. The end of that part of their relationship ended, we learn, when Charlie convinced his slower thinking brother to end his promising boxing career by taking a dive against a lesser fighter, no doubt for the benefit of Johnny Friendly.

The root cause of their split has been the patronage and greed of Johnny Friendly. By mid film, the brothers are almost completely divided by Terry's emerging moral sense and Charlie's very real concern that Terry's awakening may turn Friendly's wrath on both of them.

Finally, Charlie Malloy is placed in the unenviable position of trying to bridge the widening gulf between Terry and Johnny Friendly. In the end, when he realizes it cannot be done, he does the right thing and places his loyalties with his brother.

In the meantime, Charlie and Terry are trapped by fear of Johnny Friendly, as is virtually everyone else on the waterfront, a fear is shown by the intimacy between the players in close shots filmed in cramped spaces and leaves the impression of being trapped (hence Edie and Terry inside the pigeon's cage)

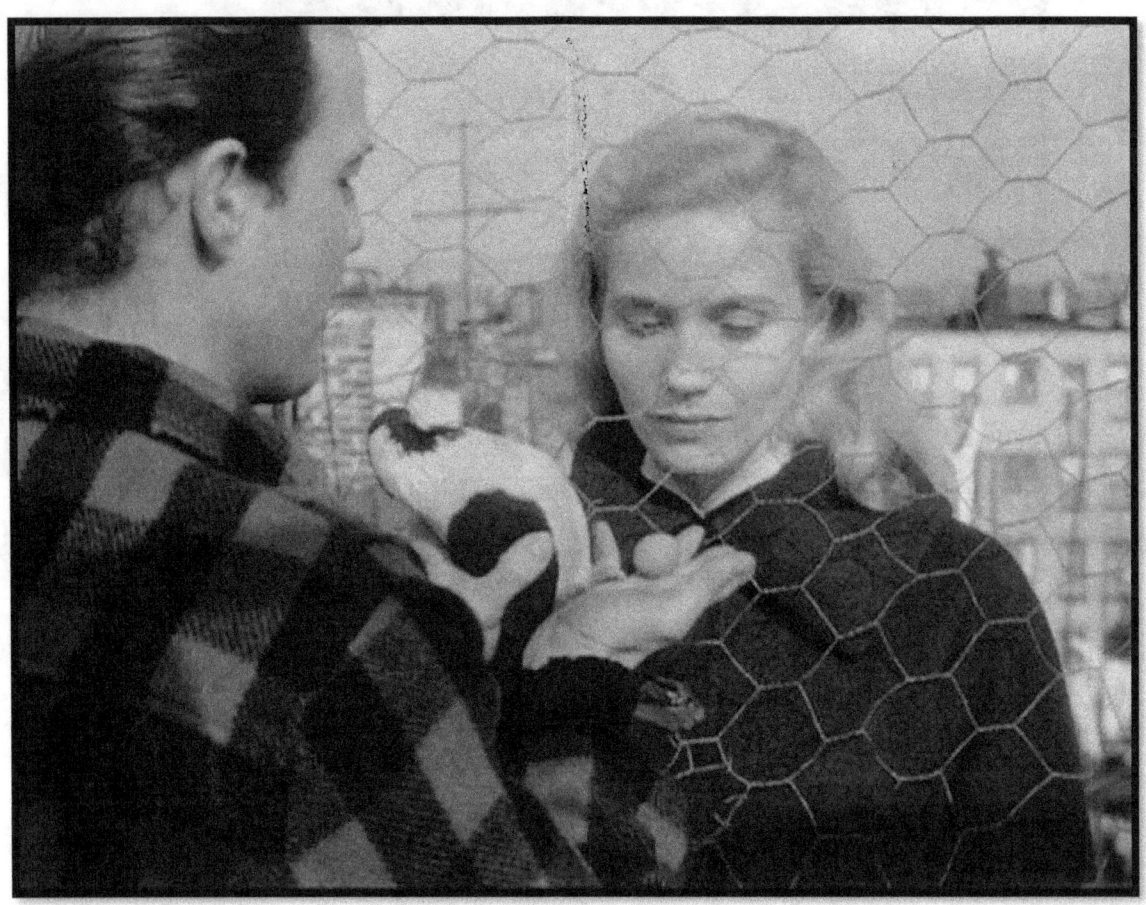

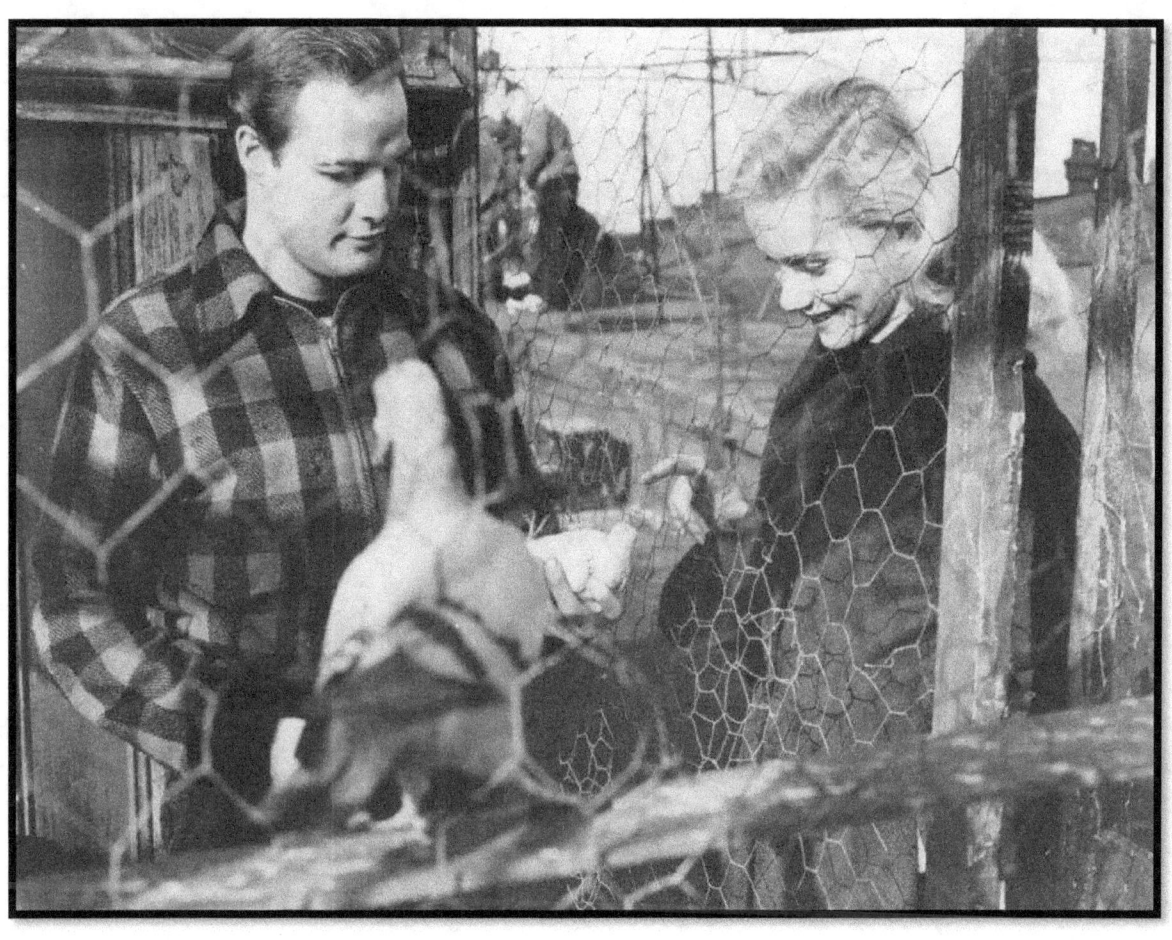

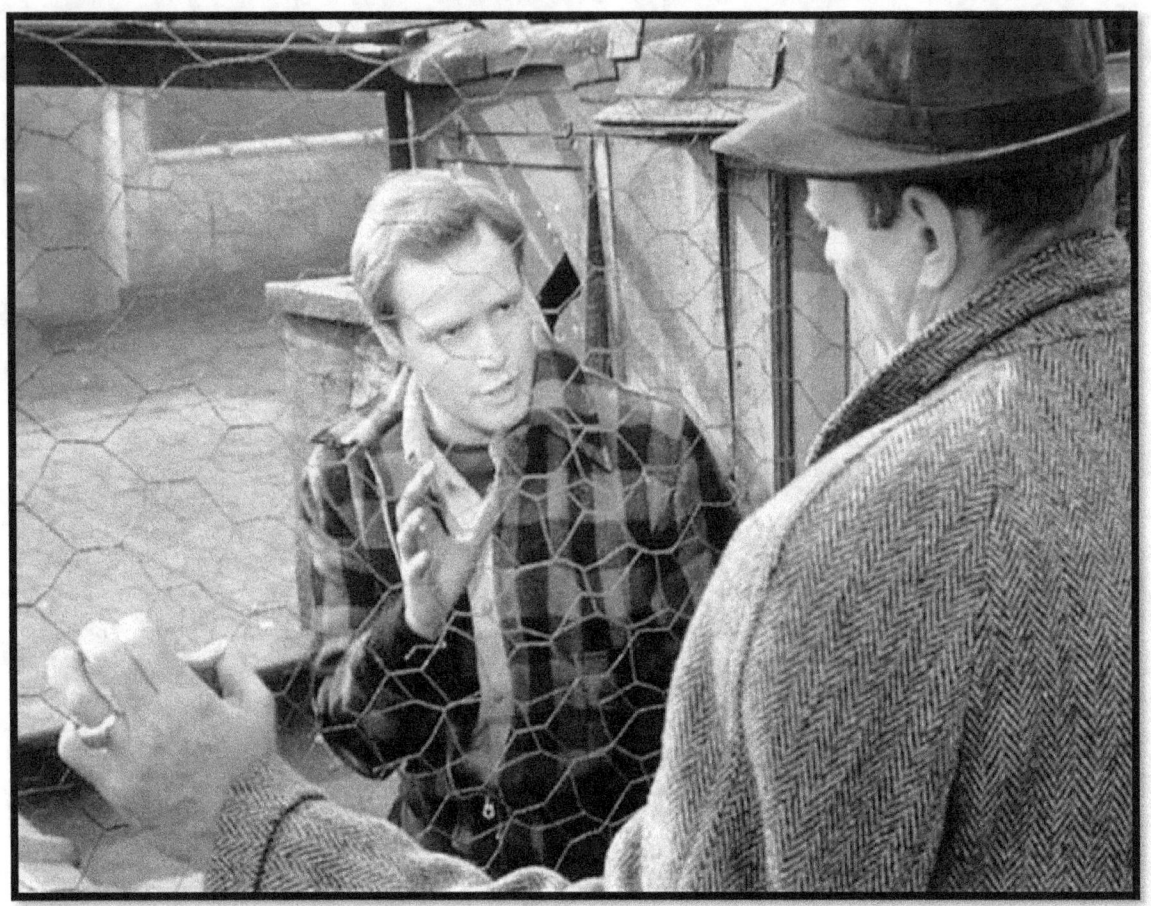

The close shot also establishes the closeness and intimacy of the characters through touching, giving the viewer the knowledge that these people have known each other for decades. Charlie and Terry touch from there very first scene together, Pop Doyle shows his affection for his daughter, Father Barry embraces Edie over her brothers body, Johnny Friendly bear hugs Terry. The dock workers shake hands, roughhouse with each other.

These scenes show that there is a true affection between Terry Malloy and brother Charley. Considering the circumstances of their lives, poverty and orphanages, their relationship on some levels is admirable. However, the quick impression is that while Charlie may be his actual brother, the Johnny Friendly gang is his extended family and Johnny Friendly is the father, even bragging that he took Terry to ball games and prizefights when Terry was a child.

Terry feels a tremendous amount of loyalty to Johnny Friendly and Charlie, enough to ignore their exploitation of or even to throw the fight of a lifetime away to please them. Even with the affection between Friendly and the brothers, when Charley Malloy learns Johnny Friendly is willing have Terry killed, the room becomes deathly silent, broken only by Johnny Friendly gangster named Barney, who, reading the racing form, asks, in the background, "Who do you like in the third?"

The scene was probably created on shooting day since it is not in any of the production notes or scripts and it is extremely effective, especially the counter point by the Barney character.....murder, even the murder of one of their own, means nothing to the mobsters. Race results are more important. Nevertheless, for the first time, seemingly, Charley Malloy understands how bloodless Johnny Friendly can be.

The scene in Johnny Friendly's bar shows Kazan's theatrical background through its staging and in the obvious comfortable performances of his stage trained actors. The entire scene looks as though it were shot on a theater stage. Although Johnny Friendly and his men look, act and talk like anyone else on the waterfront, unlike the other townspeople, they dress well, they have cash and, at least by waterfront standards, they have class and glamour, from their fresh haircuts to their three-piece suits.

The film gives a brief glimpse of a Bill McCormick-like character in the very end as "Mr. Big" when we see a shot of a tabloid-style newspaper with a headline that Johnny Friendly will be indicted for murder. Then, just after the hearings, we see a "Mr. Big" watching the hearings on television and instructing his servant not to take calls from Johnny Friendly with the line "If Mr. Friendly calls I'm out" One interesting explanation of the line "If Mr. Friendly calls I'm out" is that it referred to New York Mayor William F. O'Dwyer, who announced, after one of the waterfront hoodlums threatened to talk about what he knew about the true control over the docks, that he would not seek re-election.

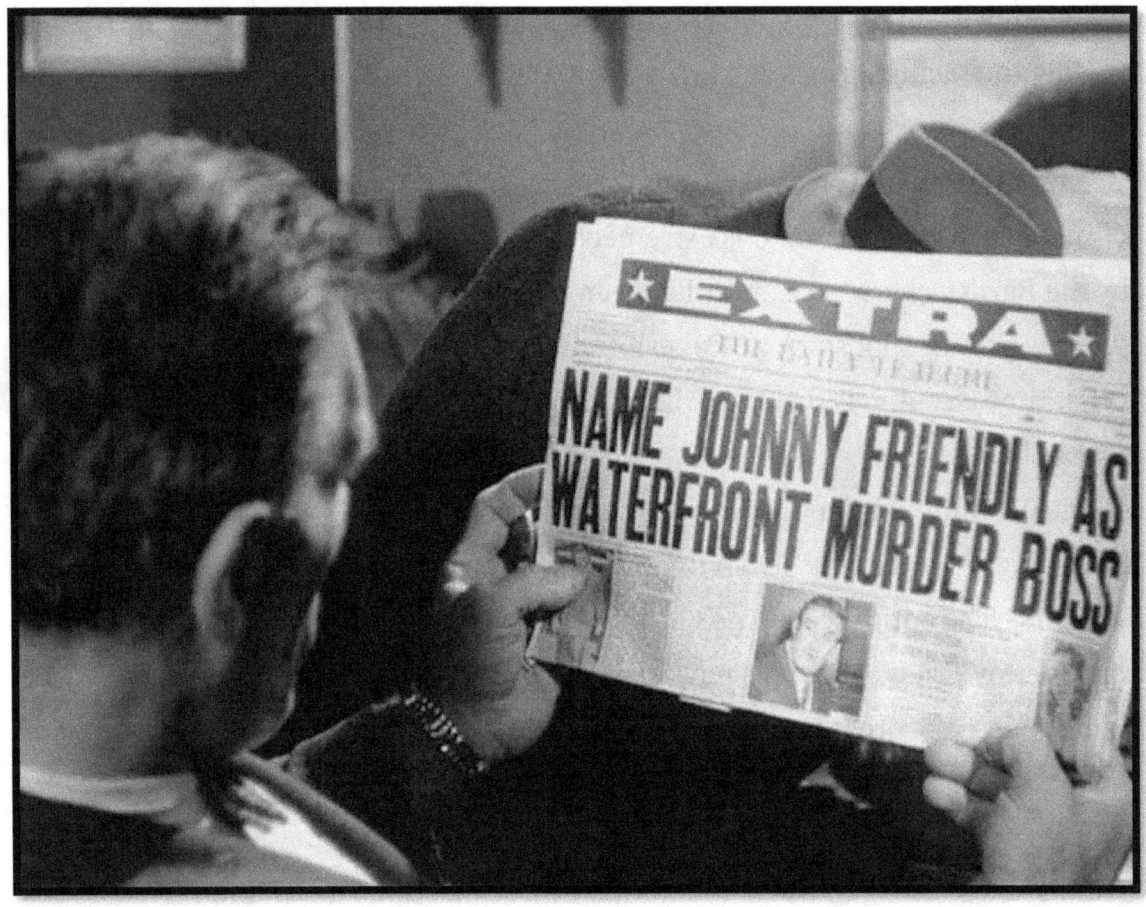

According to underworld scuttlebutt, O'Dwyer, the former New York District Attorney who later met his downfall due to corruption charges, had worked with the mob and Tammany Hall to insure corruption on the docks continued. After the hoodlum in question died in the electric chair without talking, O'Dwyer changed his mind and announced that he would in fact, run.

Supposedly, during that time, McCormick refused to take O'Dwyer's calls and Waterfront's screenwriter Budd Schulberg later used a part of the incident in the film. In the original script, Mr. Big played a slightly larger role. He also kills himself when the Crime Commission story breaks. Oddly, a Ryan like character is not mentioned or portrayed in the film.

The *Waterfront* script, although alluring to the fact that gangster Johnny Friendly is part of a larger organization, never touches on the Mafia theme or the political clout that the Mob would need to continue its stranglehold on waterfront.

As portrayed in the film, in reality the union locals were run across ethnic lines, with Italian gangsters controlling locals with mostly Italian-American members and Irish hoodlums controlling those portions of the docks worked by Irish-Americans.

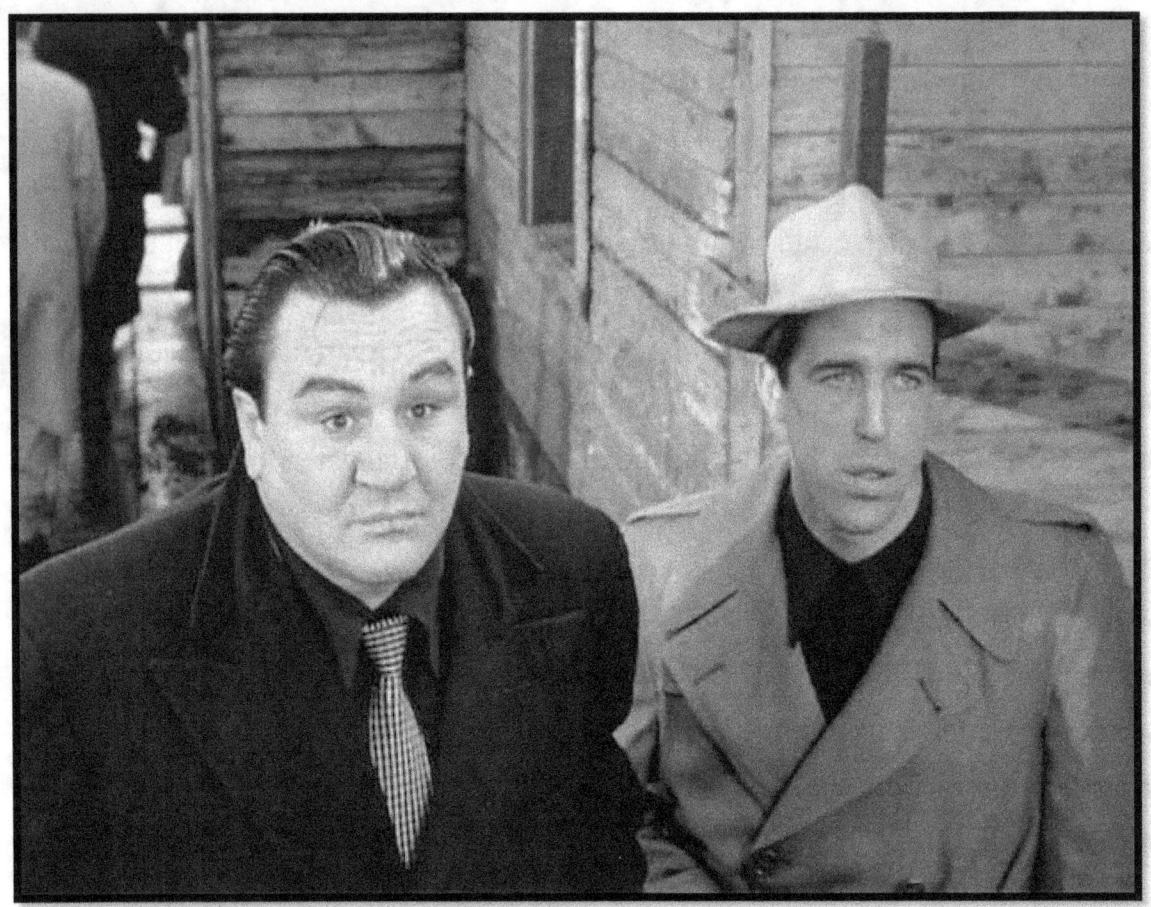

In that, the Johnny Friendly gang of hoodlums was most likely based on the Hell's Kitchen gang, mostly Irishmen, (They would eventually become known as the Westies) a violent fraction that more or less fell under Mafia Don John Gotti's influence at the end of the 20th century.

Although, according to Schulberg, Cobb's character was supposed to be based on ILA official Michael Clemente, a member of the Genovese crime family. In 1979, Clemente and other members of the Genovese family were indicted for corruption and racketeering on the New York waterfront.

Kazan's very accurate portrayal of the shape up in *Waterfront*, capturing the desperation, violence and degradation in the practice, stunned and appalled 1954 America. It was not supposed to happen here. Schulberg and Kazan made it clear to the American public that it was happening here and that the brutality and injustice of the shape up's were real and not a Hollywood fabrication used to dramatic effect. The public was outraged.

Although a definitive link cannot be made between the films portrayal of the shape up and the closing of the practice by local, state and federal investigators, it was only after Waterfront's premier that the degradation ceremony was officially ended, even Father Corridan and a series of others had tried for two decades to end before the film was written.

The film also made another clear statement; the Mafia controls the docks because the Mafia had the power. It was dramatic statement in 1953 America, a nation almost completely without knowledge of the Mafia or a national organized crime group. Schulberg linked the organized crime structure by connecting the dots; exploitation of the workers was a direct result of organized crimes influence over even the smallest detail on the docks.

A substantial amount of credit belongs to Schulberg who, disgusted after watching an actual shape in Brooklyn with Father Corridan in 1951, penned a quick article on what he had seen on the waterfront for the *New York Times*, *Sunday Magazine* titled "Joe Docks, Forgotten Man of the Waterfront". He wrote about the shape up's at dawn on the docks where hiring bosses picked the men to work that days four hour shift depending upon his mood and how much money they were willing to kick back to him. Schulberg also alluded to the practice repeatedly in the shooting script.

In Schulberg's directional hints in the script for the shape up scene, he captures its full degradation by describing the scene as "animalistic and barbaric." His camera is careful to show the reaction of Father Barry and Edie as they watch.

This scene also introduces the films only African American player Don Blackman, a professional wrestler who was well known by sports fans in the 1940s and 1950s. Blackman played the role of Luke, the sympathetic dockworker. He had one line. He also appeared in the 1958 release of Hemingway's work, The Old Man and the Sea, Affair in Trinidad (1952) The Egyptian (1954) The Witch Doctor (1953) and Scream, Blacula, Scream! (1973)

The depiction of a lone African-American on the docks is not inaccurate. As the film grows older, the reality of the century old struggle and animosities between working class Irish and Blacks in New York, grown out of a desperate struggle for the lowest paying jobs available, and grows dimmer. It leads modern viewers to believe that the lone African American speaking role in the film was tokenism, which it was not.

By 1953, when the film was made, the New York Irish, although far outnumbered by Italian Americans, were still a presence on the waterfront as is witnessed by the Irish American killer employed by the Anastasia mob to keep the locals in line. As a result, social war between the New York Irish and Blacks was very much alive and in place on the piers in 1953 and the Irish, who populated the hiring bosses as well as the dock workers, simply locked the Blacks out.

Throughout the film, the viewer needs adjust Waterfront to its time, which is unfortunate because it causes the film to lose some of its edge that it had when it first appeared in theaters.

As Schulberg pointed out "This is a movie of the '50's, reflecting a time when Blacks were not in the work gangs except in the lowest pissant jobs. I took a slight liberty in putting my friend, ex-fighter Don Blackman, in it. Incidentally, today's Jersey waterfront, under the Genovese family, has a white local and a black local, both run by racketeers, dangerous men."

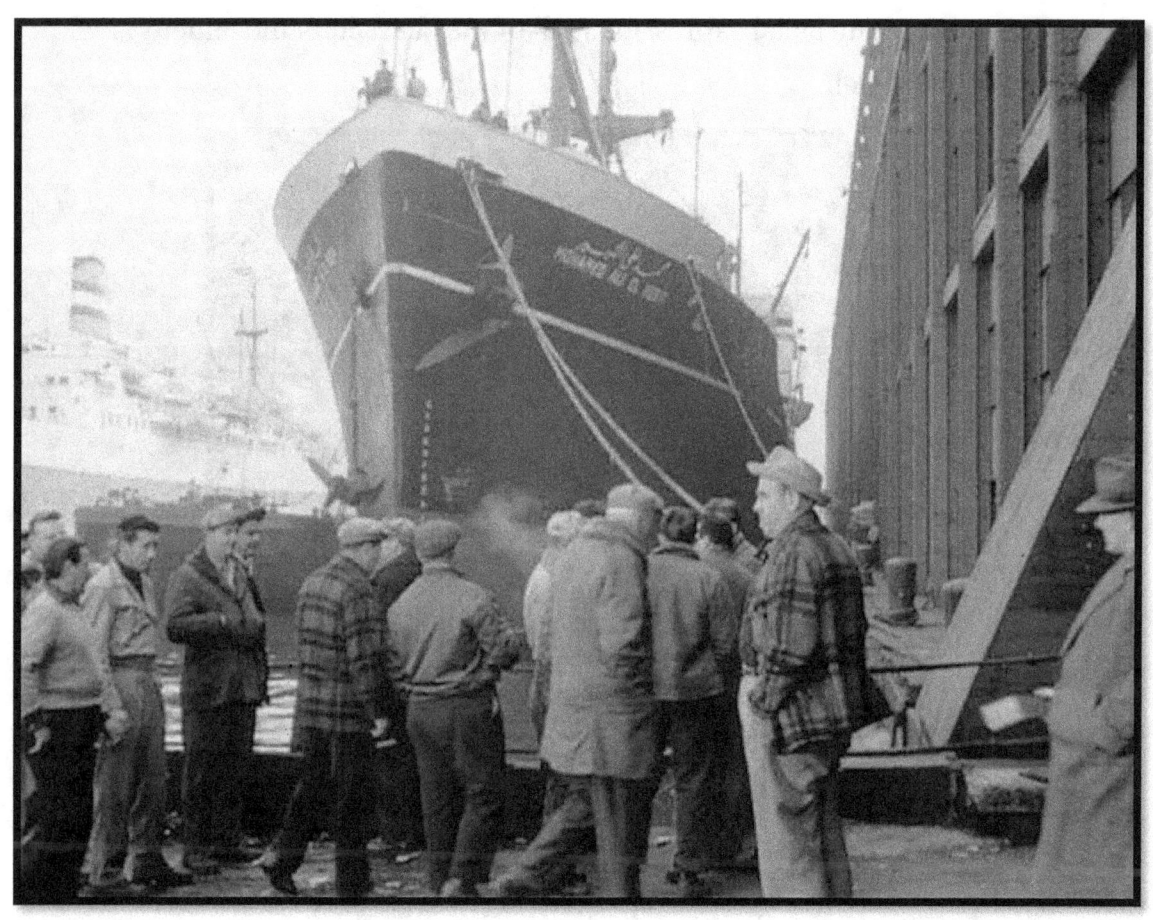

    Boris Kaufman, the films cinematographer captures the degradation of the shape up scene from camera positioning. When Big Mac, the supervisor and one of Johnny Friendly's gang, blows his whistle to call the workers to shape up, Kaufman's camera is behind Big Mac's enormous figure, obscuring the longshoremen. There is no doubt of his ultimate importance on the docks. He has the power on the docks the dock workers have none.

During the scramble for work-tags, Kaufman brings the camera low to the ground, capturing desperate facial expressions; all of the characters movement is downward towards hell itself.

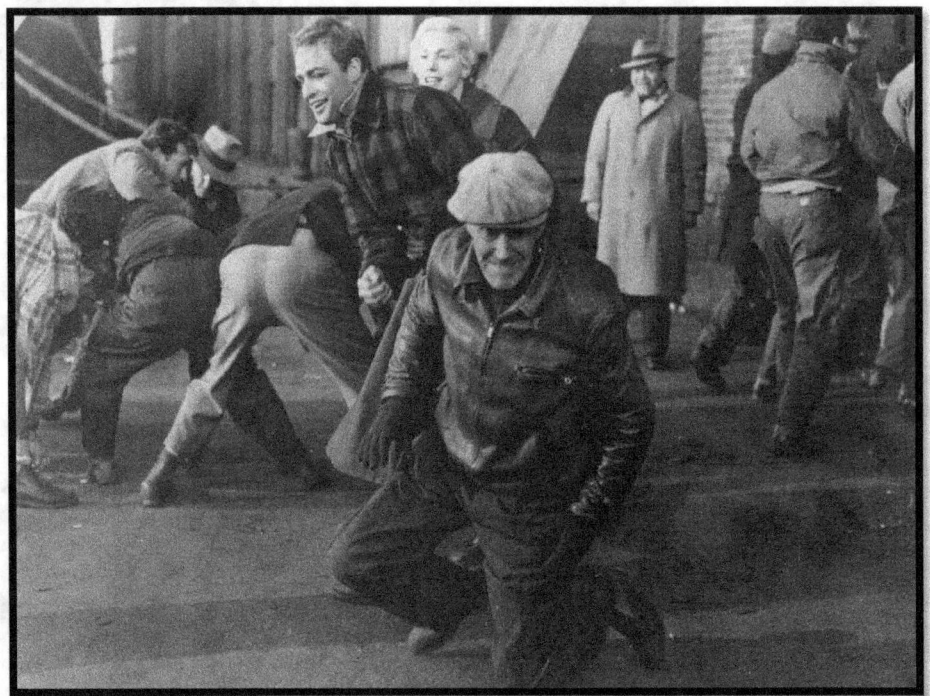

The downward position is used again later in the film after the fight scene and the deposed Johnny Friendly is pushed into the water from the docks, into the depths of hell as it were. This act balances Friendly's murder of Joey Doyle (who is pushed from a rooftop). Clever scripting allows a second balance Joey Doyle's father pushes Friendly into the water.

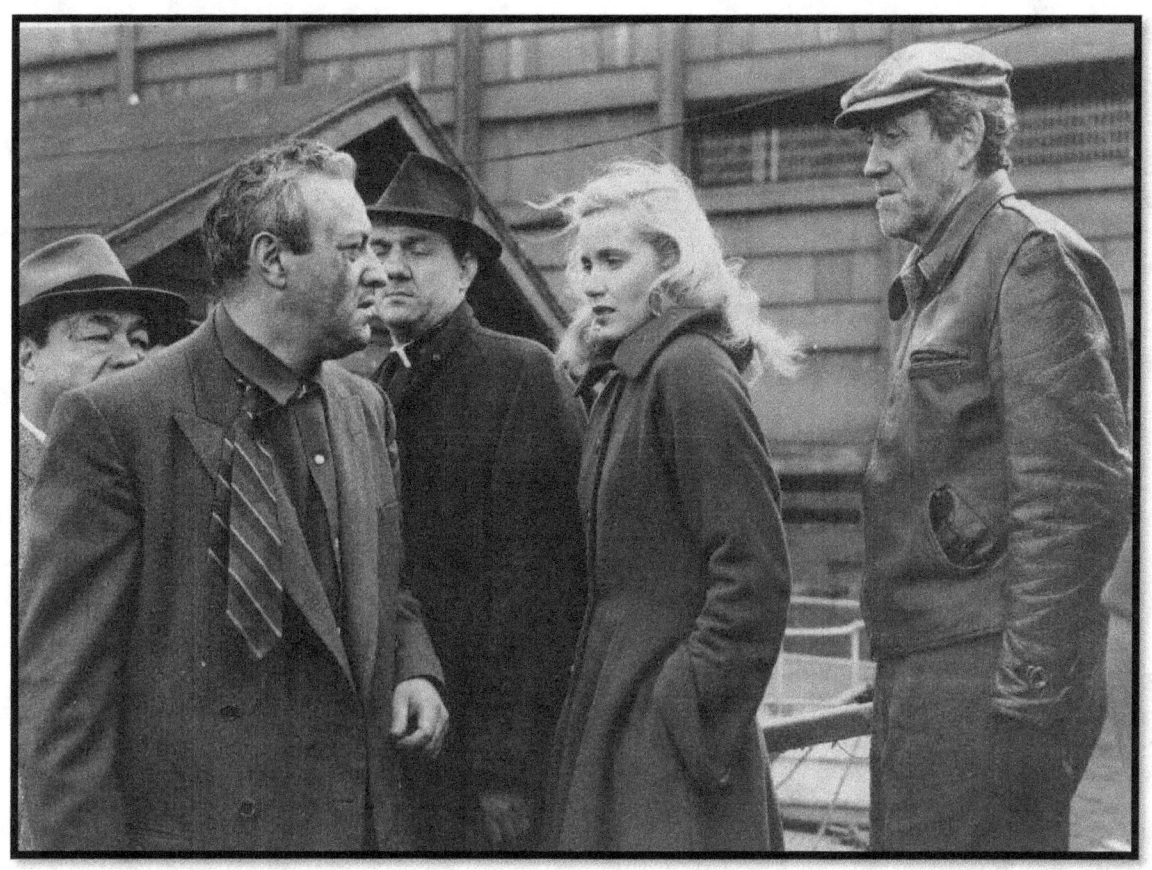

For the shot where Edie joins the fray to get a work chit for her father, Kaufman shots her within the chaos of the fray. When Edie tries to wrestle the tag away from Terry Malloy, he easily overpowers her, muscle and brawn rule on the docks. After Terry learns that she is Joey Doyle sister, he meekly surrenders the chit and the films conflict, muscle versus morality, is established.

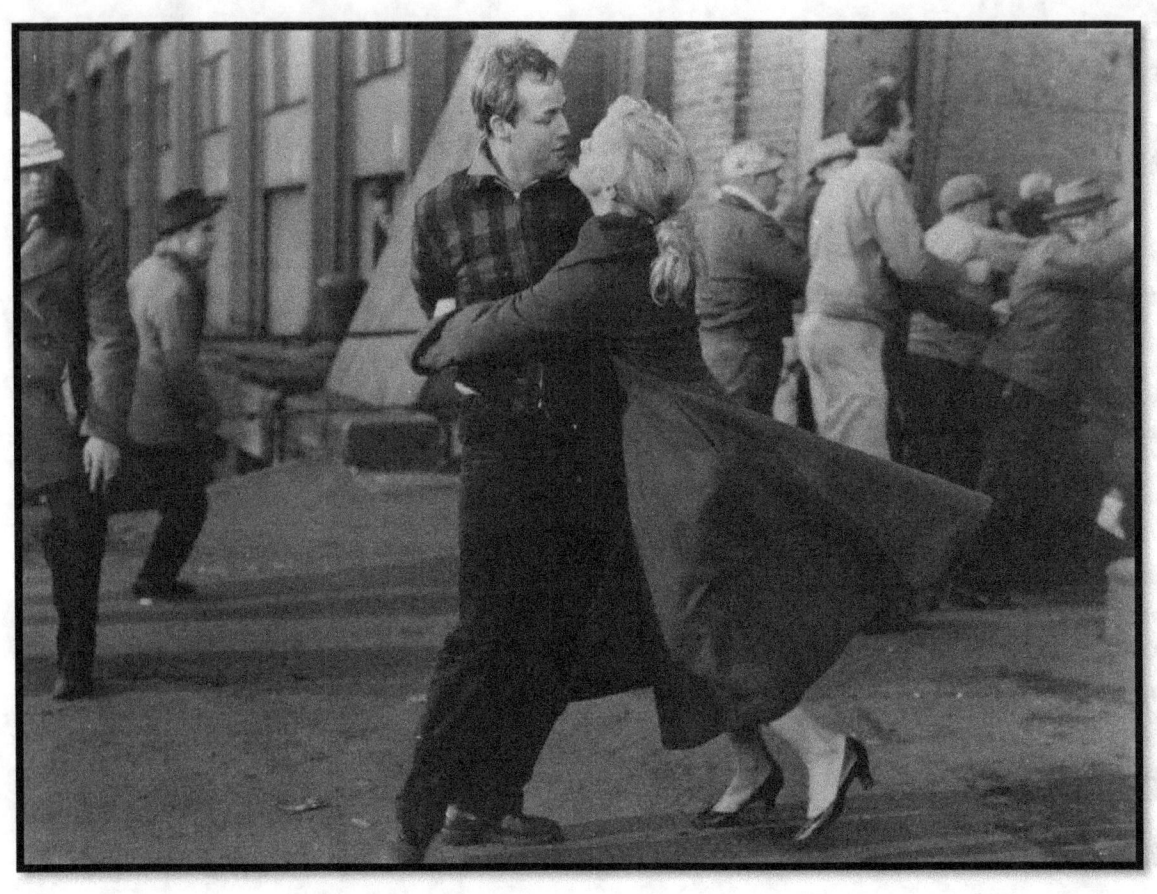

THE CINEMATOGRAPHY OF BORIS KAUFMAN

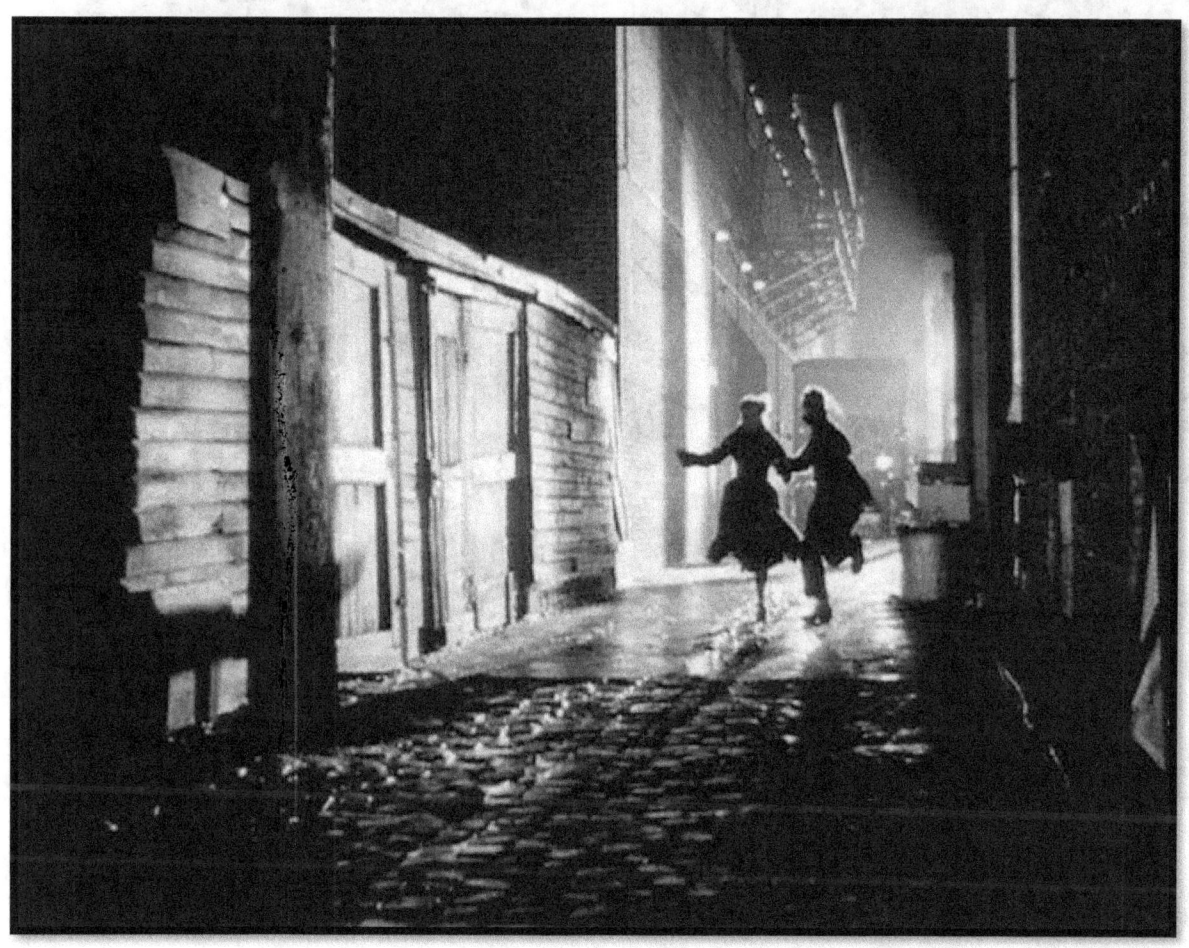

The films Cinematographer would be the talented, highly respected and legendary Boris Kaufman who had been hired by Kazan after a recommendation by filmmaker Willard Van Dyke. Schulberg said, "Boris was a great artist. He did a beautiful job under difficult conditions. The weather was cold and overcast.

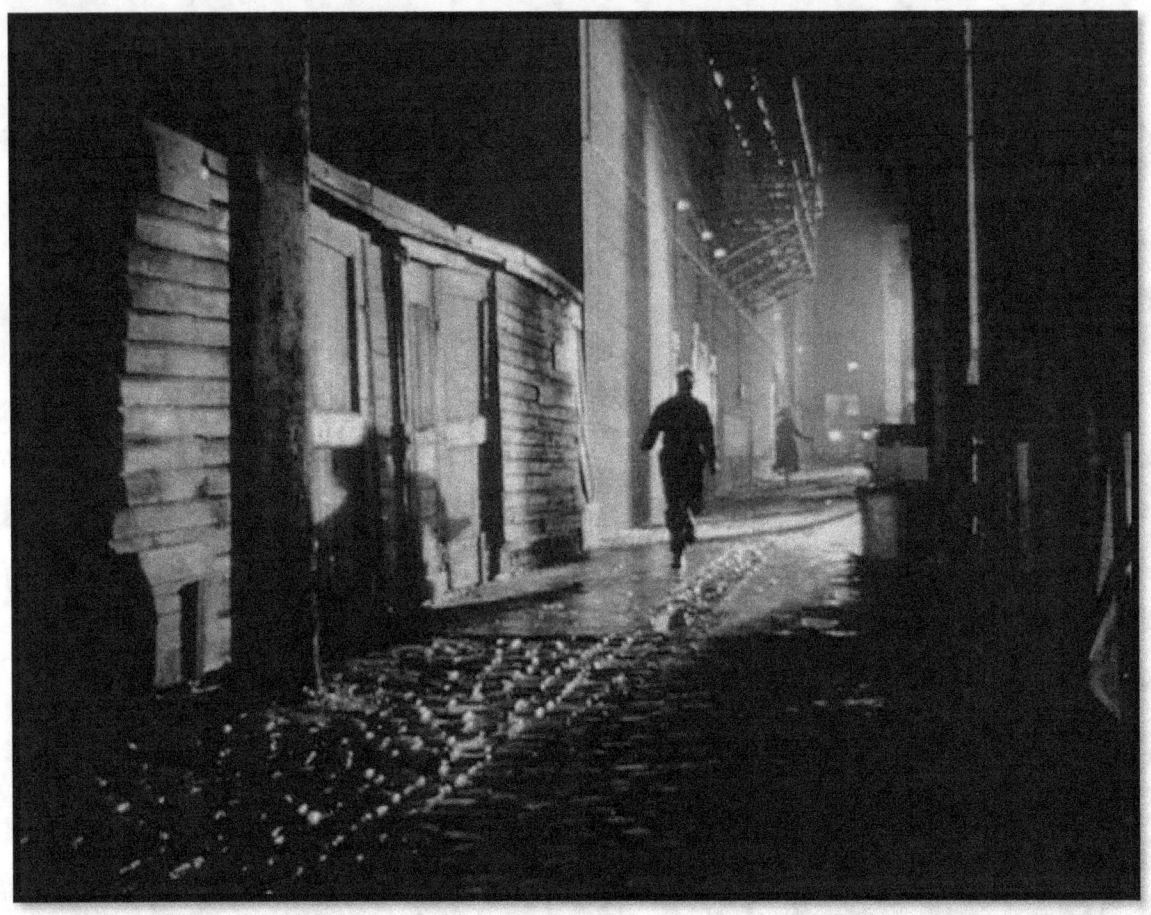

We rushed to shoot the film in 35 days. Cheap is fast. Every day costs money. Spiegel, the producer, was on Kazan's tail to go faster. We were pleased by the way, the film turned out. Everybody was against it. We overcame all the obstacles."

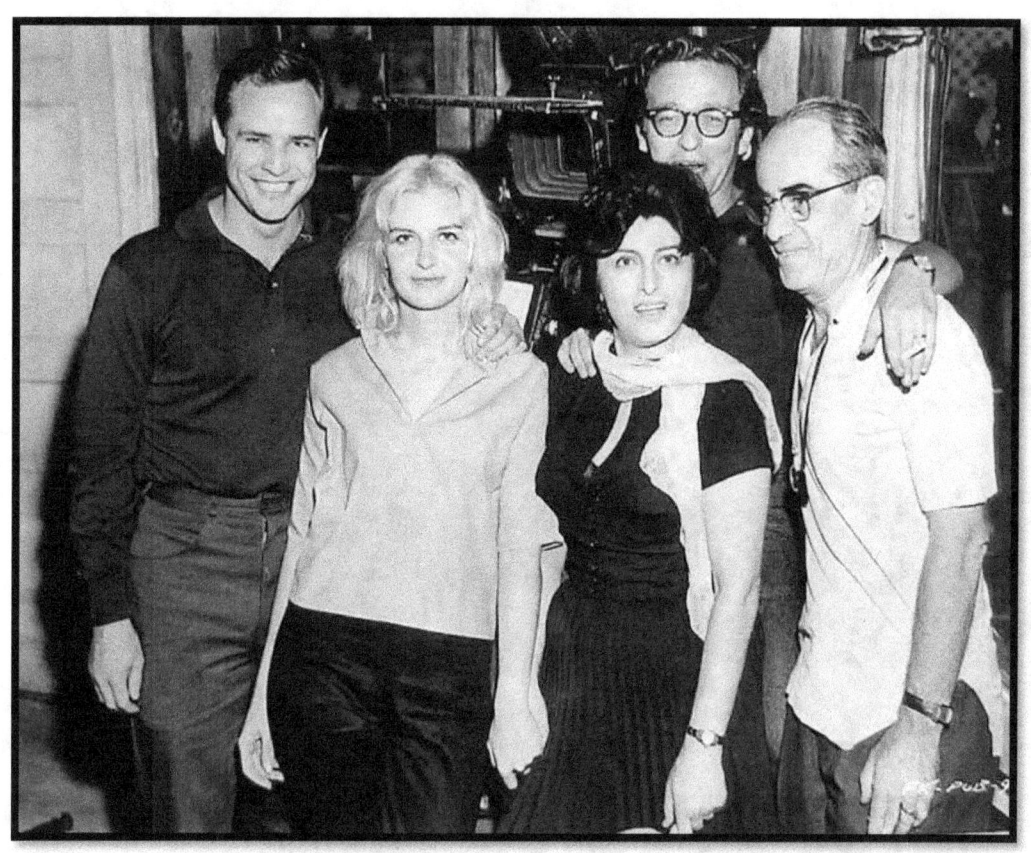

Brando, Joanne Woodward, Anna Magnani, director Sidney Lumet and Boris Kaufman on the set of The Fugitive Kind

Kaufman strongly believed that image and theme in a film must be united and that belief is displayed in the visual continuity from scene to scene, all of it flawless, which was the cinematographer's primary concern.

Since Kazan shot *Waterfront* in story sequence, (Shooting each scene as the viewer would see it) continuity became a lesser issue for Kaufman, freeing him to concentrate on constancy in lighting, an ongoing problem in outside, winter shooting so to get evenly defused lighting, Kaufman had the crew burn trash cans with dried wood (less smoke).

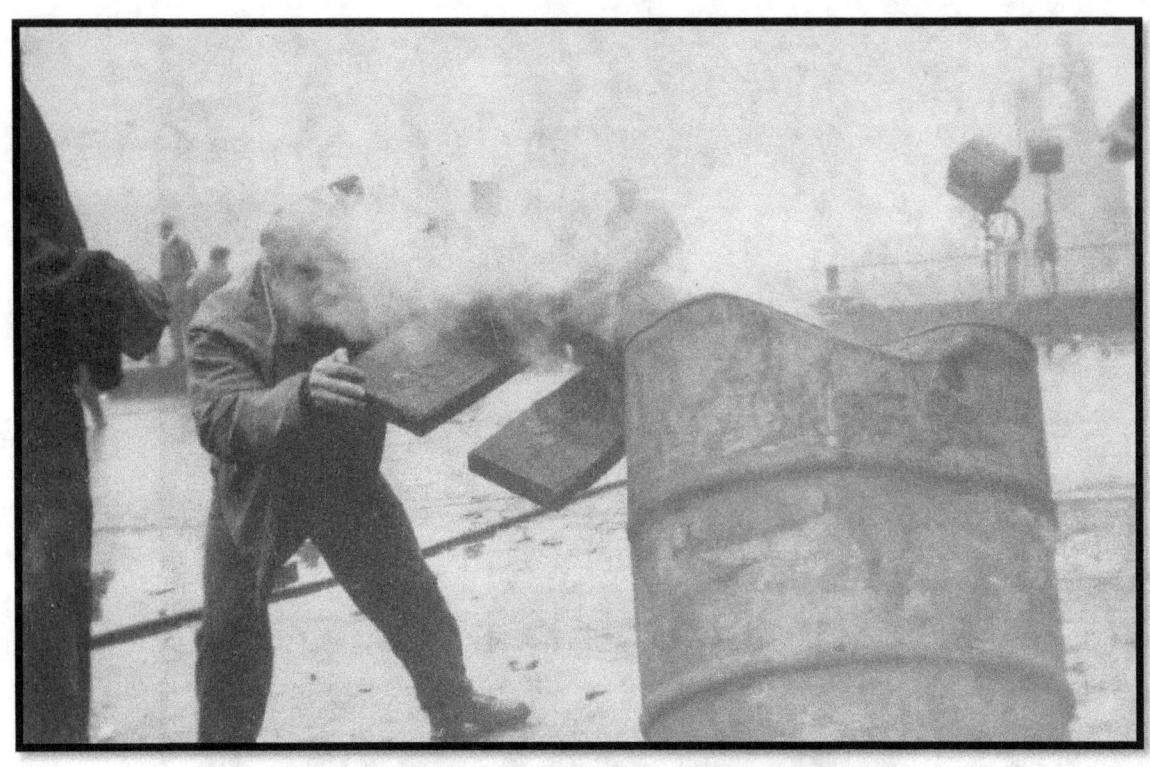

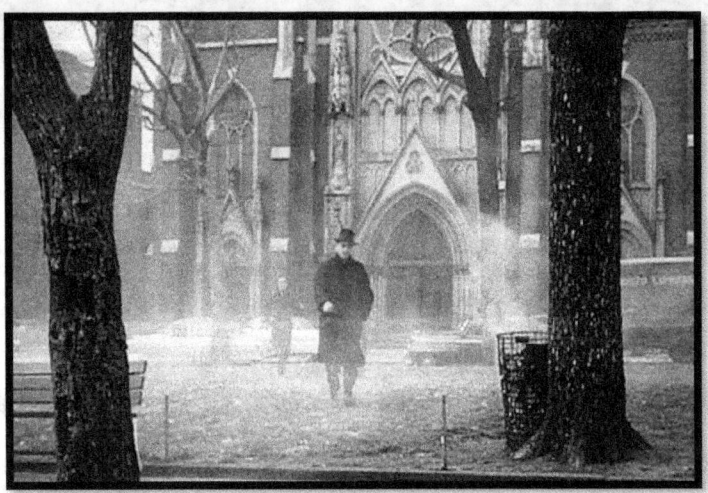

Throughout each of the three parts of the film, Kazan and Kaufman used camera angles that emphasize entrapment, solidified by the setting of laundry

252

hanging on lines, which form diagonals that intrude on human space, alleyways with blinding lights and diffused lighting that emphasizes moral confusion.

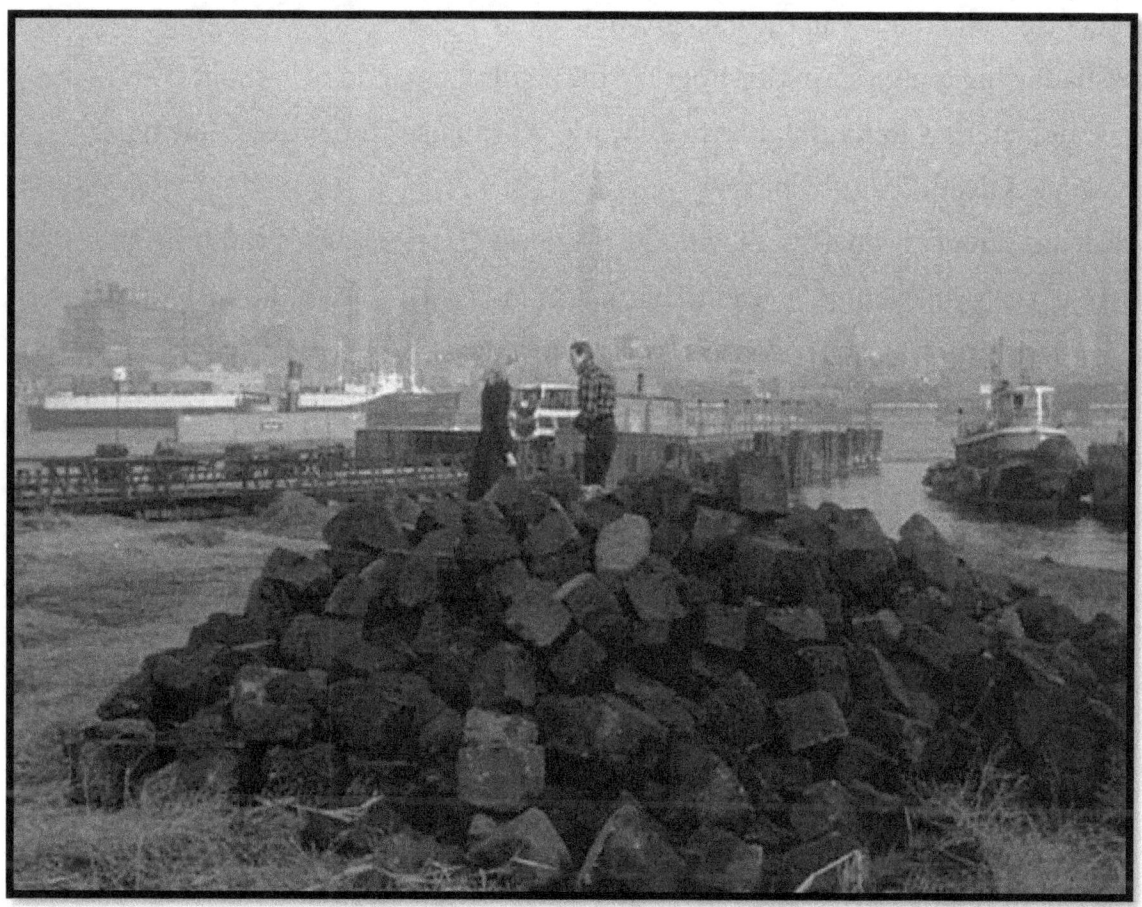

One of the better moments of camera styling in the film, in this case taking precedence over acting and scripting, is the fantastic scene where Terry confesses his role in Joey Doyle's murder to Edie. The viewer doesn't hear the confession or Edie response because Kazan allowed it to be drowned out by the scream like whistle from a nearby ship, in effect, drowned out by the waterfront as was the life of Joey Doyle. The viewer hears one of two words but the scene is impressionistic, relying on the depth of the actors reactions to the words, the acting accentuated by the sounding of a pounding press machine somewhere in the background. Edie leaves Terry alone on a hell like pile of black rocks, a flame of fire shooting into the sky in the background.

Foreshadowing is also sprinkled liberally in the film, all of done without dialogue and left only to Kaufman camera work. Kazan uses the foreshadowing in Joey Doyle's death scene by having

Doyle leans out of his apartment window to answer Terry Malloy's call from the street, a call that will eventually lead to his death. It is used a second time later in the film when Terry leans out of Edie's window to answer a dark call from the street, which leads to the discovery of his brother's corpse. The tilt to the roof to Doyle's apartment reveals that Joey is in trouble (although this simply happened and not scripted)

Again, he uses a macabre foreshadowing for the death of Kayo Dugan who wishes that the dock workers could unload crates of Irish whiskey instead of bananas, which they unload every day.

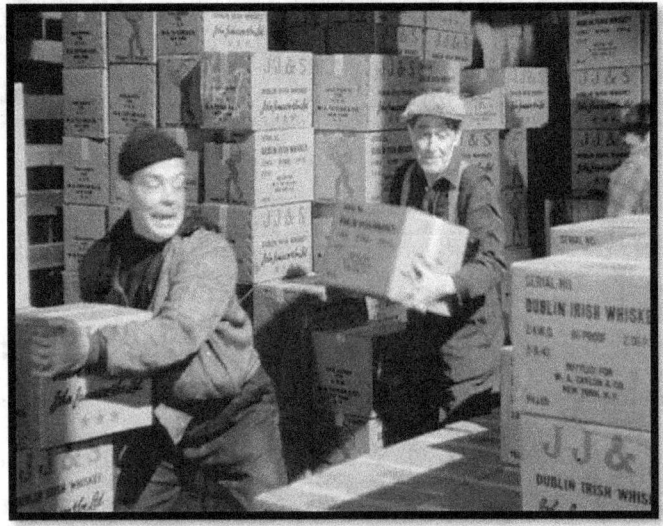

The day a ship finally arrives with a cargo of Irish whiskey is the day the gang murders Dugan on the job—by dropping a crate of whiskey on his head. He also uses the dead Joey Doyle's leather jacket to signal both death and resurrection. After Joey Doyle's murder, Pops Doyle gives Joey's jacket to Dugan, suggesting that perhaps now Dugan has a mark on him.

After Dugan's murder, the jacket is given back to Edie who give the jacket to Terry who does not wear it, perhaps out of guilt. Only when he exonerates his guilt by testifying, in the final scene at the docks, does he wear Joey's jacket.

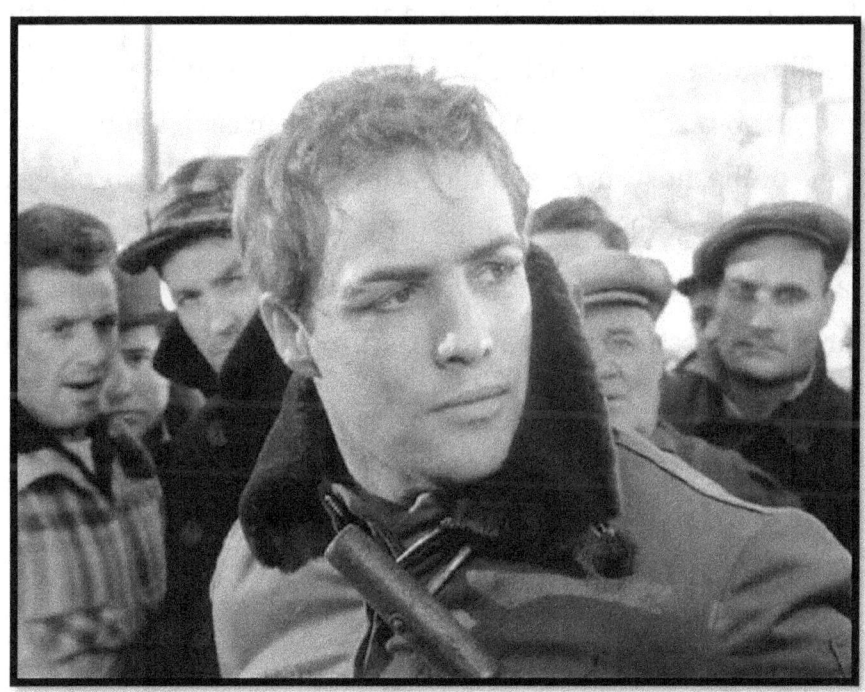

One area of the film that made Spiegel happy was the cost of film. The film is shot in black and white for its realism and social class and because Italian neo-realism, began to dictate an expectation that black and white was somehow more appropriate for social realism than color was.

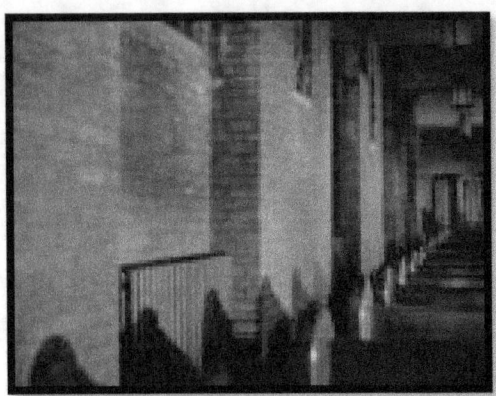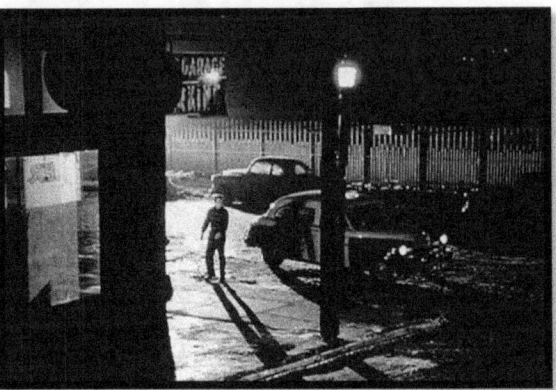

It was effective for all of those reasons, but it was also cost effective. One of the original reasons the film was shot without color was that there had been a hope that Zanuck, whom they wanted to finance the film, would envision another *Grapes of Wrath*, one of the most successful films Hollywood had ever produced.

Oddly, moviegoers today view black and white as too realistic which was the mood that Kaufman wanted, he preferred black and white to color because he believed it better brought across the concept that the director and screenwriter had in mind.

Black and white also gave Kaufman wider exposure latitude, and the ability to work in unprepared locations where he frequently used long shot, deep focus photography that situated the workmen versus the harbor.

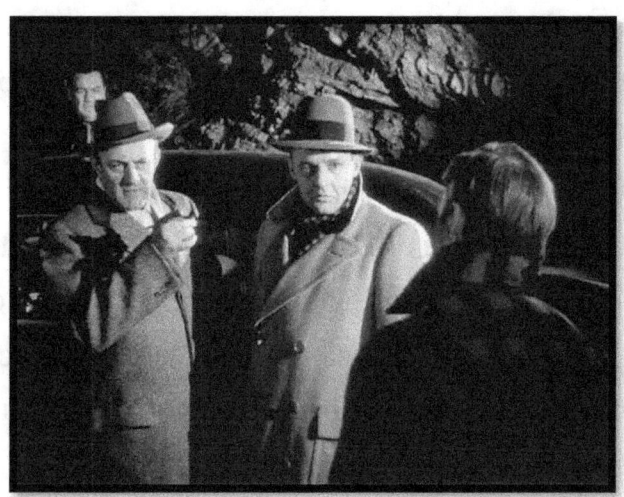

Kaufman used low angle versus high angle shots of the various characters. Terry Malloy, as an example, is never shot against an open sky until he makes the decision to challenge Johnny Friendly. After that, he is joined with Father Barry against the sky whenever he attempts to inspire workers to make spiritual choices.

The garish lighting in the back alley when Terry discovers his murdered brother effectively expresses the good/evil polarity of Terry's situation at that point in the narrative and the scene prior to that, when Terry and Edie are almost run down by a truck has a Film noir lighting scheme.

The gangsters and their world are depicted with high contrast, low-key photography, again reminiscent of film noir style. Kazan and Kaufman used suggestive framing when Malden as Father Barry, is lifted from the cargo hold with Kayo Duggan's corpse, above the men, towards heaven as if Duggan reward for his testimony and Barry's reward for his sermon, are to be brought into heaven. (in reality, it was the only way out of the cargo hold, the exit door to the hold was too narrow to lift the body through)

Kaufman preferred early morning and late afternoon shooting. It gave him natural light sources such as soft shadows and dimly lit objects would be better the black and white hues in the film stock.

Clear days were better for Kaufman to create the films distant shots because the natural light and distance would smooth over the harsher edges of the object, but clear days were far and few between during the short time that the crew was in Hoboken. Conversely, Kaufman preferred cloudy days to shot the actors close up, when the defused lighting would better bring across the actors features.

Although the camera work is one of the key elements to films success It's presence in such abbreviated form shows that it has been given short shrift, along with makeup, lighting, and costume design.

Kazan stressed actors-on-screen over camera work, he wanted the actors work to be the center of the film, not Kaufman's camera angles, as a result, while there is some wonderful camera work by Kaufman, intense close up's or dramatic long shots are rare.

The most frequent shot in the film are two-shot angles (Two actors in one shot at midrange) or in wider shots to show the characters positioning which Kazan used show the dynamics of the waterfront hierarchy. Johnny Friendly is usually shown in alone with his men in the background. As the film progresses, Terry Malloy, who is at first shot close to Friendly and his men, is gradually (starting with his condemnation to the cargo holds by Friendly for missing Kayo Duggan's testimony) between the Friendly gang and the longshoremen.

Waterfront's Art and Set Director was Canadian Richard Day, who had begun his film career in 1918 under the director Erich von Stroheim and would win, in the total of his career, seven Oscars for art direction and set design. Day's cathedral alter set for the 1928 film, *The Wedding March*, was so beautiful that the films cinematographer Hal Mohr, asked that it be kept up after filming so he could use the set for his own wedding. Day had worked with Kazan on *Streetcar* but in his work on Waterfront, he created and discovered locations that captured the psychological and physical needs of the film.

In Day's locations, after working closely with Boris Kaufman and Kazan, the city is confined in fences and walls and as a result, the charters are confined, their city is a dingy, dangerous place filled with threatening alleyways, crowded spaces and lights that pierce and blind the cast and the viewer.

Space is intruded upon by fog and steam engulfs the streets and set the tone for the characters state of mind. The Hoboken Day delivers sees Manhattan across the river as almost a golden city far beyond the reach of these mere longshoremen who exist in near poverty and filth. Almost all of Kaufman's distant shots are of an open space (And usually aerial) from the rooftop of Terry's apartment house. Those shot, always leaving a romantic image, suggest escape if only temporary, from the problems on the dirty streets below.

SCRIPT CHANGES

The Script supervisor was Roberta Hodes. Her counterpart as dialogue supervisor was Guy Thomajan who had been a stage manager on several of Kazan's plays in the 1950s. He also played the overwhelmed postal clerk in Miracle of 34th Street as well as a bit role in Kazan's *Panic in the Streets* and the role of Artoff in the *Pink Panther*.

Hodes oversaw several changes in the script including the scene where Terry takes Edie for a drink at a corner bar. As she leaves the bar, she walks through a wedding reception. Depending upon who tells the story, the wedding party, which was Polish and not Irish despite the music, was real. The bar owner had double booked the bar that night with both the wedding and film crew.

Kazan said that he improvised the wedding scene at the last second and then improved it over a period of days as a means to bring Edie and Terry in close contact. The completed script touched on corruption on the waterfront, at some point during the rewrites, corruption took a back seat to the moral struggles of Terry Malloy.

Another script adjustment came at the film opening. In the original script, the audience was to see Joey Doyle being pushed off the roof. Kazan didn't like, it was too real and to intense telling Spiegel and Schulberg that the audience would understand the scene without acting t through and that often what the audience imagined was far worse than what they saw.

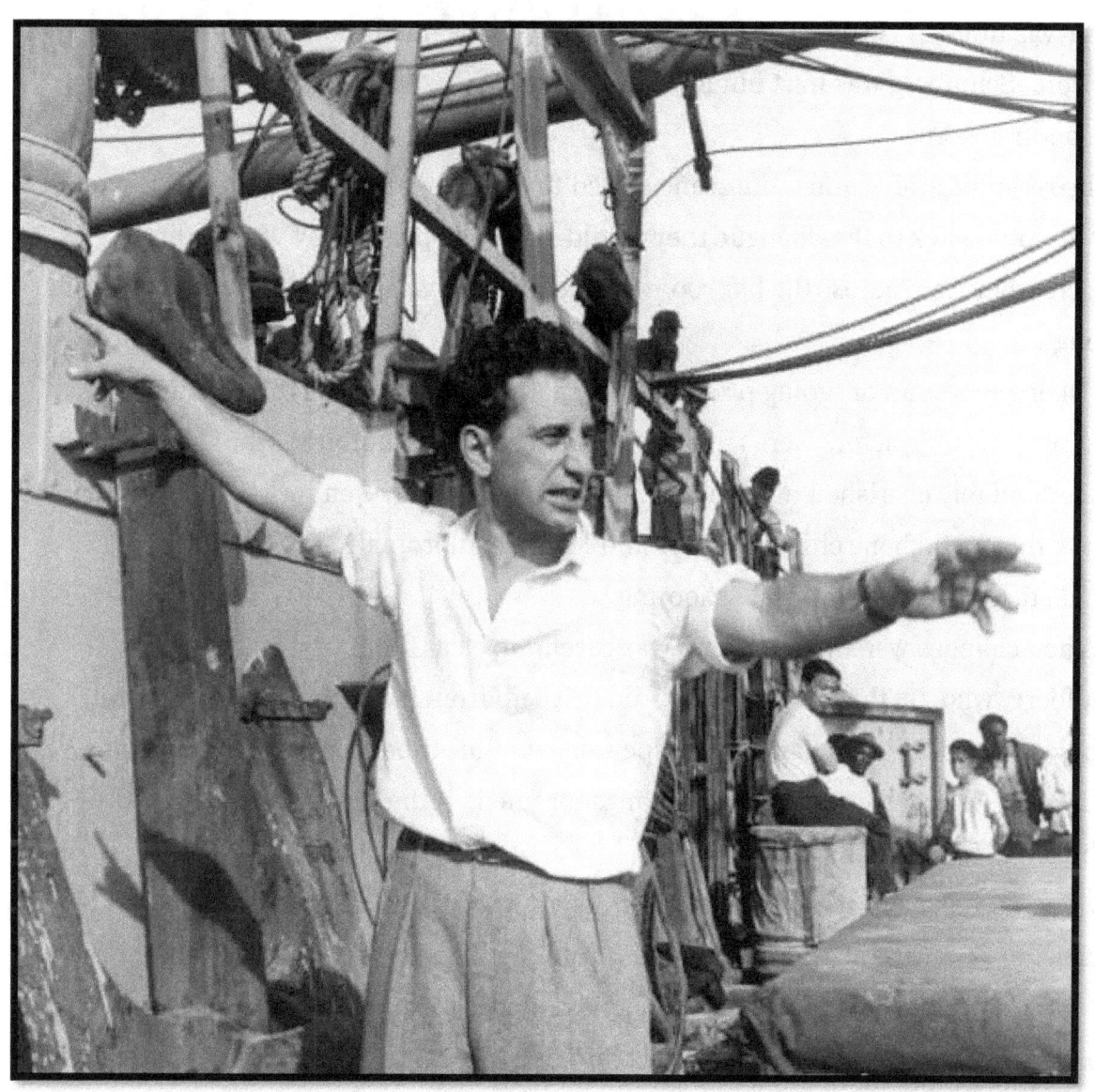

Kazan on the set of *Panic in the Streets*.

Another change, of sorts, came in the bar room scene where Terry, carrying a pistol, is confronted by Father Barry. Schulberg's directive dialogue called for a heart wrenching scene between the two characters which Kazan felt was not needed he sensed that the timing of the film required action. That night when the

261

scene was filmed, Kazan asked Schulberg to stay in his hotel room and not be on location. Schulberg was hurt but followed on the request and stayed away from the shooting scene.

The reason Kazan wanted the scene closed to Schulberg was that although the actors would stick to the dialogue they would shout the beautifully written lines at each other from across the bar room instead of softly speaking their way through it.

Dialogue was an on-going problem, especially when the film's director and most of its leading actors were from the method school. Schulberg, who understandably cherished his dialogue, rarely came to Hoboken for shooting during that awful bone chilling winter and Kazan had promised him that he would stick close to script while shooting.

When changes were made, Kazan was careful to clear them first with Schulberg, who, on the few occasions, did drive up from his Pennsylvania farm to Hoboken to discuss the changes, but spent most of his time drinking with his tour guide and friend, Brownie, and other longshoremen, in the dingy bars that lined Hoboken's town center.

Otherwise, aside from occasional input, there was little room in the script for improvisation by the actors. Kazan and Schulberg worked in the old Hollywood system of screenwriting and shooting, camera angles were written into the script to better display what the character was thinking in a certain shot, which was also written into the script. With Kazan on the writing team, the direction was written into the script. In the early days of Hollywood the writer produced a script with directions on how it would be shot and how that shot would translate into what the actor was supposed to be thinking or feeling in a scene....emotional stage directing. Some directors, like John Ford, followed the screenwriter's directions right down to the last letter.

There was some improvising. Kazan, once an actor in the Group Theatre, was considered to be an actor's director and was heavily influenced by Stella Adler, a noted actor of the stage in the 1940s who had also been a part of the Group Theatre, with Kazan and Lee Strasberg. She was also Marlon Brando's acting teacher.

Kazan had also worked with Brando at the Actors Studio as well as on other films and knew his actors talents and the benefits of improvisation in his acting and occasionally he did let Brando glide on his own such as in the "white glove" scene where Eva Marie Saint accidentally dropped one of her white gloves in a scene.

Brando picked it up to hand it back to her and then used it as a tool. His seemingly unconscious fiddling with the glove throws off the entire rhythm of the scene and adds to the unexpected nature of each step. It creates a second dynamic. Although the glove was dropped by accident by Eva Marie Saint the actress, it gave the illusion that her character, Edie Doyle, was nervous and unsure of what she wanted.

Kazan said that the glove gives the young couple an excuse to remain together for several more minutes. Recent events and their social differences (she is on her way out of the docks and Terry is going nowhere) keeps them apart but their feelings for each other, their attraction, keeps them together. Terry tries on Edie's glove as if he were trying on her values. As Johnny Friendly's dupe in the ring, he had worn black boxing gloves, as a man in the midst of changing forever he tries on the white glove of moral values. In a later scene, Edie wears the same white gloves when Terry confesses his role in her brother's murder.

The usual Hollywood offering of American's positive outlook of the workplace is missing from the film. In *Waterfront*, virtually all of the dialogue about the workplace is negative, the workers, hardened and stoic, are alienated and spill out sarcastic remarks about their work and their status. Pop Doyle talks about how one of his arms is longer than the other because of years of swinging a hook. Stealing from the cargo loads by the workers is commonplace.

Kazan wants the viewers to feel that the working man is exploited, at least on the docks, which they were. While Kazan, through Father Barry, argues for decency and humanity in the work place, it is obvious to the viewer that these men would never die for their jobs, as Terry Malloy is later willing to do, further underlying that the battle between Terry and Johnny Friendly is personnel. The films incredibly powerful dialogue was a result of Schulberg's ear for capturing the longshoreman's color and use of idiom.

Schulberg said, *"One thing you do in writing dialogue is that you make up as little of it as you can and you listen as much as you can.*

Watching it this evening, I was reminded how many times something in there was not really written by me, I simply wrote down what they were actually saying.

The scene in the hold, after Dugan gets killed, Father Barry comes down and when he talks about Christ and the shake-up that was something that I actually heard. When I heard the real waterfront priest talk about that Christ is here and he carries a hook and he sees the men who get passed over and who gets the jobs and the wine and I was just so amazed by it that I just had to try and put this old sermon, or whatever you call it, in the film.

Dialogue, you try to build your characters... if you try to get an idea about who you're writing about, then you listen to that person or those people. When Charlie gets killed, the ordinary cliché or Terry would be "I'll get em or I'll kill em" or something like that, but I actually heard a longshoreman say "I'll take it out of their skulls!" And it just rang a bell, a loud bell, that's the line I should use. I won't use "I'll get em if it's the last thing I do" or some such line, I'll say what

264

I heard my friend the longshoreman say, "I'll take it out of their skulls".

So, a lot of dialogue comes out of listening, carefully, to the characters and getting an ear for how they talk and plus, you have to shape your scenes and build your scenes on all of that. I find it very, very valuable, I think.

Schulberg recruited a longshoreman to coach Midwesterner Brando on the proper New Jersey accent for Terry Malloy. One of the unintended lighter moment of the films is brought around by Jocko, the Bartender who calmly and professionally tells an armed and bleeding Terry Malloy "He's not here right now." when Terry asks for Johnny Friendly. This is a clear example of Schulberg's mastery of dialogue. It is rarely expository and when it is, it is because it is the natural way for the character to talk.

The films characters, through the dialogue, generally avoid stereotype. Malden's Father Barry is a chain smoking short-tempered man with outward disdain for Terry. Kazan has Terry breaking the Production Code rules shouts at the priest, "You go to hell." That line in itself was risky, but the fact that Terry yells the words to a Catholic priest made it worse, so Kazan asked for an exemption of the Production Code rules by censor Joseph Breen that had been in effect since the mid-1930s as the Motion Picture Production Code. Producers submitted their films to the MPPC to get the seal of approval to show that the film was in compliance.

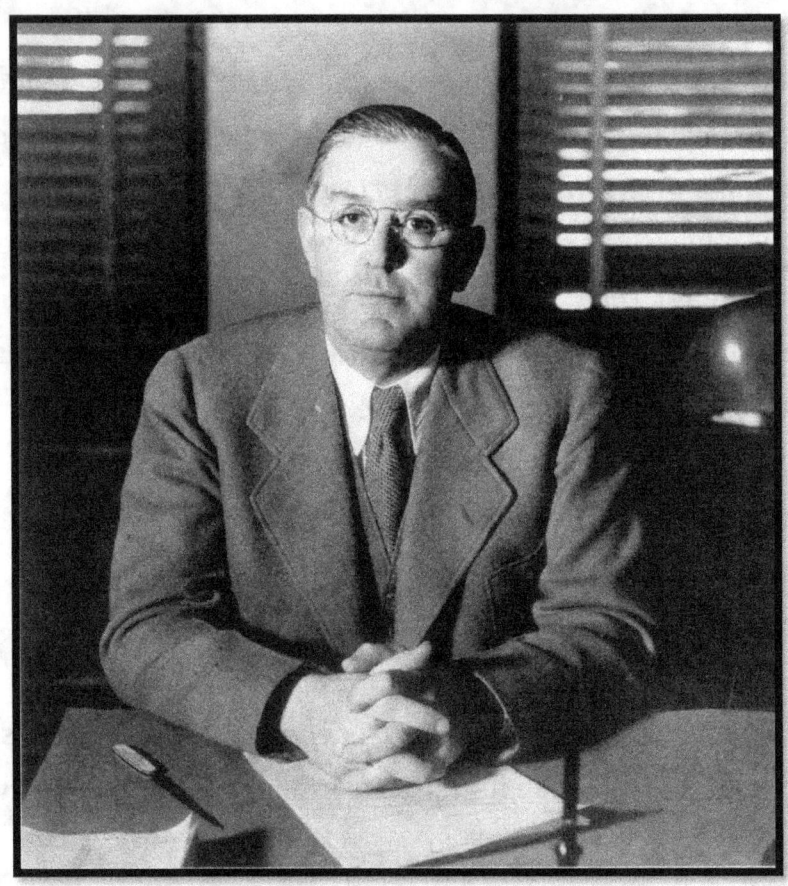

The very unpopular Mr. Breen

While it looks almost commonplace today in 1953, having a Catholic Priest light a cigarette in public was no doubt mean to shock. (Although the real Father Corridan was a chain smoker)

Oddly, the criticism from Catholic circles came not for the cigarette but for the scene where Father Barry walks into Johnny Friendly's bar and orders a beer. Kazan, who was already on thin ice with both the MPPC and the Catholic Church for *Street car named Desire* thought it best to seek out Breen's approval for the scene.

MAKE UP AND CUSTOME

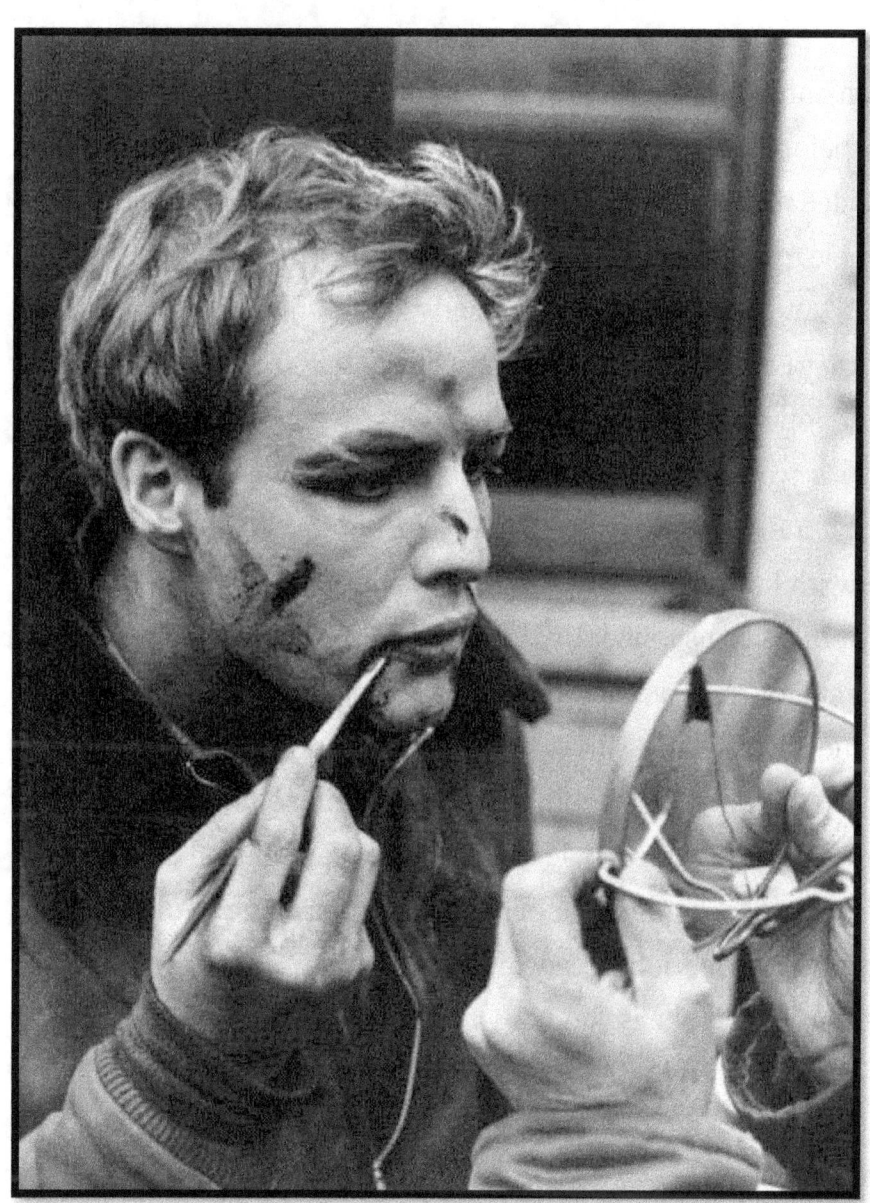

Costume design would be Anna Hill Johnstone. In her spectacular career, Johnstone was highly regarded for her keen eye (It was Johnstone who accompanied Schulberg to the stage play where Eva Marie Saint was playing) and the ability to dress the cast accurately in common clothes to portray the common person. She did an outstanding job on Brando's wardrobe.

On the Sunday before shooting began, Brando wanted to be sure he fit into Hoboken and decided to go for a stroll dressed in character as Terry Malloy. "Let's walk the whole town," he told Schulberg. They dropped into a crowded local bar for a beer "And" said Schulberg "Nobody knew who he was." Halfway through the walk they came across a gaggle of teenage schoolgirls who walked right past the most popular star in the world without noticing who he was." A tribute to Johnston's eye for detail.

Makeup and elaborate costumes were sparse. Brando wears the same simple lumberjack's coat with holes in the elbows throughout the entire film. Its checkerboard pattern helps us to identify him in any crowd and sets him apart as different. In several scenes, Eva Marie Saint's close ups show the effects of the cold on her eyes and cheeks.

Kazan used the few changes in custom to signify shifting emotions. Throughout most of the film, Edie Doyle is shown is a plain button down overcoat, her hair pulled back reflecting her convent upbringing. Towards the end of the film, she is shown briefly in a white slip, her hair flowing freely. The transformation is surprising, she is suddenly feminine shape, the demure Catholic schoolgirl although still present in the line spoken, is gone.

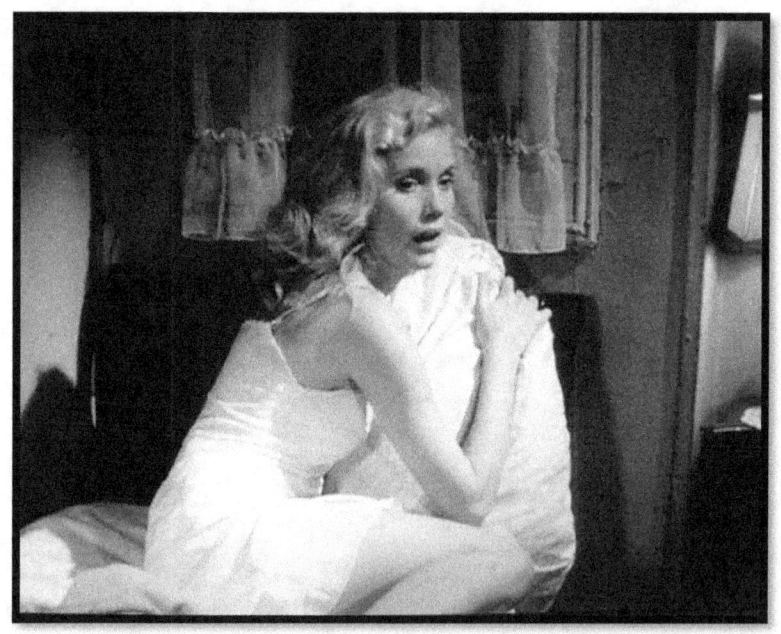

In that scene, shot inside the Doyle's apartment, set director Richard Day is mindful of Edie's position in the film as the moral compass.

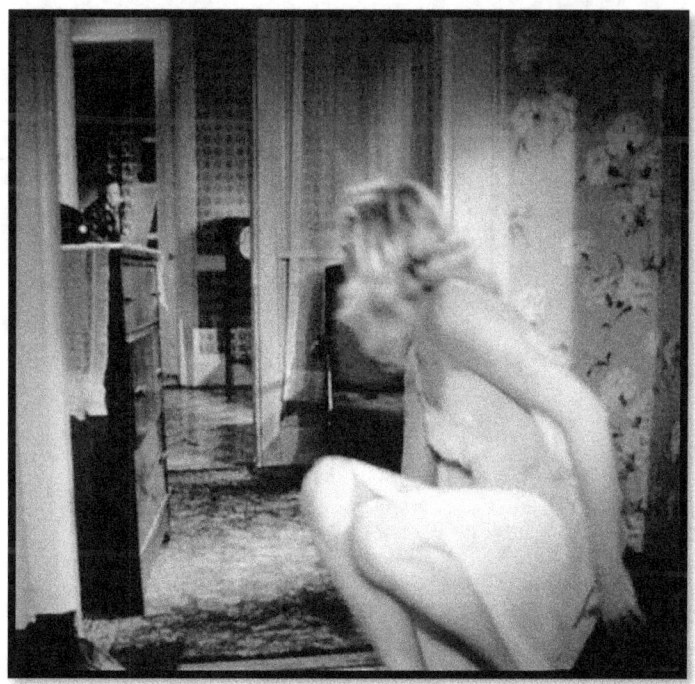

Aside from the white slip, white-blonde hair that gives Edie and angelic look, Day was careful to make sure that the walls of the cramped apartment are soiled and stained. He has placed a crucifix in two rooms.

THE TAXI SCENE
Late November 1953

"To grasp the full significance of life is the actor's duty, to interpret it is his problem, and to express it his dedication." **Brando**

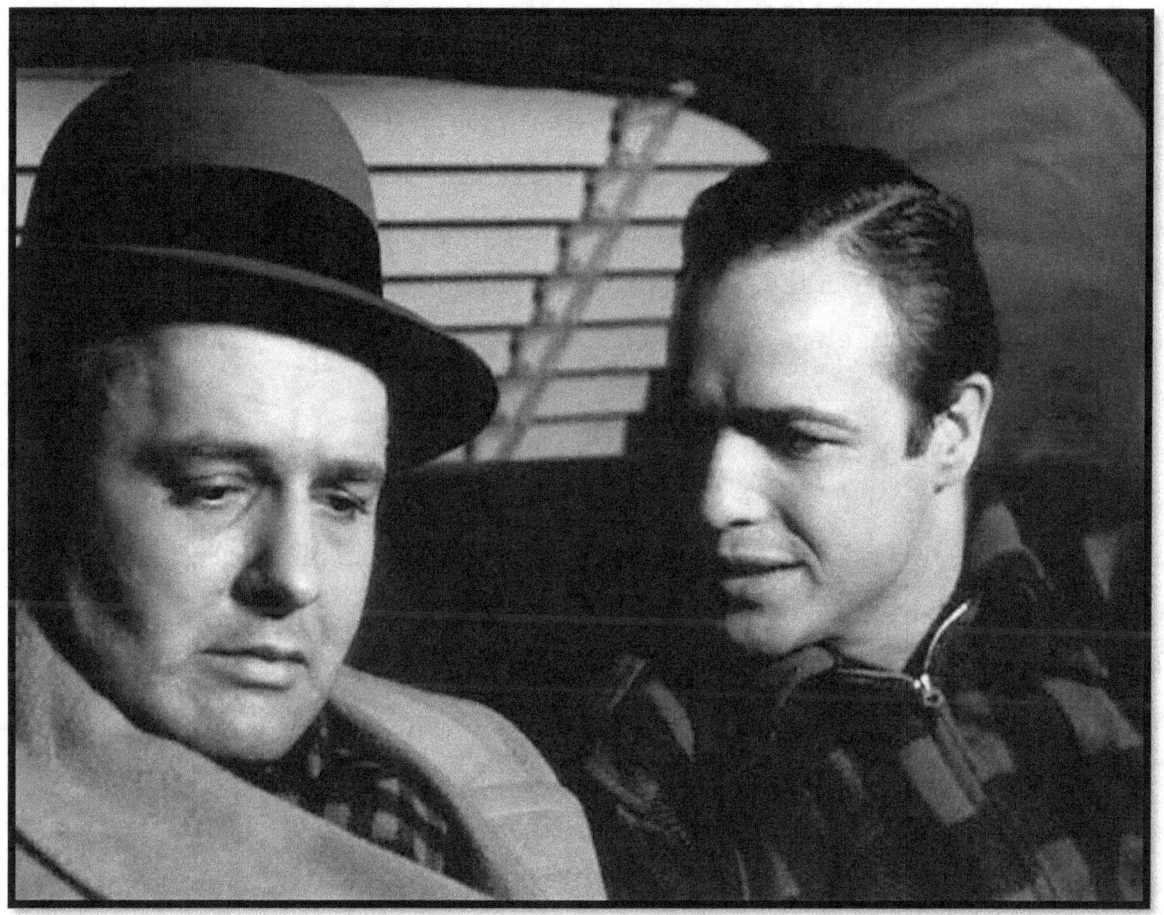

One of the most famous scenes in the history of the American cinema is also one of the simplest: two brothers, talking in the back seat of a cab. While the scene is powerful on its own, it is also the pivotal emotional point in the movie, releasing all the conflict that precedes it, the vocalization of all that is pent up between the two brothers throughout their lives. Terry pours out everything that haunts him, motivates him and causes the apprehension and self-doubt in his life. It is the scene of scenes, the most triumphant expression of failure in American movies.

Kazan had requested the scene be done in an actual taxicab while it was driven through actual Manhattan traffic. Spiegel thought that too expensive, and again and as usual without first conferring with Kazan, he redirected the shoot to the inside of a studio, where, instead of a taxicab, Kazan found the shell of a taxicab. Actually only half of the shell. In the final cut, the cabs driver is actually sitting on a wooden stool supported by phone books. Kazan angrily confronted Spiegel over the set and Spiegel, ever the salesman, draped his arms around the director and cooed, "Darling, you're a genius! You can fix it, you are brilliant! You can fix anything! This is nothing!"

Frustrated and angry, Kazan then asked for a projection unit that would show traffic through the cabs window. Again, Spiegel cut costs and no projection unit arrived. Desperate, Boris Kaufman hammered simple Venetian blinds across the cab shells rear window. A crew was brought in to shake the fake cab to make it look like it was rolling through traffic while flashlights waved across the blinds gave the illusion of passing cars.

Just as the taxi scene was about to be filmed, Brando looked at his watch and said, "I have to leave. Its 4:00 o'clock and I have to see my psychiatrist" 51 and simply walk off the set. So again, Kazan or his assistant directors read Brando's lines to a much hurt and humiliated Rod Steiger "Rod" said Schulberg "felt humiliated, second fiddle, all of that, and would never stop talking about it" 52

Year later, Steiger said, "I thought to himself "You son of a bitch, I got a little bit of talent too, I'll show you" 53 and gave one of the best performances of his life.

Although the taxi car scene is obviously a process shot (A scene shot with technical or mechanical help to enhance the setting) the dialogue and acting is so good, the process is irrelevant.

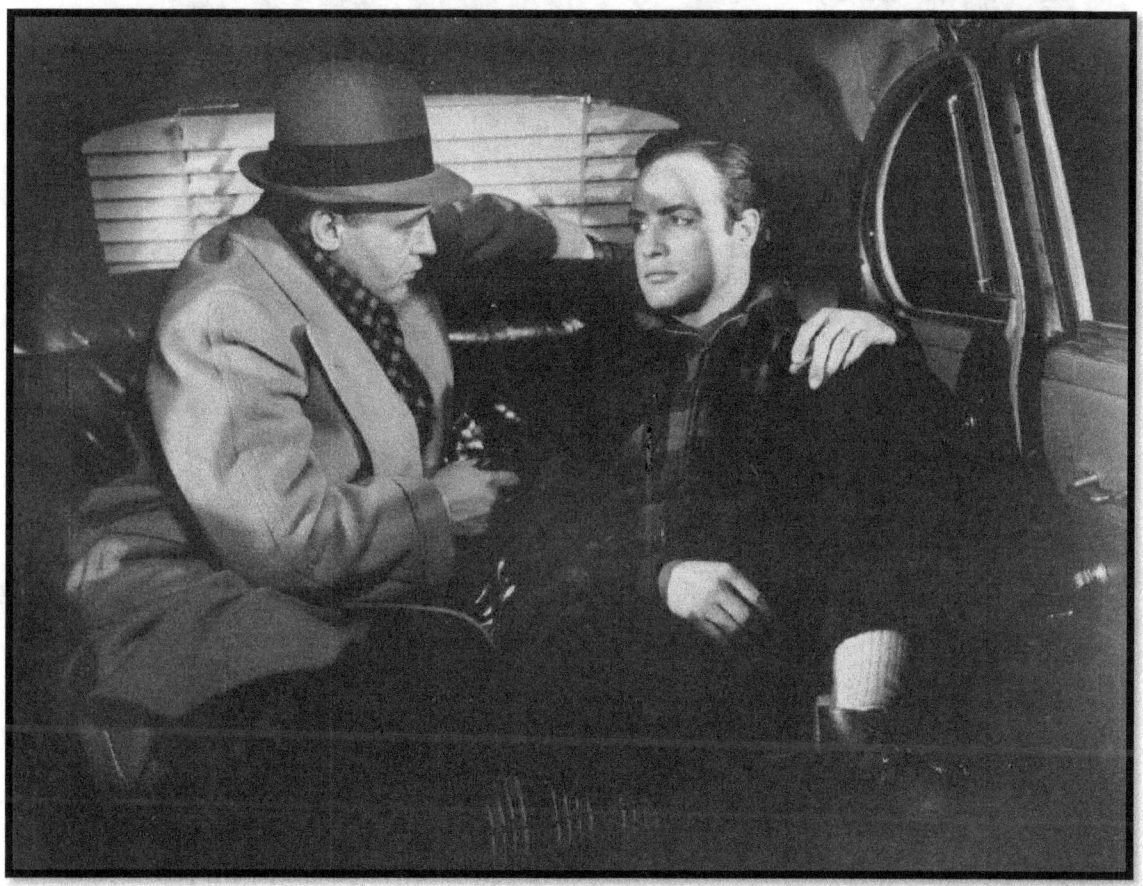

Brando read his lines and started to improvise by asking Steiger "What do you think about the Yankees this year?" to which a dumfounded Steiger answer, "What the hell are you talking about?" and Brando replied "How's Mom?" Steiger went silent and as a result, the set went silent until Kazan yelled out "Bud" (his name for Brando) "Knock off the shit"

In the part in the scene where Steiger's character pulls a pistol on Brando's Terry Malloy and Terry gently pushes it away, admonishing his brother sadly,

Brando claimed that he improvised the scene because he did not feel that Steiger's character would pull a gun on his own brother.

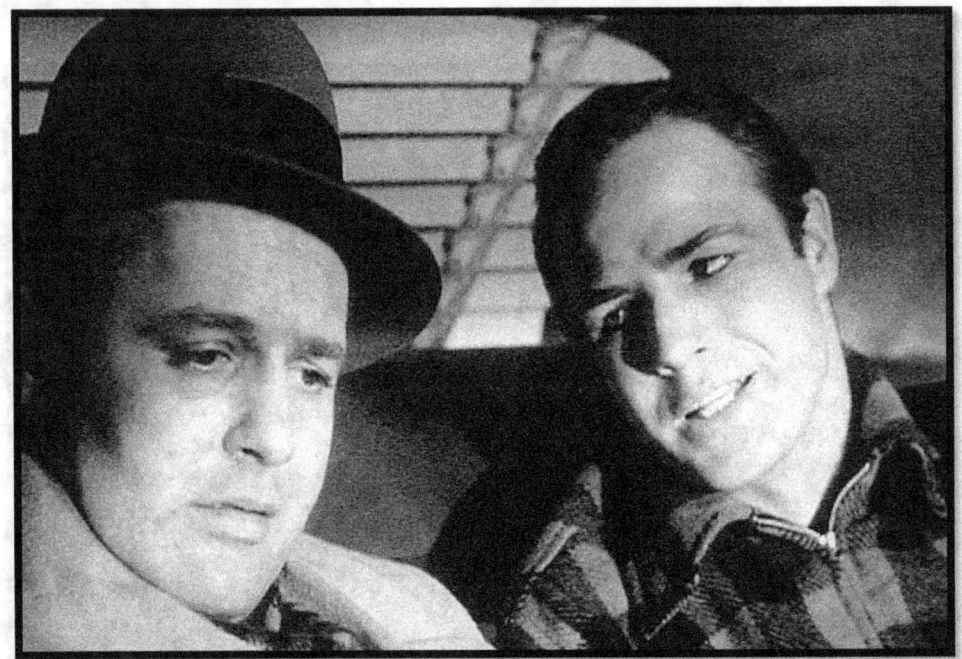

"Marlon did not improvise it" Schulberg insists, "That is a grand myth. During the filming, he would improvise a word here and there, but he did not change lines. He was good about it. Much later, Brando said he had improvised the cab scene. That's absolute nonsense. The scene was intact before we sent him the script."

Still, Brando did complain enough to Kazan that it was unbelievable that his brother, who cared deeply enough for his brother to die for him, would do such a thing. He and Kazan argued about this until finally Kazan said, "All right, wing one."

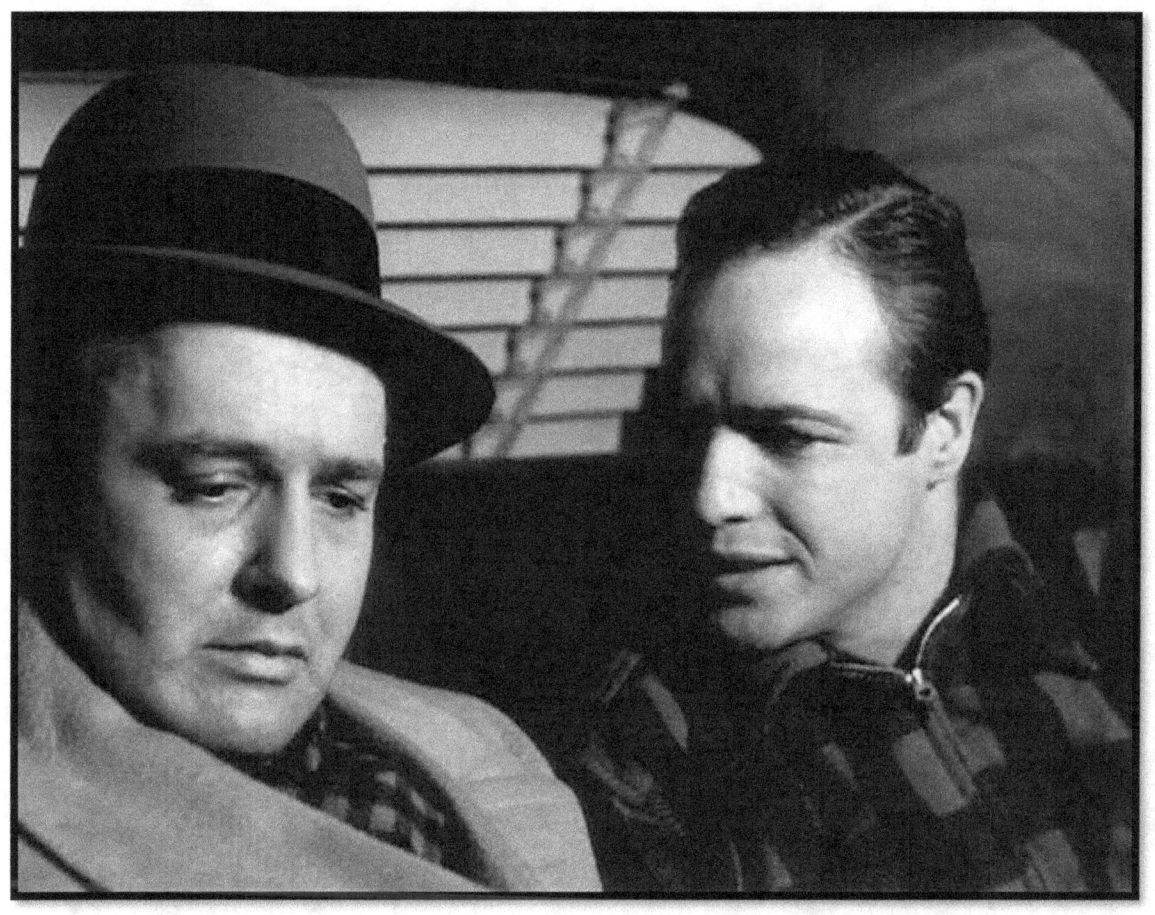

Brando and Steiger improvised parts of the scene, to a more believable scene, which Brando described; *When my brother flashed the gun in the cab, I looked at it, then up at him in disbelief. I didn't believe for a second that he would ever pull the trigger. I felt sorry for him. Then Rod started talking about my boxing career. If I'd had a better manager, he said, things would have gone better for me in the ring. "He brought you along too fast." "That wasn't him, Charlie," I said, "it was you. Remember that night at the Garden you came down to my dressing room and said, 'Kid, this isn't your night.' MY NIGHT! I could have taken Wilson apart. So what happened? He gets the shot at the title outdoors at*

a ballpark and what do I get? A one-way ticket to Palookaville. You was my brother, Charlie, you should have looked out for me a little bit. You should have taken care of me better so I didn't have to take the dives for the short-end money . . . . I could have had class. I could have been a contender. I could have been somebody instead of a bum, which is what I am, let's face it. It was you, Charlie

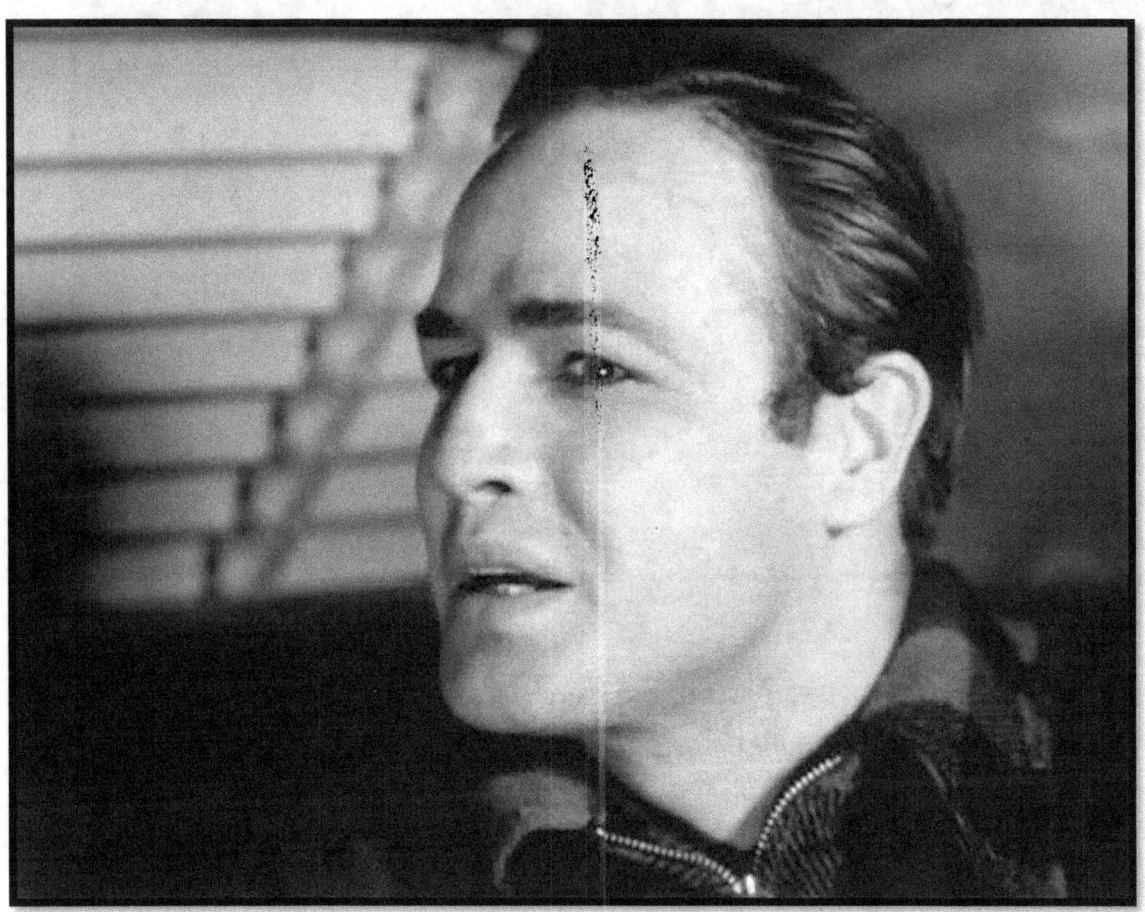

Budd Schulberg recalled, "He was a dream to work with, but there was one bone of contention. Word came to me that Marlon didn't like the taxicab scene, where Marlon's brother Charlie (Rod Steiger) is trying to convince him not to testify to the Waterfront Crime Commission and Terry/ Marlon is protesting that that's the story of his life, doing favors for the mob that sapped his pride and his manhood – they even made him take dives in the ring when he might have been, if not a champion, at least a contender, "somebody, instead of a bum". I got mad. "Gadg, you like the scene, I like it, and Spiegel likes it, what the hell doesn't he like about it?" Kazan said he didn't know. Brando wasn't so good with words. All he said was he can't play it.

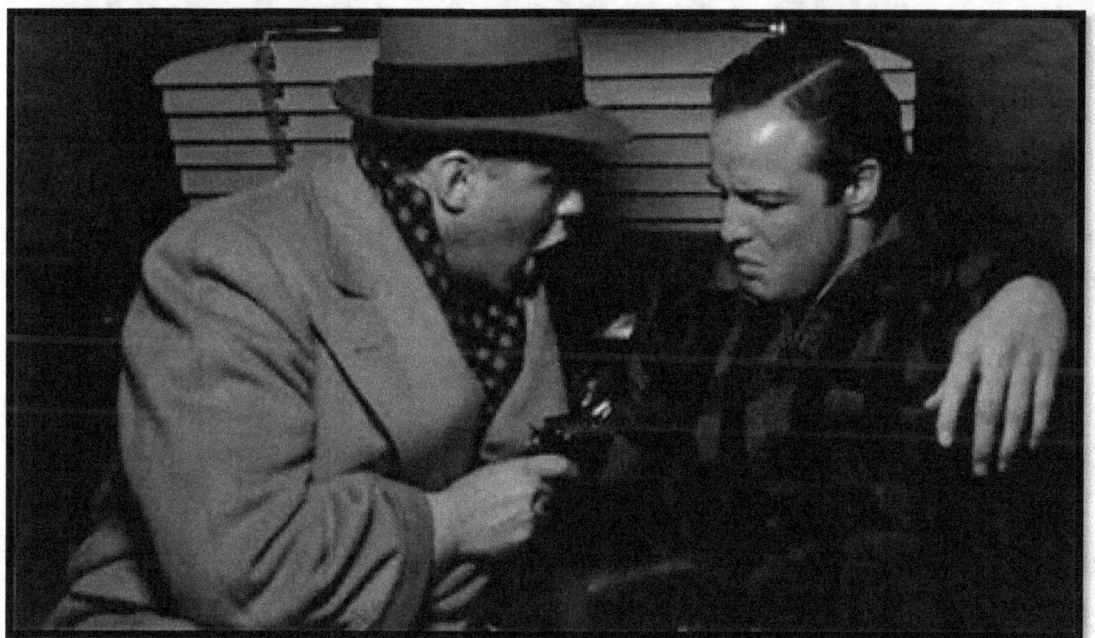

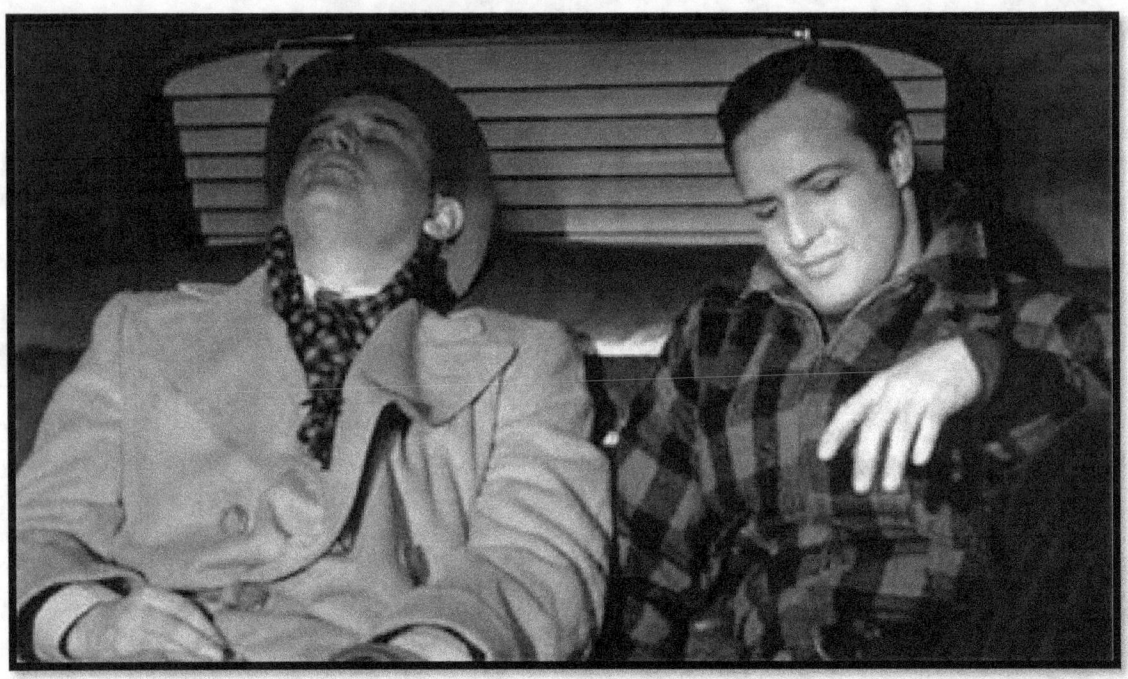

I insisted we all sit down together. Kazan agreed to set it up. I was living on a farm in Pennsylvania but I drove into the city for the meeting. But when I got to town I found it had been called off, a two-and-a-half hour drive. I drove in again next day. Same thing.

The meeting had been cancelled. I would return to my little bar-house on the farm and drown my frustration. After the third meeting fell through I asked my pal Kazan what was wrong. He told me the truth. Spiegel had bent himself in two to inveigle Brando into playing the role, he knew how protective I was about the script and he feared a face-off between Marlon and me might give Marlon an excuse for walking away.

So he went into production with me still seething and nothing resolved. A few days later we were up on the tenement roof shooting a scene when our script girl mentioned to me that Marlon had been complaining to her about the taxicab scene. I started to raise my voice and Kazan came over and asked me to be quiet. "At the lunch break let's go down in the kitchen (of the tenement flat we were using) and settle this damn thing." So there we were, just the three of us, no Spiegel, thank God, and Kazan said ``Okay, Marlon, let's have it. What the hell's wrong with the taxi scene you keep complaining about. We're getting ready to shoot it and you say it's not playable?"

"Look, `` Marlon said, ``I've got all that stuff to say to Rod about his being my brother and he shoulda have looked out for me, I've got a big speech there, I could have been a contender, I could have been somebody, well, you tell me how I can say all that if Rod's got a gun pointing at me?"

Kazan said, "Look, what if you just reach out and push the gun down, and then pick up the dialogue?"

"Oh, that will be fine," Marlon said. The scene proceeded as written. In the filmed version of the scene, Terry slowly brushes the gun aside and moans "Oh Charlie" with an echo of sadness that still reverberates today.

Adding to the scene was the cramped space of the back of the cab. Brando and Steiger were both large men, virtually unable to move their bodies in the seat and so they emphasized their emotional filled lines with a complete symphony of facial expressions with the implication that the two brothers know the end is near and are mourning the loss of the live between them. However, Terry suffers the most. He had nothing to start with and now the one dependable love in his life, his brother, has fallen away. One by one, Terry Malloy's childhood hero, are turning into weak little men.

At the end of that scene, once Terry is out of the cab, Charley barks at the driver "Take me to the Garden." The next several seconds are chilling, although almost overwhelmed by the musical score, when the driver pulls into a building garage and Charlie Malloy's killers are seen through a dimly lit window.

Nehemiah Persoff was a student in Kazan's classes at the Actors Studio. One day, Kazan came by and playfully griped Persoff in a headlock and told him "I have a scene for you" and told him to report to a CBS network owned studio on 58th and 9th Avenue, a place Persoff remembered had once been a Borden Milk factory.

Aside from that, all Kazan had told the young actor was that he would be paid the standard $75 for the scene. When he arrived, Steiger and Brando were finishing their scene in the back of the cab, but Persoff, who had never been on a movie set before was more interested in the camera work then the dialogue. When it was his turn to enter the scene, he would sit on a wooden milk cart in front of a fake steering wheel Kazan stuck his head into the window and whispered to Persoff about Steiger's character "He just murdered your mother"

The taxi scene brings the film to its turning point and establishes an acceptable balance between good versus evil. Prior to the scene Terry has already begun to change. The reoccurring reference throughout the film of "bum" as a motif is one of the motivating factors that push him to win his internal conflict with himself and the external conflict with those around him. From the very first scene of the movie, Terry fights the label of bum, in his case, establishing a small step towards self-respect and dignity. However, throughout most of the film he does not act as a man of self-respect. He acts like a bum, a spiritual bum. This changes permanently inside the taxi.

Up to this point, Terry is a loser, the forces of goodness are represented by Edie and Father Barry. The forces of darkness are found in Johnny Friendly and Terry and his brother hold the spiritual middle ground. Now that Terry has questioned his values and loyalties that he has decided not to be a bum, Charlie is forced to question his own values and loyalties. His decides on the side of brotherly loyalty. The choices that they, Charlie and Terry, make will directly affect both good and evil sides it will do away with the ambivalent middle ground in the film.

Their choices will change the oppressed and ambivalent dock workers propelling them to act against the mob (in effect, evil) Now it is clearly established that the Malloy's are no longer frozen in the middle as Johnny Friendly's pawns. Both understand that there will be consequences for their actions (Hence, Charlie hands Terry the pistol for protection)

The poignant message and magnificent performances in the emotionally charges taxi scene reminds the viewer that this is a benchmark film worthy of its praise and ranking. While the scene is a masterpiece of filmmaking and script writing however, Kazan was modest over the scene "The only thing I can take credit for in that scene" he said later "was being smart enough not to yell cut"

THE HUAC
Fall, 1950

"The closer a man approaches tragedy the more intense is his concentration of emotion upon the fixed point of his commitment, which is to say the closer he approaches what in life we call fanaticism" **Arthur Miller**

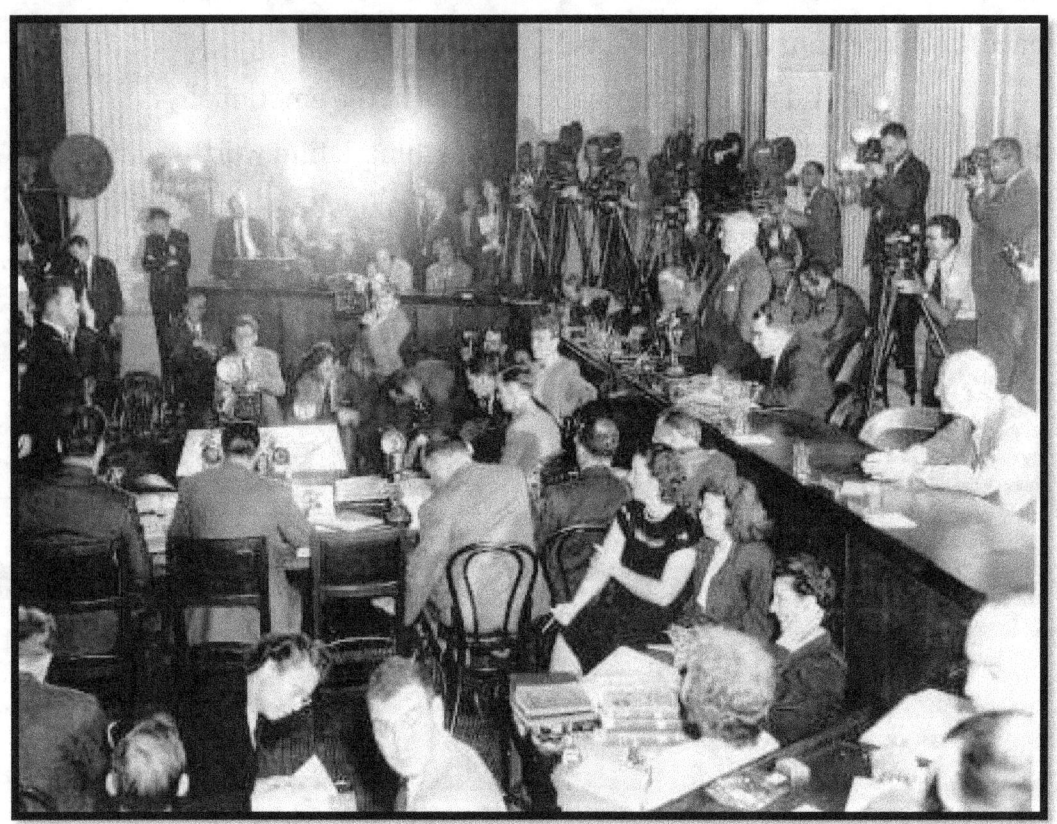

Washington's assault on Hollywood, in the form of the House Un-American Activities Committee (HUAC) and other weapons, was born out of the cold war which began, more or less, on March 12, 1947 when President Harry Truman, in keeping with the Truman Doctrine, requested $400 million in aid from Congress to combat communism in Greece and Turkey.

282

The doctrine was an answer to the growing power of the Russian Soviet Union, which had already spread out into Eastern Europe, followed by the June 1949, Chinese Communists victory over Chiang Kai-shek's Nationalist forces.

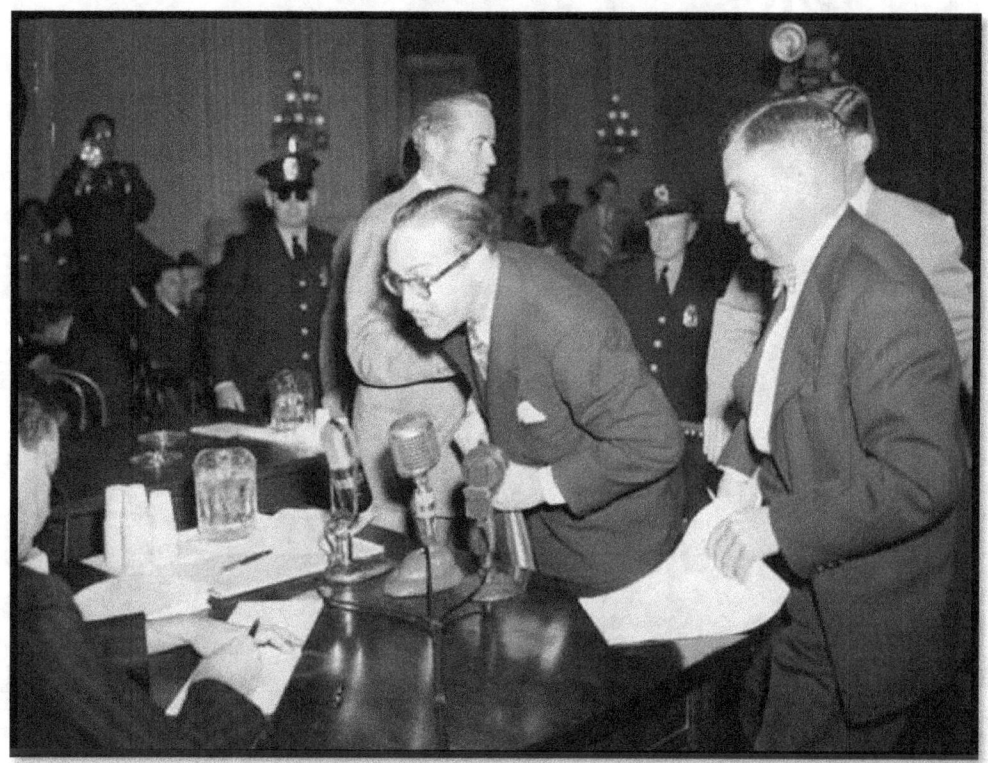

Writer Dalton Trumbo (leaning forward) at the hearings.

Two months later, while the world watched, Mao traveled to Moscow, where he negotiates the Sino-Soviet Treaty of Friendship and Alliance. A year later, on June 25, 1950, North Korean Communist forces, armed and trained by Mao's generals, crossed the 38th parallel and invaded democratic South Korea. Two days later, Truman ordered U.S. forces into South Korea to repel the attack.

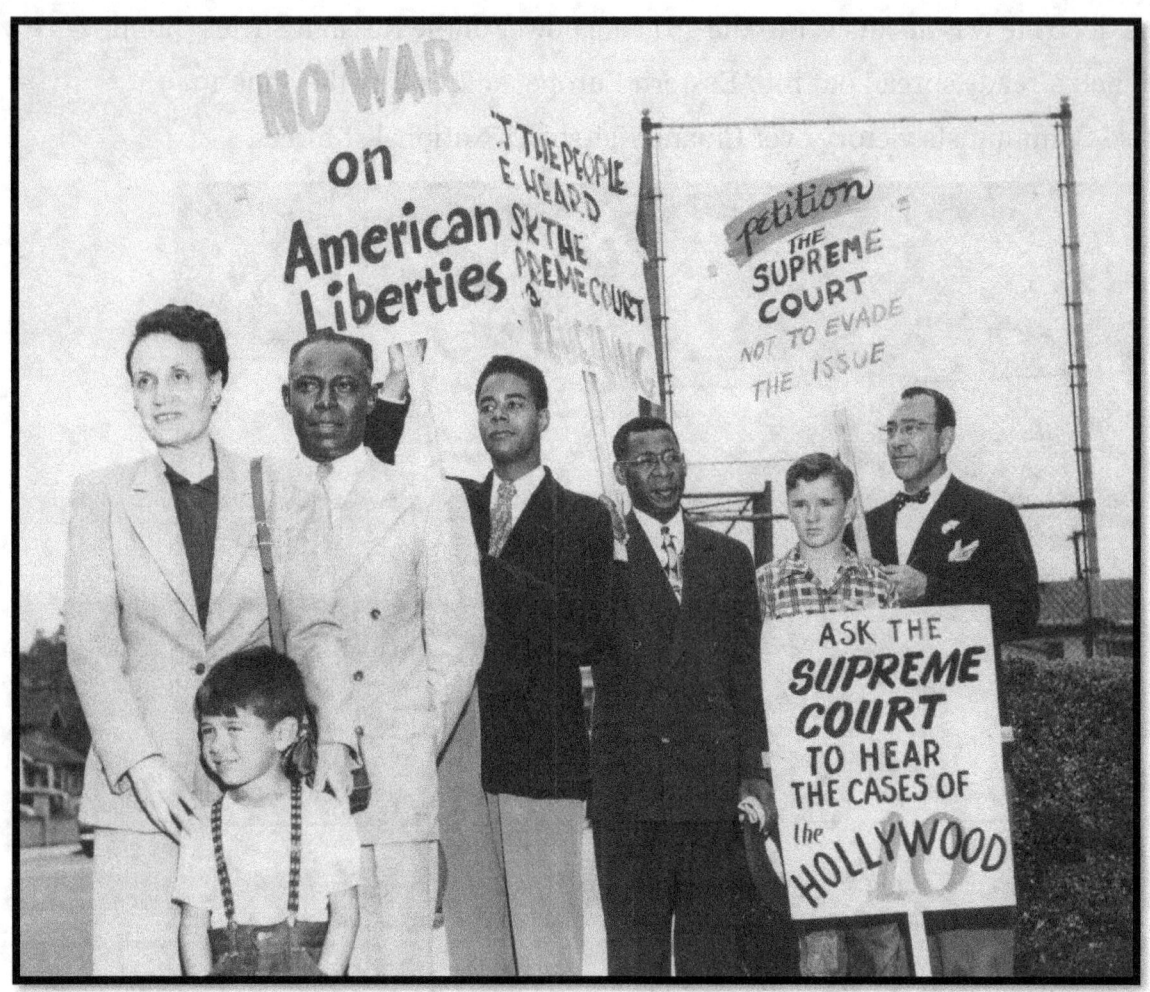

Within the United States, paranoia spread based in an absolute conviction that there was an enemy within the republic, that the Communists had established a firm foothold within the United States government and other circles of power, and were using that influence to erode democracy. Daily events, either by happenstance or unwittingly created through self-will, seemed to confirm the paranoia that thousands, perhaps tens of thousands, of Communist sleeper agents were active with the American boarders.

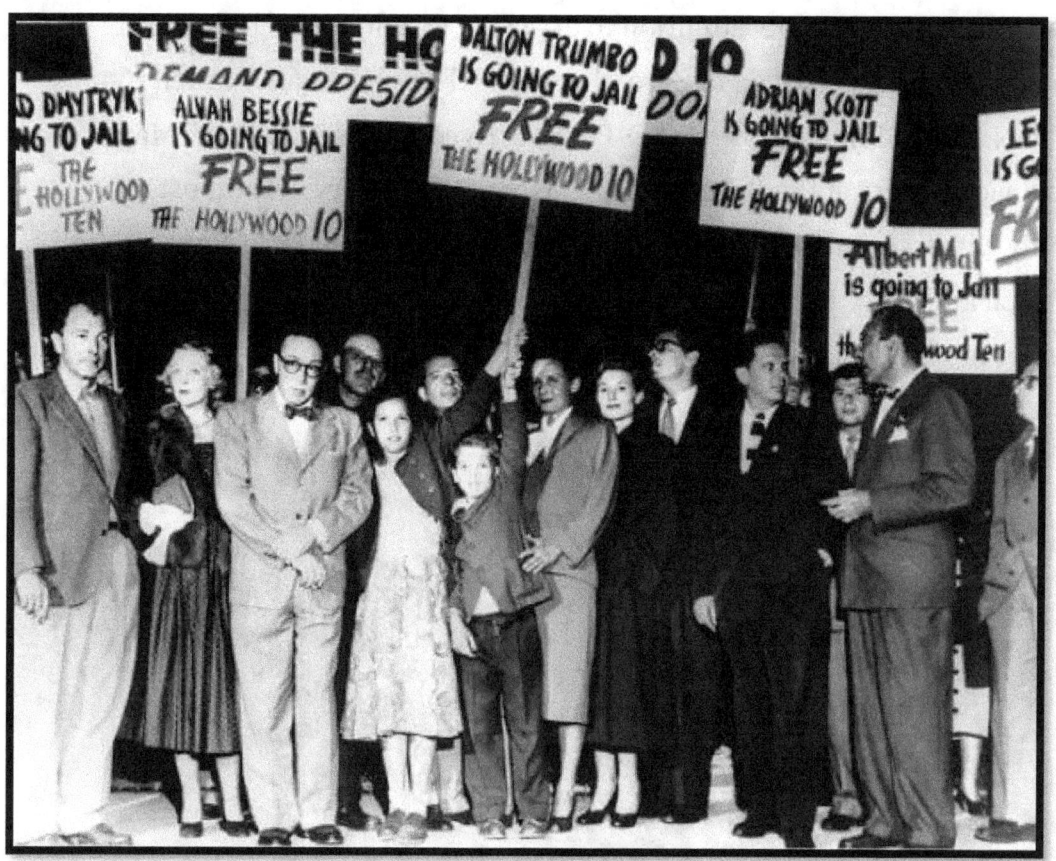

On November 1, 1952 the United States exploded the first hydrogen bomb at a test site in the Marshall Islands. This was followed, less than a year later; by the Soviets announce their first test of a hydrogen bomb. It was learned later that The secrets on the bombs preparation were passed along to the Russian by a 19 year old American Scientist. They had our bomb.

The devastation at Hiroshima was a recent memory for world They could end the world and its formula had been given to them by one of our own. There had to answers. To find them, Congress increased the investigative powers of the once virtually toothless Special Committee on Un-American Activities, the HUAC.

In 1947, the HUAC turned its attention to exposing Communists' influence in the movie industry. Amidst much fanfare, the new HUAC chairman, Parnell Thomas, (R-N.J) and John McDowell, (R-Penn) arrived in Los Angeles in May and set up headquarters at the Biltmore Hotel where they interviewed most of their friendly witnesses, mainly from the MPA and Studio head Jack Warner who identified each and every person on his studio's payroll he suspected of being a communist or of harboring left wing sympathies.

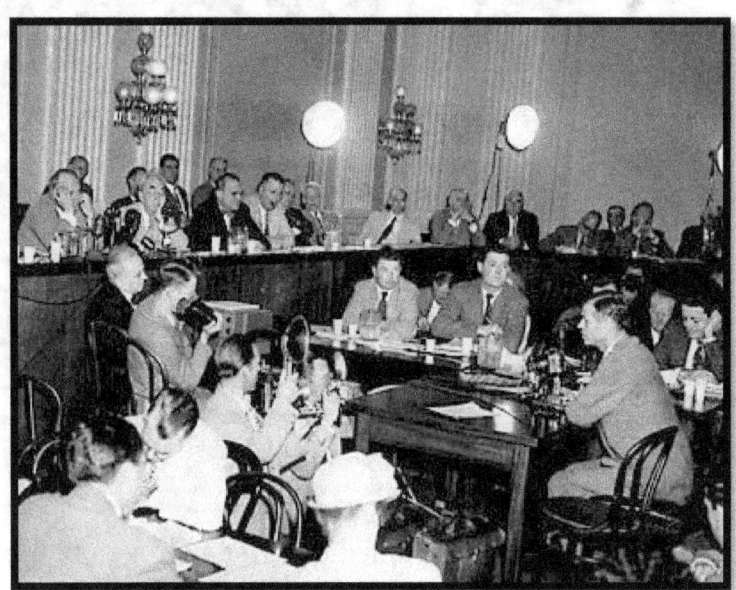

While it true that the HUAC also launched multiple investigations into Communist infiltration of organized labors, the Federal government, Hollywood was the focus of their main assault.

The industry had just released a series of films filled with liberal sentiment and the Film Noir style, then all the rage, had taken on a disparaging view of life under any system of government. Also, there was, it should be said, at least a modicum of factual substance to the committee's charges. But it really had nothing to do with Communists as much as it had to do with political opportunism and an assault on Liberalism. The cold warriors intended to set an example in Hollywood with HUAC and discourage any moves by Hollywood to make films advocating social change at home or critical of foreign policy.

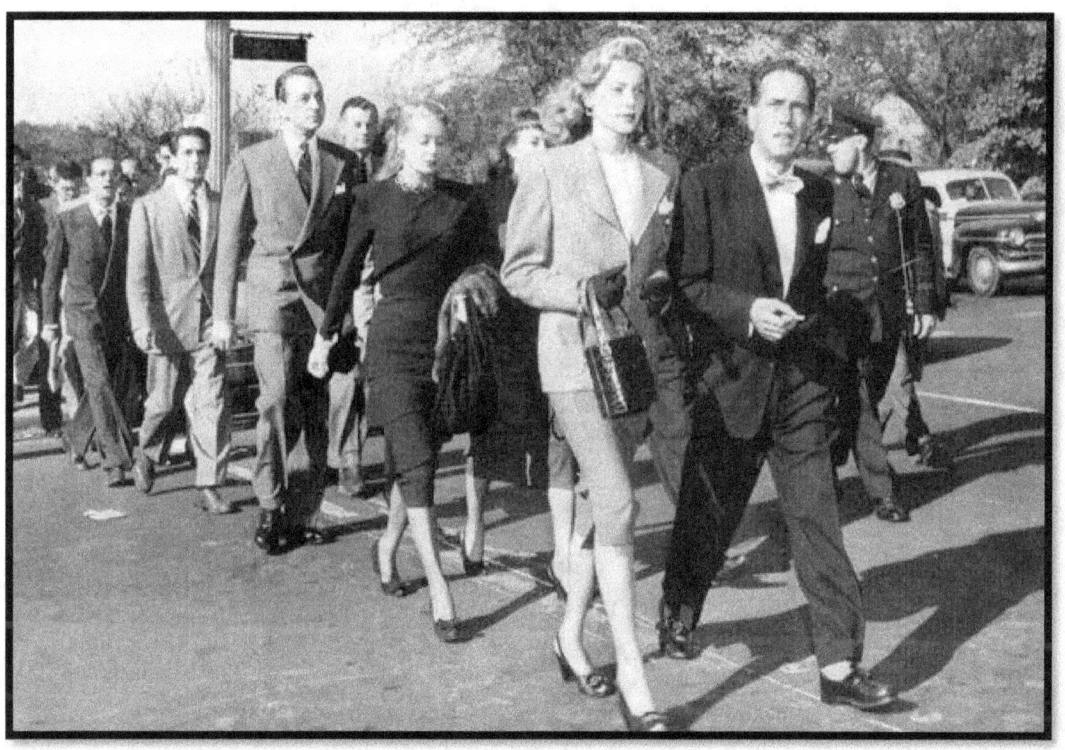

Actor march on the Congress to protest the HUAC investigations

The HUAC's operating theory was that Communists had established a significant base in Hollywood and were using that foothold to place subversive messages into films, discriminating against those who in the industry who opposed them and were placing negative images of the United States in films that would have wide international distribution.

It was a good theory, but it simply wasn't based in any fact or reality. At the time, Hollywood was, and had been since its start, an industry controlled from top to bottom by a handful of hard-nosed businessmen who ran the industry as a Money making entertainment outlet and nothing else. Most, like, Darryl Zanuck, were involved with every step of the film making processes, from beginning to end.

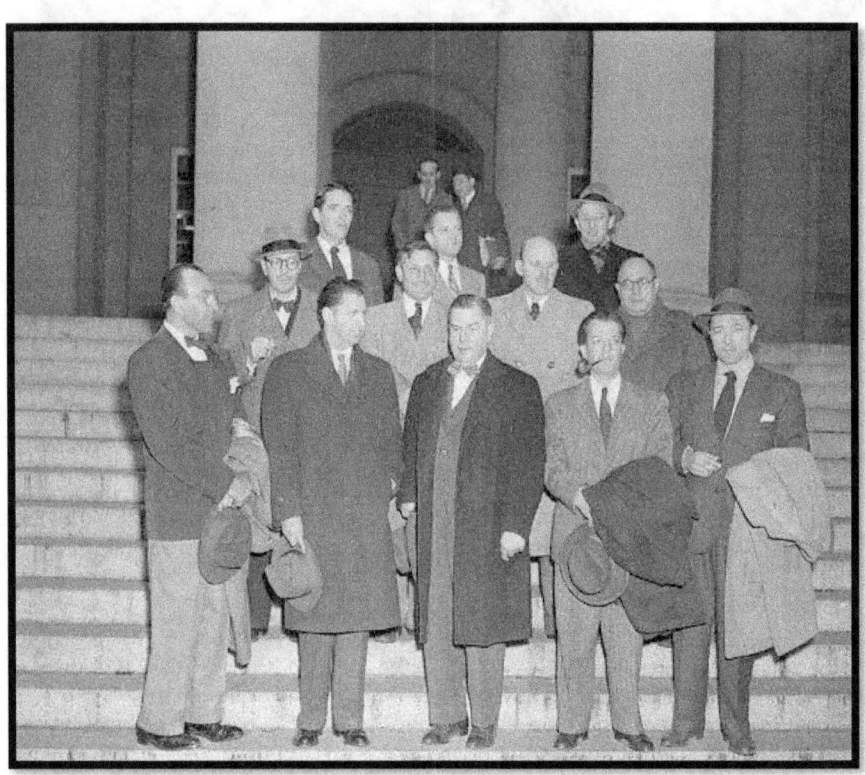

The Hollywood Ten

The fact was that the studios fell clearly on the side of the US Government in terms of creating propaganda for the world to see. But films and propaganda weren't really what the committee was after. In reality, its primary target was the ultra-liberal Screen Writers Guild, founded only in 13 years before in 1933. John Howard Lawson - later one of the Hollywood Ten - was the leader of the guild.

Although he denied being an active communist at the time (He didn't deny that he had been one in the past) he was certainly a leftist, as were a great many other unions and union members of the period (including a young Jimmy Hoffa) And although they left wing, they were not necessarily communists.

What the Committee wanted to prove, in fact, needed to prove, was that "card-carrying party members dominated the Screen Writers Guild, that Communists had succeeded in introducing subversive propaganda into motion pictures, and that President Roosevelt had brought improper pressure to bear upon the industry to produce pro-Soviet films during the war."

While it was certainly true that Hollywood in general and the Writers Guild in particular, held more than the national average of members of the Communist party, the bulk were inactive members. Regardless, they were within their rights to be members of whatever political party they so choose. Many had joined the party as part of a lofty and well-meaning set of ideals, especially those who came to adulthood during the great depression as an answer to the increasing economic inequity in the nation. But most, put off by the party's iron fisted rule, son became disenchanted and moved along to other beliefs.

The HUAC didn't care about lost ideals and disenchanted dreams. Hollywood, even Hollywood scriptwriters, caught the public's attention and kept the public's attention. Hollywood was good for the business of red hunting.

"Don't look for any so-called corrective legislation to result from the forthcoming Un-American Activities Committee investigation of Communism in Hollywood" Newsweek Magazine wrote on September 15, 1947 "Primarily the committee is fishing for headlines. By citing specific examples of Communist influences in movie scripts, the group hopes to alert the public to them."

For Arthur Miller, the hearings were "The inquisition." for Ellen Schrecker they were "a symbolic ritual". Victor Navasky more aptly described them as "degradation ceremonies."

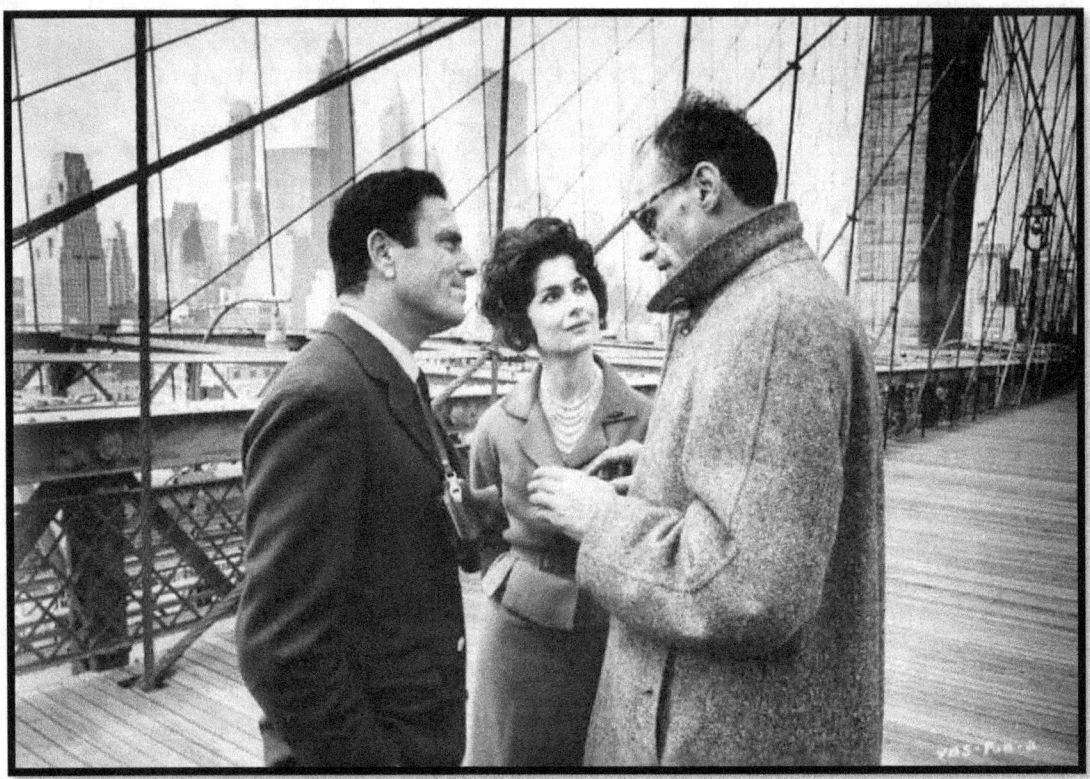

Miller, far right on the scene of *A View from the Bridge*

Not that the committee needed the hearings, in almost every case, they already had the names that they demanded. The Committee, run by the ultra-right wing, was determined to find Communists in Hollywood and to punish them, or, at the least, make an example of them.

While those who refused to testify before the Committee were punished by banishment, financial and professional ruin, (or some by suicide) for those who did testify the punishment was no less severe. Such was the case of *Waterfront's* future star, Lee J. Cobb.

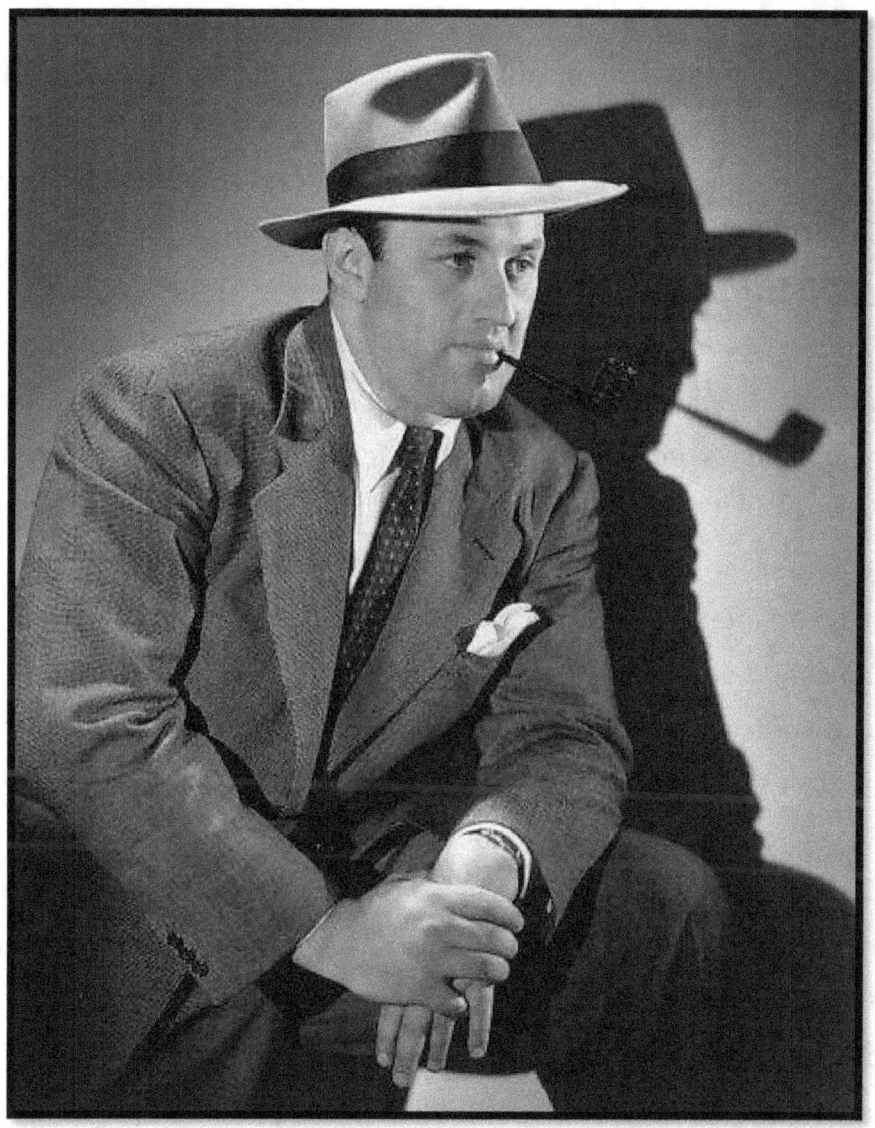

Lee J. Cobb

Cobb joined the Group Theater in 1935 where he appeared with Elia Kazan in the highly successful Clifford Odets play, *Waiting for Lefty*. Success came in

1947, when Henry Miller chose him to play the lead role of Willy Loman in *Death of a Salesman*, directed by Elia Kazan. That was followed up by his highly acclaimed work on the 1948 classic, *Call Northside 777*. By the start of the 1950's, Cobb was headed towards the height of his career. Then he was named as a communist at the HUAC hearings and called in to give his testimony. After refusing for two years to appear before the committee, on June 23, 1953, not only did he appear secretly before the HUAC, but also named names, some twenty in all. Cobb recalled: *The HUAC did a deal with me. I was pretty much worn down. I had no money. I could not borrow. I had the expenses of taking care of the children. Why am I subjecting my loved ones to this? If it's worth dying for, and I am just as idealistic as the next fellow. But I decided it wasn't worth dying for, and if this gesture were the way of getting out of the penitentiary, I'd do it. I had to be employable again. When the facilities of the government of the United States are drawn on an individual, it can be terrifying. The blacklist is just the opening gambit - being deprived of work. Your passport is confiscated. That's minor. But not being able to move without being tailed is something else. After a certain point, it grows to implied as well as articulated threats, and people succumb. My wife did, and she was institutionalized.*

The rumor around town was that Cobb had paid the HUAC twenty-five thousand dollars, through his lawyer Martin Gang, to keep his testimony a secret. If he did pay the money, it was pointless, the committee released the text anyway and the results on Cobb were devastating. Renowned for his insecurities and vanity, he had few friends in Hollywood. When his testimony became public, what few friends he did have in the industry abandoned him. His wife left him and work stopped coming his way. He was trying to support himself and his two children "On thin air and a dream" He considered filing for bankruptcy "I was in" he said "a low mental state" Waterfront would be his saving role.

KAZAN AND SCHULBEG BEFORE THE HUAC
Winter, 1952

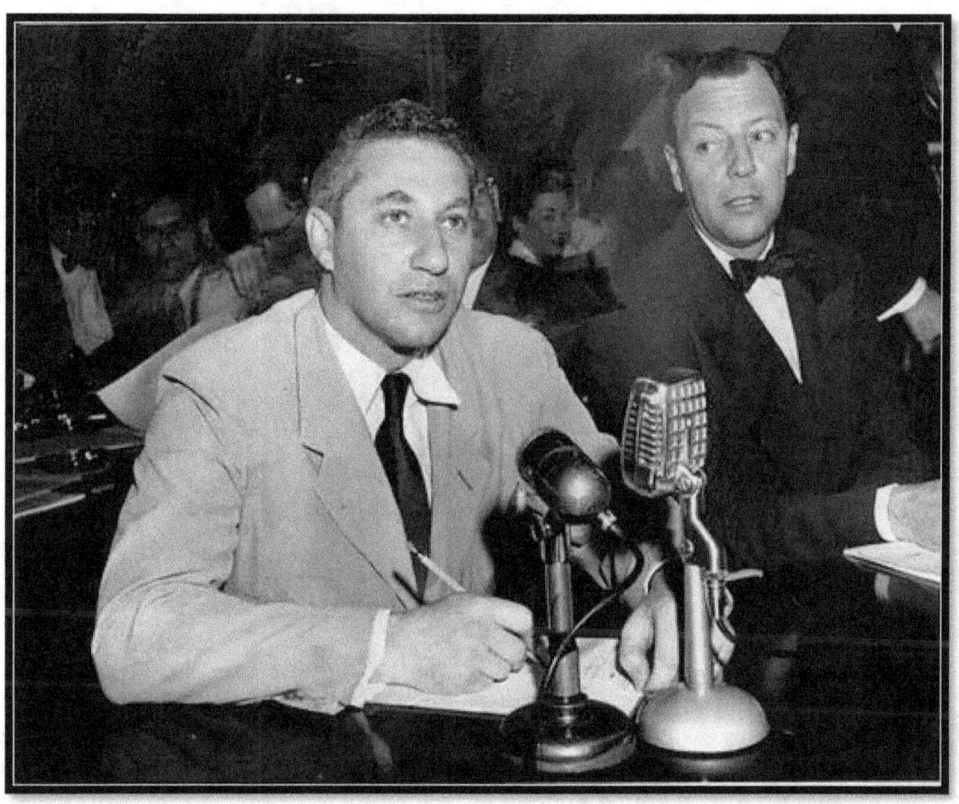

"...in the final tally we were all victims...None of us-right, left, or center, emerged from that long nightmare without sin." **Dalton Trumbo**

"Is it possible to succeed without an act of betrayal?" **Jean Renoir**

As expected, the HUAC subpoenaed Kazan to testify about his background as an active member of the Communist Party. Some in Hollywood suspected that the egotistical Kazan testified to get even for old slights, real or imagined, mostly from the Group Theatre crowd who now populated Hollywood, because they refused to recognize him as a great artist. Others, like Walter Bernstein guessed that Kazan cooperated because of his need to fit into main line Wasp society.

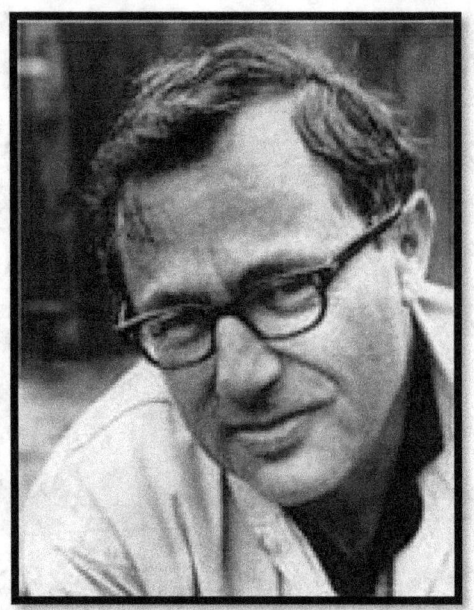

Bernstein

"The fact that his wife was a Protestant with three last names tells us something. He was insecure about his entrance into American proper society. Refusing to testify would amount to another instance of being cut off, or cutting himself off, making himself rejected, lumping himself willingly with the undesirables. Not to do that was of primary importance to him. Gadge (Kazan's nickname) was not in that sense a rebel at all and he never had been"

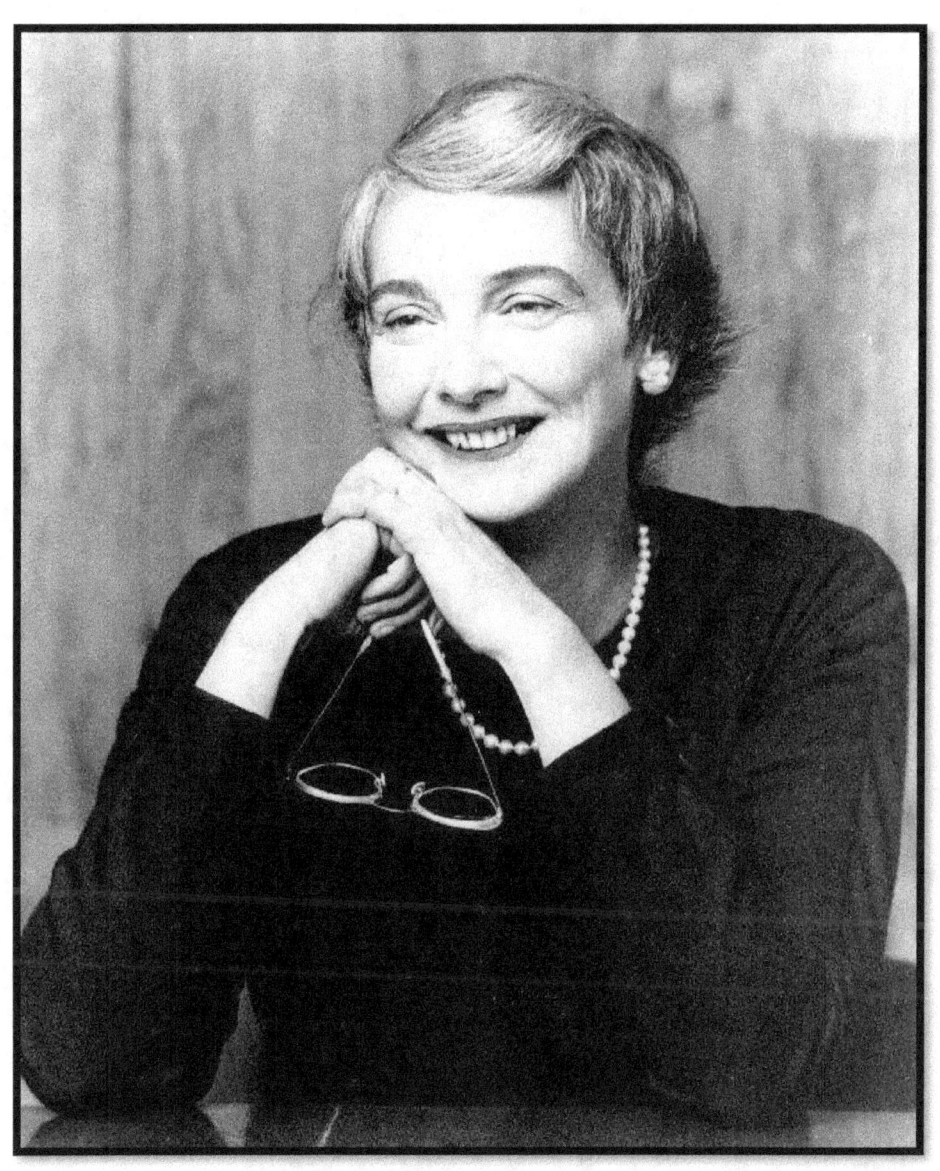

Molly Kazan, Elia's wife.

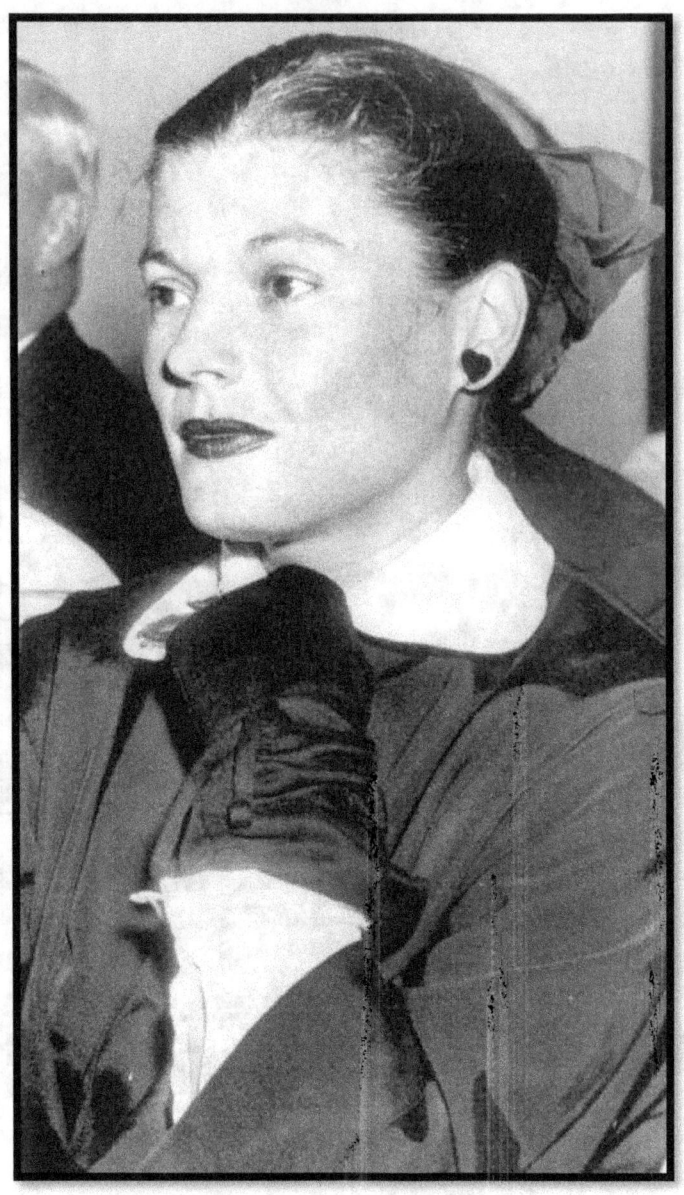

Jigee Schulberg watches her husband testify

Years later, when Hollywood elite went up in arms over Kazan receiving the Lifetime Achievement Award, Rod Steiger made the absurd statement that he when he accepted the role, and all during shooting, that he wasn't aware of the director cooperation with HUAC. "It was like I found out my father was sleeping with my sister", he said. "What he (Kazan) did was despicable. It wasn't like a man got into a position where he couldn't pay the rent, feed his family, he just panicked. He was already a millionaire in the theatre, he didn't need to do another film again, he named names just because he wanted to do movies, and that's that"

In all fairness, Kazan had good reason to be concerned. Between March 1947 and December 1952, some 6.6 million-government employees were investigated and collected background data on 60,000 citizens, which it then turned over to their employers.

At least 15,000 federal employees were fired or forced to resign by government loyalty boards. Approximately 20 percent of the working population had to take an oath or receive clearance as a condition of employment.

One hundred and ten men and women were subpoenaed during the second set of HUAC hearings from 1951 to 1953; fifty-eight turned informer. Thirty-one of them were prominent in Hollywood and had at least four film credits to their names. Those thirty-one persons gave the HUAC an average of 29 names to the committee.

To hesitate in cooperating was to ends one's career. Actor Larry Parks, the first Hollywood witness reduced himself nearly too groveling and pleading in face of the committee's demand for names. He identified 10 individuals. Still he paid a high price for his hesitation. The morning after his testimony, the headline in the Los Angeles Examiner screamed, "Parks loses $75,000 screen role" His career was over. Parks testimony was intended to be a lesson to all others who refused to cooperate.

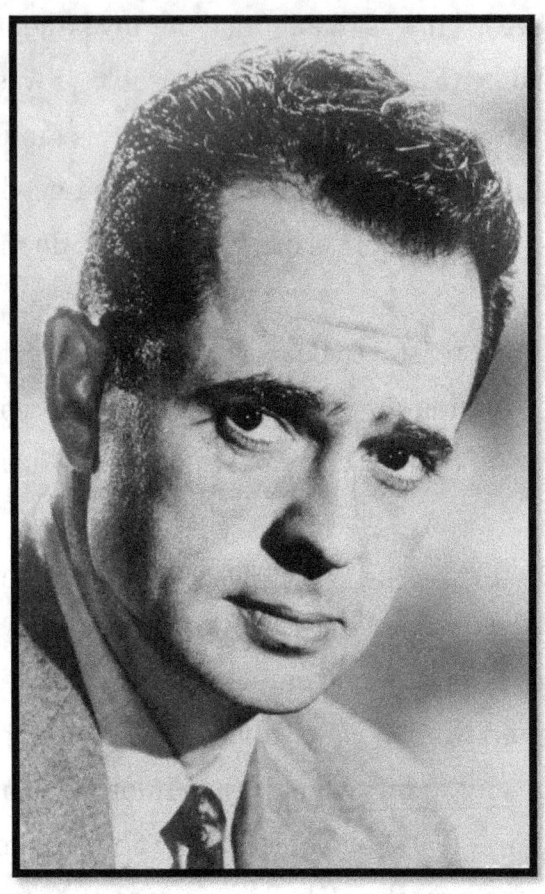

Parks

When Kazan appeared before the House committee on January 14, 1952, he told the committee investigator Raphael Nixon that he would "cooperate in every way about myself but would not discuss others."

Nixon did not pressure Kazan to name names merely advised him "to reconsider whether I wanted to withhold names from the committee." During the hearing, Kazan still refused to name names. This meant that he would be called back - and next time it would be a public session, a degradation ceremony as it was called.

Over the next few months, Kazan was a tormented soul. He felt sick, he could not sleep and he was edgy. He had convinced himself that he would not be a cooperative witness, telling his analyst that he was willing to give up filmmaking, and go back to working at the theater, since he would undoubtedly lose his job if he did not name names. On the other hand, he had become a fervent anti-Communist and believed that the Communist Party was a thoroughly organized, worldwide conspiracy. So he cooperated.

Kazan had enormous stature as an artist and intellectual. His decision to collaborate with the witch-hunters had far-reaching consequences. One director-victim told Victor Navasky, for his book *Naming Names*,

"If Kazan had refused to cooperate ... he couldn't have derailed the Committee, but he might well have broken the blacklist. He was too important to be ignored. Probably no single individual could have broken the blacklist in April 1952, and yet no person was in a better strategic position to try than Kazan, by virtue of his prestige and economic invulnerability, to mount a symbolic campaign against it, and by this example inspire hundreds of fence sitters to come over to the opposition." ....maybe.

He did the pragmatic thing. Every major studio, which in those days had a virtual lock on financing and distributing films, every major film union and most of the big name stars, stood against the Communists. Kazan was a director. He knew no other line of work. He decided to name names. However, every one of the Communists Kazan named had already been identified as a Communist by other witnesses. None of the people he named worked in the film industry. They were theater professionals in New York. Kazan's testimony destroyed no Hollywood careers.

If he did not cooperate, at the least his career was over, at the most he would go jail. He doubted that any of his "Comrades," as he sarcastically called them, would have done the same for him, if the roles had been reversed and decided, "I would give up my film career if it was in the interests of defending something I believed in but not this."

Kazan denied that he testified for the money but rather that he made his decision based on personnel experiences. However, Lillian Hellman, a questionable source at best (Hellman, who also appeared before the committee but refused to answer questions. She would later called Kazan a scoundrel and a man who lacked the courage to stand up for what she called "the right of each man to his own convictions." claimed that Kazan told her, "I earned over $400,000 last year from theater. But [Twentieth Century-Fox president Spyros] Skouras says I'll never make another movie [if I don't cooperate]."

In addition, he later told Theater producer Kermit Bloomgarden that Skouras and J Edgar Hoover had pressured him to give names 'I've got to think of my kids.' Kazan told Bloomgarden who claims to have retorted 'This too shall pass, and then you'll be an informer in the eyes of your kids, think of that.'" Bloomgarden was correct.

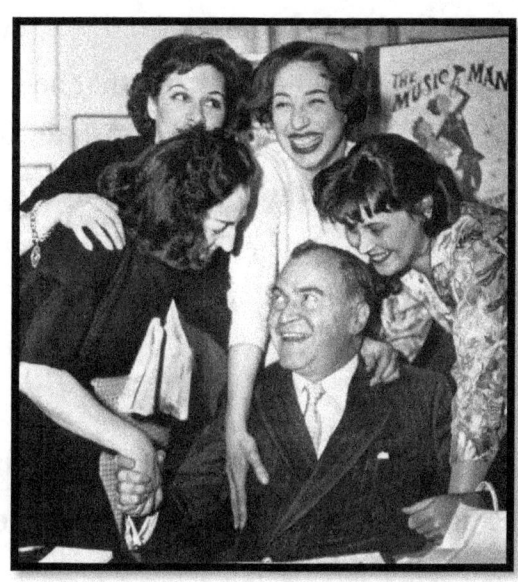

Bloomgarden

In 2004, Kazan's son, Nicholas, refused an offer from Schulberg to attend a fiftieth anniversary tribute to Waterfront in Hoboken where it was filmed. The son wished to have no part of his father's legacy as a man who cooperated with the HUAC and that it would be too painful for him to attend.

Instead, Kazan insisted that he testified out of conscience, not self-interest, doing the right thing, he said, motivated him to speak before the Committee. Waterfront's scene of Terry Malloy standing alone before a government body to betray his former friends and colleagues is framed in the same way; he does it because of his conscience, which insists that he must do this thing, no matter how it makes him look to others. One would have to be naïve to ignore the obvious connection and Kazan's statement, consciously or subconsciously, in defense of his actions.

When he returned to the studio, people ignored him, they crossed the street to avoid meeting him, he got crank phone calls and he got hate mail. He worried, constantly, over what he done. The backlash on Kazan from Hollywood was severe. It was not only that Kazan had named names, but that he had made a complete break from the pack, he condemned American communists, said they were part of a conspiracy, were dangerous to the American way of life. It had made his case eloquently and with passion and he would live to pay for it.

*****

Schulberg also had his own story to tell about the HUAC although his testimony before the committee did not seem to have the lifelong negative effect on him as it did on Kazan.

Like Kazan, Schulberg had been branded as a Red to the HUAC by his enemies in Hollywood. They had both been active members of the party in their youth. In 1934, Budd Schulberg and childhood friend Maurice Rapf joined a group of other Dartmouth Students for a three-month summer trip to the Soviet Union, sponsored by the Communist National Student League. The boys returned to the states, their heads shaven to rid them of the lice they had caught on the trip, and hailed the Communist system as the way of the future.

The HUAC never subpoenaed Schulberg, but knowing that informers had already given his name as a member of the Communist party, Schulberg contacted the HUAC and notified them that he would appear on his own, sending a telegram to the HUAC.

"I have noted" his telegram read "the public statement of your committee inviting those named in recent testimony to appear before your committee. My recollection of my communist affiliation is that it was approximately from 1937 to 1940. My opposition to communists and Soviet dictatorship is a matter of record. I will co-operate with you in any way I can".

On May 23, 1951, the HUAC took Schulberg up on his offer. A few days before he appeared before the committee Schulberg had his Paul Moss call Schulberg's childhood friend and college roommate writer Maurice Rapf.

"I'm calling on behalf of BWS" Moss said referring to Schulberg by his initials because he was positive that either Schulberg, his or Rapf's lines were bugged by the FBI.

"He's going to testify tomorrow" Moss continued "and he wants you to know he's going to do everything in his power to avoid implicating you" and then added that he would also not name a mutual friend, a professor at Dartmouth. Schulberg testified that he had been a member of the Communist Party from 1937 through 1939, that it had been a youthful indiscretion and that he had left the party because he "did not like the way its members tried to tell him how to write my books."

When asked to name names of communists in Hollywood, Schulberg named fifteen people: "They had all been named - there wasn't much new I could add. I expressed doubts [about naming names] - it would be inhuman not to. However, I truly felt the Communist Party was a menace. It was hard for me to see myself doing anything to help the Communist Party."

Schulberg testified that he was introduced into the party by Ring Lardner Jr. Lardner insisted it was the other way around and never forgave Schulberg for telling that to the committee.

The HUAC wasn't at all satisfied with Schulberg's testimony. They brought up the fact that Schulberg had been the leader of a committee that had attacked the HUAC. Did he still think that the HUAC was wrong in what it was doing, they asked Schulberg, who successfully danced around the question.

Unlike Kazan and Cobb, Schulberg never had any regrets over his actions . "First, you argue inside yourself." he recalled "Second, you go out of the

Party...Third, you realize you have not been true to yourself.... he would not be true to himself if he did not speak out on something he thought was a scourge." As for those who held him in contempt, especially toward the playwright Lillian Hellman. "She would excuse any cruelty done by the Russian government, in the name of Communism. They question our talking. I question their silence. There were premature anti-fascists but there were also premature anti-Stalinists."

"These people (those he named), if they had it in them, could have written books and plays. There was not a blacklist in publishing. There was not a blacklist in the theatre. They could have written about the forces that drove them into the Communist Party. They were practically nothing written. Nor have I seen these people interested in social problems in the decades since. They're interested in their own problems and in the protection of the Party."

It didn't matter what he thought of Hellman or anyone else. As far as Hollywood was concerned, he was out. He was shunned by the Hollywood left and became a pariah to their admirers. According to Maurice Rapf, Schulberg's father encouraged him to testify to clear the family name "He was talked into it and he did" Rapf said "Just like Kazan" and that the Dartmouth faculty, where Schulberg had been a favored son, "was horrified by his testimony"

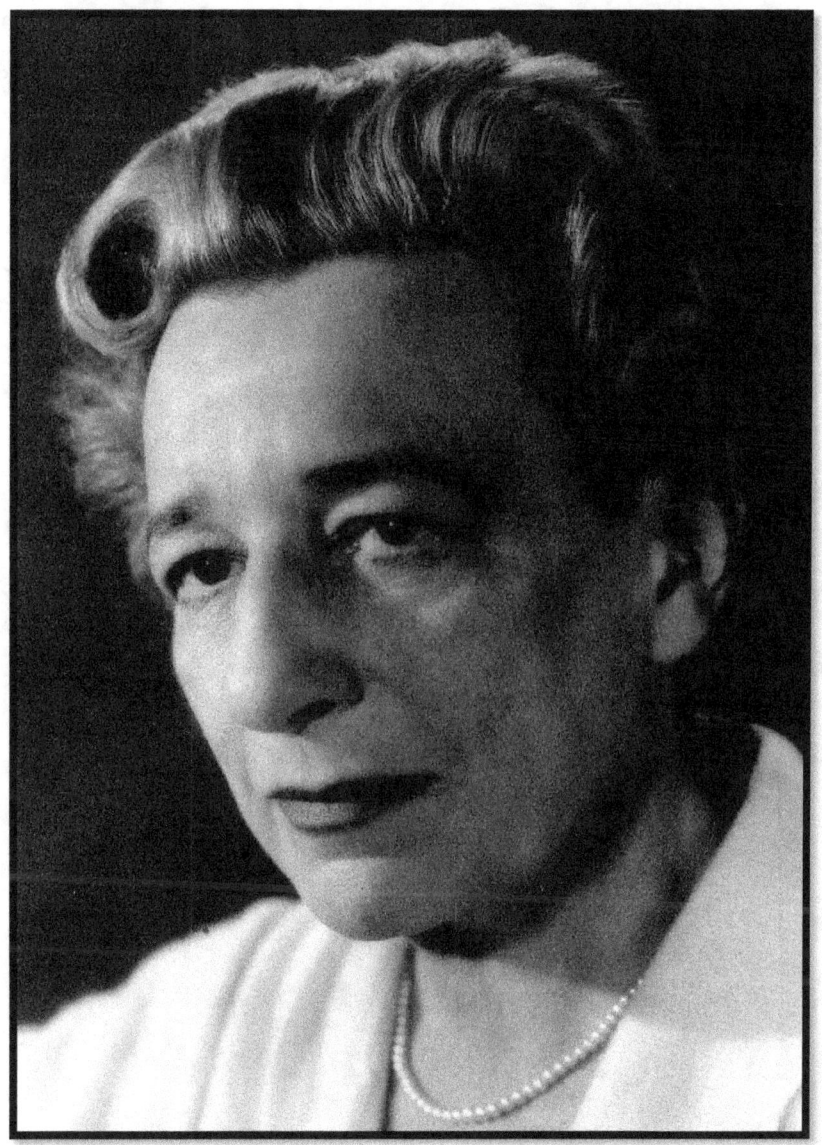

Hellman: She would excuse any cruelty done by the Russian government, in the name of Communism.

As far as Hollywood's social set was concerned, he was out. He was shunned by the Hollywood left and became a pariah to their admirers. However, the effect was not the same on Schulberg as it was on Kazan or Cobb, largely because he truly and sincerely did not care what the film community thought of him. Born and raised into the studio system he had watched as that same system used his father, one of its creators and founders, and then spit him out.

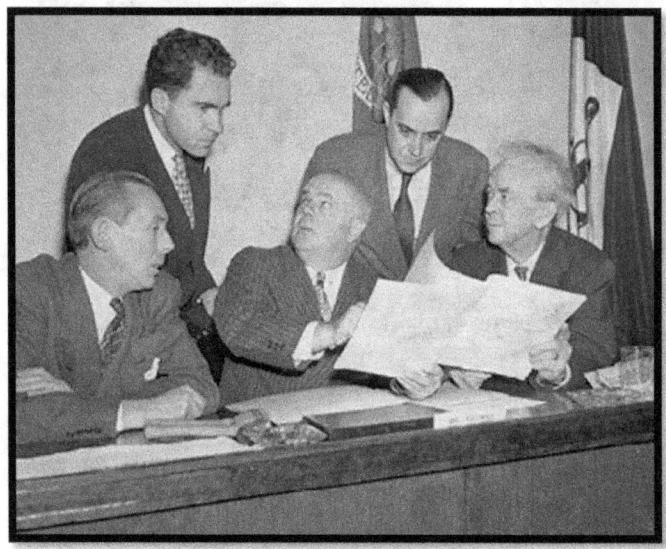

The HUAC

THE FILM AS AN ALLEGORY FOR THE HUAC

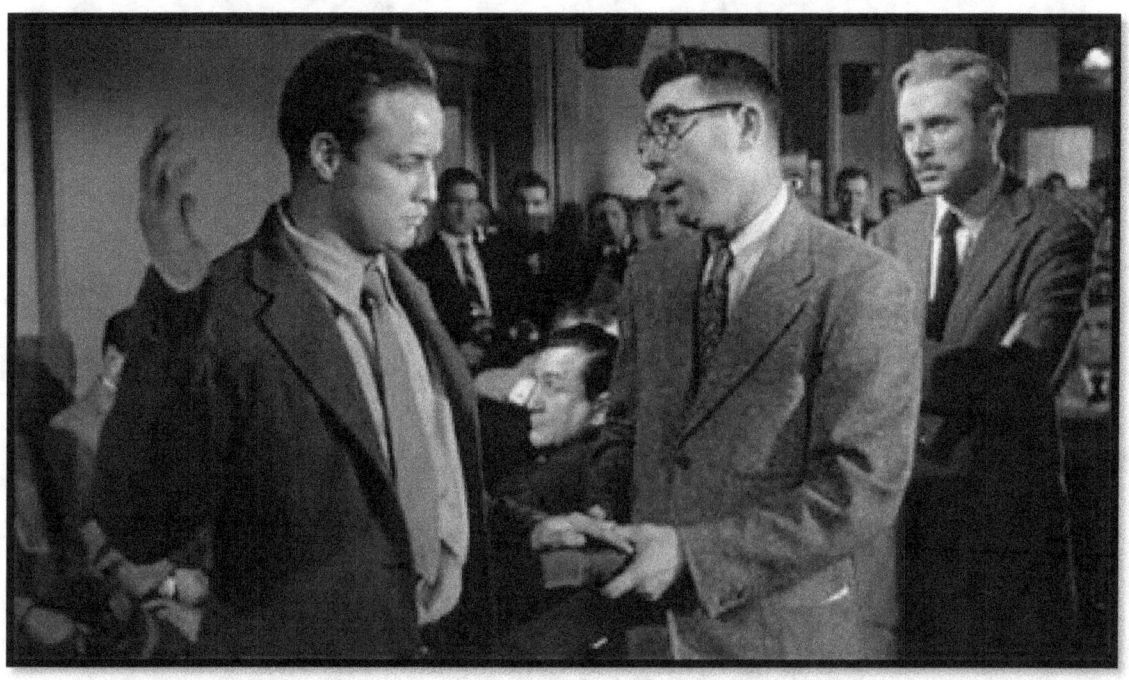

"When critics say that I put my story and my feelings onto the screen, to justify my informing, they are right." **Kazan.**

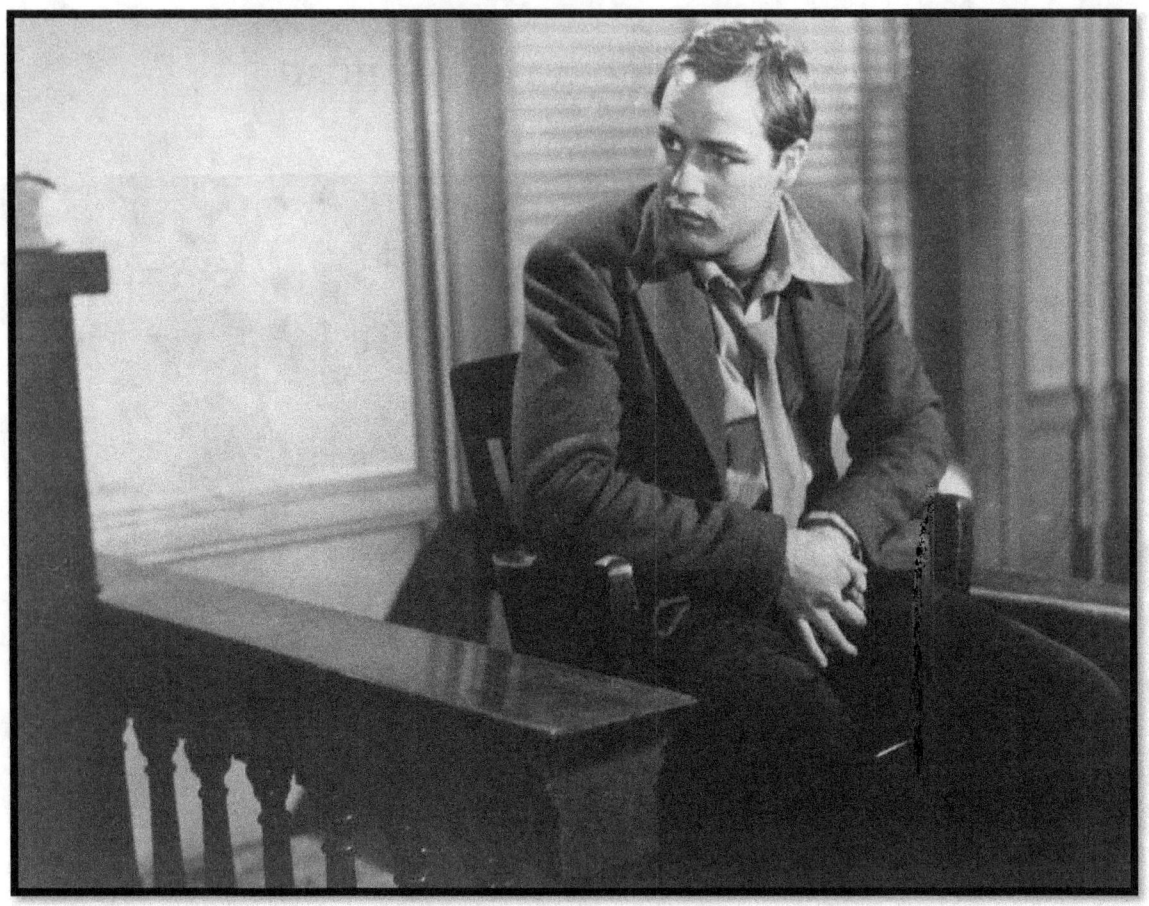

Kazan testified with defiance and attacked his past commitment to the communist cause with a vengeance. He never apologized for his actions unlike others who cooperated and later explained that they had only done so to save their careers. Acceptably repentant, they were allowed by their peers, begrudgingly, back into the Hollywood fold.

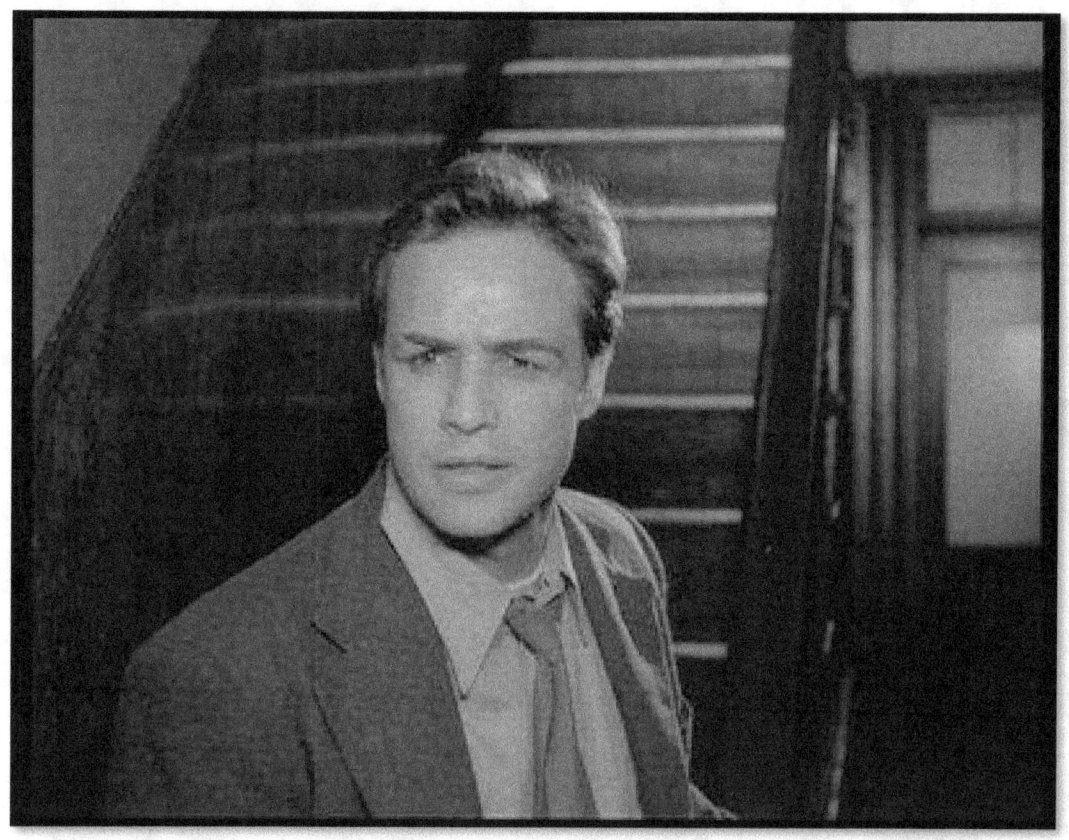

Kazan was not only unrepentant for his testimony he took out a full-page ad in the *New York Times* urging others to follow his lead thereby insisting not only in the rightness of his beliefs for himself but for everyone else.

That clear cut steadfastness to an ideal of complete righteousness in ones cause and an unwavering commitment to absolute individualism, is not only shown in Waterfront, it is the backbone message of the film.

To see the allegory as little more than Kazan's need to justify his actions is to lose the point that art has every right to be a political and social power. That we may agree or disagree with a particular social or political message in one work does not make the message right or wrong but it does fulfill the artists intent; to bring the viewer to question long held truths, to inspire debate. In this, Kazan fulfilled his obligation as an extraordinarily gifted artist.

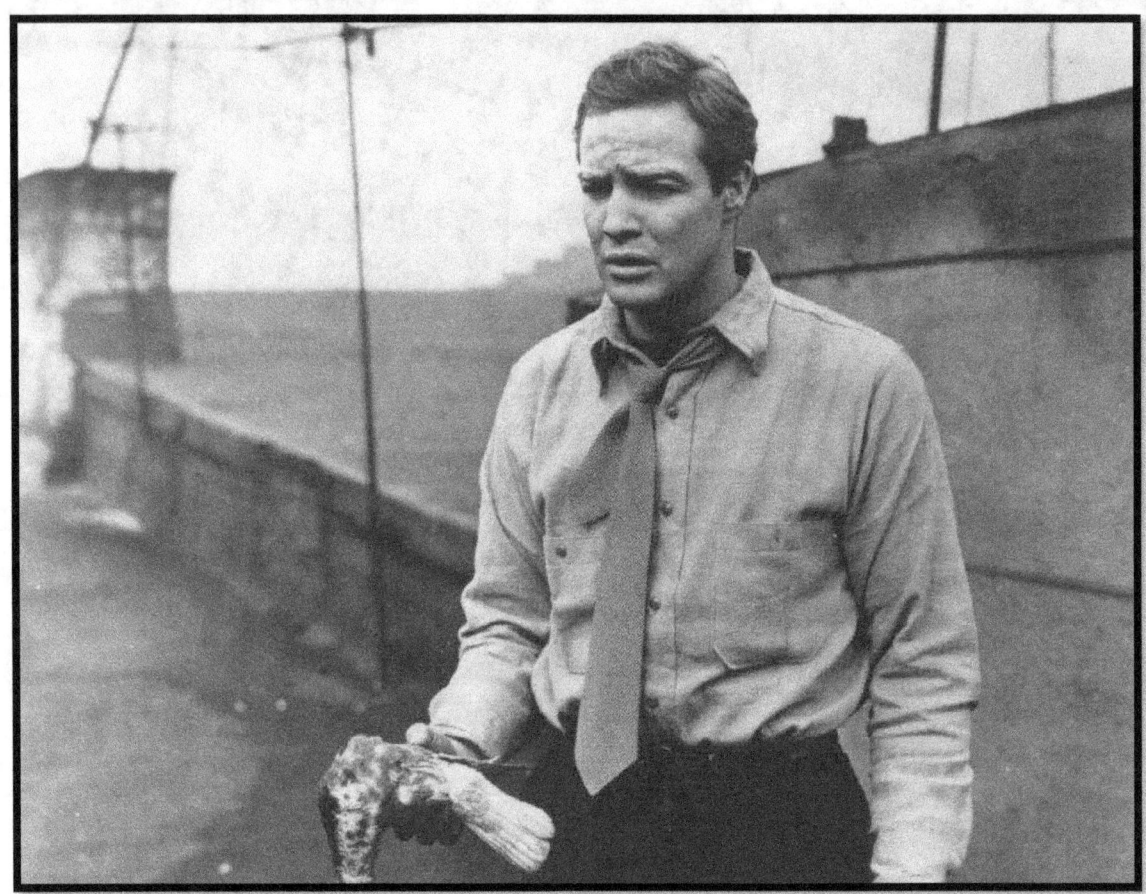

The question of whether the script for Waterfront and the eventual film Schulberg and Kazan produced was an allegory for the McCarthy era, has become a favorite topic for film students across the generations, since, clearly, Waterfront represented for Kazan an opportunity to exorcise, by proxy, his personal demons. Kazan never denied that the film is intended to justify his testimony to the House Un-American Activities Committee (HUAAC) never denying his intention to strike back at those who had ostracized him in the aftermath of his testimony. At the time Schulberg, despite the mountain of evidence to the contrary, has always denied the allegory. Both men are correct in their beliefs.

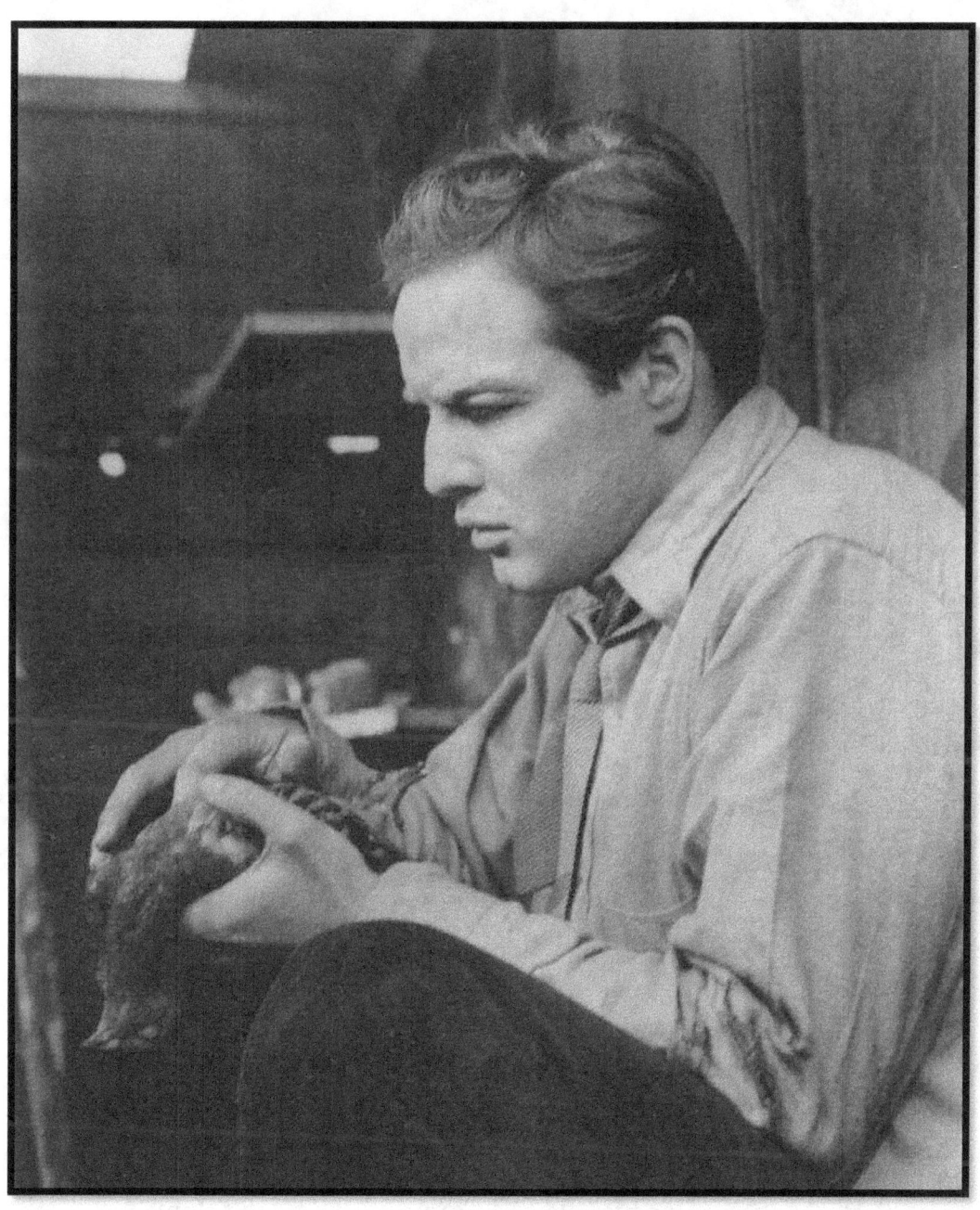

Kazan used Schulberg's literate, well-constructed screenplay Brando's empathetic performance, cinematic languages of editing, camera work, and performance as a blue print to convince the viewer of the rightness of Terry's actions.

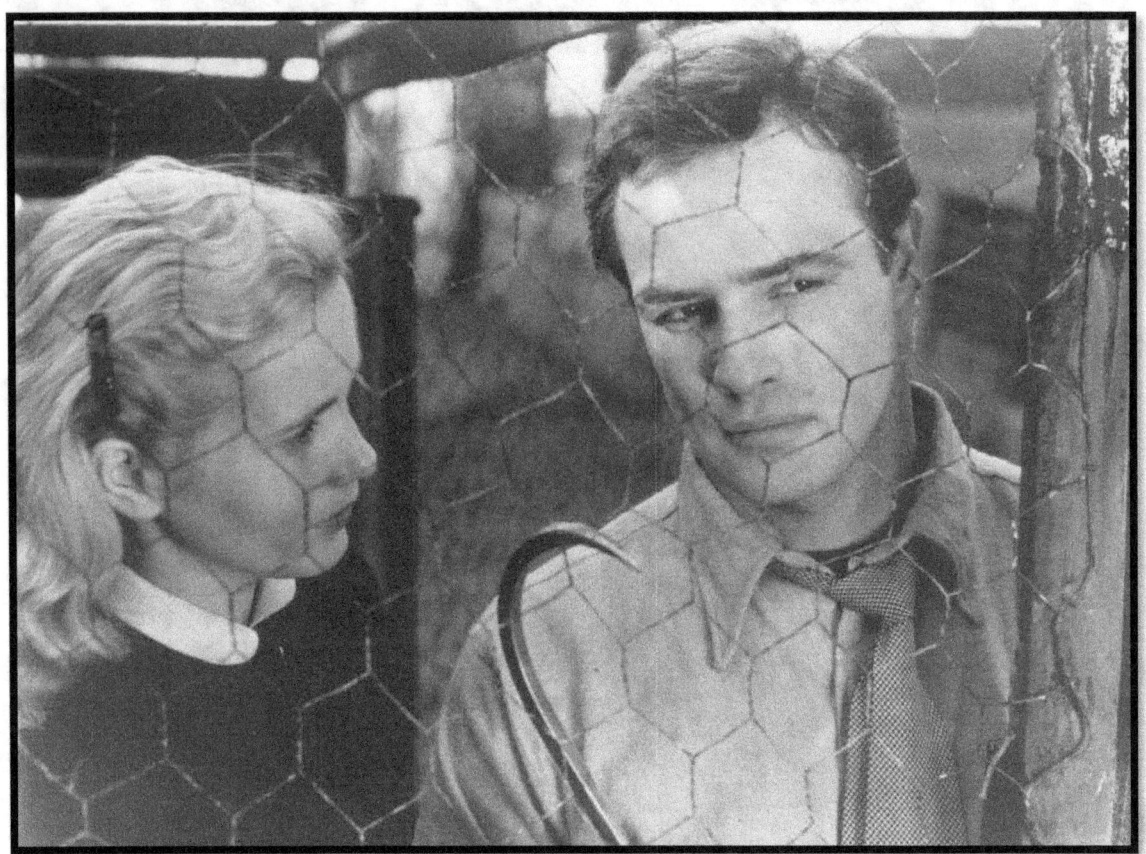

Terry is a rat but a rat with honor. The fact that he would use the script as a weapon underlines the moral ambivalence Kazan had. His willingness, like the stage character Willy Loman that dominated so much of his life, to avoid a moral stance by creating himself into a victim.

As Kazan told the HUAC, regarding his role as a Communist, "I don't think there is anything in my life towards which I have more ambivalence." Later he compared that statement to Terry Malloy, the films hero "(Malloy) felt as I did. He felt ashamed and proud of himself at the same time. He wavered between the two.... He felt like a fool, but proud of himself.... That kind of ambivalence.'

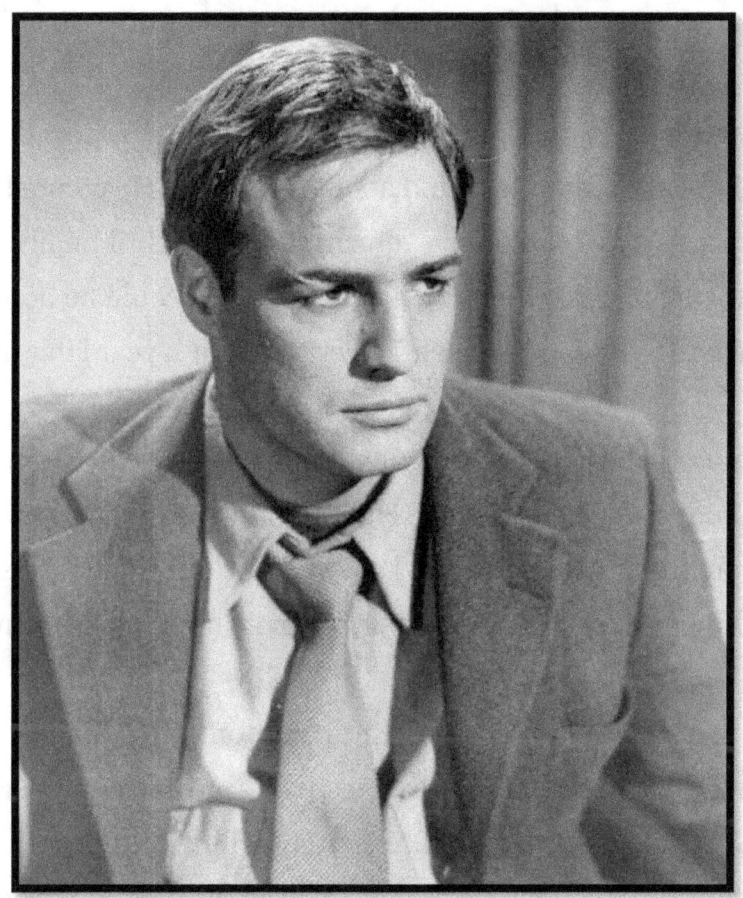

He saw himself as trapped between two powers, an oppressive and dictatorial Communist Party and federal government gone out of control in its campaign to crush an opposing ideology.

In Kazan the immigrant's view, neither one of these sides, who for him were nothing more than points of view that would never be resolved, deserved his allegiance. It had nothing to do with his honorable intentions, success, with getting ahead and staying ahead. Those two ideologies could do nothing to fend of the ghosts that haunted him. However, the HUAC's iron grip on the studios, the weight and power of the federal government, could end his career and then his honorable mission, to get ahead, his understanding of what America was, would have been all for naught.

During and directly after his testimony, Kazan made it a point to show that he had changed his mind about Communism and about testifying. He pointed out many times that it was a slow, painful often agonizing process, until finally and dramatically, he saw the light of truth and then and only then, could he not remain silence, in much the same route taken by Terry Malloy a year later in script and film.

Often overlooked in this subject is screen writer Schulberg's role in creating the allegory. Schulberg had his own demons with Hollywood. The industry had sucked the marrow from his father's bones and spewed him out when it was finished with him and Budd himself was, by 1952, virtually unemployable in Hollywood as well.

Soon after the film was released, when it became common gossip among Hollywood liberals that the film was intended to justify Kazan and Schulberg's testimony to HUAAC. Schulberg denied it immediately calling the allegory theory as the stuff of film schools. It was his view that the film was a "gangster story" and that he resented it being seen as a political statement. One of his few public statements on the issue was that fate of the Czechs, whose democratic regime had been crushed by the Russians in 1948, meant more to him than that of Stalinists in Hollywood.

He also dismissed the notion that friendly HUAC witness Lee J. Cobb's character, Johnny Friendly was created to draw a parallel between Johnny Friendly, a bloodless gangster and Stalin. "I never thought of Johnny Friendly as anything like Stalin," he said" They were both bad guys but on a different level. Stalin was killing millions--Johnny Friendly was killing a score"

While it is true that Kazan probably spiked the *Waterfront* script with allegories, it is doubtful that Schulberg did not at least know that the similarities were present in the script.

While it may not have been an allegory for Schulberg, it certainly was for Kazan. For him the films theme had little or nothing to do with gangsters. Instead, it was about "a man who has sinned and is redeemed" *Waterfront*, he said, was his story. For him, Terry Malloy, the films hero played by Brando, had broken what Kazan called the ultimate childhood taboo "Don't snitch on your friends" or as he put it later, Malloy was "A rat, or for intellectuals, an informer"

For Schulberg to be ostracized by Hollywood was meaningless. For Kazan, apparently, it meant everything and he clearly intended to have the last word and Waterfront gave him the vehicle to do that. Kazan never denied his intention to strike back at those who had ostracized him for his testimony, writing in his autobiography *A Life*, "When critics say that I put my story and my feelings onto the screen, to justify my informing, they are right."

Kazan, with Schulberg, had built the Terry Malloy character around the true-life story of a dockworker named Anthony de Vincenzo, known around the docks as Tony Mike. Schulberg had introduced Kazan to de Vincenzo while they were preparing the first draft of the Waterfront script. Kazan recalled: *"Tony Mike de Vincenzo had his own pier once, been the hiring boss there in Hoboken" His friends and relatives had been, and some still were, part of the mob exploiting the longshoremen.*

Tony Mike had not only seen the corruption, not only known all about the rackets, but also had probably at one time, benefited from them. The, apparently, the injustice got to be too much for him. He began to feel himself the victim, not the benefactor. He also began to be threatened when he did not go along with the racket bosses asked him to do. He resented being bullied as much as he scorned the dishonesty. He started to balk.

Suddenly, he was on the other side, and the racket life he once accepted as inevitable on the waterfronts was beginning to threaten his family. That he would lose his job as pier boss was certain. He was blacklisted by the mob. The best he could do was a job as a supervisor of the Hoboken sewer system at $3,500 a year. He quit and was reduced to selling newspapers at a street stand. He still dressed as a hiring boss, wore his snap-brim felt hat and topcoat, but he was making a humiliating living.

Then came the big step, one that may have surprised even Tony Mike. When he was subpoenaed to testify before the Waterfront Crime Commission about the corruption, he had seen and how it worked, who 'took' and how much, Tony Mike told the truth as no one had before.

He named names. When he did that, he broke the hoodlum law of silence: If you want to live, don't talk. He was called a rat, a squealer and a stoolie. He was ostracized then threatened. Friends he's had for years didn't talk to him. Along with this isolation in shame, which had become his life, he was the object of threats to himself and his family.

Everyone in Hoboken was certain he's pick up a newspaper soon and read that Tony Mike had 'disappeared'. Then another paper, a few days later, would break the news that Tony Mike's body had been dredged up from the bottom of the river. This was the classic story of the labor informer, squealer, and rat. Budd knew when he had a live one; he sought the friendship of de Vincenzo.

When Tony Mike invited us to dinner at his house, we jumped at the chance. It was a heavy, pungent Italian meal that was served us, pasta and peppers with meat loaded sauces and red wine. Tony Mike told us about his experiences. If you want to live, the mob had warned him, don't talk. He'd talked. He was still alive, but he knew that the last man who'd opened New York's waterfront rackets to view was found dead in a lime pit.

At a certain point, I remember well, he told us he's so feared for his safety and his family's, that he decided to carry a pistol, and when he saw our faces the suspicion that he was over dramatizing himself, he reached into his clothing and pulled out a handgun and laid it on the table, where it remained as we finished our meal.

I doubt that Budd was affected as personally as I was by the parallel of Tony Mike's story. His reaction to the loss of certain friends was not as bitter as my own. He had not experienced their blackballing as frequently and intensely as I had in the neighborhood known as Broadway. I believe that Budd regarded our waterfront story with greater objectivity, an objectivity that I appreciated. But I did see Tony Mike's story as my own, and that the connection did lend the tone of irrefutable anger to the scenes I photographed and to my work with actors. When Brando, at the end, yells at Lee J. Cobb, the mob boss "I'm glad what I done...you hear me? Glad what I done!" that was me saying, with identical heat that I was glad I testified as I had. So when critics say that I put my story and my feelings on the screen, to justify my informing, they are right. That was transference of emotion from my own experience to the screen is the merit of those scenes.... I was preparing a film about myself.

It was then that I amassed the weight of determination that made it possible later for me to endure every kind of discouragement and rejection and, when so many people tried to kill the film, never let it be canceled, even when our producer didn't back me with the help he should have given me, not to waver, not on this film, because it would mean that I was wavering on myself"

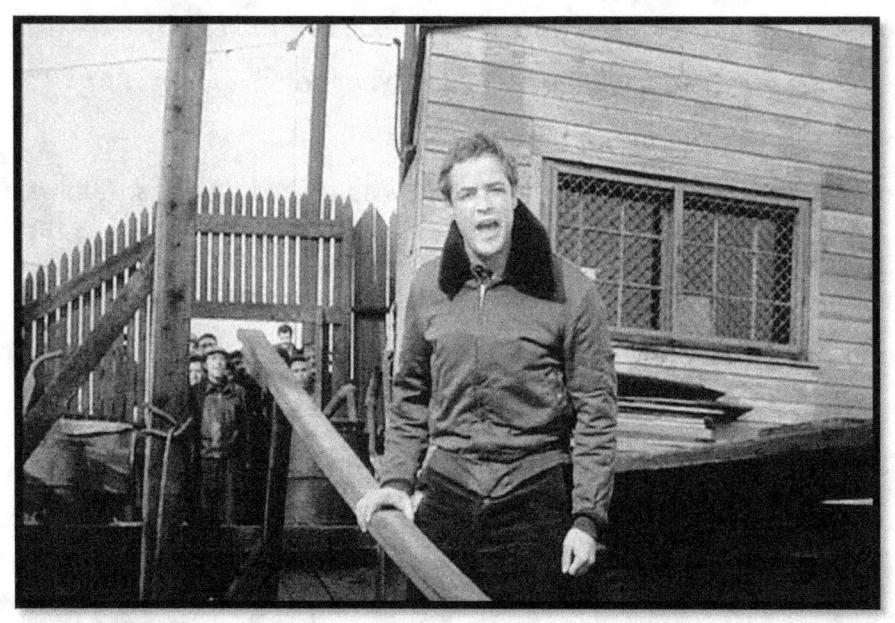

"I'm glad what I done...you hear me? Glad what I done!"

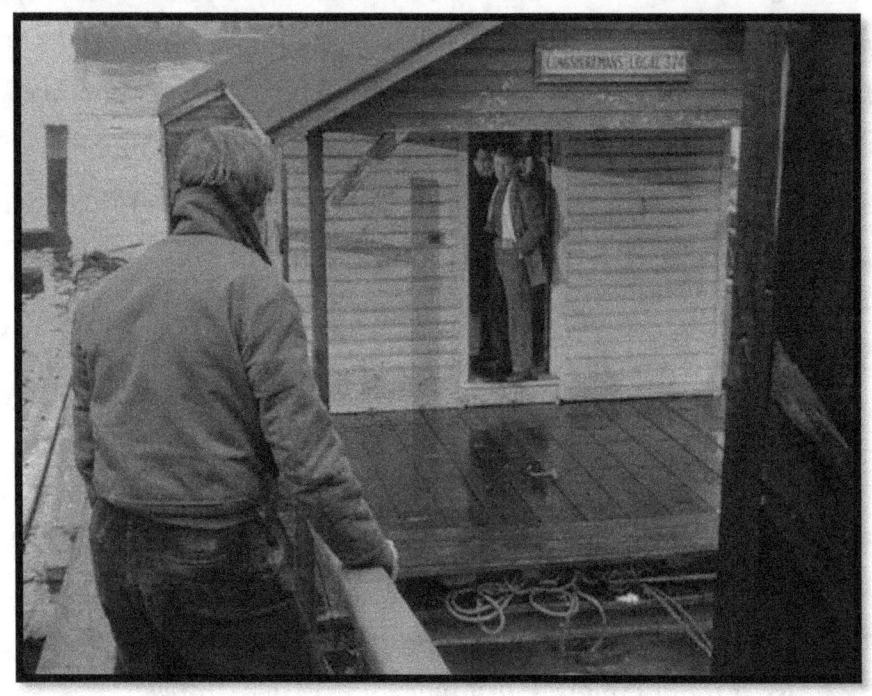

To assure that the allegory was fulfilled, after the contracts were signed, Kazan introduced Brando to Tony Mike. Brando studied and then created his role, modeling his characterization on Tony Mike De Vincenzo.

The hearing before the Crime Commission, another "testimonial" scene in the film also reflects Kazan's experience before the HUAC. In the film, the states chief investigator thanks Terry for his testimony, explaining that he has made it possible for decent people to work on the waterfront again. At Kazan's hearing, Representative Francis E. Walter said essentially the same thing as appears in the script.

"Mr. Kazan, we appreciate your cooperation with our committee. It is only through the assistance of people as you that we have been able to make the progress that has been bringing the attention of the American people to the machinations of Communist conspiracy for world domination."

When asked about the allegory, Waterfront's star, Marlon Brando said "I didn't realize was that *On the Waterfront* was really a metaphorical argument by (Kazan) and Budd Schulberg; they made a film to justify finking on their friends"

While many scoffed at Brando's remarks, it is entirely possible that Brando's failure to see any connection between Kazan's informing and his own character's behavior is logical because the situations between Terry Malloy and Elia Kazan were so very far apart.

For Kazan's detractors the notion that Waterfront captures metaphorically the truth of Kazan's relationship to the Communist Party and the HUAC is still seen as self-serving rubbish. For them, the idea that the film somehow brings out the dilemma facing Terry Malloy/Kazan is not found because neither Malloy nor Kazan truly faced any moral ambiguity. If Terry Malloy does not testify against Johnny Friendly, the mobsters will murder him as they already murdered his brothers. For him, its life and death.

The fictional circumstances in Waterfront hardly resemble the reality that Kazan and Schulberg faced. In his detractor's view, by naming names, Kazan joined the mobsters, the bad guys who had formed a political lynch mob. For them, Terry Malloy's experiences have more in common with those who were blacklisted over those who accepted the blacklisting and profited greatly from it. One is a story of dirt poor courageous man who stands on the truth of his principles the other is the tale of a wealthy and talented man who unashamedly surrendered without a fight.

Terry's decision to testify does nothing but injure Johnny Friendly, a thug killer who clearly gets what he deserves. If testimony was an allegory for Kazan's real life actions, there is a substantial difference. In the reality of the HUAC hearings, Americans were injured, they fled their homelands, some for the remainder of their lives, others were jailed some killed themselves. However, as Brando pointed out, the most damage inflicted by Kazan's testimony was on Kazan himself. "Kazan" and "informer" became forever inseparably linked.

For decades Kazan neither denied nor admitted that the role of Terry Malloy as defacto martyr and hero who justified his actions before the committee. However, undeniably the films promotes forgiveness and atonement for past sins although English film critic Lindsay Anderson took the religious aspects a step further and noted that the Brando character is made into a "Jesus like" figure at the end of the film, leading the fallen and once blind workers, back to the docks. He also called the script "fascists"

While *Waterfront's* symbolism was initially lost on Brando, it was quickly observed by Hollywood. To which Kazan answered: "When people said there are some parallels to what I had done, I couldn't and wouldn't deny it. It does have some parallels. But I wasn't concerned with them nor did I play on them.

They were not my reason for making the film. I had wanted to do a picture about the waterfront long before any of the HUAC business came up"

For Kazan, although he had enormously successful career, he was never fully accepted by Hollywood after his testimony and for the remainder of his life he seemed stranded in moral doubt over what he did. The way Terry is shunned by the boy from his old rooftop gang, following his appearance before the Crime Commission, reflects Kazan's own experiences following his testimony.

Of course, to be shunned in Hollywood has its own meaning. The Blacklisted screenwriter Walter Bernstein recalls that after Kazan's HUAC appearance, the actor James Dean made a loud statement about his contempt for what Kazan did and vowed never to work with him.

Then Kazan offered Dean a role in *East of Eden*. Bernstein ran into Dean on the street and asked about his once resolute stance on Kazan, but the actor simply shrugged and said, "He made me a star"

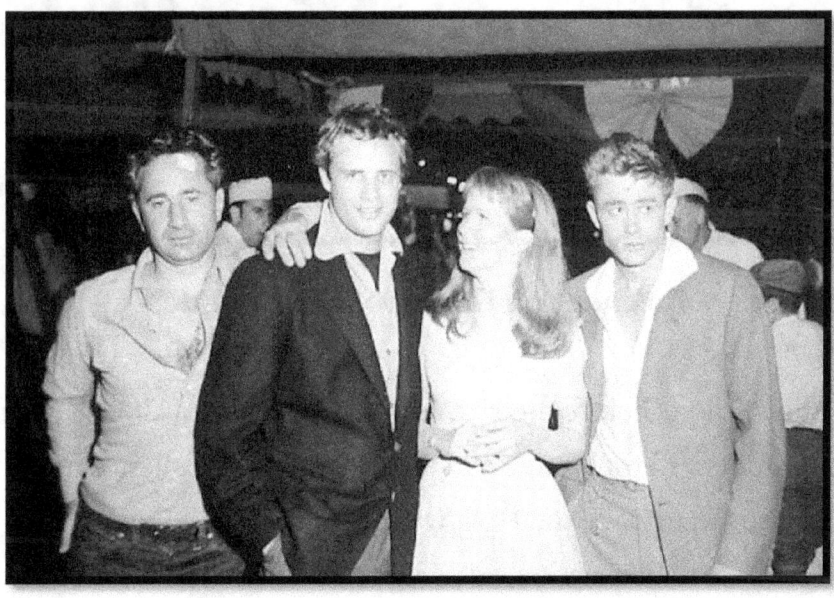

Kazan, visitor Marlon Brando, Julie Harris and James Dean pose on the set of East of Eden

Kazan's desire to justify himself pushes him in the film to change the context of informing: Terry Malloy testifies of murder, while Kazan named fellow members of the Communist Party cell that he belonged to sixteen years before, and left acrimoniously. When Terry approaches the union shack and tells Friendly that he is 'glad what I done to you', there is clearly a sense of Kazan's feelings about the Communist Party.

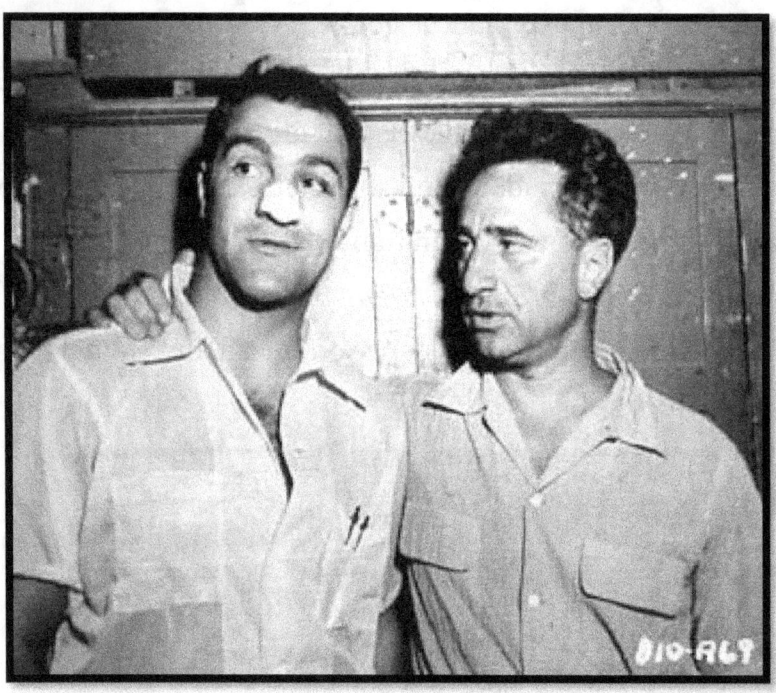

With Rocky Marciano on the set of *East of Eden*

For Kazan, giving testimony before the HUAC broke the code of silence in the Hollywood Left community. In the film Kazan transformed their silence into the longshoremen closed world, who, lie the Hollywood left, tried to portray their silence, their unwillingness to take action, as part of a moral code, "D and D" deaf and dumb but Father Barry, the films religious voice and the government, the films secular voice, will have none of it. For him, they are morally ambiguous.

322

However, to some degree, right or wrong, there was a truth to the largely Irish and Italian belief in the "D and D" code. On the real waterfront, a place where European ethnicity was strong, testifying did take on the form of a subculture sin. At that point, 1954, history was less than 75 years away from an Ireland dominated by British colonial rule where an "informer" was the lowest possible creature to walk the earth. The same held true in Southern Italy, where, throughout most of its history, the government was as repressive as any organized gang of criminals. The Omerta was alive and well.

Terror of breaking the code kept the code alive. Certainly, the actual events on the waterfront, the complete domination by the Mafia and the thorough corruption of the union, never would have succeeded without the code of deaf and dumb.

The waterfront, in actual events and in the film, is a place of dismal poverty and both renderings are essentially a story of the poor exploiting the poor. If one did break the code, endangering their lives, where would they go?   The options for the working poor are limited. Kazan, who set the religious and moral authority in the film, has none of it. He bluntly points out, throughout the film, that deaf and dumb is moral cowardice. Schulberg's script is no less forgiving.

The phrase "D and D" is so commonplace on the docks that phrase comes easily to one and all, from Father Barry to the Waterfront Crime Investigator to John Friendly. For Kazan there is nothing noble in the phrase. He portrays it repeatedly to be a form of oral slavery for the workers who blindly accept the docks for what they are and the code of the docks, D and D, for what it is.

Terry's transformation involves breaking the code of the docks and thinking for himself thereby claiming his identity as his own. He is no longer a slave to a worn out code, he can think for himself and as he thinks, therefore he is. Having been born into a world of socialized evil, where money and power is king and Johnny Friendly is a giant among men, the D and D was the accepted norm. In a sense, he is born again when he realizes, when he sees the inherent in being deaf and dumb and can now hear and speak the words of truth.

THE AMBIGUOUS END

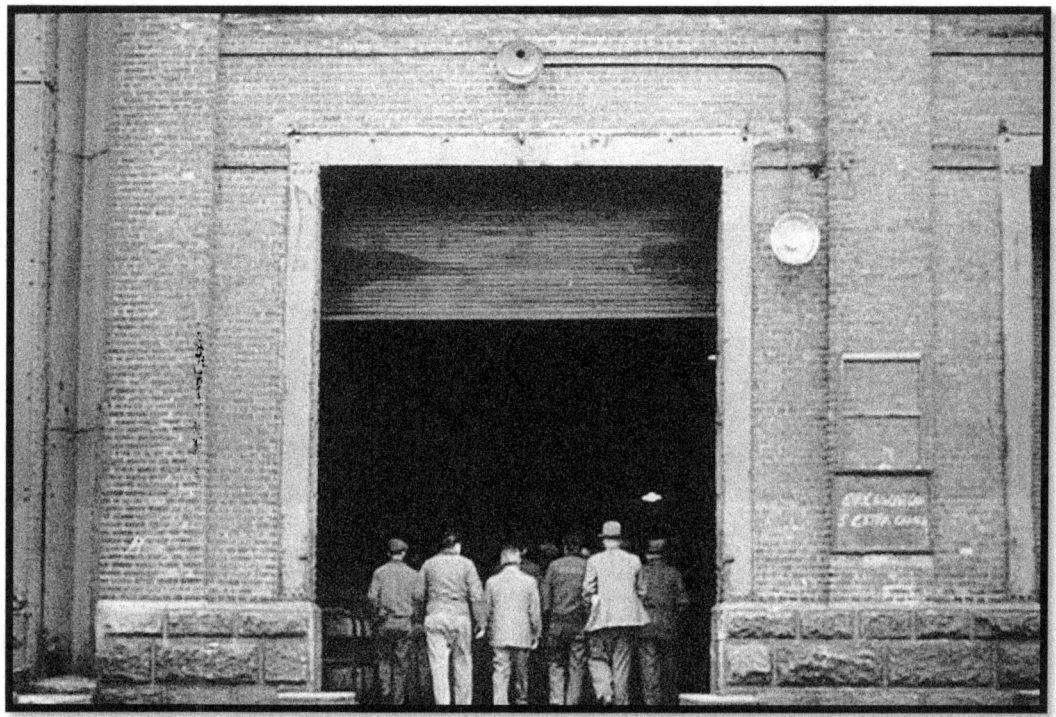

The films ending has left generations of viewers perplexed. If nothing else, the ending fits to the Hollywood dictate that a film must end with dramatic action, in this case a fistfight between a former prizefighter and a gangster.

From the scenes prior to the required Hollywood fistfight scene, it is obvious that Terry has won. He has ruined Johnny Friendly. We see a shot of a tabloid-style newspaper with news that Johnny Friendly will be indicted for murder. Then, just after the hearings, we see a "Mr. Big" watching the hearings on television and instructing his servant not to take calls from Johnny Friendly.

This is followed by a scene inside the gangster's waterfront shack where Johnny Friendly takes the guns from his thugs and says, "I'm on the hot seat. We're a law abiding union." It is obvious his power is diminishing. In fact, Johnny Friendly is only true loser in the film overall. Like Father Barry and Joey Doyle and even Terry's brother, in the end, the characters are pure of soul and essentially good.

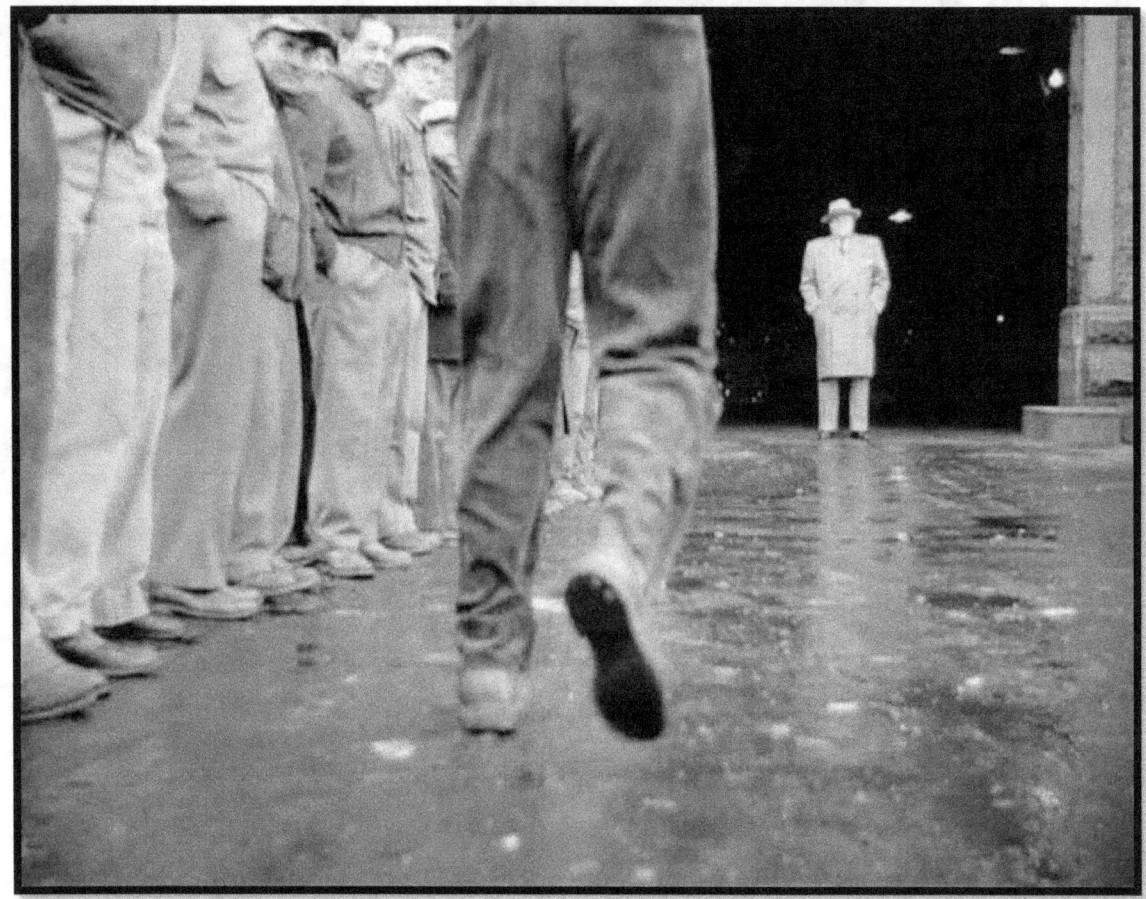

While Friendly is the films real loser, the longshoremen are not portrayed as empowered by Johnny Friendly's loss. In the final shot, a gigantic steel gray door shuts as the workers march in to the cargo bay, led by a beaten and bloody Terry. He carries a hook over his shoulder as Christ carries a cross and he is wearing

Joey Doyle's jacket, the now sacred jacket of morality. Terry is bleeding from the head reminiscent of a Christ's bleeding from the crown of thorns. In a broad overhead shot, they, the work crews and Terry, enter a warehouse and are seemingly devoured by the building while the giant doors, like the gates of heaven, slams down in the face of a defeated Johnny Friendly. (most of the final scene was shot at 7:00 PM, in the dark)

The films theme suggests that Kazan felt a need to assert the right of the individual's conscience over the body of the whole. There is no ambiguity in what Terry Malloy did, in testifying about Johnny Friendly or facing him down on the docks, it was clearly the right thing to do. In the end Terry win's the girl and the respect of the Priest and his fellow workers. Informing has elevated him to a new status. It also helps that those on his side include a Catholic priest and a kind-hearted teacher trainee, winning over the audience's sympathy.

Kazan's interpretation of ending is based on the Longshoremen's plight at that point in time. He knew that the mob still ran the unions and little had changed. "The workers" he said, "gather around Terry, as if they were going to continue their struggle. They have to work for a living they're not going into some intellectual state of withdrawal from it. It was as close as I could get to what actually happened on the waterfront."

Kazan followed the allegory to the end of the film with Terry's final walk to work. The walk has suggestions of religious symbolism (The hook slung across the bloodied shoulder etc.) following his fight with Johnny Friendly, was seen by the British film director Lindsay Anderson as fascist, involving a sudden transfer of loyalty to a new leader by the watching, apathetic crowd. There has not been a real change on the waterfront. Terry Malloy is hardly a leader. He is in it for himself. He does not want to change things. He simply wants to get along and go along, much like the conformity of the times. Terry/ Brando act out Kazan's conformity in the very last scene when Terry enters the warmth of the warehouse with the other longshoremen; he is coming in from the cold, just as Kazan had done.

For him, the workers are easily pulled around the docks like sheep at the whim of the next powerful leader because they have little else on their mind except their own well-being, which was, on the waterfront of 1954, essentially true. (Beaten and battered, Terry Malloy makes the long walk from the docks to the warehouse, the Kazan version of Christ's long walk to Calvary, his loading hood and all it symbolizes as his cross)

Kazan said that he was being true to what the reality of the moment was "What we intended to show at the end was that the workers there had found, or thought they'd found, a new potential leader. He had almost been killed remember? And very often, in the labor movement, a new movement starts with the death of a person, through the memory of a martyr." 68 However, it is doubtful that the beating Terry takes in the final scene inspired the workers to overthrow a corrupt union leader.

In the film, nothing is resolved in the end. Kenneth Hey, in his analysis of Leonard Bernstein's score for the film, points out that on the soundtrack the climatic image of Terry reporting for work, the music is indeterminate by not resolving the final chords.

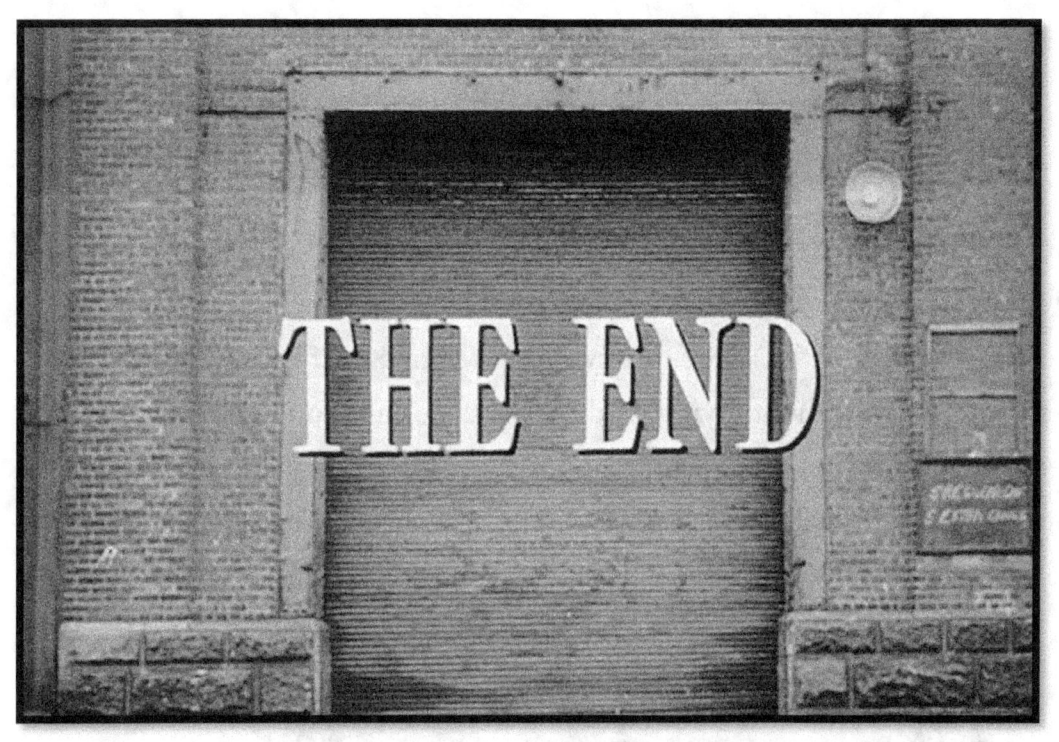

THE MUSICAL SCORE
DECEMBER 1953

Even with Kazan's excellent direction for the film, Spiegel was still very worried that the film would flop at the box office. Columbia looked at the final rushes and was less than enthusiastic. Harry Cohn watched the film and walked out of the viewing room without saying a word to Kazan. Based on that report, Spiegel decided that the film needed a lift, and without consulting with Kazan hired Leonard Bernstein to do the score for the film.

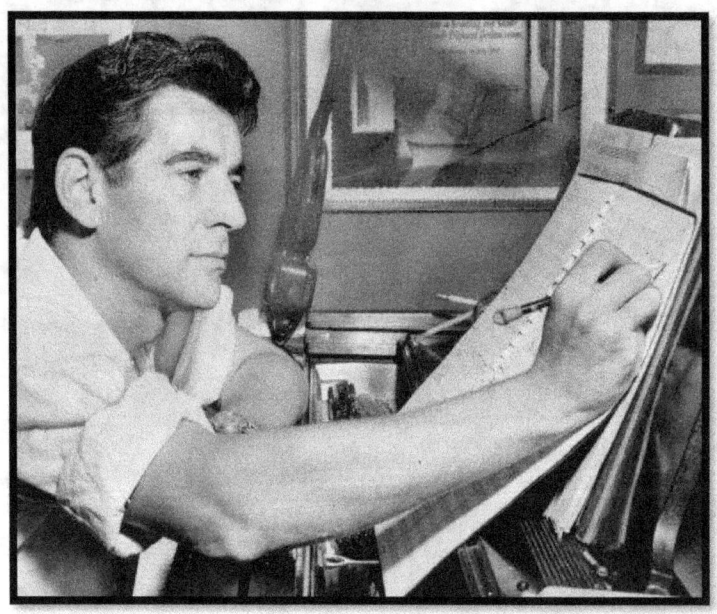

Bernstein

Spiegel reached his dismal judgment after viewing a rough cut of the film in a private screening with the director and star. He brought Bernstein along to introduce him and the idea of snapping and dramatic film score to Kazan.

From the start of the film until its end, Spiegel, an actor in his own right, would bury his head in his hands and moan "This is awful! This is the worst picture ever made!"

Brando, ever sensitive to any criticism of his work got up and walked out. Karl Malden found him later and asked "Don't you think this is a great film? We're done something important here" Brando shrugged "In and out, in and out" Bernstein good heartedly told the director that it was good film, Spiegel screamed "Good? This is a great picture!"

The Harvard educated Bernstein was certainly qualified for the job. He appointed assistant conductor of the New York Philharmonic in 1943. He made his professional conducting debut on November 14, 1943 (without even rehearsing the orchestra because there had not been enough time) and was the first American-born and American-trained conductor appointed music director of the New York Philharmonic and to conduct at Milan's La Scala Opera House.

Even without Spiegel's medaling, Kazan had a good reputation as a director who understood the importance of music in film and was responsible for bringing first-rate composers to Hollywood to score his films.
Kazan's first choice to write the films score was Alex North, who had written the 1951 score to *A Streetcar Named Desire*.

The much revered North was on his way to changing the way composers wrote for the screen. His score for Streetcar fit the film perfectly without getting in the way of the story and its characters in music written from the heart, with soul and passion. His film scoring
was an innovation, he took a deep psychological approach to understanding the overall film and to each of its characters before starting the score. Equally important, he wrote the score economically, in quick, lean points within a fine texture.

His music for Kazan's *Streetcar* remains instinctively on the mark, straightforward while hitting the mark in a highly sophisticated way. North explained the score as "the ambivalent nature of human behavior" North refused to take Kazan's call due to his testimony before the HUAC.

Bernstein received the finished print of the film in the spring of 1954. He screened the film over 50 times, selecting and timing scenes that seemed to need music. Bernstein's music for *Waterfront* is mediocre although in many circles the score is highly regarded, especially by film historians. Bernstein was new to the genre and there was precious little time for him to develop a strong working relationship with his director.

The gossip in Hollywood was that Kazan had made a mistake in hiring Bernstein for the score that the composer was in overhead. However, the proof is that he did in fact know what he was doing even though at times the music is intrusive and inept.

The almost overpowering opening scene sound track is filled with a mad rush of frantic percussion while the visual only shows a group of men swaggering out of a wooden shack. In fairness, the opening score was obviously intended to be asynchronous with the picture as a whole. But without any knowledge of the men in the scene, who they were and what they did, the viewer holds back deciding, making the music confusing rather than enlightening. Even later, when the longshoremen are beaten as they flee from Father Barry's church after a meeting, Bernstein inserted a rhythmical brass into a scene that called for any but that.

Perhaps because of a lack of experience, Bernstein did not attempt to write around the dialogue. The result is that the music's volume is repeatedly lowered at every line and then raised again until the next line. Several times during editing, bits of the score were snipped or reduced in volume, which threw

Bernstein into a rage, but it had to be done, otherwise the score would have drowned out the dialogue.

Bernstein blamed some of the scores flaws on Kazan's post production decisions, with Kazan refusing to give up a single line from Brando at the cost of the score. However, in the end, Bernstein's score does what it's supposed to do when it's supposed to do it, it adds tension or tenderness at the right moments, it adds continuity to a film that is intentionally weak on structure. The score leaves the impression of being important hence, the subject at hand in the film is important.

The film sounded different because of Leonard Bernstein's only film score, which used discordance to point up the scenes on the roof. "And" said Kazan "when we got all those Oscar nominations and we won... all those Oscars, we were really amazed that Bernstein was left out completely. However, the score was not left out, it will always be there. Occasionally it's played in philharmonic programs and it was the only one he did and he did one hell of a job at that. That was in the mixing. As the writer of the picture, as much as I admired the score, there were times that I thought it was maybe it was a little bit... too loud."70

THE OSCARS

1954

"Every great work of art has two faces, one toward its own time and one toward the future, toward eternity." **Daniel Barendoim**

"When we were done," **Kazan said**, "I knew we had a pretty good film, but I wasn't absolutely sure what we had"

What they had was a masterpiece. They had created was, arguably, the greatest American film ever made.   The essence of Waterfront's success was the essence of success for the decades other big film, *Marty* a wonderful, timeless love story about acceptance and change.

Each film was directed by artists interested in telling a small, interesting and well-written story, which introduced new faces to the screen and were filled with emotional intensity that the average filmgoer could understand.

The Post War socially conscious writers and directors wanted a less escapist production and to distance themselves from the quickly dying old authoritarian studios. While Sam Spiegel, Kazan, Schulberg and Brando were ultimate Hollywood insiders, the circumstances of the films birth allowed the creative personnel more autonomy even under the strict filming schedule.

They had created a "message film" that relied on field research, a film based on living, otherwise unromantic people, a film determined to show the underbelly of the rising cost of organized crime in America and its effect on the working man. The finished product sounded different, it looked different and it was not Hollywood.

Waterfront set the new standard for the genre of co-operative New York style filmmaking. Kazan used method actors and redefined the masculine role in film presenting a hero drenched in self-doubt. The film innovation and daring would influence an entire generation of filmmakers and actors.

Waterfronts stars, particularly Malden, Cobb and Brando, who came out of Kazan's Method acting school, turned the world of film on its ear and acting on the big screen would never be the same again. The movies realism, told through the script, the cinematography and the acting, leaped out at the viewers. The dreariness of the distant New York docks, the haggard faces of the laborers created bleakness that gave the film a sense of alienation and realism rarely captured on the screen. *On the Waterfront* opened in October of 1954 at the Astor Theater to sensational reviews and grossed over $9.5 million in its initial release.

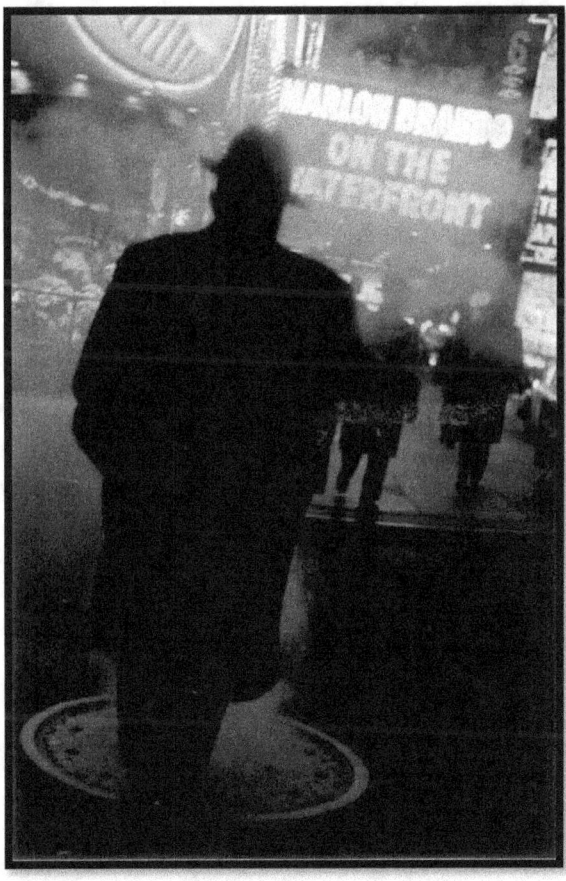

By later blockbuster standards, it seems like a paltry figure. By way of comparison, in that year, a loaf of bread cost 15 cents, a gallon of gas 21 cents and a new, three-bedroom home in the suburbs sold just under $22,000

On the second day of its low-key premier, three hundred people lined up for the first showing at 9:00 AM. The line made the afternoon papers. The film was barely mentioned.

Kazan left his Manhattan hotel room and walked down to the Astor to see crowds lined up to see his film. He noticed that most of the ticket holders in line were the types not normally attracted to his films, working people and "tough guys"

Even Spiegel stopped complaining when the film started to catch on with the youth market. Kazan and Schulberg were astounded by the public's reaction to the film. They went over it time and again and were never able to conclude exactly what was about the film that made it so magnificent. The only person involved with the film who was not surprised at its instant success was the increasingly despondent Father Corridan who said that the film's success was what God wanted.

When *Waterfront* started to rain cash, the lawsuits followed. The first from Anthony (Tony Mike) de Vincenzo, whom Kazan and Brando had based the model of the character of Terry Malloy on. De Vincenzo sued Columbia Pictures and Sam Spiegel for $ 1,000,000 for invading his right to privacy. He won a small settlement. Tony Mike died in late November, 1983, at age 74, after a bout with cancer

Frank Sinatra sued next, for $500,000, followed by the Siodmak suit and the precursory suits from several dock workers' unions under the ILA because they felt that the film depicted the honor of its locals.

When the Oscars nominations were announced, *On the Waterfront* was named for eight awards in total. The nominations included Best Picture, Best Actor (Brando), (Best Actress went to Grace Kelly in *The Country Girl*) Best Supporting Actress (Saint), (Best Supporting Actor went to Edmond O'Brien in *The Barefoot Contessa*) Best Director (Kazan), Best Story & Screenplay (Schulberg), Best Editing, Best Cinematography (Kaufman actually won for Best Black and White Cinematography, color went to Milton Krasner for *Three Coins In The Fountain*) and Best Art Direction-Black & White. (Richard Day) Nominated but not winning were Malden, Cobb and Steiger-each for Best Supporting Actor and Leonard Bernstein for Best Music. Only *Gone with the Wind* and *From here to Eternity*, at that point, had matched Waterfront in the number of nominations.

At the 1955 Golden Globes Award, the film took Best Motion Picture, Drama, Best Director, Best Motion Picture Actor, Drama (Brando) Best Cinematography, Black and White (Boris Kaufman)

At the 1954 New York Film Critics Circle, the picture took Best Film Best Director, Best Actor (Brando) and at the 1954 National Board of Review, it took Best Picture, for the 1955 Directors Guild of America the film won Outstanding Directorial Achievement in Motion Pictures and Best Assistant Director (Charles H. Maguire)

The 1955 Writers Guild of America awarded the film with Best Written America Drama, Screen (Budd Schulberg)

At the 1954 Venice Film Festival, it took the Italian Film Critics Award (Kazan) and the Silver Lion (Kazan) and was nominated for the Golden Lion (Elia Kazan)

At the 1955 British Film and TV awards, the film took Best Foreign Actor (Brando) and nomination for Best Film from Any Source and Most Promising Newcomer (Eva Marie Saint) Bernstein's score was nominated but his competition was fierce.

The Oscars Schulberg wrote *and the unexpected box-office success were sweet revenge on the studio's that had turned us down. When the film was released and we realized to our amazement we had a hit on our hands, and critics were beginning to mention it as having an outside chance for some Oscars, Marlon piped up on the West Coast by saying he thought the whole Oscar thing was ridiculous.* "Actors don't need awards, they just need the satisfaction of doing a job.

The two Dragon-ladies at the Hollywood Gates, Louella Parsons of the Hearst papers and Hedda Harper of the Los Angeles Times, teed off on Marlon. "If that's the way he feels about our cherished Oscars, he doesn't deserve your votes, etc."

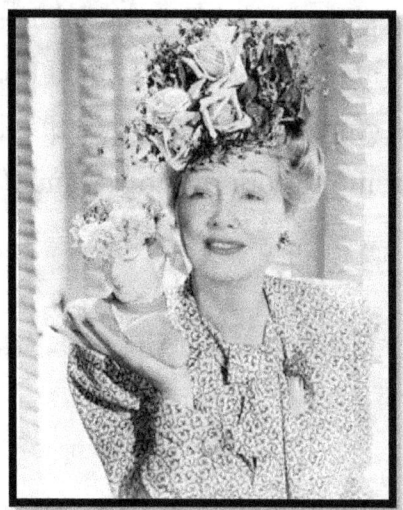

Hedda Harper

Kazan and I, and Spiegel, were worried. Schulberg said "the last thing we needed was Marlon turning the Academy against us. Spiegel and Kazan had an idea. Brando was now very fond of Roger Donoghue and he seemed to like me. So why don't we fly out to Hollywood and try to persuade Marlon to stop baiting Louella and Hedda. So out we went and our appeal to Marlon was basic: Marlon was an underdog man. He had always identified with the oppressed. With the native Americans and with the blacks, he with "`the people" under the heel of tyrants and the ruling class. Well our movie was an underdog, a movie made in the east on a pressing social theme that no big studio wanted to touch. Were there underdogs any more under than the longshoremen being kicked around by the mob? Those men, whom he had met and admired, were rooting for our picture. They felt it could actually help them bring about their much hoped for reforms on the dock. Marlon listened. We weren't asking him to go out and campaign for our picture or for himself, we told him, all we asked to do was just shut up and not provoke Louella and Hedda. But now Marlon swung 180 degrees in our direction. He offered to come with us to the Foreign Critics Association Golden Globe Awards that preceded and sometimes set the tone for the Oscars. He came resplendent in his tux and charmed everybody

As for Eva Marie Saint's Oscar nomination that had been a ploy by the producers, who wrongly assumed she would not get the award, but the publicity would be good.

After *Waterfront's* success and nominations, Schulberg wrote a piece for the Times and retold the story of how Zanuck had turned the picture down. The following morning he was attacked by a long, drawn out telegram from Zanuck explaining how deeply hurt he was over the piece and felt that at the least, Schulberg and Kazan should have thanked him for his contributions to the film. The ceremonies were held at the magnificent Pantages Theater in Los Angeles on March 30, 1955, at 7:30 PM, with simulcast from NBC studios in New York.

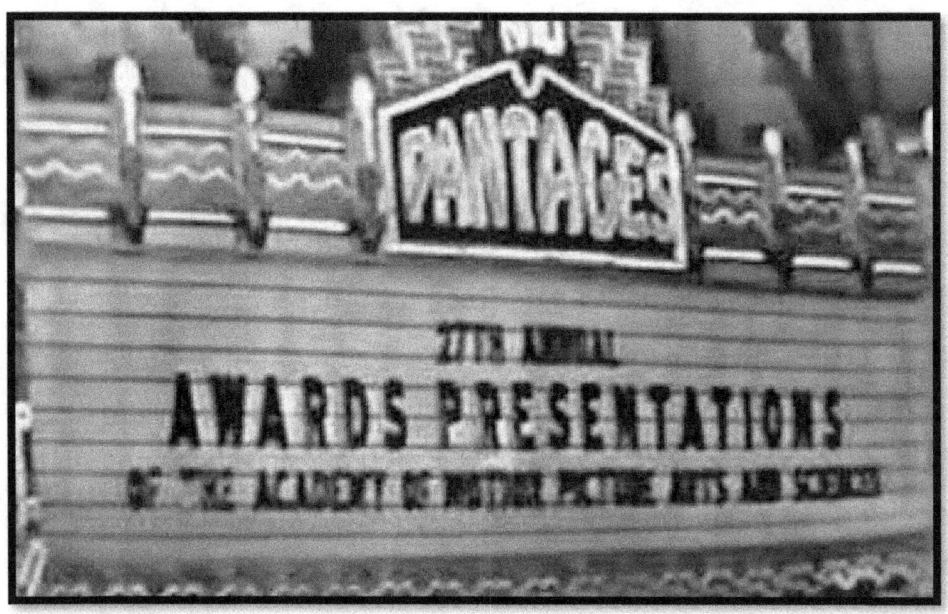

The hosts were Bob Hope and Thelma Ritter. Brando dressed in a tuxedo and looking bewildered, arrived with his secretary, agent, business manager, Aunt and his father, who quickly became lost in the crowd sending the star into a small panic.

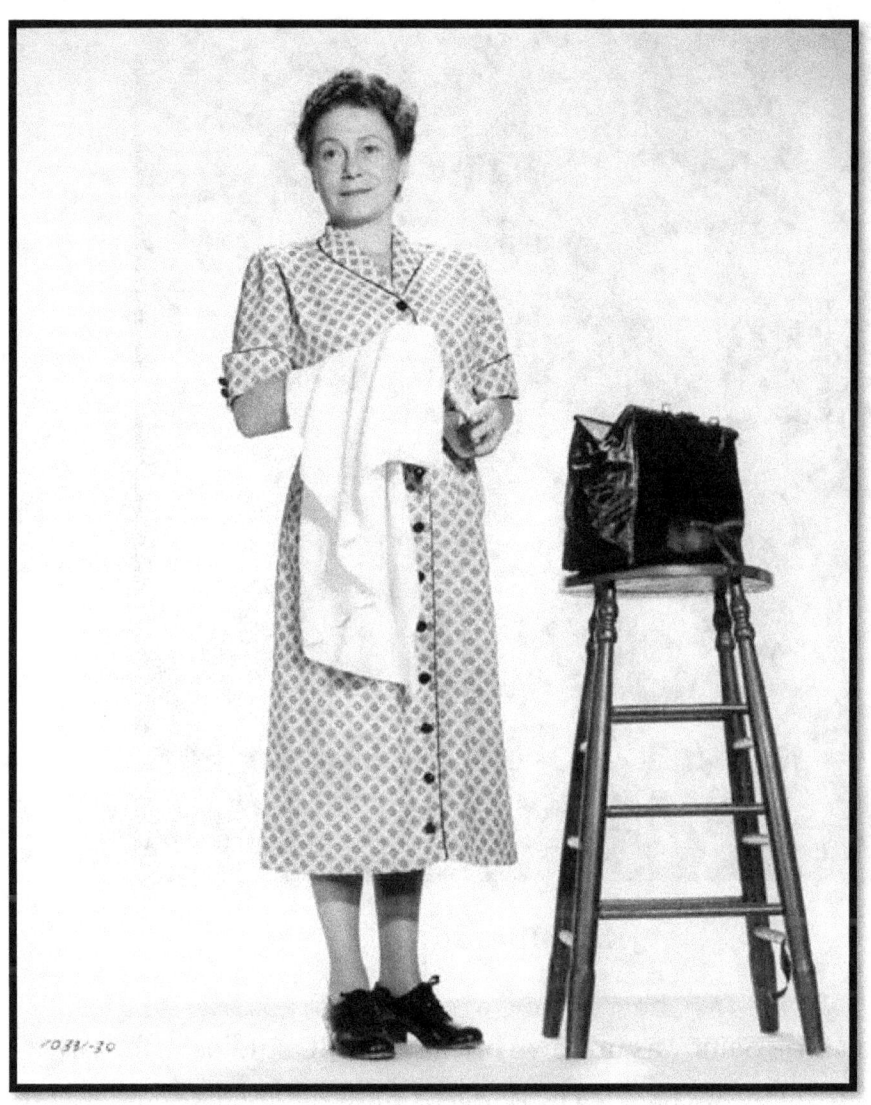

Thelma Ritter, from *Rear Window*

Rod Steiger, nominated for Best Supporting Actor, showed up with his date, Best Supporting Actress nominee, Katy Jurado, who was dressed in a flaming red Dior gown, which sprouted four enormous red roses across the neckline.

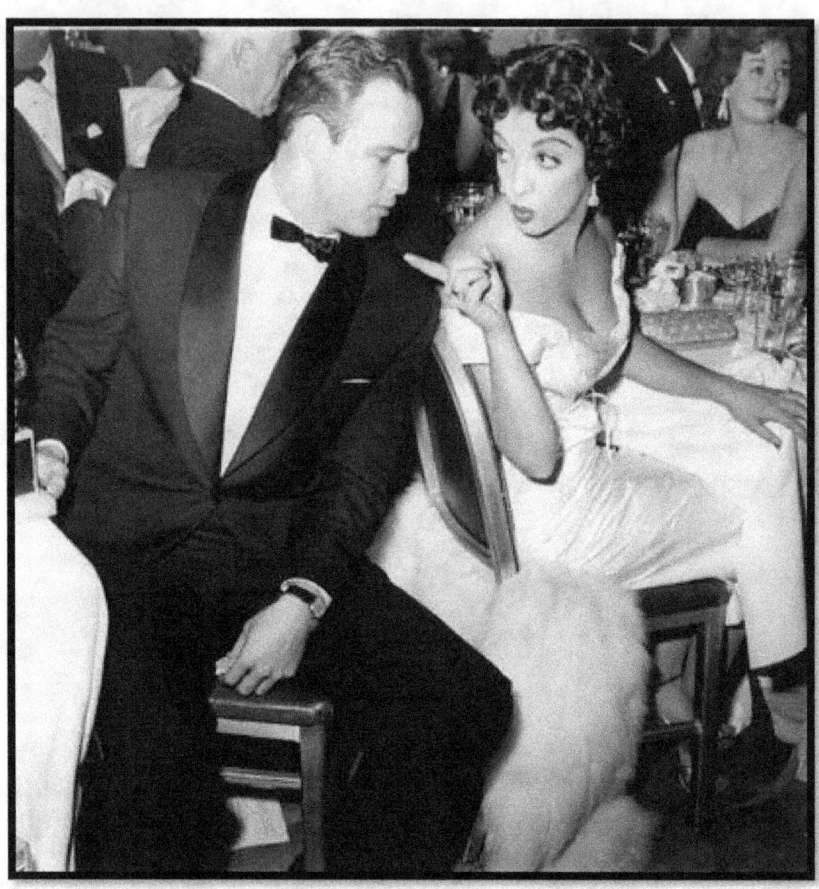

Katy Jurado

A pregnant Eva Marie Saint was in New York at the NBC studios with Karl Malden. She would follow up her role in *Waterfront* in the 1957 drama, *A Hatful of Rain,* which dealt with the then sensitive issue of drug addiction, followed by a role in Hitchcock's film *North by Northwest* in 1959 with Cary Grant and with Paul Newman in Otto Preminger's *Exodus* in 1960.

Brando took the stage and announced Best Director, Elia Kazan. After he presented the award, Brando walked behind stage for a smoke. When he attempted to return to the theater a member of the Warner Brothers Security Force, who demanded to see his identification, stopped him.

"But I'm Marlon Brando" the actor said

"Yeah and I'm Humphrey Bogart" said the guard "Let's see some ID"

Karl Malden announced that *On the Waterfront* had won Best Picture and an emotional Budd Schulberg, toasted his father "Because of my old man, this little fellow gives me an added kick tonight"

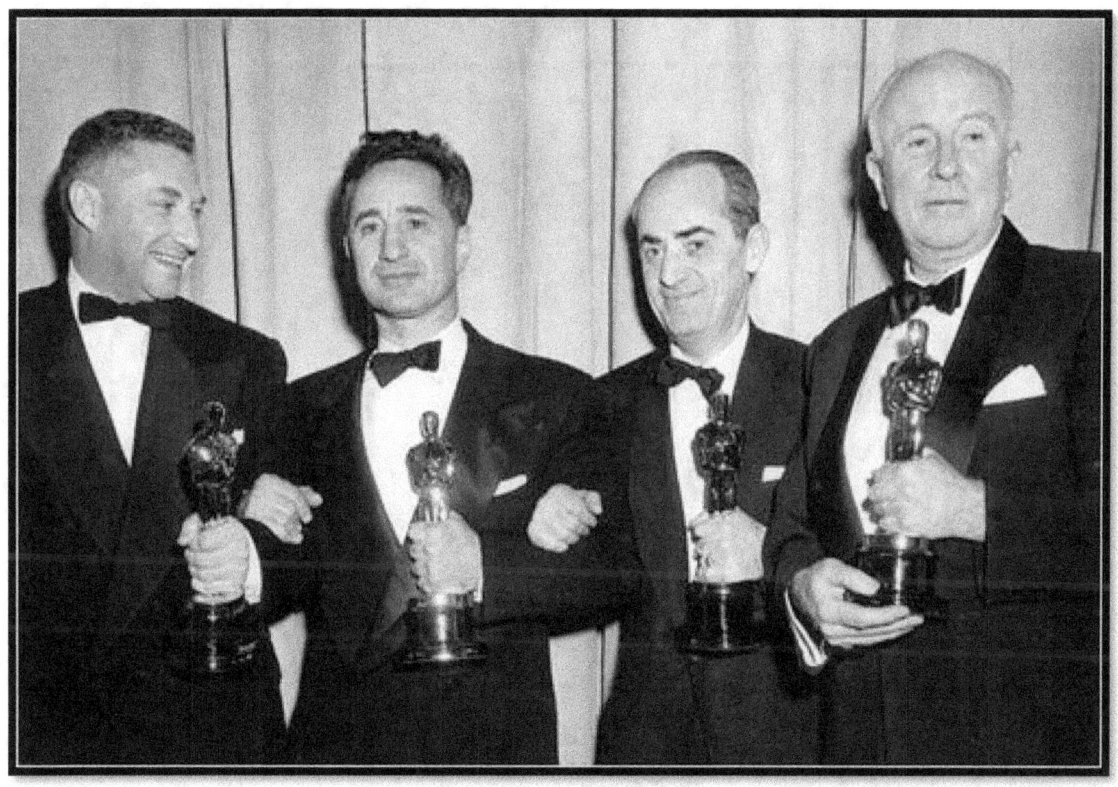

Kazan accepted his Oscar from New York, placing it face down when he made his acceptance speech. "I was tasting vengeance that night and enjoying it. On the Waterfront was my own story; every day I worked on that film, I was telling the world where I stood and my critics to go fuck themselves"

Years later, Kazan amended the statement "A New York picture," Kazan recalled, "made inexpensively by a lot of people like Sam Spiegel, who was a clown, and I, who was persona non grata, and Budd who wasn't anything much then either. The fact that we beat them all was a great pleasure to me."

Before the Best Actor award was announced, actor William Holden, who had not been permitted to make an acceptance speech when he won Best Actor the year before, took the stage and said, "As I was going to say last year..."

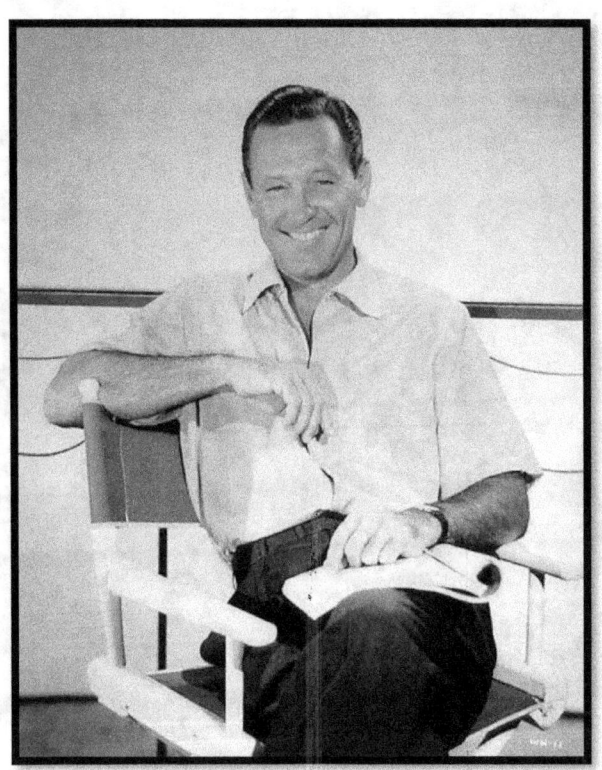

William Holden

Bette David, who would present Best Actor, strode on to the stage dressed in what one paper called "a sort of jeweled space helmet and matching shoes"

The two nominees, Bing Crosby, the strong favorite who was accompanied by his 21 years old date, and Brando, were sitting within inches of each other, but had not spoken.

As the winner was called, Brando chewed gum and looked half-asleep. When his name was called, he took the gum out of his mouth, stuck it on his chair, shook Crosby's hand "Congratulations" said "Thanks" replied Marlon who walked to the stage.

As he watched his sun run up the stairs to the stage, Brando father turned to the person sitting next to him and said, "You know, he's a good boy"

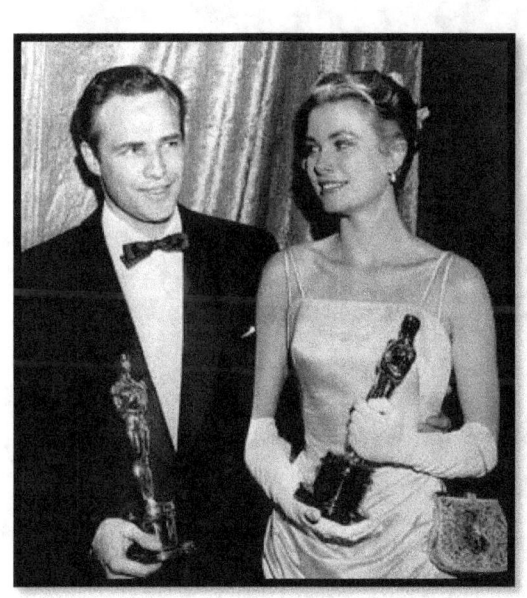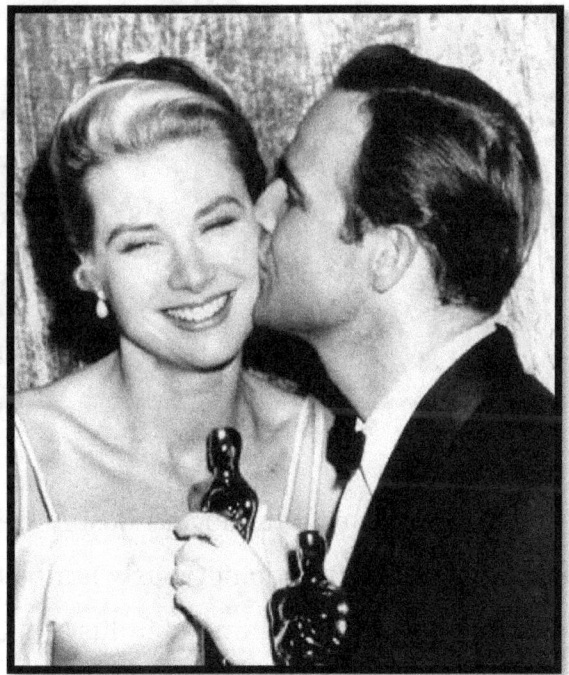

Brando's acceptance speech was brief. "Thank you very much. Uh, it's much heavier than I imagined. Uh, I, uh, I had something to say and uh, I can't remember what I, uh, was going to say for the life of me. I don't think that, uh, every in my life have so many people been so directly responsible for my being so very, very glad. It's a wonderful moment and a rare one and I am certainly indebted. Thank you."

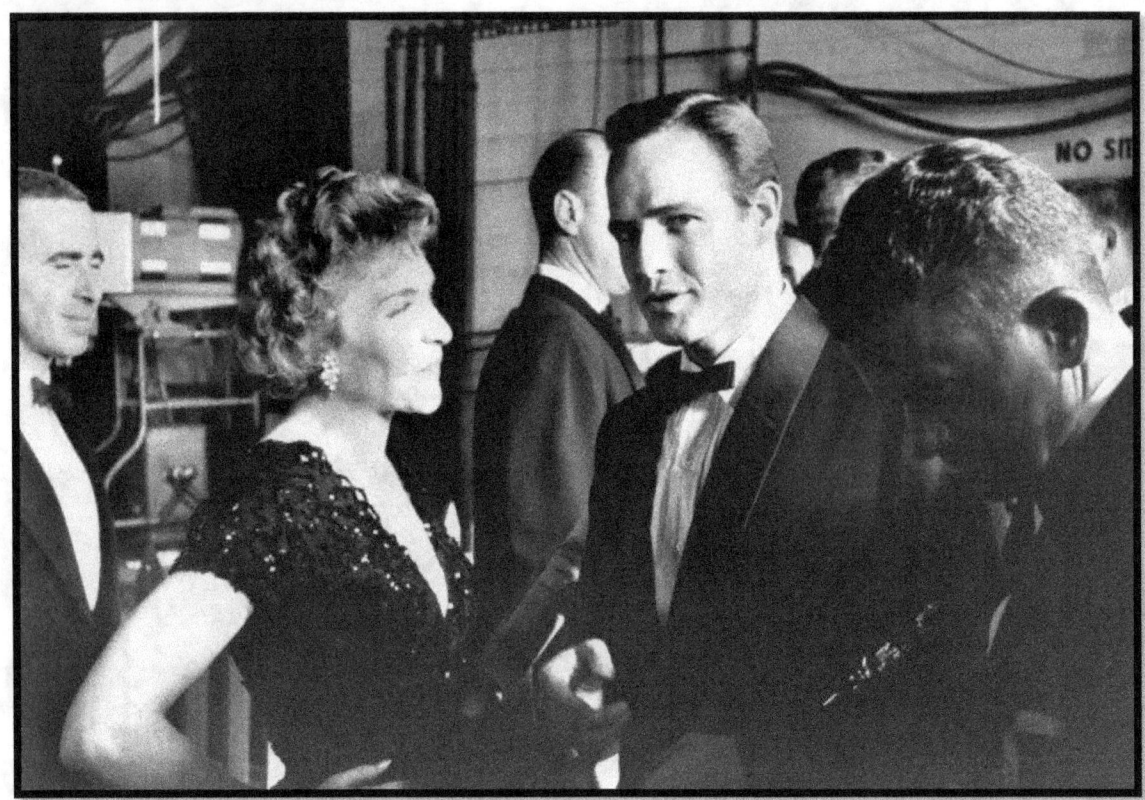

   When the show was over, Brando and Best Actress award winner Grace Kelly posed for photographs. Brando nervously fumbled with a cigarette, crushing it out when a cameraman asked him to put his arm around Kelly, which he did. A photographer yelled out for Brando to kiss Kelly, which he did, twenty times and then went around the room kissing all of the women including gossip writer Hedda Hooper. Recognizing her, he stepped back and then shook her hand.
 At a post-Oscar party at his agent's house, Brando sat on a couch and sipped champagne from a coffee mug until he fell asleep. Eventually Brando simply lost the Oscar from Waterfront. Many years later, it reappeared at an auction house in

London. Brando protested its sale and the item was removed from the block, however, he never got the Oscar back. The person who had placed it up for sale had it in his possession and insisted that Brando had given it to him.

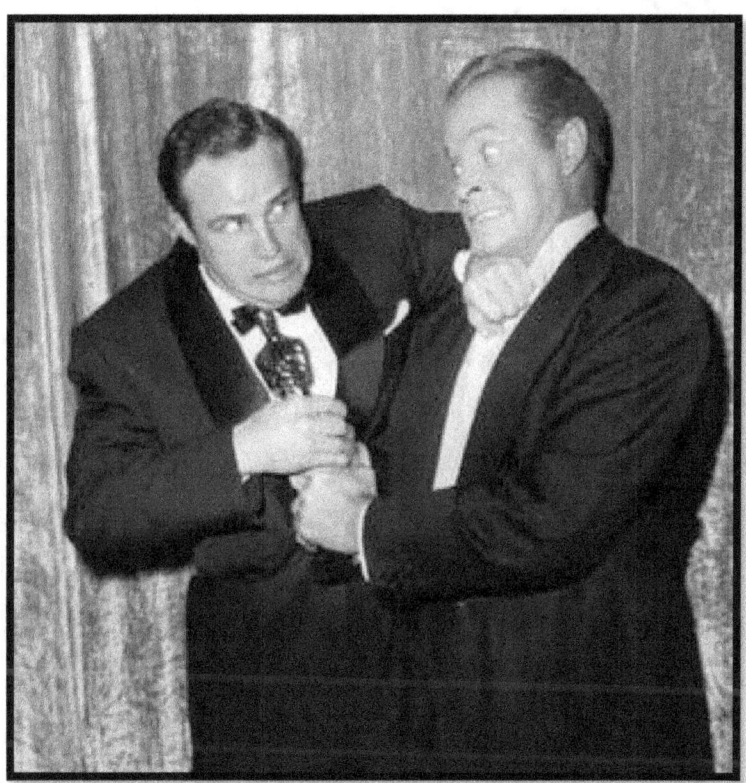

Epilogue

Like the film's ending, in reality on the real Waterfront, nothing was resolved although the film did play a crucial role in making changes in the unions. Schulberg said one of the things he was proudest of concerning the picture was something that Father Corridan said, that once the public saw what a shape-up was really like, the mob and the stevedore companies could ever hire men like that again. That was true, the shape up ended, but as Kazan's said some fifty years after the film's release the waterfront has never got any better, it's the same now, just the same as it always was.

In 2003, in a statement that could have been uttered by Peter Pantos in 1947, former New York Police Commissioner Robert McGuire, who served as the court-appointed monitor of a Bayonne local once controlled by the Genovese gang, said, "We have to get rid of the wise guys and encourage the good people to stand up"

As for Sam Spiegel, he resumed the use of his real name for his credit as producer of Waterfront instead of S. P. Eagle. The films smashing success secured his place as one of Hollywood's greatest producers. Flush with cash from *Waterfront*, he would go on to release *The Last Tycoon* (1976) *Nicholas and Alexandra* (1971) *The Night of the Generals* (1967) *The Chase* (1966) *Suddenly, Last Summer* (1959) His last film was the 1983 *Betrayal*.

He continued to live the good life, sleeping with college undergraduates and keeping steady girlfriends who were 50 years his junior. While not always admirable man, he was a man who lived life and made art on his own terms. The actor Peter O'Toole once said that "Spiegel will die in two inches of bath water" In 1985, the producer collapsed on New Year's Eve, from a heart attack, falling into the bath in his hotel room. The actor Peter Ustinov was present while a doctor tried to revive the dead Spiegel by pummeling his great chest. "Give him the kiss of life," the doctor urged Ustinov, who demurred from doing the useless act. "Alive or dead" Ustinov said, "I would not kiss Sam Spiegel."

After *Waterfront* Schulberg wrote two more films in quick succession: *The Harder They Fall,* an adaptation of his boxing novel starring Humphrey Bogart, and *A Face in the Crowd*, an indictment of the narcotic effect of television. He never won another Academy Award or wrote another novel with the depth of *What Makes Sammy Run* or another *The Disenchanted. Waterfront* was his summit.

Kazan's filmmaking took a steady decline after *Waterfront.* For him, and Schulberg, *Waterfront* represented a defining moment in their careers. The further the McCarthy years went behind him, the more it seemed to leap in front of him. In 1999, he was awarded the Academy Award for Lifetime Achievement. Two years earlier the American Film Institute had refused him a similar award because of his decision fifty years before to testify and give names before the HUAC.
The Lifetime Achievement Award divided Hollywood. Nick Nolte, Tim Robbins, Susan Sarandon, and Ed Harris, who sat out the standing ovation, hands in their laps, while, otherwise, the overall audience applauded.
Five hundred protesters gathered outside the Dorothy Chandler Pavilion where the award was given, with placards that read "Elia Kazan: Nominated for Benedict Arnold Award," "Don't Whitewash the Blacklist"
Abraham Polonsky, who claimed he had been Blacklisted, said, "I hope somebody shoots him. It will be an interesting moment in what otherwise promises to be a dull evening."

What seemed to be lost over the protest over the award, both pro and con, was that after five decades Kazan artistic message in Waterfront was still being heard, still being debated still evoking emotions, still evoking passions. His masterwork of rugged individualism continued to anger those on the left and justify those on the right. Standing on the stage that night, the now elderly Kazan appeared remarkably satisfied. Perhaps he understood what his detractors and his supporters did not understand, that his art would outlive him.

Kazan died at his home in Manhattan at age 94.

By the time *Waterfront* was released, Father Corridan's drinking, always a problem, worsened and degenerated into alcoholism. He considered himself and his work on the docks, a failure. He was completely demoralized. The evidence showed otherwise. He had fought heroically for justice on the waterfront. In less than six years, his efforts brought international attention to the outrageous working conditions of New York's longshoremen.

He inspired several congressional and State committees and commissions to investigate the waterfront, rid the docks of the shape-up, established a hiring hall and almost single handedly ran off the Communists. He could not see any of that. His problems with Cardinal Spellman worsened and he was eventually moved, banished is a better word, out of the waterfront in 1957 and assigned to a teaching position at LeMoyne College in Syracuse.

He returned to New York in the 1960s, was assigned to teach theology at Saint Peter's College, where he could east out of his classroom window and see parts of New York Harbor, the site of many battles he had fought on behalf of longshoremen. Since Corridan rarely spoke publicly of his work in the Port of New York and New Jersey and few of his students knew that he was the inspiration for the character of Father Barry. By then he was a functioning alcoholic. He ended his career, at age 73, working in hospital ministries in Brooklyn before his death in 1984, always convinced that he had lost his battle to improve life on the waterfront. Corridan's enemy in the Church, the Machiavellian Richard Cardinal Spellman, had him banished to upstate New York right after *Waterfront* was released. Father Corridan died in 1984, Budd Schulberg delivered his eulogy at the Priests funeral mass at Fordham University. There is a telling line in the film, penned by Budd Schulberg, which sums up Corridan's courageous work on the docks "You've begun to make it possible for honest men to work the docks with job security and peace of mind"

In today's film world, parts of *Waterfront* do not work as well as they once did. Occasionally the film seems contrived or overly familiar. At times, the theme was too obvious, going overboard with its preachy tone but the passion comes through. Passion never changes. The films basic theme, heroism, standing up for what one believes in the face of seemingly overwhelming opposition and for trying to change things for the better, is ageless.

Even with its few flaws, Waterfront, with its dynamic cinematic conflict and rich, textured characters, is on the AFI list of one of the top best films of twentieth century, holding position eight.

Waterfront has withstood the test of time primarily because it is a good story, brilliantly filmed, its overall grittiness, and the remarkable performances of Marlon Brando, Rod Steiger and Lee J. Cobb's. Brando's performance is still widely considered one of the greatest performances ever in film.

BIT PART PLAYERS

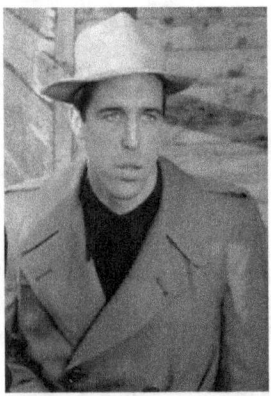

Fred Gwynne: For the role of an uneducated goon named Slim, Kazan chose six foot five actor Frederick Hubbard Gwynne, or Fred Gwynne, the son of a wealthy Wall Street broker (His mother was a cartoonist) who died from complications after routine surgery in 1932. During the war, Fred enlisted in the Navy and served on a sub chaser, on his discharge attended the New York Phoenix School of Design. The role of Slim, small as it was, was a stretch for the Groton Prep, Harvard University graduate ('51) where he performed in the drag troupe, the Hasty Pudding Theatricals and was president and chief cartoonist of The Harvard Lampoon After a successful run in *A Midsummer Night's Dream,* he moved to New York to pursue a career in films and stage. To tall and unattractive to be a leading man, he landed a supporting role in *Mrs. McThing* on Broadway, starring Helen Hayes, working part time as a copywriter for the J. Walter Thompson Advertising agency to make ends meet between assignments.
After *Waterfront*, his first film role, he landed his first major Broadway role in the musical, *Irma La Duce* where TV producer Nat Hiken who hired Gwynne to co-star as Francis Maldoon in the NBC television series, *Car 54, Where Are You?* (1961-1963)
Just before the show was canceled, one of his children drowned in the family pool. Between Waterfront and Car 54, he published his first children's book in 1958, Best in Show. In 1964, he was cast in the CBS television series, *The Munsters*, which typecast the actor for nearly two decades. In that time, he penned several more children's books including *God's First World, A Chocolate Moose for Dinner,* and *A Little Pigeon Toad.* He returned to the stage in the early 1970s, and won critical acclaim as Big Daddy in the Broadway revival of *Cat on a Hot Tin Roof* with Elizabeth Ashley and as Claudius in *Hamlet*, and the stage manager in *Our Town.* In 1976, he won an Obie Award for his performance in the off-Broadway play, *Grand Magic.*

He made a return to the screen with a small role in Bernardo Bertolucci's Luna, Ironweed, *Fatal Attraction, The Cotton Club* and *My Cousin Vinny.* Gwynne retired in the early 1992 with his wife Deborah to his farm in Rural Maryland, accepting occasional voice-over work. In the later part of the year, he was diagnosed with pancreatic cancer and died on July 2, 1993, at the age of 66. During the trial scene in Waterfront, when asked for his name Gwynne, as Slim, answers "Malden Skulovich" fellow actor Karl Malden's real name.

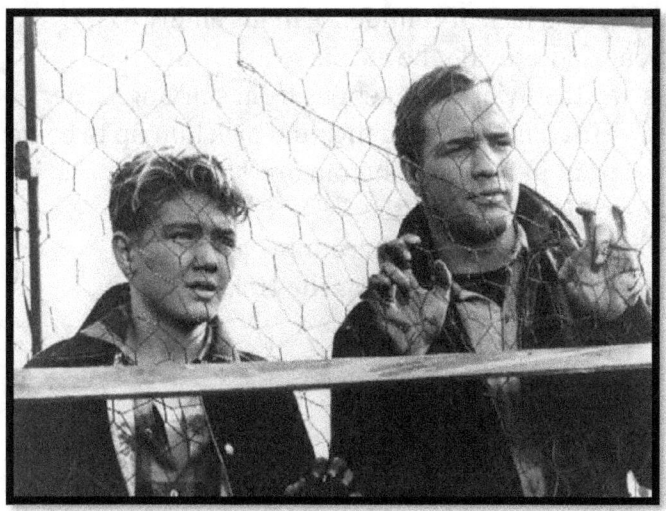

Thomas Hanley played the role of Tommy, the little boy who idolizes Terry Malloy. He was 13 years old when he ran across an assistant producer on the film installing
  Terry Malloy's pigeon coops on the roof of his apartment building. Hanley recalled;
We were alone, my mother and I. My father had been a dockworker and was murdered by the mob when I was 4 months old. We were dead broke. My mother hadn't paid the rent in eight months. Still when I found Brownie (Arthur Brown, the Assistant producer former dockworker and a drinking buddy of Schulberg's) I said, "What are you doing on my roof" here we were 8 months behind in the rent and I was calling it my roof! Brownie said that he had known my dad and that he was going to get me a part in the film. I didn't believe him. I didn't think he had that kind of pull. He paid me a couple of bucks a week to feed the pigeons but only because he thought I would tear the coop down if he didn't pay. But he got me the part.

   Brownie arranged for Hanley to be brought down to Manhattan to the Actor's Studio where Schulberg and Kazan were testing for parts. *"Kazan and Schulberg and Brando were wonderful to me. Kinder then they had to be. They were trying to help me."* In the first meeting, Kazan wanted to get a reaction out of the boy to test his acting skills. *They knew my background, and Kazan said my father was probably murdered because he was a squealer. They were trying to provoke me, and I flung a chair across the room. That's the response Kazan wanted. Marlon Brando told me to bring my mother to the set on day and I did. He told her that he had arranged for me to have an agent to help me get more roles. He was a very decent guy. To get me geared up, emotional, for the scene where I throw the dead pigeon at Marlon, Kazan and Schulberg put me in a room with a guy from the neighborhood, he had a role in the film as a cop, and I hated him. The guy made some remarks about my father and got me upset and that's how I was so emotional for the part*

  Kazan's was famous for manipulating performers to get a desired reaction. During the filming of Viva Zapata, Kazan apparently told Anthony Quinn that Brando was saying horrible things about him behind his back to heighten the conflict between their two characters on screen. The criticism of this technique, while it is necessary occasionally, but as a pattern, suggested to

353

many in Hollywood that Kazan held a cynicism and a lack of confidence in his ability to convince actors of the emotional truth of a scene and provide the means to arrive at it.

Kazan paid him $500 a week for three weeks-worth of work. "It kept us from starving.....He (Brando) was just a real regular guy," he says. "He could have had the limo pick him up to come to work every morning, but instead he took the train in from Manhattan dressed as a longshoreman. People respected that. They loved Karl Malden, too."

Hanley went on to earn his living as a dockworker. In 2005, he was running as a reform candidate for union steward in the mobbed up ILA local that still runs the Hoboken ports.

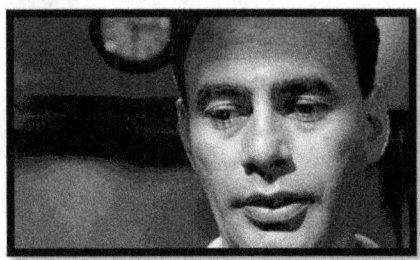

Martin Balsam, by then a veteran character actor of stage and television, made his film debut in Waterfront, (uncredited though it was) as Crime Commission investigator Gillette. Raised in the Bronx, Balsam was the oldest of three children of women's sportswear sales clerk whose motto was "All actors are bums." Regardless, after service in the Navy during the second war, Balsam joined New York's Actors Studio, supporting himself by waiting on tables and ushering at Radio City Music Hall.

Balsam followed Waterfront with a beefy role in Sidney Lumet's *Twelve Angry Men* (1957) and strong performances as the doomed soldier in Hitchcock's *Psycho* (1960), the police chief in *Cape Fear* (1962, he was also in the 1991 remake by Scorsese) and the studio chief in Edward Dmytryk's *The Carpetbaggers* (1964). In 1965, he won a well-deserved Academy Award as Best Supporting Actor for his performance as Jason Robards Jr.'s agent brother in *A Thousand Clowns*.

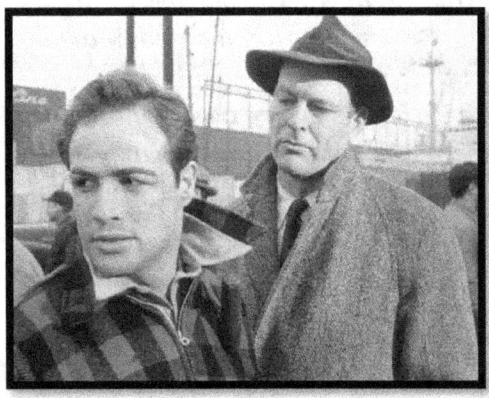

Leif Erikson played the role of the second Waterfront Crime Commission Investigator, Glover. Erikson had been a big band singer and trombone player before moving into acting in 1935 when he made his debut as a corpse in the Zane Grey Western. Erickson was under contract to Universal during the early 1940s before joining the military during World War 2 (he was injured in combat twice) although he had been in at least 20 films; Waterfront was his leading credit up until that point. He had been married to the troubled actor Frances Farmer. They divorced in 1942. A year later, she was wrongfully declared mentally incompetent in 1943 and committed to an asylum for seven years before she was released. Erickson later made it big on television on the program *The High Chaparral* (1967-71).

UNCREDITED ROLES IN THE FILM

Dan Bergin played the role of Sidney. Born in Ireland, as were several other members of the cast and crew, Waterfront was his first film. Bergin was a film editor by training.

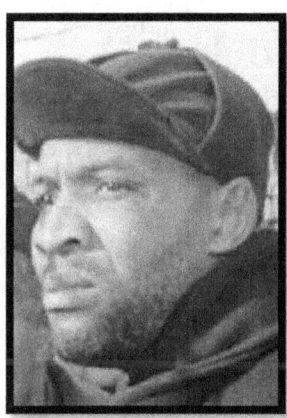

Don Blackman plays the role of Luke, the only African American in the film with a line. (Several African-Americans are pictured in the film) Blackman was a professional wrestler who landed uncredited roles in several films before *Waterfront*. Aside from *Waterfront*, he best remembered as The Doll Man in the Blacula films of the 1970s.

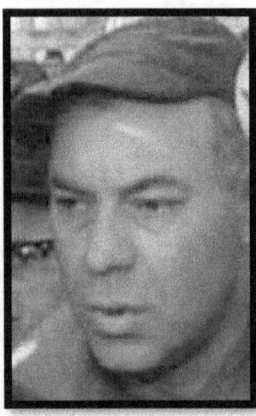
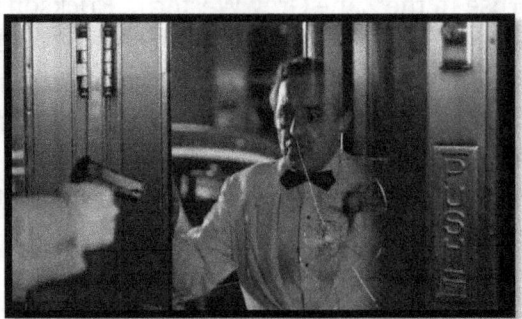

Rudy Bond played Moose. A combat infantry veteran in World War 2, Kazan introduced him to acting when he enrolled him in the Actors Studio. He went on to have a role in most of Kazan's more important productions. He later played the role of Cuneo in *The Godfather*.

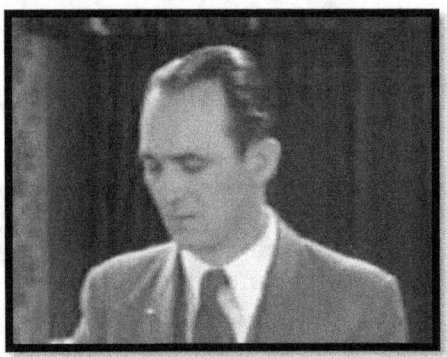

Jere Delaney had an uncredited role in the film as a dockworker. A stage actor, *Waterfront* was his last film. (Out of only three, he appeared in) He died a few months after *Waterfront* was released.

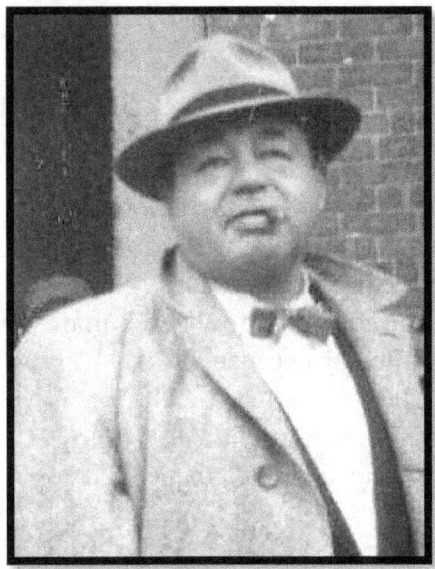

Anthony Galento The heavyweight fighter Two Ton Tony Galento (Dominic Anthony Galento) makes a brief appearance in the film as Truck, one of John Friendly's goons. Galento, who once replied to an inquiry about his thoughts on William Shakespeare by saying, "I'll moider da bum." knocked down heavyweight great Joe Louis in their 1939 title match in the second round. Louis made it to his feet on the two count and won the match.

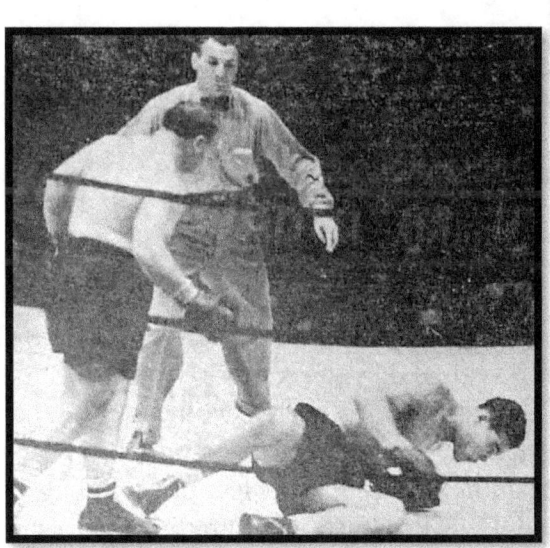

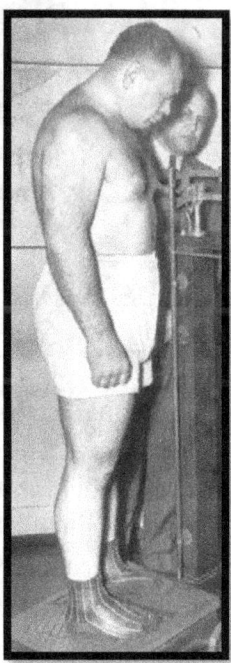

The night before the Louis fight, Tony's brother walked into his bar and asked Tony for a couple if free tickets for the fight. Tony told him to stand in line like everybody else. His brother hit him over the head with a beer bottle. The bartender stitched up the three-inch gash in his head and the Lewis fight stayed on schedule. That same night, Lewis gave him 23 more stitches in the face.

Galento, at 5 foot 9 and 250 pounds, ("A beer barrel with feet" the New York Times called him) was a Northern New Jersey hero, who took on the best heavyweights of his day including Max Bear and closed out his career with a 74-22-6 record with 51 knockouts. Galento, a notoriously dirty fighter, tormented his opponents inside and outside the ring. The usually east going Joe Lewis said that Galento was the only man in the entire sport of boxing he ever hated. He trained on beer and southern Italian food. He hated the country and refused to go into the mountains to a training camp. Instead, he did his roadwork after dark in New Jersey because, he said, "I fight at night, don't I?"

Galento would appear in two other films, *Wind Across the Everglades* and *The Best Things in Life Are Free*. Galento died on July 22, 1979 after a three-year battle against diabetes that cost him the amputation of a foot, then, later both legs.

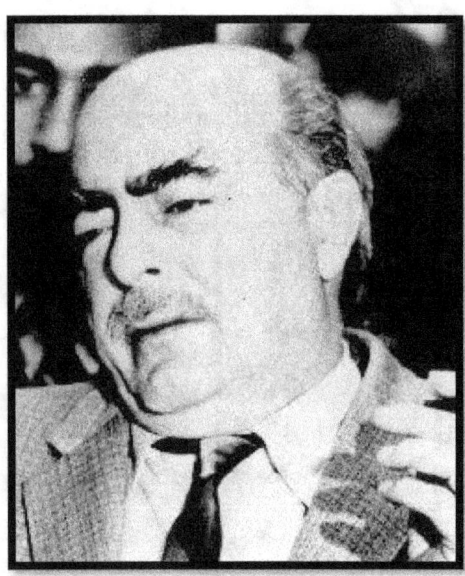

Michael Gazzo Waterfront also introduced the great actor Michael Gazzo in an uncredited bit part. He became better known as Frankie Pentangeli on the Godfather Trilogy. The film's director, Francis Ford Coppola wanted Kazan to play the role of Hyman Roth in the film, *Godfather 11*, but Kazan declined. Gazzo was also a respected acting teacher and award-winning playwright who wrote the acclaimed work *A Hatful of Rain* a portrait of a lower-middle-class worker who attempts to break his drug addiction. It was turned into a film in 1957, co-written by Gazzo. He also wrote King Creole, an Elvis Presley film. Gazzo broke into show business as a stage director and actor at the Great Neck Playhouse in New York, while studying at the Dramatic Workshop of the New School for Social Research in the mid-1940s. He had a life long association with the Actors Studio. Most of his career was spent as a writer and teacher. He came back to film in the 1971 film, *The Gang that Couldn't Shoot Straight*, based loosely on the life of gangster Joey Gallo. He received an Oscar nomination as Best Supporting Actor for his work in the *Godfather Part Two*, an award he probably should have won. (*Waterfront* extra Rudy Bond also played a role in the Godfather films, as Mafia Don Cuoneo)

Suzanne Hahn landed a bit role in the film. Then an out of work actor, she had recently graduated from LSU where her roommate was actor Joan Woodward. In mid-December of 1953, she got a telegram telling her to report to Hoboken for a work as an extra. The telegram had arrived late and Hahn assumed that she would not be hired. However, on the bus ride over to New Jersey she sat next to one of Kazan's assistant directors who was also late for work. He managed to get her a walk on role as a bar fly type who sauntered over to the jukebox and leans over it looking at the selection. The job lasted for three weeks. Three years later, she landed another role in the Broadway production of *The Three Penny Opera* where she met actor John Astin. They were married in 1956. Two of their three children are actors.

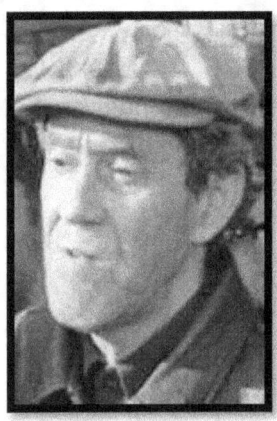

John F. Hamilton played Pop Doyle. He had been appearing in films since 1924. Waterfront was his last role. Born in Britain, Hamilton had appeared in several films as a child including one Hitchcock film, which has since been lost.

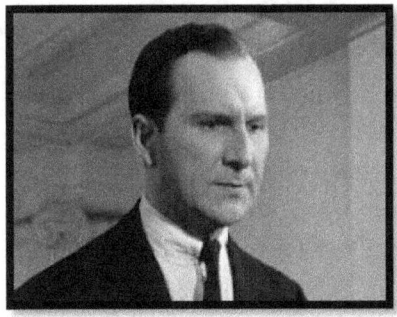

John Heldabrand played the role of Mutt. *Waterfront* was his first film. He appeared, briefly, in one other film and never acted again.

Anna Hegira (Sometimes billed as Anne) played the role of Mrs. Collins, the women in the alley. *Waterfront* was her first film. She is best known for her role as Thomna in the film *The Arrangement*

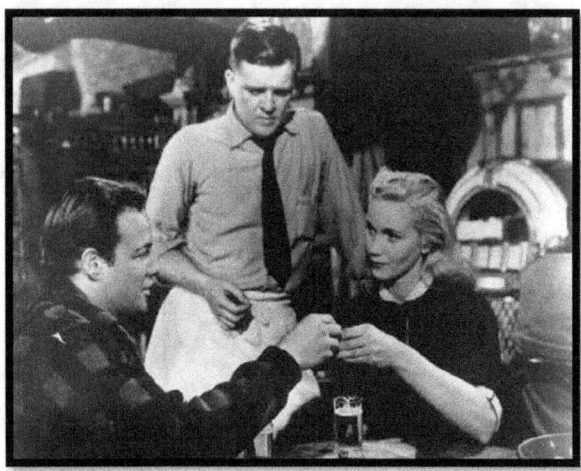

Pat Hingle (Martin Patterson Hingle) played the uncredited role of Jocko the Bartender in the scene where Terry takes Edie for a drink. "We were filming in Hoboken, New Jersey, in late fall," he recalled. They were mostly doing the waterfront scenes, but they had some interior scenes ready, in case the weather got bad. Therefore, I was there, day after day, in my apron, waiting for the weather to turn - but it never did. Anyway, I watched Kazan - and it was fascinating. He worked differently with every actor on the set, finding his own way to communicate with all of them."

He later became better known as Commissioner Gordon in the *Batman* movies. Interestingly enough Alan Napier, who played the role of Alfred the Butler on the *Batman* television series, also played the role of the Communist ringleader in John Wayne's Anti-Communist-Pro-HUAC film, *Big Jim McLean*.

Hingle was a solid character player on stage, screen and TV for over four decades. He began acting as a student at the University of Texas, made the move to New York in the late 1940s, studied at the American Theater Wing, and became Kazan's protégé at the Actor's Studio. He followed *Waterfront* with a breakthrough-supporting role in Kazan's *Splendor in the Grass* (1961), as Warren Beatty's brusque father.

Hingle appeared in a series of Clint Eastwood flicks including the conflicted police chief father of a rapist in *Sudden Impact* (1983) and as the hanging judge in Hang 'Em High (1968); He played a bartender again in *The Quick and the Dead* (1995). His other work would include roles in *Shaft* (2000) *The Grifters* (1990) *Batman* (1989) *The Falcon and the Snowman* (1985) *Nevada Smith* (1966) *The Ugly American* (1963) *Splendor in the Grass* (1961) Norma Rae, The Gauntlet, The Carey Treatment and others. *Waterfront* was his first film

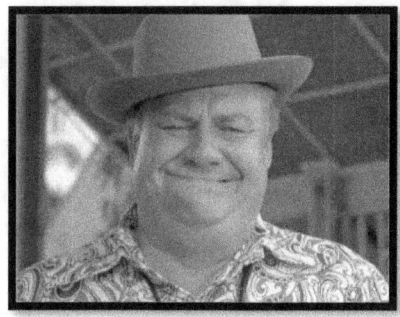

Clifton James held an uncredited role in the film. His other worked included *Bonfire of the Vanities* (1990) *Eight Men Out* (1988) *Cool Hand Luke* (1967) *The Chase* (1966) *Black Like Me* (1964) *Invitation to a Gunfighter, The Man With the Golden Gun, The Reivers The Last Detail, Will Penny, Superman II, Silver Streak* and back to New Jersey again in *Hell, Heaven or Hoboken*

Tommy Kennedy a retired Hoboken police officers was hired as an extra for the film at $7. When payday came, he was given $5. "Where's the other deuce?" I asked. "And I soon learned it was a kickback, just like the dock workers [pay] in the film. The movie's part of Hoboken history. As a cop I got stopped so many times by tourists who wanted to know where Marlon Brando fought Lee J. Cobb that I probably could've made more money as a tour guide."

Frankie Fame, an uncredited gangster, took the job because it paid "$2 an hour and a cup of coffee. I knew the heavyweight boxer Tony Galento from Jersey City. He got me into *On the Waterfront*. To this day, my kids whoop it up when they see me diving for chips in the shape-up."

Arthur Keegan played Jimmy played a dockworker. Before *Waterfront,* he had a small role in *From Here to Eternity* as Treadwell, (1953) Otherwise; *Waterfront* was his last credited film.

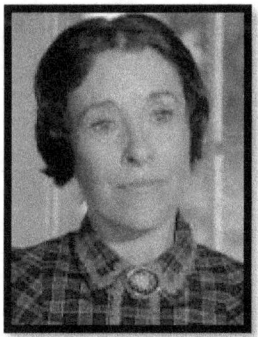

Katherine Scottie MacGregor played an uncredited role as a Longshoreman's mother. A stage actor by training she is best known for her role as Mrs. Olson on the television program *Little House on the Prairie.*

Edward McNally played an uncredited role as Terry Malloy's neighbor. *Waterfront* was his first film out of career total of 17 films.

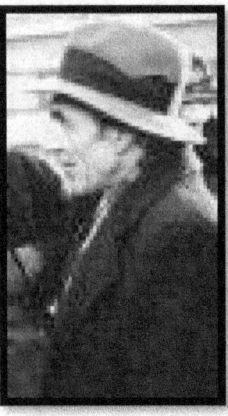

Barry Malcolm starred as Johnny Friendly's banker. Born in Ireland, he had been in films since 1923.

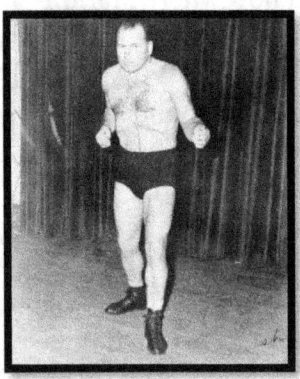

Tiger Joe Marsh (born Joseph Marusich) played an uncredited role of a police officer; however, Kazan would also cast him in bit parts in *Viva Zapata*! and *Panic in the Streets*. He also had a role in *The Joe Louis Story* (1953) Marsh was an interesting character. A Chicagoan from the wrong side of the tracks, he had been a professional wrestler, winning the World Heavyweight title in 1937. He continued wrestling into the late 1950s and later was the original model for Mr. Clean advertisements. His career had a revival in the early 1980s when he appeared on *Simon & Simon* in the role of Otto.

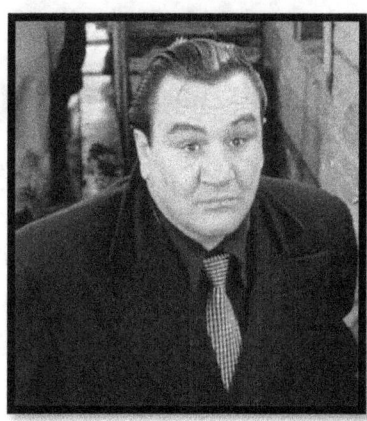

Tami Mauriello as Tillio. Mauriello was a tough, talented former light heavyweight who had failed in two courageous title attempts against champion Gus Lesnevitch, in the 1940s. After an 11 bout winning streak in the heavyweight division, Mauriello became Joe Louis's second title defense after his military service, September 18, 1946 in New York. Mauriello stunned Louis briefly with a wild right, but wound up a first-round KO victim. Tami became a boxing trivia item when he told a live network radio interviewer: "I hurt Louis, but I got too God damn careless." Tami did knock out heavy weight great Jersey Joe Wolcott, Mauriello was a close friend of Frank Sinatra. Once, during a scene that included Mauriello facing the camera, the boxer was expressionless. Kazan needed him to look angry. The five foot five and a half inch wiry director leaped from his chair, smacked the fighter as hard as he could across the face and yelled "Okay, roll em"   Mauriello was frozen for a moment, stupefied. When he regained his sense, he lunged at Kazan and had to be pulled back by the stagehands, while Kazan walked backwards away from the set explaining, "It's a method of acting Tam, that's all!"

Mike O'Dowd played Specs. He had actually worked as a longshoreman on the New York waterfront between acting gigs.

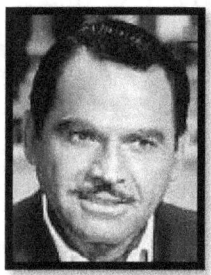

Nehemiah Persoff played the cabdriver. Born in Jerusalem, Israel he moved to the US age 9. He went on to star in Schulberg's story, *The Harder they Fall* and became the voice of Papa Mousekewitz in An American Tail: Fievel Goes West, (1991) In his career; Persoff appeared in over 500 television programs and films.

William Ramoth was a Clifton New Jersey Policeman who had fought professionally under the name Billy Kilroy. He was introduced into the New Jersey Boxing Hall of Fame in November 1978. Ramoth heard that former heavyweight contender Anthony "Two Ton Tony" Galento was in Hoboken for the filming *Waterfront* and Ramoth, who knew Galento, drove over to Hoboken to see him.

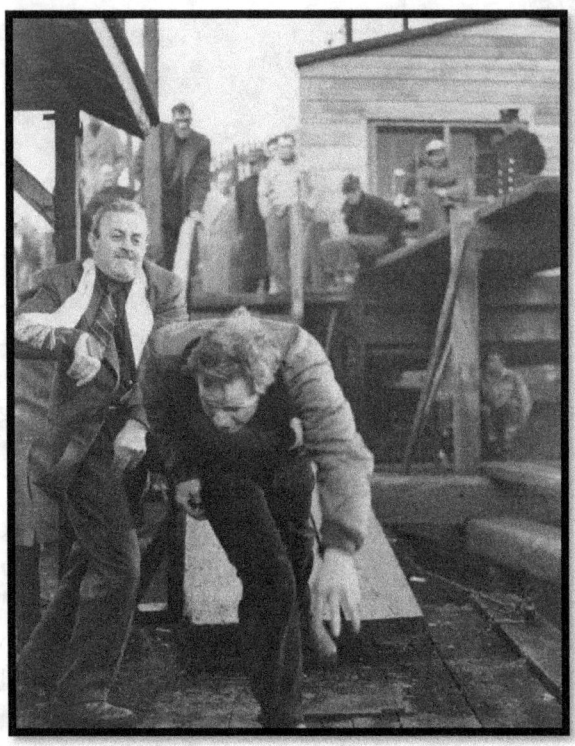

The pair was having a drink in a tavern when Kazan walked in and noticed that Ramoth, who was wearing a leather jacket, resembled Marlon Brando from a distance. He asked Ramoth if he had any boxing experience. He was hired as Brando's double for the fight scenes. Ramoth went on to do fight scenes and serve as a technical adviser in 12 more films, acting, as Paul Newman's double in The Hustler and Somebody Up There Likes Me. He also made guest appearances on several television shows, including To Tell the Truth and I've Got a Secret.

Rosie the Cat There is a scene in the film where Brando picks up Edie's cat, which earlier Pop Doyle explains, is a stray, which was taken in by Edie, and he cares for. The cats name was Rosie and it lived upstairs in an apartment above the saloon used as Johnny Friendly's bar. When the cat walked across a shooting scene in the bar, a stagehand picked it up and used it in the next scene between Brando and Saint. However, the stagehand neglected to tell the cat's owner, which caused a minor argument on the filming set.

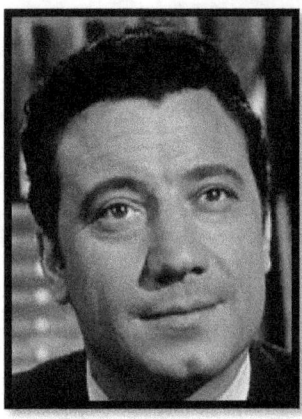

Johnny Seven (John Anthony Fetto) played an uncredited longshoreman. He would go on to appear in over 600 Television shows, 26 movies, 2 Broadway shows and Off-Broadway Shows. He is best known from the TV series *Ironside* (1967) in which he played the role of Lieutenant Carl Reese (1969-1975)

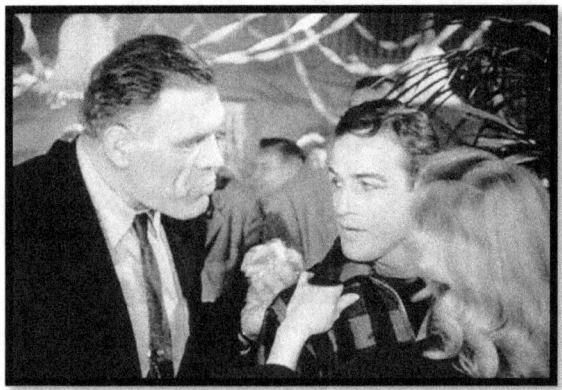

Abe Simon The role of Barney, a gangster, was played by Abe Simon, a middleweight great who lost only 3 of 31 bouts (1948-1952) and accidentally killed a fighter inside the ring with a single blow to the head. Simon had been an advisor, along with boxing great Willie Pep, on the film *Requiem for a Heavyweight*. Simon made two unsuccessfully challenges for the Heavyweight Title and was the only Jew to fight for the title. On his first attempt, he was stopped by Joe Louis in 13th round at Detroit's Olympia Stadium on March 21, 1941. In his second attempt on March 27, 1942, he was stopped again by Louis, this time in six rounds at Madison Square Garden.

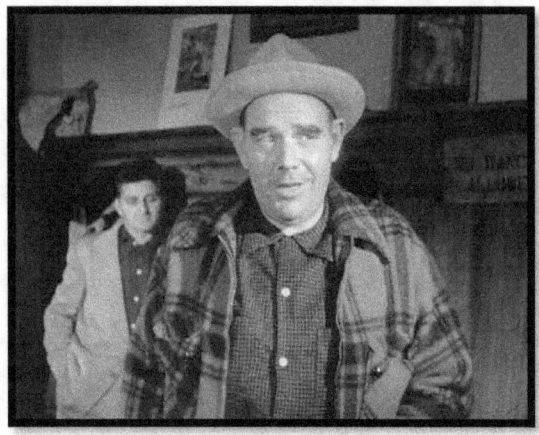

James Westerfield starred as Big Mac. A legendary character actor he would play roles in over 50 films and 75 television programs during his career. However, his first love was the stage

OTHER MEMBERS OF THE FILM AND DEVELOPMENT CREW

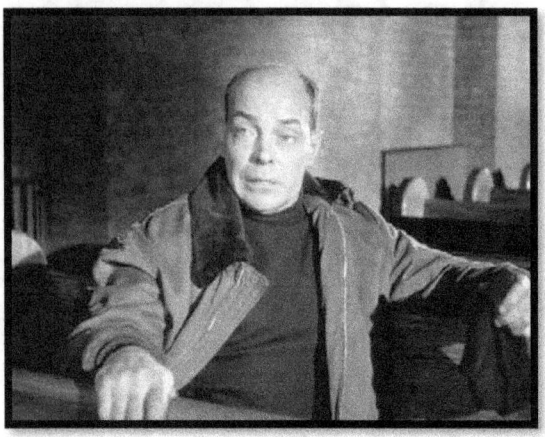

Pat Henning would play the part of Timothy "Kayo" Duggan. He had already worked with Kazan on *Man on a Tightrope* in 1953 Pat Henning would also appear in *Wind across the Everglades* and *The Cardinal*. He would become better known to Baby boomers as Sean McCoy on the Television series, Flipper. Henning, who was born in 9, died in Miami Beach in 973. One of the few professional actors in the film, his portrayal as a longshoreman is over the top, lacks sincerity and at times blatantly annoying

Howard Block was an assistant camera operator (uncredited in the film) Waterfront was his first film. He received a Life Time Achievement Award (called a Cammy) in 1998. Like so many others from the films crew, he also worked on *The Godfather*.

Robert Hodes was the script supervisor. Waterfront was his first film. He continued to work with Kazan throughout the remainder of his career.

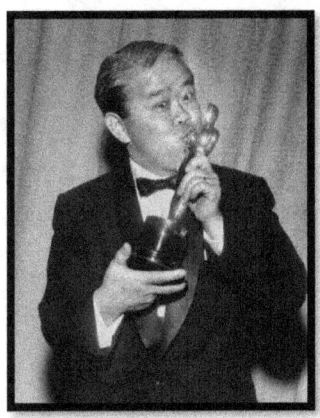

Working with Boris Kaufman was Cinematographer **Jimmy Howe**. With over 120 films to his credit, Wong is still considered one of the greatest cinematographers in the history of motion pictures. Born on August 28, 1899, in Kwangtung, China, as James Wong (He was born Wong Tung Jim but was known as Jimmy Howe during his stint at M-G-M he was given the middle name of "Wong" by the publicity department to add an exotic flair.) grew up in Washington State. He grew up with the dream of becoming a professional boxer. As a teenager, he landed a job as a delivery clerk for a commercial photographer, which, in 1917, led to an entry-level position of cutting-room helper in a studio back lot. He became a slate-boy for Cecil B. DeMille and who promoted him to assistant camera operator. By 1922, Howe was a full-fledged director of photography. In 1949, Howe was brought in to film (secretly) the screen test for Greta Garbo's proposed comeback film *La Duchesse de Langeais*. Garbo demanded the test be shot in black and white, which was granted, but there is a persistent rumor that Wong shot a second reel of the actor in color anyway. Wong perfected experimental techniques that became standard after his creative applications, especially for deep focus and used hand-held cameras, which created a unique perspective for the audience. In the boxing film *Body and Soul* (1947), he put the cinematographer on roller skates, using a small, hand-held camera to follow the action more intimately and dramatically. He was also a master of the artful use of light and shadow and his innovative yet unobtrusive camera work. He would work with some of the biggest names in the business, from Victor Fleming to John Frankenheimer. Called 'Low Key Hoe' for his unassuming style, he pioneered the use of deep-focus photography and of the hand-held camera. He was nominated for an Academy Award for his work on *Algiers*, (1938) a film produced by Walter Wanger, Schulberg's former boss on *Winter Carnival*. Algiers starred Charles Boyer and Hedy Lamarr. Followed by his 1955 win at the Academy for *The Rose Tattoo* starring Anna Magnani and Burt Lancaster, a second Academy Award for *Hud* (1963) Starring Paul Newman and a second nomination for his final film *Funny Girl* starring Barbara Streisand

Anna Hill Johnstone was the wardrobe supervisor. She also later worked on the *Godfather* films. Johnstone was actually a customer designer by trade. Johnstone accompanied Budd Schulberg to the play starring the unknown Eva Marie Saint.

George Justin would be the Production Manager. *Waterfront* was also his first film. He went on to become Vice President Production Management for Paramount Pictures, Executive Production Manager for Orion Pictures and Senior Vice President Production Management.

Kazan's Assistant director was **Charles H. Maguire.** *Waterfront* was also one of his first films. Like most of the cast and crew for Waterfront, Charlie Maguire became a Kazan regular. The director hired him again for A Face in the Crowd and Baby Doll. Maguire began his career in the film industry in the early 1950s while working as a prop man in New York's Local 52. He traveled to Hoboken, interviewed with Kazan for a job as property master, and ended up as assistant director on the film. Tutored by director Robert Aldrich, he moved to Los Angeles in the mid-'60s to find frequent work as a producer and assistant director on such films as Fail-Safe (1964) and *The Sand Peebles* (1966). Maguire would work as a director or producer on some of the best-known films of the twentieth century including *Patriot Games* (1992) *Shampoo* (1975) *The Parallax View*, (1974) *The Friends of Eddie Coyle* (1973) *The Arrangement* (1969) *I Love You Alice B. Toklas!* (1968) *Splendor in the Grass* (1961) and *The Hustler*. He continued his collaborations with Kazan until the end of their careers.

For his film editor, Kazan's chose of the best in the business, **Arthur Eugene Milford**, who had been working on his craft since 1926 and would span five decades of work before he retired. Milford entered silent films as a stuntman and title writer and graduated to an editor's position in 1926 with Two Can Play starring Clara Bow. He worked for Columbia Pictures, RKO and Republic pictures, including several Capra films including *Flight* (1929), *Platinum Blonde* (1931) and *Lost Horizon* (1937) for which he won the first of two Oscars. During the Second World War, he led the film editorial department for the Office of War Information. Afterwards, he worked for Atomic Energy Commission's film editorial department as chief Editor before returning to feature film work under Kazan. Milford went on to edited Kazan's *Baby Doll* (1956), A Face in the *Crowd* (1957) *Splendor in the Grass* (1961) Arthur Penn's *The Chase* (1966) and later worked on *Inchon* (1982) a dud financed by South Korean investors.

Mary Roach (Faye) was the hairstylist for the cast. *Waterfront* was her first film.

Fred Ryle was the make-up artist. He had been working in films since 1928.

James (Jimmy) Shield's was the films soundman. *Waterfront* was his second film

Dale Tate (Uncredited in the film) created the films titles. Tate also had an uncredited role in the film classic *The Attack of the 50-Foot Women*.

Guy Thomajan was the films Dialogue supervisor. Thomajan was also an accomplished director and actor who had roles in most of Kazan's other films

Flo Transfield was the films wardrobe mistress. She continued to work with Kazan on most of his other films.

Sam Rheiner was the films Assistant to the Producer (Sam Spiegel) *Waterfront* was his next to last film.

Arthur Steckler was the Second Assistant Director. *Waterfront* was his second film. He also went on to work in several other Kazan films.

FILM FLUBS

As it is with almost any film ever made, *Waterfront* has a handful of gaffes, goofs and flubs.

In the scene where Terry walks Edie home, just before the scene dissolves Kazan can be heard shouting "Cut!" which causes Eva Marie Saint abruptly stops and turns around to head back towards the crew area near the camera.

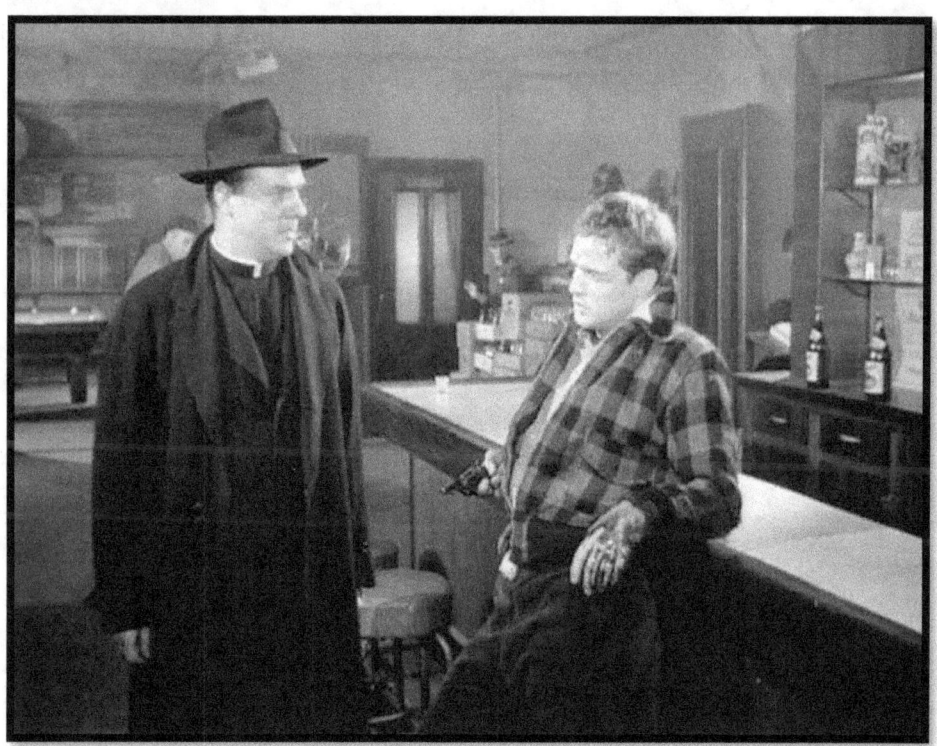

The length of the gun barrel Charley gives Terry gets larger and smaller and then smaller and larger in each scene.

When Terry exits the cab, he gets out on Charley's side rather than his own. Considering that he had his own door and how cramped the cab was, it's a wonder he would do that.

There is no explaining how or why Edie Doyle gets in the cargo hold after Kayo Duggan is killed.

When Terry is talking to Edie by the fence in the park, her hair changes from a windblown mess to a full comb out in the next shot.

When the gangster Tullio and another man enter the Johnny Friendly bar, they spot Terry Malloy sitting with a pistol. When they turn to leave Terry yells out "Stick around, Tullio." Tullio and the other man sit down sit down between Terry and the jukebox. In the next scene, which is supposed to have happened within seconds of Terry threatening Tullio, both Tullio and his friend are simply gone, vanished, without explanation. Also in the bar scene, Terry's arms are folded when viewed from behind and supporting his head when viewed from in front.

A poorly made dummy is thrown from the roof in the opening scene just as an obvious dummy is used for Terry's brother's hanging on the wall in the alley.

When Johnny Friendly climbs out of the water on to the docks, his suit and hair are perfectly dry. (Cobb was actually bald)

At the end of the film, when Terry is walking into the warehouse after his fight with Johnny Friendly, in one shot there are large puddles of water at his feet which are gone in the next scene shot shown several seconds later.

In the taxi scene, Terry's jacket is fully zippered one moment and opened the next and then closed again.

A BRIEF HISTORY OF ORGANIZED CRIME ON THE WATERFRONT

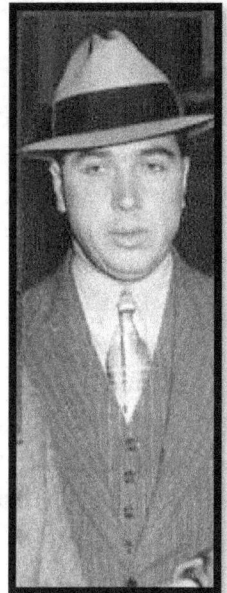 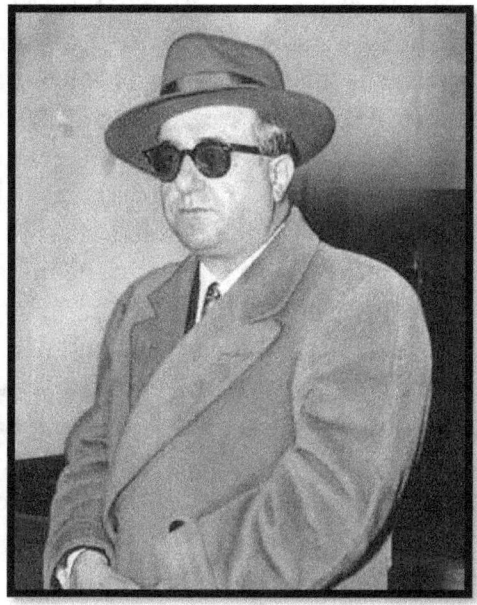 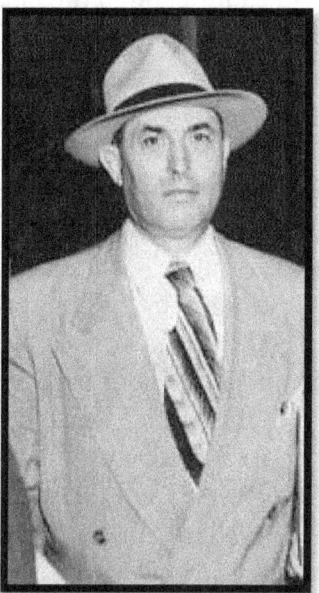

Mafia masters of the waterfront: Joe Adonis (left) The Boss, Albert Anastasia and Joe Profaci

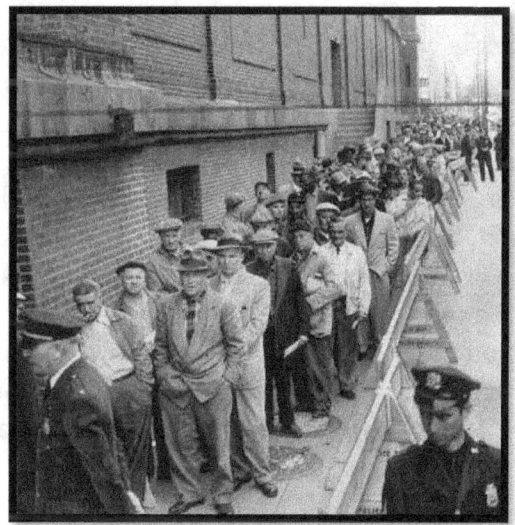

On November 12, 1953, a ship carrying canned Hawaiian fruit arrived on one of the piers run directly by the Anastasia Brothers. The local union had broken off from the ILA and switched over to the AFL union and had managed to convince the shipping line to hold off unloading the cargo for five days while they overthrew one of the Anastasia's top lieutenants, Anthony Calvo AKA Spanish Tony, out of the local. On the morning the ship was to be unloaded, the Anastasia's gather just fewer than 200 hoods to make sure the AFL rebels didn't unload the cargo. When the morning work whistle blew, the rebels, vastly outnumbered, tried to run the gangsters gauntlet on to the pier, but were beaten back. Elated, the goons cheered their fast victory. However, unknown to them, the AFL had gathered over one hundred men along Columbia Street and were marching towards the pier, armed with baseball bats. Word of the impending battle reached the police who arrived en force, 40 detectives, 5 motorcycle police officers, ten horse-mounted police, 100 police officers armed with tear gas and about 25 members of the New York Port Authority Patrol. After a brief struggle, the police pushed Anastasia's men back from the pier entrance and then provided the AFL rebels with an escort to the docks entrance. As the dock workers walked the plank onto the pier, Anastasia's men opened the battle by tossing rocks and beer bottles at the police and then rushed the dock workers. The police, backed by almost two hundred long shore and AFL men, met the gangster's head on and a half hour battle followed that sent three ILA enforcers to the hospital.

Later that evening, Albert Anastasia's brother Gerardo, called Bang Bang, led another assault on the police lines, only to be arrested along with 13 others. Tough Tony appeared a while later, telling the press that he would be back the next morning "With 10,000 longshoremen to teach these punks a lesson"

He never showed up.

On the morning of the election, professional Mafia enforcers were brought into Brooklyn from the West Side of Manhattan where they separated into gangs of four, roaming the election sites, beating up and stabbing AFL representatives and known rebels.

The rebels, backed by the Seafarers and Teamsters unions fought back. There were sporadic but bloody fights everywhere along the waterfront. In mid-morning, police stopped and searched a truck cruising the Brooklyn waterfront near mobster Mickey Bowers pistol local piers. A search of the truck found 20 sawed off baseball bats and 40 other wooden bludgeons, each two inches thick with handle grips. The driver, Seafarers representative Albert Thompson, was arrested. A few hours later, teams of long shore rebels, Seafarers and Teamsters, armed with bats, took their positions on the pistol local's piers and passed out AFL literature.

In late morning, ILA gangsters Ackaltis, Mickey and Harold Bowers, Danny St. John, Machine Gun Campbell and Johnny Keefe, raided a voting poll at Prospect Hall in Brooklyn. Three Seafarers were stabbed and four others beaten badly enough to be taken to the hospital. As a result, several hours later, the waterfront commission barred Ackaltis from any further work on the docks, but the hood had the ruling over turned by the courts

By 1956, little had changed on the waterfront. The mob still ran the ILA. Tough Tony Anastasia punched, shot and stabbed his way into control of the Brooklyn waterfront locals as he intended to do back in 1952. Mickey Bowers' mob was still in power along the piers, there were more loan sharks than ever before and too many persons looking for work, where there were fewer jobs to be had.

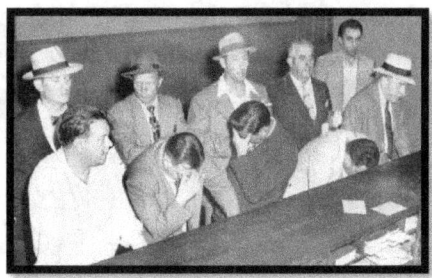 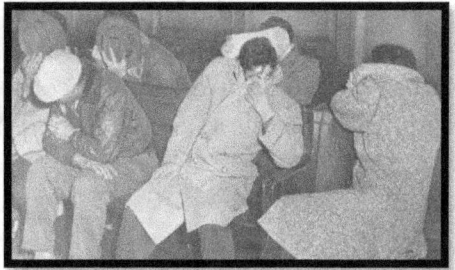

Mob loan sharks (Front row) operating on Brooklyn's waterfront

Mob Boss Albert Anastasia eventually fell from power because of plot-counter-plot Mafia power play. On October 25, 1957, the Gallo brothers, working on orders from the National Mafia Commission, killed Anastasia as he sat in the barbershop's chair at the Sheraton Hotel, a hot towel wrapped around his face. There were eleven people in the tiny shop, five barbers, a manicurist, three shoe shine boys and two customers who watched the two young hoods quickly enter the shop and put at least ten bullets into his head and neck.

In 1962, a year before he died of a heart attack, Tough Tony Anastasia told the FBI that his brother deserved to die "I ate from the same plate, I hate from the same table, we both came from the same womb. But my brother deserved to die. He killed too many men"

END NOTES

Kazan directed of 2 different actors in Oscar-nominated performances

Aside from giving Brando his start, Kazan also fueled the early careers James Dean, Warren Beatty, Lee Remick, Jo Van Fleet, Dean and Jack Palance, Barbara Bel Geddes, Dorothy McGuire, Kim Hunter, Eva Marie Saint, Julie Harris, Carroll Baker, Patricia Neal, Lee Remick and Natalie Wood their first major movie roles and redefined the craft of film acting.

John Garfield wanted the lead in *Gentlemen's Agreement* so badly he offered to change his stage name, John Garfield, for his given name Julius Garfinkle. However, the studio bosses, who were largely Jewish campaign against making the film, preferring to leave the subject alone. Instead, Garfield took a supporting role in the film at a lead star salary. Kazan later added a scene in the film, which reflects Zanuck's woes with the other studio bosses over creating the film

The line in the film ("That bird could sing but he couldn't fly") regarding Doyle's death from being pushed from a building came from actual events. Several years after the Panto killing, Reles, a member of organized crimes Murder Inc., the mob enforcement arm credited with a thousand homicides, decided to turn states evidence against the mob. Although protected by a squad of five elite members of the NYPD and one police Captain, Reles "fell" to his death out of hotel window in Coney Island. Mob boss Lucky Luciano commented, "That bird could sing but he sure couldn't fly" the words were later incorporated in to Waterfront script after Joey Doyle was tossed from the roof of his apartment building

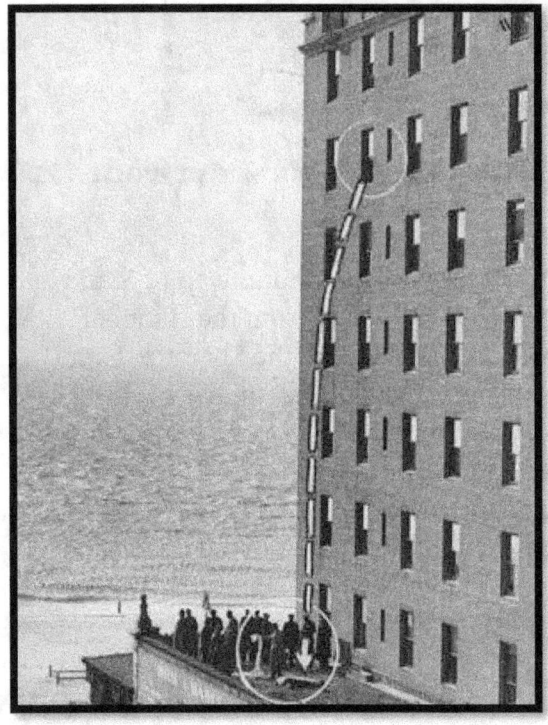 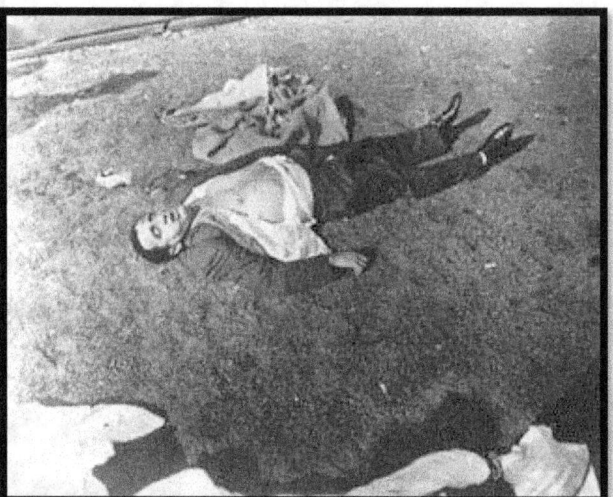

Reles dead

Harry Cohn probably understood the real waterfront better than anyone else involved in the film. He had worked at everything from pool hustler to streetcar conductor. He made his first bit of extra cash with composer Harry Ruby when they had a hit with *Ragtime Cowboy* Joe In 98, while his brother Jack, was working at Universal Pictures, Harry hustled his way into a job as a secretary-assistant to Universal's president, Carl Laemmle. In 920, the Cohn's and friend Joe Brandt struck out on their own and formed C.B.C. Productions, a film company that churned out one-reel comedies and questionable documentaries. While the industry looked down their collective noses at C.B.C, the fact was that the company was profitable. Columbia Studio's was born in 924, when the Cohn brothers and Brandt bought a tiny film studio and an adjoining apartment building in a run-down part of Los Angeles. The new company used inexpensive talent, cut corners at every possible turn, and gave the people what they wanted. That compounded with Harry Cohn's ability to get great distribution for his films, made Columbia one of the few studios to turn a profit during the Great Depression. He was the only studio president who was also head of production, which, to some degree, is what led to his unpopularity, since he scrutinized scripts and grilled writers at story conferences.

Hollywood labor activist John Weber called the IATSE under Brewer "A company union that was virtually controlled by the studios"

Another version of this was from Brewer who said that Cohn told Kazan over the phone ""Miller is a Communist. And if not, then tell me what other explanation could there be for what he did? . . . I could tell just by looking at him. He's still one of them."

Others who supported the award for Kazan were Kazan were Karl Malden, Warren Beatty, Robert De Niro, and Martin Scorcese.

Schulberg and Ray were divorced in 1944. Ray remarried screenwriter Peter Viertel and gave friendly testimony before the HUAC on June 6, 1956. She died in 1960, a recovering alcoholic, in a house fire.

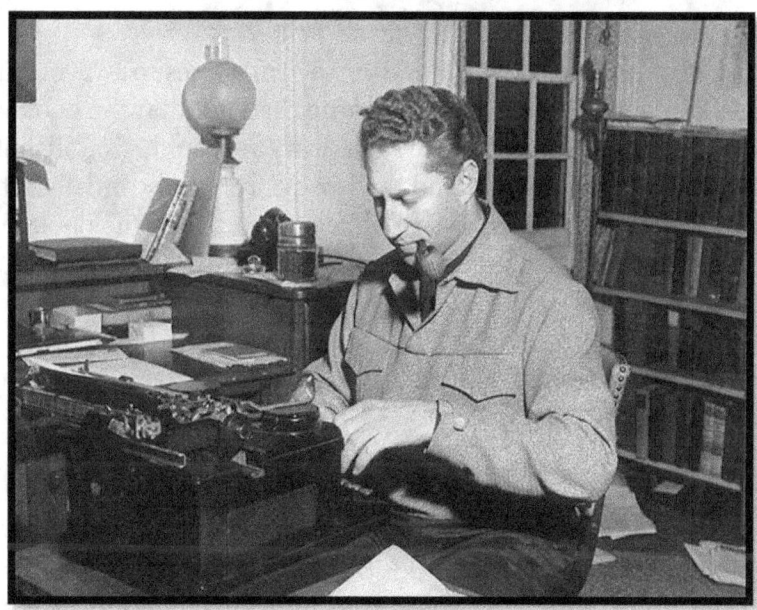

Schulberg also wrote additional dialogue for the classic film, *A Star is Born* with Ring Lardner Jr. after David Selznick secretly asked them to punch up the original script by William Wellman. Schulberg and Lardner are credited with coming up with the films best lines such as the publicity agent's remark after the alcoholic actor Norman Maine (Fredric March) has drowned. "How do you wire congratulations to the Pacific Ocean?" Lardner also contributed - uncredited again - to the dialogue in Wellman's acerbic comedy, *Nothing Sacred* (1937).

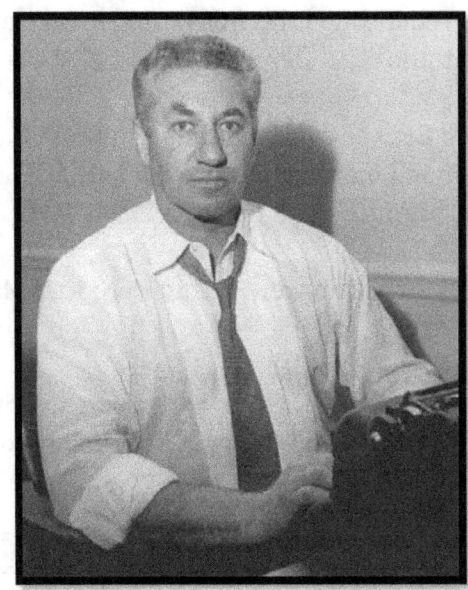

When Schulberg finished *What Makes Sammy Run* he sent copies to F. Scott Fitzgerald, Ring Lardner and Maurice Rapf and told them that his father had felt that the book was far to anti-Semitic to be published and that if they felt the same way, he wouldn't publish it. The writers disagreed with B.P. Schulberg and did not find the work particularly anti-Semitic. However, the Nazi's did. Hitler's propaganda minister Josef Gobbels republished the book in Germany, without permission, as Anti-Semitic literature. According to Maurice Rapf, 500,000 copies were printed and distributed in Nazi Germany.

In a 2004 interview with The Writers Guild East Schulberg said that, like Arthur Miller, the Panto killing got him interest in the waterfront

On January 3, 950, two years after the Mike Johnson's expose series on the waterfront appeared the *New York Sun* newspaper went out of business. Johnson was assigned to write paper obituary. It was one of the most poignant stories that he had ever written. When the paper's editor read the piece, he cried. When he noticed that Johnson had not placed his name on the article, the reporter said, "No Sun man would want a byline at that story" Malcolm Johnson won his Pulitzer Prize for the waterfront stories on the same day that Playwright Arthur Miller won his. Miller, who was preparing a film script based on Johnson's expose, said "Malcolm Johnson is the most worthy of all the Pulitzer Prize winner recognized this year"

Father Corridan, a former sales clerk, had been very successful in bringing the plight of the dock workers to the media. He had managed to have pieces written in the *World Telegram, Fortune Magazine, The New York Post, The New York Times, Look Magazine, Collier's, Jubilee, True Detective, Life Magazine, Readers Digest* and the *Brooklyn Eagle*. He had also been covered by CBS, NBC and ABC news.

The Labor School was founded in 1936 as the Xavier School of Social Studies. Located on 30 West 16th street, the parish was built in 840 with a grant of 50 cents. By 947, when Corridan arrived it had over 5,000 parishioners. Across the street from the church, at 7 West 6th, Margaret Sanger ran her birth control clinic

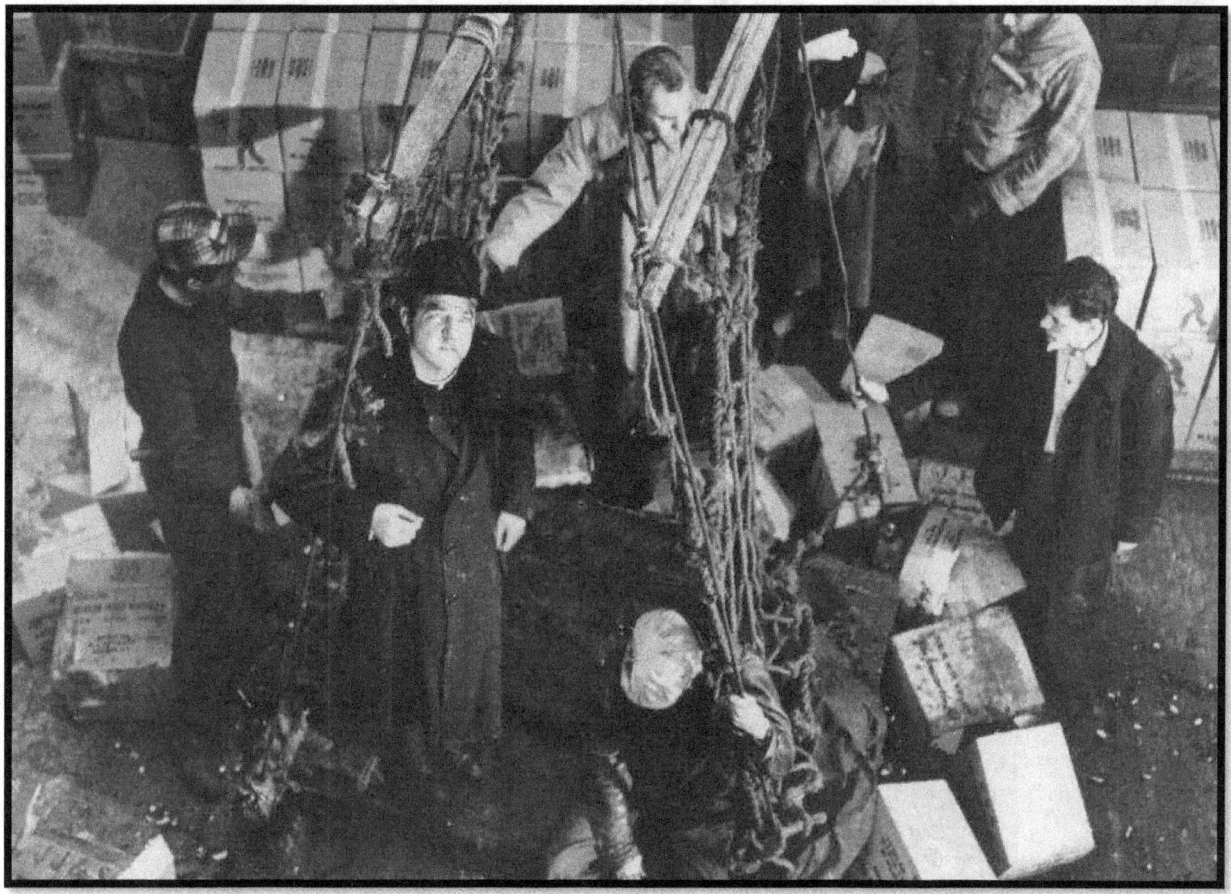

"Christ in the Cargo Hold" speech was not written by Schulberg as part of the film. In the fall of 948, Father John Corridan first delivered his sermon "Christ is in the shape up" at the Paulus Hook chapter of the Knights of Columbus in Jersey City

Killers is also echoed in Tarantino's *Reservoir Dogs*

The films name was changed from *Crime on the Waterfront* to simply On the Waterfront because there had also been a very popular radio program, *Crime on the Waterfront*, starring Mike Wallace, later of *60 Minutes fame*, as Detective Lou Kagel.

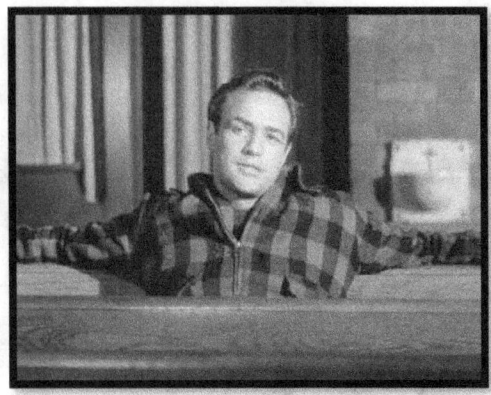 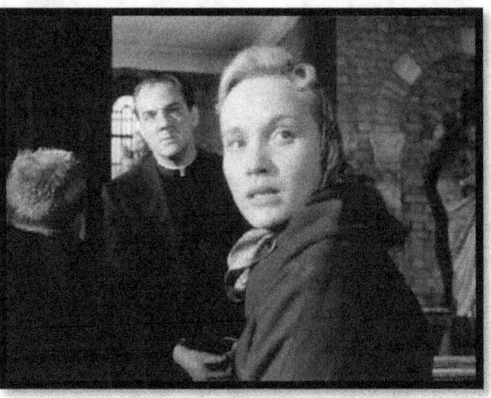

The Church meeting scene is based on actual events. The mob started to send informants to the school to watch Corridan and take the names of anyone else who appeared there regularly.

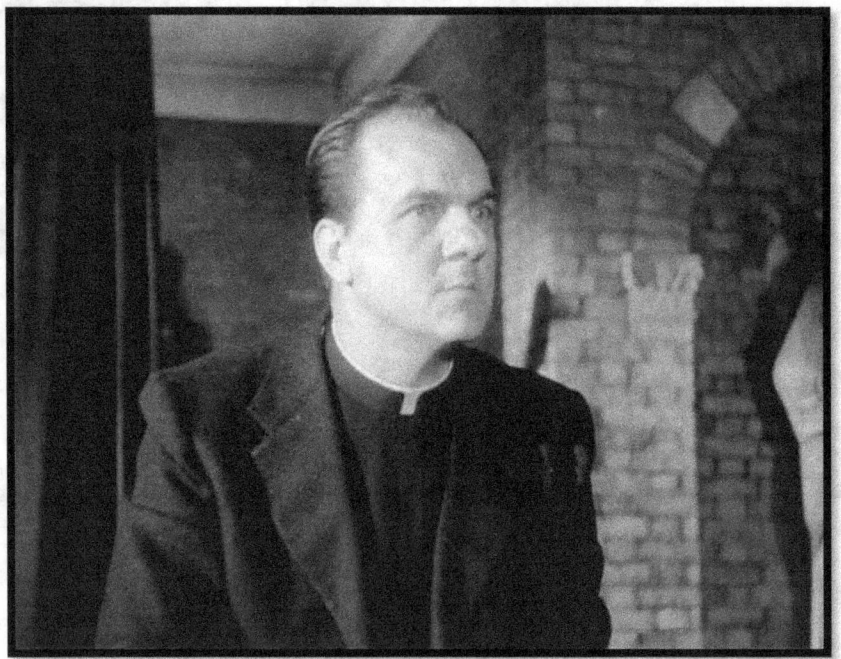

Eventually it became unsafe for dock workers to attend the classes and more often than not, the dock workers had to sneak in through a back door to avoid being seen by informants and union enforcers. Once, after Corridan found a pair of thugs waiting outside the school, he told them "If anything happens to the men I'm trying to help here, I'll know who's responsible, and I'll personally see to it that they are broken throughout this port. They'll pay and I'll see that they pay. Now get lost" Kazan is one of the dock workers in the church scene.
He sits in a pew, to Malden's right and later to Malden's left, inappropriately wearing a hat.

Zanuck later tried to get Kazan to approach AFL president George Meany to give assurances that he wouldn't cause trouble for the film, however, Kazan refused.

378

The Stranger, (946) an Orson Welles' film, was one of the best of its kind, an amazing study in mendacity and evil deception The plot concerns an ex-Nazi the psychotic Fritz Kindler, with a fascination for clocks (Welles) living in the sleepy town of Harper Connecticut. Welles' performance is still outstanding Edward G. Robinson plays Wilson, a Nazi hunter. The use of the clock motif to thread together the hunter and hunted is pure Wellesion.

Carl Foreman and Michael Wilson wrote the screenplay for Lawrence of Arabia but were both blacklisted at the time. Spiegel decided to give credit for the screenplay to Pierre Boulle the French author of the novel on which the film was based. When the film won the Academy Award for Best Screenplay Based on Material from another Medium-along with six other Oscars for Best Picture, Best Director, Best Actor as well as for Cinematography, Editing, and Music-the award was accepted on behalf of Boulle (who did not speak English) by David Lean.

A common Hollywood rumor was that Sam Spiegel was a front on several occasions for mobster Meyer Lansky, the so-called financier of the underworld. It's not impossible. Lansky always held a fascination for films. In the late 1930s, Lansky brought the idea of investing in television to the Underworld bosses. They rejected the idea because they thought television had no future.

Sam Spiegel was probably an illegal Polish immigrant who acquired a criminal record and was deported in 1929, only to return to the United States ten years later. While hiding from the immigration department, he adopted the pseudonym S. P. Eagle although his reasoning was that "Eagle" sounded prestigious

Brando was one of a long line of actors Spiegel charmed. Sir Alec Guinness insisted to Spiegel that he wanted absolutely nothing to do with the film The Bridge on the River Kwai. Yet after a dinner with Spiegel, Guinness ended the night discussing what kind of wig he would wear for his role in the film.

Years later, Brando said, "They (the film company) had to get permission from the Mafia to shoot there. When they (The Mafia) invited (Kazan) to lunch, he dragged me along and I didn't know until afterwards that the gentleman we had lunch with was in fact the head of the Jersey waterfront" It's a good story but doubtful it ever happened. As Schulberg later commented to Joanna Rapf, "Marlon may be our greatest actor but he is not exactly a Pulitzer Prize reporter"

Although Kazan was a bit overzealous with his use of bodyguards, Hoboken was not completely free of gangsters or waterfront violence. Eight months before the crew arrived, a hood named Mike Murphy, once the ILA hiring boss on Hoboken's Pier 3, which was already dormant, rushed into the offices of ILA local 867 on River street, pulled a revolver and shot down three men, 83 year old John Nolan, an ILA organizer, Nunzio Alutto, a dock worker slated to take Murphy's place as hiring boss and Patrick Lisa, Alutto's nephew. When the shooting started, Nolan leaped behind a desk and was unharmed. Lisa leaped through a closed window but was grazed by a bullet anyway. Alutto was shot through the stomach and bled to death in St. Mary's hospital a half hour later. Murphy was eventually arrested and tried, but of course was acquitted on the charge. Otherwise, Eddie Florio controlled the Hoboken piers, a former bootlegger whose former chauffeur Joey Borelli was the city's Commissioner of Police.

Boris Kaufman was born in 1897 in what had been a part of the Russian Empire, now Poland, in Bialystock, "the most Jewish town in Poland," the Kaufman brothers would move with their family to Moscow, fleeing pogroms. The Kaufman Brothers remain the most talented group of family in cinematic history – David Kaufman (later to be known as Dziga Vertov), Mikhail and Boris Kaufman. Each of the three would take up film in their own way, Dziga as a director, with Mikhail as his cinematographer in Russia. Together their film *Man with a Movie Camera* (1929) is considered one of the most innovative and influential movies of the silent era. Vertov was known for his daring, experimental camera techniques, including rapid editing and playing film footage backward. In 1927, Kaufman immigrated to France where he became the sole cinematographer on all of director Jean Vigo's films. After service in the French Army at the beginning of World War II, Kaufman settled in the U.S.

 By the time he worked on *Waterfront*, Kaufman had crafted *Garden of Eden* (954) and would later work on The Brotherhood (1968) *Bye Bye Braverman* (1968) *The Group,* (966) *Long Day's Journey Into Night* (1962) *Splendor in the Grass* (96) 2 Angry Men (with Lee J. Cobb, 1957) *Baby Doll* (Another Kazan creation 1956) and *Singing in the Dark* (1956) Kaufman and Sidney Lumet would later create *The Pawnbroker* (1965, starring Rod Steiger) photographed black-and-white, it told the stark journey through the mind of a concentration camp survivor living in Harlem.

Marlon suspected that the chauffeur whom Sam (Spiegel) had assigned to drive him to New York would report on his conversations with whomever rode with him—on the non-Bela days, me. A year later, I had a letter from Darryl Zanuck, who was then bitter, about losing the film and anxious that I should do another for him; in that letter there is this: "When I see you personally, I will tell you what I was told by our New York lawyers regarding an affidavit they obtained from a chauffeur who overheard a conversation between Marlon and you. It was at the time, very disturbing to me and since it was in the form of a 'voluntary affidavit' I had to accept it as being at least half true."

On the symbolism of raising the dead body from the cargo hold Kazan said, "I did another thing that people took as symbolic. I guess it was. You know, when the bald-headed dockworker gets killed, down in the hold, they put him on a rack; and the priest stands there, and some people have said his soul is rising to heaven. But that's the way you get out of the hold of a boat; there's no other way. There is a narrow little iron staircase that you climb up but you cannot climb up with a dead body. But they said no, it's the priest taking his soul up to heaven. The fact is, I'm not in the least religious.

One of Spiegel's tactics, when losing an argument with his directors, was to fake a heart attack

The death in the cargo scene was accurate and death by falling cargo on a dockworker was frequent. One of the few changes on the waterfront that came after the war years was standard use of the sling load, or the standard measure of cargo in the sling, which was increased with the introduction of heavier bearing winches. Before the war, Longshoremen worked with a one-ton draft, or 2,240 pounds. After the war, there was no limit. The results were that most men over age 30 couldn't handle the weight on a continuous basis and the heavier sling loads increased the threat of serious injury one hundred fold, in part because there were no safety provisions and in part because of rotten ropes that frayed and broke, sometimes causing tons of cargo to land on three or four longshoremen at once. As a result, Long shoring held the dubious distinction of being the most dangerous occupation in the nation. Hernias, falls, cuts, fractures and death were common, in fact, expected, on a daily basis.

Writer Peter Biskind made the amusing point that when analyzing the film in terms of power, the physical bullies, the hoodlums are replaced by moral bullies, Edie and Father Barry.

Johnny Friendly's bar, as of 2005, still stands in Hoboken. Its name remains the *Cafe Elysian*, although completely refurbished and very upscale today, parts of the bar look the same as they did during filming in 1953

The playground scene as well as the park scenes between Father Barry and Terry was actually several different Hoboken parks filmed and spliced into one during the editing process. The shots taken from behind the park bench of Terry and Edie was filmed in Stevens Park.

The frontal shots were filmed four blocks away with Our Lady of Grace Church in the background

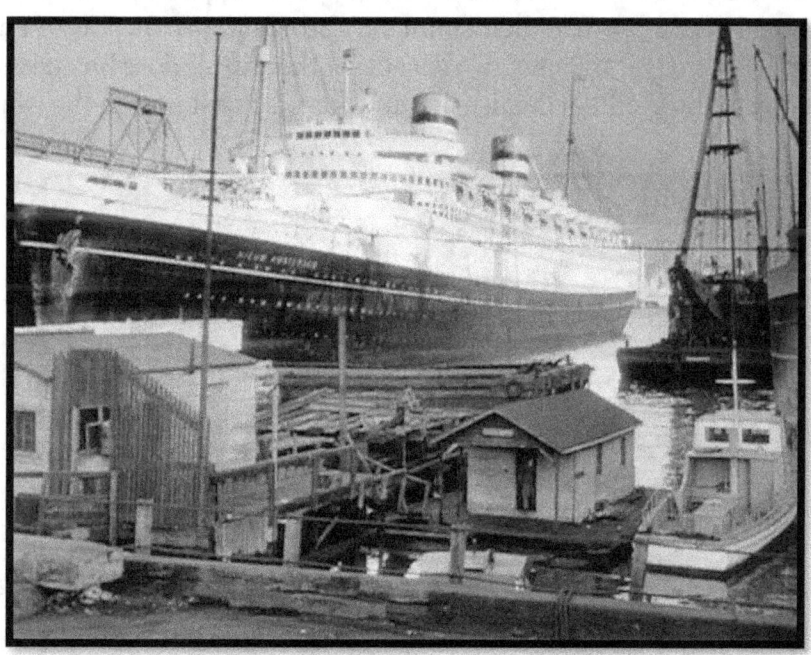

The dock used throughout most of the film was Pier C, a loading dock in Hoboken. Johnny Friendly's union office, the floating shack survived on the waterfront until 980 when it was torn

down after surviving several fires. The shack, dubbed "The Hoboken Yacht Club" was actually a private boaters club.

The shape up was finally outlawed in New York. In 95, the dock workers revolted against Boss Ryan and the ILA's rule and caused a 25-day work stoppage New York Governor Thomas ordered an investigation, the first of several. New York State Industrial Commissioner Edward Corsi headed the investigation. Heroically, Corsi extended the investigation beyond its original mandate and his final report attacked the fraudulent voting procedures which Ryan had forced into place and the absolute and complete corruption of several of Ryan's mobbed up locals. Additionally, the Corsi Report captured the public and the national media's attention, forcing Governor Thomas E. Dewey to order the New York State Crime Commission to conduct a full investigation of the ILA, which ended with the complete condemnation of both the ILA and Ryan as corrupt beyond all hope. Because of the Corsi report, in 1953, the Waterfront Commission of the New York Harbor was created with almost dictatorial powers, to do something, anything, to stunt the corruption of the ILA. Among its other reforms, the commission banned the hated shape-up.

 In one scene Big Mac, the dock supervisor suggests to Johnny Friendly that they call a work stoppage on the banana cargo because they go bad so quickly. Commercial extortion was another moneymaker on the waterfront. In the summer of 1948, the mob and corrupt officials called the ILA out on strike against the powerful *New York Daily News*, whose management had refused to pay a tribute of $00,000 on newsprint being brought in from Canada. The mob/ILA countered by demanding one dollar a ton on all newspapers shipped into the city. The paper still refused to pay and eventually had their shipments brought into the port of Philadelphia and then trucked to New York. Over the next two decades, other firm's does business on the docks followed suit, leading to the eventual demise of the largest, busiest port in the world.

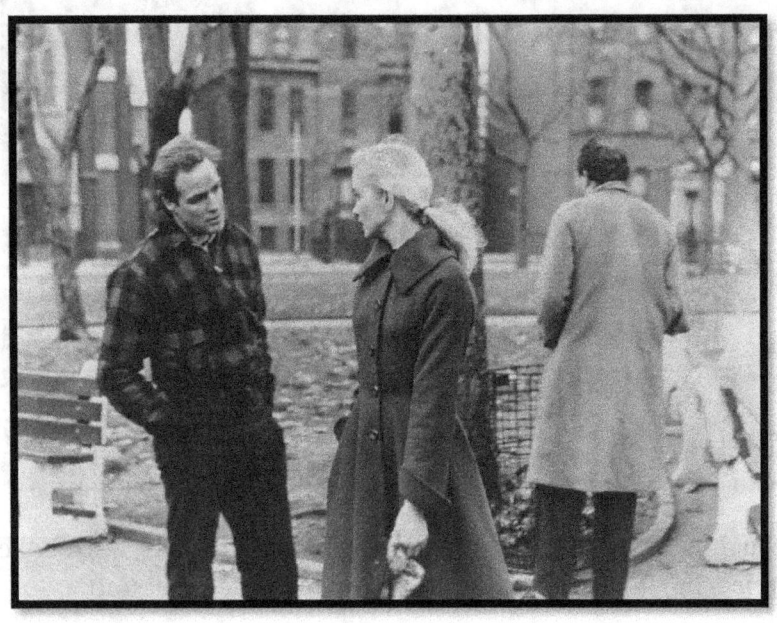

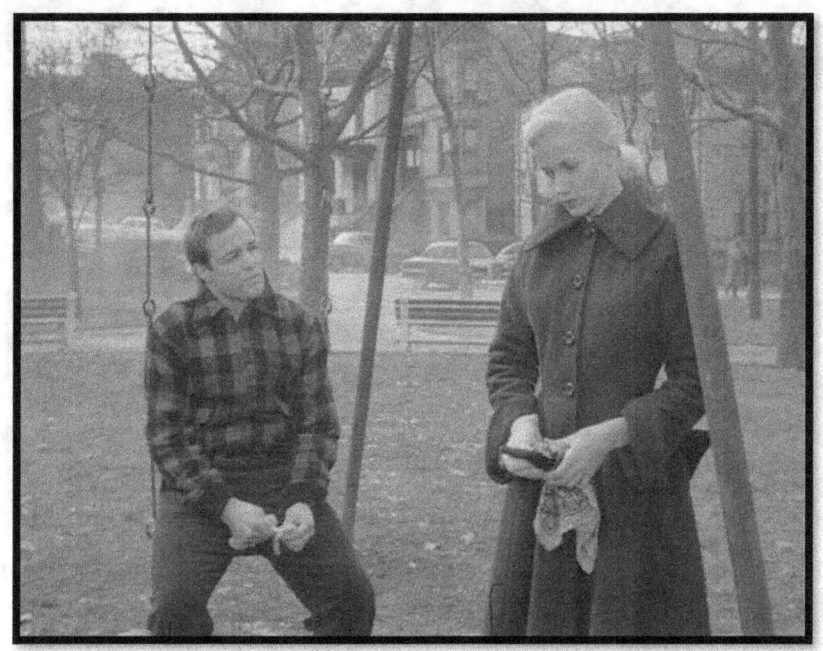

Terry wears Edie's glove in the park, was not in Kazan or Schulberg's production notes but Eva Marie Saint and Brando both recalled that they had discussed the idea before the scene.

Kazan delivered the final cut of the film to Cohn and viewed it at his home in Beverly Hills, where he kept a full sized screening room. "How much did it cost?" was the only thing he asked and then fell asleep during the screening. His only comment on one scene, wherein Brando tells priest Malden to "go to hell." Cohn to Kazan: "Boy, are you going to have trouble with the Breen Office (the then official Hollywood censor) over that "go to hell' scene. They'll never pass it." Cohn was so shocked when the Breen Office did not object to the scene that he barraged the censor with angry questions regarding other Columbia films that had been censored for what he thought were lesser offenses.

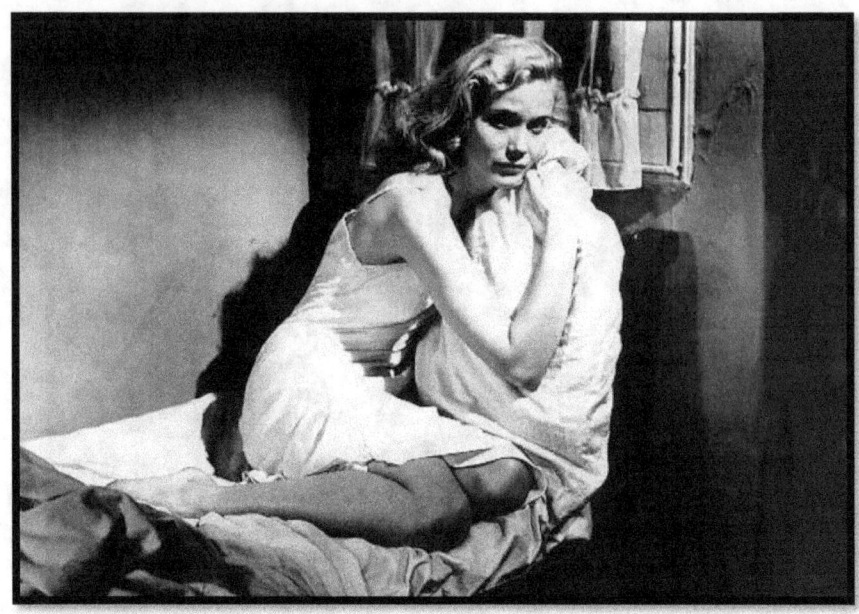

A lean blonde female in a slip or in a long, tight fitting white gown would appear in almost every one of Kazan's films. Saint was no exception.

Some years later a rumor started, perhaps by Brando himself, that Brando had read his lines from cue cards. Director Francis Ford Coppola recalled, "He felt in life you don't know your line. So why learn your lines and then try to make people feel as if they're coming to you spontaneously? He liked to struggle for the lines because that's a real thinking process. I did once say, "Gee, Marlon, you're gonna have the cue cards, they're going to see you reading them," and he said, "You remember that scene in On the Waterfront in the cab? Did you see me reading cue cards?" The implication was that he had cue cards in the cab. I doubt it. Eva Marie Saint countered that "I can't imagine that. Cue cards were never allowed on a Kazan set. Rod [Steiger] never told me that; he would have said something."

Brando was seeing the psychoanalyst to try to reconcile his success with his insecurity something he decided was a classic symptom of having been raised by alcoholic parents. He was aware that his neuroses translated into film power. Yet he always felt conflicted about his fame and money. "Acting is the expression of a neurotic impulse," he once said. "It's a bum's life. Quitting acting is a sign of maturity. The only reason I'm here in Hollywood is because I don't have the moral courage to refuse the money."

Schulberg testified that he was introduced into the party by Ring Lardner Jr. Lardner insisted it was the other way around and never forgave Schulberg for telling that to the committee.

When Schulberg flirted with communism, he was 23 years old/

In *Remembering Brando*, Schulberg said about the fight scenes:

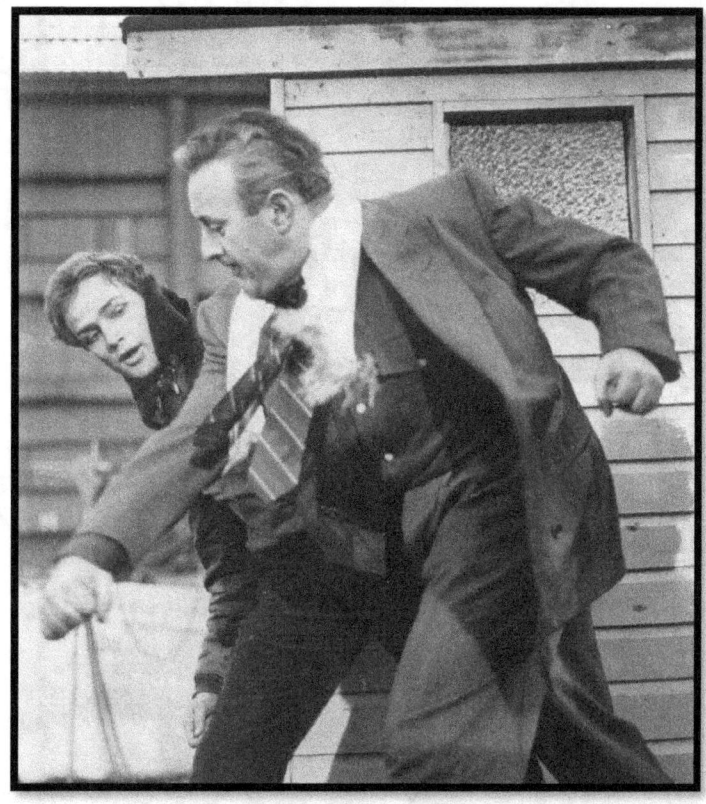

I suggested to Kazan that we bring in a professional fighter to teach Marlon how to throw punches, as well as the walk and body language of a boxer. I brought a young friend of mine, Roger Donoghue, an articulate middleweight from Yonkers whose promising career was aborted when an opponent, Georgie Flores, died after their bout in The Garden. Marlon took to Roger, got into the ring with him at Stillman's Gym, and the next day Roger rushed in with this enthusiastic report: "This kid buddy's amazing. He's such a quick study, I've got him shooting straight jabs and he's already learned how to hook off the jab! I can make a hell of a middleweight out of this kid."

"Roger," I said, "just let us get through this movie with him in it. Then you can have him back and take it from there.

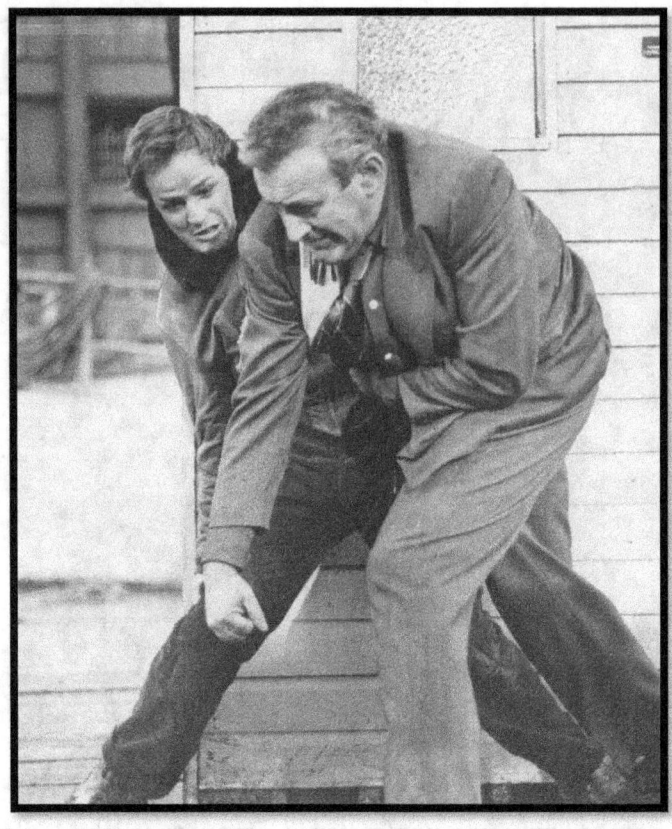

Brando liked to box. While performing as Stanley Kowalski in the stage version of "A Streetcar Named Desire," he would often persuade a member of the stage crew to spar with him in a room underneath the stage between his acts. During one of these impromptu boxing matches, with stagehand Nick Dennis, Marlon's nose was broken so badly that it literally was split across its bridge. He managed to go on stage and finish the play, but was taken to the hospital immediately after. Brando resented his good looks, or at least he said he did. He was not unhappy about the broken nose and felt that it actually improved his looks.

In the novelized version of the film by Schulberg, the mob later murders Terry Malloy.

In 995, *On the Waterfront* was produced as a stage musical. It lasted 8 weeks.

Waterfront remains one of the few films to receive multiple nominations for acting in the same category. Again, the film crosses roads with the Godfather trilogy, which also fits, into that category. The third film in the group is the 963 feature Tom Jones.

Kazan and Schulberg would need Hedda Harpers support. As her massive FBI file shows, Harper was a right wing informer for J. Edgar Hoover, she could, in 953, muster enough support to make or break a film. Hedda, oddly enough, is from the old English Saxon word Hidden knife.

Judy Garland, also nominated for Best Actress, was expecting as well and was in bed at a hospital maternity with a television crew standing by her bedside ready to film her acceptance speech live. When she didn't win, the crew left without a word.

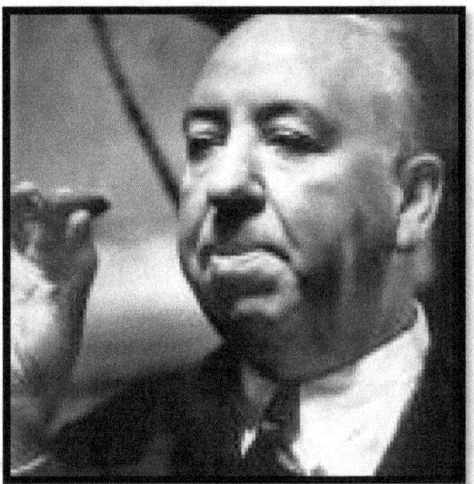

Kazan beat, among others, Alfred Hitchcock for *Rear Window*. Remarkably, Hitchcock never won any of the five Oscars for which he was nominated. He was finally granted an Honorary Oscar in 1967 .

Spiegel left behind massive apartments in New York and London, a villa in the south of France, a yacht referred to as "A floating hotel with good art work" and an extensive art collection and $20 million in cash.

TIME LINE
1948

Berlin Airlift (1948-1949) when Soviets cut off ground transportation to West Berlin.

Communists take over Czechoslovakia.

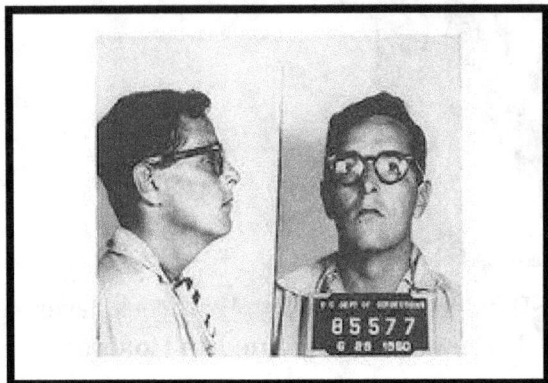

Screenwriter John Howard Lawson refused to co-operate with the HUAC and was sentenced to a year in prison.

Stalin and Tito break

Rod Steiger stars in "Philco Television Playhouse"

Independent Republic of (South) Korea is proclaimed, following election supervised by UN

Alger Hiss, former U.S. State Department official, indicted on perjury charges after denying passing secret documents to communist spy ring

A Streetcar Named Desire wins Pulitzer.

The New York- New Jersey waterfront is the largest, busiest Seaport in the world.

Joseph Patrick Ryan, AKA The King, running the New York docks as the ILA's International president.

The ILA calls a strike against the powerful *New York Daily News*, whose management had refused to pay a tribute of $100,000 on newsprint being brought in from Canada.

MGM was on the brink of financial collapse and was running at a deficit.

Father John Corridan operates the St. Francis Xavier Labor School and begins his investigation of the ILA

Wildcat strike on the New York waterfront. Strikes by the membership erupted on the waterfront in Boston, Baltimore and Philadelphia

Malcolm Johnson of the *New York Sun* newspaper, began investigating the waterfront and runs a series on the situation

Albert Maltz sentenced to nearly a year in jail for contempt of the HUAC

Father Corridan gives his speech "Christ is in the shapeup" speech Corridan at the Paulus hook chapter of the Knights of Columbus in Jersey City

Budd Schulberg meets Father Corridan

Attendance in theaters sank from 80 million per week to 60 million per week

1949

Formation of NATO.

Soviet Union tests its first atom bomb.

Federal Republic of Germany (West Germany) formed from British, American and French occupation zones.

Screenwriter Samuel Ornitz refuses to answer questions before the HUAC, sentenced to a year in prison for contempt of court.

German Democratic Republic (East Germany) formed from Soviet occupation zone.

Chinese communists win Chinese civil war. Communist People's Republic of China formally proclaimed by Chairman Mao Zedong

Berlin Blockade ends May 12, 1949; airlift continues until Sept. 30, 1949.

ILA enforcer Cockeye Dunn executed by the state of New York.

Johnny Dwyer, a rebel longshoremen leader and student of Father Corridan begins to organize the docks

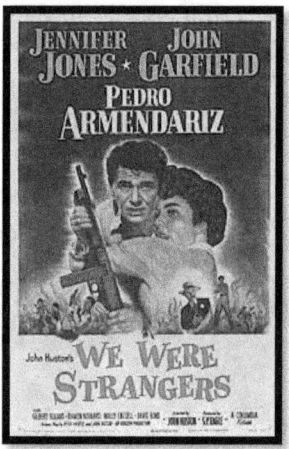

Sam Spiegel finances *We Were Strangers*. The film, set in 1933, but released in 1949, concerns a group of revolutionaries attempting to overthrow the Cuban regime. The cast is largely Hispanic and centers on a presidential assassination by a group of revolutionaries who plot to bring down their corrupt government. Two weeks after the assassination of President Kennedy in November 1963, investigators learned that Lee Harvey Oswald had watched We Were Strangers on television in October. Priscilla Johnson McMillan's 1977 book, Marina and Lee, added that Oswald had been "greatly excited" while watching the film. John Loken's 2000 book, Oswald's Trigger Films, further established that Oswald watched We Were Strangers twice in October 1963.

Malcolm Johnson wins the Pulitzer Price

Congress increased the investigative powers of Special Committee on Un-American Activities, the HUAC.

Kazan's film Pinky released

John Wayne elected president of the Motion Picture Association for the Preservation of

American Ideals, a group that cooperated freely with the HUAC.

Budd Schulberg penned a series of articles about the waterfront.

1950

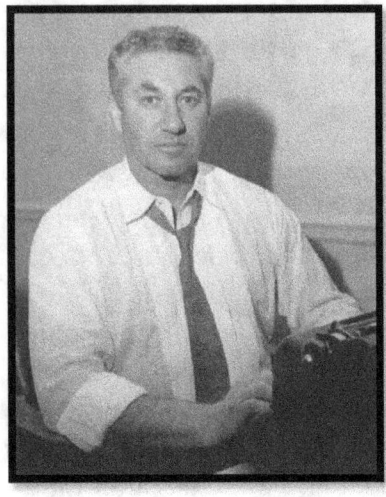

Budd Schulberg started writing the screenplay for *On The Waterfront*

Korean War begins when Communist North Korea invades the South.

Senator Joseph McCarthy Begins Communist Witch Hunt

U.S. President Truman Orders Construction of Hydrogen Bomb

Alger Hiss convicted in second trial and sentenced to five-year prison term.

Assassination attempt on President Truman by Puerto Rican nationalists

Opening of the Brooklyn Battery Tunnel cut the Red Hook neighborhood
And its 21,000 long shore residents from the rest of the borough of Brooklyn

The waterfront "Mr. Big", Bill McCormick employed thousands of longshoremen. His estimated cash worth that year was $20 million dollars.

Screenwriter and producer Adrian Scott refused to testify and was sentenced to a year in prison.

Waterfront gangster Albert Anastasia orders the murder of his boss Vincent Mangano

Father Corridan appears before the U.S. House Committee on Education and Labor and pleads for waterfront reforms.

New York Sun newspaper went out of business.

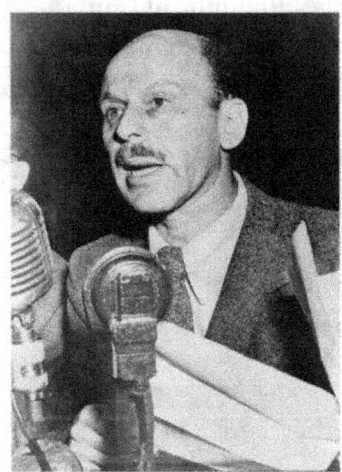

Alvah Bessie, screenwriter jailed for contempt of Congress by the HUAC

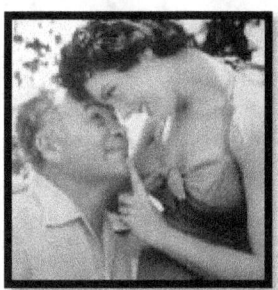

Herbert J. Biberman, director and screenwriter sentenced to 6 months in prison for contempt of Congress by the HUAC

An official Blacklist is created with the publication of Red Channels, a 213-page book of the alleged Communist affiliations of 151 actors, writers, musicians, and other radio and television entertainers.

Kazan's film Panic in the Streets is released

I Married a Communist released

Playwright Arthur Miller approached Kazan with the idea of filming a treatment about the waterfront.

Kazan and Budd Schulberg begin work on Waterfront script.

50% of all American households have a TV

1951

Julius and Ethel Rosenberg convicted of passing US atomic secrets to the Soviet Union, sentenced to death

The House on Un-American Activities Committee began its second round of hearings in Hollywood

Corridan had made a case study of Dorothy Day, a radical journalist who had become a
Catholic in 1927 and by the mid-1930s was the heart and soul of the Catholic Worker Movement, which she promoted through the extremely successful paper, The Catholic Worker, which she sold for a penny a copy.

Father Corridan and one of his followers, Christy Doran, create The Crusader, underground longshoremen's newsletter. ILA boss Joe Ryan calls the newsletter a communist publication and commissioned the creation of a counter paper, The Longshoremen's News

General Douglas MacArthur replaced as US commander in Korea.

A Streetcar Named Desire earned Kazan another Oscar and made Marlon Brando into a household name.

Color TV Introduced

Film director Edward Dmytryk, one of the original Hollywood Ten, after serving a six-month sentence in prison for contempt of the HUAC, gave the committee 26 names.

Albert Anastasia orders the death of Arnold Schuster for identifying bank robber Willie Sutton on TV

Longshoremen revolt against Ryan's rule and cause a 25-day work stoppage.

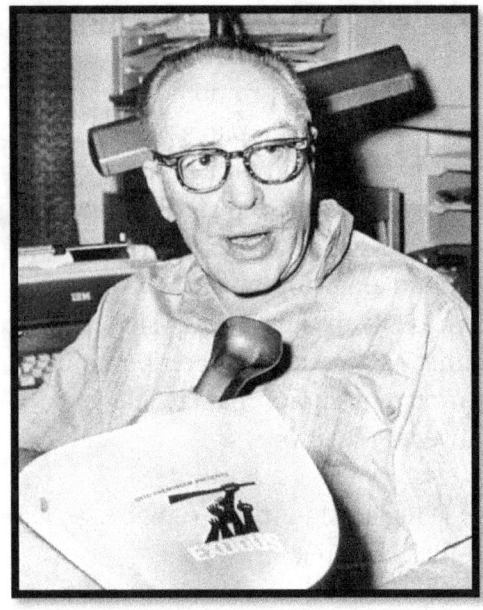

Screenwriter Dalton Trumbo refused to testify before the HUAC and was cited for contempt of Congress and served a 10-month jail.

The New York Crime Commission holds hearings in the ILA's activities on the waterfront.

Sam Spiegel finances *The Prowler* and *When I Grow Up*.

Cardinal Spellman summoned Father Corridan to his office and again questions his role on the waterfront.

Screenwriter Lester Cole sentenced to one year in federal prison by the HUAC

Budd Schulberg testified before the HUAC and named fifteen names

Actor Zero Mostel refused to testify and is blacklisted.

MGM boss Louis B. Mayer resigned, the company is near bankrupt

First British atom bomb test.

Universal sold to Decca Records

Anti-communist film My Son John released

US test first Hydrogen bomb.

Character-actor Lloyd Gough blacklisted on the basis of alleged communist ties

New York's Governor Dewey orders an investigation of the waterfront.

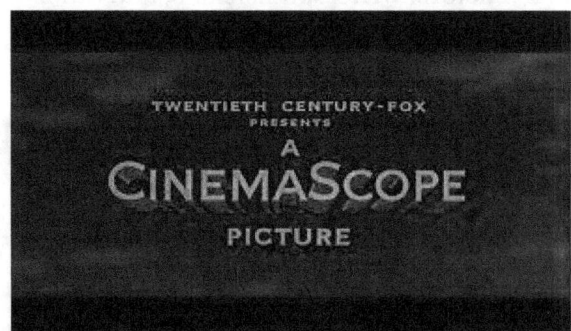

Bigger screens, 3-D, Cinemascope and VistaVision debuted

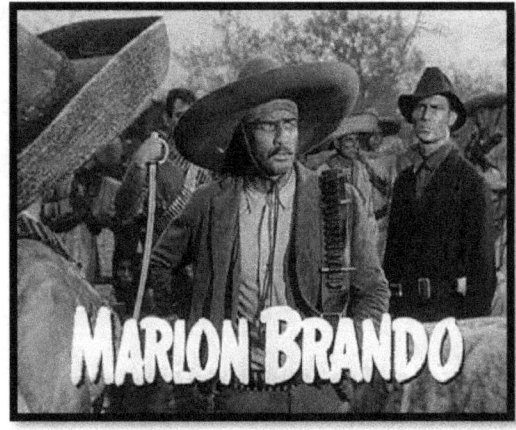

Brando and Kazan worked together on *Viva Zapata!* Brando gets his second Best Actors nomination.

Governor Thomas E. Dewey ordered the New York State Crime Commission to conduct a full investigation of the ILA

New York's conservative Cardinal, Richard Spellman, who publicly and privately questioned Father Corridan's role on the waterfront.

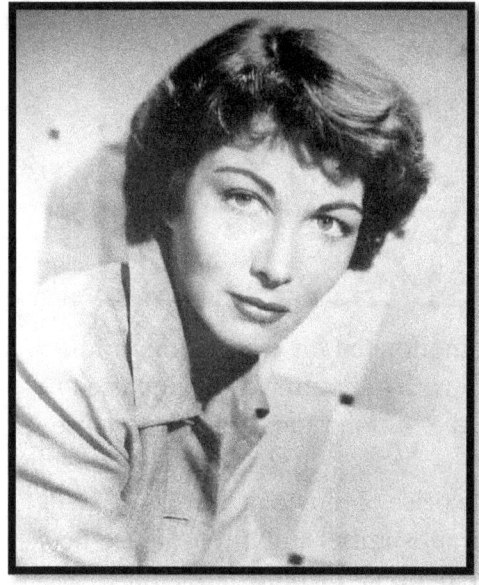

Screenwriter Arnold Manoff's wife, actress Lee Grant blacklisted for not testifying against her husband.

Kazan appeared before the House of Un-American Activities Committee

I Was a Communist for the FBI released and wins an Academy Award nomination for best documentary.

1953

Sam Spiegel in serious tax trouble.

The Waterfront Commission of the New York Harbor is created with almost dictatorial powers. The commission banned the shape-up.

RKO Studios had lost $20 million and was sold to the General Tire and Rubber Corporation.

Anti-Communist film Pickup on South Street released

Sam Spiegel finances Melba

The ILA was suspended from the American Federation of Labor

Studios ban film stars from appearing on TV

CBS and NBC inaugurated "hot kinescope" systems, which put programs on air on the West Coast at same clock hour as in the East.

Gen. Dwight D. Eisenhower inaugurated president of United States

Soviet leader Joseph Stalin dies.

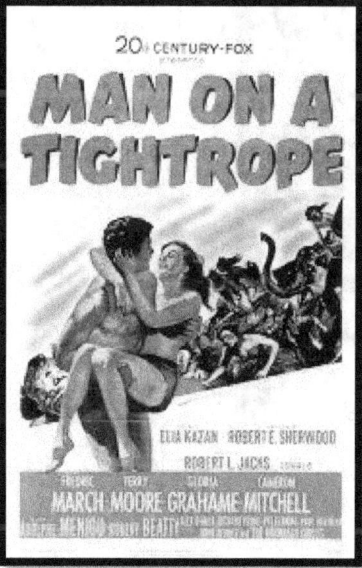

Kazan releases **Man on a Tightrope**

Korean War ends.

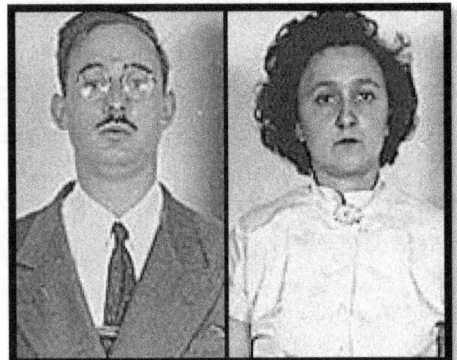

Julius and Ethel Rosenberg executed

East Berliners rise against Communist rule; quelled by tanks

There had been over 100 unsolved waterfront murders, most of them involving labor disputes.

House Committee on the Judiciary holds hearings on the ILA and the waterfront.

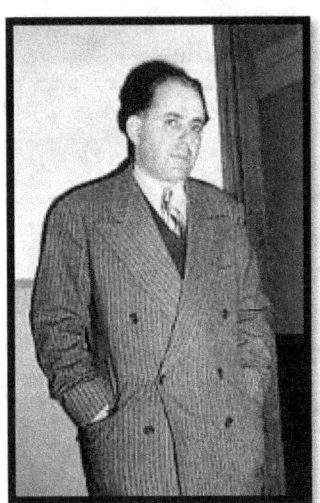

Tough Tony Anastasia was under indictment for violating a federal anti-strike indictment.

Academy Awards were televised for the first time by NBC - the broadcast received the largest single audience in network TV's five-year history.

Kazan presents the Waterfront script Darryl Zanuck who rejects it.

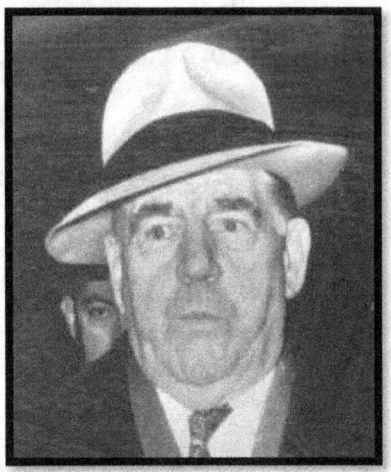

Joe Ryan indicted for theft of union funds, charged with 51 counts for having used $45,000 in union funds for personal use.

Average price of movie ticket is cost fifty cents, a substantial amount for a pre-tax average national income of less than $4,000.

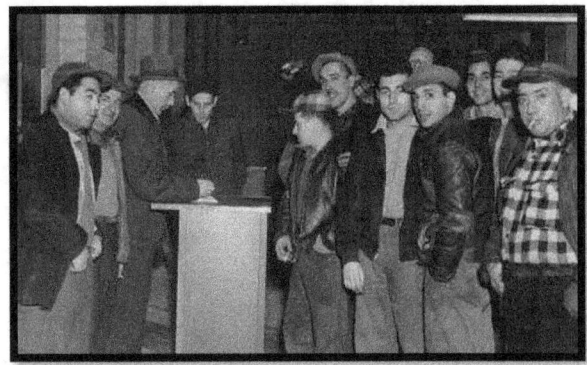

Longshoremen vote. ILA wins the election 9,110 votes to 8,791 for the reform movement

Joe Ryan forced out of the ILA

Lee J. Cobb testifies before the HUAC and named names

Sam Spiegel agrees to produce on the Waterfront.

The first issue of TV Guide was published. A year later, circulation was past 1,562,000 copies.

1954

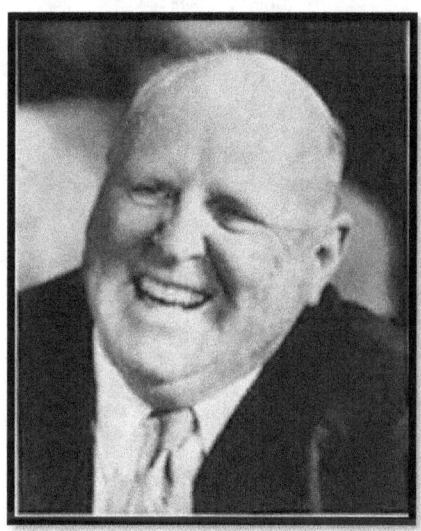

Teamster boss David Beck refused to cross the rebel's picket line. News spread and on piers up and down Manhattan, and the rebel Longshoremen came back to life.

On the Waterfront opened in October at the Astor Theater to sensational reviews and grossed over $9.5 million in its initial release.

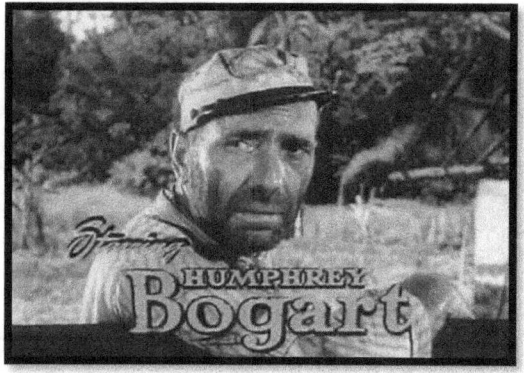

Sam Spiegel finances *The African Queen*

Actor Lee J. Cobb's wife suffers a mental breakdown.

An injunction by the National Labor Relations Board forbade ILA from striking or disrupting freight transportation. The ILA leadership responded with violence and sporadic warfare broke out on the docks

French army defeated by Vietnamese by Dien Bien Phu and agrees to independence of Vietnam. Vietnam split at 17th Parallel.

First Atomic Submarine Launched

Frank Sinatra sues Spiegel for $50,000, claiming breach of contract after retracting an offer for the lead in Waterfront

Lee J Cobb suffers a massive heart attack

Five U.S. congressmen shot on floor of House as Puerto Rican nationalist's fire from spectators' gallery; all five recover

Army v. McCarthy inquiry-Senate subcommittee report blames both sides

Soviet Union grants sovereignty to East Germany

Eisenhower launches world atomic pool without Soviet Union

Mike Brogan, an assistant hiring boss on Pier 32, murdered by the Mafia

NLRB examiner effectively overturned the ILA elections based on the findings that

they were conducted "in an atmosphere of terror, coercion, and intimidation..."

The HUAC left Hollywood after naming over 324 artists as communist Waterfront named for eight Oscar nominations.

FOOTNOTES

1) Kazan, Elia A Life. De Capo Press 1997 Pg. 540
2) Kazan, Elia A Life Pg. 542
3) Martin Robert A. Arthur Miller on Plays and Playwriting, Modern Drama 19 (1976): 375-84; reprinted in Roudané, Conversations 262-63
4) Turkus, Burton B., and Feder, Sid, Murder, Inc., New York, Da Capo Press, 1992, unabridged republication of the 1951 edition. Pg. 140
5) The Guardian Blood, sweat and fear. Friday October 22, 2004
6) Miller, Arthur. Timebends: A Life. Penguin 1995. 230
7) Miller, Arthur. Timebends: 234
8) Kazan, Elia. A life Pg.440
9) Miller, Arthur. Timebends Pg. 36
10) The Guardian Blood, sweat and fear. Friday October 22, 2004
11) Schulberg, Budd The Priest Who Made Budd Schulberg Run. Fordham May 2003, Schulberg's Speech Fordham
12) Schulberg The Priest Who Made Budd Schulberg Run. Fordham May 2003, Schulberg's Speech Fordham
13) Schulberg, Budd The Priest Who Made Budd Schulberg Run. Fordham

May 2003, Schulberg's Speech Fordham
14) Server, Lee. Writers Guild interview with Budd Schulberg, On Writing Magazine. September 2002 Volume 16
15) Server, Lee. Writers Guild interview with Budd Schulberg, On Writing Magazine. September 2002 Volume 16
16) Kazan Elia. A Life Pg 432
17) Bear, William. Elia Kazan Interviews. Jackson: University Press of Mississippi, 2000. 23
18) Kantor, Bernard R.; Blacker, Irwin R.; Kramer, Anne. "Interview with Elia Kazan." In Focus on film and theatre. Englewood Cliffs, N.J., Prentice-Hall [1974] (Series: Film focus) (Series: A Spectrum book)
19) Kantor, Bernard R.; Blacker, Irwin R.; Kramer, Anne. "Interview with Elia Kazan." In Focus on film and theatre. Englewood Cliffs, N.J., Prentice-Hall [1974] (Series: Film focus) (Series: A Spectrum book)
20) Kazan Elia. A Life Pg. 456
21) Server, Lee. Writers Guild interview with Budd Schulberg, On Writing Magazine. September 2002 Volume 16
22) Liner Notes from Studio Heritage Collection, Columbia Pictures Laserdisc. Interview with Elia Kazan
23) Kazan, Elia A Life
24) Kazan, Elia. A Life

25) Kazan, Elia A Life
26) Tallmer, Jerry. When Labor Rules the Docks. The City Paper. November 4, 2004
27) Tallmer, Jerry. When Labor Rules the Docks. The City Paper. November 4, 2004
28) Tallmer, Jerry. When Labor Rules the Docks. The City Paper. November 4, 2004
29) Server, Lee. Writers Guild interview with Budd Schulberg, On Writing Magazine. September 2002 Volume 16
30) Kazan A Life Page 515
31) Liner Notes from Studio Heritage Collection, Columbia Pictures Laserdisc. Interview with Elia Kazan
32) American Legends. American Legends .Com Budd Schulberg: The Making of On the Waterfront. Undated. Glendale, California.
33) Tallmer, Jerry. When Labor Rules the Docks. The City Paper. November 4, 2004
34) Liner Notes from Studio Heritage Collection, Columbia Pictures Laserdisc.
35) Schulberg, Budd The Great Contender Sunday Herald , July 4 2004 London
36) Kazan, Elia A Life
37) Cavassoni, Natasha. Sam Spiegel: The Incredible Life and Times of Hollywood's Most Iconoclastic Producer Simon & Schuster (April 1, 2003)

38) Kazan, Elia A Life

39) Smith Wendy, Variety April 13, 2003 Sam Spiegel

40) Liner Notes from Studio Heritage Collection, Columbia Pictures Laserdisc.

41) Malden, Karl. When Do I Start. Simon & Schuster 1997 Pg 234

42) American Legends. American Legends .Com Budd Schulberg: The Making of On the Waterfront. Undated. Glendale, California.

43) Malden, Karl. When Do I Start. Simon & Schuster 1997 Pg 37

44) Liner Notes from Studio Heritage Collection, Columbia Pictures Laserdisc

45) The Guardian, Blood, sweat and fear, Friday October 22, 2004,

46) Liner Notes from Studio Heritage Collection, Columbia Pictures Laserdisc

47) Chown, Jeffrey Visual Coding and Social Class in On the Waterfront. Northern Illinois University 2002 pg 3

48) American Legends: Interview with Budd Schulberg: The Making of on the Waterfront Americans Legends Inc. 2005

49) Server, Lee. Writers Guild interview with Budd Schulberg, On Writing Magazine. September 2002 Volume 16

50) Tallmer, Jerry The Villager, Nov. 3 2004 Screenwriter Budd Schulberg, 90, reminisces on making Waterfront

51) Liner Notes from Studio Heritage Collection, Columbia Pictures Laserdisc.

52) Liner Notes from Studio Heritage Collection, Columbia Pictures Laserdisc.

52) Liner Notes from Studio Heritage Collection, Columbia Pictures Laserdisc.

53) Liner Notes from Studio Heritage Collection, Columbia Pictures Laserdisc.

54) American Legends. American Legends .Com Budd Schulberg: The Making of On the Waterfront. Undated. Glendale, California.

55) Schulberg. The Great Contender

56) Tuohy, John W. Interviews

57) Liner Notes from Studio Heritage Collection, Columbia Pictures Laserdisc.

58) Navasky, Victor. Naming Names New York: The Viking Press, 1980 Elia Kazan and The Case for Silence Pg 356

59) Navasky, Victor. Naming Names New York: The Viking Press, 1980 Elia Kazan and The Case for Silence Pg 356

60) Navasky, Victor. Naming Names New York: The Viking Press, 1980 Elia Kazan and The Case for Silence Pg. 356

61) Kazan, A Life

62) Kazan, A Life

63) Hey, K. Ambivalence as a Theme in On the Waterfront (1954): An Interdisciplinary Approach to Film Study in Peter C. Rollins, ed., Hollywood as Historian, Revised edition, 1998.

64) American Legends. American Legends .Com Budd Schulberg: The Making of On the Waterfront. Undated. Glendale, California.

65) Kazan, A Life

66) Marlon Brando with Robert Lindsey, Brando: Songs My Mother Taught Me New York: Random House, 1994 Pg 220

67) Curnutte Daidria The Film Journal The Politics of Art: Elia Kazan and the Scandal Over On the Waterfront July 2, 2002

68) Anderson, Lindsay, "The Last Sequence of "On the Waterfront", Sight & Sound, 24, 3, 1955, pp. 127-30

69) Malden, Karl. When Do I Start. Simon & Schuster 1997 Pg. 123

70) Euroscreenwriters September 28 1998 - by Mikael Colville-Andersen

71) Kazan A Life Pg 527

72) Schulberg, Budd The Great Contender. Remembering Brando. Sunday Herald July 4, 2004

73) Kazan Pg 529

74) Kazan Pg 529

75) Cavassoni, Natasha. Sam Spiegel: The Incredible Life and Times of Hollywood's Most Iconoclastic Producer Simon & Schuster 2003 Pg. 303

76) PBS American Masters Elia Kazan November 16, 2005

SOURCES

Acker, Ally. Reel Women: Pioneers of the Cinema 1896 to the Present. New York: Continuum, 1991.

Allvine, Glendon. The Greatest Fox of Them All. New York: Lyle Stuart, 1969.

Anderegg, Michael A. William Wyler. Boston: Twayne, 1979.

Anderson, Christopher. Hollywood TV: The Studio System in the Fifties. Austin: University of Texas, 1994.

Anderson, Lindsay , "The Last Sequence of On the Waterfront, Sight and Sound Jan. Mar. 1955

Armes, Roy. A Critical History of the British Cinema. New York: Oxford University Press, 1978.

Allen, Robert C.Vaudeville and Film, 1895-1915. New York: Arno Press, 1980.

American Social History Project Who Built America? : Working People and the Nation's Economy, Politics, Culture and Society, Volume 2: From the Gilded Age to the Present, New York: 1992

Armour, Robert A. Fritz Lang. Boston: Twayne, 1977.

Auiler, Dan. Vertigo: The Making of a Hitchcock Classic. New York: St. Martins Press, 1998.

Balio, Tino, ed. The American Film Industry. Madison: University of Wisconsin Press, 1976.

_____. United Artists: The Company Built by the Stars. Madison: University of Wisconsin Press, 1976.

_____. United Artists: The Company That Changed the Film Industry. Madison: University of Wisconsin Press, 1987.

Ball, Lucile, with Betty Hannah Hoffman. Love, Lucy. New York: G. P. Putnam's Sons, 1996.

Barlett, Donald L. and James B. Steele. Empire: The Life, Legend, and Madness of Howard Hughes. New York: Norton, 1979.

Barnouw, Erik. A Tower In Babel: A History of Broadcasting in the United States to 1933. New York: Oxford University Press, 1966.

_____. The Golden Web: A History of Broadcasting in the United States 1933-1953. New York: Oxford University Press, 1968.

_____. The Image Empire: A History of Broadcasting in the United States from 1953. New York: Oxford University Press, 1970.

Barrier, Michael. Hollywood Cartoons. New York: Oxford University Press, 1999.

Behlmer, Rudy, ed. Inside Warner Bros.: 1935-1951. New York: Viking Press, 1985.

_____. Memo From David O. Selznick. New York: Viking Press, 1972.

Bennett, Joan, and Lois Kibbee. The Bennett Playbill: Five Generations of the Famous Theater Family. Octavio, NY: Holt, Rinehart & Winston, 1970.

Berg, A. Scott. Goldwyn: A Biography. New York: Ballantine, 1989.

Bergan, Ronald. Jean Renoir: Projections of Paradise. Woodstock, NY: Overlook Press, 1992.

_____. The United Artists Story. New York: Crown, 1988.

Bergman, Andrew. We're in the Money: Depression America and Its Films. New York: New York University Press, 1971.

Bergman, Ingrid, and Alan Burgess. My Story. New York: Delacorte Press, 1980.

Bernardoni, James. The New Hollywood: What the Movies Did With the New Freedom of the Seventies. Jefferson, NC: McFarland, 1991.

Bernstein, Matthew. Walter Wanger, Hollywood Independent. Berkeley, CA: University of California Press, 1994.

Bernstein, Walter. Inside Out: A Memoir of the Blacklist. New York: Alfred A Knopf, 1996.

Walter Bernstein, Inside Out: A Memoir of the Blacklist, New York: 1996

Best, Marc. Those Endearing Young Charms; Child Performers of the Screen. New York: A. S. Barnes, 1971.

Billingsley, Kenneth, Lloyd. The Hollywood Party: How Communism Seduced the American Film Industry in the 1930s and 1940s. Rocklin, CA: Prima Publishing, 1998.

Biskind, Peter. Seeing is Believing: How Hollywood Movies Taught Us to Stop Worrying and Love the Fifties. New York: Pantheon, 1983.

Peter, Biskind "The Politics of Power in 'On the Waterfront'", Film Quarterly, Fall 1975.

Bogdanovich, Peter. Who the Devil Made It: Conversations With Robert Aldrich, George Cukor, Allan Dwan, Howard Hawks, Alfred Hitchcock, Chuck Jones, Fritz Lang, Joseph H. Lewis, Sidney Lumet, Leo McCarey, Otto Preminger, Don Siegel, Josef von Sternberg, Frank Tashlin, Edgar G. Ulmer, Raoul Walsh. New York: Alfred A. Knopf, 1997.

Bordwell, David, Janet Staiger, and Kristin Thompson. The Classical Hollywood Cinema: Film Style and Mode of Production to 1960. New York: Columbia University Press, 1985.

Bowers, Ronald. The Selznick Players. Cranbury, NJ: A. S. Barnes, 1976.

Bowser, Eileen. The Transformation of Cinema, 1907-1915. New York: Charles Scribner's Sons, 1990.

Brady, Frank. Citizen Welles: A Biography of Orson Welles. New York: Charles Scribner's Sons, 1989.

Marlon Brando with Robert Lindsey, Songs My Mother Taught Me, New York: 1994

Brownlow, Kevin. Behind the Mask of Innocence. New York: Alfred A. Knopf, 1990.

_____. David Lean: A Biography. New York: Wyatt/St. Martin's Press, 1996.

_____. Mary Pickford Rediscovered: Rare Pictures of a

Hollywood Legend. New York: Harry N. Abrams, 1999.

_____. The Parade's Gone By. Berkely: University of California Press, 1968.

_____, and John Kobal. Hollywood: The Pioneers. New York: Alfred A. Knopf, 1979.

Butler, Ivan. Silent Magic: Rediscovering the Silent Film Era. New York: Ungar, 1988.

Cagney, James. Cagney by Cagney. Garden City, NY: Doubleday, 1976.

Callow, Simon. Orson Welles: The Road to Xanadu. New York: Viking Press, 1995.

Capra, Frank. The Name Above the Title. New York: Macmillan, 1971.

Carey, Gary. Doug and Mary: A Biography of Douglas Fairbanks and Mary Pickford. New York: E. P. Dutton, 1977.

Catlin, George B. The Story of Detroit. Detroit: Detroit News, 1926.

Larry Ceplair and Steven Englund, The Inquisition in Hollywood: Politics in the Film Community, 1930-1960, Garden City, NY: 1980

Chaplin, Charles. My Autobiography. New York: Simon and Schuster, 1964.

_____. My Life in Pictures. New York: Peerage Books, 1974.

Chaplin, Charles, Jr., with N. and M. Rau. My Father, Charlie Chaplin. New York: Random House, 1960.

Chaplin, Lita Grey, with Morton Cooper. My Life with Chaplin: An Intimate Memoir. New York: Bernard Geis, 1966.

Chown, Jeffrey. Hollywood Auteur: Francis Coppola. New York: Praeger, 1988.

Conant, Michael. Antitrust in the Motion Picture Industry. New York: Arno Press, 1978.

Cowie, Peter. Coppola: A Biography. New York: Charles Scribner's Sons, 1989.

Crafton, Donald. Before Mickey: The Animated Film 1898-1928. Cambridge, MA: MIT Press, 1982.

_____. The Talkies: American Cinema's Transition to Sound, 1926-1931. New York: Charles Scribner's Sons, 1997.

Crosby, Bing, as told to Pete Martin. Call Me Lucky. New York: Simon and Schuster, 1953.

Cross, Robin. The Big Book of "B" Movies or How Low Was My Budget. New York: St. Martins Press, 1981.

Crowther, Bosley. Hollywood Rajah: The Life and Times of Louis B. Mayer. New York: Henry Holt, 1960.

Culhane, John. Walt Disney's Fantasia. New York: Harry N. Abrams, 1983.

Curtis, James. Between Flops: A Biography of Preston Sturges. New York: Harcourt Brace Johanovich, 1982.

Dardis, Tom. Harold Lloyd: The Man on the Clock. New York: Viking Press, 1983.

Davis, Ronald L. John Ford: Hollywood's Old Master. Norman, OK: University of Oklahoma Press, 1995.

DeMille, Cecil B., edited by Donald Hayne. The Autobiography of Cecil B. DeMille. Englewood Cliffs, NJ: Prentice-Hall, 1959.

Dick, Bernard F. City of Dreams: The Making and Remaking of Universal Pictures. Lexington, KY: University of Kentucky, 1997.

_____. The Star-Spangled Screen: The American World War II Film. Lexington, KY: University Press of Kentucky, 1985.

Doherty, Thomas. Teenagers and Teenpics: The Juvenilization of American Movies in the 1950s. Boston: Unwin Hyman, 1988.

Donati, William. Ida Lupino: A Biography. Lexington, KY: University Press of Kentucky, 1996.

Durgnat, Raymond, and Scott Simmon. King Vidor: American. Berkeley, CA: University of California Press, 1988.

Eames, John Douglas. The MGM Story: The Complete History of Fifty Roaring Years. New York: Crown, 1975.

_____. The Paramount Story. New York: Crown, 1985.

Elsaesser, Thomas, with Adam Barker, eds., Early Cinema: Space, Frame, Narrative. London: BFI, 1990.

Essoe, Gabe. Tarzan of the Movies: A Pictorial History of More Than Fifty Years of Edgar Rice Burroughs' Legendary Hero. New York: Citadel Press, 1968.

Everson, William K. American Silent Film. New York: Oxford University Press, 1978.

Eyles, Allen. The Western. Cranbury, NJ: A. S. Barnes, 1975.

Eyman, Scott. Mary Pickford: America's Sweetheart. New York: Donald I. Fine, 1990.

Fairbanks, Douglas, Jr., and Richard Schickel. The Fairbanks Album. Boston: New York Graphic Society, 1975.

Farber, Stephen, and Marc Green. Hollywood Dynasties. New York, Delilah, 1984.

Manny Farber, Negative Space: Manny Farber on the Movies, New York: 1971

Fell, John L., ed. Film Before Griffith. Berkeley, CA: University of California Press, 1983.

Feild, Robert D. The Art of Walt Disney. New York: Macmillan, 1942.

Finch, Christopher. The Art of Walt Disney: From Mickey Mouse to the Magic Kingdoms. New York: Harry N. Abrams, 1973.

Finler, Joel W. The Hollywood Story. New York: Crown, 1988.

Fleischer, Richard. Just Tell Me When to Cry: A Memoir. New York: Carroll and Graf, 1993.

Flower, Joe. Prince of the Magic Kingdom: Michael Eisner and the Re-Making of Disney. New York: John Wiley and Sons, 1991.

Ford, Dan. Pappy: The Life of John Ford. Englewood Cliffs, NJ: Prentice-Hall, 1979.

Freedland, Michael. The Warner Brothers. New York: St. Martin's Press, 1983.

French, Philip. The Movie Moguls: An Informal History of the Hollywood Tycoons. Chicago: Henry Regnery, 1969.

Friedrich, Otto. City of Nets: A Portrait of Hollywood in the 1940's. New York: Harper & Row, 1986.

Gabler, Neal. An Empire of Their Own: How the Jews Invented Hollywood. New York: Doubleday, 1985.

Jean-Luc Godard, Godard on Godard, New York: 1972

Gallagher, Tag. John Ford: The Man and His Films. Berkeley, CA: University of California Press, 1986.

Gehring, Wes, D. Charlie Chaplin's World of Comedy. Muncie: Ball State University Press, 1980.

_____. Screwball Comedy: A Genre of Madcap Romance. New York: Greenwood Press, 1986.

Dan Georgakas, Hollywood Blacklist, from Encyclopedia of the American Left; Buhle, Buhle, and Georgakas, ed., Urbana and Chicago: 1992

Goldenson, Leonard H., with Marvin J. Wolf. Beating the Odds: The Untold Story Behind the Rise of ABC: The Stars, Struggles, and Egos That Transformed Network Television By the Man Who Made It Happen. New York: Charles Scribner's Sons, 1991.

Goldwyn, Samuel. Behind the Screen. New York: George H. Doran, 1923.

Gomery, Douglas. The Hollywood Studio System. New York: St. Martin's Press, 1986.

_____. Shared Pleasures: A History of Movie Presentation in the United States. Madison: University of Wisconsin Press, 1992.

Graham, Cooper C., Steven Higgins, Elaine Mancini, and Joao Luiz Vieira. D.W. Griffith and the Biograph Company. Metuchen, NJ: Scarecrow Press, 1985.

Grover, Ron. The Disney Touch: Disney, ABC and the Quest for the World's Greatest Media Empire. Burr Ridge, IL: Irwin Professional Publishing, 1996.

Guback, Thomas. The International Film Industry: Western Europe and America Since 1945. Bloomington, IN: Indiana University Press, 1969.

Gunning, Thomas. D.W. Griffith and the Rise of the Narrative Film. Urbana, IL: University of Illinois Press, 1991.

Hamilton, Ian. Writers in Hollywood, 1915-1951. London: Heinemann, 1990.

Hampton, Benjamin B. A History of the American Film Industry: From Its Beginnings to 1931. New York: Dover, 1970; reprinted from A History of the Movies. New York: Covici, Friede, 1931.

Haver, Ronald. David O. Selznick's Hollywood. New York: Bonanza Books, 1980.

Hay, Peter. MGM: When the Lion Roars. Atlanta, GA: Turner, 1991.

Hecht, Ben. A Child of the Century. New York: Simon and Schuster, 1954.

Henderson, Harold Paulk, The Politics of Change in Georgia: A Political Biography of Ellis Arnall. Athens, GA: University of Georgia Press, 1991.

Hendricks, Gordon. The Edison Motion Picture Myth. Berkeley, CA: University of California Press, 1961.

Hepburn, Katherine. The Making of The African Queen: Or How I Went To Africa With Bogart, Bacall and Houston and Almost Lost My Mind. New York: Alfred A. Knopf, 1987.

Heraldson, Donald. Creators of Life: A History of Animation. New York: Drake, 1975.

Herndon, Booton. Mary Pickford and Douglas Fairbanks: The Most Popular Couple the World Has Known. New York: W. W. Norton, 1977.

Higham, Charles. Merchant of Dreams: Louis B. Mayer, M.G.M. and the Secret Hollywood. New York: Donald I. Fine, 1993.

_____. Orson Welles: The Rise and Fall of an American Genius. New York: St. Martin's Press, 1985.

_____. Warner Brothers. New York: Charles Scribner's Sons, 1975.

Hirschhorn, Clive. The Universal Story: The Complete History of the Studio and It's 2,641 Films. New York: Crown, 1983.

_____. The Warner Bros. Story. New York: Crown, 1979.

Holliss, Richard, and Brian Sibley. The Disney Studio Story. New York: Crown, 1988.

Huettig, Mae D. Economic Control of the Motion Picture Industry: A Study in Industrial Organization. Philadelphia: University of Pennsylvania Press, 1944.

Hurst, Richard M. Republic Studios: Between Poverty Row and the Majors. Metuchen, NJ: Scarecrow Press, 1979.

Huston, John. An Open Book. New York: Alfred A. Knopf, 1980.

Irwin, Will. The House that Shadows Built. New York: Doubleday, Doran, 1928.

Jacobs, Diane. Christmas in July: The Life and Art of Preston Sturges. Berkeley, CA: University of California, 1992.

Jacobs, Lewis. The Rise of the American Film: A Critical History. New York: Harcourt, Brace, 1939.

James, John Douglas. The MGM Story. New York: Crown, 1976.

Jewell, Richard B., and Vernon Harbin. The RKO Story. New York: Arlington House, 1982.

Johnston, Alva. The Great Goldwyn. New York: Random House, 1937.

Kaminsky, Stuart. John Huston: Maker of Magic. Boston: Houghton Mifflin, 1978.

Kapsis, Robert E. Hitchcock: The Making of a Reputation. Chicago: University of Chicago Press, 1992.

Kazan, Elia. A Life. New York: Alfred A. Knopf, 1988.

Ephraim Katz, The Film Encyclopedia, New York: 1994

Kennedy, Joseph P., ed. The Story of the Films. Chicago: A. W. Shaw, 1927.

Keyser, Lester J. Hollywood in the Seventies. San Diego: A. S. Barnes, 1981.

Kinney, Jack. Walt Disney and Assorted Other Characters: An Unauthorized Account of the Early Years at Disney's. New York: Harmony Books, 1988.

Koppes, Clayton R., and Gregory D. Black. Hollywood Goes to War: How Politics, Profits, and Propaganda Shaped World War II Movies. New York: Free Press, 1987.

Korda, Michael. Charmed Lives: A Family Romance. New York: Random House, 1979.

Koszarski, Richard. An Evening's Entertainment: The Age of the Silent Feature Picture, 1915-1928. New York: Charles Scribner's Sons, 1990.

_____, ed. Hollywood Directors, 1914-1940. New York: Oxford University, 1976.

_____, ed. Hollywood Directors, 1941-1976. New York: Oxford University, 1977.

Kramer, Stanley, with Thomas M. Coffey. A Mad, Mad, Mad, Mad World: A Life in Hollywood. New York: Harcourt, Brace, 1997.

Kuhn, Annette. Cinema, Censorship, and Sexuality, 1909-1925. New York: Routledge, 1988.

Kulik, Karol. Alexander Korda: The Man Who Could Work Miracles. New Rochelle, NY: Arlington House, 1975.

Lahue, Karlton C. Dreams for Sale: The Rise and Fall of the Triangle Film Corporation. Cranbury, NJ: A. S. Barnes, 1971.

Lally, Kevin. Wilder Times: The Life of Billy Wilder. New York: Henry Holt, 1996.

Lasky, Betty. RKO: The Biggest Little Major of Them All. Santa Monica, CA: Roundtable, 1984.

Lasky, Jesse L., with Don Weldon. I Blow My Own Horn. Garden City, NY: Doubleday, 1957.

Lasky, Jesse, Jr. Whatever Happened to Hollywood?. New York: Funk & Wagnalls, 1975.

Anderson, Lindsay, 'The Last Sequence of "On the Waterfront", Sight & Sound

Leaming, Barbara. Orson Welles: A Biography. New York: Viking Press, 1985.

Lebo, Harlan. Citizen Kane: The Fiftieth-Anniversary Album. New York: Doubleday, 1990.

Leebron, Elizabeth, and Lynn Gartley. Walt Disney: A Guide to References and Resources. Boston: G. K. Hall, 1979.

Leff, Leonard J., and Jerold L. Simmons. The Dame in the Kimono: Hollywood, Censorship, and the Production Code from the 1920s to the 1960s. New York: Grove Weidenfeld, 1990.

Leff, Leonard J. Hitchcock and Selznick: The Rich and Strange Collaboration of Alfred Hitchcock and David O. Selznick In Hollywood. New York: Weidenfeld and Nicholson, 1987.

Le Roy, Mervyn, as told to Dick Kleiner. Mervyn Le Roy: Take One. New York: Hawthorn Books, 1974.

Lingeman, Richard R. Don't You Know There's a War On?: The American Home Front, 1941-1945. New York: G.P. Putnam's Sons, 1970.

MacCann, Richard Dyer. The First Tycoons. Metuchen, NJ: Scarecrow Press, 1987.

Madsen, Axel. William Wyler: The Authorized Biography. New York: Thomas Y. Crowell, 1973.

Maland, Charles. American Visions: The Films of Chaplin, Ford, Capra, and Welles, 1936-1941. New York: Arno Press, 1977.

Maland, Charles J. Chaplin and American Culture: The Evolution of a Star Image. Princeton, NJ: Princeton University Press, 1989.

Maltin, Leonard. Of Mice and Magic: A History of American Animated Cartoons. Rev. ed. New York: New American Library, 1987.

Maltin, Leonard, and Richard W. Bann. Our Gang: The Life and Times of the Little Rascals. New York: Crown, 1977.

Mann, Kluas Mephisto, New York: 1977

Manvell, Roger. Films and the Second World War. New York: Dell, 1976.

Marill, Alvin H. Samuel Goldwyn Presents. Cranbury, NJ: A. S. Barnes, 1976.

Marx, Arthur. Goldwyn: A Biography of the Man Behind the Myth. New York: W. W. Norton, 1976.

Marx, Samuel. Mayer and Thalberg: The Make-Believe Saints. New York: Random House, 1975.

Mast, Gerald, ed. The Movies in Our Midst: Documents in the Cultural History of Film in America. Chicago: University of Chicago Press, 1982.

McBride, Joseph. Frank Capra: The Catastrophe of Success. New York: Simon and Schuster, 1992.

McCabe, John. Cagney. New York: Alfred A. Knopf, 1997.

_____. Charlie Chaplin. New York: Doubleday, 1978.

McCarthy, Todd. Howard Hawks: The Grey Fox of Hollywood. New York: Grove Press, 1997.

McDougal, Dennis. The Last Mogul: Lew Wasserman, MCA, and the Hidden History of Hollywood. New York: Crown, 1998.

McGilligan, Patrick. Fritz Lang: The Nature of the Beast. New York: St. Martin's Press, 1997.

Merritt, Russel, and J. B. Kaufman. Walt in Wonderland: The Silent Films of Walt Disney. Pordenone, Italy: Le Giornate del Cinema Muto, 1992.

Miller, Diane Disney. The Story of Walt Disney. New York: Henry Holt, 1957.

Milton, Joyce. Tramp: The Life of Charlie Chaplin. New York: Harper Collins, 1996.

Monaco, Paul. Ribbons in Time: Movies and Society Since 1945. Bloomington, IN: Indiana University Press, 1987.

Morden, Ethan. The Hollywood Studio: House Style in the Golden Age of the Movies. New York: Alfred A. Knopf, 1988.

Mosely, Leonard. Disney's World: A Biography. New York: Stein and Day, 1985.

_____. Zanuck: The Rise and Fall of Hollywood's Last Tycoon. Boston: Little, Brown, 1984.

Musser, Charles. The Emergence of Cinema: The American Screen to 1907. New York: Charles Scribner's Sons, 1990.

_____. Before the Nickelodeon: Edwin S. Porter and the Edison Manufacturing Company. Berkeley, CA: University of California Press, 1991.

Naremore, James. The Magic World of Orson Welles. New York: Oxford University Press, 1978.

Navasky, Victor S. Naming Names, New York: 1980

Naremore, James, Acting in the Cinema, University of California Press, 1988. (Good on Brando's performance).

Neve, Brian Film and Politics in America: A Social Tradition, New York: 1992

Paley, William S. As It Happened, A Memoir. Garden City, NY: Doubleday, 1979.

Pickford, Mary. Sunshine and Shadow. Garden City, NY: Doubleday, 1955.

Poitier, Sidney. This Life. New York: Alfred A. Knopf, 1980.

Preis, Art Labor's Giant Step, New York: 1972

Ramsaye, Terry. A Million and One Nights. New York: Simon & Schuster, 1926; reprint ed., New York: Touchstone, 1986.

Rapf Joanna (ed.) On the Waterfront Cambridge: Cambridge University Press, 2003

Rebello, Stephen. Alfred Hitchcock and the Making of Psycho. New York: Dembner Books, 1990.

Robinson, David. Chaplin: His Life and Art. New York: McGraw-Hill, 1985.

_____. Chaplin: The Mirror of Opinion. London: Secker & Warburg, 1983.

Schrecker, Ellen The Age of McCarthyism: A Brief History with Documents, Boston: 1994

Andrew Sarris, Confessions of a Cultist: On the Cinema, 1955/1969, New York: 1971

Andrew Sarris, The American Cinema: Directors and Directions, 1929-1968, New York: 1968

Sanders, Coyne Steven, and Tom Gilbert. Desilu: The Story of Lucille Ball and Desi Arnaz. New York: William Morrow, 1993.

_____. Hollywood in the Twenties. Cranbury, NJ: A. S. Barnes, 1968.

Schary, Dore. Heyday: An Autobiography. Boston: Little, Brown, 1979.

Schatz, Thomas. Boom and Bust: The American Cinema in the 1940s. New York: Charles Scribner's Sons, 1997.

_____. The Genius of the System. New York: Henry Holt, 1996.

_____. Hollywood Genres: Formulas, Filmmaking, and the Studio System. New York: McGraw-Hill, 1981.

Schickel, Richard. D. W. Griffith: An American Life. New York: Simon & Schuster, 1984.

_____. The Disney Version: The Life, Times, Art and Commerce of Walt Disney. New York: Simon and Schuster, 1968.

_____. James Cagney: A Celebration. Boston: Little, Brown, 1985.

Schrecker, Ellen. The Age of McCarthyism: A Brief History With Documents. Boston: St. Martins Press, 1994.

Schulberg, Budd. Moving Pictures: Memories of a Hollywood Prince. New York: Simon & Schuster, 1984.

Schulberg, Budd, 'On the Waterfront', A Screenplay, Southern Illinois University Press, 1980.

Schumacher, Michael. Francis Ford Coppola: A Filmmaker's Life. New York: Crown, 1999.

Schwartz, Lynn, Nancy. The Hollywood Writer's Wars. New York: Alfred A Knopf, 1982.

Selznick, Irene Mayer. A Private View. New York: Alfred A. Knopf, 1983.

Sennett, Mack, as told to Cameron Shipp. King of Comedy. Garden City, NY: Doubleday, 1954.

Shale, Richard. Donald Duck Joins Up: The Walt Disney Studio During World War II. Ann Arbor, MI: UMI Research Press, 1982.

Shindler, Colin. Hollywood Goes to War: Films and American Society, 1939-1952. Boston: Routledge & Kegan Paul, 1979.

Sinyard, Neil. Silent Movies. New York: Gallery Books, 1990.

Shipman, David. The Story of Cinema. New York: St. Martin's Press, 1982.

Shows, Charles. Walt: Backstage Adventures With Walt Disney. La Jolla, CA: Windsong Books, 1979.

Sikov, Ed. On Sunset Boulevard: The Life and Times of Billy Wilder. New York: Hyperion, 1998.

Silverman, Stephen M. David Lean. New York, Harry N. Abrams, 1989.

Sinclair, Andrew. John Ford. New York: Dial Press/James Wade, 1979.

_____. Spiegel: The Man Behind the Pictures. Boston: Little, Brown, 1987.

Sklar, Robert. Film: An International History of the Medium. New York: Harry N. Abrams, 1993.

_____. Movie-Made America: A Cultural History of American Movies. New York: Vintage Books, 1994.

Smith, Albert E. Two Reels and a Crank. Garden City, NY: Doubleday, 1952.

Smoodin, Eric, ed. Disney Discourse: Producing the Magic Kingdom. New York: Routledge, 1994.

Solomon, Charles. The Disney That Never Was: The Stories and Art from Five Decades of Unproduced Animation. New York: Hyperion, 1995.

_____. Enchanted Drawings: The History of Animation. New York: Alfred A. Knopf, 1989.

Spoto, Donald. The Dark Side of Genius: The Life of Alfred Hitchcock. Boston: Little, Brown, 1983.

_____. Stanley Kramer, Film Maker. New York: Putnam, 1978.

Stanley, Robert H. The Celluloid Empire: A History of the American Movie Industry. New York: Communications Arts/Hastings House, 1978.

Sturges, Preston, adapted and edited by Sandy Sturges. Preston Sturges. New York: Simon and Schuster, 1990.

Swanson, Gloria. Swanson on Swanson. New York: Random House, 1980.

Tabori, Paul. Alexander Korda: A Biography. London: Oldbourne, 1959.

Taylor, John. Storming the Magic Kingdom: Wall Street, the Raiders, and the Battle for Disney. New York: Alfred A. Knopf, 1987.

Taylor, John Russell. Hitch: The Life and Times of Alfred Hitchcock. New York: Pantheon Books, 1978.

_____. Orson Welles. Boston: Little, Brown, 1986.

_____. Strangers in Paradise: The Hollywood Emigres. London: Faber and Faber, 1983.

Thomas, Bob. Building a Company: Roy O. Disney and the Creation of an Entertainment Empire. New York: Hyperion, 1998.

_____. Selznick. Garden City, NY: Doubleday, 1970.

_____. Life and Legend. Garden City, NY: Doubleday, 1969.

_____. Walt Disney: An American Original. New York: Simon and Schuster, 1976.

Thomas, Tony. Howard Hughes in Hollywood. Secaucus, NJ: The Citadel Press, 1985.

Thompson, Kristin. Exporting Entertainment: America in the World Film Market, 1907-1934. London: British Film Institute, 1985.

Thomson, David. Rosebud: The Story of Orson Welles. New York: Alfred A. Knopf, 1996.

Torrence, Bruce, T. Hollywood: The First Hundred Years. New York: Zoetrope, 1982.

Trethewey, Richard L. Walt Disney: The FBI Files. Pacifica, CA: Rainbo Animation Art, 1994.

Tytle, Harry. One of "Walt's Boys": An Insider's Account of Disney's Golden Years. Royal Oak, MI: Airtight Seels Allied Productions, 1997.

Trumbo, Dalton. Additional Dialogue: Letters of Dalton Trumbo 1942 - 1962. New York: M.Evans, 1970.

Udelson, Joseph H. The Great Television Race: A History of the American Television Industry, 1925-1941. Alabama: University of Alabama Press, 1982.

Vidor, King. King Vidor on Film Making. New York: David McKay, 1972.

Wallis, Hal, and Charles Higham. Starmaker: The Autobiography of Hall Wallis. New York: Macmillan, 1980.

Wapshott, Nicholas. Carol Reed: A Biography. New York: Alfred A. Knopf, 1994.

Warner, Jack. My First Hundred Years in Hollywood. New York: Random House, 1965.

Watts, Steven. The Magic Kingdom: Walt Disney and the American Way of Life. Boston: Houghton Mifflin, 1997.

Weales, Gerald. Canned Goods as Caviar: American Film Comedy of the 1930s. Chicago: University of Chicago Press, 1985.

Welles, Orson, and Peter Bogdanovich. This Is Orson Welles. New York: HarperCollins, 1992.

Whitefield, Eileen. Pickford: The Woman Who Made Hollywood. Lexington, KY: University Press of Kentucky, 1997.

Wilkerson,Tichi, and Marcia Borie, The Hollywood Reporter, the Golden Years. New York: Coward-McCann, 1984.

Williams, Henry B. Theatre at Dartmouth 1769-1914: From Eleazar Wheelock to Walter Wanger. Hanover, NH: Friends of the Dartmouth Library, 1987.

Williams, Martin. Griffith: First Artist of the Movies. New York: Oxford University Press, 1980.

Windeler, Robert. Sweetheart: The Story of Mary Pickford. New York: Praeger, 1974.

Young, Jeff (ed.), Kazan on Kazan, Faber & Faber, 1999. (Good on Kazan's directing style and approach).

Zierold, Norman. The Moguls: Hollywood's Merchants of Myth. New York: Coward-McCann, 1969.

Howard Zinn, A People's History of the United States, New York: 1980

Zinnemann, Fred. A Life in the Movies: An Autobiography. New York: Robert Stewart/Charles Scribner's Sons, 1992.

Zukor, Adolph, with Dale Kramer. The Public Is Never Wrong: My Fifty Years in the Motion Picture Industry. New York: G. P. Putnam's Sons, 1953.

The day after Kazan's testimony (April 11, 1952) was given in executive session to the HUAC, it was released to the public. The following day April 12, 1952, Kazan took an ad in The New York Times explaining his position and exhorting others to do likewise.

Newspapers/ Magazines

WEB on Kazan
Imdb.com
kirjasto
Wikipedia
PBS: American Masters
Spartacus School
Postage Paid Modern Times

OBIT: Elia Kazan, Influential Director, Dies at 94 (MERVYN ROTHSTEIN, 9/28/03, NY Times)

OBIT: Elia Kazan: Oscar-winning director of On the Waterfront who named communists to the Un-American Activities Committee during the McCarthy era (David Thomson, September 29, 2003, Guardian)

OBIT: Elia Kazan (Daily Telegraph 30/09/2003)

Elia Kazan's Landscape of Desire By A. O. SCOTT, September 30, 2003, NY Times)

Why 'Controversy' Dogged Kazan (Allan H. Ryskind, Oct 3, 2003, Human Events)

Hollywood protest at Kazan's Oscar (Tom Brook, February 22, 1999, BBC)

Washington Post: Academy Awards 1999

The Legacy of the Anti-Communist Liberal Intellectuals (Ronald Radosh, Partisan Review)

Elia Kazan's Towering Presence (Larry P. Arnn, Claremont Precepts)

Elia Kazan: Moral Hero: Kazan should be applauded for defending individual rights by testifying against Hollywood's communists. (Robert W. Tracinski, Ad Hoc Committee for Naming Names)

Justice for Elia Kazan (Glenn Woiceshyn, March 1, 1999, Capitalism Magazine)

Naming Names (Thomas Sowell, 3/19/99, Jewish World Review)

A Different Waterfront (Paul Greenburg, 3/9/99, Jewish World Review)

Kazan's Oscar: Not Too Late (L. Brent Bozell III, January 25, 1999)

Kazan and Miller: Long, Bitter Debate From the '50's: Views of Kazan and His Critics (Richard Bernstein, May 3, 1988, NY Times)

Why Elia should get his Oscar: moral and political judgments of Elia Kazan should not overshadow his art at this month's Academy Awards (Arthur Miller, March 6, 1999, The Guardian) -: The Forgotten Oscar

(Victor Navasky, March 18, 1999, The Nation)

Blacklist and Backstory: Hollywood's unexpected embrace of Elia Kazan (Jacob Weisberg, January 31, 1999, Slate)

Why Elia Kazan should not receive an Oscar: By bestowing a special honor on the director, who already has won two Oscars, the academy is glossing over history. (Steve Erickson, March 1999, Salon)

Hollywood honors Elia Kazan. Filmmaker and informer. (David Walsh, 20 February 1999, World Socialist Web Site)

And the Winner Is -- HUAC: Elia Kazan will have the statue, but the victory belongs to the blacklist (Christopher Trumbo , 3/19/99, LA Weekly)

On the Boxing Front: Writer Budd Schulberg on Contenders and Pretenders (William Gildea, June 9, 2002, washingtonpost.com)

-OBIT: Marlon Brando, Oscar-Winning Actor, Is Dead at 80 (RICK LYMAN, 7/02/04, NY Times)

The Great Contender: Remembering Brando (Budd Schulberg, 7/04/04, Sunday Herald)

OTHER SOURCES CONSULTED BY THE AUTHOR

Biskind, Peter, "The Politics of Power in 'On the Waterfront'", Film Quarterly, fall 1975.

Hey, Kenneth, 'Ambivalence as a Theme in 'On the Waterfront', in Peter C. Rollins, ed., Hollywood as Historian, Revised edition, 1998.

Kazan, Elia, A Life, 1997

Naremore, James, Acting in the Cinema, University of California Press, 1988.

Navasky, Victor, Naming Names, Viking, 1980.

Rapf, Joanna E., (ed), Handbook on 'On the Waterfront', Cambridge University Press, forthcoming.

Schulberg, Budd, 'On the Waterfront', A Screenplay, Southern Illinois University Press, 1980.

Young, Jeff (ed.), Kazan on Kazan, Faber & Faber, 1999. (Good on Kazan's directing style and approach).

Brando: Songs my Mother Taught me Random House, New York1994 Marlon Brando/ Robert Lindsey

.Buhle, Buhle, and Georgakas, ed., Encyclopedia of the American Left. Urbana and Chicago: University of Illinois Press, 1992

2. Ellen Schrecker. The Age of McCarthyism: A Brief History With Documents. Boston: St. Martin's Press, 1994

"Congressional Committees and Unfriendly Witnesses" by Ellen Schrecker

.Howard Zinn. A People's History of the United States - covering the period 1945-1960.New York: Harper & Row Publishers, 1980

Excerpts from Gordon Kahn's FBI files

"I Was A Communist For The FBI"

Movienet - Film Finders Buzz

SF Bay Guardian, October 10, 1996

Transcript of Walt Disney's testimony, 24 Oct 1947

Variety, September 13, 1996

New York Times, July 29, 1951 (Truman quote)
New York Times, November 3, 1996 (Why Lillian Hellman Remains Fascinating)

Newsweek, September 15, 1947
Newsweek, November 3, 1947
Newsweek, April 2, 1951
Newsweek, May 7, 1951
Newsweek, April 21, 1952
Newsweek, June 4, 1951
Newsweek, December 8, 1947
Newsweek, November 10, 1947
Newsweek, November 24, 1947

Fitzgerald, F. Scott. The Last Tycoon. London: Penguin Books, 1941

Mailer, Norman. The Deer Park. London: Flamingo, 1957

Schulberg, Budd. What Makes Sammy Run?. New York: Vintage, 1941

Balio, Tino, ed., The American Film Industry. The University of Wisconsin Press, 1976, 1985

Caute, David. The Great Fear. New York: Simon and Schuster, 1978

Hellman, Lillian. Scoundrel Time. Boston: Little, Brown and Company, 1976

Kazan, Elia. A Life. London: Andre Deutsch, 1988

Miller, Arthur. Timebends - A Life. London: Methuen, 1987

Navasky, Victor S. Naming Names. New York: The Viking Press, 1980

Neve, Brian. Film and Politics in America - A Social Tradition. London and New York: Routledge, 1992

Coltrane, Scott. "Gender Displaying Television Commercials: A Comparative Study of Television Commercials in the 1950s and 1980s." Sex Roles: A Journal of Research v35, n3-4 (August, 1996)

Anisfield, Nancy "Godzilla/Gojiro: Evolution of the Nuclear Metaphor." Journal of Popular Culture, Winter 1995, 29:3, pp:53+

Berger, Roger A. "'Ask What You Can Do for Your Country': The Film Version of H. G. Wells's The Time Machine and the Cold War." Literature/ Film Quarterly, vol. 17 no. 3. 1989. pp: 177-187.

Biskind, Peter "Pods, blobs, and ideology in American films of the fifties." In: Shadows of the magic lamp: fantasy and science fiction in film / Edited by George Slusser and Eric S. Rabkin. pp: 58-72. Carbondale: Southern Illinois University Press, c1985. Series title: Alternatives. UCB Main

Boddy, William Fifties Television: The Industry and Its Critics / William Boddy. Urbana: University of Illinois Press, c1990. Series title: Illinois studies in communications.

Boozer, Jack, Jr. "Entrepreneurs and 'Family Values' in the Postwar Film." In: Authority and Transgression in Literature and Film / edited by Bonnie Braendlin and Hans Braendlin. pp: 89-102. Gainesville: University Press of Florida, c1996. Main Stack PN56.A87.A87 1996

Broderick, Mick. Nuclear Movies: A Critical Analysis and Filmography of International Feature Length Films Dealing with Experimentation, Aliens, Terrorism, Holocaust, and Other Disaster Scenarios, 1914-1990 / by Mick Broderick; with a foreword by Helen Caldicott. Jefferson, N.C. McFarland & Co., 1991, c1988. Main Stack PN1995.9.N9.B76 1991 Moffitt PN1995.9.N9.B76 1991

Byars, Jackie. All That Hollywood Allows: Re-reading Gender in 1950s Melodrama / Jackie Byars. Chapel Hill : University of North Carolina Press, c1991. Series title: Gender & American culture.
UCB Main PN1995.9.S47 B9 1991
UCB Moffitt PN1995.9.S47 B9 1991

Byars, Jackie "Feminism, Psychoanalysis, and Female-Oriented Melodramas of the 1950s." In: Multiple voices in feminist film criticism / Diane Carson, Linda Dittmar, and Janice R. Welsch, editors. pp: 93-108 Minneapolis: University of Minnesota Press, c1994.
Main Stack PN1995.9.W6.M82 1994
Moffitt PN1995.9.W6.M82 1994

Corber, Robert J. Homosexuality in Cold War America: Resistance and the Crisis of Masculinity / Robert J. Corber. Durham [N.C.]: Duke University Press, 1997. New Americanists Main Stack HQ76.3.U5.C65 1997

Clark, Ginger. "Cinema of Compromise: Pinky and thePolitics of Post War Film Production." (Elia Kazan's anti-racist film, "Pinky") Western Journal of Black Studies v21, n3 (Fall, 1997):180 (10 pages).

Cox, Carole "Popular Culture: The Fifties, Hollywood and Horror Films, Art and the Old West." English Journal 76:1 (1987:Jan.) 87

Cripps, Thomas. Hollywood's High Noon: Moviemaking & Society Before Television / Thomas Cripps. Baltimore: Johns Hopkins University Press, 1997. Series title: The American moment. UCB Main PN1995.9.S6 C73 1997

Curtin, Michael. Redeeming the Wasteland: Television Documentary and Cold War Politics / Michael Curtin. New Brunswick, N.J.: Rutgers University Press, c1995. Communications, media, and culture

Main Stack PN1992.8.D6.C87 1995
Moffitt PN1992.8.D6.C87 1995

Davis, Ronald L. Celluloid Mirrors: Hollywood and American Society Since 1945 / Ronald L. Davis. Fort Worth, TX : Harcourt Brace College Publishers, c1997. Series title: Harbrace books on America since 1945.
UCB Main PN1993.5.U65 D339 1997
UCB Moffitt PN1993.5.U65 D339 1997

Dunne, Michael. "Cold War Ideology in John Ford's Fort Apache." Popular Culture Review, vol. 8 no. 1. 1997 Feb. pp: 83-95.

Evans, Joyce A. Celluloid mushroom clouds: Hollywood and the atomic bomb / Joyce A. Evans. Boulder, Colo.: Westview Press, 1998. Critical studies in communication and in the cultural industries
Main Stack PN1995.9.W3.E82 1998

Fore, Steve. "Howard Hughes' 'Authoritarian Fictions': RKO, One Minute to Zero, and the Cold War." The Velvet Light Trap, vol. 31. 1993 Spring. pp: 15-26.

Fruth, Bryan, et al. "The Atomic Age: facts and films from 1945-1965." Journal of Popular Film and Television (23:4) 1996, 154-60.

Fulford, Robert "American Demons of the 1950s." Queen's Quarterly 102, no. 3 (1995 Fall): p. 525-45

Fuller, Linda K. "The Ideology of the 'Red Scare' Movement: McCarthyism in the Movies." In: Beyond the Stars / edited by Paul Loukides and Linda

K. Fuller. pp: 229-248. Bowling Green, Ohio: Bowling Green University Popular Press, c1990
Main Stack PN1995.9.C36.B49 1990
Library has: v.[1]-5 (c1990-c1996)
Moffitt PN1995.9.C36.B49 1990

Gallagher, Brian. "Howard Hawks's The Big Sleep: A Paradigm for the Postwar American Family." North Dakota Quarterly, vol. 51 no. 3. 1983 Summer. pp: 78-91.

Gilbert, James B. "Wars of the Worlds." Journal of Popular Culture 1976 10(2): 326-336.
"Science fiction movies of the 1950's, as close examination of the cinema adaptation of H. G. Wells' War of the Worlds illustrates, were metaphoric vehicles for social commentary. They reflected the social values believed to be in hazard during the Cold War and underscore the role popular culture plays in the assimilation of values and change." [America History and Life]

Gow, Gordon Hollywood in the Fifties New York, A. S. Barnes [1971 (Series: The International film guide series) Main Stack PN1993.5.U6.G6 NRLF #: $B 384 349M

Hendershot, Cyndy. "The Atomic Scientist, Science Fiction Films, and Paranoia: The Day the Earth Stood Still, This Island Earth, and Killers from Space." Journal of American Culture, vol. 20 no. 1. 1997 Spring. pp: 31-41.

Hendershot, Cyndy. "The Bomb and Sexuality: Creature from the Black Lagoon and Revenge of the

Creature." Literature and Psychology 45, no. 4 (1999): p. 74-89

Hendershot, Cyndy. "Darwin and the Atom: Evolution/Devolution Fantasies in The Beast from 20,000 Fathoms, Them! and The Incredible Shrinking Man." Science Fiction Studies 25, no. 2 (75) (1998 July): p. 319-35

Hendershot, Cyndy. "Feminine Paranoia and Secrecy: I Married a Monster from Outer Space and Attack of the 50 Ft. Woman." Readerly/Writerly Texts, vol. 4 no. 2. 1997 Spring-Summer. pp: 71-86.

Hendershot, Cyndy. Paranoia, the bomb, and 1950s science fiction films / Cyndy Hendershot. Bowling Green, OH : Bowling Green State University Popular Press, c1999. Main Stack PN1995.9.S26.H37 1999

Katovich, Michael A; Kinkade, Patrick T "The Stories Told in Science Fiction and Social Science: Reading The Thing and Other Remakes From Two Eras." Sociological Quarterly, 34:4 Nov 1993, pp: 619+

Kneeshaw, Stephen. "Hollywood And 'The Bomb'". OAH Newsletter 1986 14(2): 9-11.
"The treatment of the atomic bomb in major Hollywood movies shifted from "bombs-create-monsters" science fiction in the 1950's to thoughtful examinations of the impact of the general nuclear energy threat in the 1960's and 1980's, while only a few second-quality movies and Planet of the Apes-style postholocaust films dealt with the bomb after the mid 1960's." [America History and Life]

Klinger, Barbara "'Local' Genres: The Hollywood Adult Film of the 1950s In: Melodrama: stage, picture, screen / edited by Jacky Bratton, Jim Cook, Christine Gledhill. pp: 134-46 London : British Film Institute, 1994. Main Stack PN1912.M45 1994

Kozak, Warren "Killer Monster Bugs from Hell! How Americans Forgot About the War and Learned to Loathe Nature. (1950s and 1960s horror science fiction films on insects) I.D. Sept-Oct, 1997 Vol/Num: v. 44, n. 5, p. 76 (4 pages)

Landrum, Larry N. "A Checklist of Materials About Science Fiction Films of the 1950's" Journal of Popular Film 1:1 (1972:Winter) 61

Larson, Mary Strom. "Sibling Interactions in 1950s versus 1980s Sitcoms: A Comparison." (family relationships in television comedies)(Processes of Communication) Journalism Quarterly v68, n3 (Autumn, 1991):381 (7 pages).

Leibman, Nina C. Living Room Lectures: The Fifties Family in Film and Television / Nina C. Leibman. 1st ed. Austin: University of Texas Press, 1995. Texas film studies series. Main Stack PN1992.8.F33.L45 1995

Leibman, Nina C. "Leave Mother Out: The Fifties Family in American Film and Television." Wide Angle, vol. 10 no. 4. 1988. pp: 24-41.

Lenihan, John H. "English Classics for Cold War America: MGM's Kim (1950), Ivanhoe (1952), and Julius Caesar (1953)" Journal of Popular Film and Television, vol. 20 no. 3. 1992 Fall. pp: 42-51.

Lucanio, Patrick. "Them or Us: Archetypal Interpretations of Fifties Alien Invasion Films / Patrick Lucanio. Bloomington: Indiana University Press, c1987.
UCB Main PN1995.9.S26 L8 1987
UCB Moffitt PN1995.9.S26 L8 1987

MacDougall, Robert "Red, Brown and Yellow Perils: Images of the American Enemy in the 1940s and 1950s." Journal of Popular Culture 32, no. 4 (1999 Spring): p. 59-75

Mannix, Patrick The Rhetoric of Antinuclear Fiction: Persuasive Strategies in Novels and Films / Patrick Mannix. Lewisburg [Pa.] : Bucknell University Press ; London; Cranbury, NJ: Associated University Presses, c1992.
UCB Main PS374.N82 M36 1992
UCB Moffitt PS374.N82 M36 1992

Marx, Samuel "The Bomb Movie." In: The Movies : texts, receptions, exposures / edited by Laurence Goldstein and Ira Konigsberg. Ann Arbor : University of Michigan Press, c1996. Main Stack PN1994.M78 1996 Moffitt PN1994.M78 1996

McGregor, Gaile. "Domestic Bliss: A Revisionist History of the Fifties." American Studies, vol. 34 no. 1. 1993 Spring. pp: 5-33.

Mellencamp, Patricia. "Five Ages of Film Feminism." In: Kiss Me Deadly:

Feminism and Cinema for the Moment. / edited by Laleen Jayamanne. pp: 18-76. Sydney: Power Publications, c1995.
Main Stack PN1995.9.W6.K57 1995

Morey, Anne. ""The Judge Called Me an Accessory': Women's Prison Films, 1950-1962." Journal of Popular Film and Television, vol. 23 no. 2. 1995 Summer. pp: 80-87.

Morris, Peter. "Salt of the Earth." In: Celluloid Power: Social Film Criticism from the Birth of a Nation to Judgment at Nuremberg. / [edited] by David Platt. pp: 485-493. Metuchen, N.J.: Scarecrow Press, 1992.
Main Stack PN1995.9.P6.C44 1992
Moffitt PN1995.9.P6.C44 1992

Neve, Brian "The 1950s: The Case of Elia Kazan and On the Waterfront." In: Cinema, politics and society in America / edited by Philip Davies and Brian Neve. pp: 97-118 Manchester, [Greater Manchester]: Manchester University Press, 1981
Main Stack PN1995.9.S6.C55; PN1995.9.S6.C5 1981b
Moffitt PN1995.9.S6.C5 1981 (another edition)

Norden, Martin F. "America And Its Fantasy Films: 1945-1951." Citation: Film & History 1982 12(1): 1-11. Considers the fantasy films produced during 1945-51 symtomatic of US social conditions; focuses on the types and roles of characters in these films, discusses the social issues raised, and briefly compares these fantasy films with the science-fiction films of the 1950's.

Perrine, Tony A. Film and the Nuclear Age: Representing Cultural Anxiety / Toni A. Perrine. New York: Garland, 1998. Garland studies in American popular history and culture UCB Main PN1995.9.W3.P49 1998

Pronay, N. "British Film Sources For The Cold-War - The Disappearance Of The Cinema-Going Public." Historical Journal Of Film Radio And Television, 1993, V13 N1:7-17.

Quart, Leonard. American Film and Society Since 1945 / Leonard Quart and Albert Auster. London: Macmillan, 1984. Series title: Contemporary United States (London, England) UCB Main PN1993.5.U6 Q3 1984

Ramsden, John. "Refocusing 'The People's War': British War Films of the 1950s." (includes appendix on the war film boom of the 1950s) Journal of Contemporary History v33, n1 (Jan, 1998):35 (32 pages).

Recchia, Edward "Film Noir and the Western. The Centennial Review vol. 40 no. 3. 1996 Fall. pp: 601-14.

Roberts, Garyn G. "Revelation, Humanity, and a Warning: Four Motifs of 1950s Science Fiction Invasion Films." Plot Conventions in American Popular Film. In: Beyond the Stars: Studies in American Popular Film 2 / edited by Paul Loukides and Linda K. Fuller. pp: 130-42. Bowling Green, Ohio: Bowling Green University Popular Press, c1990
Main Stack PN1995.9.C36.B49 1990; Moffitt PN1995.9.C36.B49 1990

Roffman, Peter The Hollywood Social Problem Film: Madness, Despair, and Politics From the Depression to the Fifties / Peter Roffman and Jim Purdy. Bloomington Indiana University Press, 1981.
UCB Main PN1995 .R63
UCB Moffitt PN1995 .R63

Rogin, Michael. "Kiss Me Deadly: Communism, Motherhood, and Cold War Movies." Representations, vol. 6. 1984 Spring. pp: 1-36.

Sayre, Nora. Running Time: Films of the Cold War / Nora Sayre. New York: Dial Press, c1982. UCB Main PN1993.5.U6 S315 1982
UCB Moffitt PN1993.5.U6 S315 1982

Sayre, Nora. "Watch the Skies." Grand Street, vol. 1 no. 2. 1982 Winter. pp: 51-58.

Shapiro, Benjamin. "Universal truths: cultural myths and generic adaptation in 1950s science fiction films." Journal of Popular Film and Television v18, n3 (Fall, 1990):103 (9 pages).

Shapiro, Jerome F. "Atomic Bomb Cinema: Illness, Suffering, and the Apocalyptic Narrative." Literature and Medicine 17.1 (1998) 126-148 UC Berkeley users only

Simmons, Jerold. "The Censoring of Rebel Without a Cause." Journal of Popular Film and Television, vol. 23 no. 2. 1995 Summer. pp: 57-63.

Smith, Judith E. "The Marrying Kind: Working-Class Courtship and

Marriage in 1950s Hollywood." In: Multiple Voices in Feminist Film Criticism / Diane Carson, Linda Dittmar, and Janice R. Welsch, editors. pp: 226-42. Minneapolis: University of Minnesota Press, c1994.
Main Stack PN1995.9.W6.M82 1994
Moffitt PN1995.9.W6.M82 1994

Sobchack, Vivian Carol. The Limits of Infinity: The American Science Fiction Film, 1950-75 / Vivian Carol Sobchack. South Brunswicks, N.J.: A. S. Barnes, c1980.
UCB Main PN1995.9.S26 .S57 1980

Strada, Michael J. "The Cinematic Bogy Man Comes Home: American Popular Perceptions of External Threat." Midwest Quarterly, vol. 28 no. 2. 1987 Winter. pp: 248-270.

Taylor, Ella. Prime-time Families: Television Culture in Postwar America / Ella Taylor. Berkeley: University of California Press, c1989.
UCB Main PN1992.8.F33 T391 1989
UCB Moffitt PN1992.8.F33 T39 1989

Throne, Marilyn "Love in the Afternoon: A Cinematic Exposure of a 1950s Myth." Literature/Film Quarterly 16, no. 1 (1988): p. 65-73

Torry, Robert. "Apocalypse Then: Benefits of the Bomb in Fifties Science Fiction Films. Cinema Journal v. 31 (Fall '91) p. 7-21.

Tibbetts, John C. "After the Fall: Revisioning the Cold --a report on the XVIIth AMHIST Conference, 25-31 July, Salisbury, MD." Historical Journal of Film, Radio, and Television 18:1, 1998, pp: 111-122

Warren, Bill Keep Watching the Skies! : American Science Fiction Movies of the Fifties / by Bill Warren ; research associate, Bill Thomas. Jefferson, N.C.: McFarland, 1982-1986.
UCB Main PN1995.9.S26 .W37 1982 V.1 (1982)

Waugh, Thomas. "The Films They Never Showed: The Flaherty-Seminar And The Cold-War." Wide Angle, vol. 17 no. 1-4. 1995. pp: 217-26.

Wells, Paul. "The Invisible Man: Shrinking Masculinity in the 1950s Science Fiction B-Movie." In: You Tarzan: Masculinity, Movies and Men. New York / edited by Pat Kirkham and Janet Thumim. pp: 181-99. New York: St. Martin's Press, 1993.
Main Stack PN1995.9.M46.Y68 1993
Moffitt PN1995.9.M46.Y68 1993

Williams, Tony. "Female Oppression in Attack of the 50-Foot Woman." Science-Fiction Studies, vol. 12 no. 3 (37). 1985 Nov. pp: 264-273.

Abrams, Brett L. "The First Hollywood Blacklist: The Major Studios Deal With The Conference Of Studio Unions, 1941-47." Southern California Quarterly 1995 77(3): 215-253.
"Traces the struggle between the conservative International Alliance of Theatrical and Stage Employees (IATSE) and the liberal Conference of Studio Unions (CSU) for control of the craftsmen employed by the motion picture studios in Los Angeles between 1941 and 1947. The

studios preferred recognition of IATSE locals, whose leaders accused the CSU of supporting communism and violence. The strikes of 1945 and 1946 brought local government, the studios, and the IATSE into a coalition against the CSU. By 1947 the CSU had lost the battle, its leaders branded as Communists and many workers siding with the IATSE just to preserve their jobs and status." [from ABC-CLIO America: History & Life]

Benson, Thomas W.; Gronbeck, Bruce E. " Thinking through Film: Hollywood Remembers the Blacklist." In: Rhetoric and community : studies in unity and fragmentation / edited by J. Michael Hogan. pp: 217-64 Columbia, S.C. : University of South Carolina Press, c1998. Studies in rhetoric/communication.
Main Stack P301.5.S63.R48 1998

Bentley, Eric Are You Now or Have You Ever Been; The Investigation of Show Business by the Un-American Activities Committee, 1947-1958 [by] Eric Bentley. New York, Harper & Row [1972]. Series title: Harper colophon books, CN 1006.
UCB Grad Svcs XMAC.B477.A73 Modern Authors Collection
UCB Main PN1590.B5 B4 1972

Bernstein, Walter. Inside Out: A Memoir of the Blacklist / Walter Bernstein. 1st ed. New York: A.A. Knopf, 1996.
UCB Main PN1998.3.B477 A3 1996
UCB Moffitt PN1998.3.B477 A3 1996

Bernstein, Walter. "Remembering the Blacklist." (excerpt from scriptwriter's book about being blacklisted in Hollywood during the 1940s and 1950s, 'Inside Out: A Memoir of the Blacklist') New York Times v145, sec2 (Sun, Oct 27, 1996):H18(N), H18(L), col 5, 20 col in. "Blacklist: memories of a word that marks an era." (excerpts from symposium 'Remembering the Blacklist' at New York Public Library for the Performing Arts at Lincoln Center, New York City, on investigations of... New York Times v143, sec2 (Sun, July 31, 1994):H3(N), H3(L), col 1, 47 col in.

Bosworth, Patricia. "Giving credit where credit is long overdue." (screenwriters once blacklisted by House Un-American Activities Committee see their screen credits restored on 24 films) New York Times v146, sec2 (Sun, April 20, 1997):H13(N), H13(L), col 1, 18 col in.

Bowman, James. "Loyalty Tests." (Anti-Communist hero Elia Kazan) American Spectator v32, n3 (March, 1999):68 (2 pages).

Bright, John Hollywood Blacklist: John Bright: oral history transcript / interviewed by Larry Ceplair ; completed under the auspices of the Oral History Program, University of California, Los Angeles. 1991.
UCB Bancroft BANC MSS 92/100 c

Biskind, Peter. "The Past Is Prologue: The Blacklist In Hollywood." Radical America 1981 15(3): 59-65. "Commentary on the recent literature on the House Committee on Un-American Activities and the blacklist of the

Hollywood 10, focusing on Victor Navasky's Naming Names (1980). The key strategy was as evident in the movie industry of the 1950's as it was during the Vietnam War: have the good dissidents turn against the bad, uncooperative ones. This betrayal would bind them more securely to the center of the political spectrum." [from ABC-CLIO America: History & Life]

Brodie, John. "Rebels Get Cause in Post-list Pix." (includes related article on re-crediting other films actually written by those blacklisted)(special section - 50th anniversary of the beginning of the... Variety v364, n6 (Sept 9, 1996):123.

Buhle, Paul. "The Hollywood Blacklist and the Jew: An Exploration of Popular Culture." Tikkun 1995 vol 10 no. 5 pp: pp. 35 September 01

Burton, Michael C. John Henry Faulk, A Biography: The Making of a Liberated Mind / by Michael C. Burton. 1st ed. Austin, Tex.: Eakin Press, c1993.
Main Stack PS3556.A92.Z59 1993

Carr, Gary L. The Left Side of Paradise: The Screenwriting of John Howard Lawson / by Gary Carr. Ann Arbor, Mich.: UMI Research Press, c1984. Series title: Studies in cinema; no. 26. UCB Main PN1998.A3 L3763 1984

Ceplair, Larry. The Inquisition in Hollywood: Politics in the Film Community, 1930-1960 / Larry Ceplair & Steven Englund. Berkeley: University of California Press, c1983.

Main Stack PN1993.5.U6.C4 1983
Moffitt PN1993.5.U6.C4 1983
Bancroft F867.M6.C4 (another edition).

Cogley, John. Report on Blacklisting. [New York]: Fund for the Republic, 1956.
Main Stack PN1993.65.U6 C63; v. 1-2 ([1956])

Cohen, Joan. "The Culture Of The Blacklist." Mankind 1978 6(3): 16-20.

Cole, Lester Hollywood Red: The Autobiography of Lester Cole. Palo Alto, Calif. : Ramparts Press, c1981.
UCB Bancroft F860 .A3C63
UCB Main PN1998.A3A12 C64

Cox, Dan "'Commie Carnival' Revisited: despite Red Scare scars, H'wood lures blacklist kids." (Hollywood)(special section - 50th anniversary of the beginning of the anti-communist blacklist/Red Scare persecutions in the US entertainment industry)(Cover Story) VarietySept 9, 1996 Vol/Num: v. 364, n. 6, p. 1 (2 pages)
"Decades later, naming names still matters; Arthur Laurents talks with Frank Rich about his play 'Jolson Sings Again' and revisits the blacklist." New York Times, sec2 (Sun, March 14, 1999):AR7(L), col 1, 25 col in.

Dick, Bernard F. Radical Innocence: A Critical Study of the Hollywood Ten / Bernard F. Dick. Lexington, Ky.: University Press of Kentucky, c1989.
UCB Main PN1998.2 .D51 1989
UCB Moffitt PN1998.2 .D5 1989

Dmytryk, Edward. Odd Man Out: A Memoir of the Hollywood Ten / Edward Dmytryk. Carbondale, IL: Southern Illinois University Press, c1996.
UCB Moffitt PN1998.3.D6 A3 1996

Dunne, Philip Take Two: A Life in Movies and Politics / Philip Dunne New York: McGraw-Hill, published in association with San Francisco Book Co., c1980
Main Stack PN1998.A3.D85

Farah, Joseph. "The Real Blacklist: True or False: The Fifties was a Period of Blacklisting and Fear in the American Movie Industry." National Review v41, n20 (Oct 27, 1989):42 (2 pages).

Federal Bureau of Investigation Confidential Files. Communist Activity in the Entertainment Industry. FBI surveillance Files on Hollywood, 1942-1958 / edited by Daniel J. Leab. Bethesda, MD: University Publications of America, c1991. 14 microfilm reels ; 35 mm.

News/Micro MICROFILM.71263
Shelved: For guide see: A guide to the microfilm edition of Federal Bureau of Investigation confidential files. Communist activity in the entertainment industry.
PN1993.5.U65 1991 GSSI Library has: reel 1-14 (c1991) Guide to this collection: PN1993.5 .U65 1991 Govt/Soc Sci

Foley, Karen Sue. The Political Blacklist in the Broadcast Industry: The Decade of the 1950s / Karen Sue Foley. New York: Arno Press, 1979, c1972. Dissertations in broadcasting Main Stack HE8689.8.F64 1979

Foreman, Amanda; Foreman, Jonathan.
"Our Dad Was No Commie." (director Elia Kazan's winning of the 1999 Oscar Lifetime Achievement award)(filmmaker Carl Foreman) New Statesman (1996) v129, n4429 (March 26, 1999):20 (2 pages).

Foreman, Jonathan. "Witch-hunt." (Carl Foreman's experience of McCarthyism and the Hollywood blacklist) Index on Censorship v24, n6 (Nov-Dec, 1995):96 (4 pages).

Fuller, Linda K. "The Ideology of the 'Red Scare' Movement: McCarthyism in the Movies." In: Beyond the Stars 5: Themes and Ideologies in American Popular Film. / edited by Paul Loukides and Linda K. Fuller. pp: 229-47. Bowling Green, Ohio: Bowling Green University Popular Press, c1990
Main Stack PN1995.9.C36.B49 1990
Moffitt PN1995.9.C36.B49 1990

Gabler, Neal. "Why the drama never ends." (honorary Academy Award for Elia Kazan, who once named names of Communist members to the House)(Column) Los Angeles Times (Sun, March 21, 1999):M1, col 1, 31 col in.

Georgakas, Dan. "The Way They Really Were." (Hollywood blacklist) Cineaste v23, n2 (Spring, 1997):28 (4 pages).

Gerard, Jeremy; Brodie, John. "H'wood Blacklistees Fought Same Battles in Gotham." (special section - 50th anniversary of the beginning of the anti-communist blacklist/Red Scare persecutions in the US entertainment industry)(Cover Story) Variety v364, n6 (Sept 9, 1996):125 (2 pages).

Goldstein, Patrick. "Film director Elia Kazan to receive Oscar, foregiveness." Los Angeles Times (Fri, Jan 15, 1999):A1, col 2, 41 col in.
Goldstein, Patrick.
"A fateful decision, damaging fallout." (decision to give lifetime achievement award to director and 'red scare' informant Elia Kazan at 1999 Academy Awards) Los Angeles Times (Tue, March 16, 1999):F1, col 1, 38 col in.

Goldstein, Patrick.
"He's been there, survived that." (filmmaker and screenwriter Abraham Polonsky)(Interview) Los Angeles Times (Wed, Jan 20, 1999):F1, col 5, 38 col in.

Gordon, Donald Hollywood Blacklist: Donald Gordon: oral history transcript / interviewed by Larry Ceplair ; completed under the auspices of the Oral History Program, University of California, Los Angeles. 1991.
UCB Bancroft BANC MSS 92/114 c

Gordon, Bernard Hollywood Exile, or, How I Learned to Love the Blacklist: A Memoir / by Bernard Gordon. 1st ed. Austin: University of Texas Press, 1999. Texas film and media studies series
Main Stack PN1998.3.G662.A3 1999

Guy, S. "'High Treason' (1951) - Britains Cold-War Fifth-Column (Film Directed By Roy Boulting)." Historical Journal Of Film Radio And Television, 1993, V13 N1:35-47.

Hamilton, Denise. "Keeper of the Flame: A Blacklist Survivor; Norma Barzman at 80, has cast off a retiring manner for an activist's role in portraying a troubled era." (Southern California Living) Los Angeles Times (Oct 3, 2000):E-1.

Hollingsworth, Mark Blacklist: The Inside Story of Political Vetting / Mark Hollingsworth and Richard Norton-Taylor. London: Hogarth Press, 1988. Series title: Current affairs.
UCB Main HD4902.5 .H641 1988

Ivins, Molly. "Johnny's Fight." (John Henry Faulk) (obituary) Mother Jones v15, n5 (July-August, 1990):8 (2 pages).

Johnson, Ted. "Little Union Unity on Subject of Commies." (special section - 50th anniversary of the beginning of the anti-communist blacklist/Red Scare persecutions in the US entertainment industry)(Cover Story) Variety v364, n6 (Sept 9, 1996):124.

Kahn, Gordon. Hollywood on Trial; The Story of the 10 Who Were Indicted. Foreword by Thomas Mann. New York, Boni & Gaer [1948].
UCB Bancroft F867.M6 K3
UCB Main PN1993.5.U6 K3 1948

Kempton, Murray. Part of Our Time, Too.(Dalton Trumbo on communism and blacklisting) Nation v268, n13 (April 5, 1999):60.

Klady, Leonard. "Pinko Stinko, 50 Years Later." (special section - 50th anniversary of the beginning of the anti-communist blacklist/Red Scare persecutions in the US entertainment industry)('Commie Carnival' Revisited)(Cover Story) Variety v364, n6 (Sept 9, 1996):1 (2 pages).

Koehler, Robert. "Kazan's HUAC testimony a permanent black mark." (Filmmaker Elia Kazan and Academy participation in blacklisting)(Brief Article) Variety v374, n2 (March 1, 1999):48 (1 page).

Kramer, Hilton. "'The Blacklist & the Cold War' Revisited." New Criterion, vol. 16 no. 3. 1997 Nov. pp: 11-16.

Kramer, Julie. "The life of the party." (Roz Roose) New Yorker v70, n48 (Feb 6, 1995):58 (15 pages). "

Leab, Daniel J. "The Hollywood Feature Film As Cold Warrior." OAH Newsletter 1985 13(2): 13-15. "[America History and Life]

Leab, Daniel J. "'I Was a Communist for the FBI' - A Classic Cold War Film and the Shadowy Figure Who Inspired It." History Today, 1996 Dec., V46 N12:42-47.

Lewis, Jon "'We Do Not Ask You to Condone This': How the Blacklist Saved Hollywood." Cinema Journal 39, no. 2 (2000 Winter): p. 3-30

Marty, Martin E. "Elia Kazan: can 'naming names' be the one unforgivable sin?" (Column) Los Angeles Times v116 (Mon, Jan 27, 1997):M1, col 1, 30 col in.

May, Lary. "Movie Star Politics: The Screen Actors' Guild, Cultural Conversion, and the Hollywood Red Scare." In: Recasting America: Culture and Politics in the Age of Cold War. / edited by Lary May. pp: 125-153. Chicago: University of Chicago Press, 1989.
Main Stack E169.12.R431 1989
Moffitt E169.12.R43 1989

McGilligan, Patrick. Tender Comrades: A Backstory of the Hollywood Blacklist / Patrick McGilligan and Paul Buhle; photographs by Alison Morley and William B. Winburn. 1st ed. New York: St. Martin's Press, 1997.
UCB Law Lib KF4298 .M33 1997
UCB Main PN1590.B5 M35 1997
UCB Moffitt PN1590.B5 M35 1997

Meroney, John. "Kazan's honor." (Elia Kazan and the blacklisting entertainment industry personalities)(Column) Washington Post (Sat, March 20, 1999):A19, col 5, 19 col in.

Mills, Michael. "Blacklist: A Different Look at the HUAC Hearings" (from: Modern Times web site)

Murphey, Dwight D.. "The 'Hollywood Blacklist' in Historical Context." The Journal of Social, Political and Economic Studies v. 18 (Fall '93) p. 327-49

Nesselson, Lisa. "Survival Instincts." (blacklistee Jon Berry) Variety v367, n6 (June 9, 1997):7 (2 pages).

Neve, Brian. "On the Waterfront." (Film in Context) History Today v45, n6 (June, 1995):19 (6 pages).

Nielsen, Michael Charles. Hollywood's Other Blacklist: Union Struggles in the Studio System / Mike Nielsen and Gene Mailes. London: British Film Institute, 1995. UCB Main PN1993.5.U6 N54 1995

O'Connor, Anne-Marie. "Blacklisted screenwriter Tarloff dies." (Frank Tarloff)(Obituary) Los Angeles Times (Mon, June 28, 1999):B1, col 1, 25 col in.

Oliver, Myrna. "Hollywood blacklist's Abraham Polonsky dies." (Obituary) Los Angeles Times (Thu, Oct 28, 1999):B1, col 6, 25 col in.

Radin, Max In the Supreme Court of the United States, October term, 1949 : no. 248, John Howard Lawson, petitioner, vs. United States of America, respondent : no 249, Dalton Trumbo, petitioner, vs. United States of America,... [S.l. : .n.], 1949 (Los Angeles : Parker & Co.). UCB Bancroft p PN1994 .R45 Radin, Max In the Supreme Court of the United States, October term, 1949 : no. 248, John Howard Lawson, petitioner, vs. United States of America, respondent : no 249, Dalton Trumbo, petitioner, vs. United States of America,... [S.l. : .n.], 1949 (Los Angeles : Parker & Co.). UCB Bancroft BOX 1474 Master Negative

Radosh, Ronald. "The Blacklist as History." New Criterion, vol. 16 no. 4. 1997 Dec. pp: 12-17. Radosh, Ronald. "Scoundrel 'Times.'" (slander case regarding a New York Times' feature article on Victor Navasky's film,'Guilty by Suspicion')(American Document) (column) American Spectator v24, n6 (June, 1991):30 (2 pages).
Red Channels: The Report of Communist Influence in Radio and Television. New York, N.Y.: American Business Consultants, 1950.
No Berkeley holdings
UCD Shields HE8698.A63
UCSD SpecColl HX83 R44 1950 Rare SRLF A 0007535131 Type EXP SRLF for loan details.
SRLF Spec.Col. HE 8698 A51r Request at UCLA Special Collections. Type EXP SRLF for loan details.
CSL State Lib 384.5 A512 Reference Center

Robb, D. "Naming the Right Names: Amending the Hollywood Blacklist." Cineaste. 1996 Volume 22 Number 2 pp: 24 UCB users only

Rosenfeld, Stephen S. "Looking back on the blacklisted." (50th anniversary of House Un-American Activities Committee's work to blacklist Hollywood writers, actors and directors)(Column) Washington Post v120 (Fri, Nov 28, 1997):A27, col 1, 17 col in.

Ross, Lillian. "Introducing the Blacklist." New Yorker v70, n5 (March 21, 1994):176 (9 pages). "Hollywood screenwriters and producers were forced to change

their scripts and general motifs during the McCarthy era of the 1940s. The classic story of the little man succeeding against the odds was considered pro-Communist." [Magazine Index]

Roth, Philip. I Married a Communist / Philip Roth. Boston : Houghton Mifflin, 1998. UCB Main PS3568.O855 I18 1998

Rothman, Cliff. "Shud He Have Been a Contendah?" (Elia Kazan) Nation v268, n13 (April 5, 1999):57 (1 page).

Rothstein, Edward. "On naming the names in life and in art." (director Elia Kazan is still pigeon-holed, scorned, for having cooperated with anti-Communist investigations by Sen. Joseph McCarthy, despite the quality of his... New York Times v146 (Mon, Jan 27, 1997):B1(N), C13(L), col 1, 27 col in.

Rouverol, Jean. Refugees from Hollywood : a journal of the blacklist years / Jean Rouverol. 1st ed. Albuquerque: University of New Mexico Press, c2000. Main Stack PN1998.2.R68 2000

Sahagun, Louis; Welkos, Robert W. "Ring Lardner Jr., Last of the Hollywood 10, Dies; Cold War: Oscar-winning writer was jailed, blacklisted for refusing to testify about his Communist affiliation." (Part A)(Obituary) Los Angeles Times (Nov 2, 2000):A-1.

Sayre, Nora. "Fifty years and counting: the power of the blacklist." (Writers Guild of America restores screenplay credits to writers who were forced to change their names in the 1950s following congressional investigation... Los Angeles Times v116 (Sun, April 13, 1997):M1, col 1, 28 col in.

Schultheiss, John. "A season of fear: the blacklisted teleplays of Abraham Polonsky." (includes filmography) Literature-Film Quarterly v24, n2 (April, 1996):148 (17 pages).

Szamuely, George. "The Way They Are." (House Un-American Activities hearings of 1951 in film; new liberal Hollywood) National Review v43, n6 (April 15, 1991):48 (3 pages).

Trumbo, Dalton The Time of the Toad; A Study of Inquisition in America By One of the Hollywood Ten. [Hollywood, Calif., Hollywood Ten, 1950?].
UCB Bancroft F867.M6T74
United States. Congress. House. Committee on Un-American Activities.
Thirty years of treason; excerpts from hearings before the House Committee on Un-American Activities, 1938-1968. Edited by Eric Bentley. New York, Viking Press [1971].
Main Stack E743.5.B4
Main Stack E743.5.B4

Vaughn, Robert Only Victims; A Study of Show Business Blacklisting. With a foreword by George McGovern. New York, Putnam [1972]
Main Stack PN1590.B5.V3 1972a

Waxman, Sharon. "Blacklist: Hollywood's raw wound; ruined artists finally get measure of

respect." Washington Post v120 (Sun, Nov 23, 1997):G1, col 1, 71 col in.

Waxman, Sharon. "For Eliz Kazan, a contentious moment of glory; blacklist meets A-list." (Academy Awards ceremony) Washington Post (Mon, March 22, 1999):C1, col 1, 19 col in.
Waxman, Sharon. "Reelpolitik at the Oscars; honor for Elia Kazan stirs up those blacklisted in McCarthy era." Washington Post (Thu, Feb 25, 1999):C1, col 5, 25 col in.

Weiner, Rex. "Hollywood Warms up to Activism." (political activism)(special section - 50th anniversary of the beginning of the anti-communist blacklist/Red Scare persecutions in the US entertainment industry)(Cover Story) Variety v364, n6 (Sept 9, 1996):124.

The Literature & Culture of the American 1950s (Professor Al Filreis, University of Pennsylvania)

Screen Actors' Guild: 50 Years: SAG Remembers The Blacklist

Blacklist: A Different Look at the 1947 HUAC Hearings (via Modern Times)

Hollywood Blacklist (from: Buhle, Buhle, and Georgakas, ed., Encyclopedia of the American LeftT, [Urbana and Chicago: University of Illinois Press, 1992])

David J. O'Brien, American Catholics and Social Reform: The New Deal

Years (New York, 1968), pp. 17, 19-20.

For studies that examine Coughlin and Day see David Brinkley, Voices of Protest: Huey Long, Father Coughlin & the Great Depression (New York, 1983); Dorothy Day, The Long Loneliness: The Autobiography of Dorothy Day (New York, 1952); William D. Miller, Dorothy Day: A Biography (New York, 1982);

Philip E. Dobson, "The Xavier Labor School, 1938-39" (n.p., undated). I would like to thank Joshua Freeman for providing me with this source.

Allen Raymond, Waterfront Priest (New York, 1955), pp. 4-5.

Daily Worker, November 19, 1948, p. 4; "Work Injuries in the United States, 1948," Monthly Labor Review, 69 (October, 1949), 385-386, 388.

Longshore Safety Survey: A Survey of Occupational Hazards in the Stevedoring Industry, National Academy of Sciences--National Research Council (Washington, D.C., 1956), p. 1.

FBI Report--Longshoremen's Strike at the Port of New York, October 2 5, 1951
Maritime Folder, Box 168, Papers of Harry Truman, Harry S. Truman Library.

Eyman, Scott. Five American cinematographers: Interviews with Karl Strauss, Joseph Ruttenberg, James Wong Howe, Linwood Dunn,

and William H. Clothier. Metuchen,
N.J. : Scarecrow Press, 1987.

Howe, James Wong. Papers of, 1930-
1970. Beverly Hills, Calif. : Academy
of Motion Picture Arts and Sciences
Library

www.ingramcontent.com/pod-product-compliance
Lightning Source LLC
Chambersburg PA
CBHW081103170526
45165CB00008B/2309